FREE Test Taking Tips DVD Offer

To help us better serve you, we have developed a Test Taking Tips DVD that we would like to give you for FREE. **This DVD covers world-class test taking tips that you can use to be even more successful when you are taking your test.**

All that we ask is that you email us your feedback about your study guide. Please let us know what you thought about it – whether that is good, bad or indifferent.

To get your **FREE Test Taking Tips DVD**, email freedvd@studyguideteam.com with "FREE DVD" in the subject line and the following information in the body of the email:

 a. The title of your study guide.

 b. Your product rating on a scale of 1-5, with 5 being the highest rating.

 c. Your feedback about the study guide. What did you think of it?

 d. Your full name and shipping address to send your free DVD.

If you have any questions or concerns, please don't hesitate to contact us at freedvd@studyguideteam.com.

Thanks again!

NCLEX PN 2020 & 2021 Study Guide

NCLEX PN Book and Practice Test Questions Review for the National Council Licensure Examination for Practical Nurses [Updated to the New Official Exam Outline]

Test Prep Books

Written and edited by Test Prep Books.

Test Prep Books is not associated with or endorsed by any official testing organization. Test Prep Books is a publisher of unofficial educational products. All test and organization names are trademarks of their respective owners. Content in this book is included for utilitarian purposes only and does not constitute an endorsement by Test Prep Books of any particular point of view.

Interested in buying more than 10 copies of our product? Contact us about bulk discounts: bulkorders@studyguideteam.com

ISBN 13: 9781628458084
ISBN 10: 1628458089

Table of Contents

Quick Overview

As you draw closer to taking your exam, effective preparation becomes more and more important. Thankfully, you have this study guide to help you get ready. Use this guide to help keep your studying on track and refer to it often.

This study guide contains several key sections that will help you be successful on your exam. The guide contains tips for what you should do the night before and the day of the test. Also included are test-taking tips. Knowing the right information is not always enough. Many well-prepared test takers struggle with exams. These tips will help equip you to accurately read, assess, and answer test questions.

A large part of the guide is devoted to showing you what content to expect on the exam and to helping you better understand that content. In this guide are practice test questions so that you can see how well you have grasped the content. Then, answer explanations are provided so that you can understand why you missed certain questions.

Don't try to cram the night before you take your exam. This is not a wise strategy for a few reasons. First, your retention of the information will be low. Your time would be better used by reviewing information you already know rather than trying to learn a lot of new information. Second, you will likely become stressed as you try to gain a large amount of knowledge in a short amount of time. Third, you will be depriving yourself of sleep. So be sure to go to bed at a reasonable time the night before. Being well-rested helps you focus and remain calm.

Be sure to eat a substantial breakfast the morning of the exam. If you are taking the exam in the afternoon, be sure to have a good lunch as well. Being hungry is distracting and can make it difficult to focus. You have hopefully spent lots of time preparing for the exam. Don't let an empty stomach get in the way of success!

When travelling to the testing center, leave earlier than needed. That way, you have a buffer in case you experience any delays. This will help you remain calm and will keep you from missing your appointment time at the testing center.

Be sure to pace yourself during the exam. Don't try to rush through the exam. There is no need to risk performing poorly on the exam just so you can leave the testing center early. Allow yourself to use all of the allotted time if needed.

Remain positive while taking the exam even if you feel like you are performing poorly. Thinking about the content you should have mastered will not help you perform better on the exam.

Once the exam is complete, take some time to relax. Even if you feel that you need to take the exam again, you will be well served by some down time before you begin studying again. It's often easier to convince yourself to study if you know that it will come with a reward!

Test-Taking Strategies

1. Predicting the Answer

When you feel confident in your preparation for a multiple-choice test, try predicting the answer before reading the answer choices. This is especially useful on questions that test objective factual knowledge. By predicting the answer before reading the available choices, you eliminate the possibility that you will be distracted or led astray by an incorrect answer choice. You will feel more confident in your selection if you read the question, predict the answer, and then find your prediction among the answer choices. After using this strategy, be sure to still read all of the answer choices carefully and completely. If you feel unprepared, you should not attempt to predict the answers. This would be a waste of time and an opportunity for your mind to wander in the wrong direction.

2. Reading the Whole Question

Too often, test takers scan a multiple-choice question, recognize a few familiar words, and immediately jump to the answer choices. Test authors are aware of this common impatience, and they will sometimes prey upon it. For instance, a test author might subtly turn the question into a negative, or he or she might redirect the focus of the question right at the end. The only way to avoid falling into these traps is to read the entirety of the question carefully before reading the answer choices.

3. Looking for Wrong Answers

Long and complicated multiple-choice questions can be intimidating. One way to simplify a difficult multiple-choice question is to eliminate all of the answer choices that are clearly wrong. In most sets of answers, there will be at least one selection that can be dismissed right away. If the test is administered on paper, the test taker could draw a line through it to indicate that it may be ignored; otherwise, the test taker will have to perform this operation mentally or on scratch paper. In either case, once the obviously incorrect answers have been eliminated, the remaining choices may be considered. Sometimes identifying the clearly wrong answers will give the test taker some information about the correct answer. For instance, if one of the remaining answer choices is a direct opposite of one of the eliminated answer choices, it may well be the correct answer. The opposite of obviously wrong is obviously right! Of course, this is not always the case. Some answers are obviously incorrect simply because they are irrelevant to the question being asked. Still, identifying and eliminating some incorrect answer choices is a good way to simplify a multiple-choice question.

4. Don't Overanalyze

Anxious test takers often overanalyze questions. When you are nervous, your brain will often run wild, causing you to make associations and discover clues that don't actually exist. If you feel that this may be a problem for you, do whatever you can to slow down during the test. Try taking a deep breath or counting to ten. As you read and consider the question, restrict yourself to the particular words used by the author. Avoid thought tangents about what the author *really* meant, or what he or she was *trying* to say. The only things that matter on a multiple-choice test are the words that are actually in the question. You must avoid reading too much into a multiple-choice question, or supposing that the writer meant something other than what he or she wrote.

5. No Need for Panic

It is wise to learn as many strategies as possible before taking a multiple-choice test, but it is likely that you will come across a few questions for which you simply don't know the answer. In this situation, avoid panicking. Because most multiple-choice tests include dozens of questions, the relative value of a single wrong answer is small. As much as possible, you should compartmentalize each question on a multiple-choice test. In other words, you should not allow your feelings about one question to affect your success on the others. When you find a question that you either don't understand or don't know how to answer, just take a deep breath and do your best. Read the entire question slowly and carefully. Try rephrasing the question a couple of different ways. Then, read all of the answer choices carefully. After eliminating obviously wrong answers, make a selection and move on to the next question.

6. Confusing Answer Choices

When working on a difficult multiple-choice question, there may be a tendency to focus on the answer choices that are the easiest to understand. Many people, whether consciously or not, gravitate to the answer choices that require the least concentration, knowledge, and memory. This is a mistake. When you come across an answer choice that is confusing, you should give it extra attention. A question might be confusing because you do not know the subject matter to which it refers. If this is the case, don't eliminate the answer before you have affirmatively settled on another. When you come across an answer choice of this type, set it aside as you look at the remaining choices. If you can confidently assert that one of the other choices is correct, you can leave the confusing answer aside. Otherwise, you will need to take a moment to try to better understand the confusing answer choice. Rephrasing is one way to tease out the sense of a confusing answer choice.

7. Your First Instinct

Many people struggle with multiple-choice tests because they overthink the questions. If you have studied sufficiently for the test, you should be prepared to trust your first instinct once you have carefully and completely read the question and all of the answer choices. There is a great deal of research suggesting that the mind can come to the correct conclusion very quickly once it has obtained all of the relevant information. At times, it may seem to you as if your intuition is working faster even than your reasoning mind. This may in fact be true. The knowledge you obtain while studying may be retrieved from your subconscious before you have a chance to work out the associations that support it. Verify your instinct by working out the reasons that it should be trusted.

8. Key Words

Many test takers struggle with multiple-choice questions because they have poor reading comprehension skills. Quickly reading and understanding a multiple-choice question requires a mixture of skill and experience. To help with this, try jotting down a few key words and phrases on a piece of scrap paper. Doing this concentrates the process of reading and forces the mind to weigh the relative importance of the question's parts. In selecting words and phrases to write down, the test taker thinks about the question more deeply and carefully. This is especially true for multiple-choice questions that are preceded by a long prompt.

9. Subtle Negatives

One of the oldest tricks in the multiple-choice test writer's book is to subtly reverse the meaning of a question with a word like *not* or *except*. If you are not paying attention to each word in the question, you can easily be led astray by this trick. For instance, a common question format is, "Which of the following is...?" Obviously, if the question instead is, "Which of the following is not...?," then the answer will be quite different. Even worse, the test makers are aware of the potential for this mistake and will include one answer choice that would be correct if the question were not negated or reversed. A test taker who misses the reversal will find what he or she believes to be a correct answer and will be so confident that he or she will fail to reread the question and discover the original error. The only way to avoid this is to practice a wide variety of multiple-choice questions and to pay close attention to each and every word.

10. Reading Every Answer Choice

It may seem obvious, but you should always read every one of the answer choices! Too many test takers fall into the habit of scanning the question and assuming that they understand the question because they recognize a few key words. From there, they pick the first answer choice that answers the question they believe they have read. Test takers who read all of the answer choices might discover that one of the latter answer choices is actually *more* correct. Moreover, reading all of the answer choices can remind you of facts related to the question that can help you arrive at the correct answer. Sometimes, a misstatement or incorrect detail in one of the latter answer choices will trigger your memory of the subject and will enable you to find the right answer. Failing to read all of the answer choices is like not reading all of the items on a restaurant menu: you might miss out on the perfect choice.

11. Spot the Hedges

One of the keys to success on multiple-choice tests is paying close attention to every word. This is never truer than with words like almost, most, some, and sometimes. These words are called "hedges" because they indicate that a statement is not totally true or not true in every place and time. An absolute statement will contain no hedges, but in many subjects, the answers are not always straightforward or absolute. There are always exceptions to the rules in these subjects. For this reason, you should favor those multiple-choice questions that contain hedging language. The presence of qualifying words indicates that the author is taking special care with his or her words, which is certainly important when composing the right answer. After all, there are many ways to be wrong, but there is only one way to be right! For this reason, it is wise to avoid answers that are absolute when taking a multiple-choice test. An absolute answer is one that says things are either all one way or all another. They often include words like *every*, *always*, *best*, and *never*. If you are taking a multiple-choice test in a subject that doesn't lend itself to absolute answers, be on your guard if you see any of these words.

12. Long Answers

In many subject areas, the answers are not simple. As already mentioned, the right answer often requires hedges. Another common feature of the answers to a complex or subjective question are qualifying clauses, which are groups of words that subtly modify the meaning of the sentence. If the question or answer choice describes a rule to which there are exceptions or the subject matter is complicated, ambiguous, or confusing, the correct answer will require many words in order to be expressed clearly and accurately. In essence, you should not be deterred by answer choices that seem excessively long. Oftentimes, the author of the text will not be able to write the correct answer without

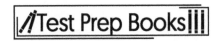

offering some qualifications and modifications. Your job is to read the answer choices thoroughly and completely and to select the one that most accurately and precisely answers the question.

13. Restating to Understand

Sometimes, a question on a multiple-choice test is difficult not because of what it asks but because of how it is written. If this is the case, restate the question or answer choice in different words. This process serves a couple of important purposes. First, it forces you to concentrate on the core of the question. In order to rephrase the question accurately, you have to understand it well. Rephrasing the question will concentrate your mind on the key words and ideas. Second, it will present the information to your mind in a fresh way. This process may trigger your memory and render some useful scrap of information picked up while studying.

14. True Statements

Sometimes an answer choice will be true in itself, but it does not answer the question. This is one of the main reasons why it is essential to read the question carefully and completely before proceeding to the answer choices. Too often, test takers skip ahead to the answer choices and look for true statements. Having found one of these, they are content to select it without reference to the question above. Obviously, this provides an easy way for test makers to play tricks. The savvy test taker will always read the entire question before turning to the answer choices. Then, having settled on a correct answer choice, he or she will refer to the original question and ensure that the selected answer is relevant. The mistake of choosing a correct-but-irrelevant answer choice is especially common on questions related to specific pieces of objective knowledge. A prepared test taker will have a wealth of factual knowledge at his or her disposal, and should not be careless in its application.

15. No Patterns

One of the more dangerous ideas that circulates about multiple-choice tests is that the correct answers tend to fall into patterns. These erroneous ideas range from a belief that B and C are the most common right answers, to the idea that an unprepared test-taker should answer "A-B-A-C-A-D-A-B-A." It cannot be emphasized enough that pattern-seeking of this type is exactly the WRONG way to approach a multiple-choice test. To begin with, it is highly unlikely that the test maker will plot the correct answers according to some predetermined pattern. The questions are scrambled and delivered in a random order. Furthermore, even if the test maker was following a pattern in the assignation of correct answers, there is no reason why the test taker would know which pattern he or she was using. Any attempt to discern a pattern in the answer choices is a waste of time and a distraction from the real work of taking the test. A test taker would be much better served by extra preparation before the test than by reliance on a pattern in the answers.

FREE DVD OFFER

Don't forget that doing well on your exam includes both understanding the test content and understanding how to use what you know to do well on the test. We offer a completely FREE Test Taking Tips DVD that covers world class test taking tips that you can use to be even more successful when you are taking your test.

All that we ask is that you email us your feedback about your study guide. To get your **FREE Test Taking Tips DVD**, email freedvd@studyguideteam.com with "FREE DVD" in the subject line and the following information in the body of the email:

- The title of your study guide.
- Your product rating on a scale of 1-5, with 5 being the highest rating.
- Your feedback about the study guide. What did you think of it?
- Your full name and shipping address to send your free DVD.

Introduction to NCLEX-PN

Function of the Test

This guide outlines the National Council Licensure Examination for Practice Nurses (NCLEX-PN) along with practice questions and answer explanations so test takers can evaluate how well they might do on the actual exam. Those who wish to begin practicing and have received a diploma as an entry-level practical/vocational nurse should sign up to take the NCLEX-PN, as the test score is used as a step toward nursing licensure. In 2018, the total number of candidates who took the NCLEX-PN was 63,049. 46,307 passed the exam, with a pass rate of 73.4%.

Test Administration

The NCLEX-PN is offered via Pearson Centers throughout the United States, Canada, Australia, American Samoa, Guam, the Northern Mariana Islands, and the U.S. Virgin Islands. Note that you must have your Authorization to Test (ATT) before you schedule your exam appointment. Once you have your ATT, test takers must visit the Pearson website and sign up to take the exam there. The testing date must be within the validity date of the ATT.

Test takers are allowed to retake the exam up to eight times a year, providing they have applied for licensure or registration through an appropriate nursing regulatory body (NRB). Test takers must wait forty-five days before they retake an exam.

For test takers in need of accommodations during the test, they should contact their individual testing program. Test takers must do this well before the testing date, as documentation is required.

Test Format

Test takers should arrive at their testing center thirty minutes before the exam with a valid ID. A signature, photograph, and palm vein scan will be taken. Note that this exam is electronic, and an on-screen calculator and erasable note board and marker will be provided.

The PN exam is four hours long and includes a tutorial and two optional breaks. Once a test taker marks a question for submission, they are not allowed to return to that question. There is a computerized survey at the end of the exam. Once finished, test takers must raise their hands in order to be dismissed by a TA.

The NCLEX-PN is divided into four Client Needs sections: Safe and Effective Care Environment, Health Promotion and Maintenance, Psychosocial Integrity, and Physiological Integrity. A table below provides a more detailed view of what is on the exam.

Client Needs Categories	Percentage on Exam
Safe and Effective Care Environment	
• Coordinated Care	18–24%
• Safety and Infection Control	10–16%
Health Promotion and Maintenance	6–12%
Psychosocial Integrity	9–15%
Physiological Integrity	
• Basic Care and Comfort	7–13%
• Pharmacological Therapies	10–16%
• Reduction of Risk Potential	9–15%
Physiological Adaptation	7–13%

Scoring

The NCLEX-PN uses Computerized Adaptive Testing (CAT) for scoring the exam. CAT works in a way that changes a subsequent question based on the way the test taker answered the previous question. Therefore, the exam is scored as the test taker submits their answers, and the test taker cannot go back to change any answers. The computer determines pass or fail based on three rules: 95% Confidence Interval Rule, Maximum-Length Exam Rule, and Run-out-of-time (R.O.O.T.) Rule. For the 95% Confidence Rule, the computer will stop giving questions once it is 95% sure you are above or below your ability to practice nursing. For the Maximum-Length Rule, the computer will disregard the 95% rule if it has not decided a pass/fail yet, and will take your final ability estimate into account. For the R.O.O.T. Rule, when you run out of time, the computer will use a set of alternate rules to determine a pass/fail grade. Scores are not released at the testing center but will be provided after the exam.

Recent/Future Developments

A Next Generation NCLEX (NGN) exam is coming soon with better questions for nurses to help them think critically and provide best outcomes for nurses, clients, and institutions.

Study Prep Plan for the NCLEX PN

1   **Schedule** - Use one of our study schedules below or come up with one of your own.

2   **Relax** - Test anxiety can hurt even the best students. There are many ways to reduce stress. Find the one that works best for you.

3   **Execute** - Once you have a good plan in place, be sure to stick to it.

One Week Study Schedule		
Day 1	Safe and Effective Care Environment
Day 2	Health Promotion and Maintenance
Day 3	Psychosocial Integrity
Day 4	Physiological Integrity
Day 5	Practice Questions
Day 6	Review Answer Explanations
Day 7	Take Your Exam!

Two Week Study Schedule			
Day 1	Coordinated Care	Day 8	Basic Care and Comfort
Day 2	Safety and Infection Control	Day 9	Pharmacological Therapies
Day 3	Practice Questions	Day 10	Reduction of Risk Potential
Day 4	Health Promotion and Maintenance	Day 11	Physiological Adaptation
Day 5	Practice Questions	Day 12	Practice Questions
Day 6	Psychosocial Integrity	Day 13	Review Answer Explanations
Day 7	Practice Questions	Day 14	Take Your Exam!

One Month Study Schedule

Day 1	Advance Directives	Day 11	Developmental Stages and Transitions	Day 21	Mental Health Concepts
Day 2	Client Care Assignments	Day 12	Health Promotion/ Disease Prevention	Day 22	Support Systems
Day 3	Confidentiality/ Information Security	Day 13	Health Screening	Day 23	Practice Questions
Day 4	Establishing Priorities	Day 14	High Risk Behaviors	Day 24	Assistive Devices
Day 5	Ergonomic Principles	Day 15	Lifestyle Choices	Day 25	Mobility/Immobility
Day 6	Safe Use of Equipment	Day 16	Self-Care	Day 26	Medication Administration
Day 7	Security Plan	Day 17	Practice Questions	Day 27	Diagnostic Tests
Day 8	Practice Questions	Day 18	Behavioral Interventions	Day 28	Basic Pathophysiology
Day 9	Community Resources	Day 19	Coping Mechanisms	Day 29	Practice Questions
Day 10	Data Collection Techniques	Day 20	Crisis Intervention	Day 30	Take Your Exam!

Safe and Effective Care Environment

Coordinated Care

Advance Directives

Advance directives, such as a **living will** or **durable power of attorney**, are forms that state a patient's choices for treatment, including refusal of treatments, life support, and stopping treatments when the patient chooses. **Do not resuscitate (DNR) status**, and its varying types, is also included in advance directives. The preoperative interview should include discussion of advance directives and DNR status. If the patient has advance directives, a copy should be placed in the medical record, and they should be reviewed by the nurse and physician. If the patient has a code status of anything other than full resuscitation, a conversation among the surgeon, anesthesiologist, and patient is necessary to discuss the patient's wishes in detail.

Older schools of thinking suggest all patients, regardless of preoperative DNR status, are considered full code while in the operating room; however, this is not true. A patient with DNR status of no intubation and no CPR may proceed with the surgical procedure if the surgeon and anesthesiologist have a conversation with the patient and a plan is agreed upon among them. Consent must be obtained by the patient if there is a change in status or a suspension of the DNR order during surgery. However, if the patient wishes to keep DNR status of no intubation and no CPR during surgery, the surgeon and/or anesthesiologist may deem the patient a nonsurgical candidate. If a patient is entering surgery with a DNR order of anything other than full code, this must be communicated to the entire surgical team and documented in the medical record. **Healthcare power of attorney** is the legal term for the person appointed by the patient to make their healthcare decisions should they become incapacitated.

Reviewing Client Understanding of Advance Directives
The role of an LPN/VN in Coordinated Care is to work in tandem with the entire health care team to make sure that the needs and choices of each patient are effectively shared and communicated across the participating departments. This involves reviewing advance directives with the patient and ensuring they understand what these directives entail. These are guideline documents utilized for instituting or continuing medical care and are a U.S. healthcare facility requirement as per The Patient Self-Determination Act of 1990. Many of the subjects they cover are delicate in nature, such as death-related legal and/or ethical matters, euthanasia, DNR (do not resuscitate) orders, organ donation, the bill or rights of a dying person, the living will of the patient, and giving over the power of attorney to a trusted person (durable power of attorney). As a result, the utmost care and empathy should be followed.

Making a note of any questions the patient asks regarding the concept of advance directives is a good way to assess their understanding of the process. For example, if a patient asks whether they are allowed to alter their directive, this raises a red flag to the nurse that they don't fully understand the process. If the patient doesn't offer any feedback voluntarily, asking them what they know about the process is a good way to determine their level of knowledge.

Advocacy

The American Nurses Association (ANA) provides this definition of nursing practice:

> The protection, promotion, and optimization of health and abilities, prevention of illness and injury, alleviation of suffering through the diagnosis and treatment of human response, and advocacy in the care of individuals, families, communities, and populations.

The ANA also addresses the importance of advocacy in its Code of Ethics, specifically in Provision 3:

> The nurse promotes, advocates for, and protects the rights, health, and safety of the patient.

The ANA Code of Ethics further states that nurses must advocate:

> with compassion and respect for the inherent dignity, worth, and uniqueness of every individual, unrestricted by considerations of social or economic status, personal attributes, or the nature of health problems.

Advocacy is a key component of nursing practice. An **advocate** is one who pleads the cause of another; and the nurse is an advocate for patient rights. Preserving human dignity, patient equality, and freedom from suffering are the basis of nursing advocacy. Nurses are in a unique position that allows them to integrate all aspects of patient care, ensuring that concerns are addressed, standards are upheld, and positive outcomes remain the goal. An experienced nurse helps patients navigate the unfamiliar system and communicate with their physicians. Nurses educate the patient about tests and procedures and are aware of how culture and ethnicity affect the patient's experience. Nurses strictly adhere to all privacy laws.

Advocacy is the promotion of the common good, especially as it applies to at-risk populations. It involves speaking out in support of policies and decisions that affect the lives of individuals who do not otherwise have a voice. Nurses meet this standard of practice by actively participating in the politics of healthcare accessibility and delivery because they are educationally and professionally prepared to evaluate and comment on the needs of patients at the local, state, and national level. This participation requires an understanding of the legislative process, the ability to negotiate with public officials, and a willingness to provide expert testimony in support of policy decisions. The advocacy role of nurses addresses the needs of the individual patient as well as the needs of all individuals in the society, and the members of the nursing profession.

In clinical practice, nurses represent the patient's interests by active participation in the development of the plan of care and subsequent care decisions. Advocacy, in this sense, is related to patient autonomy and the patient's right to informed consent and self-determination. Nurses provide the appropriate information, assess the patient's comprehension of the implications of the care decisions, and act as patient advocates by supporting the patient's decisions. In the critical care environment, patient advocacy requires the nurse to represent the patient's decisions even though those decisions may be opposed to those of the healthcare providers and family members.

Professionally, nurses advocate for policies that support and promote the practice of all nurses with regard to access to education, role identity, workplace conditions, and compensation. The responsibility for professional advocacy requires nurses to provide leadership in the development of the professional nursing role in all practice settings that may include acute care facilities, colleges and universities, or community agencies. Leadership roles in acute care settings involve participation in professional

practice and shared governance committees, providing support for basic nursing education by facilitating clinical and preceptorship experiences, and mentoring novice graduate nurses to the professional nursing role. In the academic setting, nurses work to ensure the diversity of the student population by participating in the governance structure of the institution, conducting and publishing research that supports the positive impact of professional nursing care on patient outcomes, and serving as an advocate to individual nursing students to promote their academic success. In the community, nurses assist other nurse-providers to collaborate with government officials to meet the needs that are specific to that location.

The nurse must function as a moral agent. This means that the nurse must be morally accountable and responsible for personal judgment and actions. Nurses who practice with moral integrity possess a strong sense of themselves and act in ways consistent with what they understand is the right thing to do. **Moral agency** is defined as the ability to identify right and wrong actions based on widely accepted moral criteria. The performance of nurses as moral agents is dependent on life experiences, advanced education, and clinical experience in healthcare agencies. Moral agency involves risk. It is an action that can be at odds with the traditional role of the nurse. As nurses assume more responsibility and accountability for client management and outcomes, it is essential to approach ethical dilemmas in a manner consistent with the caring component of nursing.

The role of moral agent requires nurses to have a strong sense of self and a clear understanding of the definition of right and wrong; however, nurses must also be aware that these perceptions of right and wrong will be challenged every day. In reality, nurses who act as the moral agents and are accountable for right and wrong decisions commonly encounter situations where the correct and moral action related to the patient's right to self-determination is opposed to the right and moral action with respect to competent patient care.

Client Care Assignments

Every day when the nurse reports to duty, a team of patients will be assigned to them. A caseload of patients will vary in size based on the acuity of the patients' illnesses and the unit policies that the nurse belongs to.

Acuity refers to the severity of the patient's illness. Some patients are high acuity, meaning a lot of time and resources are put into their daily routine due to the severity of their illness. Others are low acuity and do not require much oversight from the nurse to get through the day. High-acuity patients might be more difficult for many nurses because their care can often take away from the care of others. A team full of high-acuity patients, then, can be a great burden for a nurse to bear.

When patient assignments become too burdensome for nurses, those nursing-sensitive indicators are the first signs that there is a problem. When the nurse is busy with a team of high-acuity patients, it is difficult to perform all the tasks of the day, let alone perform them carefully and thoughtfully. It is then in the best interest of those making team assignments for nurses to weigh carefully the patient load and ensure equitable and fair decisions are made.

Dividing up teams of patients is often the task of the charge nurse. To fairly assign patient teams to nurses, the charge nurse must bear in mind each patient's acuity. Conflict arises when nurses feel that there is inequity in the assignment of patients and they are unduly burdened with an unfair patient load compared to other teams or units.

Nurse satisfaction directly correlates with patient care. If nurses do not feel their patient assignments are fair and the burden is too great, their performance suffers as well as their job satisfaction. Nursing performance can be linked to the following nurse-sensitive indicators: how well patient pain is managed; the presence and treatment of pressure ulcers, patient falls, and medication errors; patient satisfaction; and nosocomial or hospital-acquired infections.

Nursing staff take on many responsibilities that can be delegated to other clinical and non-clinical colleagues. However, learning how to effectively and safely delegate tasks, while still making patients feel cared for, is a skill that can take time to develop. It requires knowing not only what the needs of the patient are, but also the strengths and weaknesses of assistive personnel and how to best communicate professional needs with them. It also requires personal development in becoming comfortable with outsourcing responsibilities, as the nurse who delegates still remains accountable for the patient.

Assistive personnel may be supervised by nurses, but clinical assistive staff can provide basic medical assistance such as monitoring patients' vital signs, assisting with caretaking duties, monitoring any abnormalities or changes in the patient, maintaining a sterile and safe environment, and any other request made directly by nursing staff. Non-clinical assistive personnel, such as front desk staff, can assist with patient communication (such as wait times), managing paperwork and ensuring it is complete, and performing any other administrative task that may support the nursing staff's cases.

When nursing staff choose to delegate tasks, they may feel worried about risking their own accountability or work ethic. However, relating with assistive personnel, understanding their strengths and weaknesses, understanding their interests, and remaining transparent about the needs that are present in the department can ensure that delegated tasks are a good fit for the person who is taking the responsibility. In this regard, nursing staff take on a leadership and managerial role that requires developing their problem-solving, time management, and interpersonal skills. Some effective tools for delegation can include standardized checklists that cover the procedure that is being delegated, formal and informal meetings about assistive personnel's comfort levels and interests in performing certain tasks, and matching professional needs with individual qualifications. When delegation is effective, it can help the entire department work in a more efficient manner. Additionally, both nursing staff and assistive personnel are more likely to feel like part of a cohesive team and less likely to feel overworked or undervalued.

Client Rights

Each patient has certain rights that must be respected. When patients are admitted to a facility, they are put in a position of vulnerability. This special position of power held by the health care provider should never be abused to violate the rights of the patient. Caring for a patient is an honor, and certain rules of conduct should be followed.

The patient has the right to have health information kept private and only shared with those who are given permission to view it. The **Health Insurance Portability and Accountability Act (HIPAA)** was passed by Congress in 1996 to protect health information. The term HIPAA is often used to reference patient privacy. There are many different ways a patient's personal health information can be shared: verbally, digitally, over the phone or fax, or through written messages.

Along with protecting the patient's health information, the nurse must be respectful of the patient's privacy in general. Knocking on the patient's door before entering the room, keeping the door shut to the busy corridor outside the room, and not asking unnecessary personal questions are all ways the

nurse can extend common courtesy to the patient. The nature of the nurse's relationship with the patient is already quite personal in nature, so there is no need to exploit that relationship.

Each patient has the right to fair treatment. This means that no patient should be treated any better or worse than another patient for any reason, such as a racial bias or unfair prejudice based on the nurse's personal opinions and beliefs. Giving one patient preferential treatment over another is a violation of the patient's rights, and the nurse will be subject to disciplinary action if they are discovered to be treating patients poorly.

No patient should ever be abused or neglected. This should go without saying, but it is a patient right that is perhaps the most important. Abuse can be physical, emotional, sexual, mental, or financial. Neglect is when the patient's needs are being ignored, usually resulting in patient harm.

The patient has the **right of self-determination**, which means that they have the right to make decisions regarding their own health care. Patients are members of the healthcare team along with the doctors and nurses. What the nurse may think is the right course of action for a patient may not align with what the patient thinks is right, and that is to be respected. The healthcare team forms the plan of care and educates the patient as to what a plan entails, but it is the patient who makes the final decision to accept or reject a plan. If the patient is not capable of making their own decisions, the **power of attorney**—usually a close family member such as a wife, husband, or adult child—has the power to make healthcare decisions for the patient.

Along with self-determination, the patients also have the freedom to express themselves and their opinions. Simply being admitted to a facility does not take away their freedom of speech. Patients may have opinions about all aspects of their care, and they have every right to express these feelings. The nurse needs to be respectful, listen, and try to help when there is a problem that can be solved. Issues voiced by patients can always be escalated by the nurse, using the appropriate chain of command.

If the nurse suspects abuse or neglect, they are mandatorily required to report it to the appropriate entity. The charge nurse and/or nurse manager should be notified, so the appropriate action can be taken to right the situation. There are also hotlines that can be called, such as the National Center on Elder Abuse (1-800-677-1116).

There are different types of abuse. **Physical abuse** involves injuries to the body from punching, kicking, etc. If the nurse notes various bruises or cuts in various stages of healing without explanation, it may be a sign of physical abuse.

Sexual abuse is when sexual contact is made without the consent of one party, including rape, coercion into doing sexual acts, and fondling of genitalia. The nurse should look for unexplained bruising of or bleeding around the perineal area, new difficulty sitting or walking, or increased agitation/aggression as potential signs of sexual abuse.

Emotional abuse and **mental abuse** are not quite as obvious as physical abuse, as the damage inflicted is internal or hidden. Emotional and mental abuses are usually caused by verbal assaults. The abuser may belittle and criticize the victim to the point that the victim feels worthless, insecure, and afraid. If the nurse senses an uncomfortable relationship between an informal caregiver or family member and the patient, this should be monitored, investigated, and reported if abuse is suspected.

Financial abuse is a type of abuse in which the abuser limits the victim's access to money and financial information, sometimes stealing directly from the victim without the victim's knowledge. Being the caregiver of an older person grants a person special access to personal documents and financial resources; this privilege can be abused. If the nurse suspects that checks and other financial means meant for the patient are being rerouted and misused by a caregiver, this abuse should be reported right away.

It is the patient's right to deny treatment. Patients can deny treatment if fully informed of their medical condition and the likely outcomes resulting from the refusal. This is known as the right to informed consent. They may decide to refuse treatment because of a number of reasons, including religious or cultural beliefs, fear of the procedure or its side effects, they feel it is not necessary, or they simply do not want to do it. This right can be legally challenged if overwhelming reasons are determined to necessitate overriding the wishes of the patient, such as the endangerment of another person's life, a situation where a parent's decision threatens the life of a child, a patient stating whether they want to live, and the best interest of the public takes precedence over the patient's right. The LPN/VN needs to be able to contribute to a modified plan of care that includes these possibilities.

Collaboration with Interdisciplinary Team

Interdisciplinary rounding can provide an opportunity for team collaboration after a patient's surgery. Much like a clear hand-off process, interdisciplinary rounds reduce patient care errors, decrease mortality rates, and improve patient outcomes. Interdisciplinary rounds are an excellent place to discuss social service needs, nutritional care services, and transportation needs with all teams coordinating care for the patient in a single setting.

The patient's service needs may vary in depth for the inpatient stay and at the time of discharge; however, there should be an evaluation of these needs and a coordination of care for those services in which there is a need. Nurses document the action plan as it relates to services and requirements for the patient and collaborate with members of the interdisciplinary team to see that next steps are executed in a timely fashion. In many instances, rounding may not be possible due to the rapid pace and turnover of the medical environment, and thus, clear documentation will be an absolute must to allow for synchronous care coordination.

Nurses, physicians, surgeons, nurse aids, physical and occupational therapists, mental health professionals, and medical assistants are just some of the members who may be collaborating on the care of one patient. Perception of power between these professionals can sometimes create a stressful environment that can also affect patient outcomes. The ability of each one to collaborate with the other is imperative so that patient safety does not become an issue. Collaboration involves joint decision-making activities between both disciplines rather than nurses only following physician orders. Although each role may have a particular focus throughout the assessment and plan of care activities, they must jointly come together to formulate the best possible treatment plan throughout the treatment period. Studies show that an attentive communication style between nurses and physicians has the most positive impact on patients.

Ongoing education of physicians and nurses may be a necessity to support a collaborative environment. In addition to continuing education and in-services, job shadowing, which exposes both the nurse and physician to each one's role, can assist in promoting understanding and teamwork.

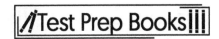

Concepts of Management and Supervision

Delegation

Nursing staff take on many responsibilities that can be delegated to other clinical and non-clinical colleagues. However, learning how to **safely delegate tasks**, while still making patients feel cared for, is a skill that can take time to develop. It requires knowing not only what the needs of the patient are, but also the strengths and weaknesses of assistive personnel and how to best communicate professional needs with them. It also requires personal development in becoming comfortable with outsourcing responsibilities, as the nurse who delegates still remains accountable for the patient.

Assistive personnel may be supervised by nurses, but clinical assistive staff can provide basic medical assistance such as monitoring patients' vital signs, assisting with caretaking duties, monitoring any abnormalities or changes in the patient, maintaining a sterile and safe environment, and any other request made directly by nursing staff. Non-clinical assistive personnel, such as front desk staff, can assist with patient communication (such as wait times), managing paperwork and ensuring it is complete, and performing any other administrative task that may support the nursing staff's cases.

When nursing staff choose to delegate tasks, they may feel worried about risking their own accountability or work ethic. However, relating with assistive personnel, understanding their strengths and weaknesses, understanding their interests, and remaining transparent about the needs that are present in the department can ensure that delegated tasks are a good fit for the person who is taking the responsibility. In this regard, nursing staff take on a leadership and managerial role that requires developing their problem-solving, time management, and interpersonal skills. Some effective tools for delegation can include standardized checklists that cover the procedure that is being delegated, formal and informal meetings about assistive personnel's comfort levels and interests in performing certain tasks, and matching professional needs with individual qualifications. When delegation is effective, it can help the entire department work in a more efficient manner. Additionally, both nursing staff and assistive personnel are more likely to feel like part of a cohesive team and less likely to feel overworked or undervalued.

Supervision

After the nurse has successfully and effectively delegated a task, the nurse then takes on the role of supervisor of the person to whom they delegated the task. Delegation requires **supervision**, to ensure the task is done appropriately and to protect the nurse's own licensure.

The key to supervision is the **follow-up**. After the task is delegated, the nurse must then make a note to investigate whether the task was done, whether it was done in a timely manner, and whether it was done correctly. Asking the person who was supposed to perform the task to report back is appropriate. All conversations and interactions must be performed professionally and with respect for both the inferior and superior party.

Many nurses were once **certified nursing assistants (CNAs)** and understand the role and responsibility of the person they now delegate to. If the two nurses were former co-workers and one has risen to the role of nurse from CNA, tensions may arise. Tensions that arise between nursing staff and those they delegate to may be resolved through careful interactions in which each party is respected and an effort made by both parties that shows they are both working hard together with the best interest of the patient at the forefront of their mind.

At times, it may be necessary for the nurse to coach and support the staff member, giving tips for better performance where appropriate. Again, this interaction must be done with professionalism and respect. It is important as an employee in any field to be receptive to constructive criticism, as well as being able to offer it when appropriate and allowing plenty of discussion on the point.

The nurse must ensure that the task delegated, such as taking vital signs or cleaning up an incontinent patient, has been appropriately documented. Documentation is necessary for legal reasons, to show that proper care was given to the patient. If the person to whom the task was delegated did not document the task, it is necessary for the nurse to confront them directly and confirm that it was done.

Recognizing and Reporting Staff Conflict

Staff conflict occurs when people have differing views or thoughts on something. Conflict on the job can be disturbing and anxiety-provoking. However, it is an inevitable part of working as a team. Recognizing and reporting it involves the following steps:

- Defining the conflict: Conflicts occur when two or more people have differing attitudes or viewpoints. Conflict can actually be helpful when it is resolved in a healthy manner, equally fulfilling to both parties, so that they both get closure.

- Evaluating the various factors that can provoke conflict: Arguments, a lack of trust, workflow disruptions, impaired interpersonal relationships, criticism of others, and frustration are examples of issues that can incite conflict.

- Recognizing the variations of personality types: It is imperative to embrace the various ways team members think and feel and how these diverse factors will affect the outcome of the conflict.

- Distinguishing types of communication: Team members can display a wide range of communicative techniques/methods during any type of interaction, but conflict can cause people to behave in varying ways, such as becoming guarded or aggressive. It is important for team members to be aware of this possibility.

- Considering the various ways to resolve team conflict: These can include the following methods:

  - Collaboration and Open Communication: Working together and maintaining an open exchange between team members helps to cultivate relationships among group members and encourages the conflicting parties to actively participate in the resolution, thus fostering a more in-depth understanding of the dispute.

  - Compromise and Negotiation: Maintaining a level playing field encourages both parties to remain confident but not belligerent, promoting equality between team members. Discussing the issue rationally allows team members to focus on common goals and interests rather than individual parties and their diverse opinions, allowing the conflicting parties to separate themselves from the conflict and the issue at hand.

  - Mediation: Sometimes one-on-one communication with each team member is required in order to discern each person's concerns, beliefs, and opinions. Once this occurs, the team can investigate resolving the conflict via methods that are satisfactory to all involved.

- Making a list of the six stages of team conflict resolution:

    o 1. Clarifying the disagreement and making sure both sides agree on the topic of the issue.

    o 2. Establishing a common goal agreed upon by those involved in the conflict.

    o 3. Discussing the various techniques the team can use to gain a common understanding.

    o 4. Defining the issues that are in the way of reaching the common goal.

    o 5. Coming to an agreement regarding the best way(s) to resolve the conflict.

    o 6. Agreeing upon a solution and deciding the responsibilities of each member.

- Acknowledging personal reactions of team members: Every team member may have a totally different response to conflict and how it is being handled by the team. These include being evasive, dominating, accommodating, collaborative, or cooperative.

- Choosing useful conflict resolution techniques: When a conflict arises, it is important to be aware of the fact that team members will have varying principles and priorities on how to settle it. Therefore, selecting the best technique for resolving conflict will depend on each situation and those involved.

- Recognize the benefits and drawbacks of team conflict-resolution strategies: This includes dealing with the issue, thinking it through, discussing it in person, using a mediator, apologizing when needed, and communicating clearly and effectively.

- Be aware of situations that typically require employee disciplinary action: Since conflict can disrupt the workflow of the whole team and covers a wide range of behaviors, sometimes disciplinary action is required.

Confidentiality/Information Security

Patient privacy and confidentiality is a constant for all healthcare providers. Given the sensitivity of medical procedures, the healthcare team must maintain strict patient confidentiality. Under the **Health Insurance Portability and Accountability Act (HIPAA)**, a patient's information is required to be protected and kept confidential regardless of the form, including electronic, written, and spoken communication. **Protected health information (PHI)** should be shared only on an as-needed and minimum necessary basis. When discussing patients or cases in settings where other personnel may overhear the conversation, the medical team should be careful not to include any PHI that may violate the patient's confidentiality. Additionally, when information is displayed electronically to families and visitors in waiting rooms, patient names should be avoided. HIPAA violations can have negative consequences for the providers and/or the facility.

The nurse plays an important role in keeping a patient's health information private. Sharing personal details—such as a patient's name, condition, and medical history—in an inappropriate way violates the person's right to privacy. For example, a nurse telling a friend who does not work in the facility that the nurse took care of the friend's aunt, without the aunt's consent or knowledge, is considered a violation of privacy. Another way a nurse could violate a resident's privacy is to access the medical record when they are not actually caring for that particular patient. For example, if a celebrity has been admitted to a different unit, and the nursing assistant accesses the celebrity's electronic health record, then they are in violation of HIPAA. Those who violate HIPAA and are caught could lose their jobs, among other punitive actions. Nurses should also ensure that other staff members—such as nursing assistants—as well as patients understand the confidentiality requirements of the facility, state, and country.

Continuity of Care

If one imagines a patient's illness as a road, what would the ideal road look like? Smooth, no potholes, appropriate signage to guide and direct the patient from illness to wellness, right? In the real world of health care, the road the patient travels from illness to wellness often has bumps and miscommunications. Things do not go as planned, missteps are taken, unexpected events and miscalculations can and unfortunately do occur.

All members of the healthcare team should be striving to provide patients with a high quality of care over time, or **continuity of care**. The patient begins their journey with an illness, at a doctor's office, convenient care clinic, or an emergency room. From there, the road proceeds through various tests and procedures to diagnose and treat the illness. Management teams that include doctors and nurses provide input into this process, and resources also contribute. The patient is at the center of the continuity of care model. In continuity of care, the whole patient is treated, not just an organ or an illness. Ideally, the community surrounding the patient is also involved in promoting good health and high quality of life.

The roots of continuity of care lie in a meaningful, long-term relationship between the patient and the healthcare provider. This relationship ensures that the patient is known. Their needs are anticipated through regular check-ups and follow-ups after the illness has run its course. The ideal is to form a firm bond of trust between the healthcare provider and the patient. This trusting relationship and deep knowledge of the case allow the provider to better advocate for the patient.

The physician or nurse practitioner coordinating care for the patient will look for ways to make the plan of care cost-effective for the patient. Tests and procedures are carefully weighed for their usefulness in the patient's case, looking for ways to eliminate wasteful healthcare spending.

The main idea behind continuity of care is to avoid what happens all too often in healthcare: fragmentation of care. The responsibility of the patient's case is often shifted from one entity to another over the course of an illness. Initially, the patient's case is handled in a primary care setting or perhaps an emergent care setting, depending on the illness. Then the patient may become hospitalized, at which point the hospitalist and various specialists step in and take over. At discharge, the patient's case is then handed over to their primary care physician and community centers. Due to this shifting of care, it becomes ambiguous just who is overseeing the patient's care. The patient has a fragmented experience rather than continuity of care.

One issue faced by healthcare providers is not having the infrastructure to effectively coordinate patient care and avoid the problems associated with fragmented care. A case manager comes into play here because their role is perfect for coordinating the patients' care as they move through the system.

Primary care physicians face a hurdle when coordinating patient care because they have limited communication with the hospital team when their patient is admitted. Nowadays, there is a team of healthcare providers called **hospitalists**, whose job it is to care for patients while they are in the hospital, but not pre- or post-admission. This is helpful because they know the ins and outs of the facility

and have good communication with the hospital's specialists and surgeons. They can all work together to get the patient in and out of the hospital relatively quickly.

A **patient-centered medical home (PCMH)** comes into play pre-admission to prevent a costly hospital visit. The idea of a PCMH is to combat fragmentation of care and promote better continuity of care for the patient on their road to wellness. The PCMH is a model of care that is well-coordinated, proactive, and centered on the patient. In this model, a patient is paired with a personal physician to oversee their care. Their family and loved ones are recruited to assist in promoting a whole patient-focused wellness plan. The PCMH moves away from fee for service; instead, it focuses on fee for value, meaning the level of success in keeping the patient healthy determines how the healthcare team is reimbursed. The patient must regularly keep in touch with their primary care physician, a factor that has been associated with better patient outcomes.

Many communities are adopting the PCMH model of healthcare, attempting to promote a better continuity of care for patients on their road from illness to wellness.

Nurses are aware that the patient often requires continued reinforcement of the educational plan after discharge, which necessitates coordination with home care services. As facilitators of learning, nurses may be involved in a large-scale effort to educate all patients. The first step of any teaching-learning initiative is the assessment of the learning needs of the participants. Specific needs that influence the design and content of the educational offering include the language preference and reading level of the participants. Nurses must also consider the effect of certain patient characteristics identified in the Synergy Model on the patient's capacity to process information. Diminished resiliency or stability, and extreme complexity, must be considered in the development of the educational plan. Nurses are also responsible for creating a bridge between teaching-learning in the acute care setting and the home environment. A detailed discharge plan, close coordination with outpatient providers, and follow-up phone calls to the patient may be used to reinforce the patient's knowledge of the plan of care.

Establishing Priorities

The ability to **establish priorities** is one of the nurse's most important skills. The nurse must be able to look at their patient load for the day, assess the needs of each patient, organize tasks in chronological order, and prioritize each task based on its importance and necessity.

When prioritizing the tasks for the day, the nurse must first employ their knowledge of the body, how it works, and what it needs to function. The nurse starts with ABC: airway, breathing, and circulation. Are any patients compromised in these respects? If so, they are immediately placed at the top of the list of priorities. If the patient cannot breathe, is hemorrhaging, or heart has stopped beating, they require the nurse's immediate assistance. The **ABCs** are considered the first priority of patient needs.

Emergency Trauma Assessment
- A: Airway
- B: Breathing
- C: Circulation
- D: Disability
- E: Examine
- F: Fahrenheit
- G: Get Vitals

- H: Head to Toe Assessment
- I: Intervention

After the ABC patient needs are taken care of, the nurse can move down the scale to the next priority. A helpful acronym to remember is **M-A-A-U-A-R**. These are considered second-priority needs.

- M is for mental status changes and alterations
- A is for acute pain
- A is for acute urinary elimination concerns
- U is for unaddressed and untreated problems requiring immediate attention
- A is for abnormal laboratory/diagnostic data outside of normal limits
- R is for risks that include those involving a healthcare problem such as safety, skin integrity, infection, and other medical conditions

Along with the ABC-MAAUAR methods of prioritization, the nurse may also utilize **Maslow's hierarchy of needs**. Maslow argues that physiological needs such as hunger, thirst, and breathing are among the first that have to be met. The same goes for patients. For example, a patient in pain needs to be addressed before a patient who needs education on a procedure that is to happen tomorrow.

After the basic physiological needs have been met, the nurse knows that on the next level of the pyramid are safety and psychological needs. Mental health fits on this tier of the hierarchy and is a crucial step toward wellness. Love and belonging follow; for this part of care the nurse can enlist the help of social services and family members. The next level of Maslow's hierarchy is "self-esteem and esteem by others." In nursing terms, this level represents the patient's need to feel they are a respected and esteemed member of the care team. The final level of Maslow's hierarchy is self-actualization, in which a person reaches their fullest potential and highest level of ability. The nurse does everything they can to help the client reach this level, pushing them to do their best and be their best at all points in the care journey.

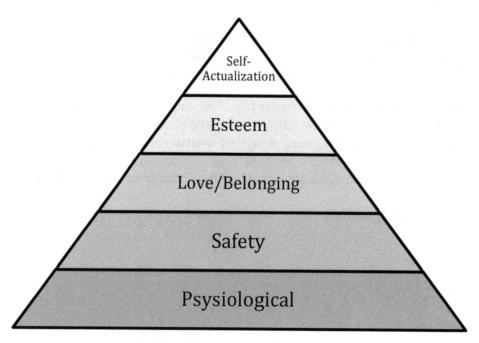

Recognizing the patient's needs and establishing priorities based on Maslow's hierarchy, the nurse can then move on to the next step of the process: after goal-setting and client care delivery comes the evaluation stage. The nurse must be continually evaluating the plan of care for each patient. The plan may need tweaking and revision throughout the day, based on how the patient responds to interventions. Quality evaluation of interventions ensures needs are being met and proper care is being delivered.

Sound nursing judgment will guide the nurse as they endeavor to prioritize and adequately meet the needs of their patients in a timely manner.

Time Management and Work Prioritization

One of the most important skills a nurse must master in the busy healthcare environment is that of time management and prioritization of tasks. The work day is filled with tasks, scheduled activities, unexpected time conflicts, and constant interruptions.

As best as the nurse can, they should have a way of planning the day. Some find it best to have some sort of written system to take notes and jot down vitals in between charting periods. Meal times can be the busiest times of day, so it should be accounted for in planning.

Countless interruptions will occur throughout the day, such as a call light going off when the nurse was planning to start a bath or a patient needing assistance to the bathroom when the nurse was planning on taking a break. It is vital that the nurse prioritizes tasks and make sure the most important tasks get done in a timely manner. It is easy to put off tasks for later that really should be done immediately, but that sort of procrastination can have adverse results. The day will be busy; that is a given. Developing one's time management and prioritization skills will help the day go a lot more smoothly.

Ethical Practice

Healthcare providers routinely face situations with patients where they must analyze various moral and ethical considerations. In the emergency department, where quick judgment and action is necessary to care and where patients are often not fully sound in body or mind, ethical dilemmas can arise without much time to process resolutions.

Nurses are held to the American Nurses Association's Code of Ethics, which states moral and ethical guidelines that nurses should incorporate into their practice. Above all else, nurses have the responsibility to do no harm while advocating for, promoting good health outcomes for, minimizing injury to, and protecting the overall health and functioning of their patients. It is important to consider the patient holistically when applying these values, such as considering what the patient may view as a good quality of life, what family values the patient holds, other family members that may be affected, legal considerations, and logistical considerations, such as how much time and medical resources are available. When patients are unable to make decisions autonomously, or even to indicate consent to treatment, nurses should act from these responsibilities to make wise and compassionate decisions on the patients' behalf.

Dilemmas that can arise for nursing staff include situations where the patient may have cultural or personal beliefs that prevent lifesaving treatment. For example, a female emergency patient may not want to be treated by any male staff, or a patient that needs a blood transfusion may not accept this procedure due to religious beliefs. In cases where the patient is able to directly communicate their wishes, the nurse may need to defer to the patient's wishes in order to preserve the patient's autonomy. This may mean providing alternative means of care, such as finding available female medical providers to assist with the female patient who does not want to be treated by male staff. It may mean withholding treatment that the patient refuses. If the patient's life is in question and rapid medical action is necessary to save the patient's life, nursing staff may need to intervene even if it is against the patient's wishes. Ethical considerations like these will vary by case and patient, and will depend on the severity of the case, the medical and personal history of the patient, and the judgment of the nurse in question. In all cases, it is ideal if the nurse and patient are able to communicate openly with each other about the case and potential medical options.

Informed Consent

Before a major medical procedure can be performed, the patient's consent must be obtained. Obtaining this consent requires educating the patient on what the procedure is, how it is performed, what types of outcomes are to be expected, and most importantly, why the procedure will be done. This process of educating the patient and getting their permission is called **informed consent**.

There are two key aspects of the term informed consent. The term "informed" implies that the patient has been given information pertaining to the procedure. This requires a conversation between the patient and their health care provider. Education must be provided to ensure that the patient has been given information about the procedure to be done as well as time to consider their options. If a patient signs a consent without having a proper understanding and comprehension of what's to be done, it is not a true informed consent.

The second part of the term is "consent." This means that the patient agrees with the plan and gives their permission for what is going to be done. Without consent, it is illegal or improper to perform certain healthcare procedures.

Consent can be given through three different avenues: implied, verbal, and written. In **implied consent**, the patient has given the health care worker permission to perform interventions on them without writing it down or saying it. This can get into a gray area on some issues, but for the most part, it's agreed upon care that is needed. For example, let's say a patient drops to the floor in full cardiac arrest. They are unresponsive. A nurse witnesses the fall and begins cardiopulmonary resuscitation (CPR) and activates the emergency response system. The patient did not say they agreed to have CPR done on them nor did they sign a document agreeing to the procedure, but it is assumed that the patient is complicit. This is due to the patient's being in danger of death and in need of swift action. On a much smaller scale, a patient coming into a doctor's office does not sign a document of consent to have their vital signs taken, yet they willingly comply with having their blood pressure taken. All parties present assume and agree upon certain procedures and thus no formal consent is required.

Verbal consent is obtained by having the patient saying something along the lines of "Yes, it is okay to do this." This is the in-between consent, slightly more formal than implied consent and less formal than the signed legal document that is informed consent.

Written consent involves a formal conversation between the health care provider, the physician performing the procedure, and the patient. It is vital that the patient is adequately educated on the procedure and has a full understanding before consenting. Obtaining consent without proper patient education is fraudulent and poor practice. Not properly informing the patient may lead to legal trouble down the road for both the nurse and the physician, not to mention potential complications following

the procedure. Above all, it is a violation of a patient's rights to not be properly informed before giving consent.

While the physician is legally responsible for satisfying all elements of informed consent, nurses are ethically responsible for assessing the patient's ability to process and understand the implications of informed consent. Nurses should ensure that the patient understands the purpose of a procedure and any possible risks, whether the physician or the nurse themselves explained the information to the patient. The nurse should also be sure the appropriate person to provide informed consent for the patient has been identified and understands the procedure. This may be the patient, his or her legal guardian, parent, etc. Nurses protect the patient's autonomy by raising these questions and concerns.

Information Technology

Information technology (IT) is a field of nursing that continues to evolve with the rest of healthcare. Nurses must not only understand the science that is associated with nursing, but they must also be able to navigate various forms of technology. While there are nurses still in the workplace who can recall what it was like to physically fill out forms and track vitals on paper, there are also nurses who have no concept of having documented their activities in these systems. All nurses must be able to function within today's technologically advanced world.

IT is important for many reasons including:

- Cost savings/reduction of costs
- Need to decrease or eliminate medication errors
- Improving documentation efficiency by removing paper charting
- Enhancing accessibility to quality health care

Medical technology needs to be fully integrated with a larger system within an institution to support the continuum of patient care. This connection provides information sharing throughout each stage of the treatment period and eventually allows for the collection of statistical data at a later date.

Next, medical technology has to support the user's ability to navigate without difficulty. The goal here is to not slow down the pace of the medical environment but allow for increasing efficiency so that technology is seamless. These qualities then allow for real-time data and real-time decision-making capabilities while reducing the risk of errors or redundancy.

There are a few gaps that remain on the IT front of the medical environment that have their roots in the **computerized physician order entry (CPOE)** arena. In some instances, CPOE software is not able to meet the needs of various interdisciplinary roles in the OR. The reason for this is that it tends to favor the inpatient setting.

Health Care Information Technology

Health care IT (HIT) has characteristics that are steeped in supporting broad processes or functions.

HIT is software that can perform operations associated with:

- Admissions
- Scheduling
- Clinical documentation
- Pharmacy

- Laboratory
- Clinical Information Technology

Clinical IT (CIT) concentrates on a particular set of clinical tasks, instruments, equipment, and imaging.

Radio Frequency Identification

Radio frequency identification (RFID) provides support for real-time surgery scheduling. This technology has been shown to drastically enhance the structure and functions within medical software. RFID functions on wireless networks and helps to "tag" items and track the movement of the items as they remain on or leave a particular unit. This may be especially important when tracking equipment or supplies that are used to care for the patient or during a surgical procedure.

Nurses will need to stay current with IT trends and engage in ongoing education and exposure to technology. Continuing education and training can be accomplished through independent reading, e-learning, and live classroom instruction.

Finally, nurses may encounter a broad range of technologies including:

- Robots
- Medication delivery devices
- Instruments
- Biotechnology and nanotechnology
- Digital tracking
- Mobile and wireless devices
- Nurses and Informatics

Nurses may assist in the development of standards for EHR (electronic health record) or other clinically based IT systems that nurses utilize for their sphere of health care. In today's landscape, many nursing applications fall into a variety of categories including:

- Internet-based patient education systems
- EHR
- Telemedicine and telenursing

These systems have the capacity to exchange information and enable the decision-making process to progress along the continuum.

Some nurses possess a master's degree in informatics and also work in a variety of roles to assist with development of clinical systems designed to support nurse activities including:

- Business or clinical analyst
- Project management
- Software developer

These systems are designed to accommodate patient education resources, nursing procedures, and critical pathways, to name a few.

Nurses may also serve in the role of perioperative robotics nurse specialist. As robotic surgery utilization continues to evolve into standard practice, the robotics nurse specialist supports a variety of tasks ranging from scheduling maintenance to assisting during surgery.

Legal Responsibilities

The nurse must uphold and answer to certain legal rights and responsibilities within their profession. From simple things like managing a patient's property to more complicated issues such as reporting abuse and neglect, the nurse has a legal responsibility to act, or their license could be in danger.

Nurses need a knowledge of the common legal terminology in their practice. The following is a list of terms the nurse should know:

- **Common law**: Common law is based on legal precedents or previously decided cases in courts of law.

- **Statutory law**: These are laws based on a state's legislative actions or any other legislative body's actions.

- **Constitutional law**: Laws based on the content of the Constitution of the United States of America are referred to as constitutional law.

- **Administrative law**: For a nurse, this is a type of law passed down from a ruling body such as a state nursing association. For example, each state's nursing board passes down regulations on continuing education requirements for licensed nurses.

- **Criminal law**: This type of law involves the arrest, prosecution, and incarceration of those who have broken the law. Such offenses as felonies and misdemeanors are covered under criminal law.

- **Liability**: Nurses are liable for their actions while practicing. Thorough documentation and patient charting are important. If an act is not charted, it was not done, so to speak. Nurses must protect themselves legally to maintain their practice.

- **Tort**: In a nursing context, this legal term refers to nursing practice violations such as malpractice, negligence, and patient confidentiality violations.

- **Unintentional tort**: Negligence and malpractice may be unintentional forms of tort.

- **Intentional tort**: On the other hand, torts may be proven to be intentional, including such violations as false imprisonment, privacy breaches, slander, libel, battery, and assault. A nurse using a physical restraint without meeting protocol or getting a physician's order is guilty of false imprisonment. Slander is a form of defamation in which the person makes false statements that are verbal, and libel is written defamation.

A nurse is legally responsible for maintaining an active licensure according to their state's regulatory board's laws. Failure to maintain licensure requirements such as continuing education credits will result in disciplinary action. Nursing licenses may be revoked or suspended because of disciplinary actions.

Nurses must report abuse, neglect, gunshot wounds, dog bites, and communicable diseases. Nurses are also legally mandated to report other healthcare providers whom they suspect may be abusing drugs or alcohol while practicing, because they are putting patients and themselves at risk.

Nurses have a legal obligation to accept the patient assignments given to them, if they believe they are appropriate and it is within their scope of practice to perform duties related to these patients. However, if they are assigned tasks that they are not prepared to perform, they must notice their supervisors and seek assistance.

Laws at the national, state, and local level must be complied with by practicing nurses. Such laws include those in relation to the Centers for Medicare and Medicaid services. Another example would be adhering to local laws regarding the disposal of biohazardous waste.

Legal Reporting Obligations

Reporting patient information and work issues in a timely manner and using the correct route on the chain of command are a legal obligation of nurse. Not reporting important information could result in serious ramifications and punitive action for the nurse, up to loss of employment and/or revocation of certification. When important information goes unreported, it can result in patient harm or unresolved conflicts that turn into bigger problems to deal with later on. Addressing patient issues and resolving conflicts all start with accurate and timely reporting.

A basic definition of a **report** is the relaying of information that one has observed or heard. When this report is given to an authority figure who can intervene, it will contain different elements, such as patient name, situation, time of event, and circumstances surrounding the event.

As one shift ends and another begins, there is a **handoff report** that is given from the off-going team to the oncoming team. The nurse who has completed the shift will tell the nurse beginning the next shift all pertinent information related to each individual patient. Another type of reporting is the exchange of smaller pieces of information between members of the healthcare team that occurs throughout a shift.

In the handoff report, the nurse should strategically relay information in a simple, concise manner that is easily understood by the oncoming nurse. It can be easy to get carried away with reporting and include every little detail of the day, opinions about patients or other coworkers, and stories of particular conversations or interactions that occurred during the shift. These superfluous details should be limited, and the report should be kept to the essential items only.

Some organizations employ the **SBAR method** to help guide communication. SBAR is an acronym for situation, background, assessment, and recommendation. An SBAR report starts with the situation: why is this communication necessary? The background is a brief explanation of the circumstances leading up to the situation. The assessment is what the reporter thinks the issue is, and the recommendation is what the reporter needs in order to correct the situation.

In addition to reporting patient information, the documenting of patient information and interventions performed is also important. A patient's chart is a legal record of observations about the patient and any care given for the patient. Most facilities use an electronic health record, which the nurse will generally be trained to use as a part of new employee orientation. Documentation may include time of observation, time task was performed, what was done, how it was done, and reaction to intervention.

There are various charting systems used to document patient data by patient care facilities. Documentation requirements will be dictated by facility policy and regulatory guidelines. Two methods are used: charting by exception and comprehensive charting.

Charting by Exception

Charting by exception means that besides recording of vital signs, only abnormal findings are documented. This charting method is somewhat controversial as so much information about the patient is usually left out. It is sometimes argued that this is the safer way to chart, as only what is deviant from

normal is noted, and thus, there is less room for documentation errors. The normal is assumed, unless otherwise noted. This method also saves time, as less information needs to be documented, leaving more time for patient care.

Comprehensive Charting

Some facilities prefer a **comprehensive method** of documentation, charting everything about the patient—normal and abnormal—in a very thorough manner. This way, when the patient's chart must be reviewed, especially in the case of a safety incident (e.g., a pressure sore develops or a patient falls), all details surrounding the event should be present in the medical record. This method works as long as everything is actually documented, although it can be quite time-consuming and take away from patient care time.

Documentation provides a defense for healthcare workers and patients in the case of patient incidents to show what was done for the patient. There is an adage that says, "If it wasn't charted, it didn't happen." The nurse needs to be mindful that the medical record is a legal document—a complete, thorough, and accurate documentation of care, according to facility policy.

Performance Improvement

Performance improvement is a mechanism to continuously review and improve processes in a system to ensure that work is completed in the most cost-effective manner while producing the best possible outcomes. Healthcare facilities are constantly hoping to drive down cost and increase reimbursements while delivering the highest quality of healthcare and utilizing analytical methods to achieve this. These analyses and implementations may be done by top administrative employees at the organization and be executed across the healthcare system, or within a particular department. Leadership support is always crucial for positive change to occur and sustain itself.

All processes should be regularly monitored for opportunities for improvement. Common opportunities include areas of reported patient dissatisfaction; federal, state, or internal benchmarks that are not being met; areas of financial loss; and common complaints among staff. While multiple opportunities for improvement may exist, focusing on one at a time usually produces the greatest outcome. When choosing a process to improve, it is important to select a process that can actually be changed by the members involved (i.e., medical staff often do not have control over external funding sources). Processes where minimal resources are required for change, but that can produce positive end results, are also preferable to costlier improvements. Once the process has been selected, a group of stakeholders that are regularly involved in the process should map out each step of the process while noting areas of wasted resource or process variation. From here, stakeholders can develop a change to test.

The **PDCA cycle** provides a framework for implementing tests of change. Plan, the first step, involves planning the change. This will include accounting for all workflow changes, the staff members involved, and logistics of implementation. It should also include baseline data relating to the problem. Do, the second step, involves implementing the change. During this step, data collection is crucial. For example, if a department believes that implementing mobile work stations will decrease nurses' wait time between patients, the department should keep a detailed record of the time spent with and between each patient. Check, the third step, involves checking data relating to the change with the baseline data and determining if the change improved the process. Act, the final step, involves making the change permanent and monitoring it for sustainability.

Evidence-Based Practice

Evidence-based practice (EBP) is a research-driven and facts-based methodology that allows healthcare providers to make scientifically supported, reliable, and validated decisions in delivering care. EBP takes into account rigorously tested, peer-reviewed, and published research relating to the case; the knowledge and experience of the healthcare provider; and clinical guidelines established by reputable governing bodies. This framework allows healthcare providers to reach case resolutions that result in positive patient outcomes in the most efficient manner. This, in turn, allows the organization to provide the best care using the least resources.

There are seven steps to successfully utilizing EBP as a methodology in the nursing field. First, the work culture should be one of a "spirit of inquiry." This culture allows staff to ask questions to promote continuous improvement and positive process change to workflow, clinical routines, and non-clinical duties. Second, the PICOT framework should be utilized when searching for an effective intervention, or working with a specific interest, in a case. The **PICOT framework** encourages nurses to develop a specific, measurable, goal-oriented research question that accounts for the patient population and demographics (P) involved in the case, the proposed intervention or issue of interest (I), a relevant comparison (C) group in which a defined outcome (O) has been positive, and the amount of time (T) needed to implement the intervention or address the issue. Once this question has been developed, staff can move onto the third step, which is to research. In this step, staff will explore reputable sources of literature to find studies and narratives with evidence that supports a resolution for their question.

Once all research has been compiled, it must be thoroughly analyzed. This is the fourth step. This step ensures that the staff is using unbiased research with stringent methodology, statistically significant outcomes, reliable and valid research designs, and that all information collected is actually applicable to their patient. For example, if a certain treatment worked with statistical significance in a longitudinal study of pediatric patients with a large sample size, and all other influencing variables were controlled for, this treatment may not necessarily work in a middle-aged adult. Therefore, though the research collected is scientifically backed and evidence-based for a pediatric population, it does not support EBP for an older population. The fifth step is to integrate the evidence to create a treatment or intervention plan for the patient. The sixth step is to monitor the implementation of the treatment or intervention and evaluate whether it was associated with positive health outcomes in the patient. Finally,

practitioners have a moral obligation to share the results with colleagues at the organization and across the field, so that it may be best utilized (or not) for other patients.

Evidence-Based Practice Flowchart

Specify Research Question

Locate Potentially-Relevant Evidence

Discard Poor Evidence

Evaluate Evidence

Update Evidence

Assemble Relevant Evidence

Use Evidence to Inform Decisions

Referral Process

As patient advocates, nurses should be knowledgeable about referring clients when a need arises. The nurse is aware of many branches of the healthcare tree that are designed to assist with each patient's specific needs. A referral is a method by which the nurse contacts another member of the healthcare team to meet the patient's care needs in the most appropriate setting. This is part of care coordination and must happen throughout all stages of the client's continuum of care. Case managers play a key role in making appropriate referrals.

Referral occurs during the first stage of the nursing process: assessment. The nurse assesses the patient and identifies a need. For example, a school nurse may become aware of students who have learning or developmental disabilities. In these cases, the nurse may refer the child and their parents to a speech therapist, a language therapist, or a developmental therapist, depending on the case.

In the hospital environment, the nurse may recognize the need for an auxiliary team and refer the client to them. Such **auxiliary teams** include the palliative care and hospice team, respiratory therapy, physical and occupational therapy, and speech/language therapy. Community resources should be used when appropriate, such as extended-care therapy, social service support, and shelters for the homeless and disadvantaged. Patients may also need spiritual care, in which case clergy can be requested to make a bedside visit.

With any referral, the nurse must follow the appropriate protocols and remain within their scope of practice. Other members of the health care team such as physicians and nursing management should be consulted. Doctor's orders must be obtained where necessary.

After the referral has been made, it is vital that the nurse or case manager evaluates the patient for their response to care. Evaluation is a key component of the nursing process. Without evaluating for effectiveness, the process is incomplete. Only after evaluation has shown effectiveness and the patient is on their way to recovery can the plan of care be deemed successful.

Resource Management

As managers of client care, nurses must decide which supplies, materials, and equipment are necessary to fulfill the patient's needs as part of the preliminary and ongoing client evaluation. They do this by assessing and determining the patient's condition, at time of primary contact. This involves measuring and recording a patient's vital signs using healthcare tools such as stethoscopes, blood pressure cuffs and thermometers, as well as other patient care equipment, medical technology, and devices. After this initial determination, the next step is ensuring that the patient is supplied with the proper resources, such as patient lifts, ventilators, compression devices, or catheters.

Each nursing team member has varying skills and duties according to the training and degrees he or she received. These skill sets are matched with the client care requirements in the healthcare setting. Depending on the training received, a nurse will be licensed to handle a specific range of materials and supplies. **Nursing assistive personnel (NAPs)** are responsible for providing support services such as assistance with daily living activities, basic hygiene, and comfort care. It is important for all team members to understand how to utilize these associated materials efficiently and effectively.

Nurses should go over all the functions of the patient care materials with the NAPs. A good knowledge check is to quiz or question staff members on the various medical devices under their care. This provides an extra level of patient safety, ensuring that all team members are aware of the required equipment and how to utilize it correctly.

The term **cost-effective** can be defined as "effective or productive in relation to cost." Therefore, a **cost-benefit ratio** refers to weighing the value or likely costs of a project or plan with its desired benefit. Contrary to what might seem logical, effective patient care with a good cost-benefit ratio is not necessarily always least expensive. For example, it has been shown that the length of time between some routine tests could be altered, such as a Pap smear screening, which has been determined to be just as effective to get checked once every two years instead of annually for most women. Regardless, patient care and services must be as cost-efficient as possible while still maintaining high quality standards and client needs requirements.

As a result, providing cost-effective healthcare is often a balancing act performed by all involved. Client care planning by nurses and other members of the healthcare team is determined according to what they deem suitable, economical, and cost beneficial while still maintaining optimal care quality and results. Therefore, the nursing team must carefully select therapies, interventions, and resources that are not only cost-effective, but also the most useful and applicable based on the patient's needs.

For instance, nurses could determine the costs of patient falls within their facility and show how nursing assistance could help prevent them. Another example would be to use cost-analysis data to determine the cost benefit and birth outcome (premature vs normal births) for pregnant teens who received prenatal care in a school setting compared those who received routine care. A third example would be assessing the rate of various health issues in their communities such as smoking, car accidents, elderly injuries, teen drinking, and drug usage and determining how nursing intervention could help improve these outcomes, ultimately decreasing the rate of admissions at their facility.

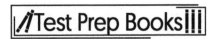

Safety and Infection Control

Accident/Error/Injury Prevention

The safety of both patients and team members is a major concern for healthcare organizations. Nurses must have an understanding and the necessary skills to prevent accidents, errors, and injuries.

The majority of accidents that occur in the older population happen in their homes, with falls being the most common accident. **Accident prevention** involves maintaining a clean home and living area and recognizing potential hazards. In addition, individuals should be knowledgeable and aware of their level of health and their own body's capabilities and weaknesses. Keeping regular appointments at the physician's office and following any medication regime correctly will keep one's health in check. It is important for people to understand and be aware of potential side effects of any medications that they may be taking. Recognizing a side effect could be a way to prevent an accident, especially if it relates to mental status or mobility. For example, blood-pressure medications have the potential to lower blood pressure to the point of the person passing out, ultimately causing a fall. Informal caregivers such as family members should check on elderly family to ensure they are able to continue taking care of themselves and to survey the home for safety hazards.

If an older adult is still living in their home, the following measures should be addressed to avoid accidents related to poisoning, burns, hypothermia, and fires. The main causes of poisoning in adults aged sixty-five and older are medicines and gases. Gases would include carbon monoxide and pipeline gases, such as propane or natural gas for heating the home. Fuel-burning devices should be checked regularly for proper functioning. Chimneys and flues should be cleaned once a year.

Older adults are often on a complicated medication regime involving multiple pills, various dosages, and the different times of the day and week that they should be taken. Medicines should be taken exactly as prescribed, and an organized schedule should be in place to prevent mistakes. One example for organizing medications is a pillbox that has individual compartments for each day of the week.

Burns and scalding in the home can be prevented if water heaters are not set too high, and if the cold water is turned on first. Kettles should be avoided if possible. If necessary, spout-filling kettles, cordless kettles, or wall-mounted heaters can be used instead. Items in the kitchen and the flow of the kitchen should allow for the least amount of distance for carrying hot food or beverages. On the stove, rear burners should be used and handles should be kept away from the edges in order to avoid accidentally knocking a pan off the stove.

An additional accident not often thought of in the older population is hypothermia, which means the body's temperature drops below 95 °F. Strategies to prevent hypothermia in the elderly include making sure the home is heated properly in colder weather, providing several layers of clothing, encouraging movement and exercise around the home to increase body heat, and making sure there's enough food and drink available.

As previously discussed, falls are the most common accident in the older adult population. Whether the person lives in their home or in a care facility, there are preventative measures that should be put into place.

Fall-prevention interventions include:

- Identification of patients at high risk for falls
- Assessment of the patient's room or environment for hazards that can be removed, such as:
  - Rugs
  - Slippery floors
  - Clutter
  - Poor lighting
- Use of assistive devices, such as:
  - Canes, used for stability
  - Walkers, used for balance because of their wide base
  - Reachers or grabbers, used to pick up items off of the floor or reach items on a shelf
  - Gait belts, used with an aide or caregiver, placed around the patient's waist to assist in walking or when standing up from a sitting position
  - Railings in bathrooms, hallways, and tubs
- Proper footwear is worn, such as rubber-soled shoes
- Staff, family-member, and patient education on fall-prevention strategies
- Assistance for patients with daily activities and routines if necessary
- Stairways that are well lit, have railings, and are lined with nonslip flooring

Fall prevention for bed-ridden patients includes:

- Keep two side rails up at all times when a patient is in bed.
- Keep the call light and personal items on a table within reach of the patient's bed.
- Place bed alarms on the patient's bed to alert the staff of any attempt to get out of bed.
- Offer toileting at least every two hours to prevent patients from getting up without assistance.

Falling with a Patient

Sometimes it becomes necessary to assist a person to the ground safely if it becomes clear that they are about to fall. When standing in front or behind the falling person, spreading one's legs apart allows for a wide base of support. Try to keep an arm under their shoulders or under their arms and ease them to the floor. Always attempt to protect their head first, and try to direct them away from hard objects, such as furniture.

Healthcare facilities should identify which patients are at a higher risk for falls, as these patients will require special fall precautions. Some facilities have signs on patients' doors that say "Fall Risk," or a patient may wear a certain color bracelet as a reminder to staff and/or family. Keep in mind that all patients are at risk for a fall, especially if they are elderly. Staff will be educated regarding how much assistance is needed for each patient. For example, patient A may be able to walk with assistance or walk with stand-by assistance. Patient B may need assistance x 2, or two staff persons, to help transfer.

Assistance for Ambulation

The types of assistance needed for ambulation are as follows:

- **Stand by assistance (SBA):** This patient does not require any assistance to move and can walk independently, though someone should be standing by to monitor. A gait belt is not required.

- **Contact-guard assistance (CGA):** This patient requires an assistant to be within reach in case of a fall. These patients can walk independently but have a high risk for falls.

- **Minimum assistance (MIN):** This patient needs a little support when moving about, and an example would be the use of a gait belt.

- **Maximum assistance (MAX):** This patient is unstable and may not be able to walk or stand without help. At least two staff persons are needed for assistance.

Patients who use assistive devices for ambulation need instruction on how to use them and may need reminders to ensure they are still using the device properly. It is important to stay with a patient who is learning to use an assistive device. A gait belt should be used while the patient is learning to use a walker.

Canes

The purpose of the cane is to help stabilize a leg that is weak. Steps for using a cane are listed below:

- Have the patient place the cane in their strong hand and move the cane out one step while stepping the weak leg out with the cane.
- With their weight on the cane, have them step out with their stronger leg.
- After each step, the patient can rest to ensure they feel balanced.

A Walker Without Wheels

A walker is used to give the patient extra stability when a patient is weak in both legs or has trouble with balance when walking. Steps for use are listed below:

- Instruct the patient to stand inside the walker while holding onto the walker with both hands.

- Have the patient lift and move the walker forward so that the back legs of the walker line up with their toes.

- With their weight on their stronger leg, have the patient take a step with their weaker leg while gripping the handrails of the walker. They should step into the center of the walker.

- Finally, their stronger leg steps up to evenly meet their other leg. They may rest in between steps if necessary.

Care must be taken to ensure that the flooring surface is flat when using a walker or a cane. Trips or falls can occur if rugs or thick carpet get caught in the walker or cane. Some walkers have wheels on the bottoms of the legs so that a patient can push the walker while walking. The wheels may be on all four legs or just the front two legs. The patient's weight is placed on the walker with their hands, and this helps with extra support as they lean forward. These types of walkers are not lifted during walking and allow for a bit faster pace. Make sure while walking that the walker does not move too far ahead of the patient.

Here are steps for moving from a chair to standing with a walker:

- Place the walker in front of the patient and have the patient place their hands on the arms of the chair.
- Assist the patient with standing up.
- Encourage the patient to place one hand at a time onto the handgrips of the walker.
- Ensure the patient feels steady and is not dizzy before walking.

Use of Crutches

Crutches can be used on a short-term basis when a patient has limitations for weight bearing on a leg. An example would be a patient that has a cast or a splint on their ankle, foot, or leg. Putting weight on an injured leg may interfere with healing and may be painful. A physical therapist will be responsible for fitting the crutches. Ensure the crutches are the appropriate length for the patient. The armpit, or axilla, rests should fit into the patient's armpit without lifting the shoulders and without causing stooping. The pads should be one to one-and-a-half inches below the axilla. If the crutches are too tall, the patient could trip over the crutches and too much pressure will be placed in their armpits. If the crutches are too short, leaning over will put unnecessary strain on the patient's back. The handgrips should also be adjusted so that the arms are slightly bent at the elbow. The grip should be comfortable.

Crutch Gaits

The **three-point crutch gait** helps with an inability to bear weight on one leg, such as with fractures, pain, or amputation.

- Move both crutches and the weaker leg forward. Then place all weight down on the crutches and move the stronger or unaffected leg forward. Repeat this pattern.
- Good balance is required for this type of gait.

The **two-point crutch gait** is used for weakness in both legs and poor coordination.

- Move the left crutch and right foot together.
- Then move the right crutch and left foot together.
- Repeat the pattern.
- This is a faster gait but difficult to learn.

The **swing-through crutch gait** helps with an inability to bear full weight on both legs.

- Move both crutches forward then swing both legs forward at the same time. The legs must swing past the crutches.
- This is the fastest gait but requires a lot of arm strength and energy.
- It will not be used in the elderly.

The **swing-to crutch gait** is used for patients who have weakness in both legs.

- Move both crutches forward.
- Put weight on both crutches and swing both legs forward together to the crutches. The legs must not swing past the crutches.
- This requires good arm strength, so it most likely will not be used for the elderly.

Standing up with crutches:

- Have the patient hold both crutches on their injured side, and then lean forward off of the chair while pushing off with their arm from the chair.
- Once standing, place the crutches under the arms.

Sitting down with crutches:

- Have the patient place both crutches on their injured side.
- Holding the handgrips in one hand, they can use their other hand to brace on the chair as they sit.

Using crutches on stairs should not be attempted until the patient is confident on level ground. Until then, or at any time, the patient can also slide up or down the stairs on their bottom. Also, the railing of the stairs can be used with one hand while holding the crutches in the other arm.

- The crutches should stay on the step the patient is standing on.
- The good leg is brought up to the next step while letting the injured leg lag behind.
- As the patient straightens up to their good leg, they should bring the crutches and their injured leg up onto the step.

Going down steps:

- Have the patient place the crutches on the next step lower and bring their injured foot forward.

- Next, the good foot is moved down to meet the crutches on the lower step. The weight is on the crutches at this time.

Transfer Devices

Nurses will be educated on the lift and transfer equipment available in their facility, and this equipment will be used every day to ensure the safety of patients and staff. Using **transfer devices** will greatly reduce the risk of lower-back stress and injury. Transfer devices eliminate manual lifting and transfers, as well as manual transfers in confined spaces, and they reduce the number of transfers needed per task. For example, it may normally take three steps to move a patient without a transfer device. With a transfer device, however, the task can be completed in only one step. Types of **protective transfer devices** include hoists, walking belts with handles (called gait belts), shower chairs, repositioning devices, and weighing devices that use slings. Examples of **repositioning devices** may be a draw sheet, a roller board, or a sliding sheet. Beds can have scales built in so that a patient can be weighed while staying in their bed. Also, there are scales that are large and wide, which will accommodate a wheelchair-bound or morbidly obese patient.

Allergic Reactions

Allergies can cause many symptoms from mild to severe. Some examples of mild symptoms might include itching, redness on the skin, hives, sneezing, runny nose, and itchy eyes. Wheezing may occur, and may be treated with a prescribed inhaler. Life-threatening allergic reactions include swelling of the tongue or throat, difficulty breathing, and anaphylaxis, which is a systemic reaction. **Anaphylaxis** is rare but can lead to death if it is not recognized and treated quickly. Allergies to foods, medications, latex, and insect bites can cause anaphylaxis. Normally a person who has serious allergic reactions will have an epinephrine pen, or "epi-pen," with them at all times, to be administered in case of a reaction. If the following symptoms associated with anaphylaxis are observed outside of a medical facility, call 911. Otherwise, report any of the following symptoms to the nurse:

- Difficulty breathing
- Swollen tongue or throat tightness
- Wheezing

- Nausea and vomiting
- Fainting or dizziness
- Low blood pressure
- Rapid heart beat
- Feeling strange or sense of impending doom
- Chest pain

Call 911 even if an epi-pen has been administered for the allergic reaction. Reaction symptoms can continue to occur, or can reoccur later.

Fire Hazards

Recognizing fire hazards in the workplace is important in the prevention of fires and the promotion of safety for patients and employees. Staff will be trained on the fire policy and regular drills should be performed so that each staff person's role is known and practiced. Below are some potential workplace fire hazards:

- Candles may not be allowed in certain facilities. If they are allowed, make sure they are never left unattended, are not within reach of children or pets, and are not placed near windows or material that could burn.

- To mitigate electrical hazards, unplug appliances and keep them clean and in good working order. If there is concern about a piece of electrical equipment that is not working properly, report it and stop using it. Keep three feet of space around heaters. Do not overload outlets with too many cords, and do not pinch cords behind devices or furniture. Do not use cords that are cracked or broken.

- Use of a stove and cooking appliances may not be allowed in certain facilities, but these guidelines are useful for anyone that may be cooking:

- Never leave cooking unattended.

- Don't cook if too sleepy or if taking medication that causes drowsiness.

- Use back burners on the stove to prevent spills and burns.

- Turn handles away from the front of the stove.

- Don't leave towels or potholders laying on the stovetop.

- Keep the oven and stove clean and wipe up spills.

- In case of a grease fire, do not use a fire extinguisher. Smother the fire in the pot or pan with a lid and turn off the burner.

- For an oven fire, turn off the oven and leave the door closed.

- For a microwave fire, leave the door closed, turn off the microwave, and unplug it.

- Healthcare facilities are smoke-free, but there may be designated smoking areas outside. Ensure that guests or employees use the appropriate area and extinguish the cigarette completely.

- Do not allow smoking near someone who is using oxygen, because oxygen is fuel for fire.

Each year, there are many structure fires in health care facilities. These fires happen in nursing homes, hospitals or hospices, mental health facilities, and doctors' offices or clinics. Cooking equipment is the primary cause of fires. Other causes of fires include clothes dryer or washer, intentional fires, smoking materials, heating equipment, electrical distribution or lighting equipment, and playing with a heat source.

Employees will be educated on the location of fire alarms, any alarm systems that are in place, sprinklers, and fire extinguishers. The danger of a fire is mainly from the smoke it creates. Smoke can travel quickly in a fire and can affect areas in a building that are not close to the fire itself. With elderly and sick patients, lack of mobility inhibits a quick escape; therefore, proper evacuation and rescue planning is essential. When responding to a fire or an alarm, always treat it as a true emergency. Call 911 even if an alarm system is monitored and activated, to ensure that help is on the way. If it is a false alarm, the fire department may still search to make sure everything is safe.

Facilitating Correct Use of Infant and Child Car Seats

As per the National Highway Safety Administration (NHTASA), car seats that are used and fitted appropriately can considerably lower infant and child death and injury in motor vehicle accidents. Estimates state that the proper use of infant and child car seats can prevent infant death by 71 percent and the death of toddlers and young children under 3 years of age by 54. percent.

It is imperative that infant seats and car seats must be not only properly installed, but also that they are the correct size for the infant/child using them in order to be effective against injures and death. For instance, rear-facing infant seats should be mounted in the back seat facing the rear of the automobile until the child is about 2 years of age and around 20 to 30 pounds. Convertible safety seats can be installed as either rear or forward facing. In most cases, regular car seat belts can be used when the child reaches at least 40 pounds and about 4 years of age. Nurses should go over these various safety regulations with patients who are parents-to-be or caring for infants or young children to make sure they are aware of the correct ways to install and use car seats.

Factors Related to Mental Status That May Contribute to the Potential for Accident or Injury

A variety of issues related to a patient's mental status can influence the potential for injury. The American Psychiatric Association's (APA) *Diagnostic and Statistical Manual of Mental Disorders (DSM) V* recognizes four main mental illness categories: Thought disorders, mood disorders, behavioral disorders and mixed mental health disorders. Agitated and altered thought processes can result from a variety of factors and causes, including hallucinations, dementia, concussions and other issues that affect the brain such as a tumor or trauma.

It is important for nursing team members to recognize the signs and symptoms of impaired cognition such as memory loss and poor hygiene, as well as signs and symptoms of acute and chronic mental illness, which could indicate conditions such as schizophrenia, depression, and bipolar disorder. Impaired cognition, also known as a disturbed thought process, interrupts and distracts a patient's mental and thought abilities, processes and activities. Attributes that could impact safety include short and/or long-term memory loss, mental conflict, a lack of understanding regarding speech and writing, confusion, disorientation, a lack of good judgment and insight, and the inability to perform the basic and vital life skills and activities. For patients with acute and chronic mental illness, it is important to oversee and gauge their safety needs and changes in terms of their mental status and behaviors at all times. This is done by evaluating the patient's mental capacity through an assessment of the way they look and behave, checking for odd thoughts or viewpoints such as delirium or delusions, their mood, and cognitive functions like alertness and memory. Checking up should be done as often as the nurse deems necessary based on the patient's past and present mental condition. This includes situations such as protecting their safety when experiencing hallucinations or delusions or during the manic phase of bipolar disorder.

Utilizing Facility Client Identification Procedures

Failing to identify patients correctly can cause mistakes and miscalculations regarding medication, transfusions, test procedures and results, procedures involving the wrong person, and discharging infants to the wrong families. It is essential for the patient to be involved in the identification process and utilizing "two patient identifiers" to improve and ensure identification dependability and consistency. Using two identifiers also helps guarantee an accurate match between the service or treatment and the patient, helping to prevent mistakes and improve patient care.

There are a number of patient identifiers depending on the healthcare facility. Some examples include: patient name, birthdate, address, phone number, Social Security Number (SSN), photograph, or their medical record number.

The nursing team must make sure that two of these above identifiers are assigned to each patient according to the facility's policy and that these same two identifiers are linked to the patient's medication, blood product, treatment, procedure, or specimen container via an attached label. It is imperative to always check a client's ID band and make sure it matches the name on the chart and the orders you are carrying out. These identifiers must be used to verify a patient's identity when admitted or transferred to another hospital or care location and prior to caring for the patient. It is important that neither identifier is the patient's room number, which could result in a patient mix-up. The nursing team also needs to be aware of how to integrate automated systems into the patient identification process if used in their facility. These are utilized in order to decrease the likelihood of identification inaccuracies and reduce medication errors. Some examples include the following:

- **Computerized provider order entry (CPOE)**: A system that allows healthcare personnel to enter and send treatment orders electronically.

- **Bar coding**: Computerized reference numbers that contain descriptive and other essential data.

- **Radio Frequency Identification (RFID)**: Wireless technology utilizing radio waves and signals to communicate data.

- **Biometric identification**: The measurement and statistical analysis of a patient's individual features for the purpose of identification.

Identifiers should be listed on an identification band (ID) applied to the patient's wrist. A separate band must also be worn to indicate any known allergies; if the patient does not have any known allergies, a band still must be worn affirming this information. If the patient is predisposed towards falling, a fall risk name band also needs to be worn. Facilities typically assign a specific color for each type of ID band. Often, name bands are white, allergy bands are red and fall risk bands are yellow. Some facilities may also stipulate the exact arm on which each band must be worn. In some facilities, a do not resuscitate

(DNR) order is also noted on a specific ID band. Since these ID bands are so important and imperative to patient safety, they are designed to be waterproof and difficult for the patient to remove.

Protecting Clients From Accident/Error/Injury

Healthcare providers and facilities must ensure that patients, visitors, and employees are safeguarded from injury. Examples of injuries that happen most frequently include burns, falls, electrical shock, accidental poisoning and disaster incidents.

Injuries involving heat can result from defective heating and cooling devices, as well as when these devices are incorrectly applied to the patient, especially when they are affected by a sensory and/or neurological issue that impedes their capacity to recognize and feel bodily harm resulting from the hot or cold therapy. Falls, both with or without injury, are a frequent and expensive accident that affect nearly every healthcare facility. As a result, all patients should undergo fall risk screening when they are admitted, as well as when their condition is flagged to indicate substantial changes in physical, psychological and/or cognitive attributes.

After undergoing the screening process, any patients deemed to be at risk for falling need to be immediately marked and documented to receive special instructions and procedures to prevent them from falling. There are a number of risk factors related to falls that are often included in a falls risk screening and assessment. These include:

- Incontinence: Patients with incontinence issues are more likely to fall than those not affected with these types of bathroom problems. This is usually a result of slipping and rushing to get to a toilet.

- Confusion: Patients who are confused may experience judgment issues and be unaware of environmental hazards that could cause them to fall.

- Poor vision: Those patients with vision issues are more likely to trip over items, especially when in an environment that is new or different. It is important that clients have their eyeglasses nearby and are urged to utilize them.

- Reaction time: Patients who experience reaction times that are slow or delayed are more likely to fall. This occurs more often with elderly patients, who may not react in time to steer clear of something that could cause them to slide or fall, such as a floor that is wet or slippery.

- Age: Patients that are at the greatest risk of falling include the elderly and young children.

- Medications: Patients taking painkillers or other tranquilizing drugs may have side effects causing them to feel disoriented due to sleepiness, dizziness, muscular weakness or orthostatic hypotension, therefore increasing the chance to falling.

- Poor muscular strength, balance, coordination, gait, and range of motion (ROM): Patients with compromised balance, coordination, ability to walk, and range of motion are more likely to fall. One effective strategy is to have them work with a physical therapist to strengthen these functions in order to prevent falls.

- Environmental hazards: The room or area occupied by the patient should be free of clutter and glare, the floor should be kept dry and clean and have adequate lighting and a working nurse call bell. These are all dangers that could exacerbate the chance of a fall. It is considered the nurse's responsibility to make sure the patient's environment is kept free of these types of environmental hazards.

- Past incidence of falls: Patients who have exhibited a prior history of falls, especially those who have fallen more often and in the recent past, are more likely to fall again.

- A fear of falling: It has been found that patients who have indicated they are afraid of falling are at a greater risk of a fall occurrence.

- Certain diseases and disorders: There are a number of diseases and health ailments that can increase the likelihood of a fall, especially those involving the musculoskeletal and/or neurological systems. These include conditions such as muscular dystrophy, Parkinson's disease and seizure disorders.

In addition to these fundamental patient-related factors, there are a number of external and environmental influences that should be considered as risk factors and need to be corrected as soon as possible:

- Insufficient patient footwear: Shoes, slippers and other footgear that do not fit properly, are slippery and/or unsafe in any other way increase the chance of a fall occurring. The items worn by patients on their feet should be skid proof, durable, safe, and the correct size. Skid proof socks are highly recommended to help prevent falls.

- Nonworking and/or incorrect usage of patient equipment: Medical equipment that is not working correctly such as a broken wheelchair or cane can lead to falls. These types of items should be reported at once and taken away for repair until they are authorized as safe to use again. Nurses also need to make sure they are aware of the correct usage of all patient equipment. A patient can fall as a result of a device, such as a mechanical lift being used improperly.

- Not receiving a response to calls for help: Nurses must answer patient calls quickly in order to avert the chance of a patient falling or suffering from some other type of accident or injury.

Besides patient risk assessment, other procedures that nurses can follow to avoid falls and decrease the level of harm caused by a fall include:

- Using supportive equipment such as walkers and canes

- Wearing padded clothing and/or placing padded gym mats next to a patient's bed to help lessen the degree of impairment from a fall when one does occur despite taking precautionary actions.

- Making sure a patient's bed is not raised too high.

- Equipping a bed or chair with an alarm to signal staff when a patient is getting up.

- Stepping up the level of patient monitoring and observation so that the patient is checked more often.

- Making sure the patient has high toilet seats and grab bars in the bathroom.

Providing Patients with Appropriate Methods to Signal Staff Members

It is important that patients have some kind of device nearby to alert nurses that they need something. This is a big step towards preventing accidents and injuries. At the same time, it is the responsibility of the nurse to answer calls for assistance right away so that the patient's needs are quickly addressed and safeguarded against some kind of mishap. The types of signal methods vary by facility and according to each patient and their situation. Nurses need to be aware of the various types and circumstances of clients under their care.

For example, although most of the time patients have the ability to contact a nurse with a call bell and light, there might be some patients who can only vocalize their calls. These types of patients should be positioned near the nurses' station or another high traffic area so they are heard and their needs addressed. Other patients may not be able to alert the nurse on their own at all. Those who are unable to alert the nurse by pressing a call signal or shouting out for help need to be located near the nurses' station or another busy place so that they can be checked frequently. In the case of a power or other failure or system breakdown that renders call bells unusable, patients should be equipped with handheld bells or buzzers to converse with the nursing staff.

Evaluating the Appropriateness of Healthcare Provider's Orders for a Patient

Nurses are responsible for executing two types of tasks: independent and dependent. Those considered independent are patient duties that do not require a doctor's order; those that are dependent are patient duties that can only be administered as per instruction from a doctor or other independent licensed practitioner.

When receiving an order, the nurse is required to make sure it is thorough, appropriate and executed quickly. Nurses should never act on any orders from a healthcare provider that are unclear or inappropriate. Instead, the nurse should follow up on any order that seems uncertain by contacting the HCP right away for an explanation.

For an order of restraints to be considered complete, it must at least include why the order is needed, the kind of restraint required, the length of time it should be used, patient actions that necessitate its usage, and the signature of the person who ordered it. An order for medication must also designate the name of the patient, the dosage, type, how it is administered and how often as well as stating why it was ordered and a signed confirmation of the person who ordered it. Any part of this process that deviates from these requirements or seems incorrect requires intervention from the nurse.

Emergency Response Plan

In the case of an emergency, a nurse must be prepared to recommend certain clients for an immediate discharge, activate the emergency response plan, and participate in disaster drills. Each facility must have plans for emergency situations, and the nurse may be a part of such planning.

Disasters can be internal or external. Examples of internal disasters include fires; violence in the workplace; failure of utilities such as water or electricity; or electrical outage or flooding in the building caused by weather disasters such as tornadoes, hurricanes, or earthquakes. An external disaster can include a serious community event in which a population sustains many injuries. Such events can include mass shootings, train wrecks, and airplane crashes. Acts of terrorism or bioterrorism can affect a facility both internally and externally. Weather events can affect a healthcare facility both internally and externally, depending on the extent of damage that occurs.

A recent example of an act of terrorism that caused a massive influx of patients to local hospitals was the Route 91 shooting in Las Vegas. This was an external event that caused the activation of certain emergency response plans to deal with the influx of incoming patients. Such events must be discussed as a potential occurrence in each facility. Healthcare facilities must put plans in place to deal with such catastrophes in a smooth, coordinated manner to effectively care for the maximum number of patients.

The hurricanes Irma and Harvey that recently struck the Gulf states are an example of an external weather situation that directly affected those communities with electrical power losses, flooding, destruction of property, and injuries and illness related to the flooding and high winds. The healthcare system must be ready for these situations with an effective emergency response plan.

One of the first steps when activating an emergency response plan is to discharge patients who are medically stable enough, in order to clear beds for incoming patients. Facilities only have a set number of beds available for patients. When the influx of patients is greater than the number of beds available, a crisis arises. When a catastrophic event occurs, the nurse is part of a triaging process that determines whether certain patients can be relocated to open beds for incoming patients. Unstable clients will stay put; they are at the top of the rung of patients to stay. Stable patients may be discharged only if it is likely they will remain stable without ongoing nursing and medical care. On the bottom rung below unstable and stable clients are ambulatory and self-care clients. These are patients who are walking around and able to independently care for themselves outside a hospital facility. Ambulatory and self-care patients will be discharged to clear beds for incoming disaster patients.

The nurse plays a key role in disaster preparedness and knowing that role is key to a successful execution of each emergency response plan. During a fire, for example, the nurse must competently implement all four elements of the **RACE** acronym, as follows:

- **R** is for rescuing all those in danger, including patients, visitors, and staff.
- **A** is for activating the alarm after those in danger have been cleared.
- **C** is for containing the fire in the smallest possible area. This is accomplished by closing all windows and doors, preventing the fire from spreading.
- **E** is for extinguishing the fire if it is small enough and the nurse can do so safely.

Concurrent with knowledge of the RACE acronym during a fire is knowledge of how to use a fire extinguisher. There are five main types of fire extinguishers: Type A, Type B, Type C, Type AB, and Type ABC. **Type A extinguishers** are used for common solids such as paper, mattresses, and clothing. **Type B extinguishers** target oil, gasoline, and grease fires, common in kitchens. **Type C extinguishers** fight electrical fires. **Type AB extinguishers** combines the roles of Type A and Type B, while **Type ABC extinguishers** combines all three. Type ABC is the most commonly seen due to its ability to extinguish all types of fire sources. This is likely the type of extinguisher located within a hospital facility for that reason.

When attempting to use a fire extinguisher, the nurse must remember the acronym **PASS**, which describes the following steps for effective use:

- **P** is for pull, pulling the pin to begin using the fire extinguisher.
- **A** is for aim, aiming directly at the bottom of the fire.

- **S** is for squeeze, squeezing the trigger to release the spray.

- **S** is for sweep, moving from side to side across the base of the fire. This will effectively extinguish the fire.

Along with knowing their role when fire threatens the safety of patients, the nurse must also know what to do when the hospital's utilities fail. Electricity powers many life-supporting machines for patients, such as oxygen delivery systems and mechanical ventilation machines. Most hospitals have back-up generators to keep these machines going when the power goes down. The nurse must alert maintenance and management immediately if the power goes off. Many hospitals have special red outlets into which important patient machinery should be plugged for just that reason.

There are times in the workplace when the nurse may encounter violence, harassment, or aggression. The source of these behavioral conflicts may be a visitor, fellow staff member, or patient. Causes of workplace violence may include delirium and disorientation, especially in hospitalized patients with illness and medication side effects in play. Visitors and family members may become disruptive for any number of reasons, including misunderstandings about care during high-stress and emotionally charged healthcare situations involving a loved one. Whatever the cause, the nurse must work to deescalate the situation verbally as well as enlisting help from team members and hospital security staff.

Each healthcare facility will have explicit guidelines that must be followed in the case of a weather emergency, such as a hurricane, tornado, or earthquake. Closing windows, doors, and curtains as well as moving patients to the appropriate predetermined safe place are all part of the nurse's role during these situations.

For all these emergencies, a chain of command needs to be established long before a catastrophic event occurs. This lays out in clear terms who is in charge during the disaster, who needs to know what, who takes on leadership roles, and so on. Clearly defining the roles of each team member and rehearsing what will happen by using emergency drills ensures that things are run smoothly and efficiently in the event of a disaster.

Ergonomic Principles

Ergonomics is the science of matching the physical requirements of a job to the physical abilities of the worker. Musculoskeletal injuries can occur if physical demands are greater than the employee's physical capabilities. Body mechanics refers to how the body moves during activities of daily living. Understanding and practicing the use of proper body mechanics is imperative to preventing associate injury. The physical requirements of a job are explained during the interview process, and the physical capabilities of the associate are assessed during the pre-employment physical examination. Education on the use of proper body mechanics begins in nursing school and continues during employment. New associate orientation should include validation of proper body mechanics.

Principles of Body Mechanics
One way the nurse can take care of themselves is to employ proper body mechanics. The job of the nurse is often highly physical in nature, with much time being spent on turning patients in bed, transferring them from the bed to the chair or bedside commode, and assisting with **ambulating** (walking) patients to the bathroom or around the unit. Moving another person, especially one with limited ability to assist, can be extremely difficult and taxing on the body.

Depending on the facility in which the nurse works, different equipment will be available to assist with moving patients. Becoming acquainted with how and when to use this equipment will be part of the nurse's training in that facility. The nurse should use this equipment whenever possible, even if it takes a little more time to do so.

Basic **safe lifting techniques** include lifting with one's legs, not one's back, avoiding twisting and awkward positions when lifting and moving the patient, and keeping the back upright as much as possible to avoid straining. The individual should make sure to keep their feet as balanced as possible and not rush lifting or moving a patient. The nurse should ask for help from other nurses whenever needed to avoid injury.

The medical environment can present potential hazards that increase risk of injury to the nurse. Examples of these are transferring the patient from the cart to the operating room bed, positioning the patient, and standing for prolonged periods. Repetitive motions, such as turning the head to one side for visualization of monitoring equipment and holding a retractor for an extended time period, can also present ergonomic hazards. Proper body mechanics should be consistently followed to prevent injury. There are three foundational principles of proper body mechanics that should be followed by nurses. First, bending at the hips and knees instead of at the waist uses the large muscle groups of the legs instead of the back muscles, and helps to prevent back injury. Second, standing with feet at about shoulder-width apart helps to reduce risk of injury by providing foundational support. Finally, the nurse should keep the back, neck, pelvis, and feet aligned when turning or moving. Twisting and bending at the neck and waist can increase risk of associate injury.

As a standard of care, many healthcare institutions have mandated use of **safe patient mobilization (SPM) equipment** in an effort to reduce associate injuries, as well as to promote patient safety. SPM equipment in the medical environment can be used during patient transfers and positioning. Slide sheets are often used in patient transfers. These sheets are placed underneath the patient prior to lateral or vertical transfer. They decrease the surface tension, making transfers easier for the associates. However, since the slide sheets do decrease surface tension, they must be removed after use, so that the patient is not at risk of sliding off the operating room bed. Inflatable blankets can be placed under the patient to assist in lateral transfers, as well. When engaged, the forced air blanket helps to support the weight of the patient, making lateral transfers easier. The mattress should be deflated after completion of transfer. Another type of SPM equipment is lift equipment. **Lift equipment** works by placing a sling under the patient's limb or underneath the entire patient, connecting the sling to the lift machine, and programming the machine to lift the body to the desired height. The weight limits of these machines vary, so the nurse must ensure the patient's weight does not exceed the weight limit set by the manufacturer.

Injury Prevention

A member of the healthcare team who is not careful could easily become injured, potentially resulting in physical harm, missed days of work, lost wages, and medical bills. Nurses are at high risk for injury due to the amount of lifting they do during a shift. Using the appropriate lifting techniques can help prevent an injury to the back and strains or sprains to the joints of the body. The nurse should employ assistive devices such as gait belts and mechanical lifting devices whenever possible. It is important to ask for help whenever necessary to prevent injury. The following depicts eight steps to use when lifting a heavy object:

1. Plan for lift and test the load
2. Ask someone for help

3. Get a firm footing
4. Bend your knees
5. Tighten stomach muscles
6. Lift with legs
7. Keep the load close to you
8. Keep your back straight

Handling Hazardous and Infectious Materials

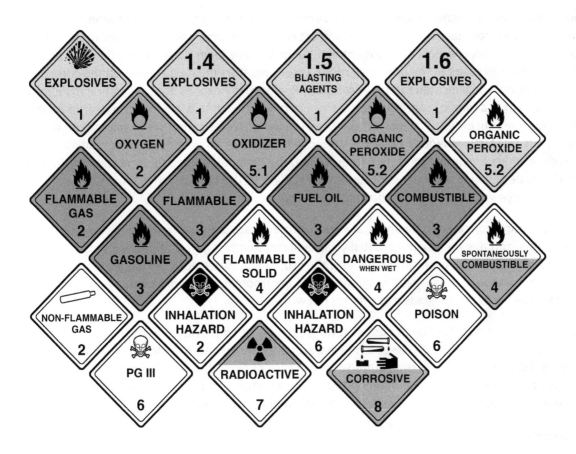

According to the Institute of **Hazardous Materials Management (IHMM)**, a hazardous material is defined as "any item that has the potential to cause harm to humans, animals, or the environment, either by itself or through interaction with other factors." A hazardous item may be biological, chemical, radiological, and/or physical in nature. Agencies such as the United States Environmental Protection Agency (EPA) and the Occupational Safety and Health Administration (OSHA) provide regulation and guidelines as to how hazardous materials are handled.

Hazardous materials in the medical environment can include biological, chemical, radiological, and physical hazards. Biological hazardous materials are commonly referred to as **biohazards**. These are materials that present a threat to the health of living things, primarily humans. Biohazards are typically introduced into the medical environment in the form of patient body fluids and excreta. Examples of biohazardous materials are blood, body fluids, viruses, and bacteria. Items in the medical environment that have been exposed to biohazardous materials are considered to be biohazardous as well, until the decontamination process is completed. For example, used surgical instruments are considered biohazardous until they have been cleaned of bioburden and sterilized.

Chemical hazardous materials in the medical environment include solid, liquid, or gas materials that pose a threat to health. Primarily, solid and liquid chemical hazards include materials used to clean, disinfect, and sanitize the medical environment. They may also include cytotoxic and chemotherapy medications. Gas chemicals are primarily anesthetic gases. Containers for chemical hazards are labeled with symbols representing the type of potential hazard, along with instructions for steps to take in the event of exposure.

Radiological hazards found in the medical environment are seen in the forms of thermal, radioactive isotopes, and electromagnetic radiation. The most common thermal radiological hazard is in the form of laser. The use of lasers exposes the patient and the healthcare team to risk of eye damage, as well as increasing the risk of fire in the operating room. Laser operators must be trained on the correct usage of the laser, along with indicated safety precautions. Radioactive isotopes are used in brachytherapy. **Brachytherapy** is a form of cancer treatment where radioactive beads are inserted near or inside a cancerous tumor in order to deliver a high dose of radiation to the tumor while sparing the surrounding healthy tissue. **Electromagnetic radiation** is seen in the form of X-ray and ultraviolet radiation. During a procedure where electromagnetic radiation is used, the patient is protected by shields and/or drapes specifically designed to minimize exposure to the radiation. The perioperative team utilizes shields, gowns, and eyewear to minimize radiation exposure.

Physical hazards also exist in the medical area. Autoclaves are used to steam sterilize surgical instruments, and this steam can potentially cause burns. Removing surgical instruments straight from the autoclave can cause burns to the hands if the proper gloves are not used. Liquid on the floor can cause someone to slip or fall, causing injury. Handling carbon dioxide tanks or cryogenic material can cause severe burns to the hands if gloves are not worn.

The types of hazards should be discussed at the beginning of employment in the medical environment. This should include identifying the potential hazards and known hazards, steps to minimize exposure to them, and discussing the necessary steps to take in case of exposure. Healthcare facilities are required to provide **materials safety data sheets (MSDS)** and keep them in a central area. For most healthcare facilities, education on hazardous materials management is done on an annual basis.

Home Safety

The nurse works to promote patient safety by ensuring their home environment is safe. The nurse will begin this process by first assessing the client's home for safety opportunities. This can be done by walking through the client's home taking mental and written notes as well as interviewing the patient and their caregiver.

The patient themselves must be assessed for their ability to live safely in their own home. Patients with dementia, Alzheimer's, and other cognitive dysfunctions present more of a risk to themselves than a patient whose cognitive faculties are well intact. The nurse may assess whether the patient is able to live independently, need constant supervision, or need assistance with only a few daily activities. An important consideration is how well the patient can follow their own medication regime. The nurse should consider whether the use of divided days-of-the-week pill boxes would be appropriate, for example. Once the client's cognitive function is assessed and addressed, the nurse can then move on to ensuring the external environment is safe.

The external environment of the patient's home poses many potential safety hazards. The patient may live in a multiple-story house, in which case the stairs present a fall risk for elderly and deconditioned patients. A hand rail may be helpful if it is not already present, as well as safety treads on the staircase. Some patients with chronic conditions that restrict them from climbing up and down stairs may require a chair elevator. The nurse can connect the patient and their family to community resources for such items.

The lighting in the home is as important as the lighting in a hospital room. One of the classic fall prevention tips in the hospital is to ensure the patient's room is adequately lit both in the daytime and at night. The same goes for the client's home. The nurse needs to ensure nightlights are available in rooms that the client may need to ambulate across during the night, such as the bedroom. Visits to the bathroom should be unencumbered and easily navigated, without fall risks in the way. Due to medication and chronic illnesses such as heart failure, visits to the bathroom often increase in the elderly patient, thus increasing fall risk.

The nurse should discourage the use of throw rugs in the homes of patients at risk for a fall. This type of rug can easily catch the client's foot, throwing them off balance and potentially causing a fall.

The house should be well kept, clean, and sanitary. If the client is not able to keep up with their normal housekeeping duties, assistance should be sought. The nurse can, again, connect the client to community resources in this case. Perhaps a church friend, community volunteer, or local housekeeping service may be used if affordable for the client. A cluttered home may present a fall risk, and it also negatively affects the mental health of the client, causing anxiety and depressive symptoms.

Some clients, such as those with diabetes, may have syringes to administer insulin that will need proper disposal. The nurse may provide the client with a sharps container for syringe disposal as well as educating the patient on proper syringe hygiene and disposal. The nurse should ensure that the client understands these concepts to prevent at-home injuries.

Food hygiene is an important topic to address with the client if they are still preparing their own food. Hand hygiene before, after, and during food preparation is vital to preventing the spread of food-borne illnesses. The client should be educated on the proper handling of meats, ensuring that they not only perform frequent hand hygiene, but that they properly sanitize surfaces that raw meat touches, such as cutting boards.

The nurse needs to assess household alarms such as fire, smoke, and carbon monoxide alarms and ensure that they have fresh batteries and are in working order. The client should be educated to monitor these alarms as needed so they are ready to go in the case of a fire or carbon monoxide leak.

Patients receiving oxygen therapy should be educated on proper oxygen use and maintenance of their oxygen tank. They will be taught not to smoke while receiving oxygen, because this is a fire hazard. They will also need to monitor the tank's gauges to make sure they know when they are running low on oxygen and need a replacement tank.

Least Restrictive Restraints and Safety Devices

Restraints can be defined as any device, material, or equipment that is attached to the body and intentionally limits a person's ability to move freely. Restraints, when applied properly, cannot be easily removed or controlled by the person. In addition to physical form, restraints can also be emotional, chemical, or environmental. Use of restraints is very controversial due to the ethical issue of personal freedom. These are a temporary solution to a problem and must always be used as a last resort. Restraints are used to limit a patient's movement to prevent injury to themselves or others, and they always require a physician's order.

Types of restraints include:

- Physical: vests, wrist restraints, straps, or anything that confines the body
- Emotional: verbal cues or emotions used to coerce the patient to act a certain way
- Environmental: side rails, locked doors, closed windows, locked beds
- Chemical: any medication used to change a patient's behavior

The medical doctor or practitioner is responsible for ordering the use of restraints. Nurses and caregivers are responsible for applying restraints safely and for the management of a patient with a restraint. After an order is given and a restraint is applied, the physician must visit the patient within twenty-four hours of placing the order to assess its further necessity.

Alternatives to Restraints

Other methods must be tried before restraints. They include:

- Talking with the patient about being cooperative
- Using distractions such as television, music, knitting, and folding towels or cloths
- Placing the patient within view of a caregiver, such as near the main desk
- Having someone sit with the patient
- Moving the patient to a quiet area
- Ensuring that the patient's bathroom needs are being met
- Ensuring personal items are within reach

When to Use Restraints

Each facility will have a specific protocol that must be followed for restraint use. Circumstances under which restraints are used include:

- Signs of patient aggression toward self, staff, or other patients
- Interference with important medical devices, such as an IV or a catheter
- Patient movements that are potentially harmful to their health, or may cause further injury
- Potential for a patient to interfere with a procedure

Applying Restraints

- Always follow the facility's restraint policy.

- Obtain an order from a physician or medical practitioner unless it is an emergency situation.

- Obtain consent from the patient or from next of kin if the patient is not capable of understanding.

- Explain to the patient what is going to happen, even if the patient is unable to understand due to confusion or dementia.

- Always monitor the patient per facility policy—check the positioning of the restraint every thirty minutes and remove every two hours for range of motion. Remember to reposition the patient and offer toileting every two hours.

- Explain the need for restraints and how long the restraints will be used.

Applying Physical Restraints

Vests have holes for the arms and the opening crosses in the back. The straps will be secured on either side of the bed or chair, depending on the patient's location. Tie it in a quick-release knot to a lower part of the bed that does not move. Make sure that two fingers fit underneath the vest on the patient's chest, so that it is not too tight.

Wrist or ankle restraints are cloths that wrap around each wrist or ankle. They have a strap that is tied to a lower, immovable part of the bed or chair. Tie it in a quick-release knot. Ensure the restraints aren't too tight and that the patient's arms or legs aren't in an awkward position. Usually a pillow will be placed under the arms and/or the knees and heels.

Legal Implications in the Use of Restraints

If restraints aren't used correctly or are used for the wrong reasons, the patient's family can take legal action against the facility. A patient in restraints becomes completely vulnerable and may feel helpless. They are at a greater risk of sexual abuse, elder abuse, psychological abuse, or violence from other patients.

Possible injuries from restraints can include:

- Broken bones
- Bruises
- Falls
- Skin tears or pressure sores
- Depression or fear due to lack of freedom
- Death from strangulation

Reporting of Incident/Event/Irregular Occurrence/Variance

If there is an unanticipated or adverse event, the nurse should follow the facility's policies and procedure for reporting and documentation. One of the first activities, of course, after the patient is stable, should be to inform the respective manager or charge nurse of the event. The facility may have internal processes to follow as well to ensure they are protected as best as possible from medicolegal action.

One of the more common reportable events that the nurse will be involved in is an incorrect count. In the event of an incorrect count, the circulator should make attempts to recover the missing item. The circulator should also follow the facility's policies and procedures; at some facilities, X-ray may not be required for needles smaller than a certain size because they are typically not visible on X-ray. If an intraoperative X-ray is required for a potentially retained object, the team should ensure that the integrity of the sterile field is maintained because the X-ray may be performed prior to full closure of the incision.

Following reasonable attempts to recover the potentially retained object, the circulator should complete the necessary documentation in the patient's chart, such as which count is incorrect, what actions were taken to recover the object, and who was notified. In addition to the documentation in the patient record, the facility's policies may require reporting of the incident in an internal system. This allows the facility to gather additional data that may not be appropriate for the patient record. In the event of a retained foreign object, the facility can use this information to determine if all appropriate actions were taken.

Safe Use of Equipment

Nurses should assure that all equipment that is to be used is safe and functioning properly. The use of medical devices, including equipment used in the operating room, is regulated by the United States Food and Drug Administration (FDA). The Joint Commission (TJC) and the Centers for Medicare and Medicaid Services (CMS) also provide oversight on the proper use of surgical equipment. Both TJC and CMS require the presence of manufacturer's instructions for use (IFU) to be present in areas where the equipment is used. Prior to surgical equipment being used on patients, the IFU are established by the device manufacturer. It is important for care providers to use the equipment only per manufacturer guidelines, since these guidelines are the ones tested and approved as safe for patient use by the FDA. If a safety concern regarding the equipment arises, the FDA recalls the product until the safety issue is resolved. For example, if a specific type of surgical guidewire breaks off at the tip and causes patient harm, the product may be recalled and pulled from circulation until further investigation.

The product manufacturer's IFU indicates if the equipment poses a fire, electrical, laser, or radiation hazard. If the product does pose one of these hazards, the IFU indicates the type(s) of hazard and the recommendations for protecting the patient and equipment users from the hazard. For instance, if the product poses a fire hazard, the IFU contains information stating which type of fire extinguisher should be available. Also, the IFU states whether to have liquid (sterile water or sterile saline) on the surgical field as a precautionary measure.

TJC and CMS observe infection control practices such as chemical disinfection and sterilization of surgical instruments during site visits to ensure healthcare facility compliance. If disinfection and sterilization are not performed according to manufacturer guidelines, the cleanliness/sterility of the surgical equipment cannot be verified. Manufacturer instructions for use should be available in each area where surgical equipment is used. Many healthcare facilities utilize OneSOURCE, an online database of manufacturer instructions for use. Since OneSOURCE is an electronic database, the contents are updated automatically, eliminating the need to update unit-based binders.

Security Plan

Within the healthcare facility, maintaining a strong **security system** is vital for patient and staff safety. The nurse will likely be trained in and involved with the hospital's security team, playing an active role in promoting a safe environment.

There are many ways a hospital can be threatened. A baby may be abducted from the hospital nursery, a hacker may breach the hospital's firewall and access private patient data, a violent person may enter the hospital and begin shooting people, a patient may run away, or a person may make a bomb threat. Whatever the threat, the facility will likely have a plan in place to quickly deal with the threat and neutralize it.

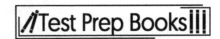

The nurse may be involved with a hospital security planning team. These types of teams meet to discuss potential threats and draw up a plan. The nurse can voice their opinion and contribute helpful ideas to effectively deal with the situation. The security team can share key tips with the rest of the staff based on their training and experience. These tips benefit the overall security of the facility. Planning, training, and drills all ensure that if a threat were to happen, the team is ready to respond.

Within the hospital, there are various methods of alerting the staff to a security breach. There may be alarm systems, announcements made over a PA system, or a text alert system on the staff's phones that notifies everyone of the situation. Many hospitals have closed circuit television security monitoring systems that employ cameras and video screens to monitor high-risk areas such as entrances and isolation rooms for violent patients. Certain security doors may be used to keep areas of the hospital off-limits to visitors or can close off areas of the hospital as needed.

Many hospitals use identification badges and bands to identify who is who and ensure only authorized persons and personnel are in certain areas. For example, the mother and father of a baby often get a special ID band identifying them as such, ensuring that no one else is permitted access to a baby, in case they might attempt an abduction.

If the nurse receives a bomb threat over the phone, they should attempt to stay on the line with the person making the threat as long as possible. The nurse may alert other staff of the bomb threat to get the security team in action, while trying to collect as much data on the perpetrator as possible. This information can include sound of their voice, whether they are male or female, and any other information the nurse can get out of them such as their location, the bomb location, and their motive. The nurse may even be able to deescalate the situation over the phone if they remain calm and collected, but the situation should be handed over to the experts on the security team as soon as possible.

Standard Precautions/Transmission-Based Precautions/Surgical Asepsis

Infection prevention is an important theme in healthcare, particularly in the surgical patient population. A main focus of nurses is protecting patients and healthcare associates from transmission of infectious organisms. Standard precautions are applied during direct patient contact and the patient's environmental contact. Standard precautions are followed universally by healthcare providers, and they are the foundation for preventing disease transmission in all healthcare settings. Included in standard precautions are hand hygiene, **personal protective equipment (PPE)**, environmental control, and sharps safety. Hand hygiene is the gold standard for preventing disease transmission. In compliance with standard precautions, the nurse performs hand hygiene before and after patient contact, before and after applying exam gloves, after touching anything in the patient's environment, before eating, and after using the restroom. PPE protects the nurse from coming into contact with the patient's bodily fluids and other potentially infectious material.

Examples of PPE are gloves, masks, gowns, shoe covers, and eye shields. Surfaces in the patient environment are laden with bacteria and other infectious agents. Environmental contamination is directly linked to pathogen transmission and **hospital-acquired infections (HAIs)**. Reusable laundry and textiles should be changed and laundered between each patient and in a healthcare-accredited laundry facility. Syringes and needles should be limited to single-patient use in compliance with evidence-based care related to infection control. Sharps should include safety devices, when possible. Angiocaths (IV needles) and surgical blades are available with built-in safety features that cover the sharp when not in use, decreasing the change of needle-stick exposure to patient body fluids. Transmission-based precautions are to be used with patients with known or suspected infection with highly transmissible pathogens. These are to be used along with standard precautions.

Transmission-based precautions are classified in three ways: contact, droplet, and airborne. **Contact precautions** are used with patients infected or colonized with microorganisms transmitted by direct or indirect contact. These include *Clostridium difficile (C. diff),* methicillin-resistant *Staphylococcus aureus* (MRSA), and vancomycin-resistant *Enterococcus* (VRE). When caring for these patients, the nurse dons a gown and gloves prior to entering the patient room. The PPE is discarded immediately prior to leaving the patient room, and hand hygiene is performed immediately. Droplet precautions, in addition to standard precautions, are used if a patient has a confirmed or suspected infection transmissible through respiratory droplets. PPE associated with droplet precautions are gloves, gown, and mask. The patient is also placed in a single-patient room. Influenza and respiratory syncytial virus (RSV) are indications for droplet precautions. Airborne precautions are taken when providing care to a patient with known or suspected infection transmissible via airborne route. The patient's respiratory particles are airborne for prolonged time periods and are carried by normal air currents. PPE for these patients includes gloves, gown, and surgical mask with respirator level of N95 or higher. The most common airborne-transmissible infections are tuberculosis, measles, and varicella.

Spread of Disease-Causing Organisms

Microorganisms that cause infection can be spread by touching surfaces, equipment, people, and bodily fluids, as well as by breathing in **airborne droplets**, such as those that exit the nostril when a person sneezes. Touching infectious microorganisms followed by contact on the hands, face, mouth, eyes, or with food can spread the germs. A clean environment and good handwashing not only protect healthcare workers from infectious germs, but protect the patients as well. Infections can spread from patient to patient, from caregiver to patient, and vice versa.

There are three types of infections: viral, bacterial and fungal. **Fungal infections** are caused by spores of fungus that usually affect the skin but also can be inhaled and cause respiratory infections. Examples of fungal skin infections include Athlete's foot, ringworm, and yeast infections. Fungal infections can be spread by touching the lesion or skin area that is infected.

Bacterial infections and **viral infections** are caused by microbes, or microscopic organisms. Both of these types of infection can produce similar symptoms, including:

- Coughing and/or sneezing
- Inflammation (swelling)
- Fever
- Vomiting
- Diarrhea
- Fatigue

Bacteria and viruses are both too small to see without a microscope, but they differ in how they infect the body. Bacteria are complex and can reproduce or multiply on their own. They can live in extreme environments, such as heat and cold, and can infect both the bodies of animals and humans. Bacterial infections are usually localized or found in contained areas of the body, such as the sinuses (sinus infection). Most bacteria are harmless and actually necessary to the body. One example is the bacteria in our gut, which is important for digesting food. Bacterial infections are treated with antibiotics, which will either kill the bacteria or stop the growth of the bacteria that has entered the body.

There are many different types of bacterial infections. Some common bacterial skin infections include cellulitis, folliculitis, impetigo, and boils. Foodborne bacterial infections usually cause vomiting, diarrhea, fever, chills, and abdominal pain. Harmful bacteria may be in raw meat, fish, eggs, and poultry, and in unpasteurized dairy products. The bacterial growth can be caused by unsanitary food preparation and handling.

Sexually-transmitted bacterial infections include chlamydia, gonorrhea, syphilis, and bacterial vaginosis. There are many additional types of infections, such as otitis media (ear infection), urinary tract infections, and respiratory tract infections. Infections in the respiratory tract can be from bacteria or a virus, and they can cause a sore throat, bronchitis, sinus infections, tuberculosis, or pneumonia.

Viruses are different from bacteria in that they need another cell in order to reproduce, or multiply. They attach to a cell in the body and change the cell to make more of the virus. Eventually, the original body cell dies. Viral infections do not respond to antibiotics and are more difficult to treat. Unlike bacteria, most viruses cause infection. The common cold is most often caused by a virus in the rhinovirus family and is an example of a mild virus. An example of life-threatening viruses is the human immunodeficiency virus (HIV). Vaccines do a good job of protecting against viruses such as polio, chicken pox, influenza, and measles. There are antiviral drugs available to treat certain viruses.

Common types of respiratory viruses include influenza-causing viruses, respiratory syncytial virus, and rhinoviruses, which are most often the cause of the common cold. Viral skin infections can include Molluscum contagiosum (small, harmless bumps on the skin), herpes simplex virus-1 (cold sores), and varicella zoster virus, which is similar to the chickenpox. Foodborne viral infections are the most common cause of food poisoning and can include the hepatitis A virus, norovirus, and rotavirus. Viruses that are transmitted sexually include human papilloma virus, hepatitis B, genital herpes (herpes simplex-2), and HIV. Other types of viruses include Epstein-Barr, West Nile, and viral meningitis.

Bacteria and viruses can be spread by:

- Droplet contact from coughing and sneezing
- Contact with infected people
- Contact with infected animals, like livestock, pets, fleas, and ticks
- Contact with infected surfaces, like tabletops or railings
- Contact with contaminated food or water

Microbes can cause acute infections, chronic infections, or latent infections. **Acute infections** last for a short period of time and **chronic infections** can last for weeks, months, or years. **Latent infections** may not show any symptoms at first and then may reappear, or show up after months or years.

Handwashing with soap and water is the number one way to prevent the spread of germs. The soap removes the visible dirt and invisible germs from the hands, and the water rinses them off.

Handwashing steps:

- Remove any jewelry or watches and pull long sleeves up past the wrists.
- Turn on the water and use warm water.
- Place soap in one hand and rub for at least twenty seconds.
- Make sure to rub the top and palms of the hands. Rub between the fingers and around the nails.
- Wash above the wrists.
- If there was contact with bodily fluids, wash for at least one minute.

- Be sure not to touch the sides of the sink during the process (the washing process would then need to be repeated).
- Rinse hands with fingers facing down so that the soap and germs run off, rather than back up the arms.
- Dry hands with a paper towel, or clean hand towel.
- Use the towel to turn off the faucet.

When to perform handwashing:

- After using the bathroom
- After sneezing or handling tissues
- Before and after eating
- Before entering a patient's room
- Before and after feeding a patient
- Before and after performing a procedure on a patient
- Before and after coming in contact with a wound
- After coming in contact with dirty linens or clothes
- After coming in contact with bodily fluids of any kind (blood, urine, vomit, mucus, or stool)
- After leaving a patient's room

Cleansing the hands with an alcohol-based hand sanitizer is also available in healthcare facilities, but it is best to wash with soap and water. Hand sanitizers can get rid of many, but not all, microbes. For example, clostridium difficile, commonly referred to as **c-diff**, is a microbe that is not killed by alcohol-based sanitizers. A c-diff infection causes a patient to have copious amounts of watery diarrhea. In addition to standard infection-prevention precautions, the nurse must wash hands with soap and water before and after caring for a patient with c-diff.

Hand sanitizer should not be used when the hands are visibly soiled, or if bodily fluids have been touched. After several uses of hand sanitizer, oils build up on the hands and should be removed by washing with soap.

Educating patients about cleanliness and proper handwashing will also help prevent the spread of disease. Make sure to assist patients with washing their hands, or use a soapy washcloth on their hands throughout the day, especially after toileting and prior to eating. Proper handwashing in the community reduces the number of people who get sick with diarrheic illnesses and respiratory illnesses, such as colds.

Isolation Techniques

One unfortunate downside of staying in a healthcare facility is the chance of contracting a healthcare-related infection. According to the World Health Organization (WHO), many of these can be prevented through the use of appropriate isolation techniques.

The types of infections that necessitate isolation are those that are easily transmitted and accessible to those with compromised immune systems, making it difficult for them to fend off the infection. C. diff and influenzas are the most common illnesses that are transmitted in healthcare settings. Therefore, nurses should be especially aware of these types of patients and conditions, for example, patients with an existing bloodborne disorder, such as HIV, hepatitis B or TB. In these cases, isolation safeguards may be necessary so that the person is not exposed to common pathogens, such as a cold.

Isolation techniques are categorized into one of five types:

- **Contact precautions**: Conditions with a high risk of contract transmission that often warrant isolation include C. diff, the Herpes simplex virus, scabies, MRSA, and fungal infections. This technique includes wearing gloves, using a face shield, wearing a mask, covering your shoes, washing your hands, and immediately reporting any exposure.

- **Droplet precautions**: These involve diseases spread by coughing or sneezing such as influenza, rhinovirus, pertussis, and group A streptococcus. Precautions include wearing a mask, wearing goggles, and removing protective gear and washing your hands after leaving the patient's room.

- **Airborne precautions**: Airborne infections are those that incorporate pathogen spores or dehydrated nuclei, such as Aspergillus or tuberculosis, and have a range distance of more than 10 feet. Patient isolation involves keeping them in a negative-pressure room with a lower pressure ventilation system that prevents airborne pathogens from escaping, wearing an appropriate respirator, and disposing of protective gear in an adjacent room.

- **Neutropenic precautions**: These are used in patients who have a comprised immune system resulting from a low number of neutrophils in their immune system, such as AIDS patients or those taking immunosuppressants. It is important to keep contaminants out of these patient's rooms, which may involve donning protective gear, washing hands prior to entering, and screening any items such as food or gifts.

- **Radiation precautions**: Radiation safeguards are comparable to neutropenic precautions because they also involve the possibility of a comprised immune system. When a patient is undergoing radiation therapy, time limits may be enforced for both visitors and healthcare staff to limit their exposure. The use of gowns, shoe covers, or other protective gear may be required. An exposure-guideline chart should be placed on or near the patient's door.

Practice Questions

1. Which of the following is the best way to prevent the spread of infection?
    a. Keeping the mouth covered when coughing or sneezing
    b. Disinfecting shared patient equipment
    c. Proper handwashing with soap and water
    d. Avoiding contact with infectious patients

2. What are the correct steps to follow when using a fire extinguisher?
    a. Pull the pin, Squeeze the handle, Aim the nozzle, Swirl around the fire
    b. Pull the pin, Aim at the base of the fire, Squeeze the handle, Sweep from side to side
    c. Squeeze the handle, Aim at the base of the fire, Pull the pin, Sweep from side to side
    d. Stand back, Pull the pin, Squeeze the handle, Sweep from side to side

3. When preparing to transfer a patient from their bed to a wheelchair, what is the first step to take?
    a. Ensure that the bed is locked.
    b. Inform the patient about what is going to happen.
    c. Get another staff member to help.
    d. Have the patient sit up in bed.

4. When attempting to lift something heavy, which of the following should not be done?
    a. Keep the legs straight and bend over to use back muscles.
    b. Spread legs apart and bend at the knees.
    c. Stand close to the object.
    d. Use only feet and legs to turn.

5. An aide is caring for a patient in their home. Which of the following items should the aide recognize as a fire hazard?
    a. Multiple electrical cords plugged into a power strip
    b. A pack of matches on a coffee table
    c. A potholder lying on the stove
    d. A toaster left out on the counter

6. Of the following patients, which one has the highest risk for skin injury?
    a. An elderly woman in an assisted-living facility who ambulates with a cane
    b. An eighty-year-old man in the hospital recovering from hip surgery
    c. A seventy-year-old man hospitalized for pneumonia
    d. An elderly woman who is incontinent of stool, and who is showing signs of confusion

7. Which of the following is not a preventative measure for pressure-ulcer formation?
    a. Padding bony areas on the body
    b. Repositioning the patient at least every two hours
    c. Keeping the patient in a sitting position while in their bed
    d. Changing soiled linens and clothing promptly

8. An aide is caring for a patient with a known respiratory infection. The patient is on droplet precautions. What is the minimum PPE required when caring for this patient?
    a. Gloves, gown, N-95 respirator
    b. Gown, eyewear, gloves, and a disposable mask
    c. Gloves and a disposable mask
    d. Disposable mask, sterile gloves, and eyewear

9. During lunchtime in the dining area, an aide notices a patient grabbing their throat. What should the aide's first action be?
    a. To call for help
    b. Have the patient stand up
    c. Ask the patient if they are choking
    d. To try to open the patient's mouth

10. Of the following tasks, which one is not considered "dirty"?
    a. Changing a diaper
    b. Assisting with oral care
    c. Changing a wound dressing
    d. Helping a patient get dressed

11. An aide enters a patient's room in response to the call light and sees a fire behind the television. What is the aide's first action?
    a. Activate the fire alarm.
    b. Use the nearest fire extinguisher.
    c. Move the patient to a safer location away from the room.
    d. Smother the fire with a blanket.

12. Which of the following is not a risk factor for falls in the elderly?
    a. Using a cane to walk
    b. Inadequate lighting in a room
    c. Muscle weakness
    d. Slower reflexes

Answer Explanations

1. C: All of the answer choices are types of standard precautions, but research has shown that handwashing is the best way to prevent the spread of germs.

2. B: Use the acronym PASS to answer this question. The pin should always be pulled first. Choices *A*, *C*, and *D* are not listed in the correct order or with the correct wording. The correct directions and order are: Pull the pin, Aim at the base of the fire, Squeeze the handle, and Sweep from side to side.

3. B: Anytime a task or procedure is about to occur, the patient should be informed first. All of the other options are part of the procedure, but the first step is to explain the task to the patient. Another staff person may not be needed, the patient may not be able to sit up in bed on their own, or they may wonder why they are being asked to sit up.

4. A: When lifting a heavy object, the lower back should not be strained; therefore, bending over and using the back muscles should be avoided. Choices *B*, *C*, and *D* should be done when lifting. Stand close to the object, bend at the knees with legs apart, and use feet and legs to turn if needed.

5. C: Anything flammable that is on top of a stove should be moved off of the stove surface to avoid a fire if the burners are turned on. Keep in mind that this patient is in their own home. All of the other choices are acceptable and pose no immediate fire hazard. Multiple cords should be plugged into a power strip, and a toaster left on the counter is not a hazard. The pack of matches on the table could be a hazard, but the patient is still living independently and may still be capable of using matches correctly. If there are no children in the home, the matches are not of immediate concern.

6. D: An elderly woman who is incontinent with stool will need frequent linen changes and cleansing of her bottom. The constant moisture has a very high potential for causing skin breakdown. In addition to her bottom, she is showing signs of confusion, which means she may become agitated and unaware of her surroundings, leading to potential bruises or tears on her extremities from the bed. The other patient scenarios described are also at risk for skin injury. However, with the information given, *D* is the patient with the highest risk.

7. C: Keeping a patient in a sitting position in their bed puts extra pressure on their coccyx and bottom due to gravity; therefore, this option is not a preventative measure for pressure-ulcer formation. Choices *A*, *B*, and *D* are interventions that should be done to help prevent pressure ulcers.

8. C: Gloves and a disposable mask are all that are required for droplet precaution; however, additional PPE may be used if desiring extra protection. The key word in this question is *minimum*. Choice *A* is not correct because an N-95 mask is not required. Choice *D* is not correct because sterile gloves are not needed and eyewear is optional. Choice *B* would give the most coverage for protection but it is not the minimum PPE required.

9. C: The first thing to do is to check to see if the patient is choking. They may nod their head if they are asked about choking, and they will not be able to talk. If the person is choking, help them stand up so that the Heimlich maneuver can be started. Choice *A*, calling for help, would not be necessary unless the person becomes unconscious or if help is needed with the Heimlich. Choice *D* is incorrect because it is not appropriate to look in the person's mouth for a lodged piece of food, as the nurse could make the obstruction worse, as well as waste precious time.

10. D: Helping a patient get dressed is not considered a dirty task unless the clothing is soiled with any bodily fluid. *A*, *B*, and *C* are all tasks that involve bodily fluids and are considered dirty. Clean tasks should be performed first, followed by dirty tasks.

11. C: Use the acronym RACE to answer this question. The information given in the question leads to the fact that the patient is in the room, and that there is probably an electrical fire. The first action should be to rescue the patient by removing them from the room. Next, activate the fire alarm and then contain the fire by closing the door to the room. Extinguish the fire with the appropriate extinguisher if available. Choice *D*, smothering the fire, is not appropriate for an electrical fire.

12. A: Use of a cane is not a risk factor for falls in the elderly. A cane would actually benefit a person by giving them extra stability when walking. Poor lighting is a risk factor because it could cause someone to stumble over items on the floor or cause an imbalance by bumping into unseen furniture. Muscle weakness and slower reflexes are also risk factors for falls in the elderly.

Health Promotion and Maintenance

Aging Process

Across the lifespan, from conception to birth, infancy to school-age, adolescence to adulthood, and middle age to death, the human experience is not unique. Like most other mammals, humans are said to be sentient beings, in possession of all of the five senses and self-awareness. With self-awareness comes the realization of one's own mortality. The aging process is linear, beginning at the moment of birth. Distinctly, the aged population is generally said to include those over the age of sixty-five. Although many expect to see a marked decline in physiological and neurological functioning, this is not necessarily the case. Depending on individual lifestyle choices, high-risk behaviors, and adherence to annually recommended health screenings, the aging process can be uneventful.

For all patient populations, one of the most important topics to discuss is their diet. Especially for older adults, proper nutrition is critical. Income fluctuations due to retirement or lost income from a deceased or divorced spouse may affect the grocery budget. Vitamin deficiencies can quickly become problematic, resulting in a brief or prolonged hospitalization. Neurological concerns may also affect memory, and patients may simply forget to eat. Simple questions regarding favorite meals, restaurants, or eating preferences can yield answers. It is important to note that missing meals can also become commonplace if a depression diagnosis exists. Inserting a brief depression inventory early in the visit may reveal the major reason for the patient's current health status and uncover areas of concern regarding daily nutrition.

Exercise is also a crucial piece of the assessment puzzle when discussing healthy lifestyle choices. Chronological age is not synonymous with physical decline, and patients should be encouraged to continue with exercise as tolerated. Simply walking daily for 30 minutes, broken into segments if necessary, is a great starting point. Weight-bearing exercise, isometrics, swimming, yoga, Pilates, or Tai-Chi all provide patients with the opportunity for gentle movement if some mobility issues exist. If needed, physical or occupational therapies can aide in the restoration of mobility and should be suggested after injury or with sedentary patients. Older patients must be reminded that retirement is not a signal to simply age, but the opportunity to age well.

Apart from the maintenance of diet and exercise is the importance of socialization and hobbies. Aging can be an isolating experience, especially as adult children move away and manage separate families. Less time may be spent with extended family and, once retired, the older adult may see less need for meeting new people in general. It is important for the nurse to assess the patient's perceived need for companionship. What do they do for fun? How do they unwind? Do they have a bucket list and what's on it? These types of open-ended questions not only create dialogue but can quickly become a goal-setting session.

When discussing high-risk behaviors with members of the aged population, it is imperative that the nurse include sexual activity. Although thought to be less sexually active than younger patients, this age group has seen a dramatic increase in sexually transmitted disease (STD) in recent years. Many have lost a spouse or life partner to death or divorce, and experience bouts of profound loneliness and sexual frustration. Although some may be seeking to remarry, most are interested in companionship and may not consider STDs to be a major concern. It is not as necessary to discuss birth control with a postmenopausal woman or elderly man as it is to discuss chlamydia, gonorrhea, herpes, and HIV. A

simple question regarding intimate partners or social life will likely yield more information that the nurse can use to gently introduce the subject.

Nurses must carefully assess the likelihood of the progression of both medical and mental health concerns. Historically, the longer an individual manages chronic disease, the more complicated the illness becomes. More biological systems are impacted, leading to further physiological compromise. For example, diabetes mellitus, if managed well over a number of years, may still result in renal, visual, and cardiovascular complications in later years. The nurse must discuss basic diabetic care with the patient at every encounter. Annual eye exams, podiatric care, consultation with a diabetic nutritionist or dietician, and adhering closely to the diet plan, are all essential.

An additional, distinctive aspect of the aged population is neurological decline. Alzheimer's disease and dementia are said to contribute to a majority of hospitalizations and nursing home placements. Nurses must be familiar with a brief neurological assessment, also referred to as a **mental status exam**, in order to provide appropriate care. It is also necessary to assess the patient frequently for abrupt decline in functioning. Patients have a tendency to be forgetful, combative, and/or behave in a childlike manner. Neurological compromise can affect balance and gait, often resulting in falls and injury. Careful consideration to the safety of the patient's home environment is critical. Caregivers must be educated, trained, and prepared regarding the signs and symptoms of neurological impairment, along with appropriate interventions. It will also be necessary to discuss or review end-of-life care plans.

One final integral piece to the assessment of the older adult is preparation for the treatment and care of the patient and the family at the end of life. Some patients may have previously determined their preferences for end-of-life and palliative care. Obtain a copy of all advance directives and review for accuracy with the patient or caregiver. Does the patient possess the ability or desire to make changes to the documents? Are the primary and secondary proxy agents present or readily available if needed for consultation? The nurse must approach the discussion of comfort care with an awareness of the appropriate parties to include from the patient's preferred circle of confidants. If the nurse is unfamiliar with these topics, enlisting the assistance of a chaplain, social worker, or hospice care professional is vital. Respite care, bereavement counseling, and support-group referrals also are essential for the patient and family to ease their transition through the dying process.

Ante/Intra/Postpartum and Newborn Care

Excellent nursing care prior to, during, and immediately following childbirth is essential. Pregnancy as a medical state comprises several distinct stages: antepartum, intrapartum, postpartum, and newborn care. **Antepartum care** can be defined as care during pregnancy. During this period, the pregnant patient must be assessed periodically for appropriate fetal growth, responsiveness in-utero, and the mother's overall health status. Any fluctuations in these areas signal the potential for maternal or fetal distress. It is necessary to obtain a complete medical, gynecological, and obstetrical history. The nurse must be aware of any sexually transmitted diseases, previous abortions or full-term pregnancies (gravida), any complications, and the number of vaginal and cesarean births (para), as well as estimated date of delivery (EDD) and current birth plan.

The term **intrapartum care** refers to care provided during childbirth. Pregnancy is a progressive medical state; nursing care during the intrapartum period is based on all information gathered during the antepartum period. The mother and fetus are monitored simultaneously for signs of distress. Although continuous fetal monitoring is the standard of care, intermittent auscultation is acceptable if performed hourly. On average, fetal heart tones range from 120 to 160 beats per minute (bpm), with periodic accelerations over 160 bpm denoting a positively responding fetus. The nurse must be equipped to discuss preferred treatment for uterine contractions and provide emotional support during delivery. Once cervical dilation reaches 10cm, the nurse must contact the provider and begin preparations for delivery of the infant. Once delivered, the mother and infant enter the postpartum stage.

The **postpartum phase** is considered to begin immediately after childbirth and ends after six weeks. Once the infant is delivered, it becomes a second patient and must be cared for separately from the mother. The nurse must assess both patients every 15 minutes for 2 hours to confirm that both mother and infant are adjusting well. Continued hospitalization is generally no longer than one day for a vaginal birth and two to three days for a cesarean section. Upon discharge—with infant care manual, feeding plan, and patient education completed—the couplet and other caregivers return to the home environment. Within weeks, the couplet will visit the physician, for well checks. This nursing assessment includes a depression inventory and discussions of progress with infant feeding.

Infants born prior to 37 weeks' gestation are considered to be preterm and at a high risk for complications at birth and throughout infancy. Specialized care of preterm infants and those born with twice-repeated APGAR scores below 7 must occur in the neonatal intensive care unit. Well infants are roomed in with their mothers, as a couplet. The postpartum nurse must be prepared to teach the parent(s) on feeding, changing, and general care of the infant. Umbilical cord care, as well as proper cleaning of a circumcised penis, is also vital in preparation for the discharge home. Within the first 24-to-48 hours after birth, careful assessment must be performed to ascertain if the infant is not adjusting to his or her new environment.

Identifying Emotional Preparedness for Pregnancy

Pregnancies can result in a wide range of emotions and sensitivities, including happiness, dread, mood fluctuations, worry, financial uncertainties, despair, and uncharacteristic responses. These can be experienced by either parent and vary significantly among patients depending on any number of factors.

It is important for nurses to check for any warning signs such as any of the above-listed emotional cues, physical appearance, or financial situation that might signal the degree of emotional readiness of the parents-to-be and their support systems, including family and community members and systems. These types of social support systems are invaluable to patients dealing with a pregnancy. It is estimated that around half of all pregnancies are unplanned, which may involve single and/or teen mothers.

Some women may have a great deal of support and others may have little or none, especially when the father is not around and/or unwelcoming of an unwanted pregnancy. When those involved in these situations are not emotionally prepared, it is important for the nurse to support any decisions related to abortion and/or adoption that might arise.

Performing Nonstress Test

A **nonstress test** is performed in the third trimester to check the wellbeing of the baby by gauging the fetal heart rate and movements of the baby in a noninvasive way. The procedure involves placing a stretchy belt monitor around the pregnant mother's stomach and asking her to track each of the baby's movements. Sometimes this is done with a handheld clicker which the mother is asked to press each time she feels a movement. The process typically takes 20 to 40 minutes. Normal results occur when the heart rate of the fetus increases by at least 15 beats per minute over a period of 15 seconds during fetal movement. An abnormal and nonreactive test result should be noted when the heart rate of the fetus does NOT increase by at least 15 beats per minute over 15 during fetal movement.

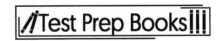

Fetal Heart Monitoring for the Antepartum Client

Antepartum monitoring (the time just before childbirth) is key to preventing fetal death and is a widely accepted tool in dealing with high-risk pregnancies or problems such as fetal distress, atypical uterine contractions, hypertension, diabetes, post-term births, and multiple birth situations.

Fetal heart rate monitoring can be external or internal. In **external heart rate monitoring**, a device such as a Doppler ultrasound is placed on the mother's abdomen to record the heartbeat of the baby. During the antepartum period, an ultrasound probe (also known as a transducer) strapped to the abdomen can be used to transmit the baby's heartbeat to a computer where the heart rate and pattern are displayed on the screen and a physical printout. **Internal heart rate monitoring** utilizes a thin electrode that is attached to the baby's scalp via the cervix to connect to a monitor to give a more accurate reading. This method is only possible if the mother's water (amniotic sac) surrounding the baby has ruptured and the cervix has opened. It is typically used when the external method of fetal heart monitoring is not giving a good reading.

Monitoring a Patient in Labor

There are two ways to monitor fetal heart rate during labor: **auscultation** is intermittently checking the fetal heartbeat, and **electronic fetal monitoring** is using electronic instruments to regularly log the fetus's heartbeat and contractions of the mother's uterus during labor. The type of monitoring typically depends on the policies of the healthcare provider and medical facility, whether the pregnancy/birth is deemed to be high-risk, and how the labor is progressing. Either method is fine as long as there are no predetermined complications or risk factors, and none arise during labor.

The mother's condition and vital signs should be assessed during the various stages of labor. These assessments should include the following:

- An evaluation of the mother's status
- An account of the mother's uterine activity
- Fetal status
- Vaginal examination and description
- Position of the baby
- Change in fetal membranes and progression of the pregnancy
- A summary of the baby and mother and the pregnancy plan, including plans for medical intervention and managing pain.

Care of Postpartum Patients

Caring for the mother after the baby is born involves checking for signs of postpartum complications such as infections and hemorrhage and making sure the baby is getting the proper nourishment from the mother, either through breast or bottle feeding. The mother's vital statistics such as temperature, blood pressure, etc. should normalize within 24 hours of the baby's birth. Atypical readings as well as symptoms such as location-specific pain, a flushed appearance, feeling hot or swollen, feeling tired, chilled or confused, exhibiting an irregular heartbeat, the malfunction of a body part or organ, unable to go to the bathroom, or gastrointestinal distress are all signals to the nurse to perform additional health checks on the mother.

Newborn Plan of Care

After the baby is born, it is important for the nurse to help a new mother and others who will be caring for the baby to understand what is involved in feeding and tending to the needs of a newborn so they feel ready to care for the newborn once they leave the medical facility. Essential points to go over with the patient and others involved in the care include the baby's dietary needs, the basics of breast and/or bottle feeding, how to care for the umbilical cord and circumcision site, how to change and secure a diaper, how to prevent life-threatening accidents, how best to answer and cope with a crying baby, as well as emotional components such as bonding and attachment.

Community Resources

Community Resources for Patients

Sometimes it is deemed necessary or at least helpful to refer a patient to a health care or other support contact following discharge from the facility. The healthcare team, including nurses, evaluate each patient accordingly and establish their needs in relation to present and possible issues.

Community resources include groups providing support for topics such as:

- Psychological care for those in a crisis situation (abuse, trauma, etc.)
- Managing anger (especially for those causing abuse)
- Social service organizations for patients without insurance and those requiring welfare aid
- Relief for caregivers who feel overburdened
- Self-help counseling support groups
- Housing assistance, including shelters for victims and children of abusive situations
- Providing transport to and from medical appointments
- Elder day care, home healthcare aid and recreational activities geared for senior citizens
- Childrearing support, including resources offering childcare and education assistance for infants, children, and teens
- Nutritional guidance to help individuals, families, and specific groups within a community attain a better dietary understanding and cope with issues such as obesity, diabetes and heart disease
- Exercise classes or programs to help promote health and fitness within a community
- Group and individual guidance for smoking cessation and substance abuse

Community Health Education

Sometimes it is the responsibility of the nurse to help devise and/or join in health educational programs in the community. These settings can vary significantly depending on the type of service offered, their degree of formality and the number of participants.

In order to correctly design a community health program, a nurse must evaluate the educational needs of those involved and come up with a plan that fulfills these requirements. Depending on the proposed strategy, the role of the nurse can range from providing in-person talks to a large community group, informing a small group of members about a specific health topic or issue, or providing personal assistance and informational sessions. It is important for the nurse to remain organized and proficient at all times no matter what the duties necessitate.

Reinforcing Teaching About Health Risks

Patients are often at risk for healthcare issues that radiate wider than their individual needs. Nurses must evaluate the awareness level of the patients under their care regarding their health risks based on their individual families, populations and communities. Each of these groups has varying facets and risk factors that could impact the patient. For example, there are many developmental transformations and milestones that affect children in a family; patients should be advised of these stages and any suitable

actions the patient can do to avoid the risk of developmental delays. The population could be impacted by the advent of an influenza outbreak, and so should be informed about the benefits of getting a flu vaccination. Communities often contain various parks and other recreational resources; these should be communicated to the patient and made aware of the benefits of exercise.

Data Collection Techniques

Collecting Data for a Health History

Nurses must perform a **health history** in order to gather essential statistics and information about present and prior health conditions, and health risks and requirements of the patient and their family. The information collected can consist of the following:

- **Primary data**: Information given directly by the patient
- **Secondary data**: Information taken from sources other than the patient
- **Subjective data**: Information that is inferred by the nurse but cannot be demonstrably observed
- **Objective data**: Data that is observed based on senses such as sight, smell or touch
- **Quantitative data**: Statistical data such as vital signs readings and lab results
- **Qualitative data**: Descriptive information such as the patient's pain level explanation

Collecting Baseline Physical Data

The nurse makes a note of a patient's baseline data following their health history but prior to their full head to toe analysis. This general survey provides a comparative starting point for the healthcare team to help evaluate condition and make care decisions. It consists of the patient's height, weight, body type, posture, walking ability, signs of pain, personal hygiene and grooming conditions, skin pallor, vital signs, oxygen levels, and the true age of the patient versus the age in appearance.

Preparing a Patient for Physical Examinations

It is important for nurses to effectively and efficiently get patients properly situated and ready for their physical examination. This includes ensuring a private setting, clarifying and emphasizing procedures, and making sure the patient is as comfortable as possible during the exam.

Documenting Findings

As is typical with all facets of nursing care, the information gathered during the patient's health history and physical examination are noted and recorded as per the guidelines and standard practices of the healthcare facility. Some facilities employ special forms to document this type of data.

Reporting Physical Examination Results

It is the responsibility of the LPN to evaluate the patient's past medical record and the results of their baseline physical exam and continually compare it to their present health situation while under their care. They should also record and convey all noteworthy results of the physical exam to the head registered nurse and/or patient's health care provider.

Developmental Stages and Transitions

Nurses must be able to recognize and document any patient data that differs from what is considered normal regarding physical and mental growth and maturity. In addition, they need to adjust the level and way they will care for the patient based on their findings. Changes that are to be expected include those associated with standard developmental stages such as puberty, menopause, pregnancy and aging. Abrupt weight gain or loss or stunted growth are not normal. Examples of atypical situations that would signal a problem and should be reported by the nurse include when a girl menstruates early (10 years or younger), a woman entering menopause at a young age (early 40s), teenage pregnancy, or severe weight loss, the latter of which could be a sign of anorexia, bulimia, or other malnutrition reasons.

Nurses should evaluate how anticipated changes in body image may influence the patient's quality of life and daily activities. These can include feelings and thoughts that strike during puberty, menopause, pregnancy, and as part of aging. If the nurse has any reason to believe that the patient cannot adapt or cope properly, this evidence should be established, noted, and reported so that the healthcare team can alter the patient's care strategy in order to manage these issues. Nurses can ask the patient how they perceive themselves in terms of body image, how they think they look to others, how the changes in their body make them feel, and how long they have felt this way. Signs that a patient may be having body image issues can include the following:

- Trying to cover the body or specific area in question
- Refusal to acknowledge the change
- A decline in personal hygiene
- Social withdrawal
- Obsession with the body or body part
- Poor self-esteem

Erikson's Psychosocial Stages of Development

Erikson's Psychosocial Stages of Development is an alternative to Freud's psychosexual stages. According to Erikson's epigenetic principle of maturation, human beings pass through eight developmental stages, each of which build upon the preceding stages and set the groundwork for the stages that follow.

All eight stages are present at birth but remain latent until both an innate schedule and an individual's cultural upbringing cause a stage to begin to unfold.

An individual does not have to "master" a stage in order to proceed to the next stage, and the outcome of a particular stage may later be changed by an individual's life experiences.

As with Freud's theory, Erikson proposed that each stage of development is characterized by a crisis; however, for Erikson, the crisis involves a conflict between the needs of the developing individual and the needs of society.

Successfully mastering a stage and its psychosocial crisis leads to the development of a healthy personality and possession of basic virtues.

Erikson's theory centers on the development of ego identity, or a sense of self that is acquired by interacting with the social environment.

Self-Image Throughout the Life Cycle

Self-image has to do with how people view themselves. This concept includes **self-esteem**, whether a person has feelings of high or low worth. The concept of self evolves throughout the life span, but it always plays a significant role in a how a person functions in life.

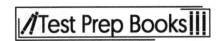

Infancy: The ego is in charge. The baby thinks primarily of basic needs, such as food or warmth.

Childhood: In early to middle childhood, children tend to rate themselves higher than peers in terms of talents and intellect. As middle school approaches, there is a decline in self-evaluations. This could be related to feeling unattractive due to physical changes or being teased or bullied by peers in that age group.

Adolescence: In the early stage of adolescence (ages nine to thirteen), another drop in self-esteem occurs. This is thought to be related to the need to let go of childish pleasures, such as a beloved toy or previous interests, and step up to the plate of becoming a more responsible person. This can be a painful sacrifice for some youth. The next drop in self-worth occurs at the end of adolescence and beginning of young adulthood (ages eighteen to twenty-three). It is during this period that the young adults realize that they truly are responsible for their own lives, yet they have not yet achieved a sense of mastery in the academic or vocational world. They are fearful and full of doubt about the ability to be successful as an independent adult.

Adulthood: Studies indicate a small but steady increase in self-image by mid-twenties. In general, during this period, men tend to have higher self-esteem than women. Persons who live in poor socioeconomic conditions tend to have lower self-esteem than their more financially stable peers. As later adulthood nears (the seventies), women tend to catch up with men in terms of how they evaluate themselves. Women in their eighties tend to have a more positive self-image than male counterparts. As a general rule, for both genders, there is a gradual increase in one's sense of self-worth throughout the life span until late middle age. Research shows that most adults' self-image peaks at around age sixty.

Influence of Age on Behaviors and Attitudes

There are various, and sometimes conflicting, hypotheses with regard to how and whether attitudes change with age.

- **Impressionable-years hypothesis**: The environment and socialization that people experience when they are young shape their worldviews and have a profound effect on their attitudes for the remainder of the lifespan.

- **Increasing persistence hypothesis**: People exhibit flexible and impressionable thinking when they are younger but become increasingly inflexible with age.

- **Life-long openness hypothesis**: People exhibit flexible and impressionable thinking throughout the lifespan, and their attitudes are dependent upon evolving life circumstances.

Some changes in behavior and thinking may be related to the changes that older adults often experience as they navigate their later years. For example, they may experience a loss of independence due to impaired health or a loss of identity and confidence as they cope with retirement. People who have always had difficulty with change are particularly likely to experience negative effects of change during older adulthood.

Examples may include somatic complaints, denial that change has occurred, feelings of powerlessness, rigid thinking, isolation, anger, depression, grief, or regression to earlier behavior.

Barriers to Communication

There are several different types of communication, including verbal, written, and nonverbal. **Verbal communication** occurs when two parties are speaking out loud; this can be in person, through video technology, or over the phone. **Written communication** can be through physical or digital writing or printing, such as e-mails, faxes, and instant messages. **Nonverbal communication** is transferred through one party's observations of the other party's body language and facial expressions.

Good communication depends on a number of factors. Do the speakers speak the same language? Language can be a barrier to communication and can be overcome with a translator. Sometimes, a family member can help with communication. Cultural barriers exist in communication as some cultures have certain beliefs about how one should talk, who should do the speaking, and how much one should speak.

The nurse should be careful not to create **nonverbal barriers** to communication with patients and coworkers. An example of a nonverbal barrier is the nurse having a personal smartphone in hand and scrolling through social media while a patient or coworker is trying to talk to them. This action suggests the nurse is not paying attention and does not care about what is being said, which inhibits good communication.

Physical barriers to communication may exist, such as a patient having a speech, hearing, visual, or other sensory impairment. The patient may have cognitive difficulties understanding basic communication, brought on by illness, change in level of consciousness, or dementia.

Barriers to Learning

Facilitation of learning refers to the process of assessing the learning needs of the patient and family, the nursing staff, and caregivers in the community, and creating, implementing, and evaluating formal and informal educational programs to address those needs. Novice nurses often view patient care and patient education as separate entities; however, experienced nurses are able to integrate the patient's educational needs into the plan of care. Nurses are aware that the patient often requires continued reinforcement of the educational plan after discharge, which necessitates coordination with home care services.

As facilitators of learning, nurses may be involved in a large-scale effort to educate all patients over 65 admitted to the nursing unit about the need for both Prevnar 13 and Pneumovax 23 to prevent pneumonia. In contrast, nurses may provide one-on-one instruction for a patient recently diagnosed with diabetes. The first step of any teaching-learning initiative is the assessment of the learning needs of the participants. Specific needs that influence the design and content of the educational offering include the language preference and reading level of the participants. Nurses must also consider the effect of certain patient characteristics identified in the Synergy Model on the patient's capacity to process information. Diminished resiliency or stability, and extreme complexity, must be considered in the development of the educational plan. Nurses are also responsible for creating a bridge between teaching-learning in the acute care setting and the home environment. A detailed discharge plan, close coordination with outpatient providers, and follow-up phone calls to the patient may be used to reinforce the patient's knowledge of the plan of care.

Successful learning plans for staff members and colleagues also consider the motivation of the participants to engage in the process. Successful facilitators include a variety of teaching strategies to develop the content and evaluate learning, in order to address adult learning needs and preferences, such as preferred language and reading level. Research indicates that when adults do not have a vested interest in the outcomes of the teaching/learning process, they may not participate as active learners.

The remaining element of successful facilitation of learning is the availability and quality of learning resources. There is evidence that individuals with different learning styles respond differently to various learning devices. The minimum requirements for successful facilitation of learning include the skilled staff to develop the educational materials, paper, a copy machine, and staff to interact with the patient in the learning session.

Barriers to the facilitation of learning must be anticipated and accommodated. Changes in the patient's condition commonly require reduction in the time spent in each learning session due to fatigue. Cognitive impairment can impede comprehension and retention of the information and will require appropriate teaching aids. The learning abilities of the patient's family members must also be assessed. Adequate instruction time might be the greatest barrier. Learning needs are assessed and discharge planning is begun on the day of admission; however, shortened inpatient stays require evaluation of the patient's comprehension of the plan of care.

Health Promotion/Disease Prevention

Two of the most important aspects of providing exceptional nursing care are health promotion and disease prevention. Both are integral to ensuring the physical and psychological wellbeing of individuals, groups, and the community at large.

Health promotion can be loosely defined as the direct or indirect presentation of information, specifically designed to influence behaviors that are expected to result in positive health outcomes. When presented directly, the instruction may be in written form such as brochures, books, or articles in magazines or newspapers. Historically, these publications were typically available in physician's offices, clinics, and hospitals. For nurses, health promotion is no longer relegated to easily discarded brochures or pamphlets. With the introduction of the Internet, information targeting healthy activities can be found instantly after several keystrokes. Nursing interventions can be provided via webinars, face-to-face coaching sessions, telephonic care, and social media sites. These mediums allow the nurse to contact thousands of individuals at once and increase exposure.

Indirect presentation of healthy lifestyle choices often occurs through billboards, signage, or posters in physicians' offices, as well as strategic mention or product placement in movies and television shows. Increasing numbers of "reality TV" stars can be seen holding bottles of a specific brand of vitamins or diet pills, or leaving a restaurant noted for healthy dishes. Albeit not as successful as the direct-to-consumer approach, this allows for health promotion to sneak in the back doors of viewers' minds, slowly affecting their daily habits. Traditionally, nurses are not involved in this type of health promotion, but nurses can use this type of behavior when interacting with patients. Ensuring that hand washing posters are present in restrooms, display cases of vitamins and supplements in the office waiting area, and sponsorship or participation in local health fairs all support higher awareness.

In an effort to actively guide the **prevention of disease**, community health nurses employ numerous tactics. Each strategy is specific to a particular population to intervene at several stages of the disease process.

Primary prevention consists of the nursing strategies implemented to prevent the onset of a particular disease process. One well-known example of primary disease prevention is the "say no to drugs" movement. Nurses in this campaign can specifically target young children and teens to prevent their initial use of drugs with the use of buttons, posters, commercials, and rallies. **Secondary prevention** focuses on the early detection of disease and prevention of considerable damage from the disease process. Using the same example, "pill checks" at rave parties would represent secondary prevention. Nurses and often paraprofessionals attend parties with teens to test the pills of party goers. This is done onsite, in the presence of the user, explaining what is found in the pill and offering to discard it. Finally, tertiary prevention efforts with this same patient population would be nursing interventions implemented in drug treatment centers, clinics, and detox units in the hospital. These nurses work with the patients actively addicted to substances and collaborate to manage their disease.

Risk Factors for Disease

The nurse gathers information and evidence regarding a patient's **risk factors** for disease from their health history upon admission to the facility, during their physical exam, and through the duration of their care. Risk factors are influences that could trigger a health-related issue such as sickness, infection, disease or some other aliment. They can be inherent, such as high blood pressure, which increases the likelihood of other disorders; or external, such as smoking, which increases the risk of lung cancer. Certain risk factors can be diminished or eradicated, especially those related to lifestyle habits such as poor diet, smoking or drinking.

Immunizations

Some types of vaccinations are obligatory as per the CDC (Centers for Disease Control and Prevention) and state regulations, such as childhood inoculations to prevent communicable diseases; others are voluntary but CDC-recommended, such as adult vaccinations for pneumonia.

Nurses need to have a working knowledge of the various immunization laws and endorsements for the age group under their care. For example, when working with young patients, nurses must know the CDC's schedule for childhood immunizations. They also need to be aware of CDC-recommendation vaccinations for adult patients who are considered at-risk for various illnesses when under their care. For instance, elderly patients with a risk respiratory disease should get the pneumonia vaccine and an annual flu shot.

The CDC has some contraindications and safeguards for certain vaccines that nurses need to be aware of. For instance, second doses of the hepatitis and DTaP vaccines should not be given when the person has had an anaphylactic episode after the first dose. They should also be used with caution on patients who have a serious illness with or without a fever. It is important for nurses to be aware that there are many myths and rumors constantly circulating about vaccines and to address any patient concerns empathically in order to reassure any apprehensive patients.

Hearing Aids, Dentures, and Eyeglasses

Patients who have difficulty hearing may require a referral to an audiologist who may then fit them with a hearing aid. Hearing aids, along with glasses, should be kept in a safe place when not in use. Small assistive devices such as hearing aids, dentures, and eyeglasses can easily be lost in the linens when they are changed or carried away with the food tray if they are left on top. The nurse and nurse's aid should work with the patient and family to ensure that these items are stored properly to avoid losing them. These items can be very difficult to track down if lost in the linens, in a bedside waste basket, or on the food tray. They are often very expensive to replace for the patient.

Health Screening

Historically, nurses have been primarily responsible for conducting **health screenings**. Every biological system within the human body should be screened periodically to ensure that it is operating at optimal levels. At the start of every developmental stage, it is recommended that patients be screened and, if

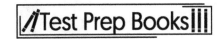

found deficient, treated and monitored for progress. Health screenings are suggested based on chronological age to guide both individual treatment and trends for developing community outreach. Armed with the data, nurses collaborate with patients, providers, and caregivers to formulate an effective treatment plan.

Nurses working within the community health sector also utilize health screenings to guide disease-prevention efforts on a larger scale. Nurse researchers can use the data to aide in the creation of medications and advertisement campaigns to target those individuals on the borderlines of a particular disease process. Further, community-health nurses can conduct health screenings to identify gaps in access to healthcare, barriers to care, and disease maintenance. Once the information is disseminated to surrounding healthcare providers, clinics, and local government officials, the community-health nurse can begin the dialogue to effect policy changes. More engagement with health fairs, educational seminars, and print and social media campaigns may also result from health screenings.

Overall, health screenings are an integral piece of the healthcare puzzle. As nurses, it is often necessary to discuss the importance of annual health-screening recommendations upon each patient encounter. If patients reject or accept the recommended testing, they become aware of any present risk factors. Nurses can probe for information as to their ambivalence. For example, while completing a depression screening, a nurse can determine if an individual is at risk for depression. A patient who scores higher on the questionnaire can reveal if the answers are an accurate representation of daily high-risk behavior, or situational in nature.

Nurses are required to educate, prep, and help clients when undergoing a screening exam. These preventative procedures are designed to detect diseases, infections, and other health ailments in their initial stages. Examples include colonoscopy screenings, Pap smears, mammograms, and ultrasounds. Nurse responsibilities include evaluating the results of the screening test and then following up with the patient. They also communicate results to the patient's doctor and make sure they are documented on the patient's medical record as per the facility's specific guidelines and practices.

A **mammogram** involves compressing the patient's breasts between two plate-like surfaces to expand the breast tissue area. An X-ray then displays images of the breasts via a computer screen so they can be checked by a doctor for signs of cancer. Nurses can help patients prep for this exam by advising them to schedule it during a time their breasts are likely to be less tender (e.g. not right before their period), not to use deodorant before the screening as it can obscure the image, and making them feel comfortable the day of the exam.

During a **colonoscopy**, a doctor uses a long, flexible tube to look inside a patient's colon for abnormalities. This screening procedure requires the patient to be sedated and follow a liquid diet and take a preparatory course of drinkable laxatives starting the day before. Nurses can help advise patients regarding the specific prep involved and also about any discomfort they might feel during and after the procedure.

Pap smear screenings scrape cells from the cervix to check for precancerous or cancerous cell abnormalities. For this test, the doctor inserts a speculum into the patient's vagina to widen the vaginal walls and provide easier access to the cervix. Nurses can help prep patients by advising not to schedule the exam during menstruation since it can skew results, to avoid sexual activity, to avoid using a douche or spermicidal products the day before the test, and help keep the patient relaxed the day of the test.

Cancer Screening

Cancer screening tests relevant to several organ systems have effectively decreased the incidence and mortality of cancer in those systems. Common screening tests include the PAP test for cervical cancer, colonoscopy for colon cancer, and mammography for breast cancer. Recently, screening for lung cancer with advanced computed tomography (CT) technology in patients with a history of smoking has been proposed, in an effort to identify lung cancers at an earlier stage that may be treated more successfully. Conversely, the research indicates that there is insufficient evidence to support any relationship between decreased disease incidence and morbidity and the prostate-specific antigen test (PSA) measurements for prostate cancer, or the annual full-body skin assessments by a dermatologist. In addition, there are no screening tests available for ovarian cancer.

Osteoporosis Screening/Bone-Density Scan

Osteoporosis is the "thinning" of the bone, which most commonly affects postmenopausal women. The degree and progression of the changes associated with osteoporosis can be measured by the bone-density exam, which compares a patient's test results with the results of younger patients who are disease free.

Domestic Violence Screening and Detection

The efficiency of domestic violence screening and detection is often hampered by the reluctance of the abused individual to report the abuse. Institutions and insurance companies have included routine assessment questions related to a patient's perceptions of personal safety; however, the widespread acceptance and effectiveness of these measures are not known.

High Risk Behaviors

High-risk behaviors can be defined as actions that have a high probability of yielding a negative consequence. Nurses must develop a rapport with patients in an effort to create open communication so the patient will be more likely to reveal conduct that could have detrimental health outcomes. This technique can also encourage patients to ask questions about their risky behaviors. The nurse can then use the established rapport to discern if the patient's level of comfort and commitment to the behaviors is amenable to change.

One of the most effective methods of encouraging open communication with patients is motivational interviewing. Nurses use motivational interviewing to assess, collaborate, plan, and implement treatment with patients. There are five major components of motivational interviewing: express empathy, illustrate incongruity, manage resistance, encourage self-validation, and promote independence. The nurse can employ these steps when combatting ambivalence to change. For example, when working with a patient who is considering smoking cessation, begin with simple statements regarding the difficulties involved with quitting. This often results in the patient remarking about the number of attempts to quit, along with reasons why his or her prior attempts did not end in success. Next, draw from earlier statements concerning lifestyle choices, the patient's own reasons for quitting, and the potential for negative outcomes. In the next step, the nurse can tie the elements together, choosing carefully which area of resistance to target. What might the patient gain from quitting? What are the potential barriers to success from the patient's viewpoint? Asking these open-ended questions will help patients draw their own conclusions, validating the ability to self-navigate through possible obstacles. Once able to verbalize how the desired outcome could be achieved, the patient has managed to break through his or her own resistance, and the groundwork has been set for more internal dialogue.

Lifestyle Choices

Traditionally, nursing interventions are designed to target the **lifestyle choices** that affect disease processes. During every patient encounter, the nurse must ask open-ended questions in order to determine which interventions should be implemented. The acronym **SMART** (specific, measurable, attainable, relevant, and timely) is a concise reference for patients. When it is clearly what the main objective is, the likelihood of achieving that goal is increased.

When addressing multiple issues, choose one area with the highest likelihood of success to build momentum and patient confidence in the process. For example, when discussing diet, it is important for the nurse to first establish what the patient's current diet and exercise plan includes. This dialogue will open the door to likes, dislikes, preferred cooking methods, and diet history. As the discussion expands, inquire about budgetary constraints and access to healthy food options. Once eating habits are known, define daily scheduling conflicts that may become barriers to success. Create a contingency plan, with multiple options. Another major area of importance for lifestyle choices is exercise. Upon reviewing current diagnoses, medications, and any mobility or chronic pain concerns, the nurse can partner with the patient to formulate a reasonable plan. Set a specific goal on the type and duration of exercise; measure steps or activity as accurately as possible with a pedometer. Can they commit to exercise daily? What is an appropriate form of exercise? Maintain the stance of advocate and collaborator to preserve patients' autonomy and validate their experiences whenever possible.

Some types of contraception are not recommended because of the patient's lifestyle choices, agreement level, or a medical condition. For instance, women who smoke and are predisposed to deep vein thrombosis should not use oral contraceptives because they are at risk for blood clots and strokes. Nurses need to be able to identify and convey anticipated consequences of contraception to the patient. These can include being aware of the different family planning methods best suited to the patient's needs and situation, the absence of unplanned pregnancies, the ability to plan a pregnancy until the patient feels the time is appropriate, and participating in a relationship that is sexually satisfying without being afraid of getting pregnant.

When patients exhibit the necessity and wish for contraception, nurses need to remain impartial in their encouragement, no matter their personal thoughts or principles on the topic. Some patients will be eager to discuss the possibility of contraception and others may be hesitant to discuss sexuality and family planning topics. In these circumstances, it is imperative for nurses to develop a level of trust with the patient and encourage them to be able to talk about their viewpoints without feeling judged or ashamed. When discussing these topics with a patient, the nurse needs to convey the advantages, dangers, cost, accessibility, and possible impediments and contraindications of the different types of contraception.

Self-Care

The job of a nurse is physically, mentally, and emotionally stressful. The strain of moving and lifting patients, along with going from room to room constantly answering the needs of the patients for a long shift, can be physically exhausting. One must organize one's time, prioritize tasks, answer questions, and have countless conversations with the healthcare team and patients and their families, all of which can take a mental toll. Dealing with patients who are sick, in pain, suffering, and, in some cases, facing death, can drain a nurse's emotional reserves, which can quickly lead to burnout if left unaddressed. Being aware of this potential for overall fatigue is the first step to managing stress and maintaining one's own health.

It is important that a nurse knows how to cope with the effects of stress positively. **Negative coping mechanisms** include unhealthy eating habits and binging behavior, abusing substances such as alcohol and drugs, acting recklessly with one's own safety, and becoming abusive in personal relationships.

Positive coping mechanisms include finding an activity to engage in to unwind and relieve stress in a healthy way. Activities such as daily exercise, spending quality time with friends and family, cooking, yoga, biking, and hiking are all ways to deal with the stress of a demanding job in a healthy way.

The nurse should be careful not to work too many hours as well. It can be tempting to take on extra shifts continually to earn extra money for gifts, vacations, or simply to pay the bills and support a family. These extra shifts and long hours can put a nurse in a danger zone if they are using up too much mental, physical, and emotional energy. It is better to be well rested and have adequate mental and physical energy for a shift than to put the patient and oneself at risk for harm.

Being properly nourished, getting adequate exercise, and maintaining healthy sleep habits will all positively contribute to a nurse's health. The nurse's health is vital to helping their patients regain or maintain their own health and, thus, should be made a high priority. If one needs help learning healthy eating habits, meal planning, how to get involved in an exercise program or routine, or other methods of managing stress, many facilities have programs to help guide employees toward better health. There are a plethora of available online resources aimed at improving one's health as well.

Practice Questions

1. When performing HS oral care for a patient with dentures, which action should the nurse take?
    a. Remove the patient's dentures, clean them with cool or tepid water, place them in a denture cup with cool or tepid water or denture cleaning solution, and leave the cup on the bedside table within the patient's reach.
    b. Remove the patient's dentures, clean them with hot water, place them in an empty denture cup, and leave the cup on the bedside table within the patient's reach.
    c. Remove the patient's dentures, wrap them in a paper towel, and place them on the bedside table within the patient's reach.
    d. Remove the patient's dentures, clean them with cool or tepid water, wrap them in a washcloth, and leave them by the sink until the patient is ready for AM care.

2. A nurse is providing AM care to a patient who has suffered a stroke and has right-sided weakness. When dressing the patient, which action should the nurse take?
    a. Before dressing the patient in the new clothing, the nurse should remove all of the patient's old clothing to prevent cross contamination.
    b. The nurse should first undress and redress the patient's upper body, then undress and redress the patient's lower body.
    c. When removing the patient's pants, the nurse should remove the pants from the left leg first and then the right leg.
    d. When redressing the patient in clean pants, the nurse should place the left leg in the pants first and then the right leg.

3. A nurse is assisting a diabetic patient with breakfast. The patient is scheduled for heart surgery in the afternoon. Which breakfast tray is appropriate for this patient?
    a. Coffee, apple juice, lime gelatin, and clear broth
    b. Coffee with sugar substitute, oatmeal, scrambled eggs, and bacon
    c. Coffee with sugar, grits, egg white omelet, and a cup of fresh fruit
    d. This patient should not receive a breakfast tray.

4. A patient is experiencing diarrhea and complaining of lightheadedness when standing. The patient is normally able to ambulate to the bathroom without assistance. What's the first action a nurse should take?
    a. Encourage the patient to drink lots of fluids to prevent dehydration.
    b. This is normal, and the nurse should do nothing.
    c. Provide the patient with additional washcloths, soap, and towels for perineal care.
    d. Place the call bell within reach and instruct the patient to call for assistance before getting out of bed.

5. A nurse is providing AM care to a comatose patient. The patient has been immobile for several weeks and is at risk for muscle atrophy and contractures. What action should the nurse take in caring for the patient?

    a. Passive range of motion exercises should be done with the patient.

    b. Perineal care should be provided, but a full bed bath should be avoided due to the patient's risk for pressure sores.

    c. Before providing oral care, the head of the patient's bed should be flat, and the patient's head should be turned to the side to prevent aspiration.

    d. The patient should be encouraged to do active range of motion exercises while lying in bed.

6. Studies have shown that which of the following practices has the most positive impact on patients?

    a. Personalized comfort measures in their post-operation room, such as a favorite snack or book

    b. Internet and television access during their clinical stay

    c. An attentive communication style between their nurses and physicians

    d. Visible operation and safety checklists that staff members regularly check and notate

7. Which of the following are vulnerable populations at high risk of being abuse and neglect victims?

    a. Dogs, fish, and gerbils

    b. Immigrants, women, and minority races

    c. Children, women, and the elderly

    d. Children, pets, and immigrants

8. A nurse is planning the daily care schedule for an older patient with limited mobility. The patient has physical therapy at 10:00 am and occupational therapy at 2:00 pm. Which schedule is most appropriate?

    a. The nurse will provide AM care at 8:00 am and afternoon care at 3:00 pm.

    b. The nurse will provide AM care at 8:00 am and afternoon care at 4:00 pm.

    c. The nurse will provide AM care at 9:00 am and afternoon care at 4:00 pm.

    d. The nurse will provide AM care at 9:00 am and afternoon care at 3:00 pm.

9. A nurse is caring for a patient who doesn't have pressure sores but is at risk for them due to immobility. How often should the patient be repositioned?

    a. Because the patient doesn't have pressure sores, it's not necessary to reposition them.

    b. The patient only needs to be repositioned when they express discomfort.

    c. The patient should be repositioned at least once every two hours.

    d. The patient should be repositioned each time perineal care is provided.

Answer Explanations

1. A: The patient's dentures should be removed, cleaned with cool or tepid water, and then stored in a denture cup with cool or tepid water (or denture cleaning solution) within the patient's reach. For Choice B, dentures should never be cleaned with or stored in hot water since hot water can damage them. In Choice C, a patient's dentures should never be stored in a paper towel because they could accidentally be thrown away. Dentures should always be stored in a denture cup. In Choice D, if a patient is unable to put their own dentures in their mouth, or the patient doesn't wish to keep them within reach, storing them by the sink is acceptable. However, they should never be stored in a washcloth. A washcloth can be used to handle dentures while cleaning them to prevent accidental damage, but dentures should always be stored in a denture cup.

2. C: When dressing a patient with a weakness or paralysis on one side, the weak side should always be undressed last and redressed first. In Choice A, unless the patient has soiled his clothes, it's unnecessary to remove all of their clothes prior to redressing them. The patient should be covered up as much as possible to avoid discomfort and/or overexposure. For Choice B, the order of the upper- and lower-body dressing is unimportant as it relates to the patient's right-sided weakness. There might be a valid reason to start with the upper body, but it isn't related to the right-sided weakness. In Choice D, this is the opposite order. The nurse should place the right leg (the weak side) into the pants first.

3. D: A patient scheduled for surgery in the afternoon would be NPO (nothing by mouth) status, so they would not be allowed to have any food or beverage. Choice A is an example of a clear liquid diet, which would not be appropriate for a patient with an upcoming surgery. This diet is more appropriate for a patient post-surgery, before progressing to a regular diet. Choice B is an appropriate diet for a diabetic patient, but this patient is scheduled for surgery in the afternoon and should be NPO. Finally, Choice C is an example of a heart-healthy diet, which may be appropriate for the patient after being cleared to eat solid foods post-surgery.

4. D: The *first* action the nurse should take is to give the call bell to the patient and instruct them to call for assistance. If a patient is experiencing lightheadedness, they're at risk for a fall. Patient safety is the number one priority. In Choice A, if not contraindicated, the patient should be encouraged to drink lots of fluids, but this is not the first action the nurse should take. In Choice B, the findings should be reported to the nurse; however, the nurse should not leave the room before placing the call bell within reach of the patient and instructing them to call for assistance before getting out of bed. In Choice C, the patient might require additional supplies for perineal care, but this isn't the first action the nurse should take.

5. A: "Muscle atrophy" is the weakening of a muscle, and a "contracture" is the shortening of a muscle. Both conditions are due to immobility. Therefore, passive range of motion exercises (unless contraindicated) should be done with the patient. In Choice B, patients at risk for pressure sores can have full bed baths, but the nurse must thoroughly dry the patient's skin to prevent breakdown. For Choice C, the nurse would be expected to provide oral care to the patient, and the patient's head should be turned to the side (if possible) to prevent aspiration. However, unless contraindicated, the head of the patient's bed should be elevated for oral care. For Choice D, active range of motion exercises are those performed by the patient independently. A comatose patient is unable to perform active range of motion exercises, so passive range of motion exercises must be performed by the nurse.

6. C: Patients respond favorably to positive intrapersonal communication between their attending nurses and physicians. The other options may be nice for patients, but studies indicate that nurse and physician relationships have the most impact on a patient's overall experience.

7. C: Children, women, and the elderly are vulnerable populations due to tendencies to be physically weaker than their attackers, possibly disabled, unable to communicate, or dependent in some other way.

8. B: Older patients need time to rest between activities, so adequate rest intervals should be allotted when planning a patient's schedule. Providing AM care at 8:00 am would give the patient time to rest before going to physical therapy, and providing afternoon care at 4:00 pm would give the patient time to rest after returning from occupational therapy. In Choice A, providing afternoon care at 3:00 pm doesn't give the patient an adequate rest period after occupational therapy. For Choice C, providing AM care at 9:00 am doesn't give the patient time to rest before physical therapy. In Choice D, providing afternoon care at 3:00 pm again doesn't give the patient an adequate rest period after occupational therapy.

9. C: Even if no pressure sores are present, all immobile patients should be repositioned at least once every two hours. For Choice A, the patient should be repositioned at least once every two hours to prevent pressure sores from developing. Again in Choice B, an immobile patient should be repositioned at least once every two hours. However, if the patient expresses discomfort, the nurse can reposition the patient even if they were repositioned less than two hours ago. For Choice D, while it might be appropriate to coordinate care in this manner, again the patient should be repositioned at least once every two hours whether or not any other care is being provided.

Psychosocial Integrity

Abuse/Neglect

Abuse and neglect can take many forms and affect people of various demographics. Children, women, and the elderly tend to be the vulnerable victim populations. Abuse and neglect cases can often put the victim in the emergency room, so nurses and other medical personnel should be aware that they likely will come across these unfortunate situations, and intervention may be necessary. It is important to know how to spot abuse and neglect cases for legal and ethical reasons.

In children, abuse and neglect can come from a biological or adoptive parent, guardian, close adult in the child's life, or stranger. Younger children are the most vulnerable individuals in this demographic. This is because they may not be able to speak, defend themselves, or understand that they are being abused, or they may be fearful of reporting a caregiver.

Child abuse can be emotional, such as refusal to provide affection or emotional comfort, criticizing the child in a cruel or unusual manner, or administering humiliation or shame tactics. Child abuse may be hard to detect or penalize legally. Physical abuse of a child involves intentional acts of physical violence that could result in injury. Sexual abuse of a child includes sexual acts or interactions by an adult; even if the child provides consent, it is considered abuse, due to the emotional and mental immaturity of the child. In the United States, legal age of consent varies by state. Signs of abuse in children can include physical indicators, such as cuts, bruises, genital pain or bleeding, and persistent yeast infections. There can also be behavioral indicators, such as slow development, aggression, anxiety, suicidal tendencies, fearful natures, antisocial or awkward behavioral habits, statements describing inappropriate physical or sexual interactions, visibly unusual relationships or interactions with a parent or caregiver, and a lack of desire (or even refusal) to go home.

Child neglect refers to a parent, guardian, or other caretaker's inaction to provide basic care such as food, water, education, medical and dental treatments, safe supervision, and clean and safe living accommodations. Signs of neglect in children can include chronic illness, malnutrition, lack of personal hygiene, above-average school absenteeism, anxiety and depression, and substance abuse.

A single sign may not mean that abuse or neglect is present, but it should be taken seriously by asking further questions and potentially seeking resources, such as legal and social support agencies, to prevent further abuse. Most states require that knowledge of potential abuse or neglect be reported to legal and child protective services. The process of reporting varies by state, and practitioners should familiarize themselves with abuse- and neglect-reporting practices of the state in which their nursing services will be provided.

Domestic violence between adult partners, also known as intimate partner violence and abuse, is also a common form of abuse that can require emergency department visits. While this type of abuse can be experienced by partners of either gender or orientation, it is most commonly inflicted by male partners on female victims. Physical indicators of abuse from a partner include marks such as bruises, black eyes, genital or anal damage, scratches, and welts. Behavioral indicators include a fearful nature, low self-esteem, isolation, anxiety, depression, constant excuses for the abusing partner's dangerous actions, and suicidal tendencies. Again, the presence of one sign may not indicate that abuse is occurring, but it can be a call to action to provide resources for the victim's safety.

Elder abuse and neglect may occur by family members or other caregivers. Elderly people are vulnerable, as they may be physically weak or have other physical and mental limitations, handicaps, or disabilities. Signs of abuse in elders are similar to those seen in children but can also include the occurrence of adult-minded activities that happen without the elder's consent, such as mishandled financial transactions or healthcare fraud. Physical indicators of abuse in the elderly include bruises, broken bones, and signs of physical restraint. Behavioral indicators include poor relationships with caregivers, anxiety, depression, and a fearful nature. Indicators of neglect in the elderly include missed or improper medication administration, signs of poor hygiene, genital or anal rashes, and malnutrition. Unfortunately, many signs of elder abuse and neglect are similar to signs of dementia, a natural reaction to ailing health, and other behaviors commonly exhibited by this age demographic. Therefore, due diligence by nurses and medical personnel is necessary. All states have elder abuse prevention laws, though procedures for reporting may vary by state, so it is important to know the process for the state in which nursing services will be administered.

Behavioral Interventions

The overall theme of any effective nursing intervention is the implementation of behavioral change to produce healthy outcomes, called **behavioral intervention**. Nursing interventions combine medical and psychosocial interventions to guide patients to live healthier lives. The most successful nursing interventions to promote disease prevention also incorporate the utilization of the patient's support network, stress-management techniques, building effective coping skills, and encouraging healthy lifestyle choices. The best illustration of how all of these components can produce the greatest impact is depicted in the following example.

Consider a nurse providing intensive case management to a morbidly obese patient seeking bariatric surgery. The incidence and prevalence of morbid obesity is rapidly increasing as the number one cause of adverse health conditions in the United States. Despite primary, secondary, and tertiary health promotion efforts, the waistlines of Americans are continuing to grow at exponential rates. Disordered eating, sedentary lifestyle, poor impulse control, and inaccurate perceptions about how to maintain a healthy diet are commonplace. It is essential that the nurse providing case management services to patients seeking morbid-obesity surgery create a specialized treatment plan to help ensure the patient's success.

After conducting the history and physical interview, it is determined that the patient recently received a dual diagnosis of type II diabetes and hypercholesterolemia. With a family history of both parents diagnosed with diabetes and hypertension, there is some concern that the disease will progress rapidly. Newly diagnosed, the patient has not yet been prescribed daily oral medications. Instead, the attending physician has ordered a case management consultation for the patient to discuss morbid-obesity surgery. In this instance, the nurse will assume the role of case manager with the final result being to recommend or deny the request to approve the patient as a candidate for bariatric surgery.

Although the primary mechanism remains under investigation, bariatric surgery has been said to resolve myriad obesity-related comorbidities. As the body mass index of Americans has grown, physicians have observed an inverse relationship with healthy lifestyle choices. Studies have shown that both type II diabetes and hypercholesterolemia are among the main diseases that significantly contribute to the development of cardiovascular disease. These conditions often require extensive, ongoing treatment. Many patients reach a state where traditional medical treatment becomes ineffective in the daily management of their symptoms. As the disease state progresses, dietary interventions also become ineffective. Surgeons who regularly perform bariatric procedures have found that it is the combination

of substantial dietary restriction and increased physical activity that can lead to an almost complete resolution of disease. For these reasons, thousands of patients make the decision to pursue bariatric surgery.

Once the initial assessment is completed, the next task for the nurse is to verify the eligibility requirements dictated by the patient's insurance carrier. The nurse will contact the patient's health insurance provider and obtain an explanation of benefits. This information will help the nurse prepare the patient to complete any required criteria. This is an integral step to ensuring that surgery can be approved. Without clear direction, the treatment plan is incomplete. It is customary for the patient to be required to receive diagnostic testing, meet with a dietician, and complete a psychological evaluation to confirm his or her readiness to succeed after surgery. The nurse will then discuss the benefit criteria with the patient to assess the patient's commitment to the process. The final step in this preliminary phase is to obtain both written and verbal agreement from the patient to receive and actively participate in medical case management.

During the engagement phase of treatment planning, the nurse will begin to utilize the SMART goal-setting process. This type of behavioral intervention focuses on the presentation of the problem, developing a solution to the problem, and outlining the necessary steps to resolve the problem. Additionally, this technique encourages patients to brainstorm ways to meet their own needs. For this scenario, the nurse will describe the criteria that must be completed in order for the patient to be approved for bariatric surgery, along with any associated timeframes within which those criteria must be met.

In most cases, patients must complete a physician-supervised lifestyle modification program, for a specific number of weeks. The nurse will ask the patient what steps can be taken to adjust his or her lifestyle in order to satisfy that requirement. Patients can work with a nutritionist, dietician, or their primary care physician. How will those appointments be scheduled, and with whom? What specific lifestyle modifications will the patient need to make and why? What will it look like when the changes have been made? Does the patient believe that they can make the necessary lifestyle modifications? Do the changes seem appropriate, based on the patient's previously stated goals and needs? How long will it take? These questions lead to the development of SMART goals.

SMART goal setting requires a series of question-and-answer sessions. This technique will continue for each objective, in an effort to guide the patient to lead the treatment-planning process. If goals are ambiguous, the patient will not understand what to do. Goals are not measurable if there is no way to track progress. Goals must also be practical in their application. The goal must make sense to the patient and contribute to the overall completion of the desired outcome. The patient must be able to see the big picture and have a clear understanding of how and why all of the tasks are interdependent.

It is also necessary for the nurse to periodically check in with the patient to determine if each task is being completed according to the timeline. Creating a plan in this way will affect how the patient thinks about goal setting in general. It is important for the nurse to allow the patient to take responsibility for completing each task. The patient will monitor his or her own progress and troubleshoot with the nurse as needed. This technique is self-empowering for the patient and reinforces the self-determination necessary for goal setting in the future.

Behavioral Strategies to Decrease Anxiety

If a patient is showing signs of or exhibiting anxious behavior, a nurse can evaluate their symptoms and come up with a suitable coping strategy. Behavioral strategies to decrease anxiety include:

- Cognitive reframing: educating the patient about how to replace negative thoughts with positive ones
- Deep breathing
- Progressive relaxation: tightening and releasing the body's muscles
- Meditation
- Prayer
- Reminiscence therapy: sharing life remembrances with other people
- Validation therapy: resolving disagreements and concerns through therapy
- Writing their thoughts in a journal
- Guided imagery: visualizing a comforting scene
- Music therapy
- Biofeedback: connecting the patient to a special machine to see various vital statistics when exposed to stress items
- Mindfulness: having an awareness of one's setting
- Setting priorities
- Talking positively about one's self
- Medication

Reminiscence Therapy, Validation Therapy, and Reality Orientation

Reminiscence therapy is designed to boost the feelings of self-worth and importance of a person suffering from anxiety. Nurses can help the patient cope with their anxiety by listening to their personal narratives, memories, and other recollections, giving them the chance to go over past events and explain how they experienced and handled stressful incidents.

Nurses can also participate in **validation therapy**, helping patients deal with tension and worry alongside a therapist who specializes in identifying and sympathizing with anxiety-ridden patients, justifying and supporting struggles and concerns.

Reality orientation is meant to help people whose anxiety stems from feelings of confusion or bewilderment gain improved mental and psychomotor function. It helps foster an awareness of various environmental factors impacting the patient, such as their identity, a sense of time, and their surroundings. The nurse can help do this by focusing on factors that are contributing to the patient's disorientation, such as the time of day, month and year, their personal situation, and the current weather. Utilizing items such as calendars, electronic reminders, and clocks can be useful.

Chemical and Other Dependencies

Substance abuse is defined, most simply, as extreme use of a drug. Abuse occurs for many reasons, such as mental health instability, inability to cope with everyday life stressors, the loss of a loved one, or enjoyment of the euphoric state that the overindulgence in a substance causes. Abused substances create some type of intoxication that alters decision-making, awareness, attentiveness, or physical impulses.

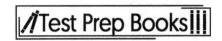

Substance abuse results in tolerance, withdrawal, and compulsive drug-taking behavior. Tolerance occurs when increased amounts of the substance are needed to achieve the desired effects. Withdrawal manifests as physiological and substance-specific cognitive symptoms (e.g., cold sweats, shivering, nausea, vomiting, paranoia, hallucinations). Withdrawal does not only happen when an individual stops abusing the substance, but also occurs when he or she attempts to reduce the amount taken in an effort to stop using altogether.

Some of the most commonly abused substances include the following:

Tobacco
People abuse tobacco either in cigarette, cigar, pipe, or snuff form. People report many reasons for tobacco use, including a calming effect, suppression of appetite, and relief of depression. The primary addictive component in tobacco is nicotine, and tobacco smoke also contains about seven hundred carcinogens (cancer-causing agents) that may result in lung and throat cancers, as well as heart disease, emphysema, peptic ulcer disease, and stroke. Withdrawal indicators include insomnia, irritability, overwhelming nicotine craving, anxiety, and depression.

Alcohol
Some individuals need a drink to "smooth out the edges," as it is a CNS depressant, which tends to calm and soothe and lower inhibitions. However, it also slurs speech and impairs muscle control, coordination, and reflex time. Alcohol abuse can cause cirrhosis of the liver; liver, esophagus, and stomach cancers; heart enlargement; chronic inflammation of the pancreas; vitamin deficiencies; certain anemias; and brain damage. Physical dependence is a biological need for alcohol to avoid physical withdrawal symptoms, which include anxiety, erratic pulse rate, tremors, seizures, and hallucinations. In its most serious form, withdrawal combined with malnourishment can lead to a potentially fatal condition known as **delirium tremens (DTs)**, which is a psychotic disorder that involves tremors, disorientation, and hallucinations.

Other Prescriptions
Prescription medications, such as anti-anxiety, sleep, and pain medications.

Marijuana
Marijuana is considered the most frequently abused illicit drug in the United States. General effects of marijuana use include pleasure, relaxation, and weakened dexterity and memory. The active addictive ingredient in marijuana is tetrahydrocannabinol (THC). It is normally smoked (but can be eaten), and its smoke has more carcinogens than that of tobacco. The individual withdrawing from marijuana will experience increased irritability and anxiety.

Cocaine
Cocaine is a stimulant that is also known as "coke," "snow," or "rock." It can be smoked, injected, snorted, or swallowed. Reported effects include pleasure, enhanced alertness, and increased energy. Both temporary and prolonged use have been known to contribute to damage to the brain, heart, lungs, and kidneys. Withdrawal symptoms include severe depression and reduced energy.

Heroin
Also known as "smack" and "horse," heroin use continues to increase. Effects of heroin abuse include pleasure, slower respirations, and drowsiness. Overdose and/or overuse of heroin can cause respiratory depression, resulting in death. Use of heroin as an injectable substance can lead to other complications

such as heart valve damage, tetanus, botulism, hepatitis B, or human immunodeficiency virus (HIV)/AIDS infection from sharing dirty needles. Withdrawal is usually intense and will demonstrate as vomiting, abdominal cramps, diarrhea, confusion, body aches, and diaphoresis.

Methamphetamines
Also known as "meth," "crank," and "crystal," methamphetamine use also continues to increase, especially in the West and Midwest regions of the United States. A methamphetamine is categorized as a stimulant that produces such effects as pleasure, increased alertness, and decreased appetite. Similar to cocaine, it can be snorted, smoked, or injected and eaten as well. Like cocaine, it shares many of the same detrimental effects, such as myocardial infarction, hypertension, and stroke. Other prolonged usage effects include paranoia, hallucinations, damage to and loss of dentition, and heart damage. Withdrawal symptoms involve depression, abdominal cramps, and increased appetite.

Nursing interventions for the individual addicted to tobacco, alcohol, and other drugs centers around the prevention of relapse, and treatment depends on the individual and the substance that is abused. Behavioral treatment assists with recognition of abuse triggers, habits, and drug cravings, as well as providing the tactics to help one cope with these issues. A physician may prescribe nicotine patches for the tobacco abuser and methadone or Suboxone to manage withdrawal symptoms and certain drug yearnings.

Non-Substance-Related Dependencies
Even some behaviors—such as exercise and work—are recognized as positive behaviors, but when taken to extremes, unpleasant consequences develop. For example, exercise addiction, in its least damaging form, may create anxiety when physical or weather conditions prevent participation. In more extreme cases, certain athletes will continue to train in spite of illness or injury, exacerbating the physical problem and sometimes causing permanent disabilities.

Overworking—sometimes referred to as "workaholism"—may also be viewed as positive by some standards. In the end, however, those working many hours of overtime may result in a life out of balance. They may also be using work as a means to avoid other responsibilities, such as family life. It can create stress and low energy, and it can lead to physical and emotional problems.

Sexual addiction, also known as hypersexuality, involves a preoccupation with sexual pleasures that can manifest itself in a multitude of ways. These behaviors prove harmful to themselves and potentially other people. One example is pornography. Those addicted to pornography find that having close and intimate contact with their long-term partner is less exciting than viewing stimulating films or pictures. This creates intimacy problems and difficulty in one's primary relationship. The Internet has made it easier for people to access these materials, sometimes at no cost, creating a greater number of persons who view it addictively.

Gambling addiction may involve a desire for the adrenaline rush of making bets or a cycle of losing money via gambling and then gambling more to try to make up for previously lost money.

Overeating, based upon the number of obese and overweight persons in our culture, is on the rise. Some people use food much in the same way that others use alcohol or drugs—to feel a sense of pleasure or to numb feelings of depression or anxiety. The consequences of obesity are numerous from a social and physical standpoint, with the most severe of these being at higher risk for heart disease or stroke.

Some individuals are addicted to self-harm in the form of cutting, scratching, or mutilating themselves. This is often described as a means to bring relief from emotional pain as one focuses on the physical sensation of pain to distract from the emotional sensation. It may also be a type of self-punishment. Some people have scars from this compulsion. Others may contract infections. It is theorized that persons who self-mutilate are at higher risk of suicide than those who do not, making it a possible precursor to suicidal ideations.

Risk-Taking Behavior

Risk-taking behaviors such as driving fast or engaging in substance use, may lead to car accidents or overdoses, respectively. Yet, they may bring about positive feelings in the moment. This includes the thrill of a fast ride or the high one gets from drug use. Given that risk-taking behavior is potentially dangerous, some people wonder why anyone would take part in such conduct. On one hand, such behavior puts those who engage in it in harm's way, but, on the other, it gives participants the chance to experience an outcome they perceive as positive. Sigmund Freud theorized that this was related to an innate drive within human beings to seek experiences that put them close to death, for the adrenaline high one might feel. Risk-taking behavior can be a singular diagnosis or it can be part of the symptomology of other conditions such as PTSD.

Risk-taking behavior includes having sex with strangers, often with no protection against sexually transmitted diseases or unplanned pregnancies. Risk-takers also enjoy gambling, typically losing more than they can handle. These individuals may also take part in extreme sports or recreational activities.

Some research indicates that men tend to be risk-takers more than women. But both male and female risk-takers share the same personality traits, such as impulsive sensation-seeking, aggression-hostility, and sociability, one study found. Genetics play a role in risk-taking behavior. Identical twins separated at birth tend to engage in risk-taking behaviors at high rates. Testosterone appears to play a role as well, which is why there's a gender imbalance in the people most likely to take part in risk-taking behaviors.

Coping Mechanisms

Unpack **coping mechanisms**, and you will find at their core a whole-hearted but poorly defined resistance to change. Effective stress management combined with adaptive coping skills are directly related to the execution of a treatment plan. It is the acquisition and application of adaptive coping skills that promotes overall wellbeing. If coping skills are maladaptive, no matter how applicable the treatment plan is, there will be no effect if the patient is ill-equipped to navigate the stages of change. It is essential that the nurse work collaboratively with the patient and other members of the healthcare team to formulate a treatment plan that is based on patient-centered care.

Consider how a nurse working in an inpatient mental health unit would respond during the assessment of a teenage girl admitted for observation after a suicide attempt. The initial physical assessment uncovers evidence of what appears to be a series of self-inflicted cuts, in various stages of healing, on the patient's inner thighs. A thorough interview with the teen reveals that the patient has been cutting herself in response to bullying from fellow residents in her boarding school. The teen also reported that the bullying has occurred for several years and had escalated to threats of physical harm. School officials were notified, and the students were expelled. Despite the fact that the offending students no longer attend the school, the patient has been unable to relinquish cutting herself. Self-injurious behaviors have increased in the last 48 hours, after the teen ended a long-term romantic relationship.

According to the patient, the break-up created feelings of hopelessness and overwhelming depression. In a deep state of depression, the student swallowed a bottle of Tylenol, hoping to end the pain. The admitting diagnosis of the attending physician is depression, with a rule-out diagnosis of bipolar disorder.

On an inpatient unit, there is often an interdisciplinary team assembled to develop a collaborative treatment plan. Although the therapist and social worker will conduct additional interviews with the patient, it will be necessary for the nurse to formulate nursing diagnoses and interventions that complement the overall plan of care. In this case, the most appropriate nursing diagnosis would be: risk for harm associated with feelings of hopelessness secondary to the diagnosis of depression. Suitable interventions would be centered around the application of the adaptive coping skills learned through ongoing individual and group therapies while admitted to the inpatient unit. The nurse will dispense antidepressant medications prescribed by the attending physician, reinforce the techniques demonstrated in therapy, and guide the patient to begin safety planning.

Patients can suffer from poor body image perception due to any number of traumatic incidents such as an accident, physical disability, hair loss due to cancer treatments and body altering surgeries such as a mastectomy or orchiectomy. It is important for nurses and other healthcare team members to help them cope with these thoughts and feelings. The first step involves performing a total evaluation of the patient's perceived body image, then devising a coping strategy. This plan can include reassuring the client to talk about how they feel about the change in their body and their subsequent negative feelings such as despair, rage, desperation, and incompetence, helping educate the patient on fostering body image self-awareness and worthiness, and highlighting the positive attributes, strengths, and capabilities, rather than the changed body element.

Types of Coping Skills
- **Self-Soothing**: Comforting the self through the five senses
- **Distraction**: Taking mind off the problem for a while
- **Opposite Action**: Doing the opposite of the initial impulse that's consistent with a more positive emotion
- **Emotional Awareness**: Tools for identifying and expressing one's feelings
- **Mindfulness**: Tools for centering and grounding the self in the present moment
- **Crisis Plan**: Support and resource information for when coping skills are not enough, such as therapist, family, friends, or a crisis team

The nurse must also remain aware that the stress of managing emotional turmoil can create feelings of powerlessness and depression. The patient may have grown accustomed to denying intense feelings and instincts in an effort to be insulated from the source of pain. The goal is to focus on rebuilding the patient's coping skills from the inside out, in order to promote a sense of hope and self-determination. Discuss the difference between adaptive and maladaptive coping skills. Encourage the patient to define which behaviors they engage in that they would place into each category. What the patient perceives to be most effective is not necessarily the healthiest response. Educate the patient on how healthier choices lead to healthier outcomes.

Discuss how the self-inflicted wounds could become infected or disfiguring. Offer information on the benefits of aerobic exercise to release endorphins known to naturally elevate the patient's mood. Encourage the patient to consider journaling, writing, or creating art to express suppressed emotions. Pet therapies have also been effective in the treatment of depression, providing much-needed emotional support. Finally, encourage the patient to consider attending local support groups for

depressed teens. The communal aspect of a support group is helpful, as other teens battling depression can validate the patient's experience.

The customary discharge plan for depressed patients at risk for suicide includes several components. First, the patient must agree that they will no longer make any attempts to harm themselves in any way. Instead, the patient will create a detailed list of at least two alternatives to self-harm. The nurse must also highlight patients' current coping skills and encourage his or her ability to support themselves and to utilize their stress management skills. What are alternatives to self-harm that could produce similar feelings of release that the patient can practice? Second, the patient must verbalize understanding that any episodes of self-harm will result in immediate hospitalization. What steps will the patient take when feeling overwhelmed? Does the patient have an accountability partner? Finally, the patient will be equipped with a personalized list of contacts to utilize when stress-relieving techniques are ineffective. This list will include a 24-hour suicide hotline, as well as the contact information for the local therapist assigned prior to the patient's discharge.

Crisis Intervention

Crisis-intervention skills are an essential component of providing exceptional patient care. Crises strike unexpectedly and, by definition, necessitate immediate intervention. Nurses in particular must have robust crisis-intervention skills in order to address the myriad issues that patients and their caregivers face. Why is crisis intervention so important? Why do nurses need to acquire this dexterity? It is because proper nursing care involves the astute assessment of the patient's overall wellbeing. At some point during the provision of care to patients and families, the nurse will encounter a situation in which they will have no other choice but to intervene. This is primarily because the nurse is often on the front lines of healthcare and the first to interact with the patient. The integration of nursing care, stress-management techniques, and assisting the patient navigate through the stages of grief are of paramount importance. Not unlike every other nursing technique, crisis-intervention skills will be enhanced with repeated use and more progressive problem solving.

Consider the importance of the nurse's adaptability to crises with reference to assisting patients and families impacted by natural disasters. Upon deployment to an area destroyed by torrential rains and subsequent flooding, a nurse could encounter families in need of not only immediate medical care, but ongoing crisis intervention. In conditions such as these, patients are often overwhelmed by their physical pain as well as concerns for how to meet their basic needs for food, shelter, and clean water. Disaster relief relies on medical triage to determine the appropriate level of care needed by patients and is typically assessed based on a four-tier model. Black/blue is reserved for the deceased; red for immediate care such as chest wounds or gunshots; yellow for those with stable wounds or head injuries; green for minor injuries such as fractures or burns.

In this situation, the nurse must be prepared to rapidly assess the patient's level of injury, the most expedient treatment needed for stabilization, and move on to the next case within minutes. Does the patient or anyone in the family maintain a specific medication regimen to manage chronic illnesses? Have any doses of required medications been missed? Are any assistive devices such as hearing aids or canes needed? It is important to note that the nurse will need to focus on the medical stabilization of patients in this stage rather than delving into psychosocial and emotional trauma.

During disaster-relief efforts, nurses are normally dispatched to both acute care and follow-up care zones. Once immediate medical needs are addressed, patients are transferred to a safe holding area. This space is set aside for psychosocial triage, where patients' basic emotional and physical needs are met. Social workers and chaplains are readily available to debrief survivors. Consider the example of a nurse working with a family impacted by the previous illustration. Having lost their home and belongings and facing recovery from minor injuries, they have been transferred to the holding area for processing. The nurse in this example would receive a brief synopsis from triage, but only regarding injuries and treatment. In this stage, the nurse would obtain a brief social history, information on chronic disease, and feasible relocation options.

Then, the nurse will need to begin guiding the patients through processing the emotional trauma of the incident. Are all family members accounted for? Does anyone in the family unit manage any mental health conditions that have been triggered? What, if any, legal or illegal substances are used or abused by anyone in the family unit? These questions are to help determine if the survivors' emotional responses are directly related to the recent trauma.

Responses to acute traumatic events often mirror the typical response of those who have experienced chronic trauma. The nurse must also assess patients for underlying mental health conditions that may have been exacerbated. In this instance, the most appropriate nursing diagnosis would include ineffective coping. Typical nursing interventions would require the nurse to work with the patient to access previous successful navigation through other traumatic events. Present viable options for next steps and allow the patient the time to process the best response to the traumatic event.

Cultural Awareness

Patients will come from all backgrounds and cultures, and medical providers should be aware of the different cultural needs that may present themselves in the emergency department. **Culture** can encompass anything from a person's geographical location, race, ethnicity, age, socioeconomic status, and religious beliefs that influence the behaviors, traditions, and rituals that he or she chooses to engage in each day. It is important to note that cultural considerations will present themselves daily. Some patients may be unable to speak English and will need interpretive services. Some patients may request that only same-sex providers treat them. Respecting and attending to different cultural needs will provide the patient with a better healthcare experience, lead to increased patient satisfaction, and impact overall health outcomes.

Medical providers can show that they consider cultural differences by kindly and compassionately asking patients to share cultural viewpoints, to share aspects of the medical system and services that make them comfortable or uncomfortable, and to continuously create rapport that allows the patient to feel comfortable in voicing their concerns. Medical providers should be mindful of any preconceived notions that they hold of certain cultures, and if possible, actively work to dispel these. Medical providers should also be mindful to not make presumptions, even if those presumptions come from an intention to be empathetic. For example, a patient who looks to be of Asian descent may have been born and raised in the United States and not identify well with any part of Asian culture. Finally, many healthcare organizations offer internal trainings that cover cultural considerations and cultural diversity. For staff that feel their knowledge and experience is limited in this aspect, these trainings can provide an avenue for personal and professional growth.

Having a diverse emergency department staff can be extremely beneficial when servicing a patient demographic that encompasses many cultures. Having a medical provider who is able to relate directly with a patient's culture can make the patient feel more comfortable and open. Additionally, a diverse emergency department staff can overcome common obstacles such as language barriers or lack of

patient education. In this regard, healthcare organizations and nursing leadership should work to actively recruit a diverse workforce.

End-of-Life Care

At least once during their career, it is inevitable that a nurse will care for a patient near the end of life. Caring for patients near the end of life can occur in numerous settings. Whether on an inpatient hospice unit or in an outpatient setting, the patient's home, or a skilled nursing facility, the primary objective is to ensure that the nurse provides patient-centered palliative care. There is a stark difference between hospice and palliative care. Both of these, however, fall under the umbrella of end-of-life care. Specifically, end-of-life care includes the care that is received at the end of a patient's illness. While palliative care is considered to be basic comfort care, hospice is the more familiar term, and usually begins once all curative treatments have been stopped.

Hospice can be loosely defined as: primarily palliative and, secondarily, medical care provided to patients deemed by at least two physicians to be terminally ill, with a projected life expectancy of six months or less. This means that the primary objective of hospice care is to provide comfort care to patients. This comfort care is provided under the primary diagnosis. The secondary medical care is typically provided whenever necessary to maintain the patient's comfort. For example, consider a patient who has been receiving hospice care for a primary diagnosis of dementia for four months. Upon admission to the inpatient unit for a weekend of respite, the patient is diagnosed with a kidney infection. The elevated fever, flank pain, nausea, vomiting, and rapid heart rate detract from the patient's overall comfort. The kidney infection is considered to be secondary to the diagnosis of dementia and will be treated. Conditions that are not considered to be comfort care are curative in nature, with the primary objective to prolong life.

It is essential for the nurse to remember that when providing care to a patient who has been placed on hospice, there is always more than one patient to be considered. The spouse or significant other, as well as whomever the patient perceives to be a member of the familial unit, will also be impacted by the patient's diagnosis and subsequent death. The family dynamics will be especially important in these cases, as they must also receive extensive treatment. The nurse can expect to see caregiver burnout, family members struggling with feelings of loss, and anticipatory grief. Most notable is the prospect of funeral planning while the patient is still alive. Although it is not uncommon for the patient or family members to reach end of life without preparing for the funeral, the finality of the task must be worked through. Both the patient and the family may need the intervention of the social worker and/or chaplain in order to facilitate this discussion. It may be necessary to obtain the patient's final wishes separately from the caregiver or family, to be shared upon the patient's demise, if the stress and grief of preparing for death becomes too overwhelming.

Although the patient is still considered to be terminally ill, they will continue to have desires, hopes, and may even want to create a plan for the future. It will be necessary to coordinate the patient's care with the interdisciplinary team (social worker, chaplain, physician, and nurse). All involved will have the opportunity to review the patient's electronic medical records, as well as current diagnosis, medications, and treatment plan. It is usually the nurse who initially notices the beginning of the patient's decompensation. As it is uncommon to accurately predict the precise date of the patient's death, the patient must be guided to prepare advance directives if not completed when enrolled into hospice. The nurse must review these documents carefully, looking for information from the patient's history for evidence of being an organ donor, specific religious affiliations, or stipulations against certain visitors.

A final word regarding the compassionate care of individuals receiving end-of-life care: If the nurse is managing a patient who has specific details in the care plan, or religious beliefs that heavily impact healthcare decisions, additional consultation may be required. For example, for a patient who identifies as Jewish, he or she may prefer to assign an additional family member to sit with the patient once deceased. As this is the religious custom, the nurse must respect this as much as possible. It is imperative that the nurse seek a consultation with the available social worker, chaplain, or member of the hospital/facility ethics board for guidance if any request is questionable. If an internal or professional conflict of interest might prevent the nurse from effectively delivering care to the patient according to his or her religious beliefs, the nurse would be best served to recuse herself in the best interests of the patient.

Grief and Loss

Grief Process

Everyone grieves differently after the death of a loved one. Grief, and how it manifests itself, is different in each individual and depends on the relationship with the deceased. For some, grief will be brief, and for others, it will be prolonged. There is a general guideline for the grieving process, but it is descriptive, not prescriptive. Individuals may experience all stages in order, some stages, but not all, or switch between stages out of order at various points in time.

The **Kubler-Ross grieving model** includes five stages: denial, bargaining, depression, anger, and acceptance. For example, when a terminal diagnosis for a loved one is received, the family members may deny what is happening and not acknowledge reality. After this stage of denial, they may begin to bargain, or try to make deals with whoever they believe has the power to change the circumstances for their loved one. This could include long arguments with the healthcare team over care or praying to a higher power for a healing miracle. After bargaining, they may fall into a depression, with feelings of helplessness or powerlessness against the forces of the disease. This may be followed by a stage of anger in which they act outwardly or express frustration that they cannot change the circumstances. The last stage of grief is acceptance, and this is considered the stage in which the grieved person is finally at peace with the circumstances and can begin healing.

As mentioned before, these categories of grief are a rough guideline of what a person may experience. Grief varies in intensity from person to person and depends a great deal on the nature of the relationship with the deceased. The nurse need only be familiar with the stages in order to recognize them in family members and/or the dying person, who may go through these stages as well. If one recognizes the grief process is occurring, one is more sensitive to the needs of the grieving.

Emotional Needs of the Patient, Family, and Caregivers

Grief is a highly emotional process. The range of emotions experienced by those grieving the loss of a loved one is vast. The initial reaction of shock and disbelief may morph quickly into anger, then sadness, and even fear. Sometimes the patient or family may feel such intense emotional pain that physical symptoms such as chest pain, gastrointestinal issues, and shortness of breath may occur. The stress of losing a loved one is both physical and emotional. The nurse can recognize this and be of assistance.

The best way to help those who are grieving—whether it is the anticipatory grieving the dying patient may feel or the grief that occurs after the patient passes on—is to be there to support the family. It's incorrect to assume that one can imagine or alleviate what the grieving are feeling or thinking.

The role of the nurse is to help in any way possible, but not to offer empty optimistic statements or promises, such as "It'll be okay soon," or "You'll move on before you know it." These statements are not helpful and may aggravate the recipient. Instead, focusing on what can be done in the present to assist them is the best approach.

Grief cannot be avoided; it is a process that is different for each individual and is necessary for healing. The nurse can offer a listening ear, a hug, or a hand to hold if welcomed and appropriate, and can inquire how the patient or the family are doing. Simply asking how they are doing shows that the nurse cares and would like to be of assistance in any way possible.

Providing for the physical comfort of the grieving by offering a cup of coffee, a warm blanket, or a snack is a way to support them. The emotional pain they are going through may have caused them to ignore their own basic physical needs, such as eating and resting. Helping them focus on something besides their emotional pain can be helpful.

The nurse, doctor, and social worker will offer social services, grief counseling, and other resources that will connect the grieving to other forms of support.

Responses to Grief

Not only will each individual respond differently to grief based on personality and relationship with the deceased, but also the response will differ based on their own spiritual beliefs and cultural influences. These beliefs and influences affect how a person thinks they should act during the mourning period, what to wear, what rituals need to be performed, and what happens after a person dies.

Each individual culture will not be gone over in this discussion, as there are a multitude of variations of the death and grieving process. It is not necessary for the nurse to know each and every one, but rather have a general knowledge of differences and be respectful towards them.

Some cultures believe an outward show of emotion is appropriate and necessary. Sometimes, this entails an outward expression of weeping and wailing. Other cultures may be more conservative and think it is appropriate to be stoic, serious, and somber, without crying and losing one's composure. Some have specific rituals before and after the death, involving holy men, priests, or other clergy who prepare the person and/or the body for an afterlife. Some may not have any religious affiliation and may not believe in a life after this one.

Regardless of what cultural and spiritual beliefs are present, the role of the healthcare team is to respect those wishes as much as possible. It is imperative that the team explore the patient and family's wishes in this respect, rather than overlooking or refusing to allow them. It is always appropriate to politely ask how best to respect the patient and family's wishes when performing tasks for the dying or deceased patient. For example, some family members may prefer to clean the body themselves after death, an important ritual to express grief and ensure proper care in their view.

Each member of the healthcare team, including the nurse, needs to assess their own beliefs about death and dying. Self-knowledge on the subject is valuable as it may not be something one has consciously acknowledged. This self-assessment also helps reveal any unfair biases and prejudices towards cultures and people whose worldview is different than one's own. Discovering what one's own beliefs and others' beliefs are leads to a better understanding between groups. These groups can then begin to find ways to work together during the difficult end-of-life period.

Physical Changes and Needs as Death Approaches

As the patient approaches death, the nurse will play an important role in ensuring physical comfort. The patient may have increased pain, skin irritability, decreased control over bowel and bladder, decreased mobility, and decreased consciousness. There are concrete steps that the nurse can take to ensure the patient is as comfortable as possible during the last stage of life.

Monitoring the patient's level of pain is important. Pain medicine as necessary will be used to provide adequate comfort. The nurse should watch for nonverbal signs of pain, such as body tension, moaning, and facial grimacing.

Elimination may become difficult if the patient loses consciousness and mobility. The nurse can make elimination easier for the patient by assisting the patient to a bedside commode or bed pan, and/or checking for incontinence in order to perform perineal care to keep the patient clean and dry.

The patient's skin may become dry and brittle. Mouth breathing can cause the oral cavity to dry out quickly, sometimes called **cotton mouth**. Applying lotions, balms, and moisturizers to skin and lips, as well as making sure the oral cavity is well moisturized, are all steps that can relieve skin discomfort. Mouth sponges or swabs can be dipped in water to wet the mouth. Some patients find these sponges comforting to chew on or take a few drops of water from.

Preventing pressure ulcers or preventing existing pressure ulcers from worsening at the end of life is a consideration for nurses to keep in mind. These can cause additional pain and discomfort that might be avoided. Using pillows to prop and position at-risk areas, such as heels, buttocks, elbows, and the back of the head will help minimize pressure.

The patient will likely have difficulty regulating body temperature, and may experience periods of feeling hot, cold, or both. The patient may not be able to verbalize these needs, but the nurse can watch for nonverbal cues such as shivering or sweating. It is important to keep the patient comfortably warm or cool, using blankets and fans. Electric blankets should not be used, as the patient may not be able to verbalize if it is too hot, risking burn injuries.

Breathing may become difficult for the patient. They will likely develop increased secretions in the airway. The patient will likely be too weak to clear these secretions, resulting in a rattling or gurgling sound. Turning the patient's head to the side, providing a cool-mist humidifier (if available), and using suction equipment are all interventions that can alleviate the patient of these secretions. Depending on the facility, the nurse may or may not be able to perform the task of suctioning. The patient may be given supplemental oxygen via nasal cannula for comfort. Monitoring to make sure the prongs of the nasal cannula are in place and not causing discomfort to the patient is important.

The patient may not appear to be awake, but still may be able to hear and perceive what is going on around them. Because of this, it is always important for the nurse to identify oneself to the patient when entering the room and tell the patient what they are doing in the room. This courtesy may comfort a patient who is otherwise alone. The nurse aid should talk to the patient, provide quiet music, and keep the lighting low and/or natural. These environmental changes can all soothe the patient and should be guided by the patient and the family's wishes. Some patients may prefer a room full of visitors and others may be more private, preferring only a few close relatives and friends.

The nurse needs to be mindful of the family's needs as well. Again, their grief and emotional response in the moment may cause them to forget their own basic needs, such as eating and getting proper rest. It

is important to remind them to rest when they need to, offer them drinks and snacks as appropriate, warm blankets, and any other offering available to comfort them during this difficult time.

The end of life need not be a lonely, miserable experience, lacking warmth, thoughtfulness, and care. The nurse can assist the healthcare team in providing comfort for the patient's physical needs as well as creating a soothing environment around the patient as they approach death.

Post-Mortem Care Procedures

After the patient has passed, the first step the nurse can take is to determine the family's needs. This is a time when spiritual and cultural considerations need to be respected. Some families may linger and talk over the body for hours before leaving the room, while others may say a brief goodbye and leave. The healthcare team should determine if there are any specific burial preparations that need to be done. Funeral and/or burial arrangements, such as cremation or embalmment, will be determined.

Once these considerations are determined, the healthcare team can prepare the body. Generally, the body will need to be cleaned, as bowel and bladder incontinence happens after death. Having an assistant, usually the nurse, is necessary, as the body will be difficult to move by a single person. Any excess tubes or IVs will need to be removed by the nurse, depending on facility policy. The body may need to be placed in a body bag, if in a facility with a morgue. This can be done using the same turning and repositioning techniques used to perform bath care.

The nurse should be aware that there are sights and sounds that one might see in a dead body that might be alarming and unexpected. For example, there may be a release of air from the lungs of the body as the nurse is cleaning or turning that may sound like a gasp or cry. The body may also have muscle twitches and slight movements as the neurological and muscular systems shut down. Both of these are normal. If the nurse and/or doctor have confirmed official death, post-mortem care can proceed.

After the body has been bathed and placed in a body bag, the body will be transferred to a gurney or some sort of transport stretcher. The body is then transported to the morgue. A morgue refers to the refrigerated room where deceased bodies are held pending funeral and burial arrangements. The cold temperature drastically slows down the decomposition process in the bodies, preserving them for the funeral presentation.

Some nurses may find post-mortem care to be uncomfortable, disturbing, and even depressing. This is an initial reaction, and many adjust to it with time and experience. Dealing with dead bodies is not something that the general public is used to experiencing. The nurse must keep in mind that post-mortem care is a continuation of respecting and caring for the patient. Everyone dies, and their bodies must be taken care of afterwards. Thinking of it as an act of respect and courtesy is perhaps the best perspective. The deceased must be treated with dignity, even in death. The nurse is in the unique position to provide such dignified care to the individual.

The reason that one enters the healthcare field should stem from an earnest desire to help others and care for them in their time of need. This extends beyond their life to their death by taking care of their remains appropriately and respectfully.

Mental Health Concepts

The mental status of a patient has the potential to impact every area of his or her life, resulting in an inability to respond to any nursing intervention. Compromised mental health has been known to affect a patient's coping mechanisms, lifestyle choices, and ability to manage stress effectively. Nurses who work with patients impacted by mental illness need to maintain awareness of numerous concepts. Chief among them is the nurse's effectiveness in conducting the initial interview. It is essential to assess the patient's mood, affect, body language, and tone. Asking open-ended questions about daily living, employment, relationship status, hobbies, and habits can help the nurse determine if any socialization deficits are present. Once the patient begins to respond, this will create an atmosphere of trust, which is necessary when conducting an assessment for depression.

One of the most frequently diagnosed mental illnesses is clinical depression. Although the vast majority of those diagnosed are women, many men are now seeking support. Once the nurse has completed the depression inventory and determines that some risk for clinical depression does exist, the next step will be to discuss how the patient's symptoms affect daily life. Within the last two weeks, has the patient felt increasingly depressed, hopeless, or helpless? Has the patient struggled to fall asleep, woken up early, or slept longer than expected? Are meal times less or more frequent? Has anyone that knows the patient remarked about a change in his or her mood? Have there been sudden bouts of tearfulness, sadness, or feelings of worthlessness? Is the patient engaging in self-harm or high-risk behaviors? Has the patient considered hurting themselves? If so, is there a plan? Does the patient have access to weapons or medications, and have there been suicide attempts in the past? This line of questioning will help the nurse to determine if the patient's depression is mild and situational, which is often transient, or if the depressive state is moderate to severe, requiring more immediate intervention.

Once it is determined that the patient is not in imminent danger or planning to commit suicide, the nurse can begin discussing nursing interventions to alleviate the patient's symptoms. If suicidal ideation does exist, safety planning and hospitalization may be necessary. Utilizing motivational interviewing to reveal the patient's readiness for change, the nurse can open the discussion from where the patient sits on the continuum. This type of nursing style is often necessary to confirm the feasibility of proposed nursing interventions.

If the patient is in pre-contemplation, the earliest stage of change, they may have an awareness of the symptoms but not know that those are symptoms of depression. At this stage, information is key. The nurse can explain the symptoms of depression and should be watchful of worsening symptoms. During the second stage, contemplation, the patient is aware that the symptoms are indicative of depression but remain ambivalent about change. The nurse will continue to provide feedback regarding the patient's own words, reflecting back his or her statements. The patient may wish for change but is not yet sure if it is possible.

Once the patient reaches perception, the ambivalence has turned into acceptance and the patient feels ready to take the first step. The nurse must have resources readily available regarding how to schedule an appointment with a counselor for talk therapy or to obtain a prescription for antidepressant medications. Be prepared to answer questions about untoward side effects and how quickly the medications become effective. During the action phase, the patient may actually schedule the appointment or fill the prescription, with significant intent to continue. In this instance, the nurse must reinforce the patient's courage and utilize the SMART goal-setting technique to establish a timeline within which to act.

Maintenance occurs once the patient actually takes the medication regularly, attends counseling, and is able to verbalize that change has occurred. The nurse should be able to validate the patient's improvement and continue to offer encouragement regarding the patient's own goals. Finally, during the relapse stage, something has occurred; a substantial stressor or an unexpected disruption creates

imbalance. The patient will begin to miss numerous appointments, forget to refill prescriptions, and symptoms will resurface. At this stage, the nurse must realize that the patient may have returned to the preparation phase. They may believe that the counseling or medications were ineffective and be unsure which steps to take next. Outreach is often necessary, as the patient may be hesitant to return; depressive symptoms may also impact his or her decision making.

It is important to note that the stages of change are not linear. Patients can move along the continuum; moving between one stage and another frequently or skipping certain stages entirely is not uncommon. It is important for the nurse to remain neutral, mirroring the patient's ambivalence to allow for self-determined action.

Mood Disorders, Depression, Anxiety

A **mood disorder** is a mental health class that broadly describe all types of depression and bipolar disorders. The following are the most common types of mood disorders:

- **Major depression**: Having less interest in usual activities, feeling sad or hopeless, and other symptoms for at least 2 weeks.

- **Dysthymia**: A chronic, low-grade, depressed, or irritable mood that lasts for at least 2 years.

- **Bipolar disorder**: A condition in which a person has periods of depression alternating with periods of mania or elevated mood.

- **Mood disorder related to another health condition**: Having an acute or chronic medical illnesses can trigger symptoms of depression.

- **Substance-induced mood disorder**: Symptoms of depression that are due to the effects of medicine, drug abuse, alcoholism, exposure to toxins, or other forms of treatment.

Mood disorders may be caused by an imbalance of brain chemicals. Life events, abrupt changes in routine, and stress may also contribute to a depressed mood. Mood disorders also tend to run in families and are more intense and harder to manage than normal feelings of sadness. Children, teens, or adults who have a parent with a mood disorder have a greater chance of also having a mood disorder. Rates of depression are nearly twice as high as in women as they are in men. Once a person in the family has this diagnosis, their brothers, sisters, or children have a higher chance of the same diagnosis. Depending on age and the type of mood disorder, a person may have different symptoms of depression. The following are the most common symptoms of a mood disorder:

- Ongoing sad, anxious, or empty affect
- Feeling hopeless or helpless
- Having low self-esteem
- Feeling inadequate or worthless
- Excessive guilt
- Repeating thoughts of death or suicide
- Loss of interest in usual activities or activities that were once enjoyed, including sex
- Relationship problems
- Trouble sleeping or sleeping too much
- Changes in appetite and/or weight
- Decreased energy

- Trouble concentrating
- A decrease in the ability to make decisions
- Frequent physical complaints that don't get better with treatment
- Very sensitive to failure or rejection
- Irritability, hostility, or aggression

With a mood disorder, these feelings are more intense than what a person may feel occasionally. If these feelings continue over time, interfere with interest in family, friends, community, or work, or if there are thoughts of suicide, medical intervention is needed.

Antidepressant and mood stabilizing medicines, especially when combined with psychotherapy, have been shown to work very well in the treatment of depression. Treatment of bipolar disorder may include mood stabilizers such as lithium and carbamazepine, along with second-generation antipsychotics such as aripiprazole and risperidone. Psychotherapy is focused on changing the person's distorted views of self and the environment. It also helps to improve interpersonal relationship skills, identify stressors in the environment, and assist with avoiding them. Family therapy, electroconvulsive therapy, and transcranial stimulation may also be therapeutic.

Post-Traumatic Stress Disorder (PTSD)

PTSD is a disorder that develops in some people who have experienced a shocking, scary, or dangerous event. People who have PTSD may feel stressed or frightened even when they are not in danger. Fear triggers many split-second changes in the body to help defend against danger or to avoid it. This fight-or-flight response is a typical reaction meant to protect a person from harm. Most people recover from initial symptoms naturally but those who continue to be affected are diagnosed with PTSD.

Symptoms usually begin within 3 months of the traumatic incident, but may occur later. Symptoms must last more than a month and be severe enough to interfere with relationships or work to be considered PTSD. The course of the illness varies, and it may become chronic. Some people recover within 6 months, while others have symptoms that last much longer. Re-experiencing symptoms may cause problems in a person's everyday routine. The symptoms can start from the person's own thoughts and feelings. Words, objects, or situations that are reminders of the event can also trigger re-experiencing symptoms.

To be diagnosed with PTSD, an adult must have all of the following for at least 1 month:

- At least one re-experiencing symptom
- At least one avoidance symptom
- At least two arousal and reactivity symptoms
- At least two cognition and mood symptoms
- Re-experiencing symptoms include:
  - Flashbacks—reliving the trauma over and over, including physical symptoms like a racing heart or sweating
  - Bad dreams
  - Frightening thoughts

Avoidance symptoms include staying away from places, events, or objects that are reminders of the traumatic experience and avoiding thoughts or feelings related to the traumatic event. Things that remind a person of the traumatic event can trigger avoidance symptoms. These symptoms may cause a

person to change his or her personal routine. For example, after a bad car accident, a person who usually drives may avoid driving or riding in a car.

Arousal and reactivity symptoms include being easily startled, feeling tense, having difficulty sleeping, and having angry outbursts. Arousal symptoms are usually constant, instead of being triggered by things that remind one of the traumatic events. These symptoms can make the person feel stressed and angry. They may make it hard to do daily tasks, such as sleeping, eating, or concentrating.

Cognition and mood symptoms include trouble remembering key features of the traumatic event, negative thoughts about self or the world, distorted feelings like guilt or blame, and loss of interest in enjoyable activities. Cognition and mood symptoms can begin or worsen after the traumatic event, but are not due to injury or substance use. These symptoms can make the person feel alienated or detached from friends or family members.

Anyone can develop PTSD at any age. This includes war veterans, children, and people who have been through a physical or sexual assault, abuse, accident, disaster, or many other serious events. According to the National Center for PTSD, about 7 or 8 out of every 100 people will experience PTSD at some point in their lives. Women are more likely to develop PTSD than men, and genes may make some people more likely to develop PTSD than others.

The main treatments for people with PTSD are medications, psychotherapy, or both. Everyone is different, and PTSD affects people differently so a treatment that works for one person may not work for another. It is important for anyone with PTSD to be treated by a mental health provider who is experienced with PTSD. Some people with PTSD need to try different treatments to find what works for their symptoms. As genetic research and brain imaging technologies continue to improve, scientists are more likely to be able to pinpoint when and where in the brain PTSD begins. This understanding may then lead to better targeted treatments to suit each person's own needs or even prevent the disorder before it causes harm.

A 2012 study of 395 military veterans with PTSD found a link between risk-taking behavior and the disorder. In addition to the above forms of riskiness, vets with PTSD have a propensity for firearms play, potentially endangering their lives. People with PTSD have already survived dangerous situations, and risk-taking behavior may give such individuals the feeling that they have more control over their present circumstances than those that led to them developing PTSD. Recognizing this propensity in their personality may help patients with risk-taking behavior, thus being the first step in remediating the problem. Behavioral and cognitive therapy, as well as psychological drugs such as antidepressants, may also aid in the treatment of this behavior.

Suicidal Ideation and/or Behaviors

It is important to take people seriously when they express having suicidal thoughts. Research has shown that about one-fifth of people who die by suicide had talked to their doctor or other healthcare professional about their decision. These types of thoughts may arise in people who feel completely hopeless or believe they can no longer cope with their life situation. Suicidal ideation can vary greatly from fleeting thoughts to preoccupation to detailed planning.

According to the CDC, for every 25 attempts, there is one suicide death. Suicide is the tenth leading cause of death for all ages in the United States, and the third leading cause of death among 15 to 24 year-olds. Patients with borderline personality disorder face an extraordinarily high risk of suicidal ideation and suicide attempts. One study showed that 73% of patients with borderline personality disorder have attempted suicide, with the average patient having 3.4 attempts.

Warning signs may include hopelessness, racing thoughts, insomnia or oversleeping, mania, loss of appetite or overeating, loneliness, alcohol abuse, excessive fatigue or low self-esteem. Research has found a variety of risk factors for suicidal ideation including the following:

- Mood and mental disorders
- Adverse life or family events (divorce, death of a loved one, job loss)
- Chronic illness or pain
- Previous suicide attempt
- Military experience
- Witnessing trauma
- Family violence
- Owning a gun
- Being the victim of abuse or bullying
- Unplanned pregnancy
- Drug or alcohol abuse

An act that is intended to cause injury but not death is called a non-suicidal self-injury. An example of this type of behavior is when patients cut themselves. It is a method of relieving psychological pain through physical pain. Men are more likely than women to commit suicide, as well as more likely to abuse alcohol and drugs concurrently. Men are less likely to seek help when they are depressed. Veterans have seen an increase in suicides in recent years. It is important to note that despite these risk factors for suicide, it can occur across a wide span of age groups, genders, and life circumstances.

Some patients who are more vocal about their suicidal ideation may be crying out for help and must be taken very seriously. Treatment should include psychotherapy and antidepressants. It should be noted, however, that antidepressants sometimes have the adverse side effect of worsened suicidal behavior. Caregivers should be instructed to be watchful for deepening of depression and thus an increased risk for suicide. Suicide hotlines are available to help suicidal patients in moments of crisis.

Religious and Spiritual Influences on Health

Religious and spiritual beliefs can heavily influence a patient's decision to receive care. It is important for the nurse to determine if any specific religious or spiritual beliefs exist for the patient, and how those beliefs inform his or her decisions. Many people value certain dietary customs in accordance with their religion and strictly adhere to them. For example, for those who identify as Jewish, adherence to a strict Kosher diet is non-negotiable. Any attempts by the nurse to suggest any changes to this diet would be viewed as insensitive. It is for this same reason that religious and spiritual beliefs of any kind must be respected.

Congregants of the Church of Scientology have received significant media attention for what some perceive to be controversial beliefs. Formed by L. Ron Hubbard in the mid 1950s, this religious group focuses on the effectiveness of prayer over traditional Western medicine. Some who self-identify as a part of this group have also expressed particular mistrust of mental health practitioners in general. Although they do not forego all medical treatments, a nurse attending to patients following this religion must consider those beliefs when developing interventions and treatment plans. It may be more

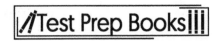

advantageous to encourage the patient to consult a church advisor and incorporate the tenants of Scientology into direct practice, if permitted.

Another religious group well known for their healthcare choices is Jehovah's Witnesses. Founded by Charles Taze Russell in the late 1800s, this group does not believe in accepting blood transfusions under any circumstances. A nurse caring for a patient who holds this belief must be prepared to discuss any viable options with the patient and church elders. Not all instances of receiving blood products are prohibited, so it will be important to confirm if the patient would consider using plasma, volume expanders, or artificial blood.

Additionally, ethical considerations regarding how to provide sensitive and compassionate care are important to highlight. It is the nurse's responsibility to seek a consultation with the unit chaplain, social worker, or facility ethics board to discuss any areas where there is a potential conflict of interest.

Not only will each individual respond differently to grief based on personality and relationship with the deceased, but also the response will differ based on their own spiritual beliefs and cultural influences. These beliefs and influences affect how a person thinks they should act during the mourning period, what to wear, what rituals need to be performed, and what happens after a person dies.

Each individual culture will not be gone over in this discussion, as there are a multitude of variations of the death and grieving process. It is not necessary for the nurse to know each and every one, but rather have a general knowledge of differences and be respectful towards them.

Some cultures believe an outward show of emotion is appropriate and necessary. Sometimes, this entails an outward expression of weeping and wailing. Other cultures may be more conservative and think it is appropriate to be stoic, serious, and somber, without crying and losing one's composure. Some have specific rituals before and after the death, involving holy men, priests, or other clergy who prepare the person and/or the body for an afterlife. Some may not have any religious affiliation and may not believe in a life after this one.

Regardless of what cultural and spiritual beliefs are present, the role of the healthcare team is to respect those wishes as much as possible. It is imperative that the team explore the patient and family's wishes in this respect, rather than overlooking or refusing to allow them. It is always appropriate to politely ask how best to respect the patient and family's wishes when performing tasks for the dying or deceased patient. For example, some family members may prefer to clean the body themselves after death, an important ritual to express grief and ensure proper care in their view.

Each member of the healthcare team, including the nurse, needs to assess their own beliefs about death and dying. Self-knowledge on the subject is valuable as it may not be something one has consciously acknowledged. This self-assessment also helps reveal any unfair biases and prejudices towards cultures and people whose worldview is different than one's own. Discovering what one's own beliefs and others' beliefs are leads to a better understanding between groups. These groups can then begin to find ways to work together during the difficult end-of-life period.

Sensory/Perceptual Alterations

Nursing interventions include a variety of holistic treatments. Among the most essential elements of nursing techniques that any nurse can employ are those associated with managing **sensory and perceptual alterations**. During the initial assessment or admission, the nurse must be diligent to perform a complete review of the patient's electronic medical record; take note of medications that mask or augment neurological deficits; and observe the patient interacting with family members, caregivers, and other medical staff. Once the nurse has been able to gather the information necessary to form an initial impression, the next step is to evaluate the patient clinically.

It is customary to perform a basic screening neurological exam at every patient encounter. Diagnoses such as Alzheimer's disease and dementia are of special note, and the nurse is to follow facility protocols for treatment of these patients. If neurological decline is detected during the initial screening, it will be necessary to assess the patient periodically and, if not specifically ordered, according to the nurse's clinical judgement.

Once the initial chart review and assessment are completed, the nurse must develop a treatment plan and nursing interventions. All have as their primary objective to maintain patient safety. Some of the most common nursing diagnoses for these patients include basic recognition of the typical safety precautions that these patients often need. Bed alarms, keeping the call light within reach, slip-resistant socks, a writing pad and pen or dry-erase board for communicating, hearing and walking aides within reach, lifting one rail of the bed to allow only one route of access, and rooming the patient closer to the nurse's station are frequently instituted. All interventions are to be provided in a calming manner, being careful not to startle the patient. It will also be necessary to be aware of distractions to the patient like ambient noise or other patients in the immediate area. Additionally, the nurse must be prepared to teach all caregivers basic diversion tactics to deescalate and soothe the patient's anxieties. Finally, take care to periodically evaluate the effectiveness of all interventions and be prepared to adjust as needed.

Stress Management

Stress management is a crucial piece of overall patient wellbeing. Poorly managed stress has the potential to cause significant health decline. When conducting an assessment, the nurse must carefully approach the topic of stress management. Since many of life's stressors cannot be completely changed, the nurse will be best served to listen actively, remarking about how certain activities or situations can worsen health conditions. Odd work hours, late night shifts, or working multiple jobs can negatively impact sleep patterns. Without restorative sleep, the patient will have difficulties focusing on treatment-plan adherence. As the lack of sleep continues, the patient can begin to lose focus on a previous goal of maintaining healthy lifestyle choices and return to easier high-risk behaviors.

Once the topic of known sources of stress has been initiated, the nurses can go one step further to inquire what steps have been taken to ameliorate those stressors. Next, the patient can be encouraged to state how they have worked to manage the stressors and what has been least effective. It is during this exchange that the patient is more likely to accept recommendations and institute them in daily life. Notably, it is also necessary to uncover sources of stress that are not readily apparent. Ask probing questions about preferred forms of stress relief and relaxation techniques. Encourage patients to seek out trusted members of their support network to communicate their needs and ask for help. Overall, a patient's ability to institute the checks and balances required to alleviate stress is crucial.

Support Systems

Another contributing factor for overall patient wellbeing is a well-functioning **support system**. Even if there is no disease process present, a support system, as defined by the patient, is vital to healthy stress and disease management. During the assessment, the nurse must ask open-ended questions about patients' support systems: What hobbies do they enjoy? How do they spend the holidays, and with

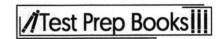

whom? Are they married or single? Do they have children? Answers to these few questions will help quickly decide if there are any gaps in socialization and open the discussion on how to fill them.

Whether it's family members, friends, or coworkers, some sort of support network usually exists for most patients. The nurse must make sure to encourage discussion about who the patient confides in and trusts. Those individuals can either add to or subtract from the patient's progression through and whole-hearted commitment to treatment. For those patients who report having no supportive network, the nurse can guide the patient toward viable options. One of the most effective and influential options would be to match the patient to a support group according to any comorbidities that they currently manage. Thousands of independent groups exist to provide a much-needed communal experience. Often run by health professionals or counselors, members of these groups can gain knowledge about their condition, daily symptom management, and possibly gain new supportive friends. Overall, the presence of a network of trusted friends and advisors is an invaluable facet of the therapeutic environment.

Family Dynamics

The term "family" holds a different level of significance to different people. No matter how the nurse chooses to define family, it is imperative that a neutral stance be maintained regarding the patient's familial network. If the nurse cannot maintain a sense of compassionate objectivity, it may cloud the nurse's responsiveness to cultural issues that affect patient care. Whenever possible, the nurse must consider that the **family dynamic** remains as the unseen influence on the patient. Stress-management techniques, as well as the cultural and familial roles assigned in the family, may have an undue influence on the patient's healthcare decisions and adherence to treatment.

A visual assessment of this dynamic can occur within several minutes. Observe how the family members interact; choices of conversation topics and responses can often reveal a great deal about who is the leader in the household. For example, upon the initial assessment of an obese teen and a morbidly obese parent, it can quickly become apparent that the dietary choices made by the teen are a mirror of those made by the primary caregiver. Both may lead a relatively sedentary lifestyle, punctuated by frequent visits to the local fast-food restaurant. As the nurse, it would be necessary to simply ask about their daily vegetable and water consumption, hobbies, or even the teen's favorite meal. During the discussion, the nurse will be better able to discuss SMART goals: specific, measurable, achievable, relevant, and timely. This type of goal setting allows for the patient to set realistic goals, with the opportunity to self-check for progress along the way.

When one member of the family is not performing at peak capacity, the dynamic shifts, causing all others to adopt different roles. If the family dynamic is cooperative, all parties will seek to reach a reasonable state of homeostasis. This means that if there is a recognized deficiency in one member of the family, each member will want to contribute to activities that will restore his or her health. This informal agreement is one of the ultimate goals of the nursing intervention. If the family dynamic is conflictual, then the parties will seek to satisfy their own needs, rather than help the ill family member achieve better health outcomes. As the nurse, it is important to utilize the familial bond, no matter the type, to influence the best result for the patient.

For the aforementioned example, the nurse would attempt to co-op the conflictual family members and align their needs with those of the patient. Offering healthier alternatives to staple meals, cheaper recipes, and suggestions for more physical activity would likely appeal to all parties. Alternatively, the nurse could propose that the teen prepare healthier meals themselves, allowing a busy parent much-needed respite from cooking daily. During the average professional nursing career, it will become clear that family members' personal health selections can derail patients' lifestyle choices. It is incumbent upon the nurse to incorporate all aspects of the patient's life in order to create the most effective treatment plan.

Therapeutic Communication

Overcoming barriers to communication requires practicing therapeutic communication. **Therapeutic communication** is a type of communication that assists the patient in the healing process rather than hindering it. There are a number of useful communication techniques the nurse can employ to aid in therapeutic communication.

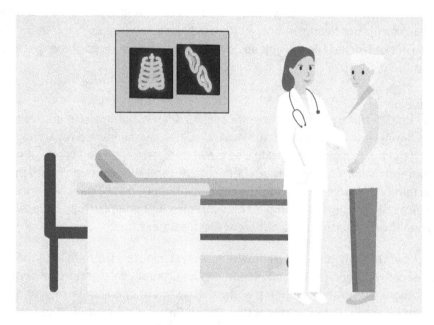

Sometimes, silence is the best way to get clarification from a patient, or simply asking them to clarify when one does not understand. Nurses may offer themselves to support the patient without providing personal details, by sympathizing and saying, "Yes, I have been through something similar." The nurse may ask the patient to summarize their thoughts or identify a theme when stories go on at length. This helps redirect communication in a positive direction.

Asking the patient how certain events made them feel is a way to investigate the patient's emotional status. The nurse may give information about their role and make observations, such as "I noticed you seem tense," to open the door to more fluent conversation. Giving the patient praise and recognition without overt flattery is a way to show support, such as complimenting a noticeable effort during a physical therapy session. The nurse may want to determine the chronological order of events, which can be helpful for reporting information.

Employing therapeutic communication aids smooth collaboration and cooperation between members of the healthcare team. Incorporating smart, simple, therapeutic communication techniques and overcoming barriers to communication are important parts of achieving this goal.

Therapeutic Environment

Within every milieu, the nurse must maintain awareness of the effectiveness of the therapeutic environment of the patient. The nurse must enter into each patient encounter with a plan to develop a

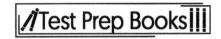

rapport as quickly as possible. A warm greeting, using Mr. or Mrs., rather than using a first name, honey, or sweetie, will imply an equal and respectful relationship. The ability to work collaboratively with the patient is the foundation of cooperative treatment planning.

Although the nurse is generally much more comfortable during the assessment, it is important for the nurse to consider that the patient may be hesitant to disclose personal information. If the patient does not trust the nurse or feels unseen, unheard, or hurried through the interaction, the environment may not feel safe. More important, when a patient does not feel safe enough to disclose, they will not share important health information, which could hinder treatment planning and adherence.

Another important aspect of the therapeutic environment for the nurse to be aware of is the treatment setting. For example, a patient in a correctional-facility hospital may be less likely to reveal sensitive information for fear of reprisal from inmates or staff. Alternatively, patients in a mental health or substance abuse treatment center may freely divulge information, as they often seek treatment of their own accord. In either instance, the nurse must utilize critical thinking to determine if the therapeutic environment is negatively impacted by the setting and seek ways to address any barriers to resolution.

Practice Questions

1. Maya eats a nutrient-rich, balanced diet and exercises vigorously for 30 minutes each day. However, she has gained almost 25 pounds over the course of four months. She has also started growing patches of facial hair. She visits her primary care physician seeking insight as to why these issues are suddenly occurring. He takes her blood pressure as they are talking and finds it to be 130/85. Maya's physician refers her to an endocrinologist, believing she is showing signs of which of the following?
   a. Bulimia nervosa
   b. Gestational diabetes
   c. Chronic kidney disease
   d. Cushing's syndrome

2. Mary is a 7-year-old in second grade. She has been absent from school nine days in one month. When Mary's teacher asks her why she has been absent or contacts her parents to ask about the absences, they all simply say she was sick and don't provide any additional information. Mary looks extremely frightened when asked about her absences. She regularly comes to school in large, baggy clothing that smells unpleasantly, and her hair always looks dirty. She falls asleep often in class, and one day her teacher saw her crying as she prepared to leave for home. Mary's teacher is probably concerned that Mary is dealing with which of the following issues?
   a. She is suffering from a hormonal imbalance or disorder
   b. She is too emotional
   c. She is hungry
   d. She is being abused or neglected by a caregiver

3. Which of the following options correctly names the type of common medication used to treat anxiety and depression?
   a. Antipsychotics
   b. Selective serotonin reuptake inhibitors (SSRIs)
   c. Norepinephrine reuptake inhibitors
   d. Homeopathic options

4. Psychosis is a common side effect of which of the following?
       I. Schizophrenia
       II. Methamphetamine, cocaine, or LSD use
       III. Bipolar Disorder
       IV. HIV antiviral medications
   a. II ad IV only
   b. I and II only
   c. I, II, and III
   d. All of the above

5. Jack and Jill are two nursing students who are on rotation in their county's emergency department. One afternoon, a woman comes into the waiting area and collapses on the floor. She says she cannot breathe and rambles about feeling blindsided. She begins thrashing on the floor and starts to sob. Upon reviewing her intake forms, Jack and Jill notice that the woman's health insurance shows she is employed, and she has not had any notable medical or mental health issues. However, she keeps mentioning that her partner has left her. Jack says, "I think she must have an undiagnosed anxiety disorder; we should look into medication options." Jill disagrees with him, saying that this seems more like which of the following?
   a. A situational crisis
   b. A case of cocaine abuse
   c. A case of intimate partner violence
   d. A nonemergency situation that they should send to the scheduling department

6. Which of the following statements is correct?
   a. Self-destruction ideation is characterized by thoughts of harming oneself, while global destruction ideation is characterized by thoughts of harming others.
   b. Suicidal ideation is characterized by thoughts of harming oneself, while homicidal ideation is characterized by thoughts of harming others.
   c. Internal ideation is characterized by thoughts of harming oneself, while external ideation is characterized by thoughts of harming others.
   d. Intrinsic ideation is characterized by thoughts of harming oneself, while extrinsic ideation is characterized by thoughts of harming others.

7. Middle school student Johnny stores an epinephrine injection pen in his locker, lunch bag, and pencil case. Johnny likely suffers from which of the following?
   a. Homicidal ideation
   b. Narcolepsy
   c. Depression
   d. A severe allergy

8. Which of the following is a commonly used anticoagulant that works by blocking the body's ability to adhere platelets together?
   a. Paxil
   b. Coumadin
   c. Heparin
   d. Thromblok

Answer Explanations

1. D: Cushing's syndrome is characterized by unmanageable weight gain, hair growth, and high blood pressure. Due to excessive production of glucocorticoid by the adrenal glands, it is an endocrine system disorder that can be managed through medication.

2. D: All the signs that Mary is showing, such as poor hygiene, absenteeism, withdrawn behaviors, and crying before going home are red flags for abuse and neglect.

3. B: Selective serotonin reuptake inhibitors (SSRIs) are a class of drugs that can treat both anxiety and depression symptoms. Therefore, brand names of this drug, such as Prozac®, Zoloft®, and Lexapro®, may be prescribed to individuals who are suffering from anxiety, depression, or a combination of both.

4. C: Schizophrenia and bipolar disorder are mental disorders in which hallucinations and delusion (key components of psychosis) are common. These characteristics can also result from mind-altering drugs, specifically methamphetamines, cocaine, and LSD. Antiviral medications used to treat HIV do not normally cause psychosis.

5. A: The patient is having many symptoms of panic, such as struggling to breathe, having difficulty controlling her emotions, and acting agitated. However, she mentions that her partner just left, and there are no other indicators of previous physical or mental health problems in her history. This is a good clue that the patient's partner's leaving is a very stressful event for her and a situational crisis that is likely causing these acute, short-term behaviors. Jack and Jill can help this patient by providing comfort, support, and counseling to help her reach a place where they can calmly discuss treatment options needed, if any.

6. B: Suicidal ideation is characterized by recurrent thoughts of suicide, ranging from passive ideation to active ideation. Homicidal ideation is characterized by thoughts or plans to kill another person or a group of people.

7. D: Severe allergies can be life-threatening and lead to anaphylaxis. An epinephrine injection pen is the first line of defense if a person comes into contact with an allergen to which he or she has a serious or life-threatening reaction.

8. B: Coumadin® is a brand name for the drug warfarin, which can be administered orally or intravenously. It works by decreasing platelet adherence to prevent clot formation. Paxil® is used to treat anxiety and depression, and Thromblok is fictitious.

Physiological Integrity

Basic Care and Comfort

Assistive Devices

The nurse may discover during assessment that the client needs an **assistive device**. There are many such devices available for a variety of different client needs. Assistive devices may generally fall into the categories of assisting with sensorial deficits or mobility deficits.

Clients with sensorial deficits may first need a referral to the appropriate party. A client with difficulties seeing may need a referral to an ophthalmologist for evaluation and a prescription for appropriate lenses.

There are four main vision problems that can be treated with corrective eyewear in mild to moderate cases: myopia, presbyopia, hyperopia, and astigmatism. More severe cases may require surgical intervention.

For the client who requires eyeglasses, the nurse must take care to protect the glasses from damage. While in the hospital room, the glasses should be kept in a safe place, such as in their case on the bedside table. Most bedside tables in hospital rooms have pullout drawers underneath that can store items such as glasses, dentures, hearing aids, and other personal effects.

Patients with blindness, who are legally blind, or who have some form of low vision, will need assistive devices to help them navigate their environment. They may also need assistance with written communications such as discharge instructions and other patient education materials. Depending on the facility, the nurse may be able to give the patient access to devices that use Braille for written communication, software for a PC or smartphone that reads aloud written instructions, and magnifiers for computer screens, phone screens, or other devices. The patient with blindness or very low vision may require a special cane, a therapy animal, or a personal assistant to help them ambulate about their room and the facility. The nurse will assess for these needs and ensure the patient has everything they need for clear communication and a safe environment during their stay.

The nurse will further assess the patient with hearing loss for any other needed interventions that might assist with communication and ease of stay. Closed captioning is available on most TV sets for most programs so the patient can fully enjoy what they are watching. The patient may be a lip-reader, in which case the nurse needs to ensure they stand directly in front of the patient, face them, and make solid eye contact when communicating important messages. The patient will need to see the nurse, specifically their lips, to interpret the message. If the nurse's face is turned away or looking down, the patient will have difficulty understanding what is being spoken to them.

The nurse needs to ensure the patient understands the message by asking questions about comprehension. Some patients with chronic, severe hearing loss may have developed a coping mechanism of pretending they understood what was said by nodding or giving a short verbal reply. They may do this because they feel embarrassed or ashamed about their hearing loss. They may also not want the further hassle of admitting they did not hear or understand what was said and needing to have the message repeated. Without further embarrassing the patient, the nurse should gently inquire about comprehension of the medications they are taking, procedures they are to go through, and if they need anything to make their stay better. Patience and thoroughness are key to ensuring the message gets delivered.

A patient with a speech-language deficit may have difficulty forming meaningful communication as well as fully comprehending the messages that are spoken to them. The nurse who assesses such a need can refer the patient to a speech-language pathologist or therapist; most hospitals have a team of these specialists. They will evaluate the patient's speech-language capabilities and recommend assistive devices as needed.

Some such assistive devices include word boards in which the patient can point to a word or picture that helps them communicate a need. The speech-therapy team will work with the patient through exercises aimed at enhancing their abilities to their greatest potential. Patients who have experienced a cerebrovascular accident or stroke often experience speech and language deficits because of the cerebral tissue damage that occurs. Not all function may be restored, depending on the patient and the extent of the stroke.

Patients with difficulties walking may require assistive devices such as a walker, cane, or wheelchair. If the nurse assesses the patient and finds that such a need is there, they may contact the physical and occupational therapy (PT and OT) teams for assistance. PT and OT work to help the patient become mobile to their greatest functioning capability as well as assisting them in performing activities of daily living (ADLs). Common ADLs that PT/OT works with the patient to perform include getting dressed, tying their shoes, and bathing and feeding themselves.

The nurse will work with the patient and encourage them to use their assistive devices as needed. The nurse ensures the patient that they, along with the nursing assistant team, are always a call button away to assist the patient in getting out of bed, walking with the use of a cane or walker, or getting them into a wheelchair. Mobility in patients is always encouraged, as it helps them heal and achieve their fullest sense of wellness, but it must always be done with safety measures in place to prevent falls and injury.

The nurse may advise the patient using a wheelchair to avoid tipping themselves out of the chair by leaning forward. Their feet should be firmly planted in the foot rests to prevent getting caught in the wheels or dragging on the ground. The brakes should be locked at all times that the wheelchair is stopped or not actively rolling to avoid slippage. The patient in the wheelchair should avoid overreaching for objects, as this may also cause them to fall out. The patient's buttocks should be positioned as far back in the seat as possible to avoid falling out.

The nurse may have a patient with a prosthetic limb. Usually these patients arrive at the hospital with their own prosthetic that they have been properly fitted for, educated on, and actively use. If the patient is a new amputee, they will need a referral to the proper prosthetics expert for fitting. Patients with prosthetics should use the proper footwear for their prosthetic as well as adequate support to prevent falls. The patient will be aware that they should not allow their prosthetic limb to become wet. Thus, they will take the limb off when washing or taking a shower. The metal components of the prosthetic will rust if exposed to water. The patient should let the nurse know if their prosthetic device feels uncomfortable, as this may be a sign of misalignment and need adjustment. If the patient is hearing unusual noises from their prosthetic such as squeaks or crunches, this may be a sign of mechanical impairment and that the prosthetic needs repair.

Patients using crutches should start walking by putting all their weight on their good leg. With the crutches firmly situated in the armpits, the patient can then lift the crutches and set them down 6 to 12 inches in front of them, lean their weight into their hands, and then step forward with the good leg. This

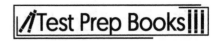

avoids putting weight on the injured leg, transferring all weight to the hands and the good leg, alternatively.

Elimination

There are many situations in a facility in which the patient is unable to **eliminate**—i.e., defecate and/or urinate—independently. Elimination is a basic and highly personal need for all people, and the nurse needs to be able to assist with this task appropriately and respectfully. Common issues in elimination are incontinence, constipation, and diarrhea. Some patients may have devices to assist with elimination, such as a colostomy, rectal tube, or urinary catheter.

Incontinence is a term meaning the patient cannot control their bladder and/or bowels. Some patients may be said to be incontinent of bowel, incontinent of bladder, or both. This can be for various reasons, including neurological impairment, such as paralysis or a physical impairment, such as a broken hip. In any scenario of incontinence, it is important to monitor the patient's elimination throughout a shift and assist when possible. If the patient is oriented enough to request help before having a bowel or bladder movement, the nurse should be as available as possible to assist. This may entail assisting the patient to the bathroom or providing a bedside commode or a bedpan.

If the patient is incontinent in bed, a partial bath will be needed along with a linen change. Checking for incontinence frequently is important, as a timely cleanup of a patient who has been incontinent is crucial to preventing skin breakdown. Proper hand hygiene needs to be performed before and after any perineal care to prevent spread of disease.

Constipation refers to a condition in which the bowels have slowed down their movement, preventing normal defecation and potentially causing discomfort to the patient. Immobility and medications may cause constipation as a side effect. Monitoring of output is one way to discover constipation, along with the patient and/or family report of bowel patterns. If constipation is suspected, the healthcare provider may prescribe a stool softener, a laxative, or—in severe cases—an enema. Soap suds and fleets enemas are commonly used types. Each institution has individual policies on who can perform enemas on patients. Other interventions used to alleviate constipation include encouraging mobility, encouraging intake of fluids when possible, and increasing fiber intake.

When the bowels are overly active and amounts of liquid stool are passed frequently, it is called **diarrhea**. Causes of diarrhea include food intolerance or allergy, infection, a medication side effect, or a reaction to a surgical procedure. A major complication of diarrhea is dehydration. Dehydration can occur rapidly in a patient with diarrhea due to loss of fluids. Intake and output need to be vigilantly monitored along with encouragement of fluid intake, if appropriate.

A **colostomy** is a surgically placed opening from the large or small intestines to the abdominal wall as a result of a bowel condition, such as colon cancer. A colostomy bag is attached to the skin around the colostomy to collect stool. Depending on how long the colostomy has been in place and how well developed the colostomy is, the patient may be able to care for their colostomy bag independently or may need varying levels of assistance from the healthcare team. Most colostomy bags are fairly easy to remove, drain, and replace when necessary.

Another assistive device for elimination of the bowels is called a **rectal tube**. A rectal tube is a tube that is inserted into the rectum to collect stool or relieve gas. At the end of the tube is a balloon that can be inflated to anchor it in place as it collects stool. The rectal tube is used in patients who are incontinent, at risk for or have skin breakdown, and/or have diarrhea. Each facility will have specific policies outlining when a rectal tube is needed. Complications, such as atony of the rectum and internal tissue breakdown, may arise when rectal tubes are in place for extended periods. The rectal tube drains into a bag that the nurse can empty and record as output in the medical record. Perineal care may be required around the site of the rectal tube if any leakage occurs.

The patient may have a urinary catheter for various reasons including immobility and monitoring of output. The catheter has an inflatable balloon at the end filled with normal saline that anchors the catheter in place as it drains urine from the urinary bladder to a collection bag. The nurse can then empty this bag and record the output in the medical record.

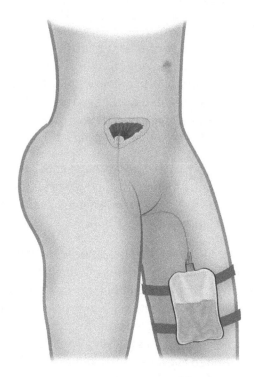

During the patient's daily bath or whenever perineal care is necessary, proper technique must be used to prevent a urinary tract infection (UTI). The nurse must follow the facility's policy regarding proper catheter care, including using warm water around the site to cleanse the urethra and always using a circular motion around the tube moving away from the patient. The nurse should never use a back and forth motion as this could introduce bacteria into the urethra, resulting in a UTI. Signs and symptoms of a UTI include fever, chills, cloudy urine, blood in the urine (hematuria), or a change in mental status. If any of these occur, the nurse should be alerted immediately.

Mobility/Immobility

Promoting Mobility and Proper Positioning

Proper positioning is important for a patient's comfort and safety. Some of the common patient positions are:

- **High Fowler's Position**: The head of the patient's bed is raised 60 to 90 degrees and the knees are either flexed or extended out straight.
- **Fowler's Position**: The head of the patient's bed is raised 45 to 60 degrees.
- **Semi-Fowler's Position**: The head of the patient's bed is raised 30 to 45 degrees.

- **Supine**: The patient is lying on their back.
- **Lateral**: The patient is lying on their side.
- **Prone**: The patient is lying on their stomach, with their head turned to the side.

When positioning a patient in bed, always raise the entire bed high enough to avoid bending over while assisting the patient. Be sure to lower the head of the bed to its lowest position before leaving the patient.

Promoting Function, Including Prosthetic and Orthotic Devices

A nurse should encourage patients to be as mobile as possible and help them correctly use assistive devices such as canes and walkers. Patients with prosthetic limbs should be given assistance with, and access to, these devices. When assisting a patient with a prosthetic limb, always note any redness or irritation that occurs where the prosthetic limb contacts the skin.

Safe Transfer Techniques

When transferring a patient, the safety of the patient and the nurse are of the greatest importance. Incorrectly performed transfers can cause injury to both. Be mindful of proper transfer techniques and body mechanics, such as keeping a straight back, bending at the knees, avoiding twisting at the waist, and, most importantly, asking for additional help if needed.

When assisting a patient out of bed, always make sure that the bed is in the lowest position. Then, assist the patient to sit upright on the side of the bed with both feet on the floor. While the patient remains in this seated position, make sure they aren't lightheaded or dizzy from the position change. If the patient needs significant physical assistance other than stabilization, an assistive device should be considered. To assist the patient in standing, the nurse should stand in front of the patient, place their knees in front of the patient's knees, and hug the patient under the arms for lifting. Then instruct the patient to help as much as possible. If transferring the patient to a chair after assisting them to stand, both the nurse and the patient should take small steps, pivoting around to the chair. Make sure the backs of the patient's knees are touching the front of the seat before lowering them into the chair.

When transferring a patient, make sure that all wheels are locked on the bed and/or chair before moving the patient.

Devices that Promote Mobility (e.g., Braces, Walkers, Wheelchairs, Gait Belt, Trapeze)

A nurse should encourage patients to use available assistive devices, such as canes, walkers, and wheelchairs. Before leaving a patient's room, make sure any assistive device that the patient uses independently is within their reach. Patients with lower-body immobility who still have upper-body strength might have a bed equipped with a trapeze. A **trapeze** is an assistive bar that hangs above the patient's bed and enables self-repositioning. Patients who are able should be encouraged to use the trapeze.

The use of assistive devices such as **gait belts** (also known as transfer belts) benefits both the nurse and the patient. When transferring or walking with a patient who needs assistance, it's advised to use a gait belt to prevent falls. When using a gait belt to assist a patient to walk, fasten the belt around their waist and hold it with both hands while standing to the side and slightly behind the patient. If the patient loses their balance and begins to fall, never attempt to catch them. Instead, continue holding the gait belt, bend at the knees, and slowly lower the patient to the floor.

Range of Motion Techniques

Range of motion exercises involve moving the body's limbs in particular ways to keep the joints healthy and flexible. Active range of motion exercises are performed by the patient independently. Passive range of motion exercises are done for patients who are unable to perform active ones. When performing passive range of motion exercises, gently guide the patient's limbs through their range of motion. Never force the limbs, as this can harm the patient.

With the patient resting in the supine position, take each joint through its range of motion. **Adduction** is the movement of a limb toward the midline of the body. **Abduction**, the opposite of adduction, is the movement of a limb away from the midline of the body.

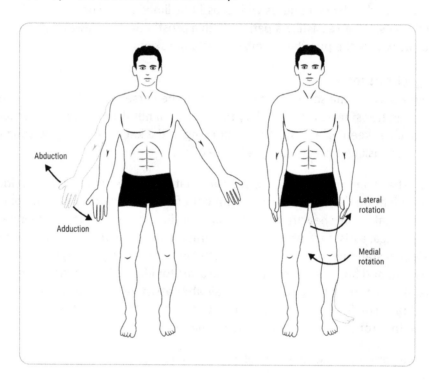

Flexion is the bending of a limb at the joint, while extension is the straightening of a limb at the joint.

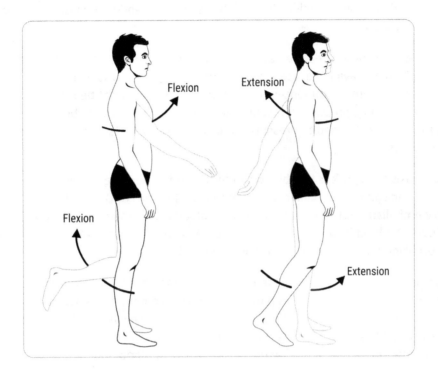

Effects of Immobility

Circulation and Skin Integrity

Patients with limited mobility are at risk for compromised circulation and/or skin breakdown. A nurse helps patients reposition themselves at least once every two hours, which prevents pressure sores and promotes adequate circulation.

Pressure sores (also called bedsores or pressure ulcers) are areas of skin breakdown that manifest when pressure on the skin minimizes circulation in that area. These usually occur over bony prominences such as the heel, ankle, coccyx, elbow, knee, or hip. Patients with pressure sores generally have some degree of immobility and are unable to reposition themselves frequently. Pressure sores are categorized by the following four stages:

- **Stage I**: The skin of the affected area is unbroken, generally red, and warm to the touch. Skin discoloration remains even after the patient is repositioned and the pressure is relieved from the site. Patients may have associated pain. Stage I pressure sores can be difficult to recognize in patients with dark skin.

- **Stage II**: Damage or loss of skin through several layers (partial thickness) with shallow ulceration of the skin, abrasion, or blistering.

- **Stage III**: Full thickness skin loss (epidermal and dermal layers) with ulceration that can be deep enough to expose fatty tissue; however, muscle, bone, and tendon are NOT visible. Tunneling might also be seen in patients with Stage III pressure sores.

- **Stage IV**: Full thickness tissue loss (epidermis, dermis, and underlying tissue damage) with deep ulceration and possible tunneling. Muscle, bone, and/or tendon are visible and palpable with Stage IV pressure sores.

To help prevent pressure sores, keep the patient's skin clean and dry, and reposition the patient at least every two hours. Whenever available, use assistive positioning devices such as pillows and wedges to help relieve pressure on bony prominences. These bony areas should not be massaged in patients who have, or are at risk of having, pressure sores. Clothing and bed linens should be straightened often to avoid wrinkles that can quickly lead to pressure sores in at-risk patients. Report any indication of skin breakdown to the nurse.

Deep vein thrombosis (DVT) refers to a blood clot in the body's deep veins, most commonly in the legs. Redness, swelling, and sometimes pain in an extremity can be signs of DVT. Patients with DVT are at risk for a **pulmonary embolism (PE)**, which occurs when a blood clot in the deep vein breaks off, travels to the lungs, and cuts off blood flow. Do not massage red or swollen areas in the extremities, as this can result in a clot breaking off and causing a pulmonary embolism.

Patients who are immobile are at an increased risk for developing DVT. If possible, patients should be encouraged to ambulate to avoid DVT. If a patient is unable to ambulate, assistance with range of motion exercises should be provided. Anti-embolism stockings (also called TED hose) and sequential compression devices (SCDs) are commonly used for patients who are confined to their beds. Both of these help to promote circulation in the lower legs and prevent blood pooling.

Elimination (Bowel and Bladder)
Immobility can lead to problems with elimination. Patients who are unable to care for their own toileting needs are at risk for incontinence. Be attentive to a patient's toileting needs and attempt to establish a routine with the patient. Immobility can also lead to constipation. If not contraindicated, a patient who is at risk for constipation should be encouraged to increase fluid intake. Patients can be reluctant to increase fluid intake because of their inability to self-toilet, so encourage the patient to increase their intake and be available for their toileting needs.

Sleep and Rest Patterns/Needs
Patients with immobility can have altered sleep patterns because of their limited ability to be physically active. Pain, discomfort, anxiety, stress, and certain medications are also common issues that can disrupt sleep. Older patients, as well as patients who are healing from illness or injury, require frequent rest and sleep periods. However, they should be encouraged to be active when they're able. Assist patients in establishing daily routines and encourage them to participate in daily living activities as much as possible. For instance, if a patient can sit in a chair for a meal rather than remaining in bed, encourage and assist them to do so. As another example, if a patient is able (with assistance) to transfer from using a bedpan to using a bedside toilet, encourage and assist them to do so. Any activities a patient can participate in will benefit their sleep, rest, and overall wellbeing. However, be attentive and careful not to overtire the patient. Any patient complaints of sleeplessness should be reported to the nurse.

Self-Image
When patients lose mobility, they can experience a sense of loss and independence. They can become isolated, depressed, and/or withdrawn and might begin to develop a negative self-image. Encourage these patients to participate in activities of daily living and give them as many opportunities as possible for autonomy.

Strength and Endurance

Patients who experience immobility can begin to lose muscle strength and endurance. If the immobile patient isn't cared for properly and their muscles aren't used, the muscles can begin to atrophy (weaken), the joints can begin to stiffen, and contractures (muscle shortenings) can develop. To prevent this from occurring, a nurse performs passive range of motion exercises with immobile patients during times of care, such as bathing and/or dressing. Patients who are able to perform active range of motion exercises are encouraged to do so.

Activity Tolerance

While patients should be encouraged to participate in activities of daily living as much as possible, be careful not to overtire them. A patient's daily routine should be planned carefully. Activities should be spaced so that there's ample opportunity to participate as well as adequate rest periods in between.

Comfort

A nurse should provide immobile patients with as much comfort as possible. Reposition patients no less than every two hours and use positioning devices such as pillows and wedges to promote proper body alignment and circulation and to reduce issues of skin breakdown.

Changes in Skin Integrity

Patients with illness, altered nutrition, decreased mobilization, and/or incontinence of bowel and/or bladder are at high risk for skin breakdown. There are some important steps a nurse can take to help prevent breakdown and promote healthy skin.

Skin health depends on adequate nutrition—especially protein intake—and proper circulation of nutrients, such as oxygen to the capillary beds near the skin's surface. Immobility and side effects of medications may cause the patients to refrain from repositioning themselves as they normally would in bed to redistribute pressure. When this happens, pressure on certain areas of the skin will cut off the supply of blood to that area. As a result, oxygen and other important nutrients will cease to nourish the area, and a pressure ulcer will begin forming.

Some common areas where pressure ulcers occur are the sacral area/lower back/buttocks and the heels. When turning and bathing, these areas need to be checked for redness, skin breakdown, and blanching, which occurs when the skin turns white when pressed, then promptly returns to its natural color. Other common areas include the ears, the back of the head, the shoulders, the elbows, and the inner knees.

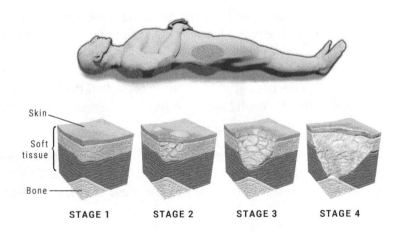

As mentioned in a previous section, there are four main stages of pressure ulcers, ranging from mild pinkness or redness of the skin to severe damage down into the fascia, muscles, and tendons. The nurse does not classify pressure ulcers, but rather observes the skin carefully for changes. Incontinence is a major risk factor for skin breakdown. The nurse may apply lotions or creams to prevent skin breakdown when providing baths and perineal care to the patient. The nurse will also turn and reposition immobile patients every two hours to decrease pressure on bony prominences. Positioning the patient's limbs and back carefully with pillows redistributes pressure.

Any changes in skin such as redness, tearing, or worsening of existing wounds would need to be reported to the nurse immediately. Some facilities may have a skin wound assessment team to oversee the care of the ulcers and recommend interventions.

Pain Management

Pain has been called the fifth vital sign. In addition to heart rate, temperature, blood pressure, and respiratory rate, the patient's experience of pain is just as vital for the healthcare team to assess, monitor, and treat.

The patient may report their pain to the nurse verbally or nonverbally. Nonverbal signs of pain the nurse can look for are facial grimacing, moaning, and tension throughout the body. Behavior that is different for a patient may also be a sign of pain. For example, the nurse may know one patient to normally be very talkative and alert, but they are instead laying silently on the bed for most of the morning, and barely acknowledging anyone entering the room. This may be a sign the patient is experiencing pain and should be investigated and reported to the nurse.

Nonpharmacological Comfort Interventions

When the nurse assesses the patient and finds they need something to alleviate a discomfort, they may first think of pharmacological interventions such as an analgesic. The nurse must also consider nonpharmacological interventions to comfort a patient, as these often come with little to none of the commonly experienced drug side effects.

There are many examples of nonpharmacological interventions the nurse may employ before turning to medication. Repositioning a patient who is feeling uncomfortable may be the first step in relieving a cramp or excessive pressure. This may involve getting the patient in or out of bed, sitting in a chair, or ambulating if appropriate. The nurse may also use pillows to prop and position the patient into a more comfortable position in the bed.

A patient may complain of being too hot or too cold. The nurse may look at what the patient is wearing and decide if additional clothing would help or if the removal of clothing items, as appropriate, would assist. Giving the patient their coat, a warm blanket from the floor's blanket warmer, or socks may comfort a cold patient. Many hospitals do not allow fans, as they are an infection control risk, but the nurse may provide other options to the patient who wishes to cool off. If the patient is not on a fluid restriction, ice chips or ice water may be helpful in refreshing them. Removing excessive blankets may cool them off as well.

The nurse can use heat and cold in even more targeted approaches to relieve pain. Application of heat, such as warm washcloths, electric blankets, and warm baths will increase blood flow to the painful area, reduce muscle spasms, slow down peristalsis, relax the smooth muscles, and even decrease stomach acid production.

Cold application, on the other hand, cannot only decrease the spasmodic activities of muscles but also cause vasoconstriction in the areas where it is applied. The application of cold items such as an ice pack, cool washcloth, and ice cubes can decrease inflammation and increase peristalsis. The application of cold items may have a longer-lasting effect than the application of heat in some patients.

The nurse should not feel uncomfortable offering therapeutic touch where and when appropriate. Most nursing schools train their students in basic massage techniques so that the nurse may use this on clients experiencing muscle tension. Massage should only be applied with the patient's consent and in an appropriate manner. The nurse may use lotion or oil if appropriate to relieve areas of muscle tension. Common areas that become tense include the neck, shoulders, and lower back. By massaging these areas, the nurse may be able to promote healthy blood flow, decrease tension, and maybe even relieve achiness that the client may be experiencing.

Some clients may request alternate therapies for **spiritual needs**. The nurse may refer the client to the appropriate entity for these interventions. For example, most hospitals offer a clergy that will come to the patient and talk with them. Patients may have spiritual issues they may want to discuss. The clergy and spiritual staff available at the hospital can address those needs, talk with the patient, and pray with them.

The nurse may use certain **psychological modalities** for relieving a patient's pain or discomfort. Distraction such as music therapy can be helpful in moving the patient's focus off the discomfort, as pain is perceived in the mind and can sometimes be overcome there as well. The nurse may educate the patient about a topic that is troubling them, thus relieving any anxiety they may feel. Simple strategies aimed at relaxation such as controlled, deep breathing may assist a patient in pain. Deep breathing causes the body to take in far more stress-reducing oxygen and release the waste product carbon dioxide, thus making the patient immediately feel better. Breathing techniques are a hallmark of natural childbirth, as the woman focuses on her breathing to work her way through each contraction. Sometimes the simple act of listening to the patient as they voice their concerns may be all it takes to alleviate their apprehension, working through the inner conflict.

There are certain relaxation strategies that may be used on patients when muscle tension is present. These fall mainly into the categories of progressive muscle relaxation, autogenic training, and biofeedback. **Progressive muscle relaxation** techniques will have the patient alternately tighten and then relax different muscle groups. **Autogenic training** involves the patient training their body to respond to verbal commands, often targeted at the breathing rate, blood pressure, heartbeat, and temperature of the body. **Biofeedback** often includes breathing exercises. The goal of all of these relaxation strategies is to promote relaxation and reduce stress.

Whichever nonpharmacological technique the nurse chooses should be selected very carefully, using critical thinking and sound nursing judgment to best serve the patient's need and alleviate their discomfort.

Nutrition and Oral Hydration

A patient admitted to a facility will often have specific nutritional needs, such as a diet modification or restriction. Conditions, such as nausea or vomiting, and equipment, such as nasogastric tubes, can further complicate the goal of maintaining adequate nutrition. The nurse should also be familiar with intravenous (IV) accesses and how to monitor them.

There are several different dietary restrictions that a patient may have depending on their condition. A cardiac diet, or heart-healthy diet, is for patients with heart conditions. This diet is generally low in sodium, fat, and cholesterol. The nurse will educate the patient about this diet, but it is important for the nurse to ensure the correct meal tray is delivered to the patient. Other dietary restrictions for health reasons include the renal diet—for patients with kidney problems or failure—a diabetic diet, which focuses on controlling carbohydrate intake, and a fluid-restricted diet for patients with heart or kidney failure.

There are cultural and religious considerations to be aware of when it comes to dietary restrictions. Some adherents of the Jewish and Islamic faiths, for example, do not consume pork products. Some Jews also do not consume meat and dairy products in the same meal. Acceptable Jewish meals are referred to as *kosher*, while in the Islamic faith, foods that are acceptable are called *halal*. Some people believe it is wrong to consume any meat and only eat non-animal foods. They are called vegetarians. Vegans do not consume any animal product of any kind, such as milk or honey.

Some patients may be lactose intolerant. Lactose is a sugar found in dairy products that can cause gastrointestinal upset to sensitive individuals. These people may need to abstain from consuming dairy products or take a digestive aid—such as the enzyme lactase—to help them digest the lactose.

There are numerous other dietary restrictions a patient can have for various reasons. The important points for the nurse are to be familiar with the patient's diet order, to ensure the correct tray is delivered, to correct a mistake made by the food service, and to ensure the patient's wishes are respected.

Illness and medications can sometimes bring on side effects of nausea and/or vomiting. The patient experiencing these side effects will likely prefer to abstain from food—called **fasting**—until the nausea and vomiting subsides. If the nausea and vomiting is short-lived, fasting is not a problem. If the fasting is prolonged, however, the patient will experience nutritional deficits and further complications.

The nurse must always assist the healthcare team in carefully monitoring all of a patient's intake and output (I&O) to ensure adequate nutrition and hydration. Any nausea or vomiting must be recorded, as well as the amount of meals eaten. The intake and output record will be tracked by the healthcare team and interventions based upon it. There are medications, such as Zofran (ondansetron), that can alleviate nausea and prevent vomiting. In the case of a patient receiving chemotherapy treatments who has constant nausea and trouble eating, there are medicines that can encourage appetite.

Some patients may have a **nasogastric (NG) tube** placed through the nose, down the esophagus and into the stomach for therapeutic or diagnostic purposes. The nurse ensures patient comfort and monitors the tube for dislodgement or displacement. The tube is usually secured in one nostril of the patient's nose with a strip of tape. Any changes in the tube must be reported to the nurse immediately.

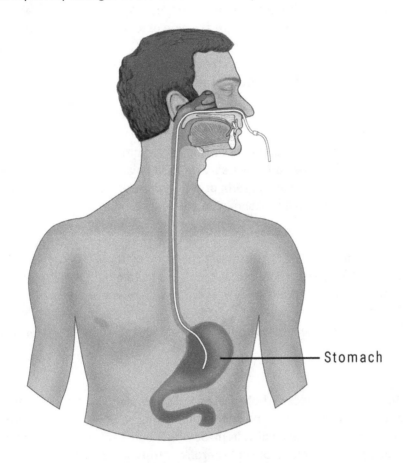

Stomach

The patient who is confused can be even further aggravated by the placement of an NG tube and may need special assistance to prevent disturbing the tube. As a last resort, a method of preserving the tube would be to put physical restraints on the patient, but only if all other options have been exhausted.

Food Nutrients

Carbohydrates
Carbohydrates are organic (containing carbon) compounds that are converted into energy for the body. They may be simple, such as refined table sugar, or complex, such as pasta, rice, and fiber.

Fats
Fats are lipid-containing compounds that are necessary for cell wall integrity, energy storage, and protection of all body organs against injury. Cholesterol is a body fat that exists in two forms: low-density lipoprotein (LDL) and high-density lipoprotein (HDL). LDLs are associated with the formation and progression of atherosclerosis, which is a build-up of lipid cells in the vasculature that results in hypertension and cardiovascular disease. Fats are also classified by the configuration of the hydrogen bonds and are classified as saturated fats, which are solid at room temperature, or unsaturated fats, which are liquid at room temperature. Research indicates that replacing saturated fats with unsaturated fats in the diet facilitates the removal of excess cholesterol from the body. Fats are contained in dairy

and animal products, nuts, and vegetable oils. Current recommendations include consuming a balanced diet that provides unsaturated fats and limited animal fats.

Proteins

Proteins are also organic compounds that contain carbon, hydrogen, and oxygen and form amino acids, the building blocks of the protein molecule. There are nine essential amino acids that must be consumed because the body cannot synthesize them. A complete protein consists of all nine essential amino acids, while an incomplete protein is deficient in one or more of the essential amino acids. Proteins are essential for all intracellular processes and as enzymes that facilitate all chemical reactions in the body. Nutritional sources of protein include animal products, dairy products, beans, and tofu.

Minerals/Electrolytes

Mineral/electrolytes are metals and nonmetals, including sodium, potassium, chloride, phosphorous, magnesium, calcium, and sulfur. They are necessary for fluid balance, transmission of nervous impulses, bone maintenance, blood clotting, healthy teeth, protein synthesis, and cardiac-impulse conduction. Minerals and electrolytes are generally consumed in adequate amounts from a balanced diet.

Vitamins

Vitamins are organic compounds that are necessary for blood clotting, immune function, maintenance of teeth, and the action of enzymes. There are two classes of vitamins. Fat-soluble vitamins, including A, D, E, and K, can be stored in excess in the body in the event of excessive intake. Water-soluble vitamins, including B-complex and C, are not stored in the body and ingested amounts greater than body requirements will be excreted in the urine. Vitamins are present in fruits, vegetables, fish, organ meats, and dairy.

Fiber

Dietary fiber is composed of complex carbohydrates and other plant substances that are not broken down by the digestive enzymes. Fiber can be water soluble or insoluble, and both forms contribute to the normal function of the gastrointestinal system. Soluble fiber that is present in oatmeal, blueberries, nuts, and beans facilitates the excretion of cholesterol, controls abrupt increases in blood glucose levels, and contributes to normal bowel function. The insoluble fiber that is present in whole grains, the skin and seeds of many fruits, and brown rice improves bowel function and also contributes to a feeling of fullness following food intake, which can lead to modest weight loss.

Water

Making up about 75 percent of the body, **water** is a vital necessity to human life. Water feeds cells and organs, creates a lubricant around the joints, and regulates body temperature. It is also important to digestion, as water moves food through the intestines.

Dietary Supplements

Dietary supplements contain various nutrients that are intended to compensate for inadequate dietary intake of those elements. These products should be used with care by anyone who also takes prescription medications because adverse interactions between the two are common.

Special Dietary Needs

Weight Control

Weight control requires a balanced diet that is calorie controlled and combined with adequate aerobic exercise. Current research indicates that the consumption of sugar and white flour, rather than dietary fats, is the greatest dietary threat to successful weight management.

Diabetes

Diabetes requires a balanced diet that is carbohydrate controlled. Diabetes may be due to a lack of insulin production by the pancreas or cellular insensitivity to the insulin that is present in the bloodstream. The controlled intake of carbohydrates limits the amount of insulin that is necessary to protect the body against the side effects of chronically elevated blood glucose levels.

Cardiovascular Disease

Cardiovascular disease most often is accompanied by excess fluid volume that is manifested by hypertension and edema. The condition requires a balanced diet that is sodium controlled, with adequate fluid intake.

Hypertension

Hypertension is associated with fluid volume excess, which means that excess dietary sodium and fluid should be avoided.

Cancer

Cancer may affect multiple body systems, which means that the diet should be balanced with additional calories to meet energy needs.

Lactose Sensitivity/Intolerance

Lactose sensitivity/intolerance results from the deficiency of the enzyme lactase, which is necessary for the breakdown or digestion of lactose, a sugar found in dairy products. This deficiency can result in stomach bloating, nausea, vomiting, and diarrhea following the ingestion of dairy products.

Gluten Free

Gluten-free diets must be free of wheat, barley, and rye in any form. This means that, in addition to bread, all processed foods must be avoided. Gluten intolerance may be a symptom of celiac disease, which affects the absorption of food in the small intestine, or an allergic response to wheat gluten; however, it is most commonly due to the lack of a necessary digestive enzyme. Possible manifestations include stomach bloating, diarrhea, fatigue, and weight loss.

Food Allergies

Food allergies can be related to one or several foods for a given patient. The allergic responses can range from mild to life threatening. The diet must be balanced and free of the allergens.

Personal Hygiene

Part of the nurse's regular assessment of the patient includes their level of **personal hygiene**. This is most important upon their initial admission assessment, as how well they are groomed walking into the facility speaks to how well they take care of themselves on a day-to-day basis at home. The nurse will very quickly be able to make a judgment about how hygienic the patient is when doing the standard head-to-toe assessment.

Components of personal hygiene include evidence of washing themselves, how they care for their feet and nails, how they dress, the cleanliness of their clothes, whether or not they have shaved, if their hair is clean and maintained, and their level of oral hygiene.

Different people uphold themselves, their families, and their households to different standards of cleanliness. Some people are more pristine, while others are slovenlier. There are certain "accepted" standards of cleanliness, but not everyone maintains every single one at all times. The nurse keeps the client's personal hygiene in the context of their physical abilities, state of illness, and cultural context. Some cultures may be used to a lower or higher level of cleanliness, and the nurse keeps this in mind when performing the assessment.

Examples of cultural differences include how often it is acceptable to bathe or shower in a week. Some cultures may stick to a daily routine, while others may think weekly is acceptable. The presence or absence of hair on certain parts of the body on males and females may be different from culture to culture. The tolerance of bodily odor may also vary as to how strong of an odor is present and acceptable. The practice of bathing or showering may be an exclusively private act in some cultures, while in other cultures it is a public, communal activity. The nurse endeavors to understand the cultural context from which their client hails.

Many nurses may dismiss oral hygiene as a low priority compared to their other daily duties with their patients, but in fact, it is a strong indicator of overall health. The oral hygiene practices of the patient should be assessed and observed, and patient education should take place where possible. It is recommended that adults and children brush their teeth twice a day and floss once a day. Mouthwash should be used as needed. All three of these items—toothbrushes, floss, and mouthwash—should be available in the patient admission kits in most facilities. The nurse can go over their use upon patient admission.

Nurses are not allowed to trim fingernails or toenails in most facilities. The main reason for this is patients with diabetic neuropathy, a common ailment among diabetics, have little to no feeling in their extremities and are prone to injury. The nurse may assist the patient in keeping their nails clean until such time as they are able to have them trimmed by the appropriate party, whether a licensed podiatrist, the patient, or a trusted family member.

The nurse will assist in other hygienic activities with the patient, depending on their functioning capabilities. Most facilities require one bath per day. This may be an independently taken bath or shower by the patient, an assisted bath, a partial bed bath, or a complete bed bath. The nurse and their assistant will help the patient complete this activity to ensure they remain clean while staying in the facility, as this promotes overall health and wellness.

Perineal care is one item of personal hygiene that the nurse and nursing assistant will ensure is completed regularly. Many patients suffer from bowel and bladder incontinence as well as often having urinary catheters and sometimes rectal tubes for the collection of urine and stool. Maintaining a clean perineal area is vital to preventing infection and preserving skin integrity.

Rest and Sleep

Sleep and rest are essential to optimal health and healing. Patients can have difficulty sleeping. Whenever possible, plan the patient's care routine to correspond with periods when the patient is awake. Care activities should be grouped together when appropriate to avoid disturbing the patient more than necessary. Although patients need adequate rest periods, they should be encouraged to get

out of bed and participate in activities when they're able, which aids in better rest. For a patient who's unable to leave their bed, encourage them to perform active, range of motion exercises.

Patients in unfamiliar surroundings, or in facilities with constant lighting and noise, can become disoriented to day and night. Provide these patients with as many environmental cues as possible, such as dimming the lights and keeping the noise level low at night, turning the lights on and opening curtains and blinds in the morning, etc. Performing activities of daily living on a set schedule can also help the patient to stay oriented.

Pharmacological Therapies

Adverse Effects/Contraindications/Side Effects/Interactions

Most of the nurse's day-to-day work will involve the administration of pharmacological and parenteral therapies as part of the patient's treatment plan. In general, **pharmacological therapy** has to do with the branch of science in which drugs are created for the use of combatting disease processes. Each of these drugs is administered into the body via pill, patch, or otherwise and has a measurable, desired effect on the body. **Parenteral therapies** are a specific mode of medication delivery via some other route than the alimentary canal, usually by a needle. This can be intravenous (IV), intrathecal, intraosseous, and subcutaneous, among other routes.

With all medication administration, the nurse must be mindful of the drug's potential adverse effects. As far as pharmacology has come in the past century, no drug has been perfected to the point of not having any potential adverse effect. An **adverse effect** is defined as a negative response to a medication that is not part of the desired effect. The chemical structure of the drug is what usually triggers these adverse effects. Adverse effects are greatly minimized by appropriate dosing for the individual patient.

Some drug side effects are quite obvious. Take, for example, warfarin. Warfarin, or Coumadin, is used to thin out the blood in patients at risk for forming deadly blood clots, such as those with atrial fibrillation. However, if inappropriately dosed and under-monitored, warfarin can cause serious hemorrhaging because of its effect on the body's clotting mechanisms and ability to achieve hemostasis. Patients taking warfarin should be carefully monitored for overdosage and signs of bleeding.

At times, a drug may cause an adverse effect when it is coadministered with some other substance that affects its chemical structure or its ability to be absorbed by the body. Narcotics, for example, should not be taken while drinking alcohol. Alcohol, a depressant, exacerbates the effect of the narcotic, also a depressant, to the point that the patient's drive to breathe and their consciousness may be completely knocked out, causing death.

Another type of adverse effect is an **allergic reaction**. Depending on the patient's unique immune system's makeup, some drugs may cause the immune system to kick into overdrive, decreasing the desired effect and adding a lot of unwanted effects. Common signs of an allergic reaction include mild reactions such as itching and rash, escalating all the way to a severe reaction such as anaphylactic shock. Anaphylaxis involves an inflammation and narrowing of the patient's airway. This makes breathing difficult and presents a life-threatening situation.

The nurse should be aware of common **contraindications** for a certain drug's use. A contraindication is a situation in which it is inappropriate to administer a drug. For example, if a patient is taking a potassium-sparing ACE inhibitor for the management of heart failure, supplementation of potassium should be avoided or only carefully done under the management of the attending physician or nephrologist. This is because the ACE inhibitor causes the body to excrete *less* potassium than it normally does, meaning supplementing potassium puts the patient at risk for hyperkalemia, a life-threatening condition that can cause heart rhythm abnormalities and dysfunction. Another common contraindication to be mindful of is the administration of Coumadin, or warfarin, with another blood thinner such as aspirin. The concurrent usage of these two medications aimed at decreasing the body's own hemostatic response can result in a life-threatening hemorrhage in the patient and should be avoided.

If the nurse ever suspects that the administration of a drug is contraindicated by the usage of another, they should always raise their concern with the ordering physician, the pharmacist on staff, and/or nursing management to confirm. It is a patient safety issue that is worth the extra time to investigate to prevent patient harm.

Adverse effects and contraindications are some of the rarer occurrences in day-to-day pharmacological therapies that the nurse will encounter. More commonly, the nurse will encounter milder, unwanted effects of drug administration called **side effects**. Most drugs have side effects or undesirable effects of administration. For example, a patient put on antibiotics for a respiratory infection may experience gastrointestinal (GI) upset such as stomachache, excessive flatulence, and diarrhea. Antibiotics destroy the native GI tract bacteria as part of their mechanism of action, which is what causes these side effects. Side effects are usually mild enough that the patient can either bear with them until they are finished taking the medication for the original cause, or the doctor may prescribe a counter drug to lessen the side effects of the original drug. As each additional drug carries with it the potential for more side effects, use of more medications should be weighed carefully as to their potential for helping the patient. The clinical judgment of the doctor and nurse and the patient's preference are all considered in these decisions.

Drug interactions are an aspect of pharmacology that the nurse must keep in mind when performing medication administration. A drug interaction may occur between many different drugs and substances. These interactions may fall into one of three categories: synergistic, antagonistic, or an interaction in which a whole new action is produced that neither substance could produce on their own.

A **synergistic interaction** is one in which the two concurrently administered substances *enhance* each other's action. Sometimes the prescriber uses the synergistic action of drugs to their advantage when the synergy would be helpful to the patient's condition. In some instances, however, synergy of two drugs is detrimental to the patient. An example of synergistic medications working in the patient's best interest would be the use of multiple antibiotics to treat an infection. Many patients with respiratory infections, such as pneumonia, will be prescribed a combination of different antibiotic therapies for two reasons. One is that the prescriber does not always know the exact causative organism of the infection and wants to wipe it out completely, and two, these combinations of antibiotics have been shown to be more effective than just using one specific antibiotic.

An example of synergistic drugs having an unwanted effect is the combination of multiple blood thinners, such as Coumadin and aspirin, that was mentioned above. In some patients' cases, the combination of the two drugs may be warranted and helpful, while in others it could have a devastating effect on the patient, resulting in a massive bleed.

Antagonistic drug interactions are ones in which the two coadministered substances cancel each other out or greatly decrease each other's potential action. Patients who are taking cholesterol-lowering drugs such as statins, for example, are discouraged from drinking grapefruit juice, as it has an antagonistic

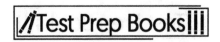

action on the statin. The grapefruit essentially absorbs all the statins before the body can, thus canceling out any positive effects they might have had for the patient, rendering them useless.

A nurse who is well-versed in pharmacological knowledge, including drug side effects, adverse effects, contraindications, and interactions, will be able to better serve and protect their patients from harm.

Dosage Calculations

The nurse administering pharmacological or parenteral therapies to the patient will often have the dosages precalculated for them; however, it is vital to have a basic knowledge of how to perform **dosage calculations** if verification or manual calculations must be done.

The place to start with dosage calculations is a working knowledge of common conversions. The following chart provides a list of conversions for the nurse to know:

- 1 liter is equal to 1000 milliliters.
- 1 gram is equal to 1000 milligrams.
- 1 milligram is equal to 1000 micrograms.
- 1 kilogram is equal to 2.2 pounds.
- 1 teaspoon is equal to 5 milliliters.
- 3 teaspoons is equal to 1 tablespoon.
- 1 kilogram is equal to 1000 grams.
- 30 milliliters is equal to 1 ounce.
- 1 tablespoon is equal to 15 milliliters.

The nurse must also know common abbreviations used in measurements, listed below:

- oz: ounce
- tbsp: tablespoon
- mL: milliliter
- kg: kilogram
- dL: deciliter
- lb: pound
- g: gram
- mg: milligram
- L: liter
- tsp: teaspoon
- mcg: microgram

Commonly encountered units of measurement within nursing include mass, volume, and time. Most hospitals use the metric system. The metric system is an internationally recognized system of measurement that provides one base unit for length, mass, and volume. Length is measured in meters, mass is measured in grams, and volume is measured in liters. Each unit can be expressed as bigger or smaller measurements in increments of 10, 100, and 1000. For example, a kilogram, the prefix "kilo-" meaning "1000," refers to 1000 grams. Other prefixes for the metric system are listed below:

- hecto-: 100
- deca-: 10
- deci-: 0.1

- centi-: 0.01
- milli-: 0.001

Converting smaller metric measurements to larger ones and vice versa requires only moving the decimal point left or right, depending on the difference in tenths, hundredths, or thousandths. For example, if a patient's height is measured as centimeters and the nurse wants to convert it to meters, they simply move the decimal point to the left two steps, as a meter is divided into hundredths when it is converted to centimeters. If the patient's measurement is 152 centimeters, the correct conversion to meters would be 1.52 meters.

One of the most frequently used calculations a nurse will need to know is the basic dosage calculation. The nurse will take the desired dose, noted as "D"; divide it by the amount of the drug the nurse has on hand, noted as "H"; multiply this total by the volume in which the drug comes (which could be tablet, capsule, or liquid form), noted as "V"; and they will arrive at the correct dose.

For example, if the nurse has an order to administer 50 milligrams (mg) of Dilantin and has a formulation of 125 mg in 5 mL, how does the nurse set up the equation? The dose, or "D," is 60 mg. The amount on hand, or "H," is 125 mg. The nurse will put D over H, divide 50 by 125, which gives her 0.4 mg. They will then multiply 0.4 times the volume in which the Dilantin is formulated in, which is 5 mL. 0.4 times 5 is 2, so the correct dosage for the patient is 2 mL of Dilantin.

Expected Actions/Outcomes

The nurse will be expected to obtain information about the client's list of prescribed medications, involving the formulary review and consultations with the pharmacist. It is vital that the nurse be able to use critical thinking when expecting certain effects and outcomes of medication administration, including oral, intradermal, subcutaneous, intramuscular, and topical formulations. Over time, the client should be evaluated for their response to their medication regime. This includes a variety of home remedies, their prescription drugs, and any over-the-counter (OTC) drug usage. The response of the client to their medications, whether therapeutic or not, should be evaluated. If adverse reactions or side effects occur, the patient's medications will need to be reevaluated and modified.

Most medical facilities have electronic health record systems that, once the client is registered for the first time, will keep track of their medication record. This will need to be modified with each doctor's visit and hospital stay, of course, but is a helpful tool in recording the client's list of medications.

With all medication administration, the nurse should keep their eye on the expected outcome. Identifying the expected outcome, or goal, of the patient's medication regime will assist in keeping the medication list as short and maximally effective as it needs to be. The expected outcome is the overarching goal and principle that will guide the healthcare team and the patient in their decision-making process.

The nurse should have access to literature that provides information about drugs, including expected outcomes, mode of action in the body, appropriate dosing, contraindications, and adverse effects. A **formulary** is an example of this type of literature that gives an official list of medicines that may be prescribed and any related information on the drug. The formulary will give both the generic and the brand name for the drug and is maintained by physicians, nurse practitioners, and pharmacists to ensure it is accurate and up to date. Drugs listed in the formulary have been evaluated for safety and effectiveness by a committee of experts to provide practitioners with those deemed best for patients.

The nurse should use one of the greatest pharmacological references available to them in the health care facility: the **pharmacist**. Most hospitals have a team of pharmacists on staff whose sole purpose is to oversee the correct dosage, administration, and usage of all the patients' medication needs. Most pharmacists have a doctorate level of education in pharmacy, which the nurse would be wise to make good use of, and often. Pharmacists are often found on the floors, overseeing correct antibiotic and other drug dosages and administration, as well as being stationed in the hospital's pharmacy, which is only a phone call away. If the nurse has a question about a medication's use for a patient, they should not hesitate to contact the pharmacist and consult them and their pharmaceutical knowledge. They are a very helpful and valuable member of the healthcare team.

The two most common routes of medication administration the nurse will encounter are oral and intravenous. There are, of course, other routes of medication administration that the nurse will need to be knowledgeable and competent in performing. Intramuscular injections are the preferred route for vaccinations such as the pneumococcal and influenza vaccines. The deltoid muscle is preferred for most vaccines, but other sites the nurse may use if necessary include the ventrogluteal, dorsogluteal, and vastus lateralis sites.

One important aspect of intramuscular injection is the Z-track technique. In this technique, the nurse pulls the skin downward or upward, injects the medication at a 90 degree angle, and then releases the skin. This creates a "zigzag," or Z-shaped, track that prevents the injected fluid from leaking backward into the subcutaneous tissue. Backward leakage of tissue may cause tissue damage, thus the usage of the Z-track technique. The nurse must avoid massaging the site, as this may cause leakage and irritation.

Prescription drugs are those that may only be prescribed by a qualified healthcare practitioner. They may be obtained with a prescription from the pharmacy and dispensed by a qualified pharmacist. **OTC medications** may be obtained without a prescription, at the discretion of the patient. **Home remedies** include any sort of tonic or home-prepared solution that the patient makes for themselves at home as a cure for an ailment. These are often made with commonly found household or pantry items. Many home remedies are unproven in their effectiveness but rather anecdotally recommended by a friend or family member, often passed down through the generations. An example of a simple home remedy is lemon juice and honey in hot water as a "cure" for a sore throat. These simple ingredients have medicinal properties that may soothe the sore throat and may be preferred by the patient to an OTC or prescription formulation for sore throats. The nurse should obtain information about any home remedies the patient may be using to get a full picture of their health and wellness habits.

Medication Administration

The nurse observes the six rights of the patient with every medication administration. The patient has the right to 1) the right medication, 2) the right route, 3) the right time frame in which the medication is to be delivered, 4) the right client to whom the medication is to be administered, 5) the right dosage, and 6) the right documentation that the drug has been administered. These rights work to ensure patient safety.

In addition to the rights of the patient, the nurse should ensure that the appropriate physician and pharmacist orders have been given. The nurse should assess the patient for any allergies. This information can be found in the patient's medical record or chart if they have been previously admitted. The allergy information on the patient should include the specific type of reaction they had, whether it was a mild rash or a severe, anaphylactic reaction.

There are several different routes by which a medication can be administered by a nurse, including the following:

Intramuscular
The provider will use an **intramuscular injection** to ensure rapid absorption of a medication into the bloodstream when the intravenous infusion of the medication is inappropriate or inaccessible. Common sites for intramuscular injection include the deltoid, vastus lateralis, and ventral gluteal muscles.

Z-Tract Injection
When injecting medications capable of causing skin irritation or discoloration in the event of leakage from the injection site, the provider will apply traction to the skin surrounding the injection site with the nondominant hand, insert the needle into the muscle at a 90-degree angle, inject the medication, withdraw the needle, and release the traction on the skin, trapping the injected solution in the muscle. This is known as a **Z-tract injection**.

Subcutaneous Injection
The provider will choose a subcutaneous site to inject medications that will absorb more slowly because of the limited blood supply in the fatty subcutaneous space. Using the nondominant hand, the provider will pinch the skin, insert the needle at a 90-degree angle into the fatty layer just under the skin, inject the medication, and withdraw the needle. It should be noted that for small children and individuals with little subcutaneous fat, a 45-degree angle is recommended to ensure the medication enters the subcutaneous tissue rather than muscle. This is known as a **subcutaneous injection**.

Oral/Sublingual/Buccal
The provider understands that the oral, sublingual, and buccal administration routes are appropriate for agents that will be rapidly absorbed into the bloodstream through the mucous membrane of the gastrointestinal tract. In addition, the sublingual and buccal routes are appropriate if the patient is unable to swallow a medication, or when the medication would be poorly absorbed or inactivated in the stomach. The provider is aware that sublingual and buccal medications are provided in tablet, film, and spray forms.

Oral administration: The provider will assist the patient to swallow oral medications that will be processed in the stomach or small intestine.

Sublingual administration: The provider will place sublingual medications under the tongue to facilitate rapid absorption of the medication into the bloodstream.

Buccal administration: The provider will place buccal medications between the cheek and the gum where the medication will be absorbed through the capillary bed.

Topical
Topical medications are applied to the skin, mucous membrane, or body tissue, and may be provided as transdermal patches; ointments, lotions, and creams; or powders. The provider will assess the administration site for local reaction, and will rotate the site as appropriate for transdermal patches. In addition, the provider will avoid personal contact with the medications that are commonly absorbed rapidly through the skin.

Inhalation

The provider understands that **inhalant drugs** are used to deliver the medication directly to the target organ, which results in more rapid and efficient local absorption of the medication, in addition to decreased systemic exposure to the effects of the medication.

The provider will use medication-specific metered dose inhalers, dry powder inhalers, or nebulizers to administer inhaled agents that may include antimicrobials and corticosteroids. The licensed provider is also responsible for verifying the patient's understanding of the proper use and administration of these medications.

Instillation (eye-ear-nose)

The provider understands that medications may be instilled into the eye, ear, or nose to promote absorption or to treat local irritation of the site. This is called **instillation**.

To instill eye drops, the provider will clear any accumulated secretions, use the nondominant hand to expose the conjunctival sac, instill the prescribed solution into the inner canthus while avoiding any contact with the eye, and use a sterile cotton ball to dry the eyelid.

To instill eye ointment, the provider will clear any accumulated secretions, use the nondominant hand to expose the conjunctival sac, apply the prescribed ointment along the sac from the inner canthus to the outer canthus while avoiding any contact between the eye and the medication container, and use a sterile cotton ball to dry the eyelid.

To instill medications into the ear, the provider will warm the solution to normal body temperature, position the patient with the head turned to the unaffected side, gently pull the ear up and back, instill the medication avoiding contact between the medicine dropper and the ear canal, place a sterile cotton ball loosely in the outer ear and instruct the patient to remain supine for fifteen minutes.

To instill nasal drops, the provider will instruct the patient to gently blow their nose, position the patient supine with the head tilted back, and instill the drops while avoiding contact between the inner nares and the medicine dropper.

Intradermal

The provider will use a 1 milliliter tuberculin syringe with a 5/8 inch 25- to 27-gauge needle to inject the prescribed medication into the interior portion of the forearm. The provider must identify the appropriate injection angle for the prescribed treatment; for example, allergy testing requires that the injection is 15 to 20 degrees, while insulin may be injected **intradermally** at 90 degrees.

Transdermal

The provider understands that **transdermal medications**, which are absorbed through the skin, provide the continuous release of a precise amount of the medication for a specific period of time. When applying a new dose of the medication, the provider will remove remaining residue from the previous dose, verify that the skin is intact and free of irritation, and sign and date the patch. Birth control pills, smoking cessation medications, pain relief agents, and nitroglycerin are some of the medications that are applied transdermally.

Vaginal

The provider understands that **vaginal medications**, which are available as suppositories, foams, ointments, and sprays, are used to alter the pH of the vagina, treat local infection, and provide comfort.

The provider will insert the suppository form into the vaginal vault where it will liquefy as a result of body temperature. The provider will apply the ointment and spray medications according to the manufacturers' directions.

Rectal

Antiemetics, analgesics, and cathartics are commonly available as suppositories. The provider will insert the **rectal suppository** above the internal anal sphincter to prevent displacement.

Injection Site

Site Selection

The provider will select the appropriate **injection site** with consideration of the age and stature of the patient and the administration requirements of the prescribed medication. The provider is aware that injection sites must be systematically rotated for medications such as insulin that are repeated daily.

Needle Length and Gauge

The provider will select the **needle gauge and length** that is consistent with the selected injection site and the administration requirements of the prescribed medication.

Medication Packaging

Multidose Vials

The provider will withdraw the calculated amount of medication from the **multidose vial** using aseptic technique to avoid contamination of the remaining solution.

Ampules

The provider will break the **ampule** using safety precautions related to glass breakage and withdraw the entire contents into the syringe. The provider will then verify that the syringe contains the calculated volume of medication, replace the needle, and administer the medication according to protocol.

Unit Dose

The provider is aware the patient's medications will most often be provided in single-dose amounts, as opposed to multidose amounts, in order to avoid medication errors.

Prefilled Cartridge-Needle Units

The provider is aware that injectable medications may be provided as **prefilled cartridges** with attached needles. Depending on the manufacturer, a nondisposable holder will be provided for the cartridge. The provider must verify that the prefilled cartridge contains the calculated dose.

Powder for Reconstitution

The provider will inject the prescribed amount of diluent into the vial, mix the solution, and withdraw the calculated amount of medication.

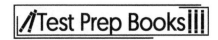

<u>Six Rights of Medication Administration</u>
As mentioned above, the **six rights of medication administration** must be addressed for every medication dose. The provider will:

- Use two means of identification (ID) to verify the right patient, which can include the patient's verbal report and the agency ID band.

- Verify the prescription and the medication as provided by the pharmacy.

- Compare the route of administration documented in the medication record with the original prescription.

- Verify the time schedule as documented in the medication record.

- Calculate the correct dose and verify the result with another provider as required by agency policy.

- Document the administration of the medication and the patient's response in the medication record according to agency policy.

Pharmacological Pain Management

Pain is the most commonly seen symptom in the emergency department, as most emergency situations cause patients to have a high level of pain. However, since cases in the emergency department often vary widely in scope and every patient will have a different personal threshold for pain tolerance, best practices are difficult to develop when it comes to **pain management**. It is often done on a case-by-case basis. However, when a patient's pain is not managed in a way that seems appropriate to that individual, it can cause patient and family dissatisfaction in the healthcare organization. As a result, medical staff must try to provide effective and safe pain management options that can make the patient comfortable at the present time, but that also do not cause harm over time. In some cases, like a sprained muscle, ice therapy and time can provide adequate pain management. More serious cases, defined as pain that does not subside after an objectively reasonable period of time for the injury, may require topical, intramuscular, or oral pain medication. These can include stronger doses of common over-the-counter pain medications, or prescription pain medications.

Prescription pain medications, especially opioids and muscle relaxers, are known for causing debilitating addiction, so when prescribing them to a patient, the lowest dose and dosing frequency necessary should be utilized. Additionally, patients should be closely monitored for their reactions to their pain medications. Finally, some individuals who are addicted to prescription pain killers and muscle relaxers may feign injuries in order to receive another prescription. Therefore, all patients' medical histories should be thoroughly evaluated to note their history of pain medication usage. Patients should also be assessed for showing any signs of drug abuse history and withdrawal symptoms (such as damaged teeth, shaking, and agitation).

Procedural sedation allows patients to remain somewhat alert during medical procedures that may be uncomfortable but not unbearably painful, such as resetting bones. Unlike general anesthesia, where patients are completely sedated and do not feel any sensations, procedural sedation allows patients to be somewhat conscious and aware of bodily functions. It can be utilized with or without pain-relieving medications. Practitioner awareness is crucial when administering procedural sedation, especially when pain relief is also utilized. Recently, overuse and improper use of common procedural sedation agents,

such as propofol, and common pain relief medications that are often used in conjunction, such as fentanyl, have caused high profile deaths.

Reduction of Risk Potential

Changes/Abnormalities in Vital Signs

One of the most basic nursing skills is obtaining and analyzing vital signs. Heart rate, blood pressure, breathing, and temperature are clues that must be interpreted to evaluate a patient's functioning status. Alterations in the vital signs must be carefully monitored to stay on top of the patient's condition and ensure timely and effective interventions take place.

The patient's **heart rate**, measured in beats per minute, tells the nurse a lot about the heart. In an adult, the normal heart rate is 60 to 100 beats per minute.

There are certain points in the body where the pulse can be felt, or palpated. **Palpable pulse points** include the carotid in the neck, the brachial near the elbow, the radial and ulnar on either side of the wrist, the femoral in the groin, the popliteal behind the knee, the posterior tibial behind the ankle, and the dorsalis pedis on top of the foot. The nurse uses these palpable peripheral pulse points to assess and count the heart rate on the patient. The location at which the nurse obtains the pulse is up to their discretion and based on the specific patient's situation. A radial pulse is the most commonly used in a stable, uncomplicated patient. A patient who is in critical condition with weakened blood circulation to the periphery of the body may need a femoral or carotid pulse taken, as these are closer to the heart and more detectable in situations of lowered cardiac output. The brachial pulse is the one that is measured when blood pressure is taken using an arm cuff.

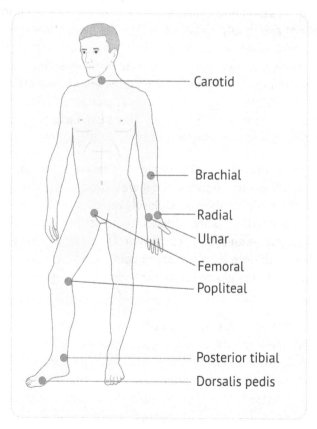

After the location of the pulse is decided and the nurse is palpating with the two-finger technique, the nurse will note the quality of the pulse. Qualities of the pulse can be faint, weak, strong, or bounding. The nurse grades the pulse on a scale of +1 to +4, with 1 indicating a faint pulse and 4 indicating a bounding pulse.

A pulse that is greater than 100 is called **tachycardia** and can arise from any number of causes. Exercise can raise the heart rate above 100 but is not considered abnormal or pathological, as it returns to normal at rest. Tachycardia without exercise and accompanied by other symptoms may be suggestive of a disease state at work and should be investigated.

Common causes of tachycardia include anxiety, medication side effects, street drug use, anemia, overactive thyroid, fear, stress, heart attack, or heart failure, among many others.

Bradycardia is the term for a heart rate that is less than 60 beats per minute. In some patients, this may be a normal finding. Patients who are experienced athletes often run bradycardic. This is because they have strengthened their heart through exercise to the point that their heart beats more efficiently with fewer beats, delivering adequate blood supply to the tissues and organs of the body. Bradycardia noted in a patient without a history of bradycardia, accompanied by other troublesome signs such as a decreased level of consciousness and hypotension, should be evaluated for probable causes and treatment.

Bradycardia may be caused by an underactive thyroid, infections of the heart, coronary artery disease, normal aging processes, medications for heart failure and hypertension, and hyperkalemia, to name a few.

The blood pressure is a vital sign that indicates how strongly the heart is pushing the blood through the circulatory system. **Blood pressure** is measured as a systolic number over a diastolic number. The systolic number represents the pressure at which the heart chambers are contracted, and the diastolic number represents the pressure when the heart chambers are at rest. Blood pressure is measured in millimeters of mercury (mmHg), as that is what the original sphygmomanometer, or blood pressure cuffs, used to determine a pressure reading.

In general, normal systolic ranges are between 100 and 120 mmHg, and normal diastolic ranges are between 60 and 80 mmHg. Between 120 and 139 mmHg systolic and 80 and 89 mmHg diastolic is considered prehypertensive, and 140 mmHg or greater systolic and 90 mmHg or greater diastolic is considered hypertensive.

Blood Pressure Levels	
Normal	systolic: less than 120 mmHg diastolic: less than 80mmHg
At risk (prehypertension)	systolic: 120–139 mmHg diastolic: 80–89 mmHg
High	systolic: 140 mmHg or higher diastolic: 90 mmHg or higher

Like tachycardia and bradycardia, hypertension and hypotension may arise from many different causes. Accompanying symptoms and patient history are key factors to consider when assessing changes in blood pressure.

Some patients may run a low blood pressure without any other accompanying symptoms, and that is to be noted as their normal, but no treatment is necessary.

Orthostatic hypotension is a special type of hypotension that occurs when the patient changes position. This occurs most commonly when they change from a seated position to standing. The patient will experience profound dizziness and unsteadiness, which is why orthostatic hypotension may lead to falls, and the patient should be cautioned to change positions slowly. Orthostatic hypotension may be measured by taking the patient's blood pressure first when lying down, then sitting up at the edge of the bed, and then a final reading while they are standing. If they are truly experiencing orthostatic hypotension, their blood pressure readings will trend downward significantly over the course of the three readings. Orthostatic hypotension is often a side effect of medications for hypertension.

A severe form of hypotension is shock, in which the body is no longer delivering an adequate supply of blood with its oxygen and nutrients to the vital organs of the body. The patient in shock will need immediate treatment and fluid resuscitation.

Low volume of blood, as occurs with a hemorrhage or a dehydrated state, will lead to low blood pressure. Blood transfusions, fluid resuscitation, and possibly blood pressure-raising medications such as intravenous (IV) dopamine may be necessary to correct hypovolemic hypotension.

A patient's **rate of breathing** should be between 16 and 20 breaths per minute and can be observed and counted simply by looking at the patient's chest for a rise and a fall. Tachypneic patients are those who are breathing at a rate greater than 20 breaths per minute. Patients with bradypnea, on the other hand, are those who are breathing below 16 breaths per minute.

Apnea is an absence of breathing and may occur during a normal sleep cycle, but prolonged and repeated occurrences of apnea are problematic and may suggest a disease process such as obstructive sleep apnea.

A patient may be tachypneic because of a blood clot, pneumonia or other respiratory infection, anxiety, asthma, chronic obstructive pulmonary disease (COPD), or diabetic ketoacidosis. Patients may be bradypneic because of an overdose of alcohol or narcotics, increased intracranial pressure, obesity, an underactive thyroid, a brain lesion, or many other causes. The nurse will look for accompanying symptoms and read through the patient history to help accurately evaluate the cause of the breathing abnormality.

The body regulates its temperature through a process called **thermoregulation**. The normal body temperature is right around 98.6 degrees Fahrenheit, give or take a degree depending on the patient's own normal.

Hyperthermia is a temperature that is above normal and may indicate an infection-fighting fever or a heat-induced condition such as heat stroke. Excessive sweating, confusion, and decreased level of consciousness may accompany hyperthermia and should be treated by making efforts to get the patient cooled down.

Hypothermia occurs when the body cannot produce enough heat to replace the heat it has lost, such as if a patient is in a harsh, cold environment without adequate warm clothing or a source of heat such as a furnace. Patients who are older, taking certain medications that interfere with the body's ability to regulate its temperature, have spinal cord injuries, are intoxicated with drugs or alcohol, or are very

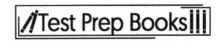

young are particularly susceptible to hypothermia and should take extra caution when exposed to very low temperatures.

Diagnostic Tests

A **diagnostic test** is one in which the result is hoped to assist in making a diagnosis of the patient's condition. The diagnostic test will reveal the patient's strengths and weaknesses and provide the clinician with data about the patient's condition.

There are many different diagnostic tests available for innumerable patient conditions. Different mediums are used to diagnose conditions, including blood work, ultrasound technology, X-rays, procedures that put cameras in the body to visualize internal structures, and more.

A female patient who has discovered a lump in her breast may be scheduled for a **mammography**. This type of diagnostic procedure is a type of X-ray that visualizes the tissue of the breast. This can help identify lumps that the patient or the practitioner is not able to palpate. The generally agreed-upon guideline for mammography is for it to be performed once every year or two after the age of forty for early breast cancer detection.

Patients with certain heart conditions may have an **echocardiography** performed. An echo, as it is commonly referred to, visualizes the structures and chambers of the heart through ultrasonography. An echo technician will use a small probe called a transducer to emit sound waves into the chest that create a sonographic image of the heart. Gel is applied to the skin of the chest to allow the transducer to easily glide back and forth as different aspects of the heart are visualized. Clots, holes, and any structural abnormalities will be identified during the echo. The official reading and interpretation of the echo images will be performed by a cardiologist after the tech has taken the images.

The **complete blood count (CBC)** is a type of diagnostic test that requires a small vial of blood to be drawn from the patient. The blood is sent to the lab, and the components of the blood are measured. The CBC measures red blood cells (RBCs), white blood cells (WBCs), hemoglobin, hematocrit, and platelets. This simple test can give the clinician a quick look at the body's oxygen-carrying capacity, immune function, and clotting capability all in one go.

For a patient with symptoms related to the gastrointestinal (GI) tract, the endoscope is a handy diagnostic tool to visualize the internal environment of the stomach and intestines. Generally, there are two types of scope: upper endoscopy and lower endoscopy. An **endoscopy** is a procedure in which a flexible tube with a camera, light, irrigation, and instrument ports are inserted for visualization of the GI tract. The patient receiving an upper GI endoscopy will require IV sedation as well as topical anesthetics applied to the throat. Lower endoscopy generally requires anesthesia as well, except for anoscopy and sigmoidoscopy, which do not travel as deeply into the body. Biopsy of tissue may be performed during a scope. As well as diagnosing certain conditions such as colon cancer, peptic ulcers, and other mucosal lesions, the scope may be performed for therapeutic reasons such as removing foreign bodies, hemostasis of bleeding lesions, debulking of tumors, placement of stents, placing a feeding tube, reduction of volvulus, and decompression of a dilated colon. Common hemostatic methods include placing hemoclips, injecting hemostatic drugs, thermal coagulation, variceal banding, and sclerotherapy.

Look at the image of a **colonoscopy** below:

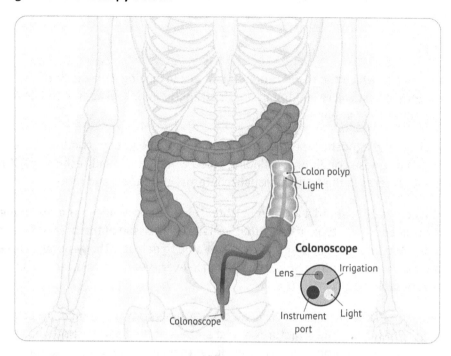

One of the most regularly performed diagnostic tests is the computed tomography scan. It may be referred to as a **CT or CAT scan**, but the meanings are all the same: a test in which a region of the body is scanned and images are obtained using radiography. The patient lays on a sliding table that moves them in and out of a circular opening in which the scanner is housed. As the patient moves through the scanner, an X-ray source and X-ray detector spin around the patient in a circular motion, taking images of the inner structures of the patient's body. These images are then sent to a computer, which makes a composite of all the images into 3-D images to be viewed and interpreted by a qualified radiologist. There are variations on how the CT can be taken, including stopping the patient for each scan or slice or keeping the patient in motion for a spiral CT, but the basic concept is the same.

CT scans may be noncontrast or with contrast. With IV or oral contrast, the patient drinks or is injected with a barium-based solution, targeted at whichever body tissues need imaging, and picked up by the X-ray during the scan. Contrast is often contraindicated in patients with renal failure, as their kidneys are unable to metabolize the substance. Contrast CTs are used to visualize tumors and inflammation and assess the vascular system for pulmonary emboli, aneurysms, or aortic dissection, among many other purposes.

Electrocardiography (EGG/ECG)

To perform a **standard 12-lead EGG/ECG**, the provider will:

- Verify the order and obtain all equipment before approaching the patient.
- Explain the procedure to the patient and assist him/her to a supine position.
- Expose the limbs and the chest, maintaining appropriate draping to preserve patient's privacy.
- Clean the electrode sites with alcohol and remove excess body hair according to agency policy.
- Attach electrodes to appropriate anatomical positions.
- Attach machine cables to the electrodes.
- Enter the patient data and calibrate the machine as necessary.

- Request that the patient does not move or speak.
- Obtain an artifact-free tracing.
- Remove the electrodes and residual conductive gel.
- Return the patient to a position of comfort.
- Submit the tracing for interpretation.

Correct Placement of EKG Leads

The accuracy of the tracing is dependent on correct lead placement; therefore, the provider will position the chest leads as follows:

- V_1 - right sternal border at the level of the fourth intercostal space
- V_2 - left sternal border at the level of fourth intercostal space
- V_3 - centered between V_2 and V_4
- V_4 - the midclavicular line at the level of the fifth intercostal space
- V_5 - horizontal to V_4 at the anterior axillary line
- V_6 - horizontal to V_4 at the midaxillary line

The provider must attach the limb leads to the extremities, not the torso. In addition, the provider must avoid large muscle groups, areas of adipose tissue deposit, and bony prominences when placing the limb leads on the four extremities.

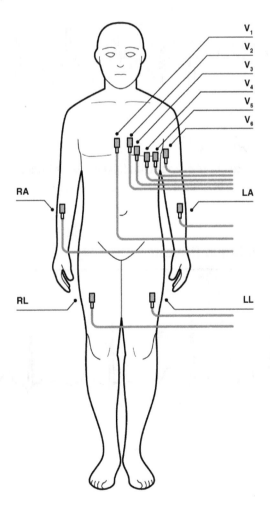

Patient Prep

In order to ensure an accurate tracing, the provider will:

- Explain the procedure to the patient.
- Expose the chest as necessary.
- Clip or shave excess hair as consistent with agency policy.
- Wipe the skin surface with gauze to decrease electrical resistance.
- Remove excess oils with alcohol wipe if necessary.
- Verify that the electrode is intact with sufficient gel.
- Attach the electrodes as appropriate.
- Complete the tracing.

Recognizing Artifacts

Artifact is most often the result of patient movement while the tracing is being recorded, and the provider must be able to differentiate between the artifact and lethal arrhythmias. Artifact is most often evidenced by a chaotic wave pattern that interrupts a normal rhythm, as shown in the figure below.

EKG Artifact

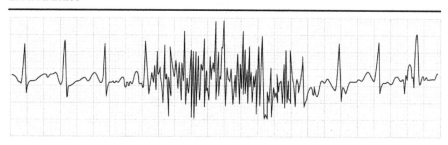

Recognizing Rhythms, Arrhythmias

Normal Sinus: The rhythm originates in the sinoatrial (SA) node as indicated by the presence of an upright p wave in lead 2. A p wave precedes every QRS complex, and the rhythm is regular at 60 to 100 beats per minute.

Normal Sinus Rhythm

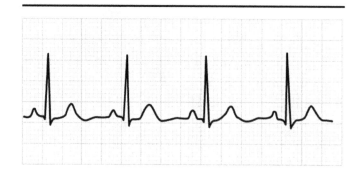

Sinus Tachycardia: The rhythm originates in the SA node as indicated by the presence of an upright p wave in lead 2. A p wave precedes every QRS complex, and the rhythm is regular at a rate greater than 100 beats per minute.

Sinus Tachycardia

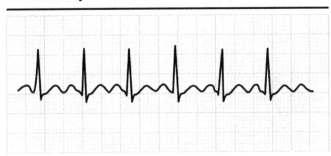

Sinus Bradycardia: The rhythm originates in the SA node as indicated by the presence of an upright p wave in lead 2. A p wave precedes every QRS complex, and the rhythm is regular at less than 60 beats per minute.

Sinus bradycardia

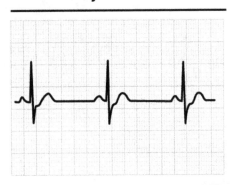

Atrial Fibrillation: The SA node fires chaotically at a rapid rate, while the ventricles contract at a slower but inefficient rate in response to an impulse from an alternative site in the heart. Individual p waves are not visible due to the rapid rate, and the QRS complexes are generally wider than the QRS complexes in the sinus rhythms.

Atrial Fibrillation

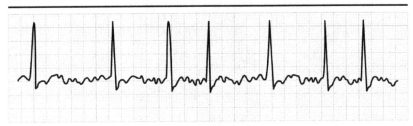

Complete Heart Block: The SA node generates a p wave that is not transmitted to the ventricles. The ventricles respond to an impulse from an alternative site, and the resulting complex has no association with the p wave. This condition requires immediate intervention.

Complete Heart Block

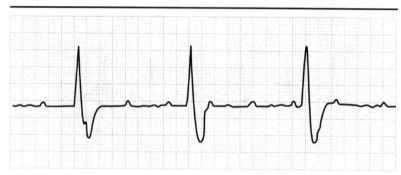

Ventricle Fibrillation: There is only erratic electrical activity resulting in quivering of the heart muscle. Immediate intervention is necessary.

Ventricular Fibrillation

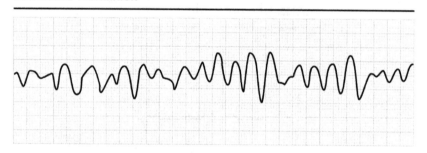

Rhythm Strips

The provider can use a 6- to 10-second strip of cardiac activity to identify the heart rate and rhythm. The ECG paper is standardized to measure time from left to right, with each small box equal to 4/10 of a second, which means that each large box is equal to 1/5 of a second and the time elapsed between the black ticks is 3 seconds. The provider calculates the heart rate by dividing 300 by the number of large squares between 2 QRS complexes. In the figure below, the heart rate is 300/4 = 75. Alternatively, the provider can identify the heart rate by counting the number of QRS complexes in a 10-second EKG strip and multiplying that result by 10.

The provider will assess the rhythm by comparing the distance between complexes 1 and 2 with the distance between complexes 2 and 3.

Cardiac Rhythm Strip

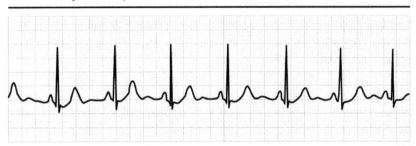

Holter Monitor

The **Holter monitor** is a portable device that is used for monitoring the EKG/ECG. The monitor may be used for routine cardiac monitoring or for diagnosing cardiac conditions that may not be evident on a single EKG/ECG tracing. The provider will attach the leads to the patient's chest, verify the patient's understanding of the process, and provide the patient with a diary with instructions to record all activity and physical symptoms for the duration of the testing period.

Holter monitor with EKG reading

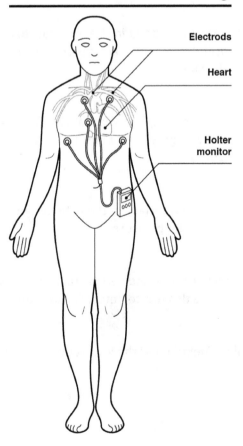

Cardiac Stress Test

The provider uses the **cardiac stress test** to identify the patient's cardiac response to the stress of exercise. The cardiac activity is recorded after the patient's heart rate reaches a target rate that is equal to 220 minus the patient's age. There are two forms of the test, which include the treadmill test and the pharmacologic test. Patients who are physically able walk on the treadmill until the target heart rate is achieved. Patients who are unable to tolerate the exercise will receive medications to raise the heart rate to the desired level. The provider will reverse the effects of these medications as soon as the appropriate tracings are obtained.

Vision Test: Color

The most commonly used test for color blindness is the **Ishihara Color Vision Test**, which is a series of circular images that are composed of colored dots. The identification of the numbers embedded in the colored plates is determined by the patient's ability to identify the red/green numbers and background. There are currently online variations of this test in addition to color testing forms that the provider may use for younger children who are not yet able to identify numbers.

Vision Test: Acuity/Distance
Snellen Chart

The **Snellen chart** contains eleven rows of letters that differ in size from row to row and is viewed from a distance of twenty feet. The resulting numbers, 20/100 for example, indicate that the patient can see objects at a distance of 20 feet that are visible to a person with normal eyesight at a distance of 100 feet.

E Chart

The **E chart** contains nine rows of letters that differ in size from row to row depicting the letter E is alternating positions. The chart is useful for children and others who are not familiar with the English alphabet. The scoring is similar to the Snellen chart.

Jaeger Card

The **Jaeger card** uses six paragraphs in differing font sizes ranging from 14 point to 3 point Times New Roman font to test near vision. The J1 paragraph at 3 point Times New Roman font is considered to equal 20/20 vision per the Snellen chart.

Ocular Pressure

The provider uses a tonometer to touch the surface of the patient's anesthetized cornea in order to record the pressure inside the eye, or **ocular pressure**.

Visual Fields

Visual fields are defined as the total horizontal and vertical range of vision when the patient's eye is centrally focused. The provider may use this test to detect "blind spots" or scotomas.

Pure-Tone Audiometry

The patient's **pure-tone threshold** is identified as the lowest decibel level at which sounds are heard 50 percent of the time.

Speech and Voice Recognition

The speech-awareness recognition (SAT), or **speech-detection threshold (SDT)**, is defined as the lowest decibel level at which the patient can acknowledge the stimuli. The test utilizes spondees—two-syllable words that are spoken with equal stress on each syllable—as the stimuli for this test.

The **speech-recognition threshold (SRT)**, or less commonly speech-reception threshold, measures the lowest decibel level at which the patient can recognize speech at least 50 percent of the time. This test also may be used to validate pure-tone threshold measurements, to determine the gain setting for a patient's hearing aid, or to provide a basis for suprathreshold word recognition testing.

Suprathreshold word recognition is used to assess the patient's ability to recognize and repeat one-syllable words that are presented at decibel levels that are consistent with social environments. Human-voice recordings are used to present the words, and the patient's responses are scored. The provider may use the results of this test to monitor the progression of a condition such as Meniere's disease, to identify improvement afforded by the use of hearing aids, or to isolate the part of the ear that is responsible for the deficit.

Tympanometry

The provider uses a **tonometer** to assess the integrity of the tympanic membrane (ear drum) and the function of the middle ear by introducing air and noise stimuli into the ear. The provider then assesses the resulting waveform and records the results.

Allergy Test: Scratch Test

In a **scratch test**, the provider applies a small amount of diluted allergen to a small wound created in the patient's skin in order to identify the specific allergens that elicit an allergic response in the patient. The allergist will select up to 50 different allergens for testing, which means that the provider will make 50 small incisions or scratches in the patient's skin arranged in a grid system to facilitate the interpretation and reporting of the test results. The provider will observe the patient closely for a minimum of 15 minutes following the introduction of the allergen for the signs of an anaphylactic reaction, in addition to signs of a positive reaction. The provider will document all positive results that are evidenced by a reddened raised area that is pruritic.

Allergy Test: Intradermal Skin Testing

The provider may use intradermal injections of the allergen to confirm negative scratch tests, or as the primary method of allergy testing. Using a 26- or 30-gauge needle, the provider will inject the allergen just below the surface of the skin. The provider must closely observe the patient and record results based on the appearance of raised, reddened wheals that are pruritic.

Pulmonary Function Tests

Pulmonary function tests evaluate the two main functions of the pulmonary system: air exchange and oxygen transport. The specific tests measure the volume of the lungs, the amount of air that can be inhaled or exhaled at one time, and the rate at which that volume is exhaled. The tests are used to monitor the progression of chronic pulmonary disorders, including asthma, emphysema, chronic obstructive lung disease, and sarcoidosis.

Spirometry

Spirometry is one of the two methods used to measure pulmonary function. The provider attaches the mouthpiece to the spirometer and instructs the patient to form a tight seal around its edge. The provider will then demonstrate the breathing patterns that are necessary for successful evaluation of each of the pulmonary measurements. The spirometry device calculates each of the values based on the patient's efforts.

Peak Flow Rate
Peak flow rate is defined as the speed at which the patient can exhale. This measure is commonly used to evaluate pulmonary function in patients with asthma.

Tuberculosis Tests/Purified Protein Derivative Skin Tests
Tuberculosis tests/purified protein derivative (PPD) skin tests are screening tests for the presence of Mycobacterium tuberculosis. The provider will use a tuberculin (TB) syringe to inject 0.1 ml of tuberculin purified protein derivative, the TB antigen, into the interior portion of the forearm. The solution forms a small, round elevation or wheal that is visible on the skin surface. The patient must return to the agency for evaluation of the site between 48 and 72 hours after the injection. The provider will assess the site and document the size of any visible induration or palpable swelling. The provider will not include any reddened areas in that measurement. The provider will refer all results that exceed 5 mm for additional testing and treatment.

Blood Pressure
Technique
To obtain an accurate measurement, the provider will:

- Assist the patient to a seated position.
- Expose the upper arm at the level of the heart.
- Apply the appropriately sized cuff.
- Palpate the antecubital space to identify the strongest pulsation point.
- Position the head of the stethoscope over the pulsation pulse.
- Slowly inflate the cuff to between 30 and 40 mm Hg above the patient's recorded blood pressure (BP). If this information is unavailable, the cuff may be inflated to between 160 and 180 mm Hg.
- Note the point at which the pulse is initially audible, which represents the systolic BP.
- Slowly deflate the cuff and record the point at which the pulse is initially audible as the systolic BP.
- Record the point at which the sounds are no longer audible as the diastolic BP.

Equipment
The **stethoscope** is a Y-shaped, hollow tube with earpieces and a diaphragm that transmits the sound to the earpieces when the provider places the diaphragm against the patient's body.

The **sphygmomanometer** includes the cuff, the mercury-filled gauge, or manometer that records the patient's pressure, and the release valve that regulates the air pressure in the cuff.

Pulse

Technique

To assess the pulse the provider will:

- Expose the intended pulse point.
- Palpate the area for the strongest pulsation.
- Position the middle three fingers of the hand on the point.
- Count the pulse for one full minute.

The provider will identify the pulse points that include the radial artery in the wrist, the brachial artery in the elbow, the carotid artery in the neck, the femoral artery in the groin, the popliteal artery behind the knee, and the dorsalis pedis and the posterior tibialis arteries in the foot.

The provider will assess the pulse rate by counting the number of pulsations per 60 minutes. In addition to the pulse rate, the provider will document the regularity or irregularity and strength of the pulsations.

Height/Weight/BMI

Technique

To record an accurate height, the provider must instruct the patient to:

- Remove all footwear.
- Stand straight with the back against the wall.
- Remain still until the height is recorded.

To record an accurate weight, the provider must first zero the scale and then instruct the patient to:

- Remove all heavy objects from the pockets.
- Stand on the scale facing forward.
- Remain still until the weight is recorded.

The BMI (body mass index) is equal to:

- Imperial English BMI Formula: $weight\ (lbs) \times 703 \div height\ (in^2)$
- Metric BMI Formula: $weight\ (kg) \div height(m^2)$

For example:

The BMI of a patient who weighs 150 pounds and is 5'6" is equal to:

$$\frac{150 \times 703}{66 \times 66} = \frac{105,450}{4,356} = 24.2\ or\ 24.0$$

Equipment

Body scales may be mechanical or digital. Some digital scales also provide detailed metabolic information including the BMI in addition to the weight. Other scales can accommodate patients who are confined to bed.

Body Temperature

There are five possible assessment sites for **body temperature**, including oral, axillary, rectal, tympanic, and temporal. The route will depend on the patient's age and the agency policies. Assessment of oral temperatures requires the provider to verify that the patient has had nothing to eat or drink for five minutes before testing in order to avoid inaccurate readings.

Thermometers may be digital with disposal covers for the probe, wand-like structures that use infrared technology and are moved across the forehead to the temporal area, or handles with disposable cones that measure the tympanic temperature.

Oxygen Saturation/Pulse Oximetry

When every hemoglobin molecule in the circulating blood volume is carrying the maximum number of four oxygen molecules, the **oxygen saturation rate** is 100 percent. The normal oxygen saturation level is 95 percent to 100 percent, and levels below 90 percent must be treated.

The provider measures oxygen saturation noninvasively by the application of a pulse oximetry device, which the provider will attach to the patient's finger. The device may be used for continuous or intermittent monitoring of the saturation rate.

The **pulse oximeter** is a foam-lined clip that attaches to the patient's finger and uses infrared technology to assess the oxygen saturation level, which is expressed as a percentage.

Respiration Rate

The **respiratory rate** is counted, and the breathing pattern is assessed. The provider should ensure that the patient is unaware that the breathing rate is being counted by leaving the fingers resting on the radial pulse site while the respiratory rate is assessed.

Age-Specific Normal and Abnormal Vital Signs

Age	Temperature Degrees Fahrenheit	Pulse Range	Respiratory Rate Range	Blood Pressure mmHg
Newborns	98.2 axillary	100–160	30–50	75–100/50–70
0–5 years	99.9 rectal	80–120	20–30	80–110/50–80
6–10 years	98.6 oral	70–100	15–30	85–120/55–80
11–14 years	98.6 oral	60–105	12–20	95–140/60–90
15–20 years	98.6 oral	60–100	12–30	95–140/60–90
Adults	98.6 oral	50–80	16–20	120/80

Examinations

- **Auscultation** refers to listening to the sounds of body organs or processes, such as blood pressure, using a stethoscope.

- **Palpation** refers to using the hand or fingers to apply pressure to a body site to assess an organ for pain or consistency.

- **Percussion** refers to tapping on a body part to assess for rebound sounds. It may be used to assess the abdomen or the lungs.

- **Mensuration** refers to the measurement of body structures, such as measuring the circumference of the newborn's head.

- **Manipulation** refers to using the hands to correct a defect such as realigning the bones after a fracture.

- **Inspection** refers to the simple observation of the color, contour, or size of a body structure.

Body Positions/Draping

The provider will use proper draping to maximize the patient's privacy and to facilitate the planned procedures.

Draping Body Position

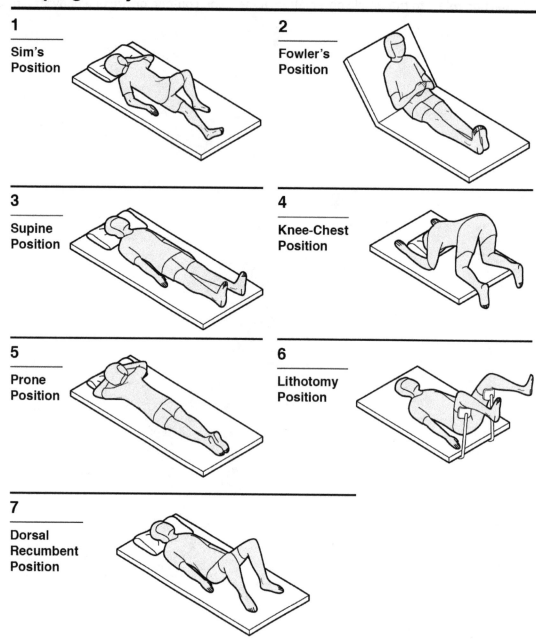

1
Sim's Position

2
Fowler's Position

3
Supine Position

4
Knee-Chest Position

5
Prone Position

6
Lithotomy Position

7
Dorsal Recumbent Position

Pediatric Exam

The purpose of the **pediatric exam** is to assess the child's growth and development and to provide family counseling regarding behavioral issues, nutrition, and injury protection. In addition, providers screen children for specific conditions at various ages to ensure that appropriate treatment is not

delayed. For instance, newborns are tested for phenylketonuria and hearing loss. Children between three and five years old are tested for alterations in vision, and school-aged children are screened for obesity.

Growth Chart
The **growth chart** is a systematic assessment of a child's growth pattern that can be compared to gender-specific norms.

The head circumference, height, and body weight are measured in children from birth to three years of age. In children older than three, the BMI is measured in addition to height and weight.

The head circumference is measured from birth to three years of age. The provider will measure the head circumference by placing a flexible measuring tape around the widest circumference of the child's head, which most commonly is above the eyebrows and the top of the ears. The provider will weigh infants lying down without clothes or diapers, and older children on mechanical or digital scales. To assess an infant's height, the provider will lay the child on a flat surface with the knee straightened and extend the flexible tape from the top of the infant's head to the bottom of the foot. The provider will position older children with their backs to a wall for an accurate measurement of their height.

Pelvic Exam/ Papanicolaou (PAP) Smear
The **pelvic exam** is done to assess the organs of the female reproductive system. The ovaries and the uterus are assessed by palpation, and the cervix is assessed by inspection. The **PAP smear** sample is a screening test for cervical cancer. The sample, obtained from the opening of the cervix, is transferred to glass slides for processing.

Prenatal/Postpartum Exams
The provider performs the **prenatal pelvic exam** to assess the development of the fetus and the status of the maternal reproductive system. The pelvic exam is done at the first visit, but is not repeated with every visit. In a normal pregnancy, it may not be repeated until the third trimester. The provider performs the postpartum exam to assess the return of the maternal reproductive organs to the nonpregnant state.

Laboratory Values

The nurse will need a savvy knowledge of common lab tests performed, why they are performed, and the normal values that are expected from the tests. These values will indicate if a disease process is at work in a body system. The nurse will need to be able to interpret that abnormality to report it to the ordering physician.

One commonly taken lab test is the serum electrolyte panel. In the body, the electrolytes work to maintain healthy cellular functions and metabolism. Electrolytes provide the structure in cell walls, generate energy for metabolic activity, transport fluid, cause muscle cell contraction, and even generate electrical impulses in the cardiac cells. Electrolytes that are often measured and assessed in the patient include sodium, potassium, magnesium, phosphorus, chloride, and calcium. The normal values of these electrolytes are listed below:

- Sodium: 135–145 mEq/L
- Potassium: 3.5–5.1 mEq/L
- Magnesium: 1.6–2.6 mg/dL

- Phosphorus: 2.5–4.5 mg/dL
- Chloride: 98–107 mEq/L
- Calcium: 8.5–10.0 mg/L

Values outside of these normal parameters may suggest an electrolyte imbalance. Hyper/hypokalemia, hyper/hyponatremia, hyper/hypomagnesemia, hyper/hypochloremia, hyper/hypocalcemia, and hyper/hypophosphatemia are all conditions that should be immediately reported to the ordering physician if they are newly developed or worsened since the last reading. Signs and symptoms accompanying these electrolyte abnormalities should also be noted and treated as appropriate.

The CBC, as noted earlier in the Diagnostic Tests section, is useful for giving the clinician a picture of the health of the circulatory system. The CBC will show if the patient is anemic, leukemic, or lacking the necessary platelets for clotting and maintaining hemostasis. The following list shows normal, expected values for each component of the CBC:

- Red blood cells: 4–5 million cells/mcL for women, 5–6 million cells/mcL for men
- White blood cells: 4500–10,000 cells/mcL
- Hemoglobin (Hbg): 14–17 gm/dL
- Hematocrit (Hct): 41%–50% for men, 36%–44% for women
- Platelets: 140,000–450,000 cells/mcL
- Mean corpuscular volume (MCV) (the size of red blood cells): 80–95

The **comprehensive metabolic panel (CMP)** is a group of lab values that are often taken together that measure how well the kidneys and liver are functioning and levels of blood sugar, cholesterol, calcium, and protein levels in the body. The electrolytes may be measured using the CMP or as part of a smaller lab test called a **basic metabolic panel (BMP)**. Though it varies based on facility, the CMP generally consists of fourteen separate lab tests, while a BMP may only contain eight separate lab tests. The practitioner will determine which of these tests to perform.

The following are normal levels found on a CMP:

- Blood glucose: 70–110 mg/dL
- Albumin: 3.4–5.4 g/dL
- Alkaline phosphatase: 44–147 IU/L
- Alanine aminotransferase (ALT): 7–40 IU/L
- Aspartate aminotransferase (AST): 10–34 IU/L
- Blood urea nitrogen (BUN): 6–20 mg/dL
- Creatinine: 0.6–1.3 mg/dL
- Total bilirubin: 0.3–1.0 mg/dL
- Total protein: 6.0–8.3 g/dL

The final lab test the nurse will need to be able to interpret is the **arterial blood gas (ABG) sample**. A commonly performed test in patients with respiratory disorders or on mechanical ventilation in the intensive care unit (ICU), this test shows the pH balance, carbon dioxide level, and bicarbonate level in the patient's blood. This test will show how well the patient's respiratory processes are performing.

Adjustments to respiratory and other therapies may be made based on it. The arterial sample is usually obtained from the radial, femoral, or brachial arteries. The following are normal ABG ranges:

- Oxygen (O2) saturation (SaO2): 94%–100%
- Arterial blood pH: 7.35–7.45
- Partial pressure of oxygen (PaO2): 75–100 mmHg
- Partial pressure of carbon dioxide (PaCO2): 38–41 mmHg
- Bicarbonate (HCO3): 22–28 mEq/L

Abnormalities in the ABGs could suggest an alkalotic or acidotic state of the patient's blood that will need correction. Reporting abnormal values to the physician and the respiratory therapist will be part of the nurse's expected duties.

Urinalysis

- **Physical (urinalysis):** The provider will perform a visual assessment of the color and turbidity of the urine sample.

- **Chemical (urinalysis):** The provider will use the reagent strip to assess the specific gravity, the pH, and the presence and quantity of protein, glucose, ketones hemoglobin and myoglobin, leukocyte esterase, bilirubin, and urobilirubin.

- **Microscopic (urinalysis):** The provider will separate the urine sediment from the fluid volume to microscopically identify the presence of RBCs, WBCs, epithelial cells, bacteria, yeasts, and parasites.

- **Culture (urinalysis):** The provider will assess the presence of infectious agents in the urine sample by inoculating the agar plates, incubating sample at body temperature, and observing and documenting any growth at 24 and 48 hours after inoculation of the sample.

Hematology Panel

- **Hematocrit (HCT):** The provider will assess the RBC count as defined by the hematocrit by placing the anticoagulated blood sample into the microhematocrit centrifuge and documenting the results.

- **Hemoglobin:** The provider will assess the amount of the hemoglobin protein that is present in the red blood cells by placing the anticoagulated blood sample into the microhematocrit centrifuge and documenting the results.

- **Erythrocyte Sedimentation Rate (ESR):** The provider will assess the ESR, which is a nonspecific indicator of inflammation, by placing the anticoagulated sample in the Westergren tube and recording the height of the settled RBCs after one hour.

- **Automated Cell Counts:** The provider will use the automated device to assess RBC, WBC, and platelet counts by preparing the sample, obtaining, and documenting the results.

- **Coagulation testing/international normalized ratio (INR):** The provider will calculate the INR, which is used to assess blood-clotting levels in patients being treated with Warfarin, according to laboratory protocol after verifying that the sample was not drawn from a heparinized line.

Chemistry/Metabolic Testing

Glucose

The provider will identify the **blood glucose sample**, which measures the amount of glucose in the circulating blood volume, as fasting or nonfasting before processing and documenting the results.

Kidney Function Tests

Kidney function is assessed by measuring the levels of metabolic waste products, including blood urea nitrogen (BUN) and creatinine, and by calculating the **glomerular filtration rate (GFR)**, which corresponds with the clearance of waste products from the blood by the kidneys. The provider will process the sample to obtain the BUN and creatinine levels. The provider will then use the creatinine level and the patient's age, body size, and gender to calculate to the GFR according to the agency-approved equation for GFR. There are four equations that may be used to calculate the GFR in adults that include the Modification of Diet in Renal Disease (MDRD), the Study equation (IDMS-traceable version), and the Chronic Kidney Disease Epidemiology Collaboration (CKD-EPI) equation.

Liver Function Tests

Elevated levels of alanine transaminase (ALT) and aspartate aminotransferase (AST), two liver enzymes, indicate acute/chronic hepatitis, cirrhosis, or liver cancer. Decreased levels of these enzymes may be due to Vitamin B-12 deficiency. Albumin, a protein synthesized by the liver that is necessary for the maintenance of osmotic pressure in the vasculature, is decreased in liver failure due to cirrhosis or cancer. The liver processes bilirubin, a waste product resulting from the normal destruction of old red blood cells, for excretion by the gastrointestinal system; however, elevated levels may be due to liver failure or transfusion reactions. The provider will verify a 10-minute centrifuge time, process the sample, and document results.

Lipid Profile

Excess dietary intact of animal fats can result in elevated total cholesterol and low-density lipoprotein (LDL) or "bad cholesterol" levels, while elevated high-density lipoprotein (HDL) or "good cholesterol" levels are the result of appropriate nutrition or the effect of cholesterol-lowering medications. Elevated triglycerides levels may result from diabetes, obesity, liver failure, or kidney disease. The provider will verify that the fasting sample was obtained before the administration of N-Acetylcysteine (NAC) or Metamizole, if indicated. The provider will then process the sample per protocol within two hours of the venipuncture and document the results.

Hemoglobin A1c

Hemoglobin A1c measures the percentage of the hemoglobin molecules that are coated or glycated with glucose. The hemoglobin molecules are located in the red blood cell, which has a lifespan of 110 to 120 days; therefore, the hemoglobin A1c test measures the average blood sugar for a four-month period. The normal A1c level is less than 5.7 percent; levels between 5.7 percent and 6.4 percent indicate prediabetes and levels greater than 6.5 percent indicate diabetes. Elevated HGB A1c levels must be confirmed with additional testing before treatment is initiated. The provider will inform the patient that fasting is not required, process the sample, and document results.

Immunology

Mononucleosis Test

The immune system produces heterophile proteins in response to the presence of the Epstein-Barr virus (EBV), the causative agent of mononucleosis. Specific tests include the analysis of the viral capsid antigen (VCA), the early antigen (EA), or the EBV nuclear antigen (EBNA). The Monospot test detects

antibodies that are not specific for mononucleosis, leading to false positive and false negative results. In addition, the Monospot test may be insensitive to the heterophile antibodies produced by children with mononucleosis. The provider will freeze the sample if processing is delayed beyond 24 hours after preparation.

Rapid Group A Streptococcus Test
Identification of the beta-hemolytic bacterium **Streptococcus pyogenes**, the most common cause of acute pharyngitis in adults and children, is obtained by using isothermal nucleic acid amplification technology. The provider will transfer the sample to the testing device adhering to proper wait-times, process the sample, and document the results.

C-Reactive Protein (CRP)
C-reactive protein (CRP) is an indicator of inflammation that is released into the bloodstream in response to tissue injury or the onset of an infection. The provider will verify that all reagents and the serum sample are at room temperature, assess the processed sample for agglutination, and document the results.

HCG Pregnancy Test
Serum levels of human chorionic gonadotropin hormone detect the presence of a pregnancy. Elevated levels may indicate a normal pregnancy, either single or multiple, chorionic cancer, or hydatidiform mole. The provider will centrifuge the clotted sample for ten minutes at room temperature, and document the results.

H. pylori
There are three testing methods for the *Helicobacter pylori* organism, including histological examination and culture of samples obtained by endoscopic biopsy, the urea breath test (UBT) that measures CO_2 levels on exhalation, and the fecal antigen test that identifies antibodies to the organism. The provider will verify that patient has avoided antibiotics and bismuth preparations for two weeks prior to the testing. The provider will process all samples according to the specific test requirements and document the results.

Influenza
Influenza testing methods include the Rapid Influenza Diagnostic Test (RIDT), and the Real Time Polymerase Chain Reaction, and the viral culture, which identify the genetic material of the virus in secretions obtained from a nasal or throat swab. The provider will process all samples according to the specific test requirements and document the results.

Fecal Occult Blood Testing
Occult bleeding is not visibly apparent, which means that detection methods rely on the chemical reaction between the blood and the testing reagents for identification of blood in a sample. For home sample collection with guaiac testing, the provider will instruct the patient to collect three samples on three different days to optimize results. The patient will secure the test card and submit it to the provider for testing. The provider will apply a guaiac solution to the sample to identify a bluish tinge in the test area, which is considered positive for the presence of occult blood.

Potential for Alterations in Body Systems

The nurse will work with patients who are at risk for an alteration in their body systems. The nurse identifies compromising patient situations that have the potential to lead to complications. These complications could include aspiration, skin breakdown, insufficient vascular perfusion, and the devastating problems that may occur when a patient has been sedentary for too long.

There are many conditions that may cause a patient to be at risk for aspiration. A patient who has suffered a stroke and has developed dysphagia, or difficulty swallowing, is immediately considered at risk for aspiration. This is because the mechanical difficulty they experience when they try to swallow can sometimes lead to leakage of the substance they are trying to swallow into their airway instead of the esophagus. Foreign substances in the airway lead to immediate difficulty breathing and respiratory distress. At this point, aspiration has occurred, and the patient needs emergent intervention to restore proper respiratory faculties.

A client with a feeding tube in place, whether nasogastric (NG) or placed via gastrostomy, is at risk for aspiration. **Aspiration** is, in fact, one of the most common complications of enteral feedings. The stomach becomes quite full with the feedings, causing gastric contents to reflux, and secretions accumulate in the pharynx where they are then aspirated. The integrity of the upper and lower esophageal sphincters may become compromised over time, contributing to aspiration risk. The patient receiving tube feedings also has the potential to have a weakened swallowing and gag reflex, contributing to aspiration risk. Clients on tube feedings should be carefully monitored for fullness of the stomach and signs of fluid buildup such as wet-sounding coughs and a rattle-like sound when breathing.

Patients who are sedated are at risk for aspiration due to their altered level of consciousness. The head of the bed should remain elevated at least 45 degrees to 90 degrees if the patient has recently received an enteral feeding to promote digestion and stomach emptying. Laying the patient flat on their back puts them at risk of aspiration.

All patients who have been immobilized by an illness are at risk for skin breakdown while in bed. The increased pressure on bony prominences that a prolonged period spent in bed creates can easily compromise skin integrity and lead to an ulceration. The nurse works to prevent pressure ulcers by keeping the client on a "turn every two hours" repositioning schedule. Every two hours, the client will be repositioned in bed, from the left side to the right side and then back again. The patient should only be positioned on their back for feedings, as this position can put quite a bit of pressure on the sacrum, an area especially vulnerable to breakdown.

There are many patient situations that may put them at risk for insufficient vascular perfusion. Patients with impaired circulation may be at risk because of hypervolemia, hypovolemia, a low amount of circulating oxygen associated with low hemoglobin counts, low blood pressure, immobilization of a limb, decreased cardiac output as seen in heart failure, and diabetes. After the nurse has identified that the client has a compromise of vascular perfusion, efforts will be made to intervene and restore normal circulation. Early mobility, in which the client is encouraged to get out of bed and get moving as soon as they are able, is vital to maintaining healthy circulation. Compression stockings are commonplace in immobile patients to artificially maintain healthy circulation.

Certain factors put a patient more at risk for developing cancer. A patient who uses tobacco or is exposed to secondhand smoke on a regular basis is at a greater risk for developing cancers of the lung, mouth, esophagus, larynx, and esophagus. Patients with a family history of a certain type of cancer such

as breast, colon, ovarian, and uterine are more at risk for developing these types of cancers. The nurse will review and record a client's risk factors for developing cancers when performing the initial admission assessment.

Potential for Complications of Diagnostic Tests/Treatments/Procedures

When a client undergoes a procedure or diagnostic test at the hospital, things do not always go according to plan. The nurse is there to assess the client when they return from their procedure to monitor them for complications. When a complication is noted, the nurse is quick to intervene, alert the attending physician, and take care of the patient to get them stabilized.

One common diagnostic procedure performed regularly at hospitals is the cardiac catheterization. Patients returning from a cardiac catherization are at risk for developing complications such as bleeding and dysrhythmias. Most facilities have protocols and checklists in place postprocedure that the nurse will follow strictly. These checklists include regular vital-sign monitoring, checking the access site for bleeding or hematoma, and cardiac monitoring for dysrhythmias. The client will be made to lay flat for a predetermined amount of time, usually six hours, so that blood flow to the accessed artery is not compromised and the access point can fully heal. Bleeding around the puncture point as well as formation of an aneurysm are other possible complications. Any abnormality will be reported to the cardiologist.

A patient who has a limb with a cast placed will be monitored for compartment syndrome. The nurse pays close attention to the limb, especially the more distal end, to ensure that adequate circulation is maintained and is not cut off by the cast placement. Assessment of pulses, whether radial or ulnar in the upper limbs or dorsalis pedis or posterior tibial in the lower limbs, will be performed to assess that circulation is not compromised.

After any test that involves incision, puncture, or any other access to the client's circulatory system, bleeding and infection are always major risks. Patients with thrombocytopenia, or a low platelet count, are at an increased risk for bleeding, as they lack the necessary component for proper hemostasis. Blood pressure monitoring is an excellent way to monitor the patient's hemodynamic status. A lowered blood pressure that is trending downward is an ominous sign that the client may be losing blood internally. Hypotension is the first step toward any sort of shock state and can lead to an interrupted delivery of oxygen to vital organs and tissues. Identifying if the client is bleeding and where the source of the bleed is will require an advanced interventional team such as a rapid-response team, usually headed by an intensivist or ICU doctor.

Along with bleeding, infection is a common complication of invasive diagnostic procedures. The nurse works to prevent infection by performing meticulous handwashing before and after client care, observing infection prevention precautions such as donning gloves and gowns in patients with communicable diseases and disinfecting equipment after use. The disposal of medical supplies in the appropriate receptacle, such as sharps in the sharps container, will assist in the goal of preventing the spread of infections. The nurse takes care to perform certain tasks using an aseptic or sterile technique, such as dressing changes, insertion of urinary catheters, insertion of NG tubes, and obtaining IV accesses.

System Specific Assessments
The nurse will need to be skilled in doing **body system-specific assessments** on clients who have undergone a diagnostic procedure or a treatment. The nurse needs to be able to use sound nursing

judgment and critical thinking to hone in on the system they need to examine based on the client's condition.

Knowledge of peripheral pulse assessment is necessary to evaluate the patient's circulatory status. Strong pulses at a normal rhythm are good; faint pulses that are either too fast or too slow are worrisome and need further evaluation. Pulses are graded on a scale of 0 to 4, 0 being absent, 1 being weak, 2 being normal, 3 being increased volume, and 4 being a bounding pulse. The pulse is assessed and documented with further action being taken if necessary.

Another way to evaluate the health of the circulatory system is to assess for and grade edema. **Edema**, a fluid accumulation in the peripheral tissues of the body, can get to a point where, when pushed down upon with a finger, the impression stays in the skin. These impressions can be graded by their depth, ranging from +1 to +4 as shown in the diagram below.

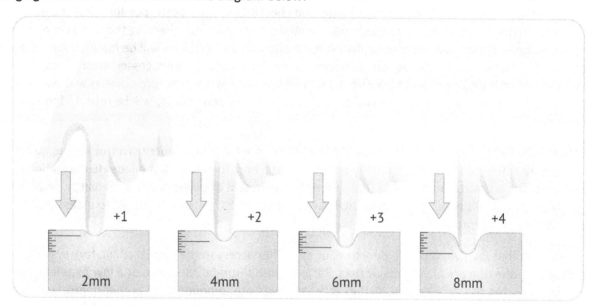

The neurological system may need specific evaluation requiring the nurse's keen assessment skills. The nurse will start by evaluating the client's level of consciousness, which is measured by interviewing the client and their knowledge of who they are, where they are, and the time. A client oriented to all three of these components is said to be oriented times three, while a client who only knows their name, for example, is only oriented times one. Commonly, this is noted in the nurse's notes as "A&OX3" or something similar. The "A" stands for "alert," as opposed to obtunded, drowsy, sleepy, difficult to arouse, and other altered levels of consciousness.

Other components of the neurological assessment include assessment of the cranial nerves, usually used on stroke assessments, motor and sensory function, pupillary response, reflexes, cerebellar function, and vital signs.

The following are the **"Five P's" of Neurovascular Assessment**:

- Pain
- Pulse
- Pallor
- Paresthesia
- Paralysis

The nurse can assess the client's musculoskeletal system by testing for bilateral strength and equality of movement. Muscular strength can be graded on a 0 to 5 scale. A patient with no visible muscle contraction is graded as a 0, a patient who has visible contraction but still no movement is graded as a 1, a patient that is contracting and trying to move but cannot overcome gravity is graded as a 2, the same without the ability to push against resistance is a 3, the same with only a limited effect of resistance on their effort is a 4, and finally, a full contraction with movement that can overcome elevated levels of resistance is a 5.

Diabetic patients have a constant battle maintaining a healthy level of blood sugar. The nurse taking care of a diabetic patient keeps a close eye on not only the patient's blood sugar but also their diabetic medications, the fluids they are receiving, and their mealtime habits. The classic symptoms of hyperglycemia are polydipsia and polyuria, where the patient drinks copious amounts of fluid and produces massive amounts of urine. Hypoglycemia symptoms reflect the interruption of blood glucose to the brain, resulting in neurological symptoms such as confusion, lowered level of consciousness, slurred speech, lightheadedness, and dizziness.

Potential for Complications from Surgical Procedures and Health Alterations

During the **surgical consent process**, surgical risks and potential complications are explained to the patient by the surgeon. The risk of complications depends on the type of surgical procedure being performed, as well as the condition and comorbidities of the patient. The perioperative environment predisposes the patient to risk of hypothermia. Per best practice guidelines, the operating room temperature should be kept between sixty-eight and seventy-three degrees Fahrenheit. Depending on the procedure, the patient may be partially clothed or fully naked. If the procedure is one hour or greater in duration, thermoregulation measures should be taken to prevent hypothermia. These measures can include warming blankets and warm intravenous fluid administration. Methods for monitoring patient temperature in the perioperative environment include temporal, esophageal, bladder, rectal, and via thermodilution catheter, which is inserted into the pulmonary artery.

Hypothermia places the patient at greater risk for developing **surgical site infection (SSI)**. Although the signs of SSI may not be apparent for several weeks postoperatively, steps in preventing SSI are implemented in the preoperative period. The Joint Commission's **Surgical Care Improvement Project (SCIP)** outlines standards around preoperative antibiotic prophylaxis and other measures to decrease risk of SSI. Major surgical procedures involving the vascular system, such as abdominal aortic aneurysm repair and open-heart surgical procedures, present the risk for high amounts of blood loss.

Hemodynamic changes often occur as a result of blood loss. **Hemodynamic changes** during the surgical procedure can include hypotension, hypertension, cardiac arrhythmias, and decreased oxygen saturation. Changes in hemodynamic stability can create the need for blood transfusion. Blood loss can lead to cardiac complications, especially in those with coronary artery disease. Patients with cardiac disease are at risk for myocardial infarction (MI) due to the surgical process. In vascular procedures, the clamping of vessels can release calcified areas or plaque into circulation, which can cause an MI or a stroke.

Venous thromboembolism (VTE) is another potential complication from surgery. VTE prophylaxis measures are implemented preoperatively to reduce this risk. Depending on the patient, these measures can include application of **sequential compression devices (SCDs)** to bilateral lower extremities. SCDs work by creating mild, intermittent compression to the extremities to prevent pooling of blood while the patient is not ambulatory. The physician may choose to order a medical VTE prophylaxis protocol. For example, the patient may receive enoxaparin (Lovenox®), a blood thinner, for a set number of doses postoperatively.

A rare yet life-threatening complication of surgery is **malignant hyperthermia (MH)**. MH is a genetic disorder that presents after exposure to anesthetic gases and/or paralytic drugs. Since MH is a genetic disorder, the preoperative interview should include questions that assess family history of MH and complications of anesthesia. If the patient indicates a history of MH or a family history of difficulty with anesthesia, the perioperative team should be prepared for MH crisis and discuss this risk with the entire perioperative team. Symptoms of MH crisis include muscle rigidity, tachycardia, rising body temperature, and rising levels of end-tidal carbon dioxide (ETCO2).

Finally, death is a potential complication of the surgery process. Risk of surgical death is related to the type of surgery and patient comorbidities. Adverse perioperative events such as dissecting a major blood vessel can also lead to death. Emergency procedures generally carry a higher risk of death than routine procedures.

Therapeutic Procedures

The nurse will need to be able to assess a client who has recently undergone a **therapeutic procedure**, apply their knowledge regarding the procedure, educate the client about aftercare, and monitor the patient post-procedure, observing the proper precautions.

Many therapeutic procedures will use anesthesia, whether local, regional, or general. **Local anesthesia** includes topical and injected anesthetics such as lidocaine and benzocaine and are common in minimally invasive procedures such as external biopsies, removals of skin lesions and moles, and dental surgeries. A **regional anesthetic** only provides analgesia to a certain part of the body and includes epidural, spinal, or paravertebral nerve blocks. **General anesthesia** renders the patient completely unconscious using medical gas or IV transfusion.

There are four stages of anesthesia: induction, excitement, surgical anesthesia, and emergence. The anesthetist carefully monitors the patient as they travel throughout these stages, maintaining them in the appropriate state of consciousness while the procedure occurs. During these stages, the client is closely monitored using pulse oximetry, blood pressure readings, measurement of heart rate and rhythm, and body temperature. The patient airway will be monitored, especially if under general anesthesia, and an artificial airway is being used such as an endotracheal tube.

All three levels of anesthesia come with their own potential complications. With local anesthetics, the patient may get too high off of a dose, or the anesthetic may be administered too rapidly. Potential complications of a local anesthetic include excitability, seizure activity, depression of the central nervous system, and respiratory and cardiac distress. Regional anesthetics can cause headache, soreness at the injection site, infection, bleeding, bruising, and low blood pressure. General sedation complications range from mild to severe, including sore throat, fatigue, and dizziness, all the way to malignant hyperthermia, respiratory arrest, cardiac arrest, and cerebrovascular accident or stroke.

Before and after the procedure, the nurse will assess the client's knowledge of the therapeutic intervention being performed, answer questions within their scope of practice, refer to the performing physician where appropriate, and educate the patient regarding the procedure. Each facility will have client education literature that can be accessed and printed out for the client and nurse's use. Informed consent will need to be obtained for most serious interventions, so this information will be useful to have on hand to answer the client's questions.

The nurse will ensure that the patient's preoperative orders are followed, such as the observance of NPO (nothing by mouth), in which the patient is not to eat or drink anything preprocedure. Any medications that are required before the procedure will be administered and documented in a timely manner. Many procedures have a pre- and postprocedure checklist that the nurse will ensure gets filled out.

The nurse will need to identify the client before and after the procedure following the two-identifier technique. Usually this involves having the client state their name and date of birth, along with a scanning of their identification band for additional identification.

The client who is to go home following a procedure will need home care instructions, such as taking care of an incision site. The nurse will educate the patient about their posthospital care. Usually, if an incision is present, there will be specific instructions as to how to keep the site clean, when the client can shower and bathe again, and how to do dressing changes. Follow-up appointments will be made to ensure the client's progress and healing.

Methods of Collection
Blood
For a venipuncture process, the provider will:

- Identify the patient, review the order, and label the collection tubes.
- Assess the nondominant hand to identify a vein that is straight and palpable.
- Wash hands and apply PPE.
- Clean the selected site with an alcohol swab per agency policy.
- Inspect the test-specific vacuum tubes and needles to verify that:
    - The tube is securely sealed and vacuum has been maintained.
    - Appropriate additives such anticoagulants or other fixatives that may be required to maintain the sample are present in the tube.
    - The chosen needle size is appropriate to the selected vein.
- Complete the venipuncture per agency policy.
- Apply pressure and a sterile dressing to the venipuncture site.
- Submit the sample for processing per agency policy.

The provider will use a capillary/dermal puncture to obtain blood from small children or when only a small volume of blood is necessary as in finger-stick puncture for blood glucose analysis.

Urine
The provider can collect a random urinalysis any time the patient voids.

To obtain a midstream/clean catch urine sample, the provider will instruct the patient to first clean the urinary meatus with the appropriate antiseptic solution, void without collecting the initial volume, and then deposit the remaining output into the container.

Before beginning the collection of a timed 24-hour collection, the provider must obtain a storage container containing any necessary preservative from the laboratory, and confirm the accommodations for refrigeration of the sample if required. The first time the patient voids, the provider will discard the specimen and record the time. All urine collected in the following 24-hour period will be collected by the provider and stored in the prepared container at the prescribed temperature.

Catheterization may be used to obtain a sterile specimen. The provider will pass the sterile catheter into the bladder to drain the urine into a sterile container, which must then be labeled and transported to the lab according to agency policy.

The pediatric urine collector is a plastic pouch attached to a foam adhesive-backed base. The provider will verify that the skin around the urinary meatus is clean, dry, and free of powder or lotions. The provider will adhere the adhesive section of the collection device over the urinary meatus and replace the patient's diaper.

Fecal Specimen
The provider will place the fecal specimen in a clean, leak-proof, properly labeled container, and promptly transport the sample to the laboratory for processing.

Sputum Specimen
The sputum specimen must contain sputum, not saliva, and it is best obtained early in the morning.

Throat Swab
After assisting the patient to a seated position in a chair or bed, the provider will use sterile swabs to remove the sample from the back of the throat while avoiding contact with the uvula and tongue. The provider will then break the tips of the swabs and secure them in the labeled collection sleeve, transport the sample to the lab according to agency policy, and document the sample collection time and site.

Genital
The provider will position the patient according to the site being sampled. The provider will use sterile swabs to sample the top of the vaginal vault for a vaginal swab, the center of the cervical os for a cervical swab, or the urinary meatus for a urethral swab. The provider will then break the tips of the swabs and secure them in the labeled collection sleeve, transport the sample to the lab according to agency policy, and document the sample collection time and site.

Wound
The provider will position the patient according to the site being sampled. The provider will remove and discard the existing dressing, use sterile swabs to obtain the sample from the center of the wound, then break the tips of the swabs and secure them in the labeled collection sleeve. Once the swabs are secured, the provider will dress the wound, ensure that the sample is delivered to the laboratory, and document the wound assessment and the sample collection time and site.

Nasopharyngeal
The provider will position the patient in a seated position with the head tilted back. After verifying the patency of the nares, the provider will insert the sterile swab 3 to 4 inches into the nasopharynx, rotate the swaps to obtain the sample, remove the swabs, break the tips of the swabs to secure them in the labeled collection sleeve, transport the specimen to the laboratory, and document the collection site and time.

Physiological Adaptation

Alterations in Body Systems

Nurses must have the ability to assess a client for alterations in their body systems. This is an inevitable occurrence, as a body system alteration is precisely the reason the client is at the hospital in the first place. The nurse will identify the body system alteration and draw up a plan of care based on their findings.

Intake and output are items that are closely monitored by the nurse to discover if an alteration in a body system has occurred. There are several types of drainage a client may experience that fall into the category of input and output. The nurse measures the drainage where appropriate and notes its appearance. Color, quantity, consistency, and any other notable characteristics are observed and documented. Types of drainage the nurse may encounter in client care include feeding tube drainage, respiratory secretions, drainage from a chest tube, rectal tube output, and urinary catheter output.

Clients with cancer may be put on radiation therapy to target and destroy cancerous tumors. This client may develop alterations in certain body systems as a result. The client is likely to become quite fatigued, as their energy is sapped by the intensity of the therapy. Weakness often accompanies fatigue. They may experience skin reactions such as a rash. The skin may become red, looking like a sunburn. The skin above the targeted location for radiation absorbs a bit of the radiation, which is why the reaction occurs. Other radiation therapy side effects may be specific to the area in which the therapy is targeted. If therapy occurs near the stomach or abdomen, for example, stomachache, nausea, vomiting, and diarrhea may occur.

If the nurse is caring for a woman who is pregnant, they will be mindful of certain body alterations associated with the prenatal period. One such complication is high blood pressure during pregnancy, called **preeclampsia**. The woman's blood pressure is carefully monitored during the prenatal period to watch for the development of this condition, which could lead to complications for both the mother and the baby. Gestational diabetes is another prenatal complication of which the nurse is mindful. Somewhere between 24 and 28 weeks, pregnant women are screened for gestational diabetes by performing the oral glucose tolerance test (OGTT). This glucose screening will identify if the woman is at risk, and treatment will follow if necessary.

Patients who are developing an infection will often have some telltale symptoms that the nurse will be watchful for. The classic signs of a localized infection on the outer surface of the body will be redness, inflammation, heat, and swelling. If the infection is systemic, within the body, the patient may have a fever, increased WBC count (or decreased if the infection has been prolonged), prodromal malaise, fatigue, chills, elevated heart rate, and even altered level of consciousness and orientation. Some infections will have specific symptoms related to the organ or tissue of the body affected. For example, a urinary tract infection (UTI) will cause the patient to have pain or burning while urinating, called **dysuria**, possibly blood in the urine, and frequent urges to void. A respiratory infection, on the other hand, will have respiratory-specific symptoms such as cough, difficulty breathing, and adventitious breath sounds on lung auscultation.

Having a basic knowledge of how an infection works, from start to finish, is advantageous to the nurse when trying to understand what is going on within the client's body. The causative organism must enter the body through some entryway: respiratory tract, break in the skin, urinary tract, IV access, GI tract, and so on. The organism then goes through what is called the "incubation period," which refers to the time that elapses between the organism entering the body and when symptoms actually begin occurring. During the incubation period, the organism is usually multiplying until it starts to have a noticeable effect on the body. Some pathogens will have a longer incubation time, while others will have shorter. Depending on the pathogen, there may be some communicability of the disease involved, in which the disease can be spread from one person to another. Therefore, observing universal precautions is vital to prevent the spread of disease. Meticulous handwashing by the nurse and all members of the healthcare team, as well as patients and family, is vital.

A full-blown infection occurs when the body's natural defenses cannot overcome the organism effectively and symptoms occur, compromising overall body function. The patient may have an elevated WBC count on the CBC, indicating the body is bolstering its immune defenses to try and overcome the infection. The final stage of the infection is when the body's immune system plus the help of medication and therapeutic interventions destroy the organism, restoring the body to natural, normal functioning ability.

Patient education is an important aspect of care that the nurse diligently performs when body system alterations occur. Helping the patient understand what is going on in their body and answering their questions is an excellent way to reduce anxiety and promote calm and understanding. Anxiety, the nurse knows, only causes additional stress in the body, which will not be conducive to healing.

When educating the patient, the nurse will talk about the body system alteration they are experiencing, using their knowledge of pathophysiology, anatomy, and physiology as well as incorporating lessons about the pharmacological interventions being used on the patient. Discussion of risk factors related to the body alterations and side effects of medication is important to include. The nurse will discuss factors that will promote healing, such as the patient getting adequate rest and early mobility. The nurse will encourage the patient to call on the healthcare team whenever a need arises, whether the need is for the nurse's aide, the nurse, or the physician. The patient should be encouraged to ask their questions and raise their concerns, as they are an important member of the healthcare team. The nurse will include information about helpful resources that the client may access such as community groups for the client's specific condition or illness, social services, and community meal or ride programs.

The following detail the basics of the body systems and their normal functions.

Integumentary

The skin or **integumentary body system** is the largest organ of the body in surface area and weight. It is composed of three layers, which include the outermost layer or epidermis, the dermis, and the hypodermis. The thickness of the epidermis varies according to the specific body area. For example, the skin is thicker on the palms and the soles of the feet than on the eyelids. The dermis contains the hair follicles, sebaceous glands, and sweat glands. Melanin is the pigment that is responsible for skin color.

The main function of the skin is the protection of the body from the outside environment. The skin regulates body temperature, using the insulation provided by body fat and the secretion of sweat, which acts as a coolant for the body. Sebum lubricates and protects the hair and the skin, and melanin absorbs harmful ultraviolet radiation. Special cells that lie on the surface of the skin also provide a barrier to bacterial infection. Nerves in the skin are responsible for sensations of pain, pressure, and temperature. In addition, the synthesis of Vitamin D, which is essential for the absorption of calcium from ingested food, begins in the skin.

Vernix caseosa is a thick, protein-based substance that protects the skin of the fetus against infection and irritation from the amniotic fluid from the third trimester until it dissipates after birth. Several childhood illnesses, such as measles and chicken pox, are associated with specific skin alterations. Acne related to hormonal changes is common in adolescents, and the effects of sunburn are observed across the lifespan. In the elderly, some of the protections provided by the skin become less effective; decreases in body fat and altered sweat production affect cold tolerance, loss of collagen support results in wrinkling of the skin, and decreased sebum secretions lead to changes in hair growth and skin moisture content.

Musculoskeletal

The **musculoskeletal system** consists of the bones, muscles, tendons, ligaments, and connective tissues that function together, providing support and motion of the body. The layers of bone include the hard exterior compact bone, the spongy bone that contains nerves and blood vessels, and the central bone marrow. The outer compact layer is covered by the strong periosteum membrane, which provides additional strength and protection for the bone. Skeletal muscles are voluntary muscles that are capable of contracting in response to nervous stimulation. Muscles are connected to bones by tendons, which are composed of tough connective tissue. Additional connective tissues called ligaments connect one bone to another at various joints.

In addition to providing support and protection, the bones are important for calcium storage and the production of blood cells. Skeletal muscles allow movement by pulling on the bones, while joints make different body movements possible.

The two most significant periods of bone growth are during fetal life and at puberty. However, until old age, bone is continually being remodeled. Specialized cells called osteoclasts break down the old bone, and osteoblasts generate new bone. In the elderly, bone remodeling is less effective, resulting in the loss of bone mass, and the incidence of osteoporosis increases. These changes can result in bone fractures, often from falling, that do not heal effectively. Muscle development follows a similar pattern with a progressive increase in muscle mass from infancy to adulthood, as well as a decline in muscle mass and physical strength in the elderly.

Nervous

The two parts of the **nervous system** are the central nervous system, which contains the brain and spinal cord, and the peripheral nervous system, which includes the ganglia and nerves. The cerebrospinal fluid and the bones of the cranium and the spine protect the brain and spinal cord. The nerves transmit impulses from one another to accomplish voluntary and involuntary processes. The nerves are surrounded by a specialized myelin sheath that insulates the nerves and facilitates the transmission of impulses.

The nervous system receives information from the body, interprets that information, and directs all motor activity for the body. This means the nervous system coordinates all the activities of the body.

The fetal brain and spinal cord are clearly visible within six weeks after conception. After the child is born, the nervous system continues to mature as the child gains motor control and learns about the environment. In the well-elderly, brain function remains stable until the age of 80, when the processing of information and short-term memory may slow.

Cardiovascular, Hematopoietic, and Lymphatic

The **cardiovascular system** includes the heart, the blood vessels, and the blood. The heart is a muscle that has four "chambers," or sections. The three types of blood vessels are: the arteries, which have a smooth muscle layer and are controlled by the nervous system; the veins, which are thinner than arteries and have valves to facilitate the return of the blood to the heart; and the capillaries, which are often only one-cell thick. Blood is red in color because the red blood cells (RBCs) that carry oxygen contain hemoglobin, which is a red pigment.

The deoxygenated blood from the body enters the heart and is transported to the lungs to allow the exchange of waste products for oxygen. The oxygenated blood then returns to the heart, which pumps the blood to the rest of body. The arteries carry oxygenated blood from the heart to the body; the veins return the deoxygenated blood to the heart, while the actual exchange of oxygen and waste products takes place in the capillaries.

The fetal cardiac system must undergo dramatic changes at birth as the infant's lungs function for the first time. Cardiovascular function remains stable until middle age, when genetic influences and lifestyle choices may affect the cardiovascular system. Most elderly people have at least some indication of decreasing efficiency of the system.

The hematopoietic system, a division of the lymphatic system, is responsible for blood-cell production. The cells are produced in the bone marrow, which is soft connective tissue in the center of large bones that have a rich blood supply. The two types of bone marrow are red bone marrow and yellow bone marrow.

The red bone marrow contains the stem cells, which can transform into specific blood cells as needed by the body. The yellow bone marrow is less active and is composed of fat cells; however, if needed, the yellow marrow can function as the red marrow to produce the blood cells.

The red bone marrow predominates from birth until adolescence. From that point on, the amount of red marrow decreases, and the amount of yellow marrow increases. This means that the elderly are at risk for conditions related to decreased blood-cell replenishment.

The lymphatic system includes the spleen, thymus, tonsils, lymph nodes, lymphatic vessels, and the lymph. The spleen is located below the diaphragm and to the rear of the stomach. The thymus consists of specialized lymphatic tissue and lies in the mediastinum behind the sternum. The tonsils are globules of lymphoid tissue located in the oropharynx. The lymphatic vessels are very small and contain valves to prevent backflow in the system vessels. The vessels that lie in close proximity to the capillaries circulate the lymph. Lymph is composed of infectious substances and cellular waste products in addition to hormones and oxygen.

The main function of the lymphatic system is protection against infection. The system also conserves body fluids and proteins and absorbs vitamins from the digestive system.

The spleen filters the blood in order to remove toxic agents and is also a reservoir for blood that can be released into systemic circulation as needed. The thymus is the site of the development and regulation of white blood cells (WBCs). The tonsils trap and destroy infectious agents as they enter the body through the mouth. The lymphatic vessels circulate the lymph, and the lymph carries toxins and cellular waste products from the cell to the heart for filtration.

There is rapid growth of the thymus gland from birth to ten years. The action of the entire system declines from adulthood to old age, which means that the elderly are less able to respond to infection.

Respiratory

The **respiratory system** consists of the airway, lungs, and respiratory muscles. The airway is composed of the pharynx, larynx, trachea, bronchi, and bronchioles. The lungs contain air-filled sacs called alveoli, and they are covered by a visceral layer of double-layered pleural membrane. The intercostal muscles are located between the ribs, and the diaphragm—the largest muscle of the body—separates the thoracic cavity from the abdominal cavity.

On inspiration, the airway transports the outside air to the lungs, while the expired air carries the carbon dioxide that is removed by the lungs. The alveoli are the site of the exchange of carbon dioxide from the systemic circulation with the oxygen contained in the inspired air. The muscles help the thoracic cavity to expand and contract to allow for air exchange.

The respiratory rate in the infant gradually decreases from a normal of 30 to 40 breaths per minute, until adolescence when it equals the normal adult rate of 12 to 20 breaths per minute. Pulmonary function declines after the age of 60 because the alveoli become larger and less efficient, and the respiratory muscles weaken.

Digestive

The **digestive system** includes the mouth, pharynx, esophagus, stomach, small intestine, large intestine, and sigmoid colon. The entire system forms a 24-foot tube through which ingested food passes. Digestion begins in the mouth, where digestive enzymes are secreted in response to food intake. Food then passes through the esophagus to the stomach, which is a pouch-shaped organ that collects and holds food for a period of time. The small intestine begins at the distal end of the stomach. The lining of the small intestine contains many villi, which are small, hair-like projections that increase the absorption of nutrients from the ingested food. The large intestine originates at the distal end of the small intestine and terminates in the rectum. The large intestine is 4 feet long and has 3 segments, including the ascending colon along the right side, the transverse colon from right to left across the body, and the descending colon down the left side of the body, where the sigmoid colon begins.

The enzymes of the mouth, stomach, and the proximal end of the small intestine break down the ingested food into nutrients that can be absorbed and used by the body. The nutrients are absorbed by the small intestine. The large intestine removes the water from the waste products, which forms the stool. The muscle layer of the large intestine is responsible for peristalsis, which is the force that moves the waste products through the intestine.

The function of the digestive system declines more slowly than other body systems, and the changes that most often occur are the result of lifestyle issues or medication use.

Urinary

The **urinary system** includes the kidneys, ureters, bladder, and urethra. The kidneys are a pair of bean-shaped organs that lie just below and posterior to the liver in the peritoneal cavity. The nephron is the functional unit of the kidney, and there are about 1 million nephrons in each of the two kidneys. The ureters are hollow tubes that allow the urine formed in the kidneys to pass into the bladder. The urinary bladder is a hollow mucous lined pouch with the ureters entering the upper portion, and the urethra exiting from the bottom portion. The urethra is a tubular structure lined with mucous membrane that connects the bladder with the outside of the body.

In addition to the formation and excretion of the waste product urine, the nephron of the kidney also regulates fluid and electrolyte balance and contributes to the control of blood pressure. The ureters allow the urine to pass from the kidneys to the bladder. The bladder stores the urine and regulates the process of urination. The urethra delivers the urine from the bladder to the outside of the body.

The lifespan changes in the urinary system are more often the result of the effects of chronic disease on the system, rather than normal decline.

Reproductive

The major organs of the **female reproductive system** include the uterus, cervix, vagina, ovaries, and fallopian tubes.

The uterus is a hollow, pear-shaped organ with a muscular layer that is positioned between the bladder and the rectum. The uterus terminates at the cervix, which opens into the vagina, which is open to the outside of the body. The ovaries, supported by several ligaments, are oval organs 1- to 2-inches long that are positioned on either side of the uterus in the pelvic cavity. The fallopian tubes, which are 4 inches long and .5 inches in diameter, connect the uterus with the ovaries.

The **male reproductive system** include the penis, scrotum, testicles, vas deferens, seminal vesicles, and the prostate gland. In addition to the urethra, the penis contains 3 sections of erectile tissue. The scrotum is a fibromuscular pouch that contains the testes, the spermatic cord, and the epididymis. The pair of testes is suspended in the scrotum and each one is approximately 2 inches by 1 inch long. The vas deferens is a tubular pathway between the testes and the penis, and the seminal vesicles are small organs located between the bladder and the bowel. The prostate gland surrounds the proximal end of the urethra within the pelvic cavity.

The main function of the male reproductive system is the production of sperm. Several million immature sperm are produced every day in the testes. The sperm are transported through the vas deferens to the penis, and the prostate gland and seminal vesicles contribute fluids that support the activity of the sperm after ejaculation.

At puberty, egg maturation, menses, and sperm production begin, and the secondary sex characteristics appear. Female fertility declines at 30 years of age, and the maturation of eggs in the ovaries ceases at menopause, which occurs at 50 years of age. Sperm production continues from puberty until death; however, after 60 years of age, the ability of the sperm to travel to the fallopian tube to fertilize an egg is decreased.

Endocrine

The glands of the **endocrine system** include the pituitary, thyroid, parathyroid, adrenal, and reproductive glands, as well as the hypothalamus, the pancreas, and the pineal body. The function of the system is to synthesize and secrete hormones that control body growth, sexual function, and metabolism, which is the production and use of energy by the body. The thyroid gland, located on either side of the trachea, regulates energy production, or the rate at which the body uses ingested food to support body functions. The parathyroid, located on the upper margin of the thyroid gland, regulates calcium levels by the activation of Vitamin D, which increases intestinal absorption of calcium, and by regulating the amount of calcium that is stored in the bones or excreted by the kidneys. The adrenal glands, located on the upper margin of the kidneys, consist of the adrenal cortex and the adrenal medulla. The hormones secreted by the adrenal cortex are necessary for life and include: cortisol, or hydrocortisone, which regulates the breakdown of proteins, carbohydrates, and fats for energy

production and the body's response to stress; corticosterone, which works with cortisol to regulate the immune system; and aldosterone, which contributes to blood-pressure control. The adrenal medulla secretions, including adrenaline, regulate the body's reaction to stress known as the fight-or-flight response. The ovaries secrete estrogen and the testes secrete testosterone, which regulate sexual maturation and function. The pancreas, located in the right upper quadrant of the abdomen, secretes the insulin that regulates blood sugar, in addition to other hormones that regulate water absorption and secretion in the intestines. The pineal gland, located in the center of the brain, secretes melatonin, which regulates the circadian rhythm or sleep cycle.

The nervous system connects each of these glands to the hypothalamus and the pituitary gland. The hypothalamus senses alterations in hormone secretions in all of these organs and conveys those messages to the pituitary gland, which then stimulates each specific organ to either increase or decrease secretion of the relevant hormone. This feedback system is necessary for homeostasis.

Sensory
The **sensory organs** include the eyes, ears, nose, tongue, and skin, and they contain special receptor cells that transmit information to the nervous system. The eyes receive and process light energy. The ears process sound waves and also contribute to the maintenance of equilibrium. The nose senses odors and the tongue senses taste. The skin responds to tactile stimulation, including pain, hot, cold, and touch. Internal organs also sense pain and pressure. The brain is responsible for processing all of these sensations.

The senses of touch and smell are active in the fetus and continue to mature after birth. Touch is especially important for infants. The elderly experience a decline in the acuity of all of the senses; however, eyesight and hearing are most commonly affected due to the effects of chronic diseases such as hypertension and diabetes.

Respiratory Problems
Some patients experiencing respiratory issues may receive supplemental oxygen. Oxygen can be administered in several different ways. The most common and minimal administration technique is via nasal cannula. The oxygen will flow through the nasal cannula into the patient's nose, and the tubing will be connected into either a mobile oxygen tank or an oxygen supply on the wall of the patient's room. Depending on the facility, there will often be a respiratory therapy team in charge of caring for patients' respiratory issues.

The picture demonstrates oxygen being administered via nasal cannula. The two prongs are placed into the nostrils of the patient.

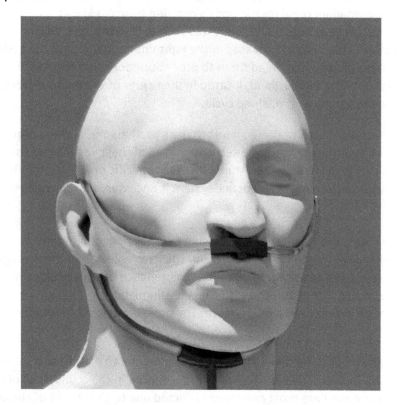

Part of the nurse's normal vital signs collection will include oxygen saturation readings. This is especially important in patients receiving supplemental oxygen and/or with identified respiratory issues. Normal values are generally considered to be 93 to 100 percent, but some patients with COPD may have a baseline saturation in the high 80s.

It is important that the aide understand the flow rate of supplemental oxygen that the patient is receiving. A typical rate is 2 to 4 liters per minute (LPM). The nurse should look for signs of hypoxia—a lack of oxygen in the body. These include decreased level of consciousness, shortness of breath, bluish lips or blueness of the extremities/nail beds (cyanosis), or unresponsiveness. Any change in respiratory status or suspected issues with oxygen administration should be reported to the nurse or respiratory therapist immediately.

Finally, the nurse must be familiar with IV (intravenous) accesses. IVs are used to administer medicine and fluids. Signs that an IV access is compromised are redness around the site, patient discomfort, bruising, and leakage. Any changes in IV access, IV pump alarms, and patient complaints should be reported to the nurse immediately.

Basic Pathophysiology

Pathophysiology refers to changes in the body due to a disease process. The patient's history of chronic and acute disease is discovered during the preoperative patient interview and chart review. Understanding the pathophysiology of the patient's disease process (or processes) empowers the nurse to know if assessment findings are congruent with the disease process or if findings are indicative of something else. For example, if a patient has 2+ pitting edema with a history of CHF, the nurse may

suspect the edema is secondary to a CHF exacerbation and investigate further by auscultating lung sounds and consulting with a cardiologist. It is also important for the nurse to consider the pathophysiological processes associated with the patient's scheduled procedure. The nurse should note that although the scheduled procedure may be minor, the patient's diagnosis may be quite serious. If the patient is having a PowerPort insertion, the surgery process is minor. However, the patient may have a diagnosis of stage IV lung cancer, and this is quite serious. Understanding this, the nurse may allow more time for the patient to verbalize feelings and provide emotional support for the patient.

Illness Management

There are certain client situations that indicate a worsening of their illness. The nurse needs to be prepared to identify this worsening and report it immediately to the attending practitioner. A solid knowledge of disease processes must be applied when managing patients' illnesses. The nurse must also be able to educate the patient regarding their condition and the management thereof. Certain interventional skills such as gastric lavage may be required for management of the patient's illness.

Any patient condition that involves a sudden compromise of airway, breathing, or circulation must be reported immediately. Swift intervention is needed to prevent long-term damage or fatality. Airway, breathing, and circulation are referred to as the patient's "ABCs" for short, and their management is at the top of the nurse's assessment checklist.

In addition to addressing the patient's ABCs, the nurse will also prioritize their care based off Maslow's hierarchy of needs. The nurse will recall that, according to this hierarchy, the patient must have physiological needs, such as hunger and thirst, met before higher priorities such as safety, esteem, and self-actualization may be met.

Determining the type of illness is key to creating a strategy to manage it. The client may suffer from chronic diseases such as heart failure, COPD, or diabetes. They may be engaged in a battle with mental illnesses such as anxiety, depression, and bipolar disorder. Depending on the client's unique profile, the nurse will identify their needs and determine a care plan that will assist them in managing their illness effectively.

A change in the client's baseline functioning status is any symptom, blood test, or behavior that trends significantly different from their normal. Some clients have abnormalities as their normal, such as a low blood pressure, low pulse oxygenation, heart dysrhythmia such as prolonged QT segment, or a "normal" level of confusion in dementia patients. The nurse goes off their initial assessments of the patient as well as the patient's medical record and family reports to determine if a notable change is taking place and needs reporting.

The nurse closely monitors the patient's response to interventions that are intended to be therapeutic. The patient may have an unexpected and unwanted response to medications and other therapies. Side effects, adverse reactions, and allergic responses all fall into this category of unwanted response to a pharmacological therapy. A patient receiving mechanical ventilation via an endotracheal tube may become agitated and aggressive, as this type of therapy can be highly irritating. The nurse sees this unwanted response and uses tools such as sedation, within the ordered parameters, to soothe the patient and return them to the therapeutic response.

Using their knowledge of pathophysiology, the nurse works to effectively manage the client's care and prevent complications. Using the example of the patient with diabetes, the nurse knows that tight management of blood glucose is a high priority. The nurse knows that these patients, depending on the cause of their diabetes, have a tough time using the body's insulin to regulate glucose in the bloodstream. The nurse monitors the client's intake at mealtimes, measures blood glucose regularly, administers diabetic medications in a timely manner so they will have maximal effectiveness, and keeps a close eye on the patient when they must be NPO or off the floor for procedures, as these are prime occasions for the patient to have a hypoglycemic event.

The nurse must manage not only one client's illness but often is working to manage an entire caseload of clients all at the same time, depending on what type of unit they are working in. Caseloads of patients require exceptional time management and organizational skills from the nurse. The nurse must be able to prioritize client needs effectively to meet them in a timely manner.

Client education performed by the nurse is a way the nurse may enable the patient to become independent in their own illness management. The patient can then feel more comfortable making informed decisions and speaking up about their care. The nurse answers the client's questions, addresses their concerns, and informs them about therapies and medications. Part of this patient education is assessing what specific education the patient needs. Some clients are very much informed about their condition and treatment modalities, while others may be healthcare illiterate, meaning they do not know very much about their condition or their options in managing it. Based on the nurse's assessment of the client's educational needs, the nurse will formulate their educational plan.

There are certain cases of client illness in which the nurse will need to perform **gastric lavage**. *Lavage* means a cleaning or rinsing out, while *gastric* refers to the stomach. The patient will be placed in high Fowler's position while an NG tube is inserted. This tube is carefully measured from the nose of the client to their earlobe and then to the tip of the xiphoid process. This point is then marked on a piece of tape. Water-soluble gel is applied to the tip of the tube before insertion for lubrication. The client will be instructed to look upward to create a hyperextension of the neck. The tube is advanced into the nares until resistance is met at the nasopharynx. The nurse expects that the client's gag reflex will kick in as well as watering of the eyes. The client will take small sips of water to open the epiglottis at which point the nurse will then be able to advance the tube all the way down to the stomach. Placement is assessed via pH test of aspirated gastric contents from the tube and/or obtainment of chest X-ray. The nurse will secure the NG tube using tape to the client's nose and a safety pin to the client's gown. After correct placement is confirmed, the nurse may use the tube to lavage the client's stomach. This will be done according to the ordering gastroenterologist's preferred method but usually includes the instilment of a solution, clamping of the tube for a determined amount of time, and then removal of the fluid later.

Fluid and Electrolyte Imbalances

Electrolytes are minerals that, when dissolved, break down into ions. They can be acids, bases, or salts. In the body, different electrolytes are responsible for specific cellular functions. These functions make up larger, critical system-wide processes, such as hydration, homeostasis, pH balance, and muscle contraction. Electrolytes typically enter the body through food and drink consumption, but in severe cases of imbalance, they may be medically-administered. They are found in the fluids of the body, such as blood.

Key electrolytes found in the body include the following:

Sodium and Chloride

Sodium (Na+) is mainly responsible for managing hydration, blood pressure, and blood volume in the body. It is found in blood, plasma, and lymph. It is important to note that sodium is primarily found

outside of cells and is accessed by a number of different systems and organs to tightly regulate water and blood levels. For example, in cases of severe dehydration, the circulatory and endocrine systems will transmit signals to the kidneys to retain sodium and, consequently, water.

Sodium also affects muscle and nerve function. It is a positively-charged ion and contributes to membrane potential—an electrochemical balance between sodium and potassium (another electrolyte) that is responsible for up to 40 percent of resting energy expenditure in a healthy adult. This balance strongly influences the functioning of nerve impulses and the ability of muscles to contract. Healthy heart functioning and contraction is dependent on membrane potential.

Sodium is available in large quantities in the standard diets of developed countries, especially in processed foods, as it is found in table salt. Consequently, sodium deficiencies (hyponatremia) are possible, but rare, in the average person. Hyponatremia can result in endocrine or nervous system disorders where sodium regulation is affected. It can also result in excessive sweating, vomiting, or diarrhea, such as in endurance sporting events, improper use of diuretics, or gastrointestinal illness. Hyponatremia may be treated with an IV sodium solution. Too much sodium (hypernatremia) is usually a result of dehydration. Hypernatremia may be treated by introducing water quantities appropriate for suspending the sodium level that is tested in the patient's blood and urine.

Chloride (Cl-) is a negatively-charged ion found outside of the cells that works closely with sodium. It shares many of the same physiologic responsibilities as sodium. Any imbalances (hypochloremia and hyperchloremia) are rare but may affect overall pH levels of the body. Chloride imbalances usually occur in response to an imbalance in other electrolytes, so treating a chloride imbalance directly is uncommon.

Potassium

Potassium (K+) is mainly responsible for regulating muscular function and is especially important in cardiac and digestive functions. In women, it is believed to promote bone density. It works in tandem with sodium to create membrane potential. Potassium is a positively-charged ion and is usually found inside cells. It plays a role in maintaining homeostasis between the intracellular and extracellular environments.

Potassium is found in all animal protein and animal dairy products and in most fruits and vegetables. Low potassium levels (hypokalemia) may be caused by dehydration due to excessive vomiting, urination, or diarrhea. In severe or acute cases, hypokalemia may be a result of renal dysfunction and may cause lethargy, muscle cramps, or heart dysrhythmia. It may be treated by stopping the cause of potassium loss (e.g., diuretics), followed by oral or IV potassium replenishment.

High potassium levels (hyperkalemia) can quickly become fatal. **Hyperkalemia** is often the result of a serious condition, such as sudden kidney or adrenal failure, and may cause nausea, vomiting, chest pain, and muscle dysfunction. It is treated based on its severity, with treatment options ranging from diuretic use to IV insulin or glucose. IV calcium may be administered if potentially dangerous heart arrhythmias are present.

1.

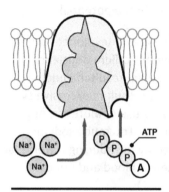

The sodium-potassium pump binds three sodium ions and a molecule of ATP.

2.

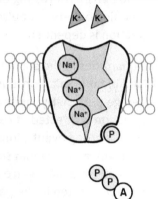

The splitting of ATP provides energy to change the shape of the channel. The sodium ions are driven through the channel.

3.

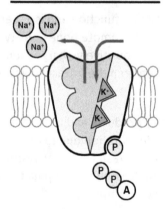

The sodium ions are released to the outside of the membrane, and the new shape of the channel allows two potassium ions to bind

4.

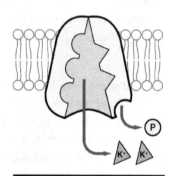

Release of the phosphate allows the channel to revert to its original form, releasing the potassium ions on the inside of the membrane

Calcium and Phosphorus

Calcium (Ca++) is plentiful in the body, with most calcium stored throughout the skeletal system. However, if there is not enough calcium in the blood (usually available through proper diet), the body will take calcium from the bones. This can become detrimental over time. If enough calcium becomes present in the blood, the body will return extra calcium stores to the bones. Besides contributing to the

skeletal structure, this electrolyte is important in nerve signaling, muscle function, and blood coagulation. It is found in dairy products, leafy greens, and fatty fishes. Many other consumables, such as fruit juices and cereals, are often fortified with calcium.

Low calcium levels (hypocalcemia) can be caused by poor diet, thyroid or kidney disorders, and some medications. Symptoms can include lethargy, poor memory, inability to concentrate, muscle cramps, and general stiffness and achiness in the body. Supplementation can rapidly restore blood calcium levels. In cases where symptoms are present, IV calcium administration in conjunction with an oral or IV vitamin D supplement may be utilized.

High calcium levels (hypercalcemia) is usually caused by thyroid dysfunction but can also be the result of diet, limited mobility (such as in paralyzed individuals), some cancers, or the use of some diuretics. Symptoms can include thirst, excess urination, gastrointestinal issues, and unexplained pain in the abdominal area or bones. Severe or untreated hypercalcemia can result in kidney stones, kidney failure, confusion, depression, lethargy, irregular heartbeat, or bone problems.

There is an intricate balance between calcium levels and the levels of phosphorus, another electrolyte. Phosphorus, like calcium, is stored in the bones and found in many of the same foods as calcium. These electrolytes work together to maintain bone integrity. When too much calcium exists in the blood, the bones release more phosphorus to balance the two levels. When there is too much phosphorus in the blood, the bones release calcium. Therefore, the presence or absence of one directly impacts the presence or absence of the other. Indicators of hypocalcemia and hypercalcemia usually also indicate low levels of phosphorus (hypophosphatemia) and high levels of phosphorus (hyperphosphatemia), respectively.

Magnesium
Magnesium (Mg++) is another electrolyte that is usually plentiful in the body. It is responsible for an array of life-sustaining functions, including hundreds of biochemical reactions such as oxidative phosphorylation and glycolysis. It is also an important factor in DNA and RNA synthesis, bone development, nerve signaling, and muscle function. Magnesium is stored inside cells or within the structure of the bones. It can be consumed through leafy greens, nuts, seeds, beans, unrefined grains, and most foods that contain fiber. Some water sources may also contain high levels of magnesium.

Low levels of magnesium (hypomagnesemia) are primarily caused by chronic alcohol or drug abuse and some prescription medications and can also occur in patients with gastrointestinal diseases (such as celiac or Crohn's). Symptoms of hypomagnesemia include nausea, vomiting, depression, personality and mood disorders, and muscle dysfunction. Chronically depleted patients may have an increased risk of cardiovascular and metabolic disorders.

High levels of magnesium (hypermagnesemia) are rare and usually result in conjunction with kidney disorders when medications are used improperly. Symptoms include low blood pressure that may result in heart failure. Hypermagnesemia is usually treated by removing any magnesium sources (such as salts or laxatives) and may also require the IV administration of calcium gluconate.

Magnesium imbalance can lead to calcium or potassium imbalance over time, as these electrolytes work together to achieve homeostasis in the body.

Hydration is critical to fluid presence in the body, as water is a critical component of blood, plasma, and lymph. When fluid levels are too high or too low, electrolytes cannot move freely or carry out their intended functions. Therefore, treating an electrolyte imbalance almost always involves managing a fluid imbalance as well. Typically, as fluid levels rise, electrolyte levels decrease. As fluid levels decrease, electrolyte levels rise. Common tests to determine electrolyte fluid imbalances include basic and comprehensive metabolic panels, which test levels of sodium, potassium, chloride, and any other electrolyte in question.

Hemodynamics

A crucial part of patient assessment and monitoring is their hemodynamic profile. **Hemodynamics** are the forces that cause blood to circulate throughout the body, originating in the heart, branching out to the vital organs and tissues, and then recirculating back to the heart and lungs for reoxygenation and pumping. There are at least three different aspects of hemodynamics that can be focused on: the measurement of pressure, flow, and oxygenation of the blood in the cardiovascular system; the use of invasive technological tools to measure and quantitate pressures, volumes, and capacity of the vascular system; and the monitoring of hemodynamics that involves measuring and interpreting the biological systems that are affected by it.

Hemodynamics can be assessed using noninvasive or invasive measures. Noninvasive measures would include the nurse's assessment of the patient's overall presentation, heart rate, and blood pressure. Invasive measurements would include inserting an arterial blood pressure monitor directly into an artery or the insertion of a Swan-Ganz catheter. The Swan-Ganz catheter, also known as a pulmonary artery catheter (PAC) or right-heart catheter, is threaded into the patient's subclavian vein, down the superior vena cava, right up to the PA. This type of catheter is used quite commonly in ICU patients. PACs give information about the patient's cardiac output and preload. Preload is obtained by estimating the pulmonary artery occlusion pressure (PAOP). Another way to assess preload is determining the right ventricular end-diastolic volume (RVEDV), measured by fast-response thermistors reading the heart rate. There is some question as to whether the use of PACs helps patients or not. Some studies suggest that the use of PACs does not reduce morbidity or mortality but rather increases these occurrences. Their use, therefore, should be weighed carefully according to the physician's discretion.

There are many different parameters to consider when assessing a patient's hemodynamics. Blood pressure is the measurement of the systolic pressure over the diastolic pressure, or the pressure in the vasculature when the heart contracts over the pressure when the heart is at rest.

Mean arterial pressure (MAP) shows the relationship between the amount of blood pumped out of the heart and the resistance the vascular system puts up against it. A low MAP suggests that blood flow has decreased to the organs, while a high MAP may indicate that the workload for the heart is increased.

Cardiac index reflects the quantity of blood pumped by the heart per minute and per meter squared of the patient's body surface area.

Cardiac output measures how much blood the heart pumps out per beat and is measured in liters.

Central venous pressure (CVP) is an estimate of the RVEDP, thus assessing RV function as well as the patient's general hydration status. A low CVP may mean the patient is dehydrated or has a decreased amount of venous return. A high CVP may indicate fluid overload or right-sided heart failure.

Pulmonary artery pressure measures the pressure in the PA. An increase in this pressure may mean the patient has developed a left-to-right cardiac shunt, they have hypertension of the PA, they may have worsening complications of COPD, a clot has traveled to the lungs (pulmonary embolus), the lungs are filling with fluid (pulmonary edema), or the left ventricle is failing.

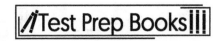

The **pulmonary capillary wedge pressure (PCWP)** approximates the left ventricular end-diastolic pressure (LVEDP). This number, when increased, may be a result of LV failure, a pathology of the mitral valve, cardiac sufficiency, or compression of the heart after a hemorrhage, such as cardiac tamponade.

The resistance that the pulmonary capillary bed in the lungs puts up against blood flow is measured via **pulmonary vascular resistance (PVR)**. When there is disease in the lungs, a pulmonary embolism, hypoxia, or pulmonary vasculitis, this number may increase. Calcium channel blockers and certain other medications may cause the PVR to be lowered because of their mechanism of action.

A hemodynamic measurement used to assess RV function and the patient's fluid status is the RV pressure. When this number is elevated, the patient may have pulmonary hypertension, failure of the right ventricle, or worsening congestive heart failure.

The stroke index measures how much blood the heart is pumping in a cardiac cycle in relation to the patient's body surface area.

Stroke volume (SV) measures how much blood the heart pumps in milliliters per beat.

The systemic vascular resistance parameter reflects how much pressure the vasculature peripheral to the heart puts up to blood flow from the heart. Vasoconstrictors, low blood volume, and septic shock can cause this number to rise, while vasodilators, high blood levels of carbon dioxide (hypercarbia), nitrates, and morphine may cause this number to fall.

The following is a list of commonly measured hemodynamic parameters and their normal values:

- Blood pressure: 90–140 mmHg systolic over 60–90 mmHg diastolic
- Mean arterial pressure (MAP): 70–100 mmHg
- Cardiac index (CI): 2.5–4.0 $L/min/m^2$
- Cardiac output (CO): 4–8 L/min
- Central venous pressure (CVP) or right arterial pressure (RA): 2–6 mmHg
- Pulmonary artery pressure (PA): systolic 20–30 mmHg (PAS), diastolic 8–12 mmHg (PAD), mean 25 mmHg (PAM)
- Pulmonary capillary wedge pressure (PCWP): 4–12 mmHg
- Pulmonary vascular resistance (PVR): 37–250 $dynes/sec/cm^5$
- Right ventricular pressure (RV): systolic 20–30 mmHg over diastolic 0–5 mmHg
- Stroke index (SI): 25–45 mL/m^2
- Stroke volume (SV): 50–100 mL/beat
- Systemic vascular resistance (SVR): 800–1200 $dynes/sec/cm^5$

Medical Emergencies

In the event of a medical emergency, there are specific steps to take depending on the situation. There will be written policies for these types of emergencies in the workplace that are used for patients, staff, and/or visitors.

Below are some examples of medical emergencies:

- Choking
- Unresponsive or unconscious person or patient
- Excessive bleeding

- Head injury
- Broken bones
- Severe burns
- Seizures
- Chest pain
- Difficulty breathing
- Allergic reactions that cause swelling and/or breathing difficulties
- Inhalation or swallowing of a toxic substance
- Accidental poisoning

Choking

If someone is **choking**, the victim will most likely grab at their throat, or they may have a cough that eventually stops, indicating blockage of the airway. If the airway is blocked, they will need the **Heimlich maneuver** to be performed immediately. Oftentimes people cough and may leave the room to get a drink or to avoid disrupting others. It is best to follow that person to ensure they are not choking.

When someone is choking and conscious, the responder, or person at the scene who witnesses and intervenes, should:

- Ask the victim if they are choking and tell them help is here.
- Assist the victim to a standing position.
- Stand behind the victim and wrap the arms around the victim's waist.
- With the hands just above the victim's belly button, place the hand in a fist with the thumb against the victim's stomach.
- Place the other hand on top of the fisted hand.
- Thrust quick, hard, and upward on the victim's stomach.
- Continue this until the food or object comes out of the victim's mouth.
- Do *not* swipe the victim's mouth with one finger, as this could push the blockage further down the airway.

If the victim is still choking and goes unconscious:

- Lower the victim to the floor, shout for help, and have someone call 911.
- Begin cardiopulmonary resuscitation (CPR) by following the basic life support steps until emergency medical services (EMS) arrives.

Unconsciousness or Unresponsiveness

If someone is **unconscious**, first try to arouse the person by shaking or tapping them. If they are indeed unresponsive, call for help, have someone call 911, and proceed to:

- Make sure the patient is lying flat and place a backboard under them for CPR.
- Follow basic life support (BLS) protocol.
- Look and listen for breathing (chest rise).
- Check for a pulse in radial artery (wrist).
- If patient is breathing, stay with them until EMS arrives. If there is a pulse but no breathing, begin rescue breaths. Give one breath every 5 or 6 seconds. Check pulse every 2 minutes.
- If no pulse, begin CPR and continue until EMS arrives.
- Direct someone else to get the automated external defibrillator (AED) as CPR is continued.

- CPR: 30 chest compressions then 2 breaths, repeat for 2-minute cycles.
- Chest compressions should be firm and deep, to the rhythm of the disco song "Stayin' Alive," about 100 beats per minute. This ensures adequate perfusion of organs with blood since the heart is not pumping on its own.
- When the AED arrives, turn it on and follow the prompts for use.

If the patient recovers, turn them onto their left side and continue to monitor them until EMS arrive. Healthcare workers will be trained and certified on BLS, CPR, and AED use.

Excessive Bleeding
For **excessive bleeding**, call for help and call 911. Then:

- Have the patient sit down or lie down.
- Use a towel or shirt to hold continuous pressure on the bleeding area.
- Elevate the area above their heart. For example, if the leg is bleeding, have the patient lie down and put their leg on a chair.
- Talk to the patient and monitor their responsiveness. Stay with them until EMS arrives.

Head Injury
Concussions, contusions, and skull fractures are all common types of traumatic brain injuries. **Concussions** occur when the brain is jarred against the skull, usually during sports, hard contact with another person, or hitting the head on the ground. Concussions can cause mental confusion and lead to disruptions in normal brain functioning. The effects of a concussion can show up immediately, or they may not show up for hours or days. Normally, concussions do not cause a loss of consciousness, so it is important to pay attention to other possible symptoms. Another type of traumatic brain injury is a contusion, which is a bruise on the brain. This bruise can swell in the brain and cause a hematoma, or bleeding in the brain. The following list includes symptoms of traumatic brain injuries:

- Confusion
- Depression
- Dizziness or balance problems
- Foggy feeling
- Double vision or changes in vision
- Tiredness
- Headache
- Memory loss
- Nausea
- Sensitivity to light
- Trouble remembering and concentrating

If a patient has a known head injury, or they stated that they hit their head, stay with the patient and call for a supervisor. Monitor the patient for mild symptoms from the list above. If the symptoms are not serious, the patient may require a visit from the physician. If the patient is elderly or has other serious health issues, hospitalization may be required to rule out more serious consequences from the head

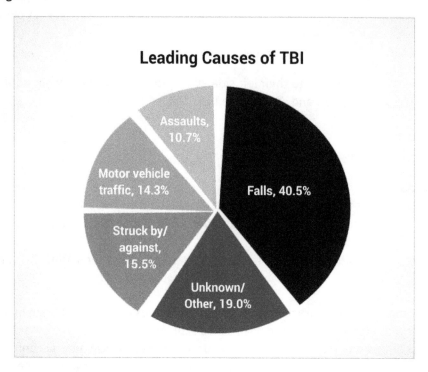

injury. The pie chart below depicts the leading causes of traumatic brain injury, with falls being the largest percentage.

Leading Causes of TBI

- Falls, 40.5%
- Unknown/Other, 19.0%
- Struck by/against, 15.5%
- Motor vehicle traffic, 14.3%
- Assaults, 10.7%

Symptoms of a head injury that are more serious and require immediate emergency treatment include:

- Unequal pupils
- Convulsions
- Fracture of the skull or face
- Inability to move legs or arms
- Clear or bloody fluid coming from the ears, nose, or mouth
- Loss of consciousness
- Persistent vomiting
- Severe headache
- Slurred speech and distorted vision
- Restlessness and irritability

If any of the above symptoms appear after a head injury, call for help and call 911.

Broken Bones (Compound Fractures)

A **compound fracture** is a fracture in which the bone is protruding through the skin. Other symptoms include pain, swelling, deformity in the fractured area, and bruising. This is the most serious type of fracture and requires immediate attention. The following comprises first aid for fractures:

- Call for help and call 911, especially if a fracture in the head, back, or neck is suspected.
- Don't move the patient unless they are in danger of further injury.
- Keep the injured area still and stay with the patient.
- Treat any bleeding by holding pressure with a towel or gauze.

- Look for signs of shock in the patient (shallow, fast breathing, or feeling faint) and lay them down with their feet elevated.
- Wrap ice packs in a towel and ice the injured area.
- Wait for EMS to arrive.

Burns

Burn injuries can range from mild to severe, but the initial treatment for all burns is the same. First-degree burns affect the top layer of the skin, second-degree burns affect two layers, and third-degree burns affect all three layers. Call for an emergency response if:

- The burn is through all the skin layers.
- The person is a baby or elderly and the burn is severe.
- The hands, feet, face, or genitals are burned.
- The burn is larger than two inches or is oozing.
- The burn is charred and leathery, or has white, brown, or black patches.

Initial treatment for all burns includes:

- Remove the source of the burn, put out the fire, smother the burning area, or have the person stop, drop, and roll.
- Remove any hot or burned clothing.
- Remove clothing that is tight and remove jewelry (burns can swell very quickly).
- Hold the burned area under cool, running water for 20 minutes.
- Use two cold cloths if running water is not available. Alternate holding them on the area every 2 minutes.
- Do not put ice on the burn.
- Keep the patient warm by covering the rest of the body.
- Wrap or cover the burn loosely with gauze, or a use a sheet for large areas.
- If EMS has been called, stay with the patient and keep them warm until help arrives.

Seizures

Seizures have many symptoms depending on the type of seizure. Some symptoms include jerking motions, shaking, unconsciousness, stiffness, and blank staring. If someone is having a violent seizure, the steps to follow include:

- Protect the victim's head by moving hard objects out of the way and placing a blanket under their head.
- Loosen clothing around their neck.
- Do not try to hold them down and do not try to put something in their mouth.
- Get help to control bystanders so that the victim has some space.
- When the seizure is over, have the victim lie on their side and make sure their airway is open.
- Call 911 if the seizure lasts more than 5 minutes, if the victim has other medical conditions, or if the person has never had a seizure before.
- People with known epilepsy may have seizures that are short and frequent, so calling 911 may not be necessary.

Chest Pain

Chest pain can be a symptom of a heart attack or other serious heart or lung condition. Prompt attention is necessary so that the person can be treated before serious heart damage or death occurs. Chest pain can also be a result of a lung infection, excessive coughing, broken ribs from an injury, anxiety, indigestion, or muscular injury. If the patient has not fallen or does not have any outward physical signs of injury to the chest area, assume that the chest pain is cardiac related. When someone complains of chest pain, do the following:

- Have the person sit down and ask where the pain is located.
- Call for the supervisor immediately.
- Assess if they have any injuries on or near their chest.
- Call 911 (if not in a medical facility) if the pain lasts more than a few minutes, or they have the following symptoms:
- Pain in the arms, shoulders, back and chest
- Difficulty breathing
- Fatigue
- Nausea
- Sweating
- Dizziness
- If there is oxygen available, a respiratory therapist or nurse will place a nasal cannula in their nose and give between two and four liters of oxygen.
- If available and the person is not allergic or taking any blood-thinner medication, the nurse will have the person chew a regular-strength aspirin. Aspirin helps the blood flow to the heart.
- Stay with the person until EMS arrives.
- If the person becomes unconscious, follow BLS guidelines and initiate CPR.

Difficulty Breathing

Breathing difficulties or shortness of breath can be caused by many factors, such as asthma, bronchitis, pneumonia, heart conditions, pulmonary embolism, anxiety, or exercise. People may occasionally have shortness of breath because of an underlying condition that is being monitored by a physician. They may take medication for this symptom and be able to continue to live relatively normal lives. However, if a person has sudden difficulty catching their breath, and it is not relieved with rest, change of position, or their inhaler medication, immediate attention is required. Do the following if a person begins to struggle with breathing:

- Call for help and have the person sit up in their chair or in their bed.

- Instruct the person to try to take slow breaths, inhaling though their nose and exhaling out of their mouth.

- Continue to talk to them reassuringly and soothingly. Anxiety can actually make breathing even more difficult.

- If their breathing becomes easier and they seem to calm down, have a physician see them as soon as possible, especially if this is something new for this person.

- If breathing continues to be difficult, call 911 (if not in medical facility).

- Place oxygen on the patient with a mask or nasal cannula, if available.

- Stay with the patient until help arrives and monitor their level of consciousness and breathing rate.

Allergic Reactions

Allergies can cause many symptoms from mild to severe. Some examples of mild symptoms might include itching, redness on the skin, hives, sneezing, runny nose, and itchy eyes. Wheezing may occur and may be treated with a prescribed inhaler. Life-threatening allergic reactions include swelling of the tongue or throat, difficulty breathing, and anaphylaxis, which is a systemic reaction. Anaphylaxis is rare but can lead to death if it is not recognized and treated quickly. Allergies to foods, medications, latex, and insect bites can cause anaphylaxis. Normally a person who has serious allergic reactions will have an epinephrine pen, or "epi-pen," with them at all times, to be administered in case of a reaction. If the following symptoms associated with anaphylaxis are observed outside of a medical facility, call 911. Otherwise, report any of the following symptoms to the nurse:

- Difficulty breathing
- Swollen tongue or throat tightness
- Wheezing
- Nausea and vomiting
- Fainting or dizziness
- Low blood pressure
- Rapid heart beat
- Feeling strange or sense of impending doom
- Chest pain

Call 911 even if an epi-pen has been administered for the allergic reaction. Reaction symptoms can continue to occur or can reoccur later.

Poisoning

Poison can be something eaten, inhaled, or absorbed in excess, or exposure to toxic substances. This type of emergency can happen to patients and employees. If there is an accidental poisoning and the person is awake and alert, call the poison-control hotline at 1-800-222-1222. Stay on the phone with poison control and stay with the victim. Try to have the following information available for the responders:

- Weight and age of the victim
- The label or bottle of the substance taken
- The time of exposure to the substance (how long it has been)
- The address of where the victim is located

If the person goes unconscious or is not breathing, call 911.

Many chemical labels, such as cleaning supplies, have warning labels and instructions for dealing with toxic exposure. The eyes may need to be flushed with water, for example. Read labels but also call for help. In healthcare facilities, protocols for chemical spills or exposure exist so that clean up and injury can be dealt with quickly. Always follow the policy provided by the facility or workplace.

Unexpected Response to Therapies

There are a vast multitude of unexpected responses that may occur during a patient's therapy. With every desired effect, there are many undesired effects that may develop. The nurse works with the healthcare team to prevent, watch for, and treat unexpected patient responses right away.

One of the most dangerous complications for a woman who has just given birth is a postpartum hemorrhage. This occurs when the uterus continues to bleed excessively, losing more than 500 mL after the baby has been delivered. An accompanying signal of postpartum hemorrhage is a drop in the hematocrit by more than ten percentage points. A postpartum hemorrhage may be primary, occurring shortly after childbirth, or secondary, occurring within twelve weeks' postpartum. Postpartum hemorrhage arises from many different causes, including abnormal uterine contractility, placental complications, injury due to caesarean section or uterine rupture, or congenital coagulation disorders.

The nurse assesses the mother for potential postpartum hemorrhage by taking vital signs, massaging the uterine fundus, and preventing bladder distention by encouraging the mother to empty her bladder regularly. Heart rate and blood pressure readings will let the nurse know whether the mother is hemodynamically stable or not. Massage of the uterine fundus encourages continued uterine contractions and prevents bleeding associated with a boggy fundus. **Boggy** means that the uterus is soft, not firm as when palpating a contracted muscle. Bladder distention can cause a displacement of the woman's uterus, which can interfere with proper contractions.

A patient receiving **total parenteral nutrition (TPN)** is at risk for the unexpected development of a pneumothorax. When the physician is inserting the catheter that will deliver the TPN, there is a potential for the catheter to enter the pleural space, causing air, fluids, or blood to leak into the pleural cavity. The potential development of pneumothorax, hemothorax, and hydrothorax is one of many reasons why checking the placement of lines in patients is a crucial first step to take before using them.

Observing a sterile technique when placing central lines, dialysis catheters, and other invasive devices into patients is critical. The nurse, as part of the healthcare team, works to ensure that a proper sterile technique is observed each time a sterile procedure is to occur. This helps to prevent infections from happening in patients during the placement of such lines. The nurse also supervises the process of disposing sharps such as needles into the proper sharps receptacle, placed in each patient's room in most facilities. Needlesticks from contaminated syringes can spread bloodborne infections such as HIV/AIDS, hepatitis B, and hepatitis C.

Practice Questions

1. What are the blood vessels called that carry blood back to the heart from the rest of the body?
   a. Capillaries
   b. Arteries
   c. Ventricles
   d. Veins

2. The nurse is taking a manual blood pressure reading from a patient who is seated in an armchair. Which of the following body positions should the nurse ask the patient to change in order to get the most accurate reading?
   a. Crossed legs
   b. Holding remote with hand not getting blood pressure reading
   c. Resting head on head rest
   d. Slouching

3. The nurse heard the doctor telling the patient how he needed to change his diet and get more exercise to better manage his diabetes. The nurse knows that the patient did not want to hear this and that the patient has been vocal in the past about not needing to change anything about his lifestyle. The nurse senses that the patient feels angry and frustrated by his conversation with the doctor. The patient is very agitated when the nurse comes to collect vital signs and tells her that he thinks she is lazy. Which defense mechanism is the patient displaying?
   a. Intellectualization
   b. Undoing
   c. Reaction formation
   d. Displacement

4. The nurse walks into the room where the patient is clutching his chest, sweating, and appears short of breath. The patient reports he is experiencing chest pain that is crushing and severe, with some pain in his left arm as well. The nurse knows that this type of chest pain is most likely associated with which following medical condition?
   a. Myocardial infarction
   b. Gastroesophageal reflux
   c. Pneumonia
   d. Pleuritis

5. The action created by a drug is known as what?
   a. Pharmacology
   b. Side effect
   c. Adverse reaction
   d. Intended effect

6. Which assessment technique would the nurse employ to obtain subjective data?
   a. Auscultation
   b. Palpation
   c. Review of allergies
   d. Patient interview

7. Which statement best describes the evaluation phase of the nursing process?
    a. Subjective, objective, and psychosocial data are gathered in this phase.
    b. Nursing diagnoses are formulated during the evaluation phase.
    c. Evaluation happens across the continuum of the nursing process.
    d. This phase often begins with educating the patient on expected outcomes.

8. A patient is admitted with prolonged vomiting, greater than 3 days. The nurse knows this patient will need what type of therapy to counteract a dangerous result of prolonged vomiting?
    a. Intravenous (IV) fluids
    b. Antibacterial medications
    c. Anti-nausea medications
    d. Physical therapy

9. The nurse walks into a patient's room and witnesses the patient violently convulsing with rigid muscles. The patient is completely unconscious. The nurse immediately recognizes this is what type of seizure?
    a. Myoclonic
    b. Absence
    c. Grand Mal
    d. Tonic

10. The nurse looks for which of the following signs that the patient is having an allergic reaction after administering a drug?
    a. Aching and stiffness
    b. Coughing and fever
    c. Fever and chills
    d. Itching and rash

11. The nurse knows that which type of the following electrolyte supplements is contraindicated if the patient is on an ACE inhibitor such as lisinopril?
    a. Magnesium
    b. Calcium
    c. Potassium
    d. Sodium

12. When administering a blood-thinning drug such as warfarin, the nurse will be mindful of which type of synergistic drug that could put the patient at risk for excessive bleeding?
    a. Aspirin
    b. Lasix
    c. Lisinopril
    d. Protonix

13. When preparing a patient for the insertion of a central venous access device (CVAD), the nurse explains that the benefits of a CVAD include all except which of the following?
    a. Easier-to-obtain frequent blood draws
    b. Administration of large amounts of medications and fluids
    c. Decreased peripheral sticks and peripheral inflammation
    d. Decreased risk of infection

14. Before using a patient's newly placed PICC line, the nurse knows which test must be performed?
    a. CT scan
    b. Chest X-ray
    c. MRI
    d. Ultrasound

15. Which of the following CVADs is an example of a nontunneled catheter?
    a. Groshong's
    b. Subclavian
    c. Small-bore
    d. Hickman's

16. The nurse has a patient who reports that he is 155 pounds. The nurse needs to record the patient's weight in kilograms. Knowing that 1 kilogram is equal to 2.2 pounds, the nurse then calculates the patient's weight to be what in kilograms?
    a. 60 kg
    b. 70 kg
    c. 341 kg
    d. 300 kg

17. The patient has an order for 240 mg of Tylenol for her pediatric patient. Tylenol comes in 160 mg per 5 mL. How many milliliters does the nurse administer to the patient?
    a. 7.5 mL
    b. 5 mL
    c. 12.5 mL
    d. 10 mL

18. Which of the following will provide the nurse with lists of generic and brand name medications, expected outcomes, and is maintained by an expert panel of medical practitioners?
    a. Patient medication list from home
    b. Facility procedure manual
    c. Formulary
    d. Electronic health record

19. When giving an intramuscular injection of the pneumococcal vaccine, the nurse selects the deltoid muscle as the site of injection. What technique can the nurse use to avoid leakage of the injected fluid into the subcutaneous tissue?
    a. Aspiration
    b. Injection at a 45 degree angle
    c. Z-track
    d. Massaging the site

20. When administering a medication, the nurse observes all except which of the following rights?
    a. Right medication
    b. Right medical facility
    c. Right timeframe
    d. Right person

21. Which term refers to a route of medication administration other than through the gastrointestinal tract?
    a. Parenteral
    b. Enteral
    c. Motor
    d. Buccal

22. The nurse is having her annual tuberculosis exam, or Mantoux test, performed. This test, which entails the injection of TB proteins or antigens, involves which route of administration?
    a. Subcutaneous
    b. Intrathecal
    c. Intradermal
    d. Sublingual

23. The nurse is assessing a patient's IV access site and finds it to be cool and swollen. The IV pump is beeping, and fluid appears to be leaking around the site. The nurse suspects which of the following IV therapy complications?
    a. Clot formation
    b. Fluid overload
    c. Infection
    d. Infiltration

24. The nurse is administering total parenteral nutrition (TPN) to the patient for the first time. He knows that he should administer the medication at which of the following rates?
    a. Slowly, at 50 percent of the prescribed dosage
    b. Quickly, at double the prescribed dosage
    c. Quickly, at three times the prescribed dosage
    d. Slowly, at 25 percent of the prescribed dosage

25. The nurse needs to assess a normal, uncomplicated patient in the doctor's office for a yearly physical. Which is the best spot to assess for this patient's pulse?
    a. Radial
    b. Femoral
    c. Popliteal
    d. Carotid

26. The patient reports that he feels dizzy and lightheaded when he stands up after sitting for a long time. What would be the appropriate intervention performed by the nurse to assess the cause of these symptoms?
    a. Taking the patient's temperature
    b. Observing the patient's rate of breathing and effort of breathing
    c. Assessing bilateral radial pulses and comparing strength
    d. Lying/sitting/standing blood pressure readings

27. The nurse is educating a female client who is to undergo a mammography. Which of the following statements would not be appropriate regarding mammography education?
    a. "This test allows the practitioner to visualize small lumps that they may not have been able to palpate."
    b. "It is recommended that you get a mammography once every year after the age of 40 for early detection of breast cancer."
    c. "The mammography is a type of computed tomography used to visualize the breast tissue."
    d. "This test takes X-ray images of the breast tissue, identifying any masses that may be cancerous."

28. A patient is admitted to the hospital from the emergency department with stomach pain and blood emesis. The nurse knows that which of the following tests is likely to be performed on the patient based on their symptoms?
    a. Sigmoidoscopy
    b. Upper endoscopy
    c. Anoscopy
    d. Colonoscopy

29. Which of the following lab values suggests the client is experiencing hypokalemia?
    a. 3.2 mEq/L
    b. 3.5 mEq/L
    c. 5.0 mEq/L
    d. 5.5 mEq/L

30. Which of the following terms refers to a state in which the client has a lower than normal count of platelet cells?
    a. Neutropenia
    b. Anemia
    c. Thrombocytopenia
    d. Leukopenia

31. The nurse in the ICU takes over for a patient who has been experiencing a respiratory acidosis. The nurse checks the daily labs and finds which of the following values that suggests the patient is still acidotic?
    a. 7.38 pH
    b. 7.25 pH
    c. 7.42 pH
    d. 7.48 pH

32. The nurse knows that all except which of the following factors put a patient at risk for aspiration?
    a. Difficulty swallowing and weakened gag reflex
    b. Liver failure
    c. Weakened upper and lower esophageal sphincter reflexes
    d. Enteral feedings

33. The nurse is assessing a patient for possible risk factors for developing cancer. The patient reports a longtime smoking habit that she has struggled to kick. The nurse knows that this risk factor puts the patient most at risk for developing all except which of the following cancers?
    a. Larynx
    b. Esophagus
    c. Lung
    d. Breast

34. The nurse caring for a patient postcardiac catheterization will perform which specific intervention to monitor for the development of life-threatening dysrhythmias?
    a. Keep the patient flat on their back for at least 6 hours postprocedure.
    b. Take regular vital signs, especially heart rate and blood pressure.
    c. Regularly observe the patient's ECG via cardiac monitoring, according to facility protocol.
    d. Regularly observe the incision site, looking for bruising, swelling, and redness.

35. A patient reports to the nurse that he is feeling anxious and dizzy, and his heart is racing. Which system-specific assessment will the nurse perform to investigate these symptoms?
    a. Assess the circulatory system by grading the patient's pitting edema.
    b. Obtain and compare bilateral peripheral pulses.
    c. Assess the patient's level of consciousness and motor and sensory function.
    d. Compare the patient's muscular strength bilaterally by having him push against resistance.

36. A patient is in the outpatient clinic for a same-day mole removal. The nurse knows which type of anesthetic is most appropriate for this type of procedure?
    a. Nerve block
    b. Local
    c. Regional
    d. General

37. The nurse assesses drainage from a client's chest tube for all except which of the following?
    a. Consistency
    b. Quantity
    c. Rate
    d. Color

38. The nurse is caring for a client who recently underwent radiation therapy to his abdomen. Based on the location of the radiation, the nurse expects which of the following side effects?
    a. Diarrhea
    b. Fatigue
    c. Trembling
    d. Muscle aches

39. A woman who has entered her 24th week of pregnancy is preparing to take the oral glucose tolerance test, which will screen for which condition of pregnancy?
    a. Hyperemesis gravidarum
    b. Preeclampsia
    c. Iron-deficiency anemia
    d. Gestational diabetes

40. The nurse has a client who has recently undergone abdominal surgery with a large incision site. The nurse knows that which of the following is *not* a sign that the wound has become infected?
    a. Redness
    b. Coolness
    c. Heat
    d. Swelling

41. When reviewing their knowledge of the stages of infections, the nurse knows that which period precedes the first symptoms of the infection?
    a. Entry of pathogen
    b. Colonization of organism
    c. Incubation period
    d. Convalescent period

42. The nurse is looking over the patient's lab values for the day. He notices that one lab parameter has gone up significantly, signaling a possible infectious process at work. Which lab parameter is he likely drawing this conclusion from?
    a. Blood urea nitrogen
    b. Hematocrit
    c. Neutrophils
    d. Sodium level

43. A patient needs invasive hemodynamic monitoring as they are being admitted to the ICU for hemorrhagic shock. The nurse will expect an order for which type of line to be inserted?
    a. PICC line
    b. Port-a-cath
    c. Dialysis catheter
    d. Right-heart catheter

44. Which of the following hemodynamic parameters is measured in beats per minute per meter squared of the patient's body surface area?
    a. Cardiac index
    b. Cardiac output
    c. Mean arterial pressure
    d. Stroke volume

45. The nurse notices a patient's medication list contains a drug that is likely to lower her pulmonary vascular resistance. Which type of medicine is the nurse likely looking at to draw this conclusion?
    a. Diuretic
    b. Morphine
    c. Nitrate
    d. Calcium channel blocker

46. A patient with a Swan-Ganz catheter in the ICU is being assessed by the nurse for the first time during the shift. The nurse notices which number on the hemodynamic profile is abnormal and needs further investigating?
  a. Mean arterial pressure: 75 mmHg
  b. Cardiac output: 2L/min
  c. Central venous pressure: 5 mmHg
  d. Pulmonary capillary wedge pressure: 6 mmHg

47. As the nurse is receiving reports on her patients for the day, she knows that which patient will take top priority in being assessed and treated?
  a. 33-year-old female who is nauseous and needs an antiemetic administered
  b. 49-year-old female who is scheduled for a cardiac catheterization and needs to sign the informed consent
  c. 55-year-old male who is being discharged later today and has a question about his care at home
  d. 78-year-old male who is complaining of shortness of breath

48. The doctor has ordered a nasogastric (NG) tube to be placed by the nurse for gastric lavage. After placing the NG, the nurse expects which of the following tests to be performed to confirm the placement of the tube?
  a. Aspiration of laryngeal secretions for pH testing
  b. Chest radiograph
  c. Abdominal ultrasound
  d. Manual palpation of the gastric body for the catheter tip

49. A client has just had a catheter placed in their chest for the purpose of total parenteral nutrition (TPN) administration. The chest X-ray shows that the catheter has slipped and caused a leakage of air into the pleural space. What is this condition called?
  a. Pneumothorax
  b. Hemothorax
  c. Hydrothorax
  d. Pneumonia

50. The nurse is caring for a woman who is 3 hours' postpartum. The nurse takes all EXCEPT which of the following actions to prevent and monitor for postpartum hemorrhage?
  a. Massage the uterine fundus.
  b. Obtain regular vital signs, including heart rate and blood pressure.
  c. Ensure that the woman avoids bladder distention.
  d. Encourage the woman to perform her Kegel exercises.

Answer Explanations

1. D: The blood vessels that carry blood back to the heart are called veins. Capillaries are where arteries and veins meet to exchange oxygen and carbon dioxide at the tissue level. Arteries carry blood away from the heart to the tissues of the body. Ventricles are a type of blood pumping chamber in the heart, although there are also ventricles in the brain that serve a different purpose.

2. A: The nurse should politely ask the patient to uncross her legs to get the most accurate blood pressure reading. Crossed legs can affect the blood pressure reading, since blood vessels can be compressed. Holding a remote, slouching, and resting the head will not compress any major arteries or veins, thus will not affect the blood pressure reading, so there is no need for the nurse to correct these positions.

3. D: The patient is displaying displacement, in which he is taking his negative feelings toward the doctor and expressing them toward the nurse, unreasonably. Reaction formation is when a person feels negatively but reacts positively. Intellectualization is when a person focuses on minute details of the situation rather than coping with the negative emotions associated with it. Undoing is when a person has done something wrong and acts excessively in the opposite way to redeem themselves of prior wrongdoing.

4. A: The chest pain described is most likely cardiac in origin, so the patient could be experiencing a myocardial infarction, or heart attack. Chest pain associated with gastroesophageal reflux is more often described as a burning sensation, without the other symptoms described. Pneumonia and pleuritis may both cause the patient to have a different type of chest pain, in which a sharp, stabbing sensation is felt upon breathing.

5. A: The nurse should review the pharmacology, or the action created by a drug, of the patient's current medications. Knowing the pharmacological effects of these medications and those of the scheduled preoperative medications can help keep the patient safe. Side effects and adverse reactions are included in the pharmacology. The intended effect does not include possible side effects or adverse reactions.

6. D: The patient interview adds subjective assessment data to the nurse's findings. Auscultation, palpation, and review of allergies yield objective assessment data.

7. C: The final phase of the nursing process is evaluation. Evaluation happens across the continuum of the nursing process, not just at the end. The nurse frequently evaluates the effectiveness of care plans, adjusts as necessary, and reevaluates. Data is collected during the assessment phase. Nursing diagnoses are formulated in the diagnosis phase. The implementation phase often begins with educating the patient on expected outcomes.

8. A: One of the most serious side effects of prolonged vomiting is dehydration, thus the patient needs fluids to restore him back to a more normal, hydrated status. Antibiotics may be used in a case of severe bacterial infection, but not likely in this case. Anti-nausea medication will likely be used to stop the vomiting but will do nothing to fix the resulting dehydration. Physical therapy is not typically necessary for such a case unless the patient was bedridden for a long time, which does not seem to be the case here.

9. C: This type of seizure with muscle rigidity, convulsions, and unconsciousness is called a grand mal seizure. An absence seizure involves a brief loss of consciousness where the patient may stare into space. A myoclonic seizure involves the body making jerking movements. A tonic seizure is characterized by rigidity and stiffness of the muscles.

10. D: Itching and the development of a rash are signs that the patient is having an allergic reaction to a medication. These two symptoms are signs that the body's inflammatory response has been kicked into overdrive because of a drug allergy. The other symptoms listed are not commonly associated with an allergic reaction.

11. C: Patients on lisinopril are at risk for hyperkalemia; thus, the supplementation of potassium is to be done under careful clinical supervision or not at all. Lisinopril causes the body to hold on to more potassium than usual, and in renal-compromised patients, the risk for hyperkalemia is ever present. The other three electrolytes mentioned can cause toxic states in the body in low and high concentrations but not as life threatening as the cardiac disturbances a hyperkalemic state can bring about.

12. A: The platelet-aggregation inhibitor, aspirin, has the potential to work synergistically with warfarin in a way that would increase the patient's risk for bleeding. Synergistic drugs work together in ways that enhance each one's individual effectiveness, sometimes for the patient's good but sometimes to the patient's detriment. Lasix, lisinopril, and Protonix are other frequently used drugs that would not work synergistically with warfarin in any significant hemostatic way.

13. D: Though there are many benefits to the CVAD, it still poses a risk for infection to the patient, even more so than a peripheral device, as it is more centric to the patient's circulatory system and vital organs. The CVAD has many benefits, including being able to provide easy access for blood draws; the capacity to deliver large amounts of blood, drugs, and fluids to the patient; and decreasing peripheral sticks and the inflammation that goes along with those. The use of the CVAD must be carefully decided, weighing the pros against the cons.

14. B: The patient must have a chest X-ray to confirm correct placement of the PICC line. Correct placement will show that the PICC line tip is resting in the distal end of the superior vena cava, right at the cavoatrial junction. The other three imaging studies are not routinely ordered to confirm PICC line placement.

15. B: A subclavian catheter is an example of a nontunneled central venous access device. Jugular and femoral lines are other examples of nontunneled catheters. Examples of tunneled catheters include Groshong's, small-bore, Hickman's, and Broviac's.

16. B: The correct conversion of the patient's weight is 70 kilograms. This answer is found by dividing the weight in pounds, 155, by the number of kilograms that are found in a pound, 2.2, which gives the nurse the correct answer. The other three answers are incorrect.

17. A: The correct answer is 7.5 mL. The answer is obtained by using the desired dose divided by the amount on hand multiplied by the volume, or the D/H x V formula. By taking the desired dose (240 mg), dividing it by the amount on hand (160mg), and multiplying it by the volume the drug is formulated in (5 mL), the nurse will then arrive at the correct dose of 7.5 mL.

18. C: The formulary is an excellent tool the nurse can access that will give them up-to-date information about drugs, their safety and effectiveness, their generic and brand names, and is maintained and updated by a team of experts. The patient medication list is a separate document and is not used for broad medication reference. The facility procedure manual will give the nurse information about how to respond to a fire and other such facility information but not information in reference to medications. The electronic health record is a document used specifically in reference to the patient but not for general informational purposes.

19. C: The Z-track technique is used to avoid medication leakage into the subcutaneous tissue. The nurse pulls the skin downward or upward, injects the medication at a 90 degree angle, and then releases the skin to create the zigzag track. Aspiration is a technique that may be used to ensure the nurse has not accidentally accessed a vein or artery when injecting but is not necessary for routine injections into the deltoid where there are no large vessels. Massaging the injection site may cause leakage and irritation.

20. B: Right medical facility is not part of the six patient medication administration rights. The six rights are the following: right medication, right route, right timeframe, right patient, right dosage, and right documentation.

21. A: *Parenteral* is the term that refers to any route outside of the gastrointestinal tract, also referred to as the *alimentary canal*. *Motor* is not a viable answer choice. *Enteral* also refers to the GI tract or intestines. *Buccal* refers to the cheeks, or inner oral cavity.

22. C: The Mantoux test, or annual tuberculosis test most nurses must undergo as part of facility policy, involves an intradermal injection of the TB proteins or antigens. The dermal layer of the skin is accessed, as opposed to a subcutaneous injection, which goes deeper into the skin. An intrathecal injection goes into the spinal canal. *Sublingual* refers to a route of administration of a drug that will go under the tongue.

23. D: The IV appears to have become dislodged, causing an infiltration of the surrounding tissues. This is marked by coolness and swelling of the site. The leaking of the fluid also suggests an infiltration of the IV site. A clot in the line would cause an obstruction to IV fluids and medications but not swelling of the surrounding tissue. Fluid overload would present systemic symptoms in the patient rather than localized swelling and coolness. An infected site would be warm rather than cool.

24. A: The TPN should be administered slowly, at 50 percent of the prescribed dosage, when beginning therapy. TPN comes with many possible complications as the body adjusts to this different source of nutrition, so starting slowly is recommended. The other three answers are incorrect.

25. A: The nurse assessing a stable, uncomplicated patient will most likely go for the radial pulse. The femoral pulse, found in the groin, would be an invasion of the patient's privacy and not appropriate for this type of routine checkup. The popliteal pulse, found behind the knee, would be an unusual and hard-to-reach spot for a routine pulse assessment. The carotid pulse is reserved for emergency situations such as cardiac arrest to assess for pulselessness before starting cardiopulmonary resuscitation (CPR).

26. D: The nurse should assess for orthostatic hypotension by performing lying/sitting/standing (LSS) blood pressure readings. If the readings trend downward significantly, up to twenty points in mmHg on the systolic side, the patient probably has orthostatic hypotension. Assessing for the patient's temperature and rate of breathing and comparing bilateral radial pulses can all be performed for the sake of having additional data but do not follow the symptoms this specific patient reported.

27. C: The mammography test is a type of X-ray, not computed tomography. While CT scans may be performed, X-rays are the gold standard for early detection of breast cancer. The patient is recommended to get the test once every year after the age of 40 for early breast cancer detection. The test can pick up masses that may not be manually palpable to the patient or the practitioner.

28. B: Based on the symptoms of stomach pain and bloody emesis that the patient reported, they will likely be scheduled for an upper endoscopy. An upper endoscopy, also called an esophagogastroduodenoscopy (EGD), visualizes the internal mucosa of the upper gastrointestinal (GI) tract. A sigmoidoscopy visualizes the sigmoid portion of the colon. An anoscopy is performed to visualize the area just inside the anus. A colonoscopy is performed to assess and intervene within the entire colon, usually used for early detection of colon cancer.

29. A: A normal range for serum potassium is between 3.5 and 5.1 mEq/L; thus, 3.2 is the correct answer. 3.5 and 5.0 mEq/L suggest a normal serum potassium. A level of 5.5 mEq/L suggests a hyperkalemic state. The nurse should report hypokalemia and will prepare to administer potassium supplementation if ordered by the physician.

30. C: Thrombocytopenia means that there are a lower than normal number of platelets in the blood. The term comes from the root word "thrombocyte." The prefix "thrombo-" means clot, and the suffix "-cyte" means cell. These cells are responsible for the body's ability to stop bleeding by forming a clot. Neutropenia and leukopenia are used interchangeably, referring to a lowered white blood cell count. *Neutrophils,* the root work for *neutropenia,* are the largest portion of the white blood cells. If the neutrophils are significantly lowered, then leukopenia results, thus the interchangeability of the words. Anemia refers to a lower-than-normal count of red blood cells and reduces the body's ability to carry and deliver oxygen.

31. B: The patient with a pH value of 7.25 is still very much acidotic and needs further therapy to return them to normal. The other values listed fall in the normal range of 7.35 to 7.45 or in the alkalotic range, which is greater than 7.45.

32. B: Liver failure is not a direct correlation with a patient's risk for aspirating. A weakened gag or swallow reflex, weakened upper and lower esophageal sphincters, and enteral feedings are all risk factors for aspiration. Patients with these risk factors should be monitored carefully during feeding times and have the head of their bed kept elevated to between 45 and 90 degrees while receiving feedings.

33. D: Breast cancer is not usually highly correlated to smoking cigarettes, although there is some evidence that smoking does not help a person's risk of avoiding breast cancer. Cancers of the mouth, throat, esophagus, and lungs are all closely correlated with a smoking habit due to their contact with the toxic inhaled smoke. The nurse notes the patient's risk factor for developing cancer in the patient medical record.

34. C: Observing and recording the patient's heart rhythm via ECG is the specific intervention necessary to monitor for the development of dysrhythmias postcardiac catheterization. All of the other interventions listed are correct postcardiac catheterization care but not specific to dysrhythmias. The nurse will keep the patient flat to assist with incision healing, take regular vital signs such as heart rate and blood pressure, and monitor for bleeding and hematoma at the incision site to evaluate the patient's overall stability.

35. B: The nurse should hone in on the cardiac system by assessing the strength and rate of the patient's pulses, comparing them bilaterally. If the rate is above normal and the quality is weak, the nurse knows that the patient's heart is working extra hard, and the reason needs to be discovered. Assessing things like pitting edema, the patient's motor and sensory function, and muscular strength are not the most precise actions the nurse can take to quickly get to the bottom of the patient's symptomology. The nurse will use sound nursing judgment to determine which assessments to make on a patient and when.

36. B: A patient who is undergoing a minimally invasive procedure such as a mole removal will only need a local anesthetic such as topical lidocaine. A regional nerve block affects only one part of the body, usually targeting the epidural, spinal, or paravertebral regions. General anesthesia is used for major surgeries in which the patient needs to be rendered completely unconscious to perform the procedure.

37. C: The nurse may assess the rate of heart beats but not necessarily drainage from a chest tube. The three common parameters for assessing drainage are consistency, quantity, and color. These are all ways to monitor and record chest output.

38. A: Based on the abdominal location of the radiation therapy, it is likely that the patient will experience gastrointestinal symptoms, including diarrhea, nausea, and vomiting, as a side effect. Fatigue, trembling, and muscle aches are possible with radiation therapy but not specific to the organs of the abdomen.

39. D: The oral glucose tolerance test is performed between the 24th and 28th week of pregnancy to screen for gestational diabetes. Hyperemesis gravidarum is a severe form of morning sickness that occurs in the first trimester but sometimes continues until the third trimester. Preeclampsia is detected through blood pressure monitoring. Iron-deficiency anemia may be detected first through symptoms of fatigue, weakness, and dizziness and then confirmed with a blood test showing a low hemoglobin and hematocrit count. These components of the red blood cells are responsible for carrying oxygen to the organs and tissues of the body and can drop during pregnancy.

40. B: The classic signs of infection are redness, heat, and swelling. If the wound is cool to the touch but appears normal otherwise, that is not suggestive of a developing infection. It may be a sign of decreased blood flow to the site, but the nurse should do a full assessment before jumping to that conclusion.

41. C: The incubation period is the point in time where the organism has already invaded the person's body through a portal of entry, is multiplying, and is getting ready to manifest the first symptoms of infection. The colonization occurs right after entry into the body where the organism takes up residence in the host and prepares to multiply. The convalescent period is when the person is recovering from the illness.

42. C: Neutrophils are the major component of the white blood cells. When their count is elevated, that means the white blood cells are hard at work fighting an infectious process. The nurse would need to investigate this conclusion further, possibly getting an order to draw some blood cultures if appropriate. Blood urea nitrogen is a waste product of the body. An elevated level would suggest failing kidneys but not an infection. Hematocrit is a component of red blood cells and is not part of the body's immune system. A high sodium level is an electrolyte abnormality that may have to do with the renal system or overall patient fluid status but not an infectious process.

43. D: A right-heart catheter, also called a Swan-Ganz catheter or pulmonary artery catheter, is threaded through a patient's central veins into the superior vena cava, terminating at the pulmonary artery. This type of catheter is used for hemodynamic monitoring, giving information about the patient's preload and cardiac output. A PICC line, or peripherally inserted central catheter, can be used for medication and fluid administration but does not give information about hemodynamics. A port-a-cath is another type of central line used for similar purposes as the PICC line and can be kept in the patient for an extended period. A dialysis catheter is a long-term access device for patients receiving regular treatments of dialysis but is not used for hemodynamic monitoring.

44. A: The cardiac index reflects the quantity of blood pumped by the heart per minute per meter squared of the patient's body surface area. Cardiac output measures how much blood the heart pumps out per minute in liters. The mean arterial pressure, or MAP, shows the relationship between the amount of blood pumped out of the heart and the resistance the vascular system puts up against it. The stroke volume measures how much blood the heart pumps in milliliters per beat.

45. D: A calcium channel blocker can lower the pulmonary vascular resistance in a patient. Diuretics, morphine, and nitrates all have potent lowering effects on the systemic vascular resistance, as opposed to the pulmonary vasculature. Knowing the hemodynamic effects certain medications have is helpful in anticipating unwanted side effects and potential drug interactions.

46. B: The patient's cardiac output is very low, suggesting a possible bleed or hypotensive crisis. Normal cardiac output falls between 4 and 8 L/min. All the other values listed are within normal range. Normal mean arterial pressure is between 70 and 100 mmHg. Normal central venous pressure is between 2 and 6 mmHg. Normal pulmonary capillary wedge pressure is between 4 and 12 mmHg.

47. D: The nurse will see the patient who is complaining of shortness of breath first. Airway, breathing, and circulation are always the highest priority for the nurse to address, as they can quickly become life-threatening situations. Maintaining proper respiration is a vital function to the patient's well-being, and stabilization is necessary immediately. The woman who is nauseous and needs antiemetics such as Zofran is the second priority, as she is actively ill and there is something the nurse can do to help her symptoms. The nurse's third priority will be the patient who needs to sign the informed consent. The nurse needs to ensure she gets that signed before the patient leaves the floor, although there are nurses in the cardiac catheterization lab who can obtain the consent if need be. The patient who has a question about discharge is the last priority, as there is no immediate threat to his health and the doctor will need to see the patient before he is discharged anyway.

48. B: A chest radiograph is the test of choice to confirm the placement of a nasogastric tube. The X-ray will show whether the catheter tip is in the gastric body or not. Aspiration of stomach contents, not laryngeal secretions, with a pH test is another, less preferred way to confirm placement. The pH test may be misleading, as there may be gastric contents farther up the esophageal canal and not necessarily within the stomach in some patients with weakened sphincters. An abdominal ultrasound may show the catheter tip, but it is not the preferred method of evaluating placement. Manual palpation of the gastric body is not a way to confirm placement, as it would be very difficult to actually feel the catheter within the stomach.

49. A: A leakage of air into the pleural cavity outside of the lungs is called a *pneumothorax*. This may happen as a complication of central line placement for TPN. Hemothorax results when blood is leaked into the pleural cavity. *Hydrothorax* refers to a leakage of water into the pleural cavity. Pneumonia is an infection that forms in the lungs as the result of an infectious organism and may cause fluid to accumulate in the bases of the lungs.

50. D: Kegel exercises are performed to strengthen the pelvic floor and prevent urinary incontinence, among many other benefits. They are not specifically targeted at preventing postpartum hemorrhage, however. All three of the other options are correct. Massaging the uterine fundus will encourage uterine contractions, which will help prevent excessive bleeding. A boggy fundus is a worrisome sign. The nurse wants to feel a firm uterus, signaling healthy contractions. Monitoring vital signs, especially heart rate and blood pressure, will keep the nurse informed about the woman's hemodynamic stability. The nurse will encourage the patient to empty her bladder regularly, as bladder distention can displace the uterus and interfere with proper uterine contractions.

Index

Dear NCLEX PN Test Taker,

We would like to start by thanking you for purchasing this study guide for your NCLEX PN exam. We hope that we exceeded your expectations.

Our goal in creating this study guide was to cover all of the topics that you will see on the test. We also strove to make our practice questions as similar as possible to what you will encounter on test day. With that being said, if you found something that you feel was not up to your standards, please send us an email and let us know.

We have study guides in a wide variety of fields. If you're interested in one, try searching for it on Amazon or send us an email.

Thanks Again and Happy Testing!
Product Development Team
info@studyguideteam.com

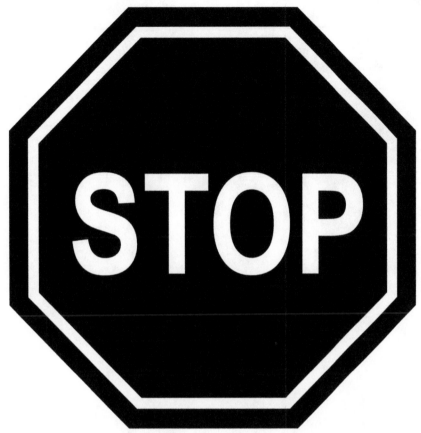

FREE Test Taking Tips DVD Offer

To help us better serve you, we have developed a Test Taking Tips DVD that we would like to give you for FREE. **This DVD covers world-class test taking tips that you can use to be even more successful when you are taking your test.**

All that we ask is that you email us your feedback about your study guide. Please let us know what you thought about it – whether that is good, bad or indifferent.

To get your **FREE Test Taking Tips DVD**, email freedvd@studyguideteam.com with "FREE DVD" in the subject line and the following information in the body of the email:

>   a. The title of your study guide.

>   b. Your product rating on a scale of 1-5, with 5 being the highest rating.

>   c. Your feedback about the study guide. What did you think of it?

>   d. Your full name and shipping address to send your free DVD.

If you have any questions or concerns, please don't hesitate to contact us at freedvd@studyguideteam.com.

Thanks again!

Amazon
5/3/2021
2020-2021

CPSIA information can be obtained
at www.ICGtesting.com
Printed in the USA
BVHW051528310321
603810BV00008B/706

Part/Chapter	Council for Exceptional Children-Division of Early Childhood	NAEYC Standards for Early Childhood Professional Preparation Programs
Chapter 5: Supporting Play for Preschool Children	**ECSE 4S1** Plan, implement, and evaluate developmentally appropriate curricula, instruction, and adaptations based on knowledge of individual children, the family, and the community. pp. 126, 135 **ECSE 5S4** Structure social environments, using peer models and proximity, and responsive adults to promote interactions among peers, parents, and caregivers. pp. 122, 126 **ECSE 7K2** Developmental and academic content. pp. 120, 130, 131 **ECSE 7S2** Plan and implement developmentally and individually appropriate curriculum. pp. 123, 128, 145	**4a** Understanding positive relationships and supportive interactions. pp. 122, 122 **4c** Using a broad repertoire of developmentally appropriate teaching and learning approaches. pp. 126, 128, 135 **4d** Reflecting on their own practice to promote positive outcomes for each child. pp. 145 **5c** Using knowledge, appropriate early learning standards, and other resources to design, implement, and evaluate meaningful challenging curricula for each child. pp. 123, 130 , 131
Chapter 6: Supporting Play in Kindergarten Classrooms	**ECSE 2S1** Apply current research to the five developmental domains, play, and temperament in learning situations. pp. 156, 160, 164 **ECSE 3S1** Develop, implement, and evaluate learning experiences and strategies. pp. 171 **ECSE 4S1** Plan, implement, and evaluate developmentally appropriate curricula, instruction, and adaptations based on knowledge of individual children, the family, and the community. pp. 171 **ECSE 5S4** Structure social environments, using peer models and proximity, and responsive adults to promote interactions among peers, parents, and caregivers. pp. 157 **ECSE 7K2** Developmental and academic content. pp. 160, 164 **ECSE 7S2** Plan and implement developmentally and individually appropriate curriculum. pp. 171	**4a** Understanding positive relationships and supportive interactions as the foundation of work with children. pp. 157, 160 **4c** Using a broad repertoire of developmentally appropriate teaching and learning approaches. pp. 160, 171 **5a** Using content knowledge and resources in academic disciplines. pp. 160, 164 **5c** Using knowledge, appropriate early learning standards, and other resources to design, implement, and evaluate meaningful challenging curricula for each child. pp. 171
PART 3: PLAY IN SCHOOL SETTINGS		
Chapter 7: Supporting Play in Primary School	**ECSE 2S1** Apply current research to the five developmental domains, play, and temperament in learning situations. pp. 191, 196 **ECSE 3S1** Develop, implement, and evaluate learning experiences and strategies that respect the diversity of infants and young children, and their families. pp. 207 **ECSE 4S1** Plan, implement, and evaluate developmentally appropriate curricula, instruction, and adaptations based on knowledge of individual children, the family, and the community. pp. 194, 208 **ECSE 5S4** Structure social environments, using peer models and proximity, and responsive adults to promote interactions among peers, parents, and caregivers. pp. 202 **ECSE 7K2** Developmental and academic content. pp. 197, 198 **ECSE 7S2** Plan and implement developmentally and individually appropriate curriculum. pp. 195, 204	**4a** Understanding positive relationships and supportive interactions as the foundation of work with children. pp. 202 **4c** Using a broad repertoire of developmentally appropriate teaching and learning approaches. pp. 191, 194, 204, 208 **5a** Using content knowledge and resources in academic disciplines. pp. 195, 197, 198 **5c** Using knowledge, appropriate early learning standards, and other resources to design, implement, and evaluate meaningful challenging curricula for each child. pp. 196, 202, 207

(Continued)

Supporting Play in Early Childhood

Environment, Curriculum, Assessment

Supporting Play in Early Childhood

Environment, Curriculum, Assessment

2nd Edition

Dorothy Justus Sluss, PhD

Professor of Early, Elementary, and Reading Education

College of Education

James Madison University

CENGAGE
Learning®

Australia • Brazil • Japan • Korea • Mexico • Singapore • Spain • United Kingdom • United States

Supporting Play in Early Childhood:
Environment, Curriculum, Assessment,
Second Edition
Dorothy Justus Sluss

Product Manager: Mark D. Kerr

Content Developer: Kassi Radomski

Content Coordinator: Sean M. Cronin

Product Assistant: Nicole Bator

Media Developer: Renee Schaaf

Market Development Manager: Kara Kindstrom

Art and Cover Direction: Carolyn Deacy,
    MPS Limited

Production Management, and Composition:
    Naman Mahisauria, MPS Limited

Manufacturing Planner: Doug Bertke

Rights Acquisitions Specialist: Thomas
    McDonough

Photo Researcher: PMG/ Venkat Narayanan

Text Researcher: PMG/ Sowmya Sankaran

Cover Image: © Susan Woog-Wagner/Photo
    Researchers/Getty Images

For product information and technology assistance, contact us at
Cengage Learning Customer & Sales Support, 1-800-354-9706

For permission to use material from this text or product,
submit all requests online at **www.cengage.com/permissions**
Further permissions questions can be e-mailed to
permissionrequest@cengage.com

Library of Congress Control Number: 2013947727

ISBN-13: 978-1-285-73515-3

ISBN-10: 1-285-73515-3

Cengage Learning
200 First Stamford Place, 4th Floor
Stamford, CT 06902
USA

Cengage Learning is a leading provider of customized learning solutions with office locations around the globe, including Singapore, the United Kingdom, Australia, Mexico, Brazil, and Japan. Locate your local office at **www.cengage.com/global**

Cengage Learning products are represented in Canada by Nelson Education, Ltd.

To learn more about Cengage Learning Solutions, visit **www.cengage.com**

Purchase any of our products at your local college store or at our preferred online store **www.cengagebrain.com**

Printed in the U.S.A.
1 2 3 4 5 6 7 17 16 15 14 13

For Maddy and Jay, who allowed me to
experience the joy of play and reminded me that
we all need to play—every day.

Brief Contents

Table of Contents

2 Play as Development 33

3 Observing and Assessing Play 57

6 Supporting Play in Kindergarten Classrooms 153

Part 3   Play in School Settings

7   Supporting Play in Primary School   189

8   Supporting Play for Children in Middle Childhood   215

9 Supporting Play for Children with Special Needs 241

Part 4 Beyond the Classroom

10 Outdoor Play for Young Children 267

Preface

Introduction

Play is fun, and for most young children, play occurs naturally. Early scholars of early childhood education recognized that children are predisposed to play—either alone or with others. For this reason, play formed the foundation of early childhood education during its infancy. Throughout the twentieth century, play was examined from a variety of disciplines using multiple perspectives. Today we know more about the benefits and value of play for young children than at any other time in history. Specifically, play contributes to cognitive, social, emotional, and physical growth and development. Support for play as a medium for learning has been established by scholars such as Piaget, Vygotsky, Bruner, Pelligrini, Reifel, Johnson, Christie, Bergen, and Smith. The most current neuroscience provides evidence for these findings. Today, high-quality early childhood education programs include courses and information about the value of play. This book was written to support the work of beginning and established teachers who want to know more about play and the implementation of a play-based program. This book was written with the needs of the following readers in mind:

- Students in early childhood education programs
- Early childhood education educators, directors, and classroom teachers
- Graduate students in education and psychology
- Parents and grandparents of young children

The Need to Play

More American children are in preschools than at any other time in this country's history. Approximately 88% of all preschool children have mothers who work outside the home (U.S. Census Bureau, 2011). The National Center for Educational Statistics (2006) reports that 36% of out-of-home care is spent in center-based care. As the traditional nursery school changes to become more focused on academic learning, play is at risk in the preschool classroom, yet play is how children learn. Play is also at risk for children over five. Many kindergarten programs are struggling to justify play. Even primary programs are affected by this focus on academic learning. Some primary programs have eliminated recess, and others have limited it to fifteen minutes at the end of the day.

It is paradoxical that although we know more about the benefits of play, teachers are challenged to justify play in today's performance-based society. This book was written to challenge this situation by providing a basis for implementing a play-based program and by providing examples of how this can be accomplished at different levels. This book is designed to provide a solid theoretical basis for play combined with program implementation for different developmental levels. The book provides a solid foundation for both beginning and returning professionals who aim to create the best possible learning experiences for children in their classroom.

Childcare Aware of America. (2012). America's most trusted child care resource. Retrieved on August 4, 2013, from http://childcareaware.org/

National Center for Educational Statistics. (2006). Digest of Education Statistics. Retrieved on July 5, 2013, from nces/ed.gov/programs/digest/d06/tables/dt06_042

U.S. Census Bureau. (2011). *Who's minding the kids? Childcare arrangements: Spring 2010—Detailed tables [Web page]. Retrieved June 7, 2013, from* http://www.census.gov/hhes/childcare/data/sipp/20 10/tables.html

Book Development

As I revised the first edition of this book, I surveyed the play landscape to assess changes that have occurred since the initial development of this book. Advocates for play are making some bold statements about the multiple values and benefits of play. At the same time, long-time scholars such as Doris Bergen, Jim Johnson, James Christie, and Anthony Pelligrini are concerned that too much is being attributed to play and that this excessive focus on the benefits of play might create a tenuous situation in the future. They remind us that care is needed in reporting research findings. It is difficult to conduct experimental research on children to prove that play impacts development. Studies such as the classic HighScope of Ypsilanti, Michigan require a great deal of time and money. For this reason, this book builds on the idea that play is *linked* to multiple benefits and positive outcomes for children while at the same time recognizing the need to always support statements with data. My goal in writing this book is to make the case for using a play-based curriculum by providing a book filled with information supported by research.

Theoretically, two major influences inform the study of play in this text. One is the view of play as progress. That is, play contributes to and fosters human growth and development. The second influence views play as valuable in and of itself. These approaches are both used to understand the value of play for young children. Although it is important to support play because it has a positive impact on development, we cannot lose sight of the value of play as a source of joy and excitement for young children.

The joy that is evident in play has influenced my professional journey. Play has always been my passion. From the time I played as a child to now, I have believed that to play is to be alive! As a classroom teacher for fourteen years, I implemented a play-based curriculum with four-year-olds, kindergarteners, and third graders in a primary school and third graders located in a classroom in a middle school. Based on my understanding of Piaget and other scholars, it seemed logical that if children naturally play and if they do, indeed, learn through play, then play should serve as the doorway to teaching and learning. Like other teacher researchers, I always watched for signs of success or failure. The success of my students year after year strengthened my resolve to place play at the core of my program. Teacher educators, reporters, and the innumerable student teachers who came through my door assured me that what I was doing was both beneficial and appropriate. My principal for so many years, Nolan Kilgore, emphasized the effectiveness of my approach.

My interest in how children learn led me out of the classroom and into a doctoral program, where I focused on how young children make sense of the world. Studying with Cosby Rogers and Janet Sawyers strengthened my view of the important role of play in learning and creativity. As I read and studied, I was primarily influenced by Piaget, Kami, Kohlberg and DeVries, and Fosnot. Later, the work of Vygotsky, Bruner, Gardner, Vivian Paley, and Tharp and Gallimore inspired my interest in sociocultural theory. Travels to the schools of Reggio Emilia, Italy, introduced me to a program that truly valued play as a legitimate activity. Teachers and parents delighted in the child's play and discovery. Everything I read and studied brought me back to play. If children learn through play, then it seems logical to use play as pedagogy.

Play as Pedagogy

If play is pedagogy, then play that dominates each age level should be used to guide curriculum development. That is, if very young children are exploring the world through sensorimotor play, it seems that encouraging practice play should be the goal of programs for infants and toddlers. In the same way, if pretense dominates the preschool and kindergarten years, then dramatic and sociodramatic play should be a major part of the curriculum. If the dominant play of primary age and middle childhood children involves games with rules, then these should be used to inform the curriculum. This approach seems logical and fully justified, yet there are no textbooks that use this approach to inform program development. This book fills this void by providing a view that uses play to inform curriculum.

Organization of the Text

The text is organized on the premise that play is pedagogy. It provides a view of play that includes all ages, birth to age twelve, and separates information in terms of age and developmental levels. This separation is designed to foster understanding of the holistic nature of play at each developmental level.

Part I lays a theoretical and empirical foundation for valuing the role of play, understanding the developmental progression of play, and knowing how to observe and assess play. Chapter 1 considers the value of play, the definition of play, and the multiple dimension of play for *all* children. It provides a look at the history of play scholarship. Although this is similar to a walk through the history of early childhood education, play is the subject of the investigation. Knowing the history of the study of play provides a foundation for implementing a play-based program. Chapter 2 looks at the benefits of play in terms of the physical, social, cognitive, and emotional domains of development. This chapter sets the stage for considering play and its multiple dimensions as a source of curriculum. Chapter 3 describes techniques for observing and evaluating play in order to access the impact of the context and interactions on outcomes. These three chapters provide empirical evidence for supporting play as pedagogy.

Part II builds on this foundation by providing information about how to design, implement, and assess programs in early childhood education (infancy through kindergarten). Chapter 4 emphasizes the importance of developing high-quality programs for infants and toddlers. As children develop, they move into preschool—the focus of Chapter 5. Follow the children from preschool into kindergarten in Chapter 6 where they learn how to conduct project-based learning (PBL).

Part III moves the reader out of the early childhood setting and into school settings. Chapter 7 shows how a play-based program can be implemented in a primary school. Chapter 8 extends this concept into middle childhood, and Chapter 9 considers the important role of play for children who have special needs.

The last section of the book, Part IV, presents two chapters devoted to play beyond the classroom. Literally, outdoor play occurs beyond the parameters of the classroom; metaphorically, the role of advocacy for children occurs outside of and beyond the classroom. Chapter 10 includes a focused look at outdoor play and the vital role of the natural environment for children. Chapter 11 looks at the impact of current trends and issues on professionalism and advocacy.

All of the chapters in this book provide necessary information for implementing appropriate, challenging play environments; curriculum; and assessments in early, primary, and middle childhood educational settings.

New Content and Special Features

The second edition of *Supporting Play: Curriculum, Environment, Assessment* builds on the first edition by updating and adding new features that are designed to increase the knowledge base of the user and to enhance the usefulness of the text.

- **NEW! Emphasis on national standards** from the National Association for the Education of Young Children (NAEYC) Program Standards and the Council for Exceptional Children—Division of Early Childhood Professional Preparation Standards (CEC-DEC). These standards are integrated throughout the text to help students make connections between the standards and what they are learning in the text. You'll find a list of relevant standards at the beginning of each chapter; standards icons within the chapter indicate where standards-related content is found; and a Standards Correlation Chart on the inside front and back covers provides a complete list of the standards listed throughout the book.

- **Learning objectives** at the beginning of each chapter correlate with main headings within the chapter and the summary at the end of the chapter. The outcomes highlight what students need to know to process and understand the information in the chapter. After completing the chapter, students should be able to demonstrate how they can use and apply their new knowledge and skills.

- **NEW! TeachSource Video** boxes highlight footage of classroom settings to help students relate key chapter content to real-life scenarios. Critical-thinking questions provide opportunities for in-class or online discussion and reflection.

- **NEW! Digital Downloads** of forms, important lists, and more are found in the text and can be downloaded from CourseMate and printed out, so students can review key concepts or use them in the classroom. (CourseMate can be bundled with the student text. Instructors, please contact your Cengage sales representative for information on accessing CourseMate.)

- **NEW! Did You Get It?** quizzes at the end of each major heading help students measure their performance against the learning objectives in each chapter. One question for each learning objective is featured in the textbook. Students are encouraged to go to CengageBrain.com to take the full quiz and check their understanding of each chapter.

- **NEW! Chapter 3, Observing and Assessing Play,** reflects the increased emphasis on using data to inform practice and understanding how to look at play.

- NEW! *chapter on middle childhood* shows how to use play to enhance the core academic areas of science, technology, engineering, and mathematics (STEM) in the elementary classroom.
- NEW *and expanded* information on current topics such as neuroscience, media, technology, special needs, gender, and cultural issues.
- NEW! *From the Experts* feature in each chapter provides depth and unique perspectives.
- Expanded PlayScapes at the beginning of each chapter are miniature case studies that focus on situations faced by families today. These stories are followed by a discussion at the beginning of the chapter and revisited in the PlayScape Reflection at the end of the chapter.
- Play Provocation, or motivation to play, is addressed at the beginning of each chapter in response to the PlayScape. This connects the reader to the case study and the new material in the text.
- A chapter summary is located at the end of each chapter. Points raised in the objectives are embedded in the chapter summary. This reinforces and confirms the students' understanding of the material.
- Key terms necessary for understanding content are provided at the end of the chapter and are located in the glossary.
- Technology and Internet Resources provide current websites and helpful computer programs related to the content of chapter.
- *New and expanded* activities

1. InClass Labs
Activities based on cooperative learning are available that require active participation.

2. Research and Inquiry
Activities that foster research and inquiry skills are designed for each chapter. This is especially beneficial for students who are interested in moving beyond the textbook.

3. Service Learning
Experiences that extend learning through service in the field are included at the end of each chapter. Interaction with schools and community agencies is an especially important part of this experience.

4. Family Connections
Activities that build relationships with families are included. These connect students with families.

5. Play Advocacy
Advocacy activities begin with awareness activities (Chapter 1) and progress to action (Chapter 11). Activities range from group presentations to community activities.

Supplements

- Online Instructor's Manual and Test Bank contains information to assist the instructor in designing the course, including sample syllabi, discussion questions, teaching and learning activities, field experiences, learning objectives, and additional online resources. For assessment support, the updated Test Bank includes true/false, multiple-choice, matching, short-answer, and essay questions for each chapter.

- **Cengage Learning Testing Powered by COGNERO** is a flexible, online system that allows instructors to author, edit, and manage test bank content from multiple Cengage Learning solutions; create multiple test versions in an instant; and deliver tests from their LMS, their classroom, or wherever they want.

- **Online PowerPoint® Slides** for each chapter assist instructors with their lectures by providing concept coverage the use of images, figures, and tables directly from the textbook.

- **CourseMate** for *Supporting Play in Early Childhood: Environment, Curriculum, Assessment*, 2nd edition, brings course concepts to life with interactive learning, study, and exam preparation tools that support the printed textbook. Students can access a new integrated eBook, Digital Downloads, flashcards, TeachSource Videos and other videos, and more. Also new is Engagement Tracker, a first-of-its-kind tool that allows teachers to monitor student engagement in the course. The accompanying instructor website, available through login.cengage.com, offers access to password-protected resources such as PowerPoint® lecture slides and the online Instructor's Manual with Test Bank.

About the Author

Dorothy Louise Justus Sluss is a Professor in the Department of Early, Elementary, and Reading Education housed in the College of Education at James Madison University. She has been involved early childhood education for over three decades. The first part of her career was spent in public schools and the second part in higher education. As a public school classroom teacher, she taught kindergarten and primary grades, and she started a program for four-year-olds in public schools. As a classroom teacher, she served as an advocate for young children through her work in numerous professional organizations.

The second half of her career was spent in higher education. She served on the faculties of East Tennessee State University, Clemson University, and the College of William and Mary. She was co-PI (principal investigator) on the grant Project TIES, Towards Inclusion in Early Childhood, and served as the initial liaison for Professional Development Schools at Mountain View and Clemson Elementary Schools. She initiated and chaired the research forum for the NAEYC Play, Practice and Policy Interest Group at NAEYC for the first decade of its sixteen-year existence. In 2013, she received the Brian Sutton Smith award for lifetime achievement in play research from The Association for the Study of Play (TASP). She was recently elected President of the Association for the Child's Right to Play, International Play Association/USA.

During her career, she has written numerous book chapters and articles that have been published in *Childhood Education, Young Children, Journal of Research in Early Childhood Education, The Allen Review,* and the *Journal of the National Association of Early Childhood Teacher Educators.*

Acknowledgments

This book is a result of many years of working with young children and their families. Like all good ideas, it took a great deal of support for this book to become reality. Special appreciation is extended to those who provided support, knowledge, and, above all, patience. Thanks to Mark Kerr, senior product manager, and his staff at Cengage Learning, who turned my ideas about a second edition into a reality, and a very special note of appreciation to my development editor, Kassi Radomski. Without Kassi, this book would never have been started, written, or finished.

My play studies have allowed me to work with some very special people. For the first edition, appreciation was expressed to the faculty, staff, and students at Clemson University and the upstate area of South Carolina. Special thanks to Clemson, Code, West End, and Ravenel Elementary Schools in South Carolina. These exceptional schools graciously allowed me to share their excellence with others. The second edition has been created in Virginia at James Madison University (JMU). Special thanks to to friends and colleagues at JMU, John Wayland Elementary School, and Winchester First Presbyterian Weekday School. I am especially indebted to family, friends, and colleagues who supported and encouraged me throughout this process.

Reviewers

I would also like to thank the reviewers of the previous edition whose suggestions and critiques provided the basis for many of the changes you see in this second edition: Jacqueline Batey, University of North Florida; Andy Beigel, Keuka College; Marilyn Bruckman, Tennessee Tech University; Susan Eliason, Bridgewater State University; Deborah Farrer, California University of Pennsylvania; Sherry Forrest, Craven Community College; Deborah Hwa-Froelich, St. Louis University; Lee Ann Jolley, Tennessee Tech University; Dennis Kirchen, Dominican University; Sharon Little, South Piedmont Community College; Rebecca Payne, John Wood Community College; Cathy Rikhye, Teacher's College, Columbia University; Angela Salmon, Florida International University; and Melinda Swafford, Tennessee Tech University.

Avenue for Feedback

Every attempt has been made to ensure accuracy throughout the book. Due to the rapidly changing nature of knowledge, some updates may have occurred. If you have suggestions, information, concerns, or questions regarding this text, please contact the author via email at djsluss@jmu.edu. Send all written comments to: Dr. Dorothy Justus Sluss, MSC 6309, 3220E Memorial Hall, James Madison University, Harrisonburg, VA 22655.

Dorothy Louise Justus Sluss

1 Theories and Foundations of PLAY

© Cengage Learning 2015

Knowing and understanding the theories and foundations of play is critically important for anyone who is interested in teaching young children. The first three chapters of this book provide a basis for knowing and understanding how to use play as pedagogy in the classroom. The first chapter focuses on making the case for play, the second chapter provides the rationale for promoting play, and the final chapter in this section focuses on developing skills in capturing the essence of children's play through observation and assessment. The three chapters in the first part make the case for play so that it can be viewed as a positive force for learning and improving the child's quality of life.

1 Valuing PLAY

STANDARDS COVERED IN THIS CHAPTER

Council of Exceptional Children—Division of Early Childhood Standards CEC DEC

ECSC 2K1 Theories of typical and atypical early childhood development

NAEYC Program Standards naeyc

1a Knowing and understanding young children's characteristics and needs

1b Knowing and understanding multiple influences on early development and learning

1c Using developmental knowledge to create healthy, respectful, supportive, and challenging learning environments

✳ LEARNING OBJECTIVES ✳

1-1 Identify current factors that affect the state of play in the United States.

1-2 List global influences that impact the play of young children.

1-3 Explain common characteristics of play.

1-4 Compare three different theories of play.

1-5 Describe the impact of culture and ethnicity on play.

PLAYSCAPE: CASE STUDY

Felicia carefully climbed the steps to the slide. When she got to the top, she slid down while laughing loudly. When she reached the bottom, she ran to the steps, climbed up the steps again, and slid down the slide again. She did this until her father intervened, "Felicia, its time to go, baby." Felicia ran to the top of the steps and shouted, "Watch me go down sideways!" She went down one more time and begged to do it again.

Explaining Play Behaviors

Felicia's behavior is familiar to many adults who remember playing until exhausted or watching others do so. Though children need little provocation or motivation to play, the slide served as a motivator for Felicia's play. Her play is further supported by her father, who placed her in a context designed to stimulate play. Felicia's play is typical of play behaviors exhibited by young children who live in areas that have accessible playgrounds and who have parents or other adults who will take them to these sites. Adults who observe children play frequently witness these paradoxical behaviors during play. Children are so tired that they cannot stand, but they cannot stop playing, and they will not stop laughing. This *pleasure*, this joy is a part of the essence of play for young children.

✳ 1-1 State of Play in America

The United States has a love/hate relationship with play, which has its roots in the founding of this country. "For a culture built as ours is, on the Protestant ethic of work and achievement, play presents a problem" (Bronfenbrenner, 1979, p. xv). We distinguish play from nonplay or work and value work more than play. This has been a concern for more than three decades. On November 20, 1989, the General Assembly of the United Nations ratified Article 31 of The Convention of the Rights of the Child. It states that:

1. Parties recognize the right of the child to rest and leisure, to engage in play and recreational activities appropriate to the age of the child, and to participate freely in cultural life and the arts.

2. Parties shall respect and promote the right of the child to participate fully in cultural and artistic life and shall encourage the provision of appropriate and equal opportunities for cultural, artistic, recreational, and leisure activity.

Acknowledgment of the value of play by so many nations is powerful. In the United States, Article 31 is supported by groups such as the National Council of Juvenile and Family Court Judges (NCJFCJ), Convention on the Rights of the Child (CRC), the International Play Association/USA (IPA/USA), and National Association for the Education of Young Children (NAEYC). To date, the United States and Somalia are the only countries that have not ratified Article 31.

David Elkind, a well-known psychologist, first expressed his concern about this valuation of work over play in *The Hurried Child* in 1981. He noted that American children are being rushed through childhood with little time to play. He again voiced concern in 1987 in *Miseducation* when he stated that children do not have time for the journey through childhood. In his twenty-fifth anniversary edition of *The Hurried Child* (2007), he focused on the impact of technology and other societal forces on the young child's world. With his book *The Power of Play: Learning Comes Naturally* (2007), he focuses on the true power of play and discusses how parents and teachers can advocate for play. Elkind's most recent admonition to parents and teachers to value play for the sake of play is as important today as it was when it was first delivered in 1981.

So, what is the state of play in America today? Is it valued? Are children playing? Factors that support play and those that are barriers to play are listed in the sections below. You can use these factors to examine play in your own community.

1-1a Support for Play

1. **Media, print, and Internet resources** There is a proliferation of play literature in the popular press and academic world that reflects an interest in play by scholars, advocates, educators, and parents (Doherty, 2012; Saracho, 2011; Wilson, 2012). Books and journals are not the only source of information. Most adults can now easily access the Internet, which extends and expands their knowledge of play levels and activities. Parents seeking additional information about development can easily access websites, such as Zero to Three, which include information about how very young children play.

2. **Research and scholarship** Three centuries of research support the value of play. Scholars of play in the twenty-first century have examined play from a variety of lens and have found a great deal of evidence to support play (Bergen, 2002; Bergen & Fromberg, 2009; Frost, Wortham, & Reifel, 2012). More recent studies in neuroscience provide evidence that play has a positive impact on neurological functioning (Buchsbaum, Bridgers, Weisberg, & Gopnik, 2012; Cook, Roggman, & Boyce, 2012; Gopnik, 2012). In the past, it was more difficult to understand how the brain worked and how play was related to overall growth and development. Today, research supports the child's natural need to play to facilitate cognitive, social, and physical growth and development.

3. **Community play spaces** Beautiful playgrounds are being developed throughout America to provide play spaces for all children (see Photo 1-1) (KaBOOM, 2013). KaBoom has recently developed a website that can locate any playground close to any location. This provides caregivers with opportunities to find play spaces as they travel and it gives parents information about playgrounds that are within close proximity of their home.

1-1 Natural spaces invite children to play and enjoy the natural environment.

4. **Children's museums** Opportunities for play are available at children's museums, and these can be located by searching the Internet for Children's Museums. Children's museums reflect the diversity of play throughout the United States. For example, themes range from apple picking in

Winchester, Virginia to sand play in Santa Fe, New Mexico to exploring the bottom of Lake Erie in Rochester, New York. The creativity and variety of the museums provide an endless venue that reflects local culture and interests.

5. **School-based play programs** Schools that include recess and play-based programs provide opportunities for formal and informal, structured and unstructured play. Many schools offer afterschool programs that include games and recreational opportunities.

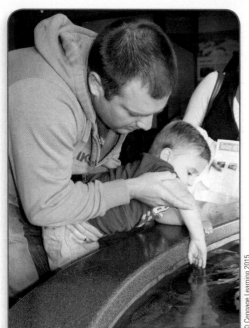

1-2 Families that participate in family play nights have opportunities to discover the world together.

© Cengage Learning 2015

6. **Professional and philanthropic organizations** Many professional organizations support play. The National Association for the Education of Young Children, Southern Education Children's Association, International Play Association/USA, Association for Childhood Education International, Alliance for Childhood, Association for the Study of Play, and Association of Children's Museums are among the professional groups that facilitate play through publications, presentations, and activities. For example, the documentary *Where Do the Children Play?* based on the work of Elizabeth Goodenough (Kupperman, 2008) had a tremendous impact on raising awareness about play places for children and was sponsored by a nonprofit organization.

7. **Families** Some families purposefully plan play nights for the family and play dates for children (Photo 1-2). These families are providing children and family members with a valuable resource.

8. **Teachers** Many teachers struggle to infuse play on a daily basis. But many provide time for recess and create play-based programs for children. They attend conferences, explore the Internet, and read articles and books in their quest for more knowledge about play. This book is designed to support the efforts of these teachers.

1-1b Obstacles to Play

Organizations that support play also recognize threats to play. Concern that the child's right to play was at risk was expressed by the International Association for the Child's Right to Play over two decades ago (Guddemi & Jambor, 1992). Unfortunately, this situation has changed little (Lester & Russell, 2010). Today, five threats to play include:

1. **Poverty and violence** Poor children who are working to sustain their own life and families do not have time or energy to play. Poverty anywhere leads to a need for life-sustaining activities such as planting or child care rather than play. According to the National Center for Poverty, there are 15 million children in the United States—21% of all children—who live in families with incomes below the federal poverty level—$22,350 a year for a family of four. Research shows that, on average, families need an income of about twice that level to cover basic expenses. Using this standard, 45% of children live in low-income families (Addy, Engelhardt, & Skinner, 2013). With so many children living in poverty, many children are focused on food, shelter, and clothing—not play. Unfortunately, poverty and violence are linked, and violence affects play. Random acts of violence in inner city and suburban neighborhoods create unsafe situations for children. This results in streets, parks, and playgrounds void of children.

2. **Changing cultural values**   Both underdeveloped and highly industrialized countries value work and view play as frivolous. Children in many underdeveloped countries are often expected to work, not play. In the same way, children in highly industrialized countries are often expected to take lessons and attend activities that will better prepare them to contribute to society and the marketplace. Young preschoolers who regularly participate in the beauty contest circuit may never have opportunities to play. Some blended families have very different values but share custody of a young child. The child may have toys from a large department store in one home, but no toys in the second home. One family may encourage play; the other may discourage play. These situations, which are becoming increasingly common, create a very difficult situation for young children who are in this situation. In the same way, children who spend their free time practicing golf, tennis, tee-ball, baseball, or dance extensively may never have time to experience the freedom of play. They may spend their time on the way to and from something that does not involve play.

3. **Media**   A 2009 Nielsen Company survey found that children between the ages of 2 and 5 spend more than 32 hours a week in front of television screens (McDonough, 2009). Scholars have found that children who are under the age of 2 do not benefit from watching television. Multimedia products designed for infants to three-year-olds do not result in learning (Richert, Robb, & Smith, 2011). Co-watching media is recommended because preschool children learn from the media if they have formed a relationship with the character, and young children view all characters on television as fictional. The media's influence on children will not decrease; it will only increase and will continue to impact children's play (see Photo 1-3).

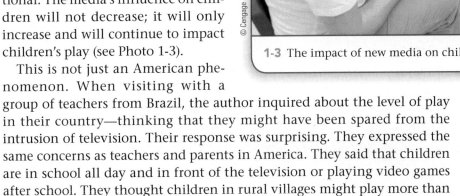

© Cengage Learning 2015

1-3 The impact of new media on children's play is yet unknown.

This is not just an American phenomenon. When visiting with a group of teachers from Brazil, the author inquired about the level of play in their country—thinking that they might have been spared from the intrusion of television. Their response was surprising. They expressed the same concerns as teachers and parents in America. They said that children are in school all day and in front of the television or playing video games after school. They thought children in rural villages might play more than children in urban settings. The answer was so similar to one given to the author by a group of teachers in the United States that it seemed surreal.

4. **Limited places for play**   Places for play are disappearing in some neighborhoods. It is not just lack of space but also the quality of the space that creates concern. Countries that have playground regulations that set standards for healthy, safe playgrounds include the United States, Canada, Scandinavia, Germany, the Netherlands, the United Kingdom, Australia, and New Zealand. Singapore, Hong Kong, and Malaysia have begun efforts to regulate playgrounds (Christiansen, 1997). Using a report rating scale,

the National Program for Playground Safety rated playgrounds in the United States as a "C." More than 200,000 playground injuries occurred from 2001 to 2008 in the United States (Olsen, Hudson, & Thompson, 2010; Wakes & Beukes, 2012).

5. **Overemphasis on academics** David Elkind joined the voices calling for reform in kindergarten and primary schools. In the foreword to *Crises in the Kindergarten* (Miller & Almon, 2009), he stated, "We have had a politically and commercially driven effort to make kindergarten a one-size-smaller first grade. Why in the world are we trying to teach the elementary curriculum at the early childhood level?" Some point to the publication of the book *Crises in the Kindergarten* as indicative of the state of play in today's kindergarten classroom. In some schools, recess has been deleted from the schedule (Henley, McBride, Milligan, & Nichols, 2007). Although the situation may not be this severe everywhere, the emphasis on academics and meeting assessment goals has led to an overemphasis on academics in many schools throughout America.

6. **Commercialization of childhood** All children, regardless of their income level, are exposed to the commercialization of play as the media, toy industry, and pay-for-play businesses are accruing profits at a staggering rate. The Campaign for a Commercial Free Childhood (CCFC) is a nonprofit group that focuses on the state of consumerism for babies and children. Our world today is filled with sources that continually attack play as well as resources that provide support for play. Many communities have businesses touted as play places for children. In reality, many of these are arcades in disguise. Is play minimized or celebrated in your community?

✳ 1-2 State of Play in a Global Society

Children throughout the world play. Play may look different in other cultures, but all children play (Lester & Russell, 2010). Children in Norway play in the snow, children in Italy play on the piazza, and children in Japan play with kites on Kodomo day (children's day). Children in Russia, Kenya, and Chile play with the people who are closest to them. They play with the sounds they can make with their mouths and with the instruments in their environments. Children throughout the world enjoy playing with water, mud, sticks, or bones—whatever adults or nature provides them in their particular region of the world.

Although it may look different, play is found in all cultures (Lancy, 2007). Play appears to be universal (Photo 1-4). For children throughout the world in both nonindustrialized and industrialized countries, play is a natural part of life. That is, "it does not take place in a vacuum; it appears in the cultural, social, and physical fabric of everyday life" (Meire, 2007). Because it is a natural part of the child's life, many of the resources that serve to encourage play in the United States can be found throughout the world. In fact, England, Wales, and Australia have national agendas for play.

1-4 Children throughout the world find ways to play.

© Cengage Learning 2015

In the same way, some of the barriers to play in the United States also exist throughout the world. For example, quiet streets are a concern in America, and in a study of four generations of play in Taishido, Japan, Kinoshita (2008) notes that "street play has almost disappeared and children now make formal arrangements for playing with friends, rather than going to favorite places in the knowledge playmates will be there" (Lester & Russell, 2010, p. 28).

Play only diminishes when social and cultural factors negatively impact it. The increasing urbanization of the world has the potential to impact play around the world (World Bank, 2009). Urban living has variability. That is, some areas will promote a high quality of life for families and children while others will not. Some of the issues that confront those who live in more urban areas include traffic, environmental hazards, violence, and accidents. In terms of the state of play in the world, children throughout the world play and they play in ways that are multidimensional and occur in a variety of contextual settings. Those who are charged with caring for children must be careful and sensitive in recognizing and valuing the many types of play.

Characteristics of Play 1-3 ✳

"What is play?" seems to be a simple question. It does not, however, have an equally simple answer (Photo 1-5). Everyone recognizes play when they see it. Listen to a caregiver's voice when he says, "Stop playing and pay attention." "Stop playing and eat your dinner." "Stop playing and listen to the story." Yet play is difficult to define, and some scholars even doubt our ability to define play (Bergen, 1988; Schlosberg, 1947). One scholar of play believed that "no behavioral concept has proved more ill-defined, elusive, controversial and unfashionable" (Wilson, 1975, p. 164). Others believe we can and must define play.

One of the first definitions of play was provided by the founder of kindergarten, Friedrich Froebel. He stated that "play is the highest expression of human development in childhood for it alone is the free expression of what is in a child's soul" (1887, p. 57). Since Froebel's definition, the literature has been replete with definitions of play. The *Oxford English Dictionary* (2013) defines play as when individuals "engage in an activity for enjoyment and recreation rather than a serious or practical purpose." Using a social constructivist or educational lens to view play, Ashiabi (2007) states that "play enables children to build and extend their knowledge and skills as they interact with their environment, with others, and on their own" (Glover, 1999).

© Cengage Learning 2015

1-5 Young children create their own reality through fantasy or pretend play.

The basis for the most respected and used definition of play was based on the work of John Huizinga (1955) and further developed by Rubin, Fein, and Vandenberg (1983). Rubin et al. viewed play as a **behavioral disposition**, as **observable behaviors**, and as **context**, and they included six factors in the disposition of play. These factors have been modified and are routinely accepted as the characteristics of play (Klein, Wirth, & Linas, 2003). Though few scholars include observable behaviors and contexts in their definition of play or in the characteristics of play, these factors have been included in the definition developed by Rubin, Fein, and Vandenberg (1983) and will be included in the definition of play used in this book. Play is a "behavioral disposition that occurs in describable and reproducible contexts and is manifest in a variety of observable behaviors" (p. 698). Although the word *dispositions* was used in the original definition, the term *characteristics* is now commonly found in the literature. More recently, children's play has been operationalized as "intrinsically motivating; pleasurable; freely chosen; non-literal; actively engaging; opportunistic and episodic; imaginative and creative; fluid and active; and predominantly for the moment and therefore concerned more with means than ends (Rubin, Fein, & Vanderberg, 1983; Sturgess, 2003)" (Ashiabi, 2007, p. 200). These main areas are considered individually in the next section.

1. **Play is pleasurable**   Play has a positive affect and is dominated by the players. They ask, "What can I do with this object" rather than "What will the object do?" (Rubin, Fein, & Vandenberg, 1983). They have the power to make the decisions. They are in control. Children may laugh, smile, or scream in delight as they show their enjoyment. They may also appear very serious but have a very contended look on their face. Children delight in play (Photo 1-6). Freud (1908/1959) and Piaget (1962) both recognized the pleasure in play. Some scholars, however, debate the inclusion of pleasure because some play is not pleasurable. Sutton-Smith calls this cruel play (1982). For example, when children play games like One Potato Two Potato, or Knuckles, a game played in the border areas between Mexico and the United States, they will play even when their hands are stinging. They are intrinsically motivated or compelled to play.

1-6 For children, play is pleasurable.

2. **Play is voluntary or freely chosen**   Play is intrinsically motivated. Children play because they want to play. Adults can assist and support play, but the motivation comes from within the child. Adults cannot make children play. It is the child who needs and chooses to play. Early educators frequently hear children say, "Make him play with me." Teachers know, however, that you cannot make children play. The urge to play comes from within the child.

3. **Play is nonliteral or symbolic**   Play involves symbolism or pretend play. It is nonliteral and carried out "as if" the activity were real. Children who use chairs to pretend they are riding on a bus are using the chairs as symbols (pivots). The child who jumps in a box held by two children and declares he is in the boat is using social pretend play. This aspect of play includes creative and imaginative behaviors that children experience during play.

4. **Play requires active engagement** Play is meaningful and requires the active engagement of the child. Children who are sitting on the periphery of the house play area (see Photo 1-7) are not playing, they are watching. Only the children involved are playing. The children are actively involved and totally absorbed in the play (Photo 1-7). The flow of the play is fluid and active; some have referred to this as improvisation as it changes quickly as the children create and re-create it together.

5. **Play is free of external rules** The rules of play are established by the children. They determine how the play will occur, who will play, what they will say, and how they will say it. They determine the acceptable and unacceptable behaviors, direct how the script will flow, and decide who will play. The child is at once the actor and director.

6. **Play focuses on means rather than end results or outcomes** The process is more important

© Cengage Learning 2015

1-7 When children are actively engaged in play, their mirror neurons are activated.

than the product. This is what distinguishes play from work. Play is opportunistic and episodic. This allows play to change at a moment's notice as children choose different goals and directions. Improvisation occurs as the children move from playing hospital to playing fire department. In play, it is the action that is important.

1-3a Play and Exploration are Similar

Play and **exploration** are often viewed as interchangeable. They are, however, distinctly different. Exploration occurs before play. Exploration has been defined as what occurs when the child is exposed to a novel object and tries to figure it out. She asks, "What can this object do?" During play she asks, "What can I do with it?" (Pellegrini & Boyd, 1993, p. 108).

Exploration is the dominant activity during the first two years of life. The infant spends most of her time engaged in exploration. The toddler spends about half of her time in exploration, whereas the preschooler spends much of her time in pretend. As the child grows and develops, exploration decreases and play increases. When a child explores, mental structures are adapted as the child's mind creates neurological pathways to accommodate new information. Play, however, allows the child to fit reality into existing structures. As practice play occurs over and over during the first two years of life, neural pathways are strengthened. In other words, during exploration, children collect data, and during play, they mess around with the data. Hughes and Hutt (1979) identified three major areas of differences between play and exploration (see Table 1-1).

TABLE 1-1 Differences between Play and Exploration

Play	Exploration
1. Positive affect	Neutral affect (cautious)
2. Creative combinations/improvisational	Stereotypical behaviors
3. Casual demeanor; heart rate is variable	Intense; heart rate is steady and concentration evident

© Cengage Learning 2015

Digital Download Download from CourseMate

1-3b Play or Playfulness?

Play has been defined as a behavioral disposition that occurs within a context that manifests itself as observable behaviors. As discussed earlier, play includes actions or behaviors that can be recognized and identified. For example, we can observe a child playing grocery store and laughing gleefully. Characteristics may include positive affect or intrinsic motivation; the context is a familiar shopping experience; and the observable behavior is pretend or **symbolic play** in a cooperative group setting or sociodramatic play. This is play.

Playfulness is not the same as play. Playfulness does not include observable behaviors. Playfulness is best described as a personality trait or internal disposition (Barnett, 1990; Liberman, 1965; Rogers, Impara, Frary, Harris, Meeks, Semantic-Lauth, & Reynolds, 1999). Components of playfulness include spontaneity, openness, communication, curiosity, emotional expressiveness, joyfulness, and humor. These traits may manifest themselves through behaviors that are culturally specific. For example, in one study of playfulness among Japanese children and American children, American children were found to be much more playful on a 31-item instrument (Rogers et al., 1999). The reason may be explained by differences between the two cultures (Tobin, Wu, & Davidson, 1989).

Einstein serves as an example of an individual who was both playful and engaged in play. When Einstein was eight, his uncle showed him a compass with a needle that always pointed north. His play with the compass stimulated a fascination with unseen forces that lasted a lifetime. He was equally playful. Eric Erikson called him the "victorious child" because he never stopped looking at the world through the eyes of a child (Rogers & Sluss, 1999).

✳ 1-4 Classical and Current Theories of Play

The plethora of studies on play today reflects the rich history of play scholarship. See Table 1-2 for a historical timeline of play scholarship. The dawning of the twentieth century brought not only studies of play, but also additional theories of play alongside theories of human growth and development. These are examined in Table 1-3.

Some of the most influential theories of play were developed by Freud, Erikson, Piaget, and Vygotsky, though none of those researchers focused exclusively on play. These modern theories differed from classical theories in one major area: Classical theories all looked at play through a biological lens and viewed physical development as a major outcome. Modern theories examined play for other benefits. Freud, Erikson, and Vygotsky all shared a belief that play allows children to engage in wish fulfillment and pretense, and these lead to social, emotional, and

TABLE 1-2 Historical Timeline of Study of Play

Theorist or Scholar	Dates	Purpose of Play	Outcome
Plato (Greece)	427 B.C.E.–347 B.C.E.	"The future builder must play at building…and those who have the care of their eduation should provide them when young with mimic tools" (Lascarieds & Hinitz, 2002, p. 10).	Occupational preparation
Johann Amos Comenius (Czech philosopher and educator)	1592–1670	Children are innately curious and different materials should be used to encourage their creativity. "They are delighted to construct little houses, and to erect walls of clay, chips, wood, or stone, thus displaying an architectural genius" (1896). He wrote the first children's book, *Orbis Sensualium Pictus, The World Illustrated* (1658/1968)	Growth and development
John Locke (English philosopher, exiled in France)	1632–1704	Children are a blank slate and can learn through play when adults use toys to teach concepts. He created the first wooden alphabet blocks: "I know of a person of great quality…who by pasting on 6 vowels (for in our language y is one) on the 6 sides of a die and remaining 18 consonants on the sides of the 3 other dice, has made this a play for children that he shall win who at one cast throws most words on these 4 dice."	Growth and development
Jean-Jacques Rousseau (French philosopher)	1712–1778	Children are innately good and nature is a primary force in learning. "You are troubled at seeing him spend his early years in doing nothing. What! Is it nothing to be happy? Is it nothing to skip, to play, to run around all day long? Never in his life will he be so happy as not" (1762).	Growth and development
Johann Heinrich Pestalozzi (Italian philosopher and educator)	1746–1827	Children should be free to explore and they learn through action (learn by doing). Wrote *How Gertrude Teaches Her Children* in 1801, in which he used Rousseau's theory to inform practice.	Play as instructional technique
Friedrich Froebel (German philosopher and educator)	1782–1852	Children learn through play. "A child who plays and works thoroughly, with perseverance, until physical fatigue forbids, will surely be a thorough, determined person, capable of self-sacrifice" (1887). Created the first kindergarten with nursery songs, gifts, and occupations.	Growth and development
Classical Theories			
Friedrich Von Schiller (German)	1892–1954	Children have too much energy, so play eliminates surplus energy.	Physical activity/development
Herbert Spencer (British philosopher)	1820–1903	First identified the notion of surplus energy theory.	Physical development
Moritz Lazarus (German philosopher)	1824–1903	Children are exhausted from work, so play allows them to regenerate energy that is used in work.	Physical activity/development

(Continued)

TABLE 1-2 Historical Timeline of Study of Play *(Continued)*

Theorist or Scholar	Dates	Purpose of Play	Outcome
Karl Groos (German philosopher)	1861–1946	Children use play to practice those instincts that they will need as adults.	Career preparation
G. Stanley Hall (American psychologist)	1844–1924	Children should engage in instinctual play that reflects their evolutionary past.	Physical activity/ development
Child Study Movement			
Patty Smith Hill (American eEducator)	1868–1946	Used G. Stanley Hall's work to develop an approach called free play. Created the first hollow wood blocks, wrote the song "Happy Birthday to You," and founded the Association for Childhood International.	Growth and development
Caroline Pratt (American educator)	1867–1954	Influenced by the work of Froebel, she created unit blocks.	Growth and development
Harriet M. Johnson (American educator)	1867–1934	Founder of Bank Street College of Education Nursery School. Wrote one of the first books on using blocks for instruction.	Growth and development
John Dewey (American educator)	1859–1952	He used play and hands-on learning as a foundation for curriculum. "In play the activity is its own end, instead of its having an ulterior result" (1913).	Growth and development
Herbert Mead (American educator)	1863–1931	Studied play and the interactions that occurred during play. Focused on play in terms of development of self.	Social and emotional development
Modern Theories of Play			
Sigmund Freud (Austrian physician)	1856–1939	Viewed play as pleasurable for social and emotional development. First to view play as providing wish fulfillment for the child.	Social and emotional development
Erik Erikson (American psychologist)	1902–1994	Believed play led to social and emotional development through mastery of psychosocial crises. Developed three levels of play.	Social and emotional development
Maria Montessori (Italian physician)	1870–1952	Developed a theory of teaching that focuses on developing the child's independence and cognitive ability through hands-on activities.	Cognitive development
Lev Vygotsky (Russian psychologist)	1896–1934	Developed a theory of play that considers the sociocultural influences on play.	Cognitive development
Mildred Parten (American psychologist)	1932–after 1932	Created a classification system for observing children during play.	Social development
Jean Piaget (Swiss psychologist)	1896–1980	Developed stages of play to align with his stages of intellectual development. Considered the role of play in the child's moral development.	Cognitive and moral development

TABLE 1-3   Classical Theories of Play (1800–1900)

Surplus Energy Theory of Play	Relaxation and Recreation Theories of Play	Practice (or Pre-Exercise Theory of Play)	Recapitulation Theory of Play
Based on the notion that children play because they have too much energy and play will rid them of the excess, this theory developed by Friedrich von Schiller (1892/1954), a German play scholar. Schiller believed that both animals and humans have a certain amount of energy necessary for survival. Since the young of both are cared for by others, they have excess energy. Thus, kittens, puppies, and children play to use up their extra energy. Schiller's theory was further supported by Herbert Spencer (1873), a British philosopher who was the first to identify this as "surplus energy" theory. He thought that in an advancing civilization, people do not have to hunt or fish for food. Since basic survival skills are met, children have surplus energy. This energy can be used for creative activities.	Based on the belief that play is necessary to reenergize human cognition. This is the exact opposite of surplus energy theory. Moritz Lazarus created this theory in Germany in in 1883. He believed that labor exhausts individuals and they need to play or engage in recreation for leisure or rejuvenation purposes. His work was extended by G. T. W. Patrick in 1916 (Rubin et al., 1983). Patrick believed that modern occupations that require mental work drain individuals of their energy. He subscribed to the idea that engaging in rigorous recreation restored balance. Hunting, fishing, and other activities necessary for survival in pre-industrial society were viewed as the antidote for fatigue.	Based on the belief that children's play "serves an adaptive purpose," this was developed by Groos (Rubin, Fein, & Vandenberg, 1983, p. 696). Carl Groos (1901) believed that children's play provides them with an opportunity to practice adult activities. Groos also thought that children's play changed as they developed, and he distinguished different stages of development. Argued against Groos's (1901) work in his (meaning Piaget's) book, Play, Dreams, and Imitation (1962).	Based on Darwinian theory, recapitulation theory is the most controversial of the classical theories. It views children as the link between animals and adult human beings. G. Stanley Hall (1916) is generally credited with this theory, though Luther Gulick (1908) made some contributions. Hall's work has come under a great deal of scrutiny due to Hall's belief in racial recapitulation. His view was criticized by the scientific community when it was published at the turn of the twentieth century. He recognized different stages of animal/human development: (1) animal stage (climbing and swinging), (2) savage stage (hunting, tag), (3) nomad stage (keeping pets), (4) agricultural or patriarchal stage (dolls or sand play), and (5) tribal stage (team games) (Hall, 1916).
Criticisms			
Surplus Energy Theory	**Relaxation and Recreation Theory**	**Practice Play Theory**	**Recapitulation Theory**
No research exists to support these claims. This theory was based on the premise that children play until exhausted and then quit, but we all know children who appear to be exhausted and then perk up when they notice something novel. This argument is circular, but not logical.	If mental work is draining, why do those who engage in physical labor also play? This does not seem rational. Second, there is little research to support this theory.	One obvious flaw of Groos's theory is that children may not be able to practice activities for adulthood because they cannot see into the future. Adults who are now using computers in offices may never have seen a computer as a child.	There is no evidence to support this theory. All children do not go through all stages. If the evolutionary process is occurring in this way and characteristics of different cultures could be transmitted, then modern society would be reflected in these stages.

(Continued)

TABLE 1-3   Classical Theories of Play (1800–1900) *(Continued)*

Current View			
Surplus Energy Theory	**Relaxation and Recreation Theory**	**Practice Play Theory**	**Recapitulation Theory**
Though this theory was developed in the early eighteenth century and discounted in the nineteenth century, remnants of it are alive and well. Those who subscribe to this theory may not be aware that they reflect a surplus energy theory of play. Many adults believe that play allows children to release energy or blow off steam.	This theory has not been substantiated by evidence but tends to have some supporters. Some businesses hold weekend outings that provide employees with an opportunity to engage in active outdoor activities.	This theory was discounted in the nineteenth century. The idea that play predisposes children to serve in specific roles as adults has a certain amount of appeal even today. This is the rationale used when parents buy four-year-olds golf clubs, fishing lines, or enroll them in tee-ball.	This theory seems odious to many to even consider. There are remnants of this theory in some of the comments made by parents when they talk about their wild children.

Digital Download   Download from CourseMate

cognitive development. More recently, theories of cognitive adaptation, arousal modulation, communication, and neuroscience have influenced the field. The most current theories will be examined in the next section.

1-4a Psychoanalytical Theory

The psychoanalytical view of play was developed by Freud and extended by Erikson. From this perspective, play benefits social and emotional development. The work of Freud and Erikson has influenced research on play throughout the twentieth century and continues to influence play therapy. Although Freud did not develop a full-blown theory of play, his writings reflect his view of the importance of play. Unlike early play scholars, he did not focus on the benefits of play for physical development. Rather, he considered the cathartic benefits of play in terms of social and emotional development.

Play, like a dream, provides wish fulfillment for the child. During play, the child fulfills his wishes by creating and controlling the environment. Wish fulfillment brings pleasure as the child creates a pretend dog that does not bite. The child is motivated to seek pleasure and avoid pain. Freud (1959) viewed the **pleasure principle** as the primary motivation for play. One caveat is that the adult can never read the mind of the child, and although psychoanalysis seems to be logical, trying to understand the unconscious motives and emotions is always risky business that should be left in the hands of trained psychologists.

Erikson studied with Freud and subscribed to a psychoanalytical view of play similar to that espoused by Freud. They differed in the area of Erikson's explanation of unconscious motivation in terms of psychosocial—not psychosexual—forces. For Erikson, play was an expressive behavior that led to social and emotional development through mastery of psychosocial crises.

Erikson recognized three major purposes of play: (1) play as ego mastery for emotional development, (2) play as social, and (3) play as a lifelong phenomenon. Play as **ego mastery** serves as catharsis. Play serves as a place where emotions can be "played out" and anxiety reduced. Erikson believed that children could master reality by planning and experimenting with "model situations in which aspects of the past are re-lived, the present represented and reviewed, and the future anticipated" (Erikson, 1977, p. 44) His view of play as beneficial for emotional development set the stage for play therapy.

1-4b Constructivist Theory

Constructivist theory considers play as an avenue for intellectual growth and development. Piaget has been the most influential theorist in this area. Because he believed that children construct knowledge through interactions with the world, this view is frequently referred to as **cognitive constructivism** (Fosnot, 1996). This approach serves as a foundation for many current preschool programs and will be further explored later in the text.

Piaget. Jean Piaget (1896–1980) was a Swiss scholar who was well known for his theories of cognitive development. He was equally well known for his contributions to play theory. As a genetic epistemologist, he initially set out to understand the development of intelligence in the young child. His quest brought him to the study of the young child's play. Though some of his methods focus on a single cultural group and have come under criticism, his book *Play, Dreams and Imitation in Childhood* (1962) remains a classic.

Piaget believed that adaptation is necessary for survival. Development occurs when children adapt to their world through systematic changes in mental structures. Play is a necessary element of development. Intellectual adaptation results from the combined opposition of two invariant processes, accommodation and assimilation. **Accommodation** occurs when children adjust their schema or mental structures to accept new knowledge. Accommodation is the action of the environment on the child (Piaget, 1962). The child transforms schemas to fit the demands of the environment. When children imitate reality, accommodation occurs. For example, the child may watch someone turn off the television. This information is accommodated in a newly created mental structure. The child may then imitate the adult and attempt to turn off the television. The child is adapting to the world (Photo 1-8). Piaget believed that assmilation and accomodation occur as the child adapts to the world, and recent scholars of brain develoment recognize the role of executive function in strengthening neuriological connections.

© Cengage Learning 2015

1-8 This child just knows it's fun to brush the goat.

Assimilation occurs when the individual fits information into existing mental structures. Assimilation is the action of the child on the environment. The child transforms the environment to meet his needs. The young child who just learned to turn off the television now has a mental structure for doing so. He imitated reality. Now if the child begins to turn off the computer also, the activity may turn into play. Assimilation occurs when the child modifies reality to meet his needs. He subordinates or modifies reality to fit his world. As the child practices turning off the television, computer, or other items, he is modifying reality to fit his view of the world. The child moves from imitation to play—from accommodation to assimilation—as he engages in practice play for the sheer joy of turning the television set off and on. Adults may not be as excited when the child begins this new play. The child, however, has increased his knowledge of the world through adaptation, and play is a major factor in his development. Both accommodation and assimilation are necessary for intellectual development. Play reflects cognitive growth and serves as a vehicle for learning.

According to Piaget, play represents disequilibrium or an imbalance in which assimilation dominates accommodation. Young children practice new behaviors through play. Watch the toddler who throws food from his high chair. The first time the food hits the floor, he is developing new mental structures for throwing food on the floor; he is accommodating. After he throws it several times, he has practiced and experienced assimilation as he strengthened his schema for objects (food) moving through space. The child will move between accommodation and assimilation as he discovers how to throw food and then realizes different strategies for throwing. The child will engage in this behavior for as long as the adult will allow, all the while practicing, playing, and learning. The initial learning that started as adaptation soon turned into play.

Piaget believed that play facilitates and follows development. He thought the child's intellectual level was reflected in her play. It is no surprise, then, that Piaget's stages of play mirror his stages of intellectual development. His three stages of intellectual development align with three stages of play. The first stage, sensorimotor development, occurs during the first two years of life, and **practice or functional play** occurs during this time. The second stage of intellectual development is the pre-operational stage, which corresponds with the beginnings of pretend and symbolism that is observed in **symbolic or dramatic play**. The third stage of cognitive development is concrete operations, and the last stage is formal operations. During these two stages, logical thinking begins and becomes stabilized. **Games with rules** begin during the concrete operation stage and become more sophisticated during the formal operations stage.

Although Piaget found these stages to be invariant and sequential in the population he examined, research has supported that children in different cultures also experience these same stages. Differences were found, however, in the influence of social norms and culture. Understanding how children develop in different cultures will add to the knowledge of how children develop their knowledge of the world.

1-4c Sociocultural Theory

Sociocultural theory considers the social, cultural, and historical factors that influence cognitive development during social interactions. Based on the work of Russian psychologist Vygotsky, this approach suggests that children construct knowledge through interactions with society and culture and is usually referred to as social constructivism (Fosnot, 1996).

Piaget and Vygotsky began life the same year, and both were constructivists but they differed greatly in their views of cognitive development and play. Lev Semenovich Vygotsky (1896–1934) was a Russian psychologist who also developed a theory of cognitive development. He believed that social-cultural and historical forces affect the child and that children learn during social interactions with an adult or more capable peer. For Vygotsky (1978), learning occurs in the zone of proximal development (ZPD). He defined the ZPD as the distance between the point of being capable of doing something with the assistance of others to the point of being capable of accomplishing the task alone. When the child who can ride a toy (pivot) with help from his parent moves to a point where he can ride the toy without assistance, the child has moved through the zone. The child developed as he moved through the zone of proximal development. Adults who provide support and guidance can create a scaffold for the child and move her to a higher level of cognitive development.

For Vygotsky, the zone of proximal development is created during play (Photo 1-9). During play, "The child always behaves beyond his average age, above his daily behavior; in play it as though he were a head taller than himself" (Vygotsky, 1978, p. 102). In contrast to Piaget, who believed that play followed development, Vygotsky believed that development occurred during play because play creates the zone of proximal development. Vygotsky believed that play has two unique purposes. The first involved pretend that happens "when the child begins to expe-

1-9 Is she pretending to be a princess? Is she preparing to take a pretend nap? Vygotsky would argue that she has created the zone of proximal development as she moves into her imaginary world.

rience unrealizable tendencies" (p. 93). Vygotsky believed that play began simultaneously with fantasy. When the toddler realizes he cannot engage in activities around him, he creates his own reality through fantasy or pretend. The child who wants to drive the car but is kept from doing so will pretend to drive. The child creates his own reality through play.

This behavior predisposes the child to abstraction. When the child pretends the stick is a horse, he engages in abstract thought. Vygotsky noted that "the child sees one thing but acts differently in relation to what he sees. Thus, a condition is reached in which the child begins to act independently of what he sees" (1978, p. 97). This capacity is necessary for instruction.

The second purpose emanates from the first and involves rules. Much representational play is rule bound—either implicitly or explicitly. When children play they will engage in specific behavior according to their own view of how the role they have assumed works. Watch a child playing in a house area. It may look like free play unfettered by rules. Closer observation may reveal a different story. If the adult tries to enter the play as the mommy, the child may cry out, "No, I'm the mommy, you can be the daddy." Some will even become upset that the daddy is not male. The child has created her own world complete with rules of behavior, and no one can enter this world of pretend unless beckoned under specific conditions. To do so may end the play. More than one student teacher has watched in shock as their attempts to extend play ended in the children dispersing and moving to another area. It is critically important that adults enter play to scaffold and support, not extinguish.

For Vygotsky, play contributed to the development of language, memory, reasoning, and social skills. His view of play as beneficial for the development of higher-level thinking and social development provided a different way of thinking about play. Rather than focus on the individual child, Vygotsky paved the way for studies of the context and interactions among children. Additional information on his view of play is available in *Mind in Society* (1978).

1-4d Arousal Modulation Theory

Arousal modulation theory views play as a behavior that occurs as a result of biological adaptation. Berlyne (1969) was the first to propose a view of play based on a behavior learning theory. He believed that the central nervous system tries to remain in a certain state of arousal. If there is too little stimulation, the child will engage in stimulus-seeking behavior or play. If too much stimulation is present, play will cease. Other scholars who have refined this theory include Ellis (1973), Fein (1981), and Shultz (1979). They believe this theory has implications for understanding and facilitating play. This theory explains why children roam from one activity to another. They are in search of additional stimulation. After children engage in an activity for a while, they will switch to a different activity or modify the activity. Children running through sprinklers will begin by running through in a rather rote way. After two or three trips, they will change how they are running and may even engage in risky behavior that leads to an injury. On the other hand, when some children are overly stimulated by too much noise or interaction, play will gradually diminish. The children seem to have a built-in moderator that causes them to seek novel or stimulating experiences when the play is dull and to close down when the play is overwhelming. This theory has not been discounted, and many teachers use it as a way to moderate activity in their classroom.

1-4e Communication Theory

Communication occurs among young animals during play. They communicate to each other that play is occurring. **Play frame** is the term that Gregory Bateson (1972) used to describe the shift from reality to play. Children enter and exit play frames by signaling to their play partner that play is beginning and play is ending (see Photo 1-10). The child who does not receive or understand the signal may disrupt play, and this is when the children will yell, "We're not playing now." Bateson's study of text and context provided a foundation for subsequent studies of communication during play.

Bateson's theory was based on his anthropological study of otter play. He believed that children create a context for play when they exchange metacommunicative signals or text that

1-10 These children are in what Bateson describes as the play frame. What signals do you think they used to signify that this is play?

© Cengage Learning 2015

conveys the message that play is occurring. Everyone involved in the play must understand the message. When children say, "This is play," they signal to others that play is occurring—that what we are doing is not real but is pretend and fun. This communication signals the other child when play begins and when play ends (Bateson, 1972).

Catherine Garvey (1977) extended Bateson's findings through her research on pretend play. She studied the child's use of language during play and developed a framework for understanding the complexity involved in the child's language. Garvey noted that a lot of the child's communication involves creating, clarifying, maintaining, and negotiating pretend play.

William Corsaro (1986) built on Garvey's work and found that children use particular communicative strategies to share their intentions with their play partner. He recognized developmental differences in the use of communication during play. Cosaro's framework for understanding the complexity of the child's language during play is currently used in research studies that involve children who speak English as a second language.

Jo Ann Farver extended Corsaro's research by examining how Mexican children communicate their messages to each other during play (Farver, 1992). Her study found that Mexican children used communication strategies very similar to participants in previous studies. She found they used more basic communication (describe actions) and less complex communication (tags). This area of study has potential for understanding how to facilitate play among children of diverse cultures and needs to be explored further by today's scholars of play.

1-4f Cognitive Adaptation Theory

More recent studies have focused on play as necessary for cognitive adaptation. This builds on the research of Piaget, but it differs in that the focus is on the child's construction of knowledge through symbols. This is called **symbolic constructivism** (Fosnot, 1996). This section begins with the work of Jerome Bruner and then discusses Leslie's theory of mind.

Bruner. Jerome Bruner (1972) viewed play as a medium for cognitive adaptation. During social play the young child can explore or try on different roles. Social and cooperative play provides a venue for developing problem-solving skills and encouraging creativity. Bruner was especially interested in play as a way immature or novice learners could safely explore their world as they prepare to assume adult roles. Bruner's early work tended to support the early practice theory of play developed by Groos. More recently, Bruner (1990) has focused on the role of narrative for development. He views children as "meaning makers" who are trying to understand their world.

1-4g Theory of Mind

Leslie (1987) was the first to link play and **theory of mind,** which describes a condition in which the child understands that the child (him or herself) has an internal mental state and that others also have internal structures (Newton & Jenvey, 2011). This occurs when the child realizes that his view is different from the view of others. This is generally most noticeable when children realize that their view of Santa Claus or other fictional characters may be different from that of others. The link to play involves social pretend play and the mental

1-11 As she plays a role, she develops her understanding of others' perspectives, which helps develop her theory of mind.

representations that occur during play. When children understand others' perspectives, they become more socially adept, and this has long-lasting effects (Photo 1-11). This theory may provide additional information about how children view the world both in and outside the realm of play, and this will add to our understanding of what is going on when the child plays.

1-4h Postmodern Theories

Postmodern theorists use critical theory to inform their research. Critical theorists believe that the individual's perspective affects his view of the situation and knowledge construction.

Gail Cannella. Gail Cannella also suggests a different method of viewing play. She is especially concerned that in America, play is viewed through a middle-class, European lens. "Applying the notion of play to all peoples in all contexts denies the multiple value structures, knowledges, and views of the world which are created by people in diverse contexts" (Cannella, 1997, p. 128).

Cannella has three major criticisms. The first involves Piaget's stages of development. These appear to be too rigid and do not reflect the realities of children in different cultures. She suggests that these stages are not separate and linear. For example, some children may play games when they are very young, but in some cultures and places, people of all ages engage in all kinds of play. Her second concern involves the view of play as object driven. For example, African American children may use more verbal than object play. Her third concern involves the use of "appropriate" and "inappropriate" to describe practices. She believes this does not provide an inclusive environment for discussion and leads to the view that one approach is the only correct approach. This perspective challenges past theories but fails to provide alternative ways to consider these issues. However, this theory benefits play scholarship because it challenges standard belief systems and creates questions for debate and discussion.

Brian Sutton-Smith. Brian Sutton-Smith has emphasized the interdisciplinary nature of play. In his pivotal paper in 1966, he pointed out that Piaget's (1962) belief that play reflects development did not equate to development. In over three hundred publications, Sutton-Smith's view of play is that it is ambiguous, difficult to define, and more difficult to capture than definitions might suggest. He warns us against overromanticizing play according to middle class values. He further argues that a great deal of play is not pleasant, nor does it lead to more positive outcomes for children (1997). For additional reading, see *The Ambiguity of Play* (1997), in which Sutton-Smith explains the rhetorics of play.

An overview of modern, current, and postmodern theories (Table 1.2) shows a steady progression from the first psychoanalytical theories to current theories. Theory-based play scholarship provides a solid basis for current and future inquiry.

1-4i Current Influential Contributions

The influence of the most recent research cannot be overlooked. Significant scholars who have contributed to play scholarship in the last part of the twentieth century include: Greta Fein (1981), who has added to the knowledge of symbolic play; Inge Bretherton (1984), who has also contributed significantly to the study of symbolic play; and Jerome Singer (1973), who conducted research in the area of imagination and pretend. Other well-known researchers include Anthony Pellegrini (1988), who investigated the benefits of rough-and-tumble play on the playground for social development and examined the relationship between literacy and play; and Kenneth Rubin and Brian Vandenberg, who co-authored with Greta Fein one of the most important articles on play (1983). These are just a few of the scholars who have been conducting research on play. The impact of brain-based research on play is yet to be realized and is discussed in the next section.

Neurological Research.   In the past thirty years, research on the brain has received attention from both the academic and public realm. In 1996, a conference titled *Rethinking the Brain* was held to discuss the implications of brain research (Shore, 1997). As a result of the conference, Rob Reiner, Michele Singer Reiner, and Ellen Gilbert developed a public awareness campaign entitled, "I Am Your Child" to communicate the importance of the first three years of life. Free videos were distributed to teachers at the NAEYC conference in Toronto, Canada, and others sold at a reduced cost to ensure that early educators could access the information. Publication of the proceedings of the conference, *Rethinking the Brain* by the Families and Work Institute (Shore, 1997) and a special edition of *Newsweek* on Your Child's Brain ensured public awareness of new research findings on the brain. This affected play studies by publicizing brain research. Shore (1997) described the findings in this way:

> At birth, the human brain is in a remarkably unfinished state. Most of its 100 billion neurons are not yet connected in networks. Forming and reinforcing these connections are the key tasks of early brain development [see Photo 1-12]. Connections among neurons are formed as the growing child experiences the surrounding world and forms attachments to parents, family members, and other caregivers. In the first decade of life, a child's brain forms trillions of connections or synapses. Axons hook up with dendrites, and chemicals called neurotransmitters facilitate the passage of impulses across the resulting synapses. Each individual neuron may be connected to as many as 15,000 other neurons, forming a network of neural pathways that is immensely complex. This elaborate network is sometimes referred to as the brain's "wiring" or "circuitry." In the early years, children's brains form twice as many synapses as they will eventually need. If these synapses are used repeatedly in a child's day-to-day life, they are reinforced and become part of the brain's permanent circuitry. It they are not used repeatedly, or often enough, they are eliminated. In this way, experience plays a crucial role in "wiring" a young child's brain. (1997, p. 17)

John Almarode

1-12 A young child's brain is activated by play.

Neuroscientists note that infants arrive ready for interaction and what happens to them makes a difference. The National Research Council Institute of Medicine released a list of four major themes based on its analysis of research on the central nervous system (Shornkoff & Phillips, 2000). The Council's researchers found that:

- All children are born wired for feelings and ready to learn.
- Early environments matter, and nurturing relationships are essential.

- Society is changing, and the needs of young children are not being addressed.

- Interactions among early childhood science, policy, and practice are problematic and demand dramatic rethinking.

These findings confirm many research studies conducted prior to the latest advancements in neurology and imaging that make these insights available. For example, many of the findings by Bowlby in the 1950s have been confirmed (Bowlby, 1988). Attachment is important for developing both emotionally and mentally. The value of adult-child interaction as the child explores his world was discussed first by Piaget (1962). These findings have implications for play. Play that occurs between the parent(s) and child or teacher and child contribute to cognitive development. A recent study confirmed these tenets by reporting that the play of fathers and mothers with their toddlers predicted fifth-grade reading and math achievement (Cook, Roggman, & Boyce, 2011).

As the market grew for anything based on the brain, so did the marketers as they realized the implications for creating a new market of consumers. DVDs, books, and toys were designed and distributed to parents during the 1990s. For example, listening to music by Mozart was associated with increased activity in the brain. Many companies sponsored the purchase of hundreds of cassette tapes, *Mozart for Babies*, that could be sent home with newborns. Providing free music for newborns is a wonderful gesture but it may not accomplish the goal of increased IQ. Gains obtained from music and movement occur during loving interactions with adults. Adults may cradle infants as they listen to a favorite song or dance around the room. This is play. When the adult who does not enjoy classical music plays it only for some intended increase in intelligence, the benefit to the child may be less than if the adult played music she enjoys. The effect of music alone is diminished by the lack of interaction from the adult. The impact of brain research is also evident in books. Titles that promote brain growth have replaced titles that promote play. For example, Jackie Silberg authored a book, *Games to Play with Babies*, in 1993. In 2000, the second edition of *125 Brain Games for Babies* was published by Grython House.

New findings in neuroscience provide support for Piaget's work and theory of mind. For example, mirror neurons react when observing actions in a way that allows the organism to imitate and react to the action (Rushton, 2011). This can help us understand the development of the mirror neurons' work in terms of mood and empathy. Sandy Twardosz (2012) recently looked at the role of neuroscience and reported that the most current findings of how the brain works support good early childhood practice, especially in the area of music.

▶️❚❚ **TeachSource** Video Case 1-1

© Cengage Learning 2015

Infancy: Brain Development

The growth and development of the young child's brain are discussed and different parts of the brain and their functions are explained.

1. How does the environment affect brain growth and development?

2. Explain the brain processing that is occurring when the six-month-old in the clip plays with the toys.

Watch on CourseMate

Did You Get It?

Piaget believed that play was _____ _____.

a. more accommodation than assimilation

b. more assimilation than accommodation

c. more equilibrium than disequilibrium

d. more interactionism than constructivism

Take the full quiz on CourseMate

Activity-Dependent Plasticity of the Brain

Dr. John Almarode, Assistant Professor, James Madison University

One summer evening, my niece (age 3) and nephew (age 5) were playing "tag" in the yard when Dylan ventured into the driveway, tripped, fell, and skinned his knees and elbows on the gravel. Without hesitation, Ava ran up to Dylan and asked if he was okay. "Dylwin, I bet that really hurt your knees." Dylan and Ava learned to use of language in a social setting through specific environmental experiences that developed during unstructured play. This social interaction and complex use of language in a social setting between a three-year-old and a five-year-old pair of siblings can be attributed to the activity-dependent plasticity of the human brain.

Activity-dependent plasticity is the capacity of the brain to change with experience or as a result of environmental conditions and influences. Plasticity occurs during normal brain development as young children experience and soak up everyday life. These experiences evoke changes at the neuronal level and influence the formation of complex neural networks of synapses. Play is a quintessential activity for activity-dependent plasticity. Put differently, the brain relies on play for learning, and this changes the brain.

This activity-dependent plasticity leads to better social, emotional, and cognitive outcomes for young

© Cengage Learning 2015

children. In the words of John Medina (2010), hooray for play!

REFERENCES

Medina, J. (2010). *Brain rules for baby. How to raise a smart and happy child from zero to five.* Seattle, WA: Pear Press.
Medina, J. (2008). *Brain rules. 12 principles for surviving and thriving at work, home, and school.* Seattle, WA: Pear Press.
Sylvester, R. (2010). *A child's brain: The need for nurture.* Thousand Oaks, CA: Corwin Press.

Dr. John Almarode is an assistant professor at James Madison University, and he is an international speaker on brain-based teaching strategies.

Play in a Changing Society 1-5 ✳

Play is valued differently in diverse cultures by groups and subgroups. Play for middle-class Americans is viewed favorably. Many middle-class parents view play as an educational activity and spend a great deal of money on educational toys. For working-class individuals, play may be viewed as frivolous. Parents who are struggling to survive may not have the time or energy to encourage play. The views of citizens of other countries are also impacted by sociocultural factors. For example, countries in Scandinavia are very committed to play and have extensive playgrounds. At the same time, citizens of Prague and Moscow are trying to rebuild their national economy and infrastructure. Another example can be found in southern Europe. Play permeates the schools of Reggio Emilia, Italy, which have been recognized for their excellent programs for infants and young children (New, 2003). At the same time, children in countries experiencing armed conflict may have little opportunity to play. Understanding that children of parents from different cultures may have different perspectives is imperative for creating a play-based program that includes children from different countries or ethnic groups.

1-5a Children with Special Needs

Play is recognized as equally important for children with disabilities or delays (Murdock & Hobbs, 2011). Programs have been developed that encourage play among children with special needs (Barton & Wolery, 2010). A play-based assessment approach has been developed that can be used with all children. The Council for Exceptional Children-Division of Early Childhood (CEC/DEC) and the National Association for the Education of Young Children (NAEYC) have collaborated to develop guidelines that benefit all children (Chandler, Cochran, Christensen, Dinnebeil, Gallagher, Lifter, Stayton, & Spino, 2012). This movement has affected classroom play, and the impact will be explored further in Chapter 9.

1-5b Technology

Advances in technology have changed play in some preschool and primary classrooms. The changes range from very positive to less than positive. For example, in some classrooms, children sit with a friend and interact with the most current video program, stop and surf the Web for an answer to a question, and then return to the video program. They create books and reports with available technology and communicate with other children around the globe. At the other end of the spectrum, some classrooms have computer programs about blocks, but no blocks. There are numerous concerns about the impact of technology on play, and these are discussed further later in the text.

Did You Get It?

The views of citizens of other countries are impacted by sociocultural factors. An example of this is:

a. Scandinavia, which has extensive playgrounds.
b. Moscow, which is rebuilding its infrastructure.
c. Iraq, which is recovering from war.
d. Prague, which is trying to rebuild their economy.

Take the full quiz on CourseMate

 PLAYSCAPE REFLECTIONS

The vignette at the beginning of the chapter depicted a child joyfully sliding while an adult watches. The slide serves as the provocation. After reading this chapter, you may realize that children enjoy play. It is also apparent that children have an almost innate need to play. The look of joy on the child's face reflects the characteristics of play that include pleasure.

The value of play is evident in the child's expression.

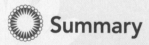 ## Summary

This chapter provided an overview of play and set the stage for the study of play in classrooms.

1-1 Identify current factors that affect the state of play in the United States.

Factors that support play in the United States include easy access to media, print, and Internet resources; an abundance of research and scholarship; great community play spaces; children's museums; school-based play programs; professional and philanthropic organizations; families; and teachers. Unfortunately, obstacles to play include poverty and/or violence; changing cultural values; limited places to play;

overemphasis on academics; and commercialization of childhood.

1-2 List global influences that impact the play of young children.

Play occurs throughout the world and reflects the unique characteristics of individual cultures.

1-3 Explain common characteristics of play.

Dispositions or characteristics of play include that it (1) Pleasurable, (2) voluntary, (3) requires active engagement, (4) is symbolic, (5) free of external rules, and (6) focuses on action rather than outcomes.

1-4 Compare three different theories of play.

Many theories have provided support for play throughout the centuries and today. Today constructivist theory, communication theory, and neuroscience provide a basis for understanding the child's need to play.

1-5 Describe the impact of culture and ethnicity on play.

Culture and ethnicity affect all aspects of children's play. As America becomes increasingly diverse, valuing different types and kinds of play will become even more important.

 # Key terms

Accommodation, 17
Assimilation, 17
Behavioral disposition, 09
Cognitive constructivism, 17
Context, 9
Dramatic play, 18

Ego mastery, 16
Exploration, 11
Functional play, 18
Games with rules, 18
Observable behavior, 9
Play frame, 20

Pleasure principle, 16
Practice play, 18
Symbolic play, 12
Symbolic constructivism, 21
Theory of mind, 21

 # Technology and Internet Resources

Play Shapers: http://www.playshaper.org.uk/ Provides an overview of how play is viewed in the United Kingdom.

White House Movement and Play Initiative: http://www.whitehouse.gov/ A national initiative to focus

on fitness was started by First Lady Michelle Obama. This program encourages movement and outdoor play.

Centers for Disease Control: http://www.cdc.gov This site describes a CDC publication that demonstrates how to create a play day for a community.

 # Activities

1. In-Class Labs

Create a cartoon that depicts either play or exploration. How can you tell that it is play? How can you distinguish exploration? How you can use your knowledge of both to encourage play?

2. Research

A. Write down your favorite memory of play. Ask an older relative or neighbor to recall her favorite play experience. How are these alike? How are they different? Talk to others who have also compared their play with those of their grandparents. Are there are any similar trends?

B. Observe a group of preschool children in a child care center or school for an hour. Write down everything that you observe. Now observe a group of children in an informal setting such as a park. Again write down everything that you see. What behaviors were similar? What behaviors were different?

C. Visit a child care center for two hours. What are the adults doing to support play in this environment?

D. Interview at least two parents of young children from another culture. What similarities do they see between the play that occurred in their native home and their child's play in the United States? What differences do they see?

E. Describe the theory that you consider most influential and discuss how it informs your interactions with children.

F. Evaluate your view of play after you reading this chapter.

3. Service Learning

1. Volunteer in a preschool for two hours. Be sure to follow center policy in terms of parking, dress, and interactions with the children. After the visit, write down as much as you can remember about the play that occurred in the classroom. Did you see support for play? Did you see children play? If so, describe their play. Which children engaged in the most play? Which children did not play? How do you distinguish play from nonplay? Does this fit with what you have read in this textbook and other sources?

2. Find a center that needs assistance repairing materials in the center. Volunteer to assist in repairing the materials and toys.

3. Volunteer to assist at a local park or playground on Saturday morning. Investigate the role of play workers in England. Would this be feasible in America? Why or why not?

4. Locate local museums and public resources that encourage play. Offer to support their facility through a service-learning project. Some groups create special displays in children's museums.

4. Family Connections

Ask a preschool teacher to distribute Table 1-4 to parents in her class. Ask them to chart how much time their children have for play during one week. The teacher can hold a meeting with parents to discuss the results of their survey and their concerns about their children. Some classes may want to develop a research project. Other classes may want to plan a meeting to discuss television alternatives, such as Family Game Night.

TABLE 1-4 Play Activities Chart

Child's Name	Play Time Indoors or Outdoors	Time Spent in Other Activities, Such as Watching Television or Playing Video Games
Monday		
Tuesday		
Wednesday		
Thursday		
Friday		
Saturday		
Sunday		
Total		

How much time does your child have to play? _____

How much time does your child spend in other activities? _____

© Cengage Learning 2015

Digital Download Download from CourseMate

 Visit CourseMate for this textbook to access the eBook, Did You Get It? quizzes, Digital Downloads, TeachSource Video Cases, flashcards, and more. Go to CengageBrain.com to log in, register, or purchase access.

 References _____

Addy, S., Engelhardt, W., & Skinner, C. (2013). Basic facts about low-income children: Children under 18 years, 2011. Fact Sheet distributed by the National Center for Poverty, Mailman School of Public Health, Columbia University.

Ashiabi, G. S. (2007). Play in the preschool classroom: Its socioemotional significance and the teacher's role in play. *Early Childhood Education Journal, 35*(2), 199–207.

Barnett, L. (1990). Playfulness: Definition, design, and measurement. *Play & Culture, 3*, 319–336.

Barton, E. E., & Wolery, M. (2010). Training teachers to promote pretend play in young children with disabilties. Exceptional Children, 77(1), 85–106.

Bateson, G. (1972). *Steps to an ecology of mind*. New York: Ballantine.

Bekoff, M., & Jamison, D. (Eds.) (1996). *Readings in animal cognition*. Cambridge, MA: MIT Press.

Bergen, D. (Ed.). (1988). *Play as a medium for learning and development: A handbook for theory and practice*. Portsmonth, NH: Heinemann.

Bergen, D. (2002). The role of pretend play in children's cognitive development. *Early Childhood Research & Practice: An Internet Journal on the Development, Care, and Education of Young Children. Spring 2002;PS 030 400.*

Bergen, D., & Fromberg, D. (2009). Play and social interaction in middle childhood. *Phi Delta Kappan, 90*(6), 426–430.

Berlyne, D. (1969). Laughter, humor, and play. In G. Lindzey & E. Aronson (Eds.), *The handbook of social psychology* (Vol. 3, pp. 795–852). Reading, MA: Adddison-Wesley.

Bowlby, J. (1988). *A secure base: Parent-child attachment and healthy human development.* New York: Basic Books.

Bretherton, I. (1984). *Symbolic play: The development of social understanding.* New York: Academic Press.

Bronfenbrenner, U. (1979). Foreward. In P. Chance (Ed.), *Learning through play. Pediatric Round Table:3* (pp. xv–xx). New York: Gardner.

Bruner, J. (1972). The nature and uses of immaturity. *American Psychologist, 27*(27), 686–708.

Bruner, J. (1990). *Acts of meaning.* Cambridge, MA: Harvard University.

Buchsbaum, D. D., Bridgers, S., Weisberg, D. S., & Gopnik, A. (2012). The power of possibility: Causal learning, counterfactual reasoning, and pretend play. Philosophical Transactions of the Royal Society, *367*(1599), 2202–2212.

Cannella, G. (1997). Deconstructing early childhood education: social justice and revolution. New York: Peter Lange.

Chandler, L. K., Cochran, D. C., Christensen, K. A., Dinnebeil, L. A., Gallagher, P. A., Lifter, K., Stayton, V. D., & Spino, M. (2012. The alignment of CEC/DEC and NAEYC Personnel Preparation Standards. Topics in Early Childhood Special Education, 31(1), 52-63.

Christiansen, M. (1997). International perspectives of playground safety. *Parks and Recreation, 32*(4), 100–101.

Comenius, J. A. (1896). *School of infancy.* Boston, MA: Heath.

Comenius, J. A. (1968). *Orbis sensualium pictus.* First English edition, Introduction by J. E. Sadler, Oxford University Press: London: Originally published in 1658.

Cook, G., Roggman, L., & D'Zatko, K. (2012). A person-oriented approach to understanding dimensions of parenting in low-income mothers. *Early Childhood Research Quarterly, 27*(4), 582–595.

Cook, G. A., Roggman, L. A., & Boyce, L. K. (2012). Fathers' and mothers' cognitive stimulation in early play with toddlers: Predictors of 5th grade reading and math. Family Science, *2*(2), 131–145.

Corsaro, W. (1986). Discourse processes within peer culture: From a constructivist to an interpretative approach to childhood socialization. In P. Adler (Ed.), *Sociological studies of children* development (pp. 81–101). New York: JAI.

Dewey, J. (1911). *Play.* In P. Monroe (Ed.), *A cyclopedia of education* (pp. 725–727). New York: Dutton.

Doherty, A. (2012). "Teacher, I showed her how to do that!": Teaching early-years children through mixed-age play. *Primary Science, 122,* 24–26.

Elkind, D. (2007). *The hurried child: Growing up too fast too soon* (25th ed.). Reading, MA: Addison-Wesley.

Elkind, D. (1987). *Miseducation: Preschoolers at risk.* New York: Alfred Knopf.

Elkind, D. (2007). *The power of play.* Philadelphia, PA: Perseus Books.

Ellis, M. J. (1973). *Why people play.* Englewood Cliffs, NJ: Prentice-Hall.

Erikson, E. H. (1977). *Toys and reason.* New York: Norton.

Erikson, E. H. (2000). *Childhood and society* (3rd ed.). New York: Norton.

Farver, J. (1992). An analysis of young American and Mexican children play dialogues. In C. Howes, O. Unger, & C. Matheson (Eds.), *The collaborative construction of pretense: Social pretend play functions* (pp. 55–66). Albany, NY: SUNY Press.

Fein, G. (1981). Pretend play in childhood: An integrative review. *Child Development, 52,* 1095–1118.

Fosnot, C. (1996). *Constructivism Theory, perspectives, and practice.* New York: Teachers College Press.

Freud, S. (1959). Creative writers and daydreaming. In J. Strackey (Ed.), *The standard edition of the complete psychological works of Sigmund Freud (Vol. IX)* (pp. 141–154). London: Hogarth. (Originally published 1908)

Froebel, F. (1887). *The education of man.* New York: Appleton.

Frost, J., & Wortham, S., & Reifel, S. (2008). *Play and child development.* Upper Saddle River, NJ: Merrill/Prentice Hall.

Garvey, C (1977). *Play.* Cambridge, MA: Harvard University Press.

Glover, A. (1999). The role of play in development and learning. In E. Dau (Main Ed.) & E. Jones (Consulting Ed.), *Child's play: Revisiting paly in early childhood settings* (pp. 5–15). Baltimore: Paul H. Brooks Publishing Co.

Gopnik, A. (2012). Nurturing brain development from birth to 3. *Zero To Three, 32*(3), 12–17.

Groos, K. (1901). *The play of man.* New York: Appleton.

Guddemi, M., & Jambor, T. (1992). *A right to play: Proceedings of the American Affiliate of the International Association for the Child's Right to Play,* Little Rock, AK: Southern Early Childhood Association.

Gulick, L. (1908). Mind and work. Garden City, NY: Doubleday.

Hall, G. S. (1916). What we owe to the tree-life of our ape-like ancestors. *Pedagogical Seminary, 23,* 94–119.

Henley, J., McBride, J., Milligan, J., & Nichols, J. (2007). Robbing elementary students of their childhood: The perils of No Child Left Behind. *Education, 128*(1), 56–63.

Hughes, M., & Hutt, C. (1979). Heart-rate correlates of childhood activities: Play exploration, problem solving and day dreaming. *Biological Psychology, 8,* 253–263.

Huizinga, J. (1955). *Homo Ludens: A study of the play element in culture.* Boston, MA: Beacon Press.

KaBOOM. (2013). It starts with a playground. Retrieved on Feb. 2013 from http://kaboom.org

Kinoshita, I. (2008). Children's use of space of the fourth generation (today) with reviewing the three generation's play maps (1982). *IPA 17th triennial conference "Play in a Changing World."* Hong Kong.

Klein, T., Wirth, D., & Linas, K. (2003). Play: Children's context for development. *Young Children, 58*, 38–46.

Kupperman, J. (Project Director). (2008). *Where do the children play?* (DVD) Metrocom International for Michigan Television.

Lancey, D. (2007). Accounting for variability in mother-child play. *American Anthropologists, 109*(2), 273–284.

Lascarides, V., & Hinitz, B. (2002). *History of early childhood education.* New York: Falmer.

Leslie, A. M. (1987). Pretense and representation: The origins of "theory of mind." *Psychological Review, 94*, 412–426.

Lester, S., & Russell, W. (2010). Children's right to play: An examination of the importance of play in the lives of children worldwide. *Working Paper No. 57.* The Hague, The Netherlands: Bernard van Leer Foundation.

Liberman, J. (1965). Playfulness and divergent thinking: An investigation of their relationship at the kindergarten level. *Journal of Creative Behavior, 1*, 391–397.

McDonough, P. (2009). *TV Viewing among kids at an eight-year high.* SVP Insights, Analysis and Policy, The Nielsen Company.

Medina, J. (2008). *Brain rules. 12 principles for surviving and thriving at work, home, and school.* Seattle, WA: Pear Press.

Medina, J. (2010). *Brain rules for baby. How to raise a smart and happy child from zero to five.* Seattle, WA: Pear Press.

Meire, J. (2007). Qualitative research on children's play: a review of recent literature. In Jambour. T., & Van Gils, J. (Eds.), *Several perspectives on children's play: Scientific reflections for practitioners* (pp. 29–78). Antwerp: Garant.

Miller, E., & Almon, J. (2009). *Crises in the kindergarten.* College Park, MD: Alliance for Childhood.

Muddock, L., & Hobbs, J. (2011). Picture me playing: increasing pretend play dialogue of children with autism spectrum disorders. *Journal of Autism and Developmental Disorders, 41*, 870–878.

New, R. (2003). Reggio Emila: New ways to think about schooling. *Educational Leadership, 60*(7), 34–39.

Newton, E., & Jenvey, V. (2011). Play and theory of mind: associations with social competence in young children, *Early Child Development Care, 181*(6), 761–773.

Olsen, H., Hudson, S. D., & Thompson, D. (2010). Strategies for playground injury prevention: An overview of a playground project. *American Journal of Health Education, 41*(3), 187–192.

Oxford English Dictionary. (2013). Oxford University Press. Retrieved on January 14, 2013 from www.oed.com

Panksepp, J. (2011). Toward a cross-species neuroscientific understanding of the affective mind: Do animals have emotional feelings? *American Journal Of Primatology, 73*(6), 545–561.

Pellegrini (1988). Elementary school children's rough-and-tumble play and social competence. *Developmental Psychology, 24*, 802–806.

Pellegrini, A., & Boyd, B. (1993). The role of play in early childhood development and education: Issues in definition and function. In B. Spodek's (Ed.), *Handbook of research on the education of young children* (pp. 105–121). New York: Macmillan Publishing Company.

Pestalozzi, J. (1894). *How Gertrude teaches her children.* Translated by Lucy E. Holland and Frances C. Turner. Edited with an introduction by Ebenezer Cooke. London: Swan Sonnenschein. (Originally published in 1801)

Piaget, J. (1962). *Play, dreams, and imitation in childhood.* New York: Norton. (Original work published in 1951)

Rantz-Smith, D. (2007). Teacher perception of play: In leaving no child behind are teachers leaving childhood behind? *Early Education and Development, 18*(2), 271–303.

Richert, R., Robb, M., & Smith, E. (2011). Media as social partners: The social nature of young children's learning from ccreen media. *Child Development, 82*(1), 82–95.

Rogers, C., Impara, J., Frary, R. ,Harris, T., Meeks, A, Semantic-Lauth, S., & Reynolds, M. (1999). *Measuring playfulness: Development of the Child Behaviors Inventory of Playfulness.* Presentation at The Association for the Study of Play Annual Conference, Santa Fe, NM.

Rogers, C., & Sluss, D. (1999). Revisiting Erikson's views on Einstein's play and inventiveness. In S. Reifel's *Play contexts revisited, Play and culture series* (Vol. 2), (pp. 3–24). Greenwich, CT: Ablex.

Rousseau, J. (1762/1991). *Emile.* Translate and annotated by Allan Bloom. London: Penguin.

Rubin, K. H., Fein, G., & Vandenberg, B. (1983). Play. In E. M. Hetherington (Ed.), P. H. Mussen (Series Ed.), *Handbook of child psychology: Vol.4, Socialization, personality, and social develoment* (pp. 693–774). New York: Wiley.

Rushton, S. (2011). Neuroscience, early childhood education and play: We are doing it right! *Early Childhood Education Journal, 39*(2), 89–94.

Saracho, O. N. (2011). *An integrated play-based curriculum for young children.* Routledge, Taylor & Francis Group.

Schiller, F. (1954). *On the aesthetic education of man.* New Haven, CT: Yale University Press.

Schlosberg, H. (1947). The concept of play. *Psychological Review, 54*, 229–231.

Shore, R. (1997). *Rethinking the brain: New insights into early development.* New York: Families and Work Institute.

Shornkoff, J., & Phillips, D. (2000). *From neurons to neighborhoods; The science of early childhood development.* Washington, DC: National Academy Press.

Shultz, T. (1979). Play as arousal modulation. In B. Sutton-Smith (Ed.), *Play and language* (pp. 7–22). New York: Gardner.

Silberg, J. (1993). *Games to play with babies.* Beltsville, MD: Gryphon House.

Silberg, J. (2000*). 125 brain games for babies.* Beltsville, MD: Gryphon House.

Singer, J. (1973). *The child's world of make-believe: Experimental studies of imaginative play.* New York: Academic Press.

Singer, J., & Singer, D. (1990). *The house of make-believe: Children's play and the developing imagination.* Cambridge, MA: Harvard University.

Spencer, H. (1873). *Principles of psychology.* (Vol. 2, 3rd ed.). New York: Appleton.

Sutton-Smith, B. (1982). Play theory and the cruel play of the nineteenth century. In F. E. Manning (Ed.), *The world of play* (pp. 103–124). West Point, NY: Leisure Press.

Sutton-Smith, B. (1997). *The ambiguity of play.* Cambridge, MA: Harvard University Press.

Sylvester, R. (2010). *A child's brain: The need for nurture.* Thousand Oaks, CA: Corwin Press.

Tobin, J., Wu, D., & Davidson, D. (1989). *Preschool in three cultures: Japan, China, and the United States.* New Haven, CT: Yale University Press.

Twardosz, S. (2012). Effects of experience on the brain: The role of neuroscience in early development and education. *Early Education And Development, 23*(1), 96–119.

United National Declaration for the Rights of the Child. Retrieved on February 2013 from http://www.ncjfcj.org/us-still-has-not-ratified-united-nations-convention-rights-child

Vygotsky, L. (1978). *Mind in society: The development of higher psychological processes.* Cambridge, MA: Harvard University Press.

Wakes, S., & Beukes, A. (2012). Height, fun and safety in the design of children's playground equipment. *International Journal of Injury Control & Safety Promotion, 19*(2), 101–108.

Wilson, E. O. (1975). *Sociobiology.* Cambridge, MA: Belknapp.

Wilson, R. (2012). *Nature and young children: Encouraging creative play and learning in natural environments* (2nd ed.). London, UK: Routledge, Taylor & Francis Group.

World Bank. (2009). *Reshaping economic geography: World development report 2009.* Washington, DC: The World Bank.

2 PLAY as Development

STANDARDS COVERED IN THIS CHAPTER

Council of Exceptional Children—Division of Early Childhood Standards CEC DEC

ECSE 2K1 Typical and atypical human growth and development

ECSE 2K6 Factors that affect mental health and social-emotional development of infants and young children

ECSE 2K7 Infants and young children develop and learn at varying rates

ECSE 3K2 Impact of social and physical environments on development and learning

NAEYC Program Standards naeyc

1a Knowing and understanding young children's characteristics and needs

1b Knowing and understanding multiple influences on early development and learning

4a Understanding positive relationships and supportive interactions as the foundation of their work with children

* LEARNING OBJECTIVES *

2-1 List the cognitive, social and emotional, communication, and physical benefits of play for infant and toddler growth and development.

2-2 Describe the types of play that dominate the infant and toddler years.

2-3 List the cognitive, social and emotional, communication, and physical benefits of play for preschoolers and kindergarteners.

2-4 Describe the types of play that dominate the preschool years.

2-5 List the cognitive, social and emotional, communication, and physical benefits of play for primary age children.

2-6 Describe the types of play that dominate the primary age children.

Lu Chen had just finished her teaching day. After picking up the groceries, she walked in her front door and was met by a shoosh and swirl as her twin girls, Wu Chon and Lu, ran through the house. They had towels draped around their shoulders and appeared to be involved in a pretend game of flying. Wu Chon ran through the house calling, "The dragons are coming, the dragons are coming!" Lu Chen's Aunt Nina looked at Wu Chon and said, "Yes they are, and they are on the patio now." Wu Chon and Lu ran outdoors to continue simultaneously searching for and fleeing from the dragons. As Lu Chen picked up the mail, she approached her aunt and asked, "Nina, do they play like this all the time when they are here?" Nina, the more experienced one, nodded, "Yes, Lu Chen, when they are not napping or sleeping. They remind me of you when you were a child. They are always busy. As soon as they return from preschool, they play." Lu Chen was delighted that her children were learning through play at school and at home.

Explaining Play Behaviors

In this scenario, we are unsure of Wu Chon's and Lu's impetus to play, but being together may explain part of the rationale for their play. The towels serve as a scaffold for the children's pretend play. Once the children have the towels draped around them, they enter the realm of pretend, and they control the play. Their play may take them upstairs or downstairs, indoors and outdoors, under the table or around the table. Are they learning anything, or is their play just a waste of their time? This is the question many parents and teachers face as they deal with play. Is play a good use of their children's time?

Play as development is fully developed in this chapter. This concept serves as a basis for examining cognitive, social, and physical development in three broad age ranges: infants and toddlers, preschoolers, and primary age children. It provides a starting point for understanding the progression of play and its subsequent benefits for human growth and development. Although generalizations are made in this chapter to provide an overview of typical growth and development, children continually progress through increasingly more complex levels of development, at different rates and various ages. Each child is different and will experience growth and development in his or her own way. For example, all typically developing children move from lying in their crib to walking upright. Some will crawl first, some will scoot, but all typically developing and most atypically developing children will walk. How this occurs varies in individual children. We begin with infants and toddlers, move to preschool and kindergarteners, and end with primary and middle childhood.

* 2-1 Benefits of Play for Infants and Toddlers (0–2)

Infants follow a predictable sequence of growth and development during the first two years. Their physical, cognitive, social and emotion, communication, and adaptive development are intertwined (Lifter, Foster-Sander,

Arzamarski, Briesch, & McClure, 2011). Growth during this period is rapid and follows a general sequence (Berk, 2012). In the same way, play begins as early as the second month of life and follows a predictable sequence (Piaget, 1951/1962). *For the first two years of life, children discover their world through play and exploration.*

2-1a Cognitive Development

The infant begins with a brain that is very plastic. Positive influences have a stimulating effect on the brain, and negative influences decrease the brain's activity (Photo 2-1). Factors that affect the child's development include nourishment, care, stimulation, and environment (Shonkoff & Phillips, 2000). The availability of play activities affects not only development but also the size of the brain. As previously reported, one study found that the play that occurs between parent and child is correlated to the child's math scores in the fifth grade (Cook, Roggman, & Boyce, 2011).

Marshall (2011) found that infant brain development is a dynamic process dependent upon **endogenous and exogenous stimulation** and a supportive environment. A critical period of brain and neurosensory development occurs during the mother's third trimester and into the infant's "fourth" trimester (first three months of life). Disruption, damage, or deprivation in the infant's social and physical environment can create permanent deficits in the developing neurosensory systems. In contrast, when the brain receives the appropriate

amount of stimulation, *the brain thrives, grows, and develops.* A study by Luby Barch, Belden, Gaffrey, Tillman, Babb, Nishino, Suzuki, and Botteron (2012) found that positive experiences were related to a healthy hippocampal development, a brain region key to memory and stress modulation. The most current research on the brain suggests that infants are born with certain neurological pathways that are hard wired and that these are strengthened through interactions with others (Gartstein, Bridgett, Young, Panksepp, & Power, 2013; Luby, et al., 2012). The infant smiles and the adult smiles back, the infant cries and the adult comforts the child, the adult plays "pat-a-cake" and the infant laughs. In this setting, the adult is fostering development because the child feels safe and secure. During the first two years, changes are occurring very quickly, and play that occurs between the adult and child provides opportunities for growth and development.

© Cengage Learning 2015

2-1 The relationship between the adult and child is a predictor for future brain growth and development.

2-1b Social Development

Infants and young children are socialized into their culture by adults and older peers. Adult-child relationships vary among cultures and ethnic groups. Western cultures tend to cultivate independence whereas some eastern cultures tend to foster cooperation (Tobin, Wu, & Davidson, 1989). This can be observed in specific caregiving patterns that include holding, sleeping, feeding, and interactions. Initial relationships are established in the microsphere with adults and may include parent(s), early educators, grandparent(s), sibling(s), and neighbors. The child will form an attachment to one of more adults. Attachment serves as the foundation for social and emotional growth and development. Honig (2002) described **attachment** as "a strong emotional bond between a baby or young child and caring adult who is part of the child's everyday life—the child's attachment figure" (p. 2). A secure attachment forms the basis of the child's sense of self and view of the world. Infants who have a caring, consistent caregiver learn to trust, and this leads to good social and emotional health.

Play can enhance attachment. When adults and infants play, babies develop knowledge of turn taking and communication signals, and they start to make sense of their world. Opportunities for fostering attachment occur when adults respond to their smile with a smile, when adults sing a comforting song and hold them as they move around the room, or when the adult plays peek-a-boo. Responsive adults who form an attachment bond with an infant during the first months will notice a difference as the child matures. Around the age of nine to ten months, the child may become anxious if the familiar caregiver or attachment figure is not available. Though this is most intense during the period from 9 months to 18 months, some older children have attachment issues, and these will be discussed later in the chapter. Positive social interactions between adults and infants lead to enhanced cognitive development.

2-1c Emotions

Erikson (1950/2000) created a lifespan perspective of social and emotional growth. During the first two years, he recognized the need for infants to develop trust rather than mistrust. A secure attachment reflects the establishment of a trusting relationship. The development of trust leads to healthy emotions. Emotional growth has frequently been linked to attachment issues. Greenspan and Wieder (2012, p. 3) identified six levels of emotional growth that lead to good mental health (see Table 2-1).

2-1d Communication

Interactions between adults and infants are necessary for the development of communication skills. The basis for language and communication is established during this adult-infant play. Some believe this is a form of game playing because of the

TABLE 2-1	Levels of Emotional Growth
1. 0–3 months:	Protection, comfort, and interesting sights and sounds *to feel regulated* and *interested in the world*;
2. 3–7 months:	Wooing and loving overtures to *fall in love*;
3. 4–10 months:	Sensitive, empathetic reading of cues to foster *purposeful communication*;
4. 9–18 months:	Admiring, organized, intentional interactions to foster *a complex sense of self*;
5. 18–30 months:	Pretend play and functional use of language to foster *emotional ideas*;
6. 30–48 months	Effective limits and use of logic in pretend play and language to foster *emotional thinking*

© Cengage Learning 2015

reciprocal nature of the interaction. Yet some scholars do not view this as game playing, but of mutually reciprocal interactive play. The adult says, "Ooh, you are soooo happy today," and the child tries to move her mouth. The adults says, "Are you ready to look at the bear?" and the infant responds with babbling sounds. This continues until the infant or the adult disengages from the interaction. Was this play or was it social interaction? It was both. As the parent engaged the child, she developed the child's knowledge of turn taking, which is necessary for both play and conversation.

2-1e Physical Development

The most rapid period of physical growth and development occurs during the first two years. Within a year of birth, the child's weight triples and he can crawl, stand, and walk. Mobility is refined and practiced during the second year of life. Two major factors that impact play during the first two years include the process of gaining teeth (7 months to 3 years) and the toilet training process (14 months to 2½ or 3 years). Both processes can limit the child's comfort level and play.

Infant and toddler movement can be divided into three stages: no mobility, low mobility, and high mobility (Wellhousen, 2002). *No mobility* is a term used to describe infants who cannot propel themselves and must be carried by adults. They discover the world by listening, looking, and touching. Low mobility infants are those who have limited mobility. Their strength is increasing and they can crawl, scoot, and begin to cruise from one place to another (Photo 2-2). High mobility infants can crawl, cruise, or climb anywhere!

Psychomotor Skills. Motor development produces the most obvious changes during the first two years. Infants begin as somewhat immobile, and by the end of the second year, any adult can attest to their mobility. Gross motor development involves the large motor muscles, and fine motor skills involve the use of smaller muscles. During the first two years, both

▶❚❚ TeachSource Video Case 2-1

0–2 Years: Fine Motor Development for Infants and Toddlers

Observing infants is so fascinating that we can easily forget the purpose of the observation.

This activity is designed to show how infants develop their fine motor skills and how play facilitates this process. View this video clip and then answer the following questions.

1. How can objects stimulate play for six- and nine-month-olds?

2. Does play affect the development of fine motor skills in young infants and toddlers?

Watch on CourseMate

2-2 Children who have opportunities to explore and play develop their locomotor skills. This child is discovering the world as he develops his crawling or gross motor skills.

© Cengage Learning 2015

are developing, but gross motor movements are more dominant. Seefeldt and Barbour (1998) described these interactions in this way.

> The baby's early movements are gross body actions, starting with the shoulders but without separate arm, hand, or finger movements. More than a year passes before the baby can make independent finger movements or oppose thumb and forefinger to grasp an object. (p. 429)

Educators can facilitate the development of gross and fine motor skills through their interactions with the children. For example, a study of children who were beginning to walk found that the most important factor is experience. Walking is a developmental process that develops with age and experience, and this has implications for practice. Early educators who provide opportunities for children to cruise and move freely are facilitating the child's physical development (Adolph, Vereijken, & Shrout, 2003).

✳ 2-2 Types of Play

Infants enter the world dependent upon their senses and physical ability to develop as human beings. Researchers tell us that some infants play within the second month of birth (Piaget, 1951/1962). Infants can see, hear, taste, touch, and smell from birth. This gives them the ability to grasp, bang, taste, and shake. Their development is directly related to their play, and their play is directly related to their development.

2-2a Practice Play

Piaget referred to the first two years of life as the **sensorimotor period**. Play that occurs during this time reflects the child's level of intellectual growth and is called practice play. During the first two years of life, functional or practice play dominates. This is not the only kind of play, however. As play develops and becomes more complex, children move from exploration and object play to language and symbolic play.

Piaget discussed six levels of practice play, and these form a framework for conceptualizing the development of play during the first two years. Shore (1997) refers to this as a "**prime time** for optimal development—periods during which the brain is particularly efficient at specific types of learning" (p. 39).

1. **Reflexive stage**   (0–1 month)

   Reflexes rule this age, and infants spend their time watching, observing, and reacting instinctively.

2. **Primary circular reactions**   (1–4 months)

   Touching becomes important as infants begin to develop their ability to cause an effect. They tend to use circular reactions when grasping and reaching.

3. **Secondary circular reactions stage**   (4–8 months)

   Reaching and grabbing skills are developing. The joy of causing an effect is evident in laughter. Doing something for the pleasure of doing it evolves at this age.

4. **Coordination of secondary schemes**   (8–12 months)

   Two factors are influential. The first is trying known actions in new situations. The child can use a previously learned behavior in a novel setting.

The second factor is mobility from one scheme to another. The child can move quickly from one action or behavior to another. Pushing and pulling objects and putting materials on their heads are fun for this age.

5. **Tertiary circular reactions**   (1 year–18 months)

Children actively explore their world. Children can stand, move, try known actions in new situations, and move from one scheme to another. This is when children will put a key in an outlet.

6. **Invention of new means through mental combinations** (18 months–24 months)

Pretense begins when the child enjoys applying schema to inadequate objects. In other words, the child enjoys pretending that one object is another.

Exploration.   During the infant's first year of life, she will spend a lot of time exploring the world through her senses. Looking and listening are most common during this time. As she grows, exploration will become more complex. For the casual observer, it is especially difficult to distinguish between play and exploration in the very young child. Is the child playing or is the child exploring (Photo 2-3)? Infants spend most of their time exploring. They use their senses to find meaning in their world. The toddler splits her time between exploration and practice play. Caruso (1984) was the first to suggest that we call it **exploratory play** due to the rapid transitions from exploration to play and back again. By the end of the second year, exploration begins to decrease and pretend begins to increase. Watch some two-year-olds as they explore a roll of toilet tissue. After figuring out how the paper can be pulled around the roll (exploration), they will pull the tissue and laugh in delight as the tissue falls to the floor (practice play), then run through the house waving the tissue like a flag (pretend). Only the child can know what is intended during her imaginary play. During this time the toddler's exploration is both a source of delight and a reason for safety concerns. The child will explore

© Cengage Learning 2015

2-3 What does this child see when he looks at the sink basin? His ability to explore his world is facilitated by the reactions of the adults around him.

the object (e.g., toy, pot or pan, or box) to figure out what it is. After the child is satisfied, she will engage in practice play, over and over. Exploration allows infants to understand the world through their physical senses, and practice play provides a venue for infants and toddlers to strengthen neurological connections.

2-2b Object Play

Object play begins when the infant can grasp objects. This usually develops around four months, when infants are in the secondary circular reaction stage. Object play becomes more complex as the child grows and develops. Children move from being conscious of only their body to being conscious of the external world as they develop and progress through the tertiary circular reactions to the invention of new means through mental combinations (Piaget, 1951/1962). Infants who lack sensory and physical capabilities to fully engage in object play may experience delays in development.

Young children begin by using one object and then proceed to the use of two or more in increasingly more complex combinations. During early object play, the object directs the infant's attention. Give the six-month-old a rattle and it is the rattle that will direct the child's interaction. Does it make a noise? Does it change when moved? The question that dominates is, "What can this thing do?" As the child matures, the child directs the action on the object. At the end of the first year, when given a pot, the toddler will put things in and take things out of it. A change occurs again by the end of the second year. The child who encounters a pot will, most likely, put it on her head. The child has moved from being guided by the object to guiding the object.

Object play generally elicits different behaviors during functional and indiscriminate play (Bjorklund & Gardiner, 2011; Rubin, Fein, & Vandenberg, 1983). During **functional play**, the child uses the object for the function that the object was intended in her culture. A drinking cup is used for pretend drinking. A toy cell phone is used as a real cell phone. The child uses the object to imitate reality. **Indiscriminant or stereotypical play** occurs when the child uses the object in an indiscriminate way—banging the cup, throwing the cell phone, and so on. This type of object play is the kind that results in such outcomes as bread being placed in the DVD player, and it is frequently a source of both frustration and amusement for young parents and early educators.

2-2c Symbolic Play

Young children begin to engage in pretend or nonliteral play around their first birthday. It becomes more complex during the second year of life. Piaget's initial work on symbolism continues to serve as the foundation for current studies. Three major elements in symbolic play occur during the first two years of life (Bretherton, 1984; Fenson, 1986): decontextualization, decentration, and integration.

Decontextualization. Decontextualization occurs when the child represents objects and actions symbolically with other objects and actions. The child's first pretense or pretend play is decontextulalized. The child may be in the middle of playing with some objects (toys) when she sees a pillow. Though she is playing on the carpet, she may place her head on the pillow as though she is going to sleep. As soon as her head touches the pillow, she will look at adults and smile because she knows it is not real. Sleeping and eating routines tend to lend themselves to the first decontexualized behaviors because they involve daily routines (Photo 2-4).

2-4 If she is pretending to eat, she is engaging in early symbolic or pretend play.

2-5 Decentration is occurring as the child focuses on the doll rather than on herself.

Decentration. Decentration occurs when the child moves from focusing on self to focusing on others. The child will begin to involve others in pretend play around 18 months (Photo 2-5). Though symbolism might be noticed around the first birthday, the child focuses on self. At one year the child might be content to pull a blanket over her head. By eighteen months, she wants to put the blanket on her head and the head of the nearest person. She begins to realize that other people are a part of the world also.

Integration. Integration involves the combination of several single schemes into a multiple-scheme play experience. The child pretends to put the doll in the bed. These behaviors are generally observed around the second birthday. Most of the play involves imitating reality and seems to follow the social conventions for the activity. This indicates that play is governed by rules. Although children develop their ability to pretend during this time, the type of play that dominates during the first two years is practice or functional play. This will change as the child grows, develops, and moves into the preschool years.

> ### Did You Get It?
> A seven-month-old's infant grabs a toy away from another child. In which stage of play is this infant?
> **a.** coordination of secondary schemes
> **b.** reflexive stage
> **c.** secondary circular reactions stage
> **d.** primary circular reactions
>
> Take the full quiz on CourseMate

Play Benefits for Preschoolers (2–5) 2-3 *

Young children continue to grow and develop during this period, though not as fast as they did during the first two years. Some children are well coordinated and can walk and run at a very early age. Others are very articulate and can solve puzzles easily. Common to all children at this age is play. Berger and Thompson (1996) called the time from two to six the **play years**. Preschoolers are in the middle of their play years. Fantasy and pretend dominate this period. Children develop play skills as they move from practice to pretend, from novice to mature play. The two-year-old who wants to throw his food from the table turns into a four-year-old who pretends the sofa is a trampoline. This progression occurs in the physical, social, and cognitive domains through different types of play and varies among different cultures, ethnic groups, and individuals. Early educators who are aware of different levels are sensitive to children and their play.

2-3a Cognitive Development

Preschool children have thought processes that have not completely matured. Piaget (1952/1974) called this the **preoperational thinking** period. Two characteristics of this age include the attribution of animistic characteristics to inanimate objects and egocentrism. Preschoolers believe they are the center of the universe. Listen to the four-year-old talk to the moon. She believes that the moon follows her from place to place. Preoperational thought signals the beginning of the ability to reconstruct in thought what has been established in behavior. These characteristics impact play, which peaks during the preoperational period.

Children at this age believe what they see and rely on their senses instead of logic. So magic is really magic to them. Paley (1981) refers to this in her classical *Walley's Stories,* when she writes about the children's discussion of the moon:

> On the other hand, when Earl mentioned the man in the moon, the children earnestly examined the issues.
>
> Earl: My cousin says you can wish on the man in the moon. I told my mother and she says it's only pretend.
>
> Wally: He doesn't have a face or a body.
>
> Lisa: Then he can't see. He's not real.
>
> Deane: But how could he get in?
>
> Wally: With a drill.
>
> … As long as children are unsure of the boundaries between fantasies and reality, they will invent supernatural beings to protect them. When part of the moon disappears, they like to think of a moon man capable of adjusting to those strange circumstances and they like to talk about their ideas. Whether they do discuss them or not depends as much on the adult reception as on their own verbal ability. (excerpted from pp. 63–65)

▶❚❚ TeachSource Video Case 2-2

2–5 Years: Piaget's Preoperational Stage

The children in this video clip are developing their capacity to think logically. No two children develop at the same rate or in the same way. Understanding how all children grow and develop, but at different times and in unique ways, provides the adult with information she can use to inform planning, teaching, and assessment.

1. How does egocentric thinking affect play?

2. What impact does conversation have on children's play?

Watch on CourseMate

© Cengage Learning 2015

2-3b Social Development

The social changes that occur from age two to five are remarkable. The child is developing his sense of self, which leads to social competence. Preschool children are moving into what Erikson referred to as the "industry versus

TABLE 2-2   Stages of Social Play (2–5 years)

Unoccupied behavior: Not involved in play, wanders around in the room.

Onlooker behavior: Observing but just watching, not playing.

Solitary play: Plays along. May be involved in very intense, concentrated play, but is playing alone.

Parallel play: Plays alone but is beside or next to other children.

Associative play: Plays with other children.

Cooperative play: Plays together in a group.

© Cengage Learning 2015

guilt" stage. They are moving from dependency on their parents to becoming autonomous individuals. Play provides an opportunity for social and emotional growth. Mildred Parten's (1932) classic study includes six levels. Preschoolers generally participate in all levels that include unoccupied behavior, onlooker behavior, solitary play, parallel play, associative play, and cooperative play. In the preschool years, unoccupied and onlooker behaviors still occur, but **parallel**, **associative**, and **cooperative play** develop at this time (see Table 2-2). **Parallel play** occurs when two children play side-by-side but do not interact with one another (Photo 2-6). This is often evident in three-year-olds.

Associative play is defined as play that occurs between two children that involves interaction. Three- and four-year-olds engage in a great deal of associative play. **Cooperative play** is generally not evident until the age of four. Cooperative play reflects the most mature level of social interactions. Cooperative play occurs when the child plays in a group that has shared goals. This involves complex social organization, which may include negotiation, division of labor, differentiated role taking, and organization of play themes.

© Cengage Learning 2015

2-6 These children are engaged in parallel play. They are aware of each other, but are playing separately.

Peer Play.   Peer play during the preschool years usually involves pretend play. Children who engage in high-quality pretense are usually well adjusted. Conolly and Doyle (1984) found that "the amount and complexity of children's fantasy play were significantly correlated with four measures of social competence: teacher rating of social skill; peer popularity; affective role-taking ability; and amount of positive social activity (e.g., expressions of friendship, invitations to play and amount of conversation)" (p. 16, 1984). Children who can engage in highly symbolic play are leaders because they not only direct but engage others in their play. One caveat is that culture may impact social interactions.

2-3c Communication

Language development during the preschool years occurs at a very rapid rate. Sociocultural influences impact the development of language. In her classic study, Shirley Brice Heath (1983) reminds us of the language differences that children bring to school. Children from lower socioeconomic homes have fewer words in their vocabulary than those from more affluent homes. Play allows children to use words in an informal situation. Play is episodic, and language is equally fluid. Play facilitates language development as children play, talk about their play, and tell stories about their play.

2-3d Physical Development

From the age of two through five, children are acquiring amazing dexterity and motor control. Their locomotor skills are also becoming more refined. **Locomotor skills** refer to skills that involve movement. These include running, jumping, hopping, climbing, skipping, rolling, creeping, crawling, climbing, stepping up and down, bounding, and galloping. The list is exhaustive. Fine motor skills are developing at a regular pace. Preschoolers enjoy and learn by working puzzles, using brushes, manipulating small blocks, working with modeling clay, zipping, and snapping.

Three- and four-year-olds are more capable than toddlers. They can walk and run easily. They can hop, jump, skip, throw a ball, climb stairs, and ride simple tricycles. During this time they are learning how to make whole or part body movements to music as they clap, turn, stamp, and move to music.

✳ 2-4 Types of Preschool Play

During the preschool years, changes in cognitive processing occur and are reflected in play. Children move from practice play to symbolic play as they develop their ability to engage in abstract thought. The literature from brain research suggests that the brain reinforces some connections and prunes others as it becomes more focused and specialized. Play allows children to develop symbolic thought necessary for higher-level thinking that involves imagination and creativity. The concept of "what might be"—that is, being able to move from perception to the concrete given, or "what is," to "what was, what could have been, what one can try for, what might happen," and, ultimately, to the purest realms of fantasy—is a touchstone of that miracle of human experience, the imagination (Singer & Singer, 1992, p. 108).

2-4a Constructive Play

One type of play that occurs during this time is constructive play; it occurs when children use materials to create (Isenberg & Jalongo, 2009). They may be creating a representation of an object or they may be just creating. When children play with play dough, build with blocks, or paint a picture, they are engaging in constructive play. Constructive play generally leads to an end product. Piaget did not believe that constructive play was play because it is more adaptive to reality. He believed that when children were exploring or constructing, they were creating new mental structures or accommodating the information. Smilansky's (1968) work recognized this as a different type of play, and now most scholars include constructive play under the heading of play as a transition stage between practice and symbolic play. Though children engage in constructive play more frequently than any other type of play in the preschool class, constructive play continues to be understudied in the preschool classroom (Sluss & Stremmel, 2004).

When a child plays with blocks, she may begin by building (constructive play). As she looks at it, she adds more blocks to the left and right side (exploration), adds more blocks (practice play), looks again, and then declares, "It's a sky-scraper and the monster is coming …" (symbolic play). Constructive play occurs as the child moves from exploration, to practice play, and then to symbolic play and repeats the cycle again. During constructive play, the child may engage in more constructive and practice play as she carries the blocks around the room. As she develops, constructive play and symbolism become more prevalent.

2-4b Symbolic Play

Symbolic play or pretend occurs when the child uses an object or action to represent another object or idea. The child might use a block to represent an airplane or lay his head down to pretend he is sleeping. Symbolism appears as early as 18 months, and dramatic play begins to develop during the second year of life. It grows more complex as the child matures, and it reaches a peak at age five or six. **Dramatic play** is viewed as an imitation of reality that includes **orderliness**, **exact imitation of reality**, and collective symbolism of play roles (Piaget, 1951/1962). Dramatic play enables children to engage in complex pretend that requires symbolic thought. Children (two- to three-year-olds) initially direct their play toward materials or objects during pretend play. As children mature (four- to five-year-olds), they include people and assume different roles (Photo 2-7). This is the most complex pretend play and is called sociodramatic play.

© Cengage Learning 2015

2-7 Levels of symbolic play can be identified during dramatic or pretend play. These children are involved in collaborative pretend play.

2-4c Sociodramatic Play

Sociodramatic play is dramatic play that occurs among two or more children who communicate verbally and then cooperatively adjust their roles during the play episode (Isbell & Raines, 2013; Isenberg & Jalongo, 2009). Sarah Smilansky (1968) found that children in other parts of the world engage in different kinds

A Teacher's Role in Facilitating Play and Development

Dr. Martha Ross
Professor Emeritus,
James Madison University

© Cengage Learning 2015

Play is as important for teachers to pay attention to as worksheets and writing journals. It is how a teacher knows what to plan next in the curriculum. Teachers are not passive in a play environment. They are constantly thinking about how to add more information, how to have children think more deeply through questioning, and how to link the child's representation of the world to more abstract levels, such as models and words. When she sees children interested in firefighters, she can read books to extend their knowledge, plan field trips or class visitors who can provide additional information and answer children's questions, and can add props to expand children's pretend play or new materials to the block area. She can observe what the children are doing and know when other types of community helpers should be added to the children's knowledge base. Teachers can also provide opportunities for children to practice the skills they are acquiring in reading and mathematics. For example, adding notebooks and paper to the kitchen area will encourage children to make grocery lists or play restaurant. Adding rulers and yard sticks to the block-building area can lead to measuring how far the car went when it went down the ramp or how tall a building is.

Teachers can also assess children's level of symbolic representation and thus their cognitive development by observing their play, by analyzing their constructions and art work, and by listening to their questions. Teachers should look for the number of symbolic actions that are involved in dramatic play, such as the use of props, the different voices used to represent different characters, the way children adapt their roles to those of other children in the group, how long the play lasts, and how clearly the characters are portrayed. In children's art, teachers look for how representational it is. Is the child naming the things he draws or paints; how detailed or how clearly do the objects resemble what they are supposed to be; how are they oriented to each other; do they float on the page or are they anchored on a line? The more detailed children's representations are, the more the child is able to use and recall the things he knows, the more mature is his cognitive development. This symbolic representation is the prerequisite to understanding the more abstract world of letters and numbers.

Dr. Martha Ross is Professor Emeritus at James Madison University, where she taught child development. She has worked in the field of Early Childhood Education for 42 years.

of social play. What begins as dramatic play turns into sociodramatic play. She described six characteristics that are typically found in sociodramatic play (Smilansky & Shefatya, 1990, p. 24). The first four are common to both dramatic and sociodramatic play. The last two occur only during sociodramatic play. They are as follows:

1. *Imitative role-play.* The child undertakes a make-believe role and expresses it in imitative action and /or verbalization.

2. *Make-believe with regard to objects.* Movements or verbal declarations and/or materials or toys that are not replicas of the object itself are substituted for real objects.

3. *Verbal make-believe with regard to action and situations.* Verbal descriptions or declarations are substituted for actions and situations.

4. *Persistence in role-play.* The child continues within a role or play theme for a period of time at least 10 minutes long.

The following are only found in sociodramatic play:

5. *Interaction.* At least two players interact within the context of a play episode.

6. *Verbal communication.* There is some verbal interaction related to the play episode.

Pretend reaches its peak at the end of the kindergarten years.

Superhero Play. Superhero play begins in the preschool years. Although it is relatively brief in duration, many adults ban this type of play in their classroom. Superhero play combines pretend play with rough and tumble play. Some teachers believe that all superhero play is linked to violent themes or aggression. Though aggression and violent themes should never be condoned or permitted, stopping play always carries the risk of diminishing play. The real message becomes, "It is only acceptable play when I say it is acceptable," and that may be a message that stops positive behaviors in addition to play.

Superhero play can be beneficial for children. It combines symbolism with a type of rough and tumble play. Children who don a cape or towel as a make-believe cape assume a role that allows them to be strong and powerful. They are developing empathy as they aid the victim of an attack. They develop symbolism when they imagine other villains. Some children will take capes to school to play out their themes. This also encourages group and cooperative play for children who may not have access to playmates at home. The same children who would never engage in sociodramatic play indoors will engage in sociodramatic play on the playground as they negotiate the role of the superhero.

Before ending superhero play, it may be worthwhile to observe the play that is occurring and decide if it is superhero play, rough and tumble play, or war play. Superhero play and rough and tumble play have positive attributes and should be encouraged. On the other hand, war play or violent themes should be approached differently, as explained in the following section.

War Play. Many adults confuse superhero play and war play. Toys that reflect war and violence have been banned in some Scandinavian countries. In contrast, in the United States, many toys such as GI Joe or action heroes are easily accessible in national chain stores. Parents who want to prevent their children from this exposure must be vigilant (Levin & Carlsson-Paige, 2006). Early educators face the same issues. Today, many teachers have a no-gun or no-war-toy rule. The recent tragedies involving guns and young children at Newtown, Connecticut have placed the issue of guns and a culture of violence in the national news.

Because preschoolers are in the early stage of pretend, they engage in dramatic play rather than sociodramatic play. Their play is very brief, episodic, and improvisational. Guiding play in a way that discourages war play for the preschool child requires sensitive, thoughtful teachers. Diane Levin (2003) recommends the following approaches to dealing with violent play:

1. Address children's needs while trying to reduce play with violence.

2. Encourage the safety of all children.

3. Promote the development of imaginative and creative play rather than imitative play.

2-4d Physical Play

Two types of physical play that develop during the preschool years include chase and rough and tumble. Both involve large muscle movement, and although adults would like to restrict these types of play to the playground, they can and do occur at any time and in any place.

Chase.   Chase involves one child running after another. With preschoolers, the chaser may become the chased within a minute with no apparent rationale. Children run for a while, rest for a while, and then run some more. Sometimes one child will become angry because the other ceases to chase. The nature of chase play is very variable at this age.

Rough and Tumble.   Rough and tumble play only occupies only about 10% of all preschoolers' behavior on the playground (Pelligrini, 2011). Because play at this age is so egocentric and short lived, rough and tumble play is brief. Additional information on rough and tumble play is provided in Chapter five.

As children develop, they move into the primary years. With their change in capabilities, their play changes. Piaget (1951/1962) would argue that this is a reflection of intelligence, but Vygotsky (1978) would disagree because he believed that play provides a platform for the development of intelligence. Regardless of the theoretical stance, children change with age, and so does their play. The next section focuses on play behaviors common in the primary school. As in the previous sections, the discussion will occur in terms of cognitive, social, and physical development.

✳ 2-5 Benefits of Play for Primary Age Children (6–8)

Children in the primary grades are generally between six and eight years of age. *Middle childhood* is the term typically used to describe the period of time between six and eleven years of age. This chapter looks specifically at children up through age eight and will use the term *primary age* to describe this age group. According to Hughes (2010), there are three major characteristics of development during this time that impact play: (1) a need for order, (2) a need to belong, and (3) a sense of self. In the cognitive domain, the child is developing logical thought and has a *need for order* and structure. Socially, the child wants to be accepted by his peers and has a *need to belong*. Emotionally, the child is in what Erikson described as the industry versus inferiority stage (Erikson, 2000). The child needs to develop confidence and a sense of self-esteem. These traits affect the type of play that occurs in the primary years.

2-5a Cognitive Development

Children develop a more organized and logical view of the world during middle childhood. Piaget (1951/1962) referred to this as concrete operational thinking. Children at this age can generally engage in decentering, reversibility, seriation, and spatial reasoning, and they are beginning to conserve. That is, they are aware that the quantity of an object may be the same although it appears in different forms. They are developing logical thinking skills. They can use specific strategies, such as mnemonics, for remembering information. They find games especially enjoyable, and this may help explain why school-age children are drawn to computer games.

Bruner (1976) wrote about the role of play in developing problem-solving skills. As children try one maneuver after another on the game board, they must revisit and reconsider their moves. Cognitive skills used and developed during board games are useful for problem solving.

2-5b Social Development

Social development changes during this time. The young child may play with others, but now the child's play will be influenced by peers, the media, advertisements, and other influences in the child's world. During this time, children are developing friends. Now their choice of games or toys may be more influenced by these factors than by their parents.

2-5c Communication

Primary age children especially enjoy word games. They will create their own words and jokes that cause them to laugh hysterically. The fact that others may not understand these jokes does not concern them, as long as their friends are laughing. Knock-knock jokes are popular during this time. Word meanings that vary across cultures may create conflict during informal interactions. Children will experiment with language that may or may not be appropriate for school.

2-5d Physical Development

Children's skills really begin to emerge during the school years. Gender differences are noticeable between the age of 6 and 8 as boys gain more height and weight than girls (Frost, Wortham, & Reifel, 2012). Environmental factors influence health, and thus play, during this time. Children who are malnourished or obese will not be able to perform at the same level as their peers. Children who have serious illnesses will also be limited by their physical capabilities. During this time, children will take risks. They may not see the car as they chase a ball, or they may not realize that they will slide into a tree. As children become more mature, they become more aware of risks but may be more influenced by peers. Those who are allowed to play still enjoy recess at this age. See Chapter 10 for a full discussion of recess.

Fine Motor. Fine motor skills become more developed during this time. Some children will become especially skilled; others will continue to develop their skills. For children who are especially coordinated, games with strings and other tasks that require hand—eye coordination will begin to take on a separate role. It is not unusual to watch a budding musician emerge as she realizes that she can reach the octaves much easier than her friend can. Many games are played that develop hand—eye coordination. In some countries, such as China and Hungary, the game of marbles is played by both girls and boys (Ulker & Gu, 2004). Today, very few children in the United States play the game of marbles. Rather they demonstrate their agility through keyboarding or video games.

Gross motor. Gross motor skills become more refined as children develop skills in running, jumping, climbing, and chasing. They ride bicycles and play tee-ball, Little League (age 8), tennis, and other sport activities. Children play games that involve both movement and thought. For example, tag, jump rope, and hide and seek all take on different levels of complexity during these years. These involve chase but can lead to rough and tumble play, which may turn into play fighting. For this reason, many schools ban chase games and rough and tumble play in an attempt to prevent aggression. This ban, however, may lead to more aggression. A brief overview is provided below and is revisited later in Chapter 10

> ### Did You Get It?
> A seven-year-old child enjoys telling knock-knock jokes. Which area of development is being displayed?
> a. social
> b. physical
> c. cognitive
> d. fine motor
>
> Take the full quiz on CourseMate

✳ 2-6 Types of Play for Primary Age Children (6–8)

Primary age children grow and develop at different rates. Whereas some may be conserving volume and mass, others may not be conserving at all. Understanding this variability provides a foundation for understanding how children of varying cognitive levels play with and without their peers.

2-6a Symbolic Play

Symbolic play or pretend decreases during this time. Piaget (1951/1962) cites three reasons for the "diminution of ludic symbolism with age" (p. 145). First, the child no longer needs the cathartic effects of play. The child finds pleasure and power in different aspects of his life. For example, the child of five who does not like leaving home to go to preschool may pretend that he has an imaginary playmate that he can control. By seven, the child will share his frustrations with his friends and then write a story about "No School Today." Second, games of make-believe become games with rules. The child who plays zookeeper at four may be more interested in playing a game of "Sorry" at seven. The world makes sense, and he has a decreased need for creating a make-believe world. The five-year-old who does not understand why he is moving to a new town may engage in pretend play or create an imaginary friend; whereas the second grader may write a story about his experience.

Symbolism in the primary grades can be observed in stories or plays that children write, in dramatic plays, or in the creation of music or art. Symbolism occurs as creative symbolism and creativity. This change in thinking also changes and alters play. Sociodramatic play becomes storytelling as children act out elaborate scripts with dolls or miniature cars. Changes in cognitive thinking affect how they learn. Jerome Bruner (1985) noted that "there is evidence that by getting children to play with materials that they must later use in a problem-solving task, one gets superior performance from them in comparison with those children who spend time familiarizing themselves with the materials in various other ways…. The players generate more hypotheses and they reject wrong ones more quickly. They seem to become frustrated less and fixated less" (p. 603). Teachers who align their teaching with the child's developmental level will need to include play in the primary curriculum.

▶❚❚ **TeachSource** Video Case 2-3

© Cengage Learning 2015

5–11 years: Gross Motor Development for Middle Childhood

Variations in gross motor skills of children in middle childhood (6–12 years) are even more evident. Some children run smoothly across the playground whereas others struggle to run without stopping to catch their breath or falling. This clip highlights the development of these skills.

1. Discuss the development of gross motor skills and how they vary from child to child.

2. The development of gross motor skills impacts other domains. What additional skills are being developed?

Watch on CourseMate

2-6b Play Rituals

Gender differences continue to be pronounced from the ages of six to eight years of age and are especially evident in their play rituals (Boyle, Marshall, & Robeson,

2003). Boys tend to engage in games that require some sort of physical interaction before, during, or after the activity. This may be a game of touch football, high five, or play fighting. Some girls play games and engage in play rituals. Play rituals are defined as activities that instill "cultural values in aesthetically satisfying behaviors" (Barnes, 1998, p. 12). Common examples of play rituals include jump rope, cheerleading, and dancing. More recently, this has been described as verbal play. June Factor describes verbal play as social, rule grounded, and often traditional (1988, p. ix.) At this age, the increase in logical thinking leads to a need for order that can be found in play rituals and verbal play. Children are especially drawn to games like One Potato, Two Potato, and games like Rock, Paper, Scissors.

2-6c Games with Rules

Games with rules occur among primary age children. Piaget established two conditions for games with rules: competition and rules. He noted that games with rules are

> *Sensory-motor combinations (races, marbles, ball games, etc.), or intellectual combinations (cards, chess, etc.) in which there is competition between individuals (otherwise rules would be useless) and which are regulated either by a code handed down from earlier generations or by temporary agreement. (Piaget, 1951/1962, p. 144)*

Games with rules have an element of competition whereas play does not. Play occurs just for the sake of the play.

Chase Games.   Chase games begin in the preschool years, escalate in primary school, and disappear by middle school (Pellegrini, 2009). Chase games sometimes include threats of kissing, themes from popular culture, traditional hide and seek, and any kind of make-believe "contamination."

Rough and Tumble Play.   The decrease in symbolic play is accompanied by a simultaneous increase in **rough and tumble play (R&T)**. Rough and tumble play is defined as play that involves running, chasing, fleeing, and wrestling behaviors. Rough and tumble includes "play face, run, chase, flee, wrestle, and open-hand beat" (Pellegrini & Boyd, 1993, p. 115). These can be defined as follows:

Play face	Wide smile or exaggerated expression
Run	Rapid sustained movement from one place to another
Chase	One child pursues another.
Flee	Rapid movement from one spot to another
Wrestle	Physical contact that involves both children in an interactive tussle
Open-hand beat	Using the open hand, rather than a closed fist, for tagging

Aggression, on the other hand, usually includes frowning, fixation, hitting, pushing, taking, and grabbing (Blurton Jones, 1972). Children take turns during rough and tumble play, and specific rules govern the play: "in R&T children learn to use and practice skills that are important for their social competence. For example, in R&T children alternate roles between the victim and victimizer. Such reciprocal role taking may be important for children's perspective-taking ability" (Pellegrini, 1988, p. 15). The differences between R&T and aggression are real. R&T, like chase, is a normal, beneficial activity for primary age children. It can and should be encouraged while simultaneously discouraging aggression.

Did You Get It?

Three children are playing with dolls and imitating their parents going to work. In what type of play are these children engaging?
a. symbolic
b. sensorimotor
c. associative
d. integrated play

Take the full quiz on CourseMate

Bruno Bettelheim (1987) points to the work of the classical theorist K. Groos and to Piaget, both of whom investigated the function of play in developing motor and cognitive and intellectual abilities. "Play teaches the child, without his being aware of it, the habits most needed for intellectual growth, such as stick-to-itiveness, which is so important in all learning. Perseverance is easily acquired around enjoyable activities such as chosen play. But if it has not become a habit through what is enjoyable, it is not likely to become one through an endeavor like school work" (p. 36). Understanding the types of play observed frequently at this age and their progression provides a background for creating and implementing programs that are appropriate for young children. This chapter provides the base for developing programs discussed in Chapters 4, 5, 6, 7, and 8.

✻ PLAYSCAPE: REFLECTIONS

Lu Chen, like Jaunita in the previous chapter, values play. However, she may not know or understand that Wu Chon and Lu are developing their large motor skills when they engage in chase games that involve running and jumping. They are also developing social skills as they interact with each other and negotiate Aunt Nina's rules. This in turn helps them to understand and adjust to their culture and society outside their home. But are they learning? Pretend play develops their ability to engage in abstraction, which is a critical skill for learning and recognizing the alphabet and numbers. The twins play at school and at home. At school, they will play with English-speaking Americans. Their play will reflect a blend of the play that the children bring to school. In contrast, at home they will be able to learn games and stories passed along from their Chinese ancestors. The transmission of culture is an important part of their life because they are the first generation in a new land. Lu Chen can enrich their lives by taking them to parks, libraries, and social and spiritual activities on the weekend. Wu Chon and Lu will be ready to learn when they enter the public school system. The wise kindergarten teacher will help Lu Chen transition the children into a setting through play. Play can serve as a conduit for transitioning from one culture to another.

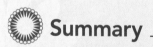

Summary

Play as beneficial for growth and development formed the core of this chapter. Although children develop holistically through play, this chapter teases it apart for the purpose of examination. The benefits of play are explored for infants and toddlers (birth to age two), preschoolers (three- to five-year-olds), and primary age children (six- to eight-year-olds). Their progress is examined in terms of cognitive, social, and physical growth. The progression of play is examined as the child moves from sensory exploration to complex games with rules.

2-1 Play benefits the cognitive, social and emotional, communication, and physical growth and development of infants and toddlers.

- Cognitive: Play facilitates healthy brain development.

- Social and emotional: Interactive play between the infant and adult enhances attachment and facilitates good emotional health.
- Communication: Interactive play serves as the basis for developing language skills.

- Physical: Play helps develop gross and fine motor skills. As the child attempts to reach a toy, she develops her ability to reach, stretch, scoot, crawl, and walk.

2-2 Describe the types of play that dominate the infant and toddler years.

- Practice, exploratory, object, and symbolic play occur during this time, and practice play dominates.

2-3 Play benefits the cognitive, social and emotional, communication, and physical growth and development of preschoolers.

- Cognitive: Play provides intellectual safety as the child interprets the world.
- Social and emotional: The goal of the play years is to develop autonomy.
- Communication: Children learn how to take turns and socially interact with others who may be different.
- Physical: Locomotor skills begin to develop.

2-4 Describe the types of play that dominate the preschool years.

- Constructive play, symbolic play, sociodramatic play, superhero play, war play, chase, and rough and tumble play.

- These are called the play years, and symbolic play dominates the preschool years.

2-5 Play benefits the cognitive, social and emotional, communication, and physical growth and development of children who are in primary years.

- Cognitive: Children develop logical thinking and problem-solving skills.
- Social and emotional: Children engage in peer interactions and develop friendships.
- Communication: Children play word games.
- Physical: Fine motor and locomotor skills continue to develop.

2-6 Describe the types of play that dominate the primary years.

- Symbolic, Play rituals, games with rules, chase games, and rough and tumble play are types of play that occur. Games with rules dominate the primary years.

 ## Key terms

 ## Technology and Internet Resources

Parenting Infants and Young Children:
https://www.childwelfare.gov/
Provides information on parenting infants and young children, including special issues such as infant crying, brain development, and sudden infant death syndrome.

Normal Growth and Development:
http://www.nlm.nih.gov
Provides information about typical growth and development.

Child Development (Center for Disease Control): http://www.cdc.gov/ncbddd/
All aspects of a child's health, from nutrition to parenting, are discussed.

Gesell Institute of Child Development:
http://www.gesellinstitute.org
This is a reliable source of information about child growth and development. There is a special emphasis on developmental stages.

✿ Activities ....

1. InClass Labs

A. As a group, create a table depicting the levels of the cognitive, social, language, or physical growth of a child. Make an accompanying table that depicts the development of play in that domain or area. What developmental factors affect play?

B. Observe a small child either in class, at an onsite lab school, or in a video clip. Where is the child developmentally? What kind of play did you observe? Does this fit the information in the textbook?

2. Research and Inquiry

A. Visit a local park. Watch the play of four- and five-year-olds. Now find some older children (six- to eight-year-olds) to observe. Is the play of younger children different from that of the older children? If so, identify the differences. Are the differences evident to casual observers?

B. Visit a local park. Watch the play of one age group. What developmental dimensions were evident? Describe their play. Does it fit with the information given in the text?

C. Piaget believed that play followed development, but Vygotsky believed that development followed play. Investigate this issue. Does play precede or follow development?

3. Service Learning

A. Volunteer in a local after school program. After you leave the center, write a description of the observed play. Did the center encourage play for different ages? If so, how? What games did you observe? Did you see "boys only" or "girls only" groups emerge in play?

B. Find out what play opportunities are available for children who are in local homeless shelters. Work in teams of four students. Each person should create a toy box for one age group. For example, each person will complete a toy box for infants, toddlers, preschoolers, and primary age children.

4. Family Connections

Choose one of the following projects:

A. Develop brochures that communicate the stages of play to parents. Place these in local medical officers and public offices that parents visit.

B. Create posters that depict different types of play (functional, constructive, dramatic, sociodramatic, and games). Place these in local grocery stores or community centers.

5. Play Advocacy

A. Ask what play arrangements are available at the local police office. Do they have Teddy bears in police cars?

B. Look at opportunities to play in the community. Are there areas of the town that are play depleted? How can communities advocate for playgrounds?

 Visit CourseMate for this textbook to access the eBook, Did You Get It? quizzes, Digital Downloads, TeachSource Video Cases, flashcards, and more. Go to CengageBrain.com to log in, register, or purchase access.

◉ References _____

Adolph, K., Vereijken, B., & Shrout, P. E. (2003). What Changes in Infant Walking and Why. *Child Development, 74*(2), 475–497.

Barnes, D. (1998). Play in historical context. In D. Fronberg and D. Bergen (Eds.), *Play from birth to twelve and beyond* (pp. 5–11). New York: Garland Publishing.

Berger, K. S., & Thompson, R. A. (1996). *The developing person through childhood.* New York: Worth.

Berk, L. (2012). *Child development.* Columbus, OH: Pearson.

Bettelheim, B. (1987). The importance of play. *The Atlantic, 259*(3), 35–46.

Blurton Jones, N. (1972). Categories of child-child interaction. In N. Blurton Jones (Ed.), *Ethological studies of child behavior* (pp. 97–129). Cambridge, UK: Cambridge University Press.

Boyle, D., Marshall, N., & Robeson, W. (2003). Gender at play: Fourth-grade girls and boys on the playground. *American Behavioral Scientist, 46*(10), 1326–1345.

Bretherton, I. (1984). Representing the social world in symbolic play: Reality and fantasy. In I. Bretherton (Ed.), *Symbolic play: The development of social understanding* (pp. 1–41) New York: Academic.

Bruner, J. (1976). The nature and uses of immaturity. In J. Bruner, A. Jolly, & K. Sylva (Eds.), *Play: Its role in development and evolution* (pp. 28–64). New York: Basic Books.

Bruner, J. (1985). On teaching thinking: An afterthrought. In S. F. Chipman, J. W. Segan, & R. Glasser (Eds.), *Thinking and learning skills* (Vol. 2, pp. 597–608). Hillsdale, NJ: Lawrence Erlbaum Associates.

Caruso, D. A. (1984). Infants' exploratory play. *Young Children, 40*(1), 27–30.

Conolly, J. A., & Doyle, A. B. (1984). Relation of social fantasy to social competence in preschoolers. *Developmental Psychology, 20*, 797–806.

Cook, G., Roggman L., & Boyce, L. (2011). Fathers' and mothers' cognitive stimulation in early play with toddlers: Predictors of 5th grade reading and math. *Family Science, 2*(2), 131–145.

Erikson, E. (2000). *Childhood and society.* New York: W.W. Norton. (Originally published in 1950.)

Factor, J. (1988). *Captain Cook chased a crook.* Australia: Penguin.

Fenson, L. (1986). The developmental progression of play. In A. Gottfried & C. C. Brown (Eds.), *Play interactions: The contribution of play materials and parental involvement to children's development* (pp. 53–66). Lexington, MA: Heath.

Frost, J., Wortham, S., & Reifel, S. (2012). *Play and child development* (4th ed.). Upper Saddle River, NJ: Merrill/ Prentice Hall.

Gartstein, M. A., Bridgett, D. J., Young, B. N., Panksepp, J., & Power, T. (2013). Origins of effortful control: Infant and parent contributions. *Infancy, 18*(2), 149–183.

Greenspan, S., & Wieder, S. (2012). *Infant and early childhood mental health.* Washington, DC: Annual Psychiatric Publishing, Inc.

Heath, S. (1983). *Ways with words: Language, life, and work in communities and classrooms.* Cambridge, UK: Cambridge University Press.

Honig, A. (2002). *Secure relationships: Nurturing infant/toddler attachment in early care settings.* Washington, DC: NAEYC.

Hughes, F. (2010). *Children, play, and development* (4th ed.). Washington, DC: Sage.

Isbell, R., & Raines, S. (2013). Creativity and the arts with young children (5th ed.). Clifton Park, NY: Delmar.

Isenberg, J., & Jalongo, M. (2009) *Creative thinking and arts based learning: Preschool thorough fourth grade.* Columbus, OH: Pearson.

Levin, D. (2003). Beyond banning war and superhero play: Meeting children's needs in violent times. *Young Children, 58*(3), 60–63.

Levin, D., & Carlsson-Paige, N. (2006). All about war play. *Scholastic Parent & Child, 13*(5), 44–47.

Lifter, K., Foster-Sanda, S., Arzamarski, C., Briesch J., & McClure, E.(2011). Overview of play: Its uses and importance in early intervention/early childhood special education. *Infants & Young Children, 24*(3) 225–245.

Luby, J., Barch, D., Belden, A., Gaffrey, M., Tillman, R., Babb, C., Nishino, T., Suzuki, H., & Botteron, K. (2012). Maternal support in early childhood predicts larger hippocampal volumes at school age. *Proceedings of the National Academy of Sciences, 109*, 2854–2859.

Marshall, J. (2011). Infant neurosensory development: Considerations for infant child care. *Early Childhood Education Journal, 39*(3), 175–181.

Paley, V. (1981). *Wally's stories.* Cambridge, MA: Harvard University.

Parten, M. (1932). Social participation among preschool children. Journal of Abnormal Psychology, *27*, 243–269.

Pellegrini, A. (1988). Elementary school children's rough-and-tough play and social competence. *Developmental Psychology, 24*, 802–806.

Pellegrini, A. (2009). *The role of play in human development.* New York: Oxford University Press.

Pellegrini, A. (2011). The development and function of locomotor play. In Anthony Pellegrini (Ed.), *The Oxford handbook of the development of play* (pp. 172–184). New York: Oxford University Press.

Pellegrini, A., & Boyd, B. (1993). The role of early childhood development and education: Issues in definition and function. In B. Spodek (Ed.), *Handbook of research in early childhood education.* (pp. 105–121). New York: Macmillian.

Piaget, J. (1952/1974). *The origins of intelligence in children.* New York: Basic Books.

Piaget, J. (1951/1962). *Play, dreams, and imitation in childhood.* New York: Norton.

Rubin, K. H., Fein, G., & Vandenberg, B. (1983). Play. In E. M. Hetherington (Ed.), P. H. Mussen (Series Ed.), *Handbook of child psychology: Vol. 4, Socialization, personality, and social development* (pp. 693–774). New York: Wiley.

Seefeldt, C., & Barbour, N. (1998). *Early childhood education: An introduction.* Columbus, OH: Merrill.

Shonkoff, J., & Phillips, D. (2000). *From neurons to neighborhoods: The science of early childhood development.* Washington, DC: National Academy Press.

Shore, R. (1997). *Rethinking the brain: New insights into early development.* New York: Families and Work Institute.

Singer, J., & Singer, D. (1992). *The house of make believe.* Cambridge, MA: Harvard University Press.

Sluss, D., & Stremmel, A. (2004). An sociocultural investigation of collaborative constructive block play. *Journal of Research in Childhood Education, 18*(4), 293–305.

Smilansky, S. (1968) *The effects of sociodramatic play on disadvantaged preschool children.* New York: Wiley.

Smilansky, S., & Shefatya, L. (1990). *Facilitating play: A medium for promoting cognitive, socio-emotional, and academic development.* Gaithersburg, MD: Psychosocial and Educational Publications.

Tobin, J., Wu, D., & Davidson, D. (1989). *Preschool in three cultures: Japan, China, and the United States.* New Haven, CT: Yale University Press.

Ulker, R., & Gu, W. (2004). *Traditional Play: Chinese and Turkish Examples*, Presentation at The Association for the Study of Play. Feb. 18–21, Atlanta, GA.

Vygotsky, L. (1978). *Mind in society: The development of higher psychological processes.* Cambridge, MA: Harvard University Press.

Wellhousen, K. (2002). *Outdoor play every day: Innovative play concepts for early childhood.* Clifton Park, NY: Delmar.

3 Observing and Assessing PLAY

© Cengage Learning 2015

STANDARDS COVERED IN THIS CHAPTER

Council of Exceptional Children—Division of Early Childhood (Birth to Eight) Standards

ESCS 8S2 Integrate family practices and concerns in the assessment process

ECSE 8S7 Maintain the interest of infants and young children in the assessment process

ECSE 8S11 Conduct ongoing formative assessments to monitor instructional effectiveness

ECSE 8S6 Gather information from a variety of sources and environments

NAEYC Program Standards **naeyc**

3a Understanding the goals, benefits, and uses of assessment

3b Knowing about assessment partnerships with families and colleagues

---

✳ LEARNING OBJECTIVES ✳

3-1 Explain the benefits of observing and assessing play.

3-2 Describe the impact of ecological factors on observation and assessment.

3-3 Explain different types of observation.

3-4 List three ways to assess cognitive development during play.

3-5 Identify Parten's six levels of social interaction during play that reflect social development.

3-6 List three areas of physical development that can be assessed during play.

3-7 Analyze the benefits of communicating observation and assessment results to families, caregivers, and colleagues.

PLAYSCAPE: CASE STUDY

Today was a long day. One of Juanita's co-workers didn't show up for work on the early shift, so Juanita had to work the main counter. Then her car wouldn't start, so she had to call her brother to pick her up. Juanita was relieved that her brother didn't complain when she asked her brother to swing by the HeadStart Center to pick up her youngest son, Roberto. When they got home, Juanita had some time with Roberto before her older children (twins) came home from school.

Roberto walked across the floor, jumped on the couch, and began to tumble. Juanita saw him as he tumbled off the couch and onto the floor. "Roberto, where do you get so much energy? You never run down. Let's go outside for a while." As Juanita walked to the playground with Roberto, she thought about how much he was like his older brothers. He loved to swing, to slide, and to run. She always enjoyed these times when she could watch him play. She had only been outside for a short while when the bus arrived, and the eight-year-old twins ran from the bus, "Roberto, let's play!" As much as she cherished her time with Roberto, she knew that he also needed time with his brothers. They would run, jump, and, maybe, even play-fight. Then they would be ready to work on their homework and go to bed. But first, they needed to play.

Explaining Play Behaviors

Why do children play? What is their provocation to play? Do they even need a provocation to play? In this case study, the couch served as the child's provocation to jump, and the playground served as an impetus for running and chasing. But why do children engage in this type of behavior? Is all play valuable? If play is beneficial, how do we know?

✳ 3-1 Observing and Assessing Play

Observation and assessment can answer this parent's concern. Although observing and assessing play are not the same, both utilize a systematic approach to "reach valid conclusions about the current functioning [of children] and their future well being" (Weis, 2008, p. 63). Observing play involves the process of looking at what the child is experiencing. Assessing play is different in that an evaluation may be made based on the collected data or artifacts. This chapter will discuss how to use both to improve the quality of life for young children. According to the NAEYC Code of Ethical Conduct and Statement of Commitment (NAEYC, 2011), there are two purposes for assessment. One is to use assessment instruments appropriate to benefit children. The second is to use the information to identify children who may need additional support and design appropriate programs to meet their needs.

Ethical guidelines require those who are charged with the care and education of young children to ensure that observations and assessments occur only for the benefit of the child or the program. Observing and assessing children during play is optimal for several reasons:

1. Play is a natural behavior or environment for children, and, as such, provides a natural context for observation and assessment.

2. Observations and assessments of play provide a mechanism for invisible assessment. That is, the child is not aware of the observation or assessment that is occurring. Assessment that occurs within the natural routine or context of the classroom allows the teacher to capture information without upsetting the child or removing her from a familiar classroom setting.

3. Teachers can collect and chart data on the developmental level of the child. These data can be used to evaluate the child's developmental level so individual needs can be met.

4. Teachers can collect and chart data on the developmental levels of children to guide program development.

5. Observations and assessments provide a written source of evidence to document the child's behaviors that can be shared with caregivers and other adults who need to know and understand the child's developmental level and progress.

Ecological Factors 3-2 ✳

naeyc
CEC DEC

Observable behaviors associated with play are affected by context. That is, factors such as culture, gender, and age influence what children do during play. "The context is conceptualized as a transaction between children and their environments" (Pelligrini & Boyd, 1993). Bronfenbrenner's ecological model provides a framework for understanding the systemic impact of culture on families and children (Bronfenbrenner & Morris, 2006). The ecological system includes the microsystem, mesosystem, exosystem, macrosystem, and chronosystem. These are explained in terms of the impact on the play of infants, preschoolers, and primary age children.

3-2a Microsystem

Factors that directly influence the child are located in the **microsystem**. These include the family, school, afterschool programs, neighborhood, and other community events (Photo 3-1). These directly influence and impact play. For example, infants primarily engage in play and exploration for the first two years of their life. Factors in the microsystem that affect infant play include the relationship between the parent(s) and child, the early educator and child, church groups and child, and neighborhood and child. Infant play will be impacted by adults who care for them.

Preschoolers will be affected by adults as well as toys and materials. Primary age children are influenced by peers,

© Cengage Learning 2015

3-1 This child is having a positive experience as he looks at his image in the mirror. His microsystem involves his family, who selected the child care center; the early educators, who created a stimulating environment; his peers or playmates, who have parents who also selected the same center; and his grandparents, who will pick him up and take him to their home for the afternoon.

3-2 Although she does not know or understand the mesosystem or what occurs when two systems intersect, elements of her microsystem (preschool, neighborhood) have changed due to the interaction of her culture (macrosystem) and the government (exosystem).

adults, parents, and the neighborhood. By the age of eight, peers have a great influence and can impact children's play both indoors and outdoors. Friends affect whether the child chooses to play computer games or outdoor rough and tumble play. Generally, many of the factors that influence play are in the microsystem, and these observable behaviors can be observed, assessed, and evaluated.

3-2b Mesosystem

The **mesosystem** involves interactions between two systems (Photo 3-2). That is, what happens in one system affects another system. A child who is forced to leave his home due to a government decision or natural disaster may be forced to relocate to a new area. The child may not be able to speak the language in his new preschool. The interactions of these factors impact play but may be invisible to the observer.

3-2c Exosystem

The **exosystem** includes systems over which the individual has minimal control. These include policies established by local governments as well as socioeconomic factors. For example, when a school board makes policies that eradicate recess in a system, play is affected. In the same way, children's socioeconomic status impacts their play. Children who have time to play may have different play skills than those who have limited access. The availability of funds impacts the number of toys, museum visits, and trips, and all these factors affect play.

3-2d Macrosystem

The **macrosystem** is composed of the larger systems of attitudes and ideology of the culture, such as traditions, beliefs, and values. For example, many Scandinavian countries view the care of young children as a community responsibility. This view of children influences the government's policies on children. Scandinavian governments view child care as a national responsibility and provide gifts and care for children when they are born. In contrast, many Americans view child care as a family issue, and this makes it much more difficult to garner support from senators and representatives and turns universal child care into a controversial issue.

Culture and tradition impact play. For example, attachment patterns that affect play are different in cultures throughout the world. Some cultures spend a lot of time holding babies; some do not. Some cultures have traditions that encourage children to explore and play independently, whereas others value the child staying close to the adult (Roopnarine, 2011). These values impact play.

Some children in America are socialized to view a police officer as someone who can help and assist them in a time of need. Children who have grown up in a repressive society may hide when a police officer visits the school and may not want to participate in play activities that involve role-playing a police officer. The tragedy in Newtown, Connecticut may serve as an impetus for changing our culture, but for now, children who live in the United States are exposed to media violence and have access to war toys. In many Scandinavian countries, media violence is limited and war toys are banned. Society's attitude toward violence affects children's play.

3-2e Chronosystem

The **chronosystem** includes sociocultural factors that impact the child over time. For example, what is the impact of the computer on play at age four, and how does that differ from the impact of the computer on play at age eight? Looking at changes over time provides additional insight.

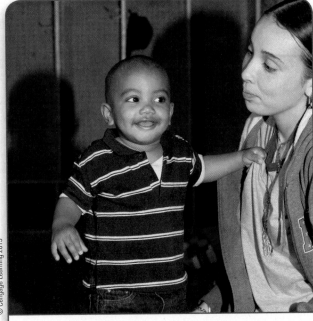

3-3 Understanding his ecological system requires knowledge of the child's family, neighborhood, and community interactions. This teacher will be able to facilitate his growth and development as she becomes more knowledgeable about the forces that impact his life on a daily basis.

Understanding the impact of culture on children and their play is necessary for observation and assessment. For example, currently 25% of the children under five are Latino (United States Census Bureau, 2012). If Congress passes an amendment to the constitution about immigration (exosystem), it may impact a large number of children in the classroom (microsystem). Completing an observation or assessment when these factors are impacting the children would result in misinformation, but these factors may not be evident immediately.

Assessing the ecology of the child requires a careful analysis of the systems that interact to affect the child's life (Photo 3-3). Those who work with young children know that when a parent is in the military and stationed out of the country, the other parent is affected, and this, in turn, impacts the child's behavior. This impact may be evident in the child's play before the child chooses to talk about her loneliness or sadness. Conducting a case study on the child's ecological setting provides a complete picture of the factors that influence the child's behavior.

Did You Get It?

Friends affect whether the child chooses to play computer games or outdoor rough and tumble play. This factor is an aspect of the child's

a. mesosystem.

b. exosystem.

c. microsystem.

d. macrosystem.

Take the full quiz on CourseMate

Types of Observation 3-3 ✳

Observations of children can be categorized in different ways depending on the structure used for data collection (Greathouse & Shaughnessy, 2010; Sattler, 2008). The least amount of structure can be found in naturalistic observations. These observations allow the observer to collect data by sitting quietly and observing the behavior or child under study. For example, a teacher may want to investigate the behavior of a child who is always involved in a conflict in the block play area. The teacher may choose to sit quietly in the area and observe what is occurring during the time preceding the altercation. In this way, he collects data that can

3-4 A careful observation of these three children reveals that they are engaged in cooperative play and that all three are actively involved. If this were an item on the checklist, cooperative play could be checked for all three children.

be used to understand the child's behavior and/or make changes in the curriculum.

The observer who chooses to watch can choose from a variety of instruments, such as checklists, rating scales, running records, anecdotal accounts, and event samplings. Several instruments can be combined to collect data, and these can be used to evaluate a single child, several children, or even a class (Photo 3-4). Some researchers, such as Ridgers, Stratton, Gareth, and McKenzie (2010), have developed instruments to collect specific information and these can be modified for classroom use.

A **checklist** is designed to record information about what the child can do at the time of the observation (see Table 3-1). When observing a group of toddlers engaged in different kinds of play behaviors, a checklist can provide a record of the social development of the child by capturing who can engage in parallel play or associative play. If some children need support in engaging other children during play, additional activities to support associative or interactive play can be added to the environment.

A **rating scale** provides a way to rate the quality of the play behavior (see Table 3-2). A rating scale has at least three categories for distinguishing the

TABLE 3-1	Checklists	
Child's Name	**Parallel Play**	**Associative Play**
Kara		
Mat		
Grace		
Jason		

Digital Download Download from CourseMate

TABLE 3-2	Rating Scale		
Child's Name	**Needs Support**	**Developing**	**Target**
Aeiden			
David			
Sydney			

Digital Download Download from CourseMate

TABLE 3-3   Running Record

Observed Behaviors	Inferences
Jaiden and Isaac are in the center playing with blocks and transportation props. Jaiden moves over to the edge of the carpet to set up a castle and says, "Don't play with my cars and trucks." Isaac replies, "I'm not. Don't take my trains." Jaiden continues to play with the cars.	The setting provides a context for play that facilitates mature play. Jaiden and Isaac engaged in associative play. The teacher may want to facilitate cooperative play as the next step.

© Cengage Learning 2015

skill level and can be created for any play behavior. The key is being able to qualify the data from simple to more complex. For example, a rating scale can be used to illustrate different levels of cognitive development reflected during play frames.

A **running record** is used to capture the behaviors in the natural setting or context of play (see Table 3-3). The goal is to record everything that is occurring without any valuation of the event. Generally, a sheet of paper is divided into two columns. The event is recorded in the first column and an interpretation is provided in the second column. Running records are created while the observer is watching the child (Photo 3-5).

Anecdotal records differ from running records in that only one aspect of the behavior or event is reported (see Table 3-4). An anecdotal record includes a beginning, middle, and end. It conveys a story of something that happened that was meaningful. For example, after watching one child bite another during play center time and responding to both the victim and initiator, the teacher may create an anecdotal record about the event so that he can recall exactly what occurred. Anecdotal records should be created immediately after the event so that the written documents reflect the event accurately (Photo 3-6).

© Cengage Learning 2015

3-5 There are multiple ways to capture and report her play behaviors. A checklist could be used to record that she is using locomotor skills to push a vehicle. A rating scale could be used to show how well she uses her whole body and both hands to move the vehicle. A running record could be used to capture her play before, during, and after she moves the vehicle through the block structure.

TABLE 3-4   Anecdotal Records

Marissa and Maria are playing in the dress-up area. Each child is wearing a dress and hat indicating that she is engaged in pretend play. Marissa and Maria have been setting the table and playing with dolls for about ten minutes when Marissa says, "You be the Mommy and I'll be the Daddy." Maria responds, "You can't be the Daddy. Only boys can be daddys." Marissa shouts, "Yes, I can!" Maria cries and leaves the center. Marissa stays in the center, and Eli enters the center.

© Cengage Learning 2015

What do you think?

Running records and anecdotal records require more time and attention than checklists or rating scales, but provide a great deal more information. Which do you prefer and why?

What do you think?

Time, event, and interval samplings allow you to examine the child's behavior in a way that minimizes subjective perspectives. Specifically, collecting behavior samples can provide a more complete picture of play behaviors. Some teachers use all three types to collect information. Which one do you think will be the most valuable to you?

3-6 Anecdotal records provide a way to capture language and interactions. Like Eli in Table 3-4, this child may be joining play that had been contentious. How he joins the group, maintains, or extends the script will determine the quality of the play.

© Cengage Learning 2015

Did You Get It?

A teacher who wants to assess the level of a child's motor development by watching the child play on a climbing frame would probably use a/n
a. checklist.
b. rating scale.
c. running record.
d. anecdotal record.

Take the full quiz on CourseMate

Behavior samplings utilize a more structured approach to capture specific information. These include timed samplings, event samplings, and interval samplings. Timed sampling involves observing every five minutes for a specific amount of time. The observer may be watching every five minutes for a period of thirty minutes. The person will watch the child for five minutes and then record the observation for five minutes. This is repeated for a set amount of time. Using this approach in the house area can provide information about collaborative pretend play that may never be captured using other methods.

Event samplings focus on observing a specific behavior. The observer may watch a child for thirty minutes and note how many times the child responds appropriately to a question or comment from another child. Event samplings can provide a record that confirms or disconfirms a teacher's assessment that a child is engaging in a specific sort of behavior.

Understanding Cognitive Development 3-4 ✳

Three major scholars—Jean Piaget (1951/1962), Lev Vygotsky (1978), and Maria Montessori (1964)—have influenced how we use observations to understand children. Piaget (1951/1962) described the stages of play because he believed that children's cognitive development was reflected in their play. Using a Piagetian perspective, looking at children's play provides a window into their mind. Vygotsky believed that children developed through play and that play served as a medium for learning. Looking at play through a Vygotskian lens provides a view of how the child is learning through play. Montessori did not advocate a theory of play. Instead she used materials that we refer to as sensory and manipulative materials to prepare the child for his role in the world. Although many of the materials that fill preschool and kindergarten classrooms were created by Maria Montessori, she was not an advocate for play. A Montessorian view of play observes the child's competency and adds a new activity or material when the child is ready to move to the next level.

3-4a Piagetian-Inspired Stages of Play

In his research, Piaget (1951/1962) described three levels of cognitive development reflected in play behaviors. He found that play becomes more complex with age. He categorized play in three major stages that include practice play, symbolic play, and games with rules.

Stage I. Sensorimotor Play (birth to age two). Play that occurs during the first two years of life when the child is in the sensorimotor stage is called **practice play** (also called **functional play** by Smilansky, 1968). The two-year-old drops a shoe in a fountain, watches the splash, and returns to put another in the water. She is engaging in practice play. This practice play allows the child to improve her gross and fine motor skills as well as strengthen neurological connections.

Practice play involves the "pleasurable repetition of skills that have already been mastered; skipping pebbles, tying and untying shoes, riding a bike" (Rogers & Sawyers, 1988, p. 15). The child engages in practice play for sheer delight and the pleasure of having an activity under control. Piaget used an example that he collected during observations of his child:

> At 2 [years]: 8 [months](2) [s]he filled a pail with sand, overturned it, demolished the sand-pie with her spade and began again, and she did this for more than an hour. ... These are experiments to see the results. (Piaget, 1951/1962, p. 115)

Two-year-olds generally delight in practice play (Photo 3-7). Practice play may look different with different objects and in different cultures, but most two-year-olds

© Cengage Learning 2015

3-7 Practice play is the dominant play during the first two years of life. This child has a toy that encourages practice play. He drops the ball, picks it up, and drops it again. This practice play allows the child to improve his gross and fine motor skills as well as strengthen neurological connections.

enjoy repetitive or practice play. Watch the child who can easily step up one stair; she begins to step up and down for no apparent reason. The child laughs as she steps up and down. Doing so meets the criteria of play. The child is not accommodating or learning new materials. The child knows how to step. The activity is under her control and is pleasurable. This fits the definition of practice play. Piaget described three levels of practice play: mere practice, fortuitous combinations, and intentional combinations. Although practice play dominates the first 18 months of life, it occurs throughout the lifespan.

Mere practice play occurs when the child is just repeating an act for pleasure; this type of play may involve physical and mental activities. For example, the toddler who pulls the paper towels from the rack does so just to watch them fall. She does not care about the number that have fallen, just the process of watching them fall. This is mere practice play.

The second level of practice play is called **fortuitous combinations**. The child engages in mere practice play and in doing so discovers a new way of putting activities together. Old schemas are used in new creations. Piaget described a behavior that is still observed in classes today:

> At 2[years]:2 [months] Y. began by emptying a box of bricks on to the floor and putting them back again. Then he amused himself by pushing one brick against another, thus moving as many as possible at once. Then he put one on top of the other and pushed them all. (1951/1962, p. 116)

Anyone who has watched children play with blocks has observed this behavior. Children start out by practicing and then figure out a more interesting way to play. Knocking down blocks after creating a structure also falls under this heading (Photo 3-8). Watch children when the adult says, "Clean-up time!" They develop very interesting strategies as they deconstruct the block structure.

The third level of practice play is called **intentional combinations**. This is the most complex level of play and occurs when new behaviors are deliberately combined. When combinations occur, the play will follow one of three directions: children will add symbolism and pretend will occur; social interactions will lead to games with rules; or real adaptation occurs and play ceases. A child who is placing blocks one on top of another moves from practice play to symbolic play when she announces, "Now this is the wall. Humpty Dumpty can sit on my wall." The child has engaged in an intentional combination and moves into symbolic or social pretend play. A checklist like the one in Table 3-5 can be used to capture the child's level of practice play.

The notion of developmental progression from the early implicit to the later explicit understanding of pretense (Photo 3-9) has been supported by a study conducted by Frahsek, Mack, Mack, Pfalz-Blezinger, and Knopf (2010). In their study, they created a standardized test for 24- to 30-month-olds that used a semistructured play setting. Their findings contribute to our understanding of the development of pretend in young children.

3-8 Watch as he pushes the blocks, stacks the blocks, and moves them across the floor. As he attempts to move the blocks, he discovers that two blocks move easily until they encounter a large quantity of blocks, at which point they move in an upward motion.

© Cengage Learning 2015

TABLE 3-5 Practice Play Checklist

	Practice Play	Fortuitous Combinations	Intentional Combinations
Lynitta			
Wyatt			

© Cengage Learning 2015

Digital Download Download from CourseMate

© Cengage Learning 2015

3-9 Pretend play moves from the implicit to the explicit. How is the teacher supporting play? Is she guiding them? Is she encouraging them? Is she assessing their dramatic play and ability to develop collaborative pretend? Whatever she is doing, it is working well because the children appear to be engaging in mature play.

Constructive play is included in Piaget's taxonomy by some scholars (Rubin, Fein, & Vandenberg, 1983). Play behaviors described by Smilansky (1968) as constructive play were viewed by Piaget (1951/1962) as an intentional combination and identified as constructive practice play—not a separate level of play. Constructive play occurs when children use materials to create or construct something. Materials used for construction include such items as blocks, paint, clay, or play-dough. Preschool and kindergarten children spend more than half their time in constructive play. Constructive play moves from simple to complex. Different levels of constructive play have been created for block play and art work.

Smilansky's other observable play behaviors—functional play, dramatic play and games with rules—are similar to Piaget's stages. Although pure Piagetians disagree with the use of constructive play as a separate category, Smilansky's view of constructive play has been generally accepted in the research literature and serves as a level of play (Drew, Christie, Johnson, Meckley, & Nell, 2008). Throughout the rest of this book, the stages of cognitive play will include constructive play as a separate category in the stages of play.

Stage II. Symbolic Play (ages two to seven). Symbolic play occurs when a child uses an object to stand for another during pretend play. Rogers and Sawyers (1988) describe it this way: "symbolic play, in which the *signifier* is separated from the *signified*. **Symbolic play** marks the beginning of representational thought through the use of substitute objects or actions" (1988, p. 17).

The signifier is the symbol or substitute object that evokes that which is symbolized. When a child picks up a block and pretends to call mom, the block is the signifier because it is a symbol that is substituted for a telephone—the signified. Howes (1992) has found that "social pretend play is salient in the formation of both social interaction skills and friendships from the toddler period into middle childhood, but that there are changes in both the forms and the functions of social pretend play across these periods" (1992, p. 3). Like practice play, symbolic play may appear different for distinct ethnic groups and cultures, but the underlying premise of abstaction is the same.

Piaget's (1951/1962) view of symbolic play is similar to what Smilansky (1968) called dramatic play, Vygotsky (1978) called pretend, and Pelligrini and Boyd (1993) referred to as fantasy. Piaget's study of symbolism is still respected and serves as the basis for a great deal of research.

1. **Stage I. (Birth to age two.)** Although practice play dominates the first two years, children begin to engage in symbolic play somewhere between ages two and three. Symbolic play begins with "projection of symbolic schemas on to new objects" (Piaget, 1951/1962, p. 121). When the young child first begins to pretend that he is sleeping or eating when he knows that he is not, symbolism is developing. The child will laugh as he "pretends" to sleep and will delight in the adult's response.

2. **Stage II. (Ages two to seven.)** The second level of symbolic play occurs "with simple identification of one object with another" (Piaget, 1951/1962, p. 123). During the early part of Level II, children benefit from props that reflect reality. Miniature phones, school buses, and dolls stimulate symbolic play or pretend for two- and three-year-olds. Between the age of three and four, children begin to engage in a closer approximation of reality. Props are an important part of play. As children increase their ability to symbolize, props that are more open ended stimulate more pretense as children attempt to make them resemble their real-life counterparts. During this time, a box can become a car, a bus, or a rocket ship. The materials serve as a scaffold for the child's mental construction. Whereas the two-year-old's play is enhanced by a replicate cell phone, the four-year-old can use a box to create a closer approximation to reality. Four-year-olds might spend time trying to paint the box or add materials to make it appear more realistic, but they have a clear idea of what they are doing. Many adults have been surprised to hear a child say, "The wing on the airplane goes here" during play with blocks that seem to look alike. Although the adult does not see what the child is constructing mentally, the child has an idea of what the plane should look like, and that is what she is determined to re-create.

Pretend play provides a conduit for bringing home experiences to school. Children assume a familiar role, such as the mom or dad, in their play in the house area. When children from other cultures or ethnic groups join the classroom, play is enriched and expanded. One early childhood professional shared a story about a group of refugee children who entered her class as a group. During the play center, they built a shrine that looked like one that they had in their home. Because there were several children in the class, they felt comfortable bringing the familiar into the unfamiliar setting of school. Sensitive teachers can extend these experiences for young children.

Piaget further differentiated the second level of symbolic play as (a) orderliness, (b) exact imitation of reality, and (c) collective symbolism with differentiation and complementary adjustment of roles. Again, sensitivity to other cultures is needed. As children attempt to re-create reality, children who have unique social and cultural histories may find adjustment difficult. Teachers who are sensitive to these differences can facilitate the child's transition into the group play setting. Piaget's differentiations are further delineated as follows:

(a) **Orderliness** refers to the ability to engage in play that follows an order. The child can develop a play script that had a beginning, middle, and end. When the child can engage in play that follows an order, the child is developing schemata that will lead to more complex thinking.

(b) **Exact imitation of reality** refers to play that imitates life. A child who has attended a family dinner that included caviar may want to pretend that she is eating caviar a certain way. She wants to re-create reality through her own lens. Her playmate may not understand her reality, and the change may create a different situation. In the same way, children who have observed video footage and/or movies of explicit sexual activities may attempt to imitate their reality. Teachers must be sensitive yet make appropriate interventions when play turns violent or aggressive.

(c) **Collective symbolism with differentiation and complementary adjustment of roles** occurs when children agree to assume different roles (Photo 3-10). Children may borrow from reality as they adjust and change the roles. This may occur at any time, but generally it happens at the end of the year in a kindergarten class. After a year of playing in different ways, kindergarten children may decide to play bus and act out driving to a field trip. They will assign roles, such as the bus driver or the teacher.

© Cengage Learning 2015

3-10 These children are engaged in cooperative dramatic play. This occurs when children agree to assume different roles. They are assuming and negotiating the roles within the play frame. Piaget referred to this as collective symbolism with differentiation and complementary adjustment of roles.

TABLE 3-6 Cognitive Play			
Observations	First Observation	Second Observation	Third Observation
Practice Play: Repeats the same play over and over			
Symbolic Play: Constructive Creates something			
Symbolic Play: Dramatic Pretends			
Symbolic Play: Sociodramatic Pretends with a group			
Games with Rules Plays games			

Narrative _____

_____

_____

Source: Based on the scholarship of Piaget (1951/1962) and Smilansky (1968).

Improvisation occurs quickly as children switch roles and change scenes. Maintaining the play theme is important, and children who cannot do so may find themselves excluded from the play.

Piaget's stages have formed the basis for a great deal of play research. Table 3-6 illustrates how Piaget's stages can be used to provide a record of the child's play.

3-11 Games with rules are important for children at this age. They move from play that involves the players creating rules that all the players follow to play that involves following rules that are a part of a game or external authority.

Stage III. Games with Rules (ages seven to eleven). Piaget viewed this stage as more developed and complex. When children move into the concrete operational stage of development, they are more interested in games with rules (Photo 3-11). Although young children may enjoy games like "Hi Ho! Cherry-O," and "Candy Land," they create their own rules. Older children adhere to external rules in that the roles are clearly defined and reality is closely imitated. Running games, board games, cards, or computer games are interesting and exciting for this age group. Second and third graders begin developing their interest in games, and this interest can be used to foster instruction.

Digital Assessment for Young Children

Susan Barnes, PhD

© Cengage Learning 2015

Early childhood educators facing increasing demands from parents, school officials, and taxpayers for evidence of the impact of their instructional practices are looking for ways to collect data to support the decisions they make. Although computer games have been used successfully to measure learning outcomes with older children and adults for many years, the research describing the appropriateness of using computers with young children is just beginning to emerge.

The benefits of using standardized computer-based assessments are well known (Drasgow & Olson-Buchanan, 1999). Objective results can be reported quickly, and it is easy to compare results from different settings. Administering face-to-face, one-on-one assessments with young children is labor intensive. As you just read in this chapter, the best assessments occur in natural settings. We understand that collecting children's work created during open-ended activities and jotting down what children say during their visits to the dramatic play center or during role-play games will yield rich, meaningful information about their development and their understandings of the content. However, creating portfolios and doing observational running records can take several weeks. It is tempting to send a group of children to the computer lab, have them all log on to a website and play a "game" that reports each child's score, and then use that information to capture information on student proficiency. It is easy to modify computer-based assessments for children with special needs by using larger fonts or including audio and video. However, those creating and using assessments to determine appropriate placements and to plan future instructions must be aware of the many factors that can influence the results.

Using computer-based games presents some special challenges, so those who are considering using those games for assessment purposes need to think seriously about the experiences and the characteristics of their young students. For example, children who have typically used the computer for entertainment or for practicing reading or math skills may not put forth their best effort or be able to persist until the end of an assessment activity, thus earning a score that is not truly reflective of their actual proficiency. Of course, children who have had more experience on the computer will perform better on computer-based assessments than those who have not had experience with computers (Li & Atkins, 2004). The widely accepted constructivist theory attributed to Jean Piaget (e.g., Hendrick & Weissman, 2006) provides teachers with a view of pre-operational children who need to be actively engaged with their world. Most computer games and assessments are limited in the level of engagement they provide. Although cognitive development is an important characteristic to consider, other developmental domains should be examined as well. Fine motor skills of young children vary widely. Whereas one child may be able to easily sort items on the screen using click and drag, a peer could require several unsuccessful attempts before being able to complete the same task.

The NAEYC (2012) position statement addressing the use of computers with young children provides some guidelines addressing appropriate practice. However, because decisions about the eligibility for services, subsequent instruction, and placements are made based on the results of assessments, it is important that everyone designing and using assessments understand the instruments, the children, *and* the interaction between the assessment and the child. Computers can serve as patient tutors, providing feedback during drill and practice, and as teacher's helper for recording, storing, and displaying assessment data results. The computer's role as the administrator of assessments should be carefully considered before any high-stakes decisions are made based on the results of the computer-based assessment. As always, many observations and data points should be used to give the best picture of the accomplishments and needs of each student.

(Continued)

REFERENCES

Drasgow, F., & Olson-Buchanan, J. B. (1999). *Innovations in computer assessment.* Mahwah, NJ: Lawrence Erlbaum Associates.

Hendrick, J., & Weissman, P. (2006). *The whole child: Developmental education for the early years.* Upper Saddle River, NJ: Pearson Prentice Hall.

Li, X., & Atkins, M. S. (2004). Early childhood computer experience and cognitive and motor development. *Pediatrics, 1*(6), 1715–1722.

NAEYC (National Association for the Education of Young Children). (2012) Technology and Interactive Media as Tools in Early Childhood Programs Serving Children from Birth through Age 8. Retrieved December 3, 2012 from http://www.naeyc.org/files/naeyc/PS_technology_WEB.pdf

Dr. Susan Barnes received her undergraduate and master's degree at the University of Michigan, where she served as the Head Teacher of International House Preschool. She completed her doctoral work at James Madison University, where she now serves as an Assistant Professor.

3-4b Vygotskian Tools of the Mind

Vygotsky believed that play freed children to do in play what they could not do outside the play frame. He believed that children created the zone of proximal development during play—that is, a zone in which children move from a point of accomplishing a task or skill with the assistance of others to being able to complete the task independently. Learning to ride a bicycle is an example that demonstrates this movement from riding with assistance to riding independently. By observing children at play, we can see what they are capable of doing with and without assistance. Those influenced by Vygotsky's view focus on observing and assessing what the child can and cannot accomplish independently.

A student of Vygotsky has extended his work to focus on tools and language. Elkonin (2005) has investigated the transitions that occur as children move from focusing on objects to fousing on people. The young child pushes a school bus across the floor. She is interested in how the bus moves across the floor. As the child becomes mature, she focuses on the stops the bus will make and the children who will board the bus. In this way, the child moves from focusing on the school bus or object to focusing on relationships (people who board the bus).

A sociocultural view of play emphasizes planning for play and language usage during play. The ability to plan play requires the child to think about how he will control his play. This can be facilitated through language used during planning and during play. Vygotsky referred to planning and language as tools of the mind. Elkonin (2005) examined how adults use language to scaffold play. These ideas served as the impetus for the work by Leong and Bodrova (2012), who developed a system for assessing dramatic play, PRoPELS, that can be used in the classroom. The assessment looks at planning for play, role-playing, props, (extended) time frame, language, and scenarios to stimulate play (Leong & Bodrova, 2012).

3-4c Montessori

Maria Montessori pioneered the use of observation to inform instruction. Although her philosophy and methods are not well understood by many early educators (Murray, 2012), Montessori believed that teachers should observe the child's use of materials to understand the child's level of knowledge and confidence in using the materials. When the child reaches a sensitive period, she moves to the next level, or challenge, as she tries to match her own readiness with the materials that are available. Montessori believed that assessment is the ongoing process of collecting, reflecting, and using information to develop rich

Did You Get It?

Piaget categorized play into which three stages?

a. cognitive, physical and social

b. planning for play, role-playing, and props

c. collecting, reflecting, and using information

d. practice play, symbolic play, and games with rules

Take the full quiz on CourseMate

portraits (Gutek, 2004). (For additional information on assessment in Montessori Schools, contact the American Montessori Society.)

Social Development 3-5 ✳

Mildred Parten first identified observable behaviors that reflect social development. In her classic study, Parten (1932) described social play behaviors of children during outdoor play. She found that social play becomes more complex with age. She classified social play in six categories: unoccupied behavior, onlooker behavior, solitary play, parallel play, associative play, and cooperative play. The first four are nonsocial, but the last three involve more complex social participation. These behaviors were originally viewed as developmental but are now viewed by some as descriptions of different play styles (Isenberg & Jalongo, 2009). These stages may look different for other cultures. Watching children at play with their peers who are members of their culture may provide information about social interactions that occur during play.

3-5a Unoccupied Behavior

During play, the child who does not play or does not seem to have a goal is engaged in **unoccupied behavior**. The child will play with her body, stand around, or walk about aimlessly. Some parents are concerned when their children display this behavior, but this is not unusual for young children.

Nor is this behavior a concern when observed in older children infrequently. If this behavior occurs on a regular basis, adults must intervene to discover the cause of unoccupied behavior.

3-5b Onlooker Behavior

Onlooker behavior occurs when the child watches, asks questions, and talks to other children that he is observing, but fails to enter play. He uses the skills of a reporter—he observes but does not become involved. This stage allows the child to choose activities with which he feels comfortable; the child may easily move to another level as he becomes more comfortable being a part of a group in a classroom setting. Children from other ethnic or cultural groups may feel more comfortable watching prior to entering play.

3-5c Solitary Play

The child plays alone and independently during **solitary play**. She may be close to others but is not aware of their activity. Solitary play dominates the first two years of life as children become fascinated and engaged with toys. Older children may also use solitary play as a method of finding solitude or for the enjoyment of playing alone. Watch an eight-year-old play with small building blocks alone. Her play may be very complex, but she may be seeking privacy and the freedom of choosing her own direction during play. We really cannot know. Although her behaviors are observable, her thoughts are not. She plays alone without referencing others. Recent studies indicate that this may reflect a higher level of play than cooperative play (Frost, Wortham, & Reifle, 2012).

3-5d Parallel Play

When the child is involved in **parallel play**, he plays alongside other children but does not engage them in conversation. The child may choose similar toys, but will not engage the other children who are in the area. This play is typical of preschoolers and may serve as a precursor for group play. It is interesting to watch this sort of play because the child may mirror what the other child does yet may never say a word.

3-5e Associative Play

During **associative play**, the child will play with other children. Conversation will occur as materials are borrowed or loaned. The children may play together if their materials intersect with the other, but they are playing independently. Although they may be playing with blocks, there is no attempt to form a group structure. They are content to work on their own creations. They may be in the house area, but they have their own script. This sets the stage for cooperative play.

3-5f Cooperative Play

Cooperative play occurs when the child plays in a group that has shared goals. This involves complex social organization that may include negotiation, division of labor, differentiated role taking, and organization of play themes. This social organization usually results in very sophisticated play and is often evident in kindergarten and primary grades. Originally viewed as the highest level of play, cooperative play may allow children who are less mature to follow the leadership of others mindlessly. This role in a group may require less maturity than self-selected solitary or associative play.

Looking at play on the playground provides a source of information about children that may aid in developing a profile of the child. A chart useful for recording social interactions during play is included in Table 3-7.

TABLE 3-7 Observing Social Play	First Observation	Second Observation	Third Observation
Unoccupied Not involved in play, wanders around room			
Onlooker Observing, but just watching, not playing			
Solitary Play Plays alone			
Parallel Play Plays beside other children			
Associative Play Plays with other children			
Cooperative Play Plays together as a group			
Other			

Narrative _____

© Cengage Learning 2015

Source: Adapted from Parten (1932).

Observing and assessing physical development during play can be accomplished indoors and outdoors (see Table 3-8). Fine motor, gross motor, and locomotor skills provide a way to discuss the behaviors that are being studied. **Fine motor skills** are used to describe how the child accomplishes tasks using her small muscles. These skills can be assessed during play activities (such as running a truck on a carpet mat), art activities, manipulative play, and sensory-motor activities. Any play activity that requires the child to use fine motor skills can be used to assess his level of development. **Gross motor skills** refer to how the child uses his large muscles. These skills can be observed by watching the child climb, walk, or use his arms during play. Any activity that involves the use of large muscles can be used to assess the level of growth and development (Photo 3-12). **Locomotor skills** refer

TABLE 3-8	Assessing Physical Development			
Child's Name	Walks with Even Gait	Hops on One Foot	Skips with Even Stride	Runs with R Runs with Even Stride
Gerado				
Marie				
Kingston				

© Cengage Learning 2015

Digital Download Download from CourseMate

© Cengage Learning 2015

3-12 Recess provides an opportunity for children to use large muscles as they develop their gross motor skills. This child is developing large muscles in his upper and lower body. Recess provides an opportunity for observing and assessing play in a more specific way.

Did You Get It?

A teacher who observes a five-year-old child swinging a bat is probably assessing the child's

a. social skills.
b. locomotor skills.
c. gross motor skills.
d. fine motor skills.

Take the full quiz on CourseMate

to the ability to move—to engage in activities such as walking, running, skipping, and hopping. Any play activity that involves movement can be used to assess locomotor skills.

✳ 3-7 Benefits of Organizing for Assessment

The key to effective assessment is keeping the parent(s) or caregivers informed and viewing them as partners in the assessment process. There are three organizational methods that can be used to organize observations and assessments for communication: case studies, portfolios, and documentation panels.

3-7a Case Study

Case studies involve the observation and assessment of a single child over a period of time. These are very time intensive but provide a view of the whole child. Observations of the cognitive, social and emotional, and physical developmental domains provide parts of a puzzle that provide a picture of the child when completed.

Conducting the case study requires observing the child for a sustained period of time. Begin the case study by asking the parent or custodian for written permission to conduct a case study. After permission is obtained from the parent, explain to the child that you would like to watch his play and ask him if he will allow you to watch his play. Children should have a voice in when and how they are observed. If the child is comfortable with the concept, develop a timeline and make a plan about how and when to capture data. For example, physical development is a good place to begin because the information is readily evident. That is, it is much more evident that a child can run smoothly across the playground than that the child engages in collaborative cooperative pretend play.

Step 1. Begin the study by collecting information about the child's contextual setting. Use Bronfenbrenner's ecological theory as a guide for data collection (Bronfenbrenner & Morris, 2006). What factors are impacting the child's behavior? What is the child's microsystem, mesosystem, macrosystem, and exosystem? A child who is living with an 80-year-old grandmother has different realities than a child who is living with two middle-class parents. Where the child lives, who cares for the child in the morning and evening, and where the child goes after school are all factors that impact the child's life. Setting the stage for the study by telling the child's story ensures that the child is viewed as an individual first.

Step 2. Collect information to make a decision about the child's physical development. Set up a plan to triangulate the data. That is, use three ways to capture information about the child. To assess physical development, we could look at (a) the physical traits of the child (height, weight, hair color, etc.), (b) gross motors skills on the playground, and (c) fine motor skills in the classroom. This yields a good overview of the child's physical growth and development.

(a) Begin the assessment by looking first at the child's height and weight. Is the child overweight or underweight? Can the child hear and see well, or are impairments diagnosed? This information provides one source of information about the child's physical condition.

(b) Look at gross motor skills. Can the child run, skip, hop, or jump? Focus on the child's strengths. What can the child do?

(c) Consider fine motor skills. Is the child right-handed or left-handed? Can she use both hands equally well? Can she write, draw, tear, or cut paper? Again, focus on what the child can do.

Step 3. Collect information to make a decision about the child's cognitive development. Set up a plan to triangulate the data by looking at the child's play level, use of books, and language usage.

(a) Play level: Using Piaget's theory as a guide, collect information about the child's play level. Is the child involved in practice play, constructive play, symbolic play, or games with rules? Watch the child over a period of three to four weeks. Use a chart to record the type of play that the child uses.

(b) Reading skills: Does the child enjoy looking at books? Does the child enjoy listening to a story? Where is the child on the reading continuum?

(c) Language skills: Does the child communicate with others? How is his receptive and expressive speech? **Expressive speech** is what children use when talking to others.

They express themselves to others. **Receptive speech** skills are used to understand what others have said. Generally, receptive speech skills are more developed than expressive speed skills. That is, it is easier to listen than talk.

Step 4. Collect information to make a decision about the child's social development. Set up a plan to triangulate the data by looking at the child's (a) play level (onlooker, parallel, associative, or cooperative play), (b) interactions with peers, and (c) interactions with adults. Additional information can be added, such as, "Does the child have a sense of humor?" "What is the proximity of the child to others throughout the day?"

Step 5. Tell the child's story by putting all the information together in a narrative.

(a) Who is the child? What do we know about this child in the context of family? Is the child experiencing overall good health?

(b) Is the child developing typically in the areas of physical, social, and cognitive development?

(c) What are the child's strengths? What are areas of concern? These areas will be used to guide plans and activities for this this child for the next few months, at which time another case study should be conducted.

3-7b Portfolios

Portfolios provide an opportunity for sharing observations and assessment information. A portfolio is a collection of pictures, observations, direct quotes, and

© Cengage Learning 2015

▶❚❚ **TeachSource** Video Case 3-1

Home/School Communication: The Parent/Teacher Conference

This video provides tips for teachers who are planning to meet parents to discuss their child. These conferences often create tension for teachers and parents because the outcome is unknown for both parties.

1. How would a discussion of the child's play with friends change this conference?

2. Look at the bonus video: Parent challenges a teacher's approach to game playing. How would you respond to this parent?

Watch on CourseMate

artifacts created by the child. Some portfolios will include inferences that the teacher is making about the child. Some centers will create portfolios for every child in the center and add to these each year.

Beginning in the infant/toddler center, the center purchases a binder/notebook for each child in the center. The infant/toddler teacher can organize the notebook (i.e., portfolio) around the developmental domains (explained in the section on case study) or around the child's play interests. As the child progresses through the center, the teachers add to the notebook. When the child leaves the center, she has a record of her growth and development.

3-7c Documentation Panels

Documentation panels provide another avenue for communicating or sharing information. Inspired by the schools of Reggio Emilia, documentation panels are a reflection of the child's play as interpreted by the teacher. These may include inferences about the child's play that link the child's behavior to theory and research.

The case study and/or portfolio only focus on one child at a time. They are very time consuming to conduct, and they are sent home at the end of each school year. In contrast, the documentation panel may focus on several children and is displayed from one year to the next so the children can see how other children have used these materials. Case studies and portfolios tell one child's story in a binder. Documentation panels tell the story of one or more children discovering their world.

3-7d Communication

The most important aspect is to keep the parents informed throughout the school term. By assessing and communicating your findings about play, you give parents the opportunity to use this information to inform their play interactions at home.

✳ PLAYSCAPE: REFLECTIONS

In the PlayScape given at the beginning of this chapter, Juanita knew intuitively that her children needed and benefitted from playing alone and with others. Skilled professionals use observation and assessment to understand the multiple outcomes of play. For example, when Juanita's son plays alone, he learns to concentrate on his own task, to work independently, and to solve problems independently. When he plays with his siblings, he learns turn taking, language, and social interaction. Children will develop their cognitive processing skills as they engage in games that require critical thinking and problem solving. Social skills will be developed as they take turns, win and lose, and resolve disputes. They develop their locomotor skills as they run, walk, jump, and skip on the playground. We can observe, assess, and document areas of growth in these areas. Professionals can use observation and assessment tools to document growth and development in a way that will allow them to understand each child's needs and to plan instruction that meets the need of the child.

Summary

3-1 Describe the benefits of observing and assessing play.

Play provides a natural environment for observation and assessment. Play-based assessment allows unobtrusive observation and assessment, which can provide the teacher with data that can be used to understand individual growth and development as well as guide program direction. Written observations and assessment provide a source of evidence that can be shared with others who are invested in the child's growth and development.

3-2 Describe the impact of ecological factors on observation and assessment.

Bronfenbrenner's ecological system provides an organizing framework for thinking about the impact of family and culture (Bronfenbrenner & Morris, 2006). The microsystem has the most influence because it directly impacts children. The mesosystem includes people and places in the microsystem that interact together, and the exosystem includes those factors that impact the child indirectly. The macrosystem reflects the impact of culture and societal structure. Understanding how different factors affect children during play or play-based assessment is critically important for those who are working with young children.

3-3 Explain different types of observation.

Naturalistic observations occur in the center or school setting. A checklist is used for acknowledging accomplishment, whereas a rating scale ranks the levels of accomplishment. A running record records every behavior that occurs, whereas an anecdotal record provides a narrative of one event. Behavior samplings provide a way to document occurrences of specific behaviors. These instruments can be used for collecting other data but are especially useful when used to collect data about play.

3-4 List three ways to assess cognitive development during play.

One approach uses a Piagetian lens that recognizes qualitatively different levels of play, which include practice or functional, constructive, and symbolic play, and games with rules. Another way to assess cognitive development is influenced by a Vygotskian perspective. Using this view, symbolism, rules created by the children, and the movement from nonskill to skill attainment are examined. Because a Vygotskian approach focuses on the child's independent attainment of skills, it is especially well suited for play assessment. Third, looking at play using a Montessori view requires a view that focuses on sensory-motor activities, self-correcting manipulation materials, and the completion of tasks.

3-5 Identify Parten's six levels of social interaction during play that reflect social development.

Parten (1932) identified different social interactions that occur during play. These include unoccupied (not involved in play, wanders around room), onlooker (observing, but just watching, not playing), solitary (plays alone), parallel (occurs when two or more children play with materials but do not disengage in social interaction even though they play on their own), associative (occurs when the child begins to play with other children), and cooperative (occurs when children work together on a common goal).

3-6 List three areas of physical development that can be assessed during play.

Fine motor skills can be assessed as children use their small motor skills to pick up small cars or to manipulate objects. Gross motor skills can be assessed as children throw, reach, or walk. Locomotor skills can be assessed as children run, hop, skip, and jump.

3-7 Analyze the benefits of communicating observation and assessment results to families, caregivers, and colleagues.

Families, caregivers, and colleagues benefit when observation and assessment results are clearly communicated. If one purpose of assessment is to inform the child's instruction, then all who surround the child must be aware of the child's strengths and limitations. Case studies, portfolios, and documentation panels provide ways to share information.

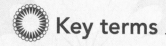
Key terms

Anecdotal record, 63
Associative play, 74
Behavior samplings, 64
Checklist, 62
Chronosystem, 61
Constructive play, 67
Cooperative play, 74
Event samplings, 64
Expressive Speech, 77
Exosystem, 60

Fine motor skills, 75
Fortuitous combinations, 66
Functional play, 65
Gross motor skills, 75
Intentional combinations, 66
Locomotor skills, 75
Macrosystem, 60
Mere practice play, 66
Mesosystem, 60
Microsystem, 59

Onlooker behavior, 73
Parallel play, 74
Practice play, 65
Rating scale, 62
Receptive speech, 77
Running record, 63
Solitary play, 73
Symbolic play, 68
Unoccupied behavior, 73

Technology and Internet Resources

Gesell Institute of Child Development http://gesellinstitute.org

A nonprofit group dedicated to preserving and extending the work of Arnold Gesell since 1950. The focus is on understanding how children grow and learn. The site offers a variety of materials for sale.

Jean Piaget Society http://www.piaget.org/

Site features a great deal of materials that extend the discussion provided in this chapter.

A three-minute video demonstrates the concept of pre-operational thinking.

National Institutes of Health http://www.ncbi.nlm.nih.gov

Site provides information on assessing different aspects of pretend play within a play setting.

Tools of the Mind http://www.toolsofthemind.org

Based on the work of Vygotsky, this site was created by Leong and Bodrova.

The site provides information on various topics.

Activities

1. InClass Lab

Divide the class into four to six groups with five people in each group. Half of the class should engage in play behaviors while the other half observes their actions. Continue this activity until all the students have engaged in this activity. Compare observations. What are the similarities? What are the differences?

2. Research and Inquiry

Two children who have Russian ancestry enter the kindergarten classroom. Shauna, the kindergarten teacher, observes their play. She notices that they play with each other, play in the home area, but do not interact with other children. Based on your knowledge of the ecological system, what factors might be affecting their play? Explain your answer.

3. Service Learning

A. Volunteer in a local afterschool program. After you leave, write a description of the play you

observed. Did the program encourage play for different ages? If so, how? What games did you observe? Did you see "boys only" or "girls only" groups emerge in play?

B. Find out what play opportunities are available for children who live in local homeless shelters. Advise the class to work in teams of four. Each team should create a toy box for one age group. For example, the teams will complete toy boxes for infants, toddlers, preschoolers, or primary age children. When finished, teams can take the materials to a local homeless shelter for use.

4. Family Connections

Choose one of the following projects: Develop brochures that communicate the stages of play to parents. Place these in local medical officers and public offices that parents visit. Create posters that depict different types of play (functional, constructive, dramatic, sociodramatic, and games). Place these in local grocery stores or community centers.

5. Play Advocacy

A. Find out what play opportunities are available for children in local homeless shelters and offer to develop additional materials. See Activity 3(b) above.

B. Ask what play arrangements are available at the local police office. Do they have Teddy bears in police cars?

 Visit CourseMate for this textbook to access the eBook, Did You Get It? quizzes, Digital Downloads, TeachSource Video Cases, flashcards, and more. Go to CengageBrain.com to log in, register, or purchase access.

References

Bronfenbrenner, U., & Morris, P. (2006). The bioecological model of human development.In R. Lerner, & W. Damon (Eds.), *Handbook of child psychology* (6th ed.): Vol. 1, *Theoretical models of human development* (pp. 793–828). Hoboken, NJ: John Wiley & Sons.

Drew, W., Christie, J., Johnson, J., Meckley, A., & Nell, M. (2008). Constructive play: A value-added strategy for meeting early learning standards. *Young Children, 63*(4): 38–44.

Elkonin, D. B. (2005). Chapter 1: The subject of our research: The developed form of play. *Journal of Russian and East European Psychology, 45*(1): 22–48.

Frahsek, S., Mack, W., Mack, C., Pfalz-Blezinger, C., & Knopf, M. (2010). Assessing difference aspects of pretend play within a play setting. Towards a standardized assessment of pretend play in young children. *British Journal of Developmental Psychology, 28*, 331–345.

Frost, J., Wortham, S., & Reifel, S. (2012). *Play and child development*(4th ed.). Upper Saddle River, NJ: Merrill/ Prentice Hall.

Greathouse, D., & Shaughnessy, M. (2010). An interview with Jerome Sattler. *North American Journal of Psychology, 12*(2), 335–340.

Gutek, G. (2004). *The Montessori method: The origins of an educational innovation.* Lanham, MD: Rowman and Littlefield.

Howes, C. (1992). *The collaborative construction of pretend play: Social pretend play functions.* Albany: SUNY.

Isenberg, J., & Jalongo, M. (2009). *Creative thinking and arts based learning: Preschool through fourth grade.* Columbus, OH: Pearson.

Montessori, M. (1964). *The Montessori method* (A. E. George, Trans.). New York: Schocken Books. (Original work published 1912).

Murray, A. (2012). Public knowledge of Montessori education. *Montessori Life: A Publication of the American Montessori Society, 24*(1), 18–21.

National Association for the Education of Young Children Guidelines for Ethical Assessment (2011) *NAEYC code of ethical conduct and statement of commitment.* Retrieved on July 3, 2013 from http://www.naeyc.org/files/naeyc/ file/positions/Ethics%20Position%20Statement2011. pdf

National Association for the Education of Young Children. (2007). NAEYC and NAECS/SDE position statement: Early childhood curriculum, assessment and program evaluation—building an effective, accountable system in programs for children birth through age 8. Retrieved on July 3, 2013 from http://www.naeyc.org/files/naeyc/ file/positions/CAPEexpand.pdf

Parten, M.(1932). Social participation among pre-school children. *Journal of Abnormal Psychology, 27*, 243–269.

Pelligrini, A. (2011). *The Oxford handbook of the development of play.* New York: Oxford University Press.

Pelligrini, A., & Boyd, B. (1993). The role of early childhood development and education: Issues in definition and function. In B. Spodek (Ed.), *Handbook of research in early childhood education.* (pp. 105–121). New York: Macmillian.

Piaget, J. (1951/1962). *Play, dreams, and imitation in childhood.* New York: Norton.

Piaget, J. (1952/1974). *The origins of intelligence in children.* New York: Basic Books.

Reifel, S. (2011). Observation and early childhood teaching: Everyday fundamentals. *Young Children, 66*(2), 62–65.

Ridgers, N. D., Stratton, G., & McKenzie, T. L. (2010). Reliability and validity of the system for observing children's activity and relationships during play (SOCARP). *Journal of physical activity & health, 7*(1), 17–25.

Rogers, C., & Sawyers, J. (1988). *Play in the lives of children.* Washington, DC: National Association for the Education of Young Children.

Roopnarine, J. (2011). Cultural variations in beliefs about play, parent-child play, and children's play: Meaning for childhood development. In A. Pelegrinni (Ed.), *The Oxford Handbook of The Development of Play* (pp. 10–19). New York: Oxford University Press.

Rubin, K. H., Fein, G., & Vandenberg, B. (1983). Play. In E. M. Hetherington (Ed.), P. H Mussen (Series Ed.), *Handbook of child psychology: Vol. 4, Socialization, personality, and social develoment* (pp. 693–774). New York: Wiley.

Sattler, J. (2008). *Assessment of children: Cognitive foundations* (5th ed.). La Mesa, CA: Jerome M. Sattler Publishers.

Sherwood, S., & S. Reifel. (2010). The multiple meanings of play: Exploring preservice teachers' beliefs about a central element of early childhood education. *Journal of Early Childhood Teacher Education, 31*, 322–343.

Smilansky, S. (1968). *The effects of sociodramatic play on disadvantaged preschool children.* New York: Wiley.

United States Census Bureau. (2012). United States Census Data, 2012. Retrieved February 2, 2013 from http://www.census.gov/#

Vygotsky, L. (1978). *Mind in society: The development of higher psychological processes.* Cambridge, MA: Harvard University Press.

Weis, R. (2008). *Introduction to abnormal child and adolescent psychology.* Thousand Oaks, CA: Sage Publications, Inc.

2 PLAY in Early Education

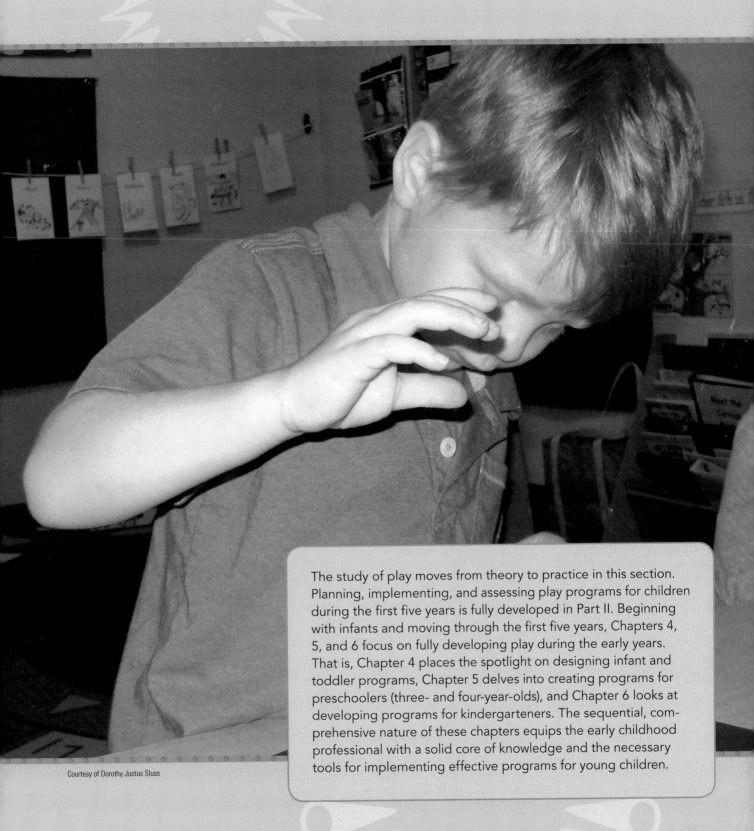

Courtesy of Dorothy Justus Sluss

The study of play moves from theory to practice in this section. Planning, implementing, and assessing play programs for children during the first five years is fully developed in Part II. Beginning with infants and moving through the first five years, Chapters 4, 5, and 6 focus on fully developing play during the early years. That is, Chapter 4 places the spotlight on designing infant and toddler programs, Chapter 5 delves into creating programs for preschoolers (three- and four-year-olds), and Chapter 6 looks at developing programs for kindergarteners. The sequential, comprehensive nature of these chapters equips the early childhood professional with a solid core of knowledge and the necessary tools for implementing effective programs for young children.

4 Supporting PLAY for Infants and Toddlers

STANDARDS COVERED IN THIS CHAPTER

Council of Exceptional Children—Division of Early Childhood Standards CEC DEC

ECSE 2K7 Infants and young children develop and learn at varying rates

ECSE7K1 Theories and research that form the basis of developmental and academic curricula and instructional strategies for infants and young children

ECSE 7K2 Developmental and academic content

ECSE 7S2 Plan and implement developmentally and individually appropriate curriculum

NAEYC Program Standards **naeyc**

4a Understanding positive relationships and supportive interactions as the foundation of work with children

4b Knowing and understanding effective strategies and tools for early education

4c Using a broad repertoire of developmentally appropriate teaching and learning approaches

✳ LEARNING OBJECTIVES ✳

4-1 List the benefits of a play-based curriculum for infants and toddlers.

4-2 Identify the factors that create a context for play.

4-3 Describe the characteristics of adults who facilitate high-quality care in infant/toddler centers.

4-4 Differentiate the progression of music development from birth to age two.

4-5 Distinguish levels of movement development from birth to age two.

4-6 Categorize levels of art development from birth to age two.

4-7 Explain characteristics of places and spaces for infant and toddler play.

4-8 Identify the attributes of a play-based program for infants and toddlers.

4-9 List the areas included in a play-based environment for infants and toddlers.

4-10 Discuss three program models.

4-11 Create activities that encourage play.

4-12 Demonstrate two ways to assess infant and toddler play.

© Cengage Learning 2015

✳ PLAYSCAPE: CASE STUDY

Natasha is concerned that her infant, Shanana, is staying in an infant/toddler center. As a single mother, her choices are limited. Natasha's mom helped her find a program that allows Natasha to take high school courses while her infant receives care in the infant/toddler center located in the building next door. After a long day at school, Natasha arrives to pick up Shanana at the center. She finds the lead teacher, Annie, playing with Shanana. As a seven-month-old, Shanana will go to anyone easily. Natasha watches Annie and Shanana, and she notices how Shanana plays. Shanana looks at the reflecting lights in the plastic toy container, reaches out to touch it, notices it rolls, and smiles. Natasha wishes she had more time to play with Shanana. But for now, she needs to pick up Shanana and head home, where her mom and sister will play with Shanana while Natasha does her homework.

Explaining Play Behaviors

Shanana is a typical seven-month-old. She is attached to her mother but enjoys interacting with other adults. Her provocation to play is the plastic bottle filled with liquid and sparkles. Because she is surrounded by females, Natasha will want to find a way for Shanana to spend some time with males, who can provide a positive role model and engage in a different type of play. Shanana is fortunate because her mother has a circle of support and will be able to engage in play that will add to the quality of her life (Bronfenbrenner & Morris, 2006).

✳ 4-1 Play-Based Curriculum in Infant/Toddler Centers

When infants and toddlers are not sleeping, they are engaged in play and exploration. Programs that meet the needs of this age group must include play and exploration as key components of the curriculum. Infant/toddler programs are, by design, different from those of preschoolers. Security is the main focus of young infants (birth to 9 months), exploration is the main theme of mobile infants (8 to 18 months), and toddlers (16 to 36 months) are continuing to focus on their identity (Zero to Three, 2012). Because of these differences, the care of infants is different from that of toddlers. Infant caregivers must be aware of stimulating without overstimulating. Programs for toddlers should not be scaled-down preschool programs. Children with disabilities or delays will require more stimulation. Children without delays will require less stimulation. Understanding this balance requires an attitude of *respect, responsiveness, and reciprocity* (Gonzalez-Mena, 2011).

Programs that support play and exploration maintain a safe, healthy, caring environment. Essential elements include movement, music, art, toys, language and literacy activities that ensure object play, motor play, social play, and symbolic/pretend play. Developmental characteristics of infants and toddlers should inform the curriculum because at this age developmental domains are so intertwined (Kaefer, 2012). Infants need a smaller space with areas for sleeping, eating, and messy activities, and they need well-defined floor-play areas. Toddlers need more space for moving and clearly defined areas for play. The unique characteristics of nonmobile infants (lap babies), mobile infants (cruisers), and highly mobile toddlers (movers) serve as a basis for developing programs and environments that reflect best practices for young children.

4-1a Benefits of Play-Based Curriculum

A play-based curriculum for very young children ensures that adults who interact with the child focus on facilitating the child's development (Marshall, 2011).

1. **Social development is enhanced** A play-based infant curriculum encourages and values adult-child interaction. The adult is the most important person in the infant's world. It is the adult who initiates the game of "look at me, laugh with me" that is so important for the development of the young human. The young child feels safe, secure, respected, valued, cared for, happy, encouraged, and reassured.

2. **Emotional development is enhanced** The young child in a play-based program is encouraged to laugh, sing, and move with others. This cultivates emotional development that is so important for brain growth and development. Young children develop confidence as they learn about themselves, others, the environment, routines, and limits.

3. **Cognitive development is facilitated** The developing brain is stimulated when infants and toddlers are encouraged to interact with others, explore, and initiate action on objects. When the infant explores the rattler or the stuffed bear, she is taking the lead in acting on the object and exploring her world. She is developing her understanding of the physics of dropping something and watching it fall. When this occurs, neurological connections are strengthened.

4. **Physical development is promoted** During play, infants and toddlers move, stretch, throw, creep, crawl, climb, walk, and run. These movements encourage the development of gross motor skills. As infants and toddlers grasp, toss, and experiment with toys, they are developing their fine motor skills as well as a respect for people and things.

5. **Language development is encouraged** When infants/toddlers play with other children, talk and laugh with adults, sing and engage in verbal play with words, they are learning the syntactical structures necessary for language development. Without necessary models, children will never develop the basic foundation for language.

What do you think?

How is brain development related to the developmental domains listed in this section? Find information in Chapter 1 that will support your perspective. You may want to review the TeachSource video, Brain Development, highlighted in Chapter 1.

Did You Get It?

At lunch time, a 10-month-old child begins to drop her cup off the high chair tray. This child is demonstrating behavior that reflects a change in her _____ development.

a. emotional
b. cognitive
c. social
d. physical

Take the full quiz on CourseMate

Creating a Context for Play 4-2 ✳

Good programs create a context for play by providing love, protection, and a developmentally appropriate pace (Photo 4-1). Alan Fogel (1998) noted that "a first-century B.C. Chinese text, *Liji (Record of Rituals)*, states, "When training is premature, nothing is gained other than a great deal of work" (Kojima, 1986, p. 44). Programs that are sensitive to the developmental needs of the very young child have specific characteristics. Studies of infant/toddler programs

4-1 Infants and toddlers thrive in an environment designed to keep them healthy, safe, and ready to play. This infant is in an environment designed to optimize play and development. Read the next section for information about how to create this environment.

Did You Get It?

Staff at a child care center engages in daily communication with parents. What indicator of high-quality care does this demonstrate?

a. Health and safety recommendations and guidelines that are rigorously followed.

b. Sensitively responsive caregivers who know each baby so well that they can anticipate the babies' needs.

c. Low adult-to-child ratios and group sizes that are strictly maintained.

d. Staff who demonstrate that strong interpersonal skills and positive communication exist and are facilitated among caregivers, colleagues, parents, and babies.

Take the full quiz on CourseMate

have found specific indicators of high-quality care that include the following (McMullen, 1999, p. 73):

- Use of developmentally appropriate practice as a philosophy in setting up the environment and developing the curriculum
- Low adult-to-child ratios and group sizes that are strictly maintained
- Health and safety recommendations and guidelines that are rigorously followed
- Staff that is knowledgeable in child development and learning specific to the infant and toddler developmental period and who know how to use this knowledge appropriately
- Administrative policies and workplace conditions that discourage staff turnover, and thus encourage consistency of caregiving for babies
- Staff who demonstrate that strong interpersonal skills and positive communication exist and are facilitated among caregivers, colleagues, parents, and babies
- Sensitively responsive caregivers who know each baby so well that they can anticipate the babies' needs, read their verbal and nonverbal cues, and consistently respond quickly in a loving and affectionate manner to meet those needs

✳ 4-3 Adult Facilitation

Next to safety, adult interaction is the most important component in the infant curriculum (Photo 4-2). When adults establish a strong relationship with the infant, there are positive outcomes for the infant (Greenspan & Wieder, 2012). Infants who do not bond to an attachment figure may be at risk even in their adolescent years (Berk, 2012). For this reason, the child care community is concerned about the high turnover rate in child care centers. Approximately one-third of all infant/toddler teachers leave every year, and one-third of those teachers are first-year teachers (NACCRRA, 2013). The effect on consistency and attachment is both regrettable and a cause for alarm.

Consistency is not the only requirement. Adults in infant/toddler centers have a complex role. Not only are they involved as a play partner during floor play, they must watch the children's reactions and assess how well they are doing. Greenspan and Wieder (2012) identified three major characteristics of those who provide high-quality care to infants and toddlers:

1. Interactive relationships that include

   - Warmth and security
   - Regulation, so the child does not become overwhelmed
   - Relatedness and engagement
   - Back-and-forth emotional signaling and gesturing
   - Shared social problem solving
   - The use of ideas in a meaningful and functional way
   - Thinking and reasoning

2. Awareness of the variation that exists in motoric and sensory capacities of individual children

3. Recognition of the interrelatedness of different developmental domains (paraphrased from Greenspan and Wieder, 2012, p. xi)

Establishing affective relationships between adults and the infants and toddlers in their care is the first step in creating an environment for play (see Table 4-1).

© Cengage Learning 2015

4-2 The adult is the most important person in the child's life. Because the brain continues to grow so rapidly after birth, adults who provide strong attachments stimulate the development of the child.

TABLE 4-1 Helping Babies Play

Birth to four months

In these early months, babies explore their new world with their eyes. The following will help babies develop this exploration:

- Provide bright, moving objects for babies to practice looking at. Mobiles should be interesting from the baby's view. Provide consistency by leaving the objects in their place so the baby begins to recognize familiar objects in the crib at home as well as in out-of-home care settings.

- Move objects close to and away from babies. Also, move your face close to and away from them. This will make a different visual impact than things that stay still; in addition, it helps babies judge the relationship between objects and between themselves and objects.

- Hold babies up to your shoulder and move them around to provide a better view.

- Show the baby in a mirror how beautiful and wonderful he is.

- Playfully engage the baby in repetitions of looking, smiling, talking, and laughing. The adult usually starts the game by smiling and talking to gain baby's attention. Experienced caregivers and parents find that tongue clicking, head shaking, moving quickly toward baby and then stopping, and repeating certain sounds are entertaining to babies. Perform in a clownlike fashion and stop to wait for baby to do her part— laughing, smiling, or moving her arms and legs in excitement. Repeat the clown show several times, each time stopping for baby to have a turn. The show stops when baby starts to look away or show other signs of fatigue, overstimulation, or lack of interest.

(Continued)

TABLE 4-1   Helping Babies Play (*Continued*)

Babies explore sound and motion, too. The following will help increase these explorations:

- Talk to babies in a playful way. Smile and repeat soft sounds again. Stop between sounds and watch for them to smile or move in response to your voice. If you get a playful response, repeat the show.

- Sing to the baby. Make up songs just for the baby. Dance with the baby nestled on your shoulder.

- Play with the baby's hands and feet, gently patting and rubbing, saying silly, soft sounds to match. "Pedal" the baby's legs for a bike ride, describing where you're going.

Four to eight months

In this stage, infants can use not only eyes and ears but hands and mouth to explore objects. The following can stimulate play for this age group:

- Keep toy safety a primary concern. Provide objects that can be held by small hands but that are not small enough to fit entirely in the mouth. Toys must be washable and made of tough, durable materials. There must be no sharp edges or points that can injure and no small parts that can come off (small wheels or buttons, for example).

- Toys that move or make a sound in response to the baby's actions are best. Look for toys that pop up, turn, honk, rattle, or play music when the baby pushes, punches, hits, or pokes at them.

- Minimize interruptions to protect babies' exploration of new objects. Watch but don't interrupt when babies are busy exploring. Also prevent other children (especially older ones) from interrupting play. Having duplicates of several toys will help prevent would-be "snatchers" from robbing the explorer.

Babies are also becoming more social at this age and will enjoy your efforts to entertain them by doing the following:

- Playing "This Little Piggy Went to Market" with their toes

- Singing special songs while changing their diapers and clothes or cutting nails

Eight to twelve months

Babies now are fully active in exploring their world. Almost all babies crawl or creep; many walk around the room holding onto furniture; some are independently walking. Babies now combine objects and practice dropping, throwing, and squeezing. The following suggestions will foster their play:

- Provide objects to put in containers and dump out. Some good containers are plastic bowls, plastic storage boxes, baskets, and shoe boxes. Make sure that items to put in the containers are small enough for small hands but not small enough to fit entirely in the mouth. Good things to put in are small clocks, yarn balls, plastic lids, and rings from stack-a-ring toys.

- Hide objects for baby to find. Hide objects under covers. At first, leave part of the toy visible or cover with a see-through material (thin scarf, plastic lid, cheese cloth). Hide the baby under a cover; look and look until the baby pops out while you ask, "Where's the baby? Where's Lucy?"

- Help babies practice sounds by repeating their sounds back—for example, dada, oh oh, and, by the end of the first year, words like *kitty*, *baby*, and *doll*. Don't limit speech to imitating babies, but extend and expand their words into sentences.

- Read to the baby.

- Provide toys that challenge the infant's skills. Children this age practice pulling, pushing, poking, and punching.

(*Continued*)

TABLE 4-1 Helping Babies Play (Continued)

- Be sure toys are in working order. Toys that don't work are just no fun. They can be very frustrating.

- Introduce toys with more than one part. Infants this age especially like things that fit inside something else.

- Stretch baby's arms above her head, asking, "How big is baby? SOOOO Big!" After a while, baby will hold up her arms to respond to your question.

- Play Pat-A-Cake, Peek-A-Boo, and Copycat with the baby.

- Children in this age group enjoy the sensory feeling of moving through space—riding piggyback, swinging in child-seat swings, riding in wagons, and dancing in an adult's arms. They and older babies also enjoy bouncing on an adult's knee to the accompaniment of a song or verse such as "This Is the Way the Lady Rides."

Twelve to eighteen months

Infants in this age group are great experimenters, trying out all their skills this way and that just to see what will happen. The first pretend play occurrs in this group when infants begin to act "as if" doing daily activities. They pretend to sleep, eat, or bathe. They then apply these acts to others and later copy others' behaviors as their own. The following suggestions will help support play for babies in this age group:

- Provide simple pictures of familiar items (laminated, covered with clear plastic, or put into zip-type plastic bags) for baby to practice naming.

- Read to the baby, talking about the book as you go.

- Provide safe places (indoors and outdoors) for moving—walking and climbing. Due to the likelihood of many falls, climbing steps should be plastic or covered with carpet. Tunnels and cabinets provide opportunities for going in, out, through, and under.

- Be the receiver of the child's pretend actions. Take a drink from the empty cup, smack your lips, and say, "Ummmmm, good." Let the child comb your hair or pretend to wash your face. Then extend the pretense to another recipient such as a doll. Support the child's language development by narrating the drama as it progresses: "Jimmy is asleep," or "Oh, I'm going to be clean. I'm getting a bath."

- Provide real-looking toys for daily activities such as eating, bathing, riding, and cleaning. Important toys for pretense at this age are dolls (realistic, representative of a variety of racial/ethic groups): daddy, mommy, brother, sister, baby; and transportation vehicles: boats, planes, cars, and trains.

Source: Excerpted with minor changes from Janet K. Sawyers and Cosby S. Rogers, Helping young children develop through play: A practical guide for parents, caregivers, and teachers. (Washington, DC: NAEYC, 1988), 13–21. Used by permission from Cosby Rogers and Janet Sawyers.

Did You Get It?

A caregiver at a child care center plays Pat-A-Cake and Peek-A-Boo with the 8-12 month-old infants. This is an appropriate activity because

a. singing special songs while changing their diapers is developmentally appropriate.

b. being the receiver of the child's pretend actions is developmentally appropriate.

c. playing Pat-A-Cake, Peek-A-Boo, and Copycat with the baby is developmentally appropriate.

d. talking to babies in a playful way is developmentally appropriate.

Take the full quiz on CourseMate

Music and a Play-Based Aesthetic Curriculum 4-4 ✳

An aesthetics-based approach to infant/toddler care can enrich the life of both the child and early educator. This approach utilizes the arts to create a beautiful, enjoyable environment. Music, movement, and art can be combined with play to foster a creative environment for learning.

Infants are born ready for music. Many interactions between parents and infants have a musical quality. When adults talk to babies, their voices have a higher pitch and phrases have distinct contours that are specific to the parents'

TABLE 4-2	Music Benefits Children in a Variety of Ways

- Children are exposed to the music of their culture and other cultures
- Children develop an appreciation for music
- Communication increases when children are singing and interacting with each other
- Social interaction increases as children sit, stand, and move together as a group
- Language develops as children use rhymes and rhythms
- Motor skills develop as children use their large and small muscles during finger-plays and dances
- Creativity develops as children play instruments, make up their own sounds and songs, and create dances
- Music provides an integrative activity that develops the whole child

4-3 The adult who sings to the infant sets the stage for the child's appreciation for music.

culture (Custodero, 2003; Papousek, 1996). Speech directed toward infants has a musical quality that may serve as a survival mechanism. Parents intuitively use music with younger children. The musical interactions that occur between adult and child foster the development of young children as they learn about turn taking, meaning making, and belonging (Custodero, 2003).

These ideas are not new. In the 1600s, Comenius (1592–1670) wrote the *School of Infancy* (1631) in which he advocated the use of music with young children. Froebel (1887/1902) valued music and incorporated it into the curriculum in the 1800s. Play, music, and movement are almost impossible to separate. All are intrinsically motivated. Some scholars believe the play that occurs between the mother and child during reciprocal interactions has a musical quality. Like play, music supports many developing skills, as listed in Table 4-2.

Music is a major component in a play-based program. Teachers who are excited about music stimulate this interest in others. Songs can be used to calm, soothe, and transition young children (Photo 4-3). Numerous recordings are available for the adult who is not comfortable singing. It is the adult's attitude toward music that is important. Too often, teachers mistakenly believe that if you do not sound like a major recording star, you should not sing. Children need interactions with adults who will sing while they diaper, sing during daily routines, and sing in response to the child's needs. Music is developmentally appropriate for infants and toddlers. The infant who responds to songs is learning both music and language. The teacher's role is to facilitate, not perform.

4-4a Stages of Development of Musicality

The stages of development of musicality are recommended as one way to think about the infant's development in the area of music. These stages include newborn, birth to six months, six to nine months, nine to twelve, twelve to eighteen months, and older toddlers (Trevarthen & Malloch, 2003).

Newborn. The newborn is receptive to sounds in the immediate surroundings, including music. Although the benefits of Mozart recordings for babies have been overemphasized by the media and marketing agencies, infants are absorbing everything from the environment. When music is too loud or abrasive, infants withdraw. When music is pleasant and melodious, they play. Daily activities can be situated within a framework of music. The teacher's hum, a peaceful musical recording, or the sounds of conversation create pleasant sounds for babies.

Birth to Six Months.   Play and music go hand in hand at this age. Beginning with **motherese, parentese, or infant-directed speech** (IDS), the child is learning how to be musical. Babies are naturally sociable and intensely aware of the feelings of those around them. The child and teacher play with music as they develop a relationship together. The child is listening to surrounding sounds. The patterns of music that the child hears provide a foundation for music as well as math. The music can be as simple as the adult's familiar song or sing-song voice when reading a story. If the child has specific lullabies or finger-plays in her culture, these can be used to enhance the musical and emotional experience for the infant.

Six to Nine Months.   Around the middle of the first year, babies develop the ability to "join in collaborative rhythmic games of toe-pointing, leg-wagging, and arm-waving, accompanied by a variety of calls, crows, and babbles" (Trevarthen & Malloch, 2003, p. 14).

This is the age when babies develop an awareness of self and others. They enjoy one-on-one play and performing in a familiar setting. As they develop an awareness of familiar and unfamiliar, they may be timid around strangers. Lullabies and interactive songs are especially enjoyable as the child interacts with adults around her.

Nine to Twelve Months.   Mouthing seems to decrease during this time as the infant's skills in reaching and grasping escalate. Infants explore and play with objects and are fascinated by those that make a gentle musical noise. This is the age when they enjoy pushing a button that will create an action. They like to shake a rattle that makes a gentle noise, and they still enjoy singing and musical activities such as Pat-A-Cake.

© Cengage Learning 2015

Twelve to Eighteen Months.   The child continues to enjoy interactive play, and now he can like games such as Peek-A-Boo. He will move as he listens to music, and he likes social interaction such as holding, rocking, swaying, and singing when he is sad or tired. At this age the child begins to enjoy games that involve abrupt movement that coincides with a chant. Pop goes the weasel is a favorite of this age.

Older Toddlers.   The toddler will mimic and participate in family and community musical rituals. They are able to chant a sing-song speech of repeated tones. Children who are in a musical environment will reflect their culture. This is the age when children will bang or hit objects to make a loud, violent noise (see Photo 4-4). At home, pots and pans are a favorite. Centers will want to provide materials that can be used in the same way, such as a drum made from an oatmeal container. Children at this age will choose certain "favorites songs" that they enjoy and ignore others that do not appeal to them.

4-4 A variety of musical materials that are safe for the toddler provide wonderful opportunities to explore sound, touch, and music.

Parents may talk about a particular song or commercial jingle that is interesting to their child at home. As children sing along, they are developing language skills as well as music skills (melody, rhythm, and expressive time).

4-4b Songs for Infants and Toddlers

Early educators must have a repertoire of available songs to sing or play in the infant/toddler room. Including songs from all cultures in the classroom will ensure a culturally enriching setting for the young child.

Lullabies.   Lullabies are found in every culture (Honig, 2002). These are often sung in a slow, gentle voice. Lullabies are soothing for both the child and adult. They provide a signal that comfort is available and sleep may soon follow. Lullabies have been transmitted orally for many centuries but are now available through books and digital recordings. Lullabies from other cultures include "Ladino lullay, Durme, Durme, Hermozo Hijico" (Sleep, Sleep, My Beautiful Little Son) (Commins, 1967), "All the Pretty Little Horses," and, of course, "Rock-a-Bye Baby."

Nursery Rhymes.   Nursery rhymes have been handed down from one generation to another. Nursery rhymes are simple and easy for the child to remember. Some of the most popular include rhymes such as:

> Peter, Peter Pumpkin Eater,
> Had a wife and couldn't keep her;
> Put her in a pumpkin shell and
> There he kept her very well.

From the Experts

Cultural Imperatives of Play in Infancy

Dr. Smita Mathur, University of South Florida Polytechnic

© Cengage Learning 2015

Culture drives play. How infants play is largely determined by their family background. That is, babies are shaped by culture-specific knowledge, attitudes, beliefs, and practice during play experiences in their everyday environments. Infants acquire a sense of self, security, attachment, and belonging as they interact in culture-specific ways with those closest to them.

Early culture-specific experiences combine with innate tendencies to set the foundation for play and related learning. The quality and quantity of play experiences in infancy are determined by the toys and other play materials available, the number and age of play partners, adults who surround the baby, and the roles assigned to the adults.

For example, in India, the daily oil massage with soft dough strengthens the foundation for strong attachment between the mother and infant. Along with the massage, the mother playfully sings to the infant. The baby reciprocates, and this sets the stage for early play. A securely wrapped infant tied to the mother's back in Nigeria finds herself in the

(Continued)

mother's environments. The constantly changing scenarios—such as walks through the marketplace, kitchen conversations with other women, and family celebrations with music and dance—all stimulate the senses and expose the infant to multiple experiences from the familiarity and personal safety of her mother's back. A stay-at-home Japanese mother who co-sleeps with her baby lays the foundation for interdependence and cohesive relationships within the family.

In contrast, families in North America take pride in fostering independence and self-reliance early in a child's life. Infants are often reared in child-centered nuclear households and positively reinforced as they assert their unique individuality. North American families also provide infants multiple opportunities to play independently with interactive toys that promote exploration and experimentation. A baby in Oaxaca, Mexico is surrounded by multi-age playmates and adults from his extended family. In this environment play and caregiving happen in unstructured settings. Babies are held close by adult caregivers and often swaddled in colorful homespun fabric. The baby's parents may hold off naming their baby until her first birthday.

These varied culture-specific environments and interactions determine the content of infants' play and set the stage for healthy social-emotional development and school readiness.

Dr. Smita Mathur graduated from Syracuse University and has worked with young children in different cultures throughout her career. Recently, she has been involved with developing educational programs for migrant children in Florida, where she is an assistant professor at the University of South Florida Polytechnic.

This poem suggests that the wife is the property of the husband and that he can use whatever force to ensure that she does as he bids. Of course, the small infant or young toddler does not understand the social issues involved in this simple rhyme, but she does internalize the words. The use of rhymes that are culturally appropriate is recommended. For example, *Mary Had a Little Jam and Other Silly Rhymes* (Lansky, 2003) is a much better choice. The new version of the old rhyme delivers a much needed message:

> Peter, Peter, sugar eater;
>   Always wanted food much sweeter.
> Adding sugar was a blunder.
>   Now he is a toothless wonder. (Lansky, 2003, p. 18)

Incorporating rhymes from different cultures is essential in today's classroom. Young children need to hear their poems, songs, and rhymes that reflect multiple cultures (see Table 4-3). Music is a powerful force for transmitting culture. When it is combined with play, it provides a powerful method of transmitting and transforming culture.

Movement in a Play-Based 4-5 ✳ Aesthetic Program

Movement and music are interrelated in humans. Movement begins in the mother's womb. Infants will react to the kinds of music they hear. They become more active with lively music and less active with slower music. Jalongo and Stamp (1997) note that "a baby's behavior is dominated by reflexes—gasping, sucking, startling at a loud noise" (p. 67). Early educators must hold, rock, and cuddle infants during this time. It is important to engage the child without overstimulating. Understanding how humans move from being nonmobile infants to highly mobile toddlers will help differentiate activities for each age.

4-5a Low Mobility (Lap Baby)

Infants are sometimes referred to as lap babies so that everyone who cares for the baby will be aware of the baby's abilities and need to be held. Some sources refer to this as "no mobility." The term *low mobility* is preferred because these babies have mobility, just not enough to move themselves across the room during the first month. Children are born with specific reflexes, including the Palmar grasp, Moro reflex, Babinski reflex, rooting and sucking reflex, hand-to-mouth reflex, righting reflex, and Tonic neck reflex. After birth, they develop reciprocal kicking, neck righting, the parachute reflex, and the Landau reflex (Berk, 2012). When babies begin making motions that are voluntary, not automatic, they will use both gross motor and fine motor movements (see Photo 4-5).

Movement need not be taught, but it should be facilitated through interactions that involve observation and support. Movement is restricted in many of the containers designed for infants (e.g., stroller, walker, car seat, and infant carrier). Although car seats are required for safety during travel and must be used properly, the overuse of baby containers is a concern.

4-5 Children will naturally move when the appropriate amount of stimulation occurs on a regular basis.

© Cengage Learning 2015

4-5b More Mobility (Cruisers and Creepers)

During the first two years of life, the child will move progressively from an infant who can be placed on a bed safely to a toddler who is beginning to walk. The progression moves from less to more complex and generally follows this pattern:

> Raising self to a prone position
> Crawling or scooting
> Pulling to sitting
> Pulling up on furniture
> Standing alone

The most current research recommends that adults place children on their backs to sleep to prevent SIDS (sudden infant death syndrome) and choking (American Academy of Pediatrics Task Force on Infant Positioning and SIDS, 2013). Many young parents are reporting that children are not crawling as early as expected or are not crawling at all. Although the data are still anecdotal, there may be a relationship between the reported late onset of crawling and the practice of not placing infants on their stomachs to sleep. Safety concerns must be given the highest priority, but teaching motor skills such as crawling is not necessary. Children will progress naturally if supported appropriately as shown in Photo 4-6.

▶❚❚ **TeachSource** Video Case 4-1

0–2 Years: Gross Motor Development for Infants and Toddlers

Before infants and toddlers can sit up, they must be able to control their neck, shoulder, and trunk muscles. What activities support movement among infants and toddlers who are beginning to sit up, crawl, and cruise?

Watch on CourseMate

© Cengage Learning 2015

4-6 Children progress from no mobility to high mobility within two years of birth. This affects play. This baby is tempted by the toy, so she is motivated to move. She is almost ready to crawl, but, like some children, she may scoot and then walk without crawling. Each child experiences this progression in her own way.

4-7 Mobility gives toddlers the freedom to move, and this movement changes their world as well as the world of the adults who surround them.

4-5c High Mobility (Toddlers and Climbers)

At or before the age of two, children climb and move rapidly (see Photo 4-7). This contributes to the concern that most adults have about this age group. Because toddlers can climb and move so quickly, they can move quickly but not always safely. For this reason, safety is a primary concern for this age group. Approximately 25% of babies climb by the age of fourteen months, and over half climb by the age of seventeen months. By their second birthday, almost all children are climbing (Readdick & Park, 1998). Once children begin walking, they must be moved into a different area of the child care center. Nonmovers and movers have different needs. Children who are mobile need an environment that will allow them to walk, jump, hop, and climb. Gates may be needed to limit access in some areas. For example, some centers separate infants and toddlers during infant floor play and toddler play center time that includes: house, block, movement, or water play. They remove them to encourage interactions at other times. Gates provide a way to control the traffic flow but should be used judiciously.

In our discussion, music and movement have been separated only for the sake of clarity. In reality, young children combine movement and music when they bounce, sway, shake, nod, tap, gallop, swing, or jump with music. Play and movement are inseparable. From the first Pat-A-Cake to the "tyke bike," motor development occurs at an amazing rate, and play facilitates this development.

Did You Get It?

Movement should not be taught, but

a. it should be demonstrated.

b. skills should be forced to be learned at certain ages.

c. it should be facilitated through interactions that involve observation and support.

d. it is wise to encourage children to perform activities before they are ready.

Take the full quiz on CourseMate

Art in a Play-Based Aesthetic Program 4-6 ✳

Infants respond to sensory stimulation at birth. Because art involves the senses, art begins at birth. Isenberg and Jalongo (2009) point out that infants can taste, see, listen, and respond to touch. Babies are capable of visual tracking

TABLE 4-3   First Patterns

○   ○

○

or following an object with their eyes within two weeks of birth. Research has established that they prefer patterned over nonpatterned, complex over simple, flashing colored lights over white light, moving over stationary, and the human face more than any other object.

The child's appreciation for art begins when he first recognizes that two dots at the top and a dot at the bottom is their parent (i.e., their parent's eyes and mouth) (see Table 4-3). This generally occurs around the age of three months. As their first recognition of patterns develops, so does their sojourn into art appreciation. Research has found that infants will spend a longer amount of time watching a face deemed attractive (symmetrical) than one that is considered less attractive (Langlois, Roggman, & Rieser-Danner, 1990).

As infants absorb knowledge from the world, they are receptors of art. They tend to enjoy colors that contrast, such as black, white, and red, rather than pastels. They do not become producers of art until they are older—although infants are observers of art when they are born.

4-6a Developmental Stages of Art

Adults who expose children to beautiful environments prepare children for an aesthetic approach to life. There has been some concern lately about when and how early to expose children to art. Art involves more than production. For the very young child, the foundation for art develops through experiences with the world. Looking at pictures and patterns, touching different objects, tasting different flavors, and experiencing a variety of materials all form a foundation for art. Toddlers playing in water run from the grass to the sidewalk and back again— all the time experiencing the unique texture of each. This is an art experience.

Newborn to Six Months.   Stimulation should be reasonable. The infant center should not be overly stimulating. Unbreakable mirrors, pictures of human faces, and contrasting colors with different shapes are recommended. Infants enjoy different materials and fabrics. Blankets that have different textures sewn together are also enjoyable. Simple paper plate puppets are enjoyable without being overly stimulating.

Infants (Six Months to Twelve Months).   At this age, babies are beginning to develop an awareness of taste and an awareness of cause and effect. Their play reflects a lot of practice. As they explore their world, babies will use food in a variety of ways. This is at once play, science, and art. Many early childhood educators discourage the use of food as art material (Isenberg & Jalongo, 2009). This author believes that babies will play with their food with no encouragement from adults; therefore, food should be provided for intake only and not for art. This is supported by the guidelines for appropriate practice (Bredekamp & Copple, 2009).

Toddlers: Twelve Months to Two Years.   Everything is a multisensory experience to a toddler. Toddlers experience sensory materials and engage fully in any activity that interests them. Isbell and Raines (2013) point out that children at this age are in the **scribble stage** of artistic development. The very first marks that young children make are **uncontrolled scribbles** and can be made with markers, crayons, or sticks in the sand. As toddlers develop fine motor skills, they move to **controlled scribbles.** They delight in marking and experimenting with designs. Other materials that are enjoyable include crayons, markers, and large paper for toddlers to explore and manipulate. Watching a toddler discover that she can draw large circles on a white wall creates a dilemma for adults. The thrill of watching a human being discover her power is mediated by the thought of repainting the wall!

Toddlers enjoy natural materials, including mud, water, sand, dirt, grass, and plants. Caution is urged because some plants are poisonous. Toddlers also enjoy shredded paper in a dry swimming pool. This provides both a sensory experience and an opportunity to repurpose paper.

Different cultures may emphasize different aspects earlier than others. In some European countries, one-year-olds work with paint, and older toddlers enjoy using clay. In the United States, paint has generally been reserved for older two- and three-year-olds (Photo 4-8). The main focus of art at this age is to expose children to a beautiful, orderly environment that allows them to fully develop their senses and to provide sensory stimulation through a variety of authentic art experiences.

Story and Reenactment.   Infants need to interact with books in a variety of ways (Photo 4-9). The essential component is the adult who reads to the infant and young child. Children benefit from hearing a variety of books read to them on an ongoing basis and having access to books. The International Reading Association (IRA) and the National Association for the Education of Young Children (NAEYC) prepared a report that outlines guidelines for literacy from birth through the primary years. Recommendations for infant literacy development reflect the views of both groups and are included in the sections that follows.

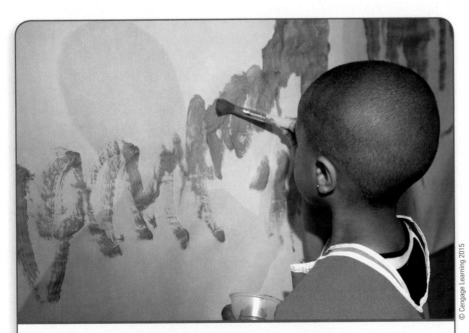

© Cengage Learning 2015

4-8 Art is a universal language. The older toddler in the picture is using a brush (instrument) to put paint (medium) on the paper (surface). Changing any of these changes the experience for the young child.

4-9 Exposing children to beautiful pictures such as those found in Eric Carle's books enhances both their art and literacy skills.

Did You Get It?

What is an appropriate art activity for an eighteen-month old?

a. tasting a variety of foods

b. exposure to red and black contrasting shapes

c. finger painting with pudding

d. playing with corn starch and water

Take the full quiz on CourseMate

Children need relationships with caring adults who engage in many one-on-one and face-to-face interactions with them to support oral language development and to lay the foundation for later literacy learning (see Figure 4-1). Important experiences and teaching behaviors include, but are not limited to the following:

- Talking to babies and toddlers with simple language, frequent eye contact, and responsiveness to children's cues and language attempts

- Frequently playing with, talking to, singing to, and doing finger-plays with very young children

- Sharing cardboard books with babies and frequently reading to toddlers on the adult's lap or together with one or two other children

Figure 4-1 Play is a major component of early literacy. When children listen to stories, they develop language and listening skills that provide scripts for play.

© Cengage Learning 2015

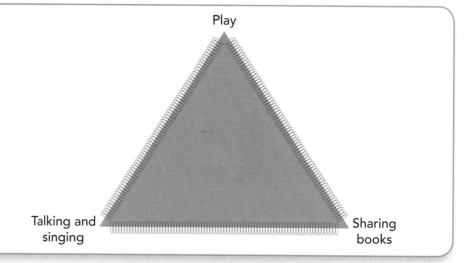

Play

Talking and singing

Sharing books

High-quality play interactions are encouraged in some centers and discouraged in others. The difference depends on the adult and the context for play that is created. If adults are overly concerned about safety issues, they may stifle the child. Yet unsafe classrooms are not an option. The early educator must create a safe environment that fosters exploration. Lowman and Ruhman (1998) refer to the multi-S approach when creating a play environment. Factors in the multi-S approach include safety and health, sanitation, stability and order, scale and comfort, simplicity and convenience, seclusion and choice, stimulation, softness, sensory appealing, soothing and sunny.

1. **Safety and health**   The younger the child, the more important the safety and health issues. Guidelines for NAEYC recommend a ratio of one adult for three infants (Bredekamp & Copple, 2009). Ensure that the room provides a safe environment with safe materials. A choke tube can be used to check small parts of toys.

2. **Sanitation**   Sanitation includes ensuring that diapering, toileting, and feeding are conducted using sanitary routines. Toys that infants mouth must be sanitized daily with a bleach solution to minimize the transmission of germs.

3. **Stability and order**   Children need a stable environment. They need to know that the toy on the shelf will be on the shelf tomorrow. The rotation of materials should happen on a slow basis. Children will become familiar with certain items and may show distress when these items are abruptly removed from the environment. Adults also benefit from order and stability in the center.

4. **Scale and comfort**   This is important in the infant room. Adults need rocking chairs in the sleeping area of the infant center. The younger the child, the smaller the space. Infants need a limited amount of space so that they can become familiar with their surroundings.

5. **Simplicity and convenience**   The space needs to be relatively simplistic. Movement patterns should allow free flow and be convenient for the child care providers. Adults who have to step over a three-foot gate throughout the day will become physically exhausted just from their movement throughout the room. Cushions can be used as barriers and are safer and easier to move.

6. **Seclusion and choice**   Since more and more children are spending more of their waking hours in group care, it is essential that they have places where they can be alone and the freedom to make that choice. Do infants have the choice of looking at a black and white spiral or a mirror? At a child care center, children cannot explore as they would at home (e.g., they can't explore their parents' kitchen cabinets), so we must create small spaces that they can explore.

7. **Stimulation**   Infants and toddlers should receive a reasonable amount of stimulation, not too much and not too little. Understanding and maintaining this balance requires the early childhood educator to have keen insight and experience. Responsive teachers make good choices for children in terms of how much stimulation is appropriate.

8. **Softness** Creating an environment that is more like home than an institution creates a pleasing environment for young children and adults. Hanging an example of a local fabric brings the culture into the center. For example, some areas have beautiful quilts; others have woven blankets or rugs. Bringing in soft items creates a more inviting space for young children.

9. **Sensory appealing** The recent emphasis on the schools of Reggio Emilia has helped focus on the value of a beautiful environment. Infants need to hear classical music, see mirrors and light throughout the room, feel different textures beneath their feet, and crawl into small spaces with mirrors that allow them to explore and experience a sense of security. Adults also enjoy and benefit from beautiful spaces.

10. **Soothing and sunny** The environment should be soothing and sunny. Over time, if young children are placed in windowless rooms with red walls and Disney characters, they may become overstimulated. The infant room should be light and bright. Too often infant centers are relegated to the basement. Natural light should flood as much of the center as possible, with the exception of the sleeping area. Windows, translucent walls, and mirrors bring light into the center. An aesthetically pleasing environment enhances the pleasure and play of both the child and adult.

✳ 4-8 Designing Environments for Infants

Creating an environment that includes all the elements described in the previous section is a challenge. How do adults design an environment that encourages play? Before beginning the design process, contact the local and state regulatory agencies. Regulations vary from state to state. In some states, licensing requirements are very rigid. In some areas, there are minimum requirements. For example, in some states, two exit areas are required. Other states require little more than covering electrical outlets. Meeting the criteria for state and local licensure is not an option. High-quality programs meet not only health and safety requirements; they meet the voluntary NAEYC accreditation requirements. The accreditation process ensures that recommended adult-child ratios are met and that optimal, not minimum, standards of care are provided. Knowledge of the state requirements and NAEYC guidelines up front will prevent problems later.

Before we consider areas for children, it should be noted that adults have needs also. Early educators who are in centers for long periods need a variety of seating and movement arrangements. A rocking chair in the sleeping or quiet area, a comfortable chair or couch with book baskets nearby, and chairs in the dining area are all appropriate for adults. According to NAEYC guidelines, the infant area should include six basic areas (Bredekamp & Copple, 2009): entrance and exit area, dining areas, diapering areas, sleeping areas, floor-play areas, and gross motor areas.

1. **Entrance and exit** The entrance and exit for parents should provide a safe, orderly environment. The entrance should be inviting to parents and should include some items, such as mirrors, that infants find interesting. A family bulletin board should be available so parents will know what is going on in the center and can communicate with others as needed. Placing the

infants' cubbies in the entryway increases efficiency. Clipboards containing information about feeding and toileting should also contain information about play or perceptual changes.

2. **Dining areas** Dining areas should be sanitary and as natural as possible. Some children who have disabilities may need special feeding arrangements. Placing five or six infants in bucket seats at a table is not appropriate; nor is placing four infants in a row in high chairs. The consumption of food should be a nutritious, enjoyable experience. Soft music in the background contributes to the ambience of the eating experience. The word *dining* has been purposefully used instead of the word *feeding*. Adults should look at their environment and consider ways to feed children with respect.

3. **Diapering areas** Diapering areas should be sanitary and close to a source of water. The placement of mirrors and wind chimes on the ceiling creates an interesting, familiar environment during diapering. This is a time when early educators talk, sing, and play special games with children. Using different songs or games with different children can add to the infant's development of self. For example, if a child has a parent from a unique cultural group, using a song from home will add to the child's comfort level.

4. **Sleeping areas** An area of the center should be set aside for rest, relaxation, and sleep. A rocking chair will allow teachers and parents to comfort the child in a relaxing atmosphere. Mothers who are nursing can enjoy the peacefulness of the area as they nurse their infant. Cribs are for sleeping and should not be cluttered with too many toys. As soon as the child is awake, he should be moved to the floor area (Gerber, 1998).

5. **Floor-play areas** The floor is the stage for play with infants. Floor play is encouraged when caregivers do the following (Gonzalez-Mena & Eyer, 2001, p. 69):

   - Separate the play space from the caregiving space. Cushions can be used to define the area, and a soft fabric should cover the floor. This can range from carpet to a blanket or quilt.

   - Make sure everything in the play space is touchable and "mouthable."

   - Include both fine and gross motor activities. Floor play provides an opportunity to use beach balls, aluminum pie pans, empty boxes, and soft cloth balls. Putting an unbreakable mirror on the floor-play area increases the child's interest in the play area. An inclined plane and bar on the side of the wall works for both crawlers and cruisers.

   - Let children find unique ways to combine toys and materials. This is the key to good floor play. Observe the children. If they are playing with scarves, let them use the scarves in any way they like, as long as it is safe. If they are playing with sensory bottles, let them roll and shake them. Let them put the scarves over the bottles, if they choose. Floor play is exploration time with objects.

   - Put out the right number of toys. The right amount varies. It is important not to overstimulate the children. They might find one or two sensory bottles interesting and stimulating. Putting five sensory bottles in the center is not appropriate. Too many toys can be confusing. It is better to have toys that can be combined and manipulated.

4-10 Play areas provide stimulation through a variety of surfaces and materials. This child is curious about the colorful materials on the wall, and this exploration will stimulate his cognitive processing, gross motor skills, and visual perception skills.

© Cengage Learning 2015

- Provide the correct balance of choices. Again, the right amount varies. A good rule of thumb for floor play is to start with two choices per child, with a limit of five choices for three children. Observe the children. Is this amount sufficient, or do they need more? Young children should not be overwhelmed by choices.

As soon as the baby begins to move on his own, place the baby flat on his tummy on a quilt with multiple colors that will interest him, and *never leave the infant during floor play.* When baby tires of looking at the materials on the quilt, place a soft textured ball or stuffed animal about five inches in front of him. Watch as he tries to move toward the ball. Be careful not to frustrate him. Adjust the distance as needed. The object of the play is fun. When the baby can reach the object and shake it, he will laugh with a sense of accomplishment.

6. **Gross motor area**   A gross motor area is a necessary part of the infant area (Photo 4-10). Children need spaces that allow them to crawl and cruise safely. A low inclined plane on the floor provides a good place for crawlers. A couch provides a comfortable place for adults and for children who are cruising. A variety of choices, including toys for pushing and pulling, should reflect the diverse abilities in the group. Daily outings in the fresh air are healthy for infants and caregivers.

✳ 4-9 Designing Environments for Toddlers

The toddler area should include six basic areas, with at least five play areas.

1. Entrance and exit
2. Dining area
3. Sleeping and resting
4. Toileting
5. Gross motor area
6. Play centers
   a. block
   b. house
   c. dramatic
   d. quiet
   e. sensory/messy
   f. water
   g. art

1. **Entrance and exit**   The entry to the center should be safe and serviceable, aesthetically pleasing, and appropriate for toddlers. Some centers place items that will attract the children's attention when they enter the center. For example, some will place unbreakable mirrors near the entry; others will place plants or aquariums that can be filled with pebbles or small rocks. In keeping with fire codes, it is important not to clutter the entry way, but it is also important to set the stage for play by providing stimulating materials in a variety of places. The entrance to the toddler area should include a place where children can place their personal belongings. A family board should be available so parents can keep current and communicate with other as needed. Placing the toddlers' cubbies near the door increases efficiency and limits messy feet to one area.

2. **Dining area**   The eating areas for toddlers should be separate and near the food preparation area. All appropriate sanitation measures should be taken in the preparation area. Rules for following hand washing should be posted so new personnel know the proper procedures. Toddlers should have the opportunity to eat on low tables with their friends and an adult. As soon as they finish, they should be able to leave the table and move to a gross motor or play area.

3. **Sleeping area**   Rest time is easier when children have a routine. When the music begins to play and the lights are dimmed, children become accustomed to what happens next: rest time. Toddlers need cots for rest. These can be stacked in one area of the room. Children who sleep on carpet on the floor can become chilled, and adults who are not on the floor are unaware of their discomfort. Children should have a stuffed animal, doll, or toy during this time to comfort and entertain them. Classical music or lullabies create a mood for rest.

4. **Toileting needs**   Toddlers are between diapers and independence. Facilities that have both a place for diapering and child-size commodes encourage toilet learning. Parents and teachers must be consistent in their practice. The ease of pull-ups is causing some children to stay in training pants longer than in the past. Some centers have even banned pull-ups because they believe that pull-ups prolong the toilet training process. Adding low, shatterproof mirrors can create an atmosphere that is pleasant and appealing.

5. **Gross motor area**   Toddlers need an area for gross motor movement. This can consist of a loft that children enter and exit through a ramp, steps to a window, steps up and down in a corner, or a beach ball. Toddlers need to move, and adults must provide safe options.

6. **Toddler play centers**   Centers first appear in the toddler room as areas. This should not be confused with the kind of center time that occurs in preschool or kindergarten. These areas provide order and assist children in choosing play. Exploration and play are dominant activities, and the interest areas should stimulate both.

   a. **Block**   The block center should have a variety of blocks on low shelves. Modern materials provide a variety of lightweight, durable materials that include soft foam, cardboard, and plastic. At this age, symbolic play is stimulated by real-life objects, so placing miniature school buses, barns, and people in the center will support play.

b. Home center Realistic home materials can contribute to the child's developing use of dramatic play. The use of real pots and pans, real dishes, and clean, empty containers is recommended. A large box placed in the middle of the house area can become a car, a truck, or a boat.

c. Dramatic Toddlers enjoy dress-up and are especially intrigued by hats. They need realistic props to encourage their play. Real materials like phones or real police hats add to the richness of their play. Safe mirrors increase opportunities to pretend.

d. Quiet zone (object play/toys/book baskets) Toddlers also need an area where they can sit and work a puzzle, look at a book, or sit in someone's lap. Baskets filled with books are convenient and very accessible; toddlers can pick up a book and return it to the basket when they have finished with the book. Soft pillows add to this center space. This quiet zone center provides a good transitioning center for the young toddler who has been accustomed to floor play.

e. Sensory (paint, sand. shredded paper) Perception skills are developing during this time. When teachers help children see differences between red and blue or blue and yellow; the child's visual perception skills are enhanced. When children play with clay, water, or mud, they are increasing both their cognitive and sensory knowledge of the world. Sand can be used both inside and outdoors. It provides an excellent sensory material for toddlers. Toys that can be used to pour, scoop, and shovel sand extend play.

f. Water zone Water play can be encouraged by using small pans of water. Safety around water is a concern at this age. Toddlers do not understand the dangers of water. They can drown in a small amount of water and will jump into a pool without understanding the consequences. Dishpans that are no more than eight inches tall can provide a safe source of water for toddlers. To prevent transmission of germs, individual tubs of water are preferable to a large water table.

g. Art Finger painting is a favorite art activity for this age. Be sure smocks are available so children don't get paint on their clothes. As discussed at the beginning of this chapter, infants and toddlers do not differentiate between edible and nonedible materials. It is confusing to use food for art, and many cultures find the use of food for art offensive. For this reason, items other than food should be considered when choosing materials for the art area.

Developing a program that includes all the areas mentioned above requires knowledge, creativity, energy, and enthusiasm. The following section provides an overview of models that can be used to develop an infant/toddler program.

Did You Get It?

Which area of the room would encourage the infant to play?

a. dining area
b. floor area
c. diapering area
d. gross motor area

Take the full quiz on CourseMate

✳ 4-10 Program Models

Components of a play-based curriculum focused on art, music, and movement have been presented in this chapter. Other program models are available for those who prefer a different curriculum framework. It would be impossible to present all the available models within the scope of this book, so representative models are briefly presented. Information included in this chapter only provides an overview of each program. For more information, contact the individual program.

- Developmental interaction model (Bank Street College of Education)
- Cognitive developmental model (HighScope)
- Constructivist (Reggio Emilia)
- Professional development programs (Creative Curriculum, West Ed program, Educaring)
- Family Child Care

Although the Waldorf and Montessori methods are appropriate models for infants and young children, they require specialized training and are not discussed in this chapter.

4-10a Developmental Interaction

The developmental interaction approach is known by many as the Bank Street approach. It is based on the philosophy that children construct knowledge through interactions with the world. Although this term was coined in the 1970s, the approach reflects the philosophy used in the Bank Street schools started in the early part of the twentieth century (Cuffaro, Nager, & Shapiro, 2000). The program for infants and toddlers is called the Family Program, and it is based on the work of Erikson (2000) and Piaget (1965). Mental health and experiential activities are the guiding principles of the program. Infants and toddlers experience a very calm, relaxed atmosphere. The curriculum consists of an even-paced daily schedule with time for playing, eating, resting, and playing outdoors. Transitions are viewed as important times for children. Faculty members are committed to minimizing difficult transitions. The Bank Street program's approach of "easing in" children new to the center is a model for appropriate child care practice: Parents commit to staying with the child until they can leave without distress. Activities available for infants and toddlers include art, blocks, sensory experiences, music, movement, and gross motor play and outings. The outings are local excursions that involve two or three children. The Bank Street approach has always used a multi-age group setting to reflect a natural social setting. This program is located in New York at Columbia Teachers College.

4-10b Cognitive Developmental

The cognitive developmental approach is also known as the HighScope program. The program was initiated as a traditional preschool program and, after the first year of struggling for a philosophy, the program decided to use a program informed by the work of Jean Piaget. This view posits that knowledge is constructed through interactions between children and adults. The child develops knowledge through "personal interaction with ideas, direct experience with physical objects and events, and application of logical thinking to these experiences. The teacher's role is to supply the context for these experiences, to help the child think about them logically, and, through observation, to understand the progress the child is making"

(Weikart & Schweinhart, 2012, p. 279). It is worth noting that HighScope is the only program model that has been validated through longitudinal studies (Schweinhart & Weikart, 2006).

The HighScope program for infants and toddlers provides a warm and nurturing environment for children under three. Active learning experiences and key experiences are designed for sensory-motor learners. The organization of space and materials, children's daily schedules, caregiving routines, and adult support based on child observation, team planning, and partnerships with parents are consistent with HighScope's Piagetian-based perspective.

Constructivist. Many Piagetian-based programs are also based on a constructivist philosophy. The example used here reflects a social constructivist model found in Italy. The infant/toddler programs of Reggio Emilia have been recognized around the world. They are referred to as *Asili Nido*, or safe nests, and serve infants from four months through three years old. The child sets the schedule throughout the day; however, lunch occurs at a specific and unchanging time each day. Most centers include a separate room for sleeping, a floor-play area, an area for diapering, a room for gross motor movement, and a place for eating/dining. The infant/toddler centers are beautiful spaces and feature areas that children can explore intently.

Relationships that develop among adults and infants are the most important part of the curriculum. The foundation for this perspective flows out of the work of Loris Malaguzzi (Gandini & Edwards, 2001). The curriculum is based on the child's needs and desires for the day. Children are valued for their many different ways of knowing the world. Those who are interested in this approach can find additional information in books such as *Bambini: The Italian Approach to Infant/Toddler Care* (Gandini & Edwards, 2001) or *Approaches to Early Childhood Education* (Roopnarine & Johnson, 2012).

4-10c Professional Development

Creative Curriculum. This training approach was developed by Amy Dombro, Laura Colker, and Diane Twister Dodge (1999) and provides a structure for developing programs. Unlike the other program models, it does not have an on-site center, nor is it associated with a university. Workshops are designed for use in professional development programs, and they rely heavily on publications. Publications are user friendly and provide a good overview of the program. Materials designed for parents are especially beneficial. The materials designed for infants and toddlers are called *Innovations* (Miller & Albrecht, 2001). Teaching Strategies, publishers of Creative Curriculum, provide training materials for practitioners and students.

The West Ed Program for Infant and Toddler Caregivers (PITC). The West Ed Program is a well-known program designed to foster high-quality infant/toddler care. West Ed proponents believe that infant care is not babysitting, nor is it a miniaturized preschool. They recognize a unique difference built on relationships and emphasize six areas: primary care, small groups, continuity, individualized care, cultural responsiveness, and inclusion of children with special needs. Ron Lally, who directs the center, has been influential in providing training throughout the United States. Indeed, West Ed training programs are located throughout the country. See the West Ed website for additional information, for the nearest training site, and for a list of recommended books and materials.

Educaring. The educaring approach was developed by Magda Gerber (1998). Professional development based on Educaring, also called Resources for Infant Caring (RIC), emphasizes the natural development of the child. This program is concerned about too much stimulation too early; it advises adults to respect and respond sensitively to the needs of the infant. Play is a major part of this program, and "wants nothing" is a term that is used frequently in this approach. "Wants nothing" refers to time spent watching and observing the infant. Advocates of this approach try to use an approach that they believe is aligned with the child's natural growth.

4-10d Family Child Care

Family centers should have similar areas and play centers as those recommended for programs outside the home. There are additional safety precautions that must be taken in home-based programs. Caregivers will need to conduct a survey of their home child care area to ensure safety. Cabinets must have secure fasteners, electrical and water dangers should be considered, and places that create a climbing or falling hazard should be removed or eliminated. All areas that the children access should be safe. Licensed public centers must follow state and local rules and regulations regarding fire codes and safety. Home centers must also comply with procedures for safety and health. As in other programs, a play-based approach is recommended.

Toys and Materials to Encourage Play 4-11 ✳

A caring relationship that leads to the child's sense of trust is a major focus during the first two years of life. Materials and toys that foster this relationship are valuable. Watch a one-year-old play with soft, cotton-filled ball. He looks at it, touches it, mouths it, throws it, and waits for someone to return it to him. He is the consummate explorer. Play materials and toys that are appropriate support and scaffold sensorimotor development. Materials or toys with contrasting colors such as yellow and red are appealing to young infants. Although very young children need few toys, by the age of one, the average child in the United States has over twenty-five toys in her collection. Duplicate toys should be available to toddlers, who should not be forced to share. Safety is a concern with children under two years in group care. Most centers have a **choke tube.** A choke tube is used to see if an item is dangerous for young children. Most commercial companies sell choke tubes. If the item fits in the choke tube, it will fit in a young child's throat and should not be used. Some centers make their own tubes out of paper towel rolls. Selecting toys and play materials to match the age and stage of the child will minimize accidents.

4-11a Infants (Birth to Four Months)

The nonmobile child benefits from materials that he can see, hear, or touch. Young infants respond to bright colors such as yellow and red and enjoy

TABLE 4-4	Play Materials for Infants to Six Months
Toys brought from home and kept in cubby to be used by the individual child only.	Soft, washable doll, stuffed animal, or attachment item from home. All should be free of plastic eyes, buttons, or materials that can be pulled off.
Toys and materials used by all children and sanitized regularly.	Soft balls and blocks, cloth balls with silky tags, and reflective plastic bottles. Rattles and toys that can be shaken, tossed, kicked, and manipulated. Floor coverings and wall hangings with contrasting colors and patterns, soft colorful scarves. *Avoid computer-enhanced toys.*

© Cengage Learning 2015

watching movement. Hanging mobiles that move and emit a gentle song are especially interesting to babies. Be wary of toys that make loud sounds or have rough edges. Safety is always paramount when selecting and using play materials. As the child grows, he explores his world and soon learns that he can cause an action when he acts on a toy. As soon as the infant realizes that he can kick or hit and create a sound or movement, he will begin to enjoy play materials. The infant does not need a large number of toys. Infants in group care need one or two items that they can bring from home that they can use exclusively. This can be placed in the infant's cubby to ensure that it is sanitary and the child has complete access to it. The center's collection should be sterilized on a daily basis to ensure good health. In these early months, babies explore their new world with their eyes and ears. See Tables 4-4 and 4-5 for things you can do to foster infants' exploration.

As the infant develops, interactions with the same, caring adults continue to be extremely important. The infant needs repetitive play and interactions to develop patterns and to understand the world that surrounds him.

Infants (eight months to twelve months) have some mobility and are beginning to discover their world on their own. They need toys that they can manipulate and explore. During this time, they can sit upright and use their

TABLE 4-5	Play Materials for Infants – Seven Months Through Twelve Months
Toys brought from home and kept in cubby to be used by the individual child only.	Soft, washable doll, stuffed animal, or attachment item from home. All should be free of buttons or materials that can be pulled off.
Toys and materials used by all children and sanitized regularly.	Soft balls, several soft blocks, reflective plastic bottles, variety of balls that make interesting noises, bells and rattles, nested and stacking materials, activity boxes with objects that can be manipulated, containers that can be filled and emptied, cars and animals to push and pull, and small cloth, plastic or cardboard books. *Avoid computer-enhanced toys.*

© Cengage Learning 2015

TABLE 4-6 Play Materials for Young Toddlers (one-year to two-year-olds)	
Toys brought from home and kept in cubby to be used by the individual child only.	Soft, washable dolls, stuffed animals, or attachment item from home. All should be free of buttons or materials that can be pulled off.
Toys and materials used by all children and sanitized regularly.	Simple, washable dolls, set of lightweight blocks, few wooden or sturdy plastic people and animal figures.
	Several types and sizes of balls, push and pull toys, riding toys, stacking and nesting toys, and a variety of books.
	Crayons and paper, sensory bins, and empty cardboard boxes.
	For 18-month-olds onward, plastic pop-off beads and stringing beads, puzzles with knobs that have 3-to 5-pieces, pegboards with variety of large pegs, and simple musical instruments.
	Avoid computer-enhanced toys.

© Cengage Learning 2015

hands. The "pincer" grasp is developing, so the child can hold things with one hand and manipulate with the other. They can stick their fingers in small places. (This is why electrical outlets must be covered.) They like to stack things and enjoy kicking and splashing (water play) during bath time. Around the age of nine to ten months, they will begin to distinguish the familiar versus the unfamiliar. One or two soft objects from home can make life better at the center. Items from home should be placed in a cubby and used by that child only. Because babies are developing object permanence around eleven months, they enjoy toys such as jack-in-the box. They also enjoy soft materials such as scarves. See Table 4-6 for activities that encourage play with infants eight-to twelve-months old.

The one-year-old is usually mobile or in the process of developing mobility. Play materials reflect this change. They climb and carry, push, and dump materials. They will move objects from one place to another. This is especially troublesome to parents when they find the keys have been carried to the trash can! One-year-olds can participate in painting and other sensory experiences. Toddlers at this stage are beginning to imitate adult behaviors and are especially fascinated by hats and empty boxes. One caveat is that toddlers who play in water should have their own small container. Plastic dishpans are ideal. Group water play in the toddler area has been identified as a source of disease transmission. Keeping children healthy who are in group care is an important goal of child care programs. So the water table should be washed out with bleach after each use, and each child must wash her hands before and after using the table.

Infants in this age group are great experimenters, trying out all their skills this way and that just to see what will happen. The first pretend play occurs in this group when infants begin to act "as if" doing daily activities. They pretend to sleep, eat, or bathe. They then apply these acts to others and later copy others' behaviors as their own. Suggestions for supporting play for these babies are provided in Table 4-7.

Did You Get It?

A simple jack-in-the-box toy, from which a clown pops up whenever a button is pressed, is most developmentally appropriate for a child who is _____, due to his or her newly developed ability to explore objects with his or her hands.

a. two-years-old.
b. two-months-old.
c. seven-months-old.
d. seventeen-months-old.

Take the full quiz on CourseMate

TABLE 4-7 Play Materials for Older Toddlers (two-year-olds)

Toys brought from home and kept in cubby to be used by the individual child only.	Soft, washable dolls, stuffed animals, or attachment item from home. All should be free of buttons or materials that can be pulled off.
Toys and materials used by all children and sanitized regularly.	Games such as lotto as well as matching games, stringing beads, puzzles with pieces that fit together, simple instrumental music set, and a variety of sturdy books.
	Dolls with simple garments and caretaking accessories, vacuum cleaner, shopping cart, plastic school buses, and figurines, hats, full-length unbreakable mirror, dress-up clothes, child-sized stove, refrigerator, and sink, table and chairs, cabinet, pots, and pans, empty food boxes such as cereal boxes that toddlers recognize easily.
	Set of unit blocks and props (wooden and plastic figures and animals, construction materials), wooden barns, assortment of farm and zoo animals, plastic nuts and bolts, empty cardboard boxes.
	Transportation vehicles such as planes, trucks, and cars that children can ride on and small replicates that they can use in block play.
	Sensory bins, crayons and paper, and art supplies such as paints, paintbrushes, chalk and chalkboard, colored paper, safety scissors, clay or dough, markers, and easels. Buckets for painting with water on the playground.
	Variety of types and sizes of balls and riding toys that are propelled by the child.
	Avoid computer-enhanced toys

© Cengage Learning 2015

✳ 4-12 Play-Based Infant/Toddler Assessment

Assessment in infant/toddler centers should reflect the philosophical approach used in the center. Programs using a high-quality approach will use a systematic, ongoing system. The Bank Street program assessment system is congruent with the Bank Street approach; HighScope has an assessment tool; and Innovations has a system for evaluating children. Reggio Emila places less emphasis on individual assessment but uses documentation to capture infant/toddler growth and development in a developmentally appropriate way. It is beyond the scope of this book to cover the many assessment tools designed for children under two. Rather, this section will look specifically at play-based assessment instruments.

Play assessment is routinely used in clinical settings. It is also used in early intervention settings. Few programs assess play. One instrument has been developed that assesses overall infant development with an emphasis on play is the Ounce Scale. Samuel Meisels, who served as president of the Erikson Institute, developed the Ounce Scale for use with infants, birth to forty-two months. The assessment is designed to reflect the developmental domains of social/ emotional, cognitive, and physical development. The Ounce program provides a venue for parents and early educators to look at the child together in an interactive manner. Assessment in infant centers is especially meaningful because this is the time when disabilities or developmental delays should be identified so intervention strategies can begin.

4-12a Ounce Scale Assessment System

The **Ounce Scale** is an observational assessment for evaluating infants' and toddlers' development over a period of three and a half years—from birth to age three and a half. Its purpose is twofold: (1) to provide guidelines and standards for observing and interpreting young children's growth and behavior, and (2) to provide information that parents and caregivers can use in everyday interactions with children. The Ounce Scale has three elements:

- **The Observation Record** provides a focus for observing and documenting children's everyday behaviors and provides data for making evaluations about development.

- **The Family Album** provides a structure for parents to learn about and record their child's development. Parents write down their child's behavior and reactions as they show children family photos, tell family stories, and ask observation questions that are the same as the ones in the caregiver's Observation Record.

- **The Developmental Profile** enables caregivers and other staff to evaluate each child's development and progress over time, and to compare their observation data to specific performance Standards.

A User's Guide, Standards for the Developmental Profiles, and Reproducible Masters are also available to assist you in implementing the Ounce Scale.

The Ounce Scale is organized around six major areas of development:

1. **Personal Connections**—*It's About Trust:* How children show that they trust familiar adults

2. **Feelings About Self**—*Learning About Me:* How children express who they are

3. **Relationships with Other Children**—*Child to Child:* What children do around other children

4. **Understanding and Communicating**—*Baby and Toddler Talk:* How children understand and communicate

5. **Exploration and Problem Solving**—*Seek and Solve:* How children explore and figure things out

6. **Movement and Coordination**—*Body Basics:* How children move their bodies and use their hands to do things

The Ounce Scale provides an interactive system of documentation, monitoring, and evaluation of development for Early Head Start programs, early intervention programs (including children at risk for special needs or those with disabilities), and other home- and center-based infant, toddler, and preschool child care in the community. The Ounce Scale provides a meaningful way to evaluate children's accomplishments, areas of difficulty, and approaches to learning. The Scale provides guidance to thinking about future goals so that family and caregivers can work together. Families and caregivers using the Ounce Scale learn to observe their children and to use this information to enhance relationships and support development.

4-12b Program Assessment

Child care program evaluation tends to be controversial (Dickinson, 2003). There is no required national system for evaluating systems, and mandatory systems vary from state to state. Infant/toddler centers are evaluated using both voluntary and mandated systems. States have specific mandated requirements for state licensing that vary in level of rigor. Some states also have systems for recognizing high-, medium-, and low-quality centers.

A voluntary system for accreditation is available through the National Association for the Education of Young Children. This system requires a commitment from the center faculty, staff, parents, and community. Centers that complete this process are listed on a national register that can be assessed online. Because it is a voluntary program, it is not mandated and is optional.

4-12c Infant/Toddler Environmental Rating Scale (ITERS)

Some child care programs use a program assessment system to determine the quality of their center. One that is well known in the field is the **Infant/Toddler Environmental Rating Scale (ITERS)** (Harms, Cryer, & Clifford, 2005). ITERS is designed to give a quick overview of quality in a center and is well known and respected in the field. Evaluators who use the ITERS must have training prior to use. Video recordings and workshops are available to those who choose to use this method. Areas included in the rating scale include the following (Harms, Cryer, & Clifford, 2005, p. 9):

1. Space and furnishings

2. Personal care routines

3. Listening and talking

4. Activities

5. Interaction

6. Program structure

7. Parents and staff

The ITERS evaluates the context for play; it does not evaluate play. Still, it is a useful instrument. Assessment is not an option for infants and toddlers; it is a necessary part of a play-based program.

Summary

4-1 List the benefits of a play-based curriculum for infants and toddlers.

Social, emotional, cognitive, physical, and language development are facilitated for infants and toddlers who are in high-quality play-based programs.

4-2 Identify the factors that create a context for play.

The use of a play-based curriculum in an aesthetic setting that uses developmentally appropriate practice; low adult-to-child ratios and group sizes; healthy, safe environments; staff who know how to care for infants and toddlers; policies to maintain committed staff; positive communication among all involved in the care of young children; and sensitive, responsive caregivers.

4-3 Describe the characteristics of adults who facilitate high-quality care in infant/toddler centers.

Traits of adults who provide high-quality care for infants and toddlers include interactive emotional signaling, understanding that all children are individuals who develop at their own rate, and understanding that the developmental domains (cognitive, social and emotional, and physical) are interrelated.

4-4 Differentiate the progression of music development from birth to age two.

Birth to six months—Infant-directed speech, melodious interactions

Six months to nine months old—Imitation and awareness of self and others. Lullabies and interactive rhymes are especially effective

Nine to twelve months—Interactions with objects that move or make a noise reaching, grasping, and exploration.

Twelve to eighteen months—Interactive games (Peek-A-Boo, Pat-A-Cake)

Eighteen to twenty-four months—nursery rhymes mimic and participate in music rituals.

4-5 Distinguish levels of movement development, birth to age two.

Low mobility (lap baby) occurs when the child is born. Because the infant is not mobile, adults must move the baby for feeding, sleeping, diapering, and playing.

More mobility (creepers and cruisers) allows the infant to move from one place to another.

High mobility (toddlers) gives the child lots of mobility as she experiments with moving quickly.

4-6 Categorize levels of art development, birth to age two.

Newborn to six months: Balanced stimulation

Infants, six to twelve months: Sensory experiences are wonderful for this age.

Toddlers, twelve months to two years: Multisensory stage, scribble stage when toddlers move from uncontrolled scribbles to controlled scribbles.

4-7 Explain characteristics of places and spaces for infant/toddler play.

Characteristics include safety and health, sanitation, stability and order, scale and comfort, simplicity and convenience, seclusion and choice, stimulation, softness, sensory appealing, soothing and sunny.

4-8 Design a play space for infants and toddlers. List the attributes of a play-based program for infants and toddlers.

Attributes include safe and healthy environment, sanitary, stable and orderly, appropriate scale and comfortable for everyone, simple and convenient, places for seclusion and privacy, stimulating activities, soft and sensory appealing places that are bright and sunny.

4-9 List the areas included in a play-based environment for infants and toddlers.

Areas for infants should include entrance and exit, dining areas, sleeping areas, floor-play areas, and gross motor areas.

Areas for toddlers should include entrance and exit, dining area, resting area, toileting area, gross motor area, and play centers such as block, home, dramatic play, sensory, quiet, water, and art.

4-10 Discuss three program models for infants and young children.

The developmental interaction model as seen at Bank Street, the cognitive development model as used by HighScope, and the constructivist approach used in Reggio Emilia schools are three popular models used in high-quality play-based programs.

4-11 Create activities that encourage play.

Materials that stimulate play include toys designed to elicit play from children at specific ages and stages.

4-12 List two assessment approaches that include play.

Two assessment programs for assessing play include Ounce and ITERS. Both approaches require specialized training. Ounce focuses on the individual child, and ITERS assesses the Program.

Key terms

Choke tube, 109
Controlled scribbles, 99
Infant-directed speech (IDS), 93

Infant/Toddler Environmental Rating Scale (ITERS), 114
Motherese or Parentese, 93

Ounce Scale, 113
Scribble stage, 99
Uncontrolled scribbles, 99

Technology and Internet Resources

Gesell Institute

http://www.gesellinstitute.org

The Gesell Institute reflects the views of Arnold Gesell, who established developmental norms for young children. He believes that children progress through increasingly complex stages.

Zero to Three

http://www.zerotothree.org

Website designed to provide information and support for families with children age three or younger. The available information is impressive and comprehensive; there are valuable links to other informational sources. Zero to Three is a nonprofit agency.

Activities

1. InClass Labs

A. Develop a table to reflect the progression of mobility from infancy through the age of two.

B. Draw a room that includes the areas recommended in the chapter. What kind of play is encouraged in each section of the room?

2. Research and Inquiry

A. Visit an infant/toddler center for two hours in the morning. Did you see play? Did you see support for play? If so, what type of play did you observe? How does this fit with the information provided in this chapter?

B. Watch a toddler play for an hour. Did you see functional play?

C. Perform an inventory of all items that facilitate play in the center.

D. What books are available on infant care in your college library? In your local library? What access do parents in different neighborhoods have to information?

3. Service Learning

A. Volunteer at an NAEYC accredited center for a day. Now, volunteer at a center that serves low-income infants and toddlers that is not NAEYC accredited. What differences did you see?

B. Visit a neonatal center in a local hospital. Volunteer to assist in rocking and holding babies. How is care provided? How does music, movement, or art impact the infant's care?

4. Family Connections

A. Create a website with links to information about infants and toddlers.

B. Plan a hands-on workshop on play and toys that you can make.

C. Create a website that includes a list of at least five things families can do to encourage toddler play.

5. Play Advocacy

A. What are the state regulations for infant care?

B. What are national issues affecting infant care?

C. What are the state and local issues affecting infant care?

D. Compare the requirements for becoming a professional beautician and infant/toddler child care provider.

E. Volunteer to hand out play brochures with other parent education materials at a local discount store or supermarket.

 Visit CourseMate for this textbook to access the eBook, Did You Get It? quizzes, Digital Downloads, TeachSource Video Cases, flashcards, and more. Go to CengageBrain.com to log in, register, or purchase access.

References

American Academy of Pediatrics Task Force on Infant Positioning and SIDS. (2013). Retrieved on July 5, 2013 from http://pediatrics.aappublications.org/content/122/Supplement_2/S113.

Berk, L. (2012). *Child Development.* Columbus: Pearson.

Brazelton, T., & Cramer, B. (1990). *The earliest relationship: Parents, infants, and the drama of early attachment.* New York: Addison-Wesley.

Bredekamp, S., & Copple, C. (2007). Developmentally appropriate practice in early childhood programs (3rd ed.). Washington, DC: National Association for the Education of Young Children.

Bronfenbrenner, U., & Morris, P. (2006). The bioecological model of human development. In R. Lerner & W. Damon (Eds.), *Handbook of child psychology* (6th ed.) (Vol. 1), *Theoretical models of human development* (pp. 793–828). Hoboken, NJ: John Wiley & Sons.

Bronson, M. B. (1995). *The Right Stuff for Children: Birth to 8.* Washington, DC: National Association for the Education of Young Children.

Comenius, J. A. (1631). *School of infancy.* Boston: Heath. (English translation:1896)

Commins, D. B. (1967). *Lullabies of the world.* New York: Random House.

Copple, C., & S. Bredekamp (Eds.). 2009. *Developmentally Appropriate Practice in Early Childhood Programs Serving Children from Birth Through Age* (3rd ed.). Washington, DC: National Association for the Education of Young Children.

Cuffaro, H. K., Nager, N., & Shaprio, E. (2000). The developmental-interaction approach at Bank Street College of Education. In J. P. Roopnarine and J. Johnson (Eds.), *Approaches to Early Childhood Education* (3rd ed.) (pp. 263–274). Upper Saddle River, NJ: Merrill/Prentice Hall.

Custodero, L. (2003). The musical lives of young children: Inviting, seeking, and initiating. *Zero to Three, 23*(1), 4–10.

Dickinson, D. (2003). Are measures of "global quality" sufficient? *Educational Researcher, 32*(4), 27–29.

Dombro, A., Colker, L., & Twister Dodge, D. (1999) *The creative curriculum for infants and toddlers* (rev. ed.) Washington, DC: Teaching Strategies.

Erikson, E. (2000). *Childhood and society.* (3rd ed.). New York: Norton. (Originally published in 1950.)

Fogel, A. (1998). *Infancy: Infant, family, and society* (2nd ed.). St. Paul, MN: West.

Froebel, F. (1887/1902). *The education of man.* (W. N. Hailmann, Trans.). New York: Appleton. (Originally published in 1826, copyright 1887.)

Gandini. L., & Edwards, C. (2001). *Bambini: The Italian approach to infant/toddler care.* New York: Teachers College Press.

Gerber, M. (1998). *Your self-confident baby.* New York: John Wiley.

Gonzalez-Mena, J. (2011). Infants/toddler care and education: Making connections—What do preschool teachers know about infant/toddler care and education?. *Exchange—Early Childhood Leaders, 33*(3), 12.

Greenspan, S., & Wieder, S. (2012). *Infant and early childhood mental health.* Washington, DC: Annual Psychiatric Publishing, Inc.

Gonzalex-Mena, J., & Eyer, D. W. (2001). *Infants, toddlers, and caregivers.* Mountain View, CA: Mayfield.

Harms, T., Cryer, D., & Clifford, R. (2005). *Infant/Toddler Environment Rating Scale (ITERs)* (rev. ed.). New York: Teachers College.

Honig, A. (2002). *Secure relationships: Nurturing infants/toddler attachment in early care settings.* Washington, DC: National Association for the Education of Young Children.

Houck, F., Signore, C., Fein, S., Ragu, T. (2008). Infant sleeping arrangements and practices during the first year of life. *Pediatrics, 122(2),* 113–120.

International Reading Association (IRA) and the National Association for the Education of Young Children (NAEYC) joint position paper. Learning to read and write: Developmentally appropriate practices for young children. Young Children, *53,* 430–446.

Isenberg, J., & Jalongo, M. (2009). *Creative thinking and arts based learning: Preschool thorough fourth grade* (5th ed.). Columbus, OH: Pearson.

Isbell, R., & Raines, S. (2013). *Creativity and the arts with young children* (3rd ed.). Clifton Park, NY: Delmar.

Jalongo, M., & Stamp, L. (1997). *The arts in children's lives: Aesthetic education in early childhood.* Boston: Allyn & Bacon.

Kaefer, T. (2012). What you see is what you get: Learning from the ambivalent environment. In A. Pinkham, T. Kaefer, & Susan B. Neuman's (Eds.), *Knowledge development in early childhood: Sources of learning and classroom implications* (pp. 3–17). New York: The Guilford Press.

Kojima, H. (1986). The history of child development in Japan. In H. Azuma & H. Stevenson (Eds.), *Child development and education in Japan* (pp. 39–54). New York: Academic Press.

Langlois, J. H., Roggman, L. A., & Rieser-Danner, L. A. (1990). Infants' differential social responses to attractive and unattractive faces. *Developmental Psychology, 26,* 153–159.

Lansky, B. (2003). *Mary had a little jam and other silly rhymes.* New York: Scholastic.

Lowman, L., & Ruhmann, L. (1998). Simply sensational spaces: A multi-"s" approach to toddler environments. *Young Children, 53* (3), 11–17.

Marshall, J. (2011). Infant neurosensory development: Considerations for infant child care. Early *Childhood Education Journal, 39*(3), 175–181.

McMullen, M. B. (1999). Achieving the best practices in infant and toddler care and education. *Young Children, 54,* 69–76.

Meisels, S. J., Wen, X., & Beachy-Quick, K. (2010). Authentic assessment for infants and toddlers: Exploring the reliability and validity of the Ounce Scale. *Applied Developmental Science, 14*(2), 55–71.

Meisels, S. (2003) *The Ounce Scale.* New York: Pearson Early Learning.

Miller, K., & Albrecht, K. (2001). *Innovations: The comprehensive infant & toddler curriculum.* Beltsville, MD: Gryphon House.

National Association of Child Care Resource & Referral Agencies (NACCRRA). (2013). Child Care Workforce. Retrieved on July 3, 2013 from http://www.naccrra.org/about-child-care/quality-matters

Piaget, J. (1965). *The moral judgement of the child.* New York: Free Press.

Papousek, M. (1996). Intuitive parenting: A hidden source of musical stimulation in infancy. In I. Delige & J. Sloboda (Eds.), *Musical beginnings: Origins and development of musical competence* (pp. 88–112). New York: Oxford University Press.

Readdick, C., & Park, J. (1998). Achieving great heights: The climbing child. *Young Children, 53*(6), 14–19.

Roopnarine, J. P., & Johnson, J. (2012). Approaches to early childhood education (6th ed.). Upper Saddle River, NJ: Pearson.

Sawyers, J., & Rogers, C. (2003). Helping babies play. Young Children, *58*(3), 52–54.

Schaefer, C., Gitlin, K., & Sandgrund, A.(Eds.) (1991). Play diagnosis and assessment. New York: Wiley.

Stonehouse, A. (1999). Play: A way of being for babies and toddlers. In E. Dau (Ed.) Child's play: Revisiting play in early childhood settings. Baltimore: Paul Brooks.

Schweinhart, L. J., & Weikart, D. P. (2006). The HighScope preschool curriculum comparison study through age 23. *Early Years Education: Major Themes in Education, 4*(2), 116.

Szanton, E. (2001). For America's infants and toddlers, are important values threatened by our zeal to "teach"? Young Children, *56*(1), 15–21.

Trevarthen, C., & Malloch, S. (2003). Musicality and music before three: Human vitality and invention shared with pride. *Zero to Three, 23*(1), 10–18.

Watson, J. (1976). Smiling, cooing, and "The Game." In J. S. Bruner, A. Jolly, and K. Silva (Eds.), Play: Its role in development and evolution (p. 275). New York : Basic Books.

Weikart, D., & Schweinhart, L. (2012). The HighScope curriculum for early childhood care and education. In J. O. Roopnarine & J. Johnson (Eds.), *Approaches to early childhood education* (6th ed.) (pp. 215–239). Upper Saddle River, NJ: Merrill/Prentice Hall.

Zero to Three. (2012). Cognitive development in the first three years of life. In C. Copple (Ed.), *Growing minds: Building cognitive foundations in early childhood* (pp. 1–12). Washington, DC: National Association for the Education of Young Children.

5 Supporting PLAY for Preschool Children

STANDARDS COVERED IN THIS CHAPTER
Council of Exceptional Children—Division of Early Childhood CEC DEC

ECSE 4S1 Plan, implement, and evaluate developmentally appropriate curricula, instruction, and adaptations based on knowledge of individual children, the family, and the community

ECSE 5S4 Structure social environments, using peer models and proximity, and responsive adults to promote interactions among peers, parents, and caregivers

ECSE 7K2 Developmental and academic content

ECSE 7S2 Plan and implement developmentally and individually appropriate curriculum

NAEYC Program Standards naeyc

4a Understanding positive relationships and supportive interactions

✳ LEARNING OBJECTIVES ✳

5-1 List the benefits of play for preschoolers.

5-2 Discuss how adult interactions impact preschoolers.

5-3 Identify the steps involved in organizing a high-quality play environment.

5-4 Explain how play is extended and expanded play through art, music, and movement.

5-5 Articulate how play supports the content areas of literacy, mathematics, science, and social studies.

5-6 Design a preschool classroom with at least five learning centers.

5-7 Compare and contrast play-based preschool models.

5-8 Describe how to assess play, organize findings, and share results.

© Cengage Learning 2015

4c Using a broad repertoire of developmentally appropriate teaching and learning approaches

4d Reflecting on their own practice to promote positive outcomes for each child

5c Using knowledge, appropriate early learning standards, and other resources to design, implement, and evaluate meaningful, challenging curricula for each child

✳ PLAYSCAPE: CASE STUDY

Rosalie just completed a great day at work. She closed a major sale for the company and picked up a $10,000 bonus. She finished some contracts on her desk, closed her email, and walked to the Corporate Child Care Center. She knew the teachers because they visited her home before she enrolled Juan in the program, and they chatted with her every day when she visited the center to drop off and pick up Juan. She liked the brightness and light that flooded the center, and she liked that she could bring Juan with her to her workplace, and that she and Juan could leave her workplace together every afternoon. As she rounded the corner, she heard laughter coming from Juan's classroom. She watched Juan from the doorway. He was putting some blocks on a large square. Jumping up, he started dancing inside the square and singing, "I'm king, I'm king, I'm king of the wild things!" As she looked at her child, she wondered where he got such notions—king of wild things! She was so impressed with his keen imagination. He was so intelligent. He might grow up to be President. She was so glad she had selected the company center over home child care. She could come by and visit between projects in the office, and she and Juan could travel together to and from work. More than anything, she enjoyed watching him play.

Explaining Play Behaviors

Juan's play was inspired by the availability of wooden blocks and the story that he had heard earlier in the day. Unaware of the story, his mother assumed that he made up his title. At this age, play takes on an added dimension as children begin to integrate physical, social, and symbolic aspects of play. These are called the **"play years"** because play informs children's view of the world and pretend play reaches its peak. During this time children play with words, toys, people, playmates, dogs, and cats, just to name a few. Anything and everything is a game as they explore and play with their world. Supporting play in preschool centers and providing support for teachers who facilitate play will be the focus of this chapter. It is important to note that three-year-olds still need special safety consideration.

✳ 5-1 Benefits of Play for Preschoolers

More American children are in preschools than at any other time in this country's history. According to the U.S. Department of Education, National Center for Education Statistics (2012), almost 60% of children under age five are cared for by someone other than their parents for an average of 30 hours a week. About

12% are in HeadStart and 44% are in other centers. As the traditional nursery school changes to become more focused on academic learning, play is at risk in the preschool classroom, yet play is how children learn.

The benefits of play for preschoolers build on the benefits of play discussed in earlier chapters. Scholars have found that play supports the preschoolers' brain development, self-regulation, and health.

1. **Brain development** (cognitive development)   Brain growth occurs most rapidly during the first three years, yet the brain continues to grow and develop rapidly during the preschool years. Specific parts or lobes of the brain are responsible for different skills, and these parts grow and develop at different rates in individual children. The prefrontal cortex, located in the frontal lobe area of the brain, is mainly responsible for a set of skills referred to as **executive function**. The executive function includes planning (conceptualizing what may occur in the future), working memory (ability to process and store incoming information), inhibitory control (capacity to monitor and control actions), goal setting (establishing objectives that will be met), and attentional flexibility (the ability to easily move from thinking about one topic or subject to another). Evidence indicates that inhibitory control is one of the first executive functions to appear during the preschool years (Zelazo & Lyons, 2011).

   A study by Qu (2011) found that children were less impulsive when engaged in co-play with other children. In the study, three- and four-year-old children engaged in play with and without a co-player. When children played with a **co-player** who shared the same goal, they were able to stay focused and meet their goals. The implication is that when children engage in co-play with others who have a similar goal, their executive function is more efficient.

2. **Self-regulation** (social, emotional, and cognitive development)   The ability to regulate one's own behavior or follow the directions of others is one of the goals of schools and society. Success in school requires that the children learn to regulate their behavior. Kelly and Hammond (2011) conducted a study to look at the relationship between symbolic play and executive function in young children. They found a correlation between symbolic play and some, but not all, executive functioning in young children. In their study, they defined symbolic play as "children's deliberate distortion of reality in play when they act as if something is the case when it is not (p. 21)." The role of executive function was examined in terms of the child's inhibition, and it was also examined generatively—that is, the child's ability to control her behavior and to generate new ideas. We are cautioned that correlation does not indicate causation, but a correlation was found between symbolic play and specific aspects of executive functioning. That is, the child's ability to self-regulate was related to symbolic play.

3. **Health** (physical development)   Obesity and childhood diabetes are at epidemic levels in the United States. The Centers for Disease Control and Prevention (CDC) (2013) reports that over 17% of children and adolescents between the ages of twelve and nineteen, or 12.5 million adolescents, are considered obese. For the first time in a decade, however, there is a decline in the number of low-income children who are obese. The CDC reports that for the period of 2003 through 2010, the number of children under four who are obese decreased from 15.21% to 14.94%. Play is a natural environment in which children can increase their physical capacity.

✳ 5-2 The Role of the Adult

Teachers play an important role in creating a high-quality play program (Photo 5-1). Interactions between the teacher and child can be organized into three distinct domains: emotional support, classroom organization, and instructional support (Downer, López, Grimm, Hamagami, Pianta, & Howes, 2012).

The first domain, emotional support that the teacher provides in the classroom, is important for the success of the young child in the classroom. This includes the relationship that the teacher has with children and their families, with colleagues, and with others involved in children's lives (Pianta & La Paro, 2003). These relationships are established throughout the day and especially through play. The teacher who pushes the child in the swing, engages in a tea party, or creates a situation that encourages children to develop a complex play script is facilitating learning and the development of new skills. Teachers who know how to foster high-quality relationships are powerful agents of change. As children move from exploration/instruction to play, the teacher stimulates or bores, facilitates or stifles, builds self-esteem or ridicules, and these interactions make a difference for life.

© Cengage Learning 2015

5-1 Creating the context for play is important. Interactions with adults, however, are even more important. The adult in this picture has created an environment (water and suds) for play and is engaging in high-quality interactions with the children. She will serve as a model for language development as she scaffolds play to a higher, more complex level.

The second domain, classroom organization, is equally important. If the teacher has the class set up to encourage autonomy, the interactions will be positive. For example, if the children can enter the room, find their own place for their materials, sign in, and move independently to a play center, interactions will most likely be positive. In contrast, if the teacher does not have a plan for the day and how routines will be handled, the teacher will spend time giving directions and explaining what will occur next. When teachers spend their time taking care of custodial issues, there is little time left for meaningful learning.

The third domain, instructional support, is key in facilitating the child's cognitive development. Specifically, the teacher can facilitate learning through positive interactions during instruction. The teacher can provide meaningful conversations during activities and experiences designed to stimulate learning. When teachers discourage children or convey that a child is not capable, children will mirror the teacher's attitude. A proactive or positive voice creates a welcoming community for learning, especially for children who are learning English (Colbert, Boyce, Obradović, Bush, Stamperdahl, Kim, & Adler, 2012; Colbert, 2012).

Other studies have found that the role of the teacher is especially important for children who are homeless, recent immigrants, or English language learners. In one study, Trawick-Smith and Dziurgot (2010) found that young children from Puerto Rico were viewed as nonplayers in the Eurocentric kindergarten classroom. They spend their day "alone, uninvolved, and looking confused and anxious" (p. 92). When their behaviors were considered in the context of the culture of Puerto Rican island culture, their play was very typical. The teacher who understands the child's culture can ease transitions into the class by adding or adapting aspects of the child's culture in the classroom. In taking these steps, the teacher can create a high-quality program. Additional suggestions for creating a high-quality program are presented in Table 5-1.

Did You Get It?

In a preschool classroom, the activity centers are arranged in advance and have the materials easily accessible to the children. This will encourage the children to:

a. have positive interactions with the teacher and their peers.

b. increase aggressive behavior among the children.

c. discourage the children from playing because there are too many choices.

d. reduce the children's aesthetic appreciation.

Take the full quiz on CourseMate

TABLE 5-1 Components of a High-Quality Program

1. Children and staff engage in meaningful interactions that provide opportunities to develop an understanding of self and others.

2. Children are encouraged to be actively involved in the learning process, to experience a variety of developmentally appropriate activities and materials, and to pursue their own interests in the context of life in the community and the world.

3. Parents are an integral part of the process. Communication with parents is based on the concept that parents are the principal influence on children's lives. Parents are well informed about and welcome as observers and contributors to the program.

4. Adults who staff the program are trained in child development and early education and who recognize and provide for children's needs. The quality and competence of the staff is the most important determinant of the quality of an early childhood program.

5. The organizational structure of the staff is designed to meet the needs of individual children and to maintain positive interactions and constructive activity among the children and staff.

6. Program administration is efficient and stable to minimize disruptions for children and their families. Effective administration includes good communication, positive community relationships, fiscal stability, and attention to the needs and working conditions of staff members.

7. The indoor and outdoor physical environments are designed to promote involvement in the daily activities and easy, constructive interactions among adults and children.

8. The health and safety of children and adults is protected and enhanced. Good programs act to prevent illness and accidents, are prepared to deal with emergencies should they occur, and educate children concerning safe and healthy practice.

9. Good nutrition and eating habits are important to the administration, staff, and parents. Mealtime is viewed as a time for enjoying food and conversation.

10. Ongoing and systematic evaluation is essential to improving and maintaining the quality of an early childhood program. Evaluation focuses on the program's effectiveness in meeting the needs of children and parents.

Adapted from B. Willer, in Reaching the full cost of quality in early childhood programs (1990), NAEYC.

Organizing for Play 5-3 ✳

The creation of the context for play requires organization. There are many ways to consider the teacher's multi-dimensional role. For the sake of clarity, these roles have been integrated in a step-by-step plan that begins with planning and then moves to evaluation and intervention in a dynamic, spiraling cycle that is continuously changing. These four main areas include planning, observing, guiding, and evaluating.

5-3a Planning for Play

This is the first and most important step and a role that many teachers relish. Planning and organizing involve orchestrating time, space, materials, and preparatory experiences. Organization is influenced by the teacher's constant reflections and ongoing reactions. If she notices an interest in dinosaurs, she may choose to make papier maché dinosaur eggs and place them in the outdoor sandbox to simulate a dig for fossils. Adding books on dinosaurs and materials for a fossil hunt will stimulate both play and learning. When time, space, materials, and preparatory experiences are optimal, play flourishes.

Time.   Time is a crucial element. Preschool children need time to become involved in play that involves more sophisticated play scripts. Some teachers think that children should move every fifteen minutes. When teachers do this, they interrupt play to the extent that the children never become involved in mature play and never develop the ability to concentrate and sustain social interactions. This teaches the child to hop from one topic to another. Children need at least thirty minutes to become engaged in play. Preschool programs by their very nature should be structured around play, and long periods of play are necessary for the development of concentration skills.

Physical Space.   Preschool children need adequate space in which to engage in a variety of activities. Research suggests that 30 to 50 square feet of useable space per child will facilitate play. Less than 25 feet per child leads to increased aggression (Smith & Connolly, 1980). Space should be set up so there are clear paths and boundaries. When children build with blocks, their play space needs to be located away from the pathway or exit. Low shelves can be used to separate different play spaces (Photo 5-2). The room needs to have a clear pathway to an exit for safety purposes. Children need clear boundaries, but they also need to be able to integrate materials when engaged in complex play. The room should have areas that are wet and dry; quiet and noisy; private and group; areas for solo play; and soft spaces. Teachers who have limited space may want to consider innovations such as a loft (with plexiglass-sided stairs or ramp), which will increase the space available.

© Cengage Learning 2015

5-2 The center's design can stimulate or detract from mature play. This center has low shelves that serve as dividers. The teacher can see what is going on in the center, but the children have a sense of privacy. They can build or play without concern that someone will run through their creations or constructions. Adults encourage play when they create the context for play.

Materials.   Selecting, rotating, and storing materials has a major impact on play. The teacher must decide what materials are developmentally appropriate for the group. Is this a good match for the age, level of development, and culture represented in the classroom? Three-year-olds will enjoy building with plastic and cardboard blocks, but four-year-olds also enjoy wooden blocks with accessories.

Materials need to reflect the culture of the classroom. Using food, such as rice, as a play material may be offensive to parents who see this as a grievous waste of food. Check to see if the children need more stimulating materials. What is going on during play? Are new materials needed to add interest or do materials need to be placed in storage? The use of prop boxes can facilitate storage and frequency of use. A **prop box** is a box that is used to store material for a specific play theme such as doctor's office, pet store, or flower shop. If materials are too difficult to retrieve, they may not be accessed as needed. Materials include purchased materials (puzzles, stacking toys, stringing toys, and nesting cups) and real materials (sand, mud, water, clay, and wood). Materials make such a difference that many preschool teachers joke about spending their mornings at the "local preschool store" (i.e., a yard sale). Table 5-2 lists some interesting play list materials.

Preparatory Experiences.   Children need experiences and activities that will extend their play. If not, children will play and replay their reality. Exposing

TABLE 5-2 Play Materials for Preschoolers and Kindergartners

- A full-length, unbreakable preschool mirror mounted on wall or in a sturdy stand
- Dolls of various ethnicities, including those of the children in the program, with clothes and caregiving accessories (e.g., bottles, blankets)
- A variety of dress-ups (with increasing levels of role-relevant details) and supporting props for various themes
- A variety of hand puppets
- Materials for constructing play scenes, including blocks and human and animal figures
- A variety of sturdy vehicles for use with blocks
- Sand and water play materials for exploration and experimentation (measures, strainers, tubes, funnels) and materials for fantasy play in sand and water
- Construction materials, including large and small wooden unit blocks, large hollow blocks, and a variety of other small materials for construction
- A variety of puzzles (fit-in, framed, jigsaw), with number of pieces appropriate to children's ages
- Beads for stringing (size depends on age); pegboards; pattern-making materials (pattern blocks and tiles, weaving materials) for older end of age range
- Dressing, lacing, and stringing materials to learn simple self-help skills and beginning sewing activities
- Specific skill-development materials that include activities related to matching, sorting, and ordering by shape, color, letter, number, and so on; equipment related to science and the natural world
- A variety of games, such as dominoes, lotto, simple card games, bingo, and first board games (with the outcomes based on chance, not strategy)
- A large variety of books appropriate to the ages, interests, and experiences of the group.
- A large variety of art and craft materials, including both graphic and plastic materials
- A standard rhythm instrument set (and instruments such as wood xylophones, if cost permits)
- Recorded music (and player) for singing, moving, and playing rhythm instruments
- Push and pull toys that support sociodramatic play (wagon, doll carriage, vacuum cleaner)
- A variety of balls for specific sports activities, such as kicking, throwing, catching, and rolling (beanbags can also be used for throwing and catching; target games can be used for the older end of the age range)
- Pedal tricycles (appropriate for children's size and age)
- Outdoor and gym equipment (e.g., climbing gym, swings, slides, ladders, seesaw by age five) proportioned to children's sizes and capabilities; also sand and gardening tools and all-weather construction equipment

Source: From *The Right Stuff for Children: Birth to 8* (pp. 26, 42, and 81), by M. B. Bronson, 1995, Washington, DC: National Association for the Education of Young Children. Copyright 1995 by the National Association for the Education of Young Children. Reprinted by permission.

children to rich literature every day and taking them on field trips gives children a base for imitating, representing, playing, and replaying newly acquired knowledge. This provides an excellent opportunity to integrate academics with play. Children need exposure to new ideas to optimize play (see Photo 5-3).

5-3b Observing

Observing provides the teacher an opportunity to look at the total picture. As a skilled observer, the teacher will see many levels of play skills. Some children will be engaging in a great deal of symbolic play. Others may be just walking

5-3 The impetus to play can be stimulated by people, experiences, materials, or stories. The book the teacher is reading to children may stimulate play in the block center or new dramatic play in the house area, which provides capes and props.

naeyc
CEC DEC

around. Another may be engaged in associative play or one may play alone. By observing the action that is occurring, the teacher will know where and when to act. The skilled teacher notices that the book center is empty or that the house materials need to be rotated. Teachers who are skillful know when to intervene and when to walk away. The teacher's knowledge of play is reflected in her observations. Time to watch play is an important and often overlooked responsibility.

5-3c Guiding Play

The teacher assumes a variety of roles during play. Research indicates that experienced teachers adjust their role to meet the needs of the children (Trawick-Smith & Dziurgot, 2011). Teachers may position themselves in or out of the play frame (Ashiabi, 2007). The term **play frame** has been used to describe an episode of play that has a definite beginning point and a definite ending point. Teachers in the play frame assume four major roles and interact in a variety of roles within these different roles.

Parallel Play. The adult can engage in a type of **parallel play**. This occurs when the teacher is near the child, but not engaged with the child. In this situation, the teacher can model play and serve as a source of security. Many teachers use this technique when a child is sitting alone, is new, or is timid. The teacher is involved in the play but not as an interactive player. This technique is equally useful for stimulating children to cross gender lines. For example, female teachers who engage in parallel play in the block area will notice more girls moving into the block area. In the same way, a male preschool teacher who cares for a baby doll in the house area might notice more boys caring for baby dolls. Teachers frequently use parallel play to foster social concepts and interactions.

Co-Play. The preschool teacher becomes a co-player when she engages in play with the child. She is careful to follow the child's lead and exit the play in a way that fits the play. Co-play is useful for extending play when it has become repetitious. The teacher must be careful to enter and exit naturally (Photo 5-4).

Understanding how to engage in co-play is important. When the adult enters the child's play, the adult and child are on a level playing field and the child can take the lead and direct the teacher. Knowing how to respond so that the child's play script is preserved without stopping or appropriating the play requires knowledge and skill. When co-play occurs appropriately and naturally, the teacher has a window into the child's mind and can learn a great deal about the child through this experience. Let's take a look at one play scene that occurred in a classroom.

Noticing that Maria and Tony were involved in another episode that has led to fights during the past week, the teacher moves over to the play area. She knocks on the pretend door and asks if she can visit a while. After she joins the children, the children ask if she wants to eat pizza with them. She agrees. Maria begins setting the table. The teacher asks if she can help prepare the pizza. Tony replies, "No, the man of the house cooks." Maria responds, "Not in my house." The teacher interjects, "Yes, I can help. I will help set the table while the pizza is cooking. Can we take turns cooking and setting the table? I will get the plates. Who will help me set the table?"

In the preceding example, the teacher's careful interjection as a co-player allowed the children to consider other roles as valuable. The teacher did not admonish the children, who reflected different cultural perspectives, but focused interest on other aspects of the play. Using the information she has gathered will allow her to plan activities and experiences that will broaden the children's knowledge of gender roles.

Play Tutor. A **play tutor** serves as a play leader, model, and scaffold for the child as the child develops his play skills (see Photo 5-5). This technique is used most in therapeutic settings or with a child who has developmental delays. Play tutoring is especially important with children who have had limited play experiences or who have developmental delays. Teachers who have participated in professional development are more supportive than those who have not participated in professional development (Driscoll, Wang, Mashburn, & Pianta, 2011). The adult's ability to scaffold play makes a huge difference for those children who are typically developing but have had limited social experiences.

Spokesperson For Reality. Inside the play frame, the **spokesperson for reality** can add to the depth of the play by extending and expanding it. Paradoxically, the spokesperson for reality can also stop the play. The outcome depends on how the teacher interjects her statements. For example, Robert and Whitney were playing together in the art area. They were pretending that everything they touched was magic. "I'm touching the glue and it's magic." "The glue touches you and it's magic." Whitney jumps

▶‖ **TeachSource** Video Case 5-1

© Cengage Learning 2015

2–5 Years: Gender in Early Childhood

In the scenario in the video, the children's conversation reflects their view of gender roles. This clip explores children's understanding of gender through conversations with young children.

1. After watching this clip, reread the section on co-play. Has your view of the scenario given (of Maria, Tony, and the teacher) changed? If so, in what ways?

2. As the classroom teacher, how could you discourage stereotypical gender play and encourage a variety of perspectives?

Watch on CourseMate

© Cengage Learning 2015

5-4 The adult in this picture is involved in the child's play. If she sits and plays, waiting for the child to mimic or join her, she is engaged in parallel play. If she plays along with the child, engaging in interactive movements and conversation, she is engaged in co-play. Only the adult knows what will extend or stop play.

5-5 These children are engaged in a game with an adult, who may assume roles ranging from co-player to play tutor or even spokesperson for reality.

up and holds the bottle over Robert's head, saying, "It's magic, it's magic." If the teacher interjects abruptly and reminds Whitney that glue should be used on paper, not on people, she stops the play. If she does not intervene, Robert will have glue on his head. If time permits, the teacher may be able to co-play and say, "Let me add the magic to my paper." This allows the play to continue. If time does not permit, the teacher must intervene as the spokesperson for reality. Even though the play has stopped, Robert does not have glue in his hair. These decisions are the most difficult to make. Sensitive teachers will consider social, cultural, and historical factors when making the decision.

Outside the Play Frame. Teachers guide play from inside the play frame by careful interactions. The play frame begins when children shift from reality to pretend play, and it ends when children shift back to reality. Children use signals to communicate the beginning and ending of play. Guidance can also be offered outside the play frame. If a child is hitting another child, the teacher must intervene. In Maslow's (1959) hierarchy, health and safety are the first basic considerations. The teacher who does not intervene sends a message that this behavior is acceptable. Safety and health issues always take precedence. Allowing children to hurt other children sends a message that it is acceptable to hurt other children. This message should not be heard by either the child inflicting or the child receiving the pain. Strategies for guiding play from outside the play frame have been suggested by Van Hoorn, Nourot, Scales, and Alward (2011). These roles include artist apprenticeship, peacemaker, guardian of the gate, spectator, matchmaker, storyteller, and scribe. Suggestions for assuming these roles are as follows:

- The artist apprenticeship facilitates play by moving materials and props. Moving a phone from the house area to the block area may allow the constructor to phone his make-believe space ship.
- The guardian of the gate protects the play by facilitating careful entry into the play.
- The peacemaker helps resolve conflicts by offering alternatives.
- As spectator, the teacher serves as an audience and offers feedback when needed.
- The teacher serves as matchmaker when she suggests that specific children play with other children.
- The storyteller provides a platform for play reenactment. Vivian Paley devoted much energy to defining the role of the storyteller in her book *Walley's Stories* (1981). This aesthetics-based approach allows children to reenact their play as a story, thus developing their literacy skills.
- As the scribe, the teacher captures what occurred during play through writing or drawings. This allows the teacher to turn the children's actions into words or pictures, which enhances communication and literacy skills.

These roles extend, expand, and support play in a way that leads to meaningful learning.

5-3d Evaluating play

Evaluating play provides teachers with opportunities to document both play and learning using authentic, ongoing assessment. Information gained through assessment can be used to guide changes and interactions. Additional observations can provide information concerning the consequences of the changes. Evaluating play involves looking at the centers and the play that is occurring at each center. First, a list of all centers in the room should be made. A tally of children in each center will reveal which centers are most popular. The number of children visiting a center should be monitored and less popular centers altered. This should occur regularly throughout the year. Doing so provides an overall profile of usage, but does not provide information about the quality of play going on in the center. Examining the quality of play that is occurring requires a different lens and is discussed at the end of this chapter.

Extending Play-Based Learning with Art, Music, and Movement 5-4 ✳

Preschool children explore and experience their world through music, movement, art, and storytelling. An aesthetics-based program provides a way to embrace both play and academics. When children create art and engage in musical activities, movement, or storytelling, they discover and strengthen their ideas, experiences, and feelings through symbols and symbolism (Isbell & Raines, 2013). Play also involves symbols and abstraction. Combining play with art, music, movement, and storytelling enhances the quality of life for preschool children as they develop their ability to engage in abstract thought.

5-4a Art

Art should be a major part of the preschooler's daily experience in school. From painting at the easels to creating with clay, children should have opportunities for art every day. When children use large pieces of paper for drawing their play, they are engaging in writing. When children paint a picture of their pretend castle—that only they recognize—they give life to their play and use their ability to abstract. Pretend play and art provide opportunities for facilitating academic skills.

Children go through several stages as they develop their artistic abilities. The first stage is called the controlled scribble stage (0–2). Most three- and four-year-olds are in the **basic forms stage** of artistic development (Isbell & Raines, 2013). They have better fine motor control and hand—eye coordination than they had when they were toddlers. They have moved beyond controlled scribbles and can repeat marks. It is not unusual to see a child at this age fill a complete page with similar marks. When drawing a story about his play, one child filled a sheet and said that he played in the ocean that day. Actually the child played at the water table, but perhaps that was his ocean.

Children's first exposure to materials will be reflected in their artistic ability. Some children at this age will still be in the controlled scribble stage (0–2) and others will begin to move into a more advanced stage. The **preschematic stage** occurs from four to seven years of age and involves the use of symbols to represent ideas, thoughts, experiences, or feelings (Isbell & Raines, 2013). This stage begins in the preschool classroom and is refined in the primary classroom.

5-4b Music

Music enriches play. Incorporating music in preschool programs can be traced to the work of pioneers in early education discussed in Chapters 1 and 4. In the 1700s, Rousseau (1762) recommended that mothers teach their children how to sing so the children could recognize meter and harmony. Froebel (1895) used songs in his kindergarten that are still being sung today. Throughout the twentieth century, music has been part of the preschool curriculum. Today, research supports the use of music in programs for young children (Bond, 2012).

The preschooler's interest in music reflects both her cultural and social background. A child's background in music is soon evident in the preschool classroom. Some children enjoy classical music and recognize Bach when they hear his music. Others may enjoy and respond to jazz, pop, country, rap, or spiritual music. Encouraging parents to bring their own music to school creates a climate of trust and respect. It also exposes all children to a variety of music and facilitates cultural interaction. One exception is the use of music with violent or offensive language. Rap music with violent themes should never be used in a center.

Three- and four-year-olds want to clap, sing, and move. They can improvise simple melodies and sustain a one- or two-tone accompaniment to a well-known song. Music contributes to the total development of the child through the development of psychomotor, perceptual, affective, cognitive, social, cultural, and aesthetic skills (Isenberg, & Jalongo, 2009).

Early Educators and Music. Music is limited in classrooms only by the adult. Early educators who are comfortable using music throughout the day to set the tone have a powerful tool. Singing in the classroom can be developed. Linda Neelly (2002, p. 81) believes that a positive attitude can be established by recognizing the following:

1. The art of singing is learned through singing.

2. Teachers should think of themselves as singers.

3. Children love to express their feelings and understandings about the world through singing.

4. Teachers should think of all children as singers. No non-singers!

5. Singing with children throughout daily routines nurtures important learning connections.

6. Enthusiastic teacher participation in singing encourages the development of children's innate musical ability.

7. Singing is developmentally appropriate practice.

Thomas Moore, a trained early childhood educator and musician, encourages teachers to embrace music and use music to foster social relationships (2002).

Songs for Preschoolers. By age three, children can name favorite tunes, recognize favorite songs, and sing. Many cultures have songs that have been passed on to the next generation identified with that culture. "Go Tell Aunt Rhody" and "This Train" are examples of songs that have been handed down in rural America. Learning songs from other cultures can facilitate multiculturalism. Learning simple songs is an exercise in both music and memory. There is a plethora of songs designed to teach concepts. Few can deny, however, the continuing influence of Ella Jenkins, who uses her music to teach about both the world and music. (Ella Jenkins has been singing songs with and for children for over fifty years. She received a Parents' Choice award and Grammy nominations before receiving a Grammy Lifetime Achievement Award in 2004.

5-4c Movement

Most preschool children can walk, hop, run, jump, gallop, skip, and climb. Movement occurs naturally when children play. Teachers can also facilitate movement through play. A position paper, "Physical Education Is Critical to Educating the Whole Child," was issued by the National Association for Sport and Physical Education (NASPE) (2011) with the intent of promoting physical education for all children. The goal of movement programs for children at this age is to produce citizens who

- Have mastered necessary physical skills
- Participate regularly in physical activity
- Understand the cost benefits of physical activities
- Recognize the long-term benefits of healthy choices (Wellhousen, 2002)

Preschool children are in the **fundamental movement phase** (Gabbard, 1992). In this stage, preschool children are developing skills that will provide a foundation for movement later. Children at this stage should be involved in both planned and unplanned activities that occur both indoors and outdoors. Teachers should provide opportunities for children to engage in a variety of activities and develop a variety of skills, including skipping, hopping, climbing safely, jumping, running, and various balancing activities. A variety of levels will be apparent at this age. Some children will have difficulty standing on one foot whereas others are very agile.

Given the number of children in care outside the home, it is imperative that children have opportunities to develop good habits for physical health. Outdoor play adds to the child's physical fitness and love of nature. Helping children enjoy movement at this age may establish patterns that last a lifetime.

What do you think?

Transitions are difficult for preschool children. Some teachers use movement or songs to transition children from one point to another. How can you use movement activities as a transition activity? How can you ensure that movement and recess are available for children every day?

Did You Get It?

After reading Eric Carle's *The Very Hungry Caterpillar*, a child paints a picture of a butterfly. This activity is

a. appropriate because preschoolers use art to communicate.

b. inappropriate because preschoolers can't paint.

c. inappropriate because preschoolers would not read that story.

d. appropriate because butterflies are pretty.

Take the full quiz on CourseMate

Play as a Medium for Learning Content 5-5 ✳

The foundation for the content areas begins at birth and develops with each passing year. Play serves as a medium for learning during this time. Children who play with blocks learn how to build and tear down their own creations. Children who ride tricycles learn to guide and control equipment. Children who play with baby dolls learn to nurture and care for the next generation. These are all valuable skills, and they all form the basis for content areas. Building up and tearing down provides practice in completing a project and turning ideas into products; operating equipment prepares the child for tool usage in other areas and develops motor skills; and understanding that all humans need care is basic for life. These skills facilitate the development of social and interpersonal skills that are foundational components for learning specific content. Core content subjects are extended and expanded through play and include language and literacy, math, science. and social studies. Details are provided in the section that follows.

TABLE 5-3 Literacy-Enhancing Activities	
Students	**Teachers**
• Enjoy listening to and talking about books.	• Enjoy reading and rereading small and large books to children.
• Understand that written words have meaning.	• Establish a language and literacy-rich environment.
• Begin writing activities.	• Encourage children to experiment with writing.
• Participate in word and rhyming games.	• Talk about letters by name and sounds.
• Begin to recognize words on labels and signs.	• Engage children in language games.
• Identify some letters and begin to make some letter-sound matches.	• Promote literacy-related play activities.

5-5a Language and Literacy

Language begins before birth; the fetus can hear its parents talking. After the child is born, she is immersed in language, and communication develops. Play provides a medium for language that may not occur in other parts of the classroom or curriculum. Developing and expanding language enhances literacy learning. When children use language during play, there is a tendency to continue the process throughout the day. The more children talk to others, the more comfortable they become with the medium of language and literacy. This is especially important for children who are reluctant to engage with others, but it is important for all children. Seeing themselves as competent and confident enhances their opportunities for literacy learning (Evans, 2012).

In the same way, literacy immersion facilitates the child's knowledge of reading. The International Reading Association (IRA) and the National Association for the Education of Young Children (NAEYC) issued a joint paper outlining guidelines for parents and teachers to encourage literacy at different levels (IRA/NAEYC, 1998). Preschoolers are in Phase I, an awareness and exploration stage. To encourage literacy in the classroom for students who are in Phase I, students and teachers should engage in literacy-enhancing activities such as those listed in Table 5-3.

Language, literacy, and play are not discrete topics in the preschool classroom. Rather, they should be integrated throughout the day. Preschool classrooms that encourage language and literacy learning through play encourage the following:

- Relationships between children and adults. For example, teachers are models for reading and writing during play, they value home language and culture, and they encourage language and literacy before, during, and after play.

- An emotional climate that encourages talking and discussion before, during, and after play.

- A print-rich play environment. For example, play centers are labeled with English and other languages used by the children; words, equipment, and materials are labeled; and signs and schedules for play centers are easily visible.

- Paper, books, and other literacy tools to extend play are available. For example, if children are playing grocery or pizza store, then ordering forms, pencils, and play money extend both literacy and mathematical learning.

- Reading a variety of high-quality books that extend the children's play interests. For example, if children have been playing with construction items in the block area, reading books that add to their knowledge of construction, building, and/or architecture adds to their depth of knowledge and can take their play to a more complex level.

- The use of resources to extend play. For example, if children are playing about creating a garden, the class can go on a field trip to a local horticulture site or store.

Play and language/literacy are natural partners when teachers observe play so that they can plan and extend learning.

5-5b Math

Play provides an optimal environment for supporting math acquisition. According to Kamii and Housman (2000), young children in the preoperational stage of intellectual development construct their understanding of the world through physical knowledge, logical-mathematical knowledge, and social-arbitrary knowledge. **Physical knowledge** is knowledge of the observable traits of an object. **Logical-mathematical knowledge** occurs when children construct a relationship between two objects. **Social-arbitrary knowledge** is knowledge that is socially constructed by society. Examples include reading from left to right, counting seven days as a week, and using the alphabet to construct words that have meaning. Reading skills can be described as social-arbitrary knowledge. Physical and cognitive skills can be learned through physical knowledge. Math skills can only be developed through logical-mathematical thinking. Young children must construct relationships within their mental structures. These skills can be developed through play.

The National Council for Teachers of Mathematics recommends a hands-on approach to math and play for preschool children (Copley, 2010). A study by Hanline, Milton, and Phelps (2010) found a relationship between block play skills and reading and math skills. Based on their findings, they recommended an approach that included both intentional use of manipulatives and opportunities for play throughout the day. Play in other areas such as sand and water provides opportunities for mathematical learning in the natural environment of play (Wallace, White, Stone, & Kastberg, 2010).

Preschool children should be engaged in play that incorporates math naturally. When children set the table in the house area, they are learning patterns and counting. When they build with wooden blocks or use interlocking cubes, they are learning geometry. When children paint, they are developing an understanding of lines, shapes, and space. When children discuss the plan for the day, they are learning about time. All math concepts that children should know can and should be taught throughout the day during play and other natural activities. It is not appropriate for children to use workbooks or worksheets in a preschool classroom.

5-5c Science

Knowledge of science is also developed through logical-mathematical thinking. Preschool children should be exposed to science in a way that is both natural and playful. Einstein noted that he never lost his ability to view the world through the eyes of a child, and Erikson referred to Einstein as "the victorious child" (Rogers & Sluss, 1999). He meant that children are naturally curious and open to new ideas. This disposition for science can and should be nurtured. Play provides a natural medium for science. When children explore the grass or other coverings outdoors, they are using their observation skills. When children ask "Why?" they are developing their understanding of how the world works. This is the first step toward developing a scientific view of the world. Teachers foster this perspective when they create a curriculum that stimulates what some call "sciencing" with young children. The basic process skills of science are nurtured through play.

It is critical that children be exposed to their immediate environment rather than the environment on the latest child's video. It might be better to assist in their knowledge of one tree rather than an entire rain forest that they may never see. Children benefit by touching and feeling items before incorporating them into their mental structures. Look around the immediate environment. What can children touch? What can they feel? Children can touch leaves, nuts, shells, cacti, rocks, sand, snow, or water. Preschool children can plant seeds in the ground, watch them grow, and even harvest vegetables from the plant. Planting seeds to take home too often results in seeds that never mature. A natural, realistic approach to science is the best approach. An inquiry-based approach that utilizes the child's natural environment is optimal for developing science skills (Photo 5-6).

© Cengage Learning 2015

5-6 Play is a natural part of scientific inquiry.

5-5d Social Studies

Social studies for preschool children is generally integrated with literacy. Lucy Sprague Mitchell's (1921). "Here and Now" approach developed in the 1920s still provides guidelines for a social studies curriculum. The **"Here and Now" curriculum** focuses on what is close to the child and reflects what ecologists refer to as microcosm. Preschool children need to understand and make sense of their immediate world before they are ready to venture into the abstract. A computer in a room for a three-year-old may change what appears to be near to the child. Still, the child needs to locate her neighborhood on a representative floor map before she is ready to recite the names of state capitals. It is well known that recall is the lowest level of knowledge acquisition, but it still seems to impress adults when children can recall obscure facts about abstract situations. Often adults discover that children have memorized the days of the week but cannot understand the concept that a visitor will appear in two days. When children learn in an authentic manner that fits their learning level, their knowledge base is much more developed.

When children engage in dramatic play, they are using their knowledge of social structure to create the script for play. This prepares them to be members of society. By taking turns during play, they learn that fairness is important; this is a major concept in a democracy. Children who spend play money in a play center learn the basics of an economy.

Social studies for preschoolers can be presented through units and projects. Units are teacher-directed studies of a theme or topic such as the farm or zoo.

The teacher selects the topic, plans and designs the unit, delivers the instruction, and generally ends with a field trip to a specific place related to the unit of study. Themes and units have been used for many years in early childhood programs. This approach is developmentally appropriate when it reflects the interest and level of the children. Units are appropriate when they are created with a specific purpose in mind and the early educator is amenable to change based on the children's interest. Many resources for units can be found on the Internet to guide unit development and implementation. For example, *Let's Find Out on Sesame Street* (2013) includes topics such as "Parks," which features a video of a park ranger. *PBS Kids* (2013) has a section for educators that features units such as Dinosaur Trains; and *National Geographic Little Kids* (2013) includes excellent pictures and video of insects (e.g., The Lady Bug) that can be used to stimulate discussion and further study.

The project approach, first popularized in the 1970s by Lillian Katz and Sylvia Chard (1989), is a well-respected approach that reflects and aligns with the children's interests. Projects are different in that they use an inquiry-based approach that contains three stages that are co-constructed with the children. The project approach also differs from a unit in that a field trip may be used at the beginning of the project to stimulate interest. When young children engage in project study, they construct knowledge through an in-depth study of a particular subject, such as the experience described in *Exploring Water With Young Children* (Chalufour & Worth, 2005). The schools of Reggio Emilia use projects as a major foundation for their curriculum (Gandini, 2008). The project approach is an optimal way for preschoolers to learn and is further explored in Chapters 5 and 6 for other age groups.

Did You Get It?

Two preschoolers take all the stuffed animals from the doll center and line them up in size order. This is a demonstration of _____ knowledge?
a. symbolic
b. sociocultural
c. logical-mathematical
d. primary

Take the full quiz on CourseMate

Designing Play Centers for Preschoolers 5-6 ✳

Centers in the preschool classroom define the play areas in a safe and orderly fashion. Every day, children should have an established, safe, and fair way to choose centers. A choice board provides a good way to select centers. Children should be able to choose another center if they are not satisfied with their initial choice. Allocating an hour for center play ensures quality outcomes from play. Ringing a bell to send children to another center disrupts play. This technique prevents the development of concentration skills. Centers can include art, music and movement, books, blocks, house, quiet, and dress-up. A sociodramatic interest center that might be a doctor's office, a grocery store, or an pizza shop should be rotated routinely. That is, although a doctor's office complete with masks and operating tables may be interesting for a week or so, it will not interest the children if left up for two months. Rotating or changing the sociodramatic center creates a novel situation that stimulates the child's interest in the area. With three- and four-year-olds, it is important to not overwhelm the child with too many choices or too much material. It is better to rotate centers and materials in and out of the classroom by placing additional materials in a nearby storage area when not in use.

5-6a Art/Messy/Writing Center

The art center can be used for multiple purposes. The art center should be near a source of water. If it is not located on a tile floor, place plastic shower curtains or

5-7 Children who have daily opportunities to paint can express their view of the world through art.

© Cengage Learning 2015

something similar under the area to facilitate clean-up. Easel painting should be available for children who choose to paint (Photo 5-7). This can be accomplished if easels remain up and materials are accessible. Painting smocks should be within reach. Hanging them on hooks close to the easels allows children to put them on by themselves. A drying rack provides a convenient place for children to dry their products. An area should be available for displaying the finished products. Tables or flat surface areas are also needed in the art area and can be used for finger painting and other activities that require drying time. Examples of great art can also be displayed in the art center. These can be collected from discarded calendars. Most preschool children enjoy the work of Monet, Picasso, and Van Gogh.

Storage shelves should be close so children can select paper, crayons, markers, and paper independently. Stamps, patterns, and templates extend choices. Many centers use the art center as a writing center so children can create books and journals in this center also. Some centers include reusable materials. Adding a bin where parents can leave recyclable materials adds to the class resources and helps parents feel involved. A parent who brings newspapers on Monday can quietly leave the papers on the shelf as she departs for her job. She has contributed to the class, and the class benefits from her donation. Preschoolers have the luxury of using the old newspapers for finding letters, cutting out pictures from advertisements, or making hats. The key to the art center is organization of materials on the child's level. Be sure to use only safety scissors, which can be stored in a plastic container or a rack for scissors.

5-6b Music and Movement

The music and movement center is especially important for children developing gross and fine motor skills. This area can be located away from the block or book areas. Most preschool children can climb stairs, walk up ramps, or dance to music. Lofts with plexiglass partitions and ladders encourage movement. Adding music items such as tamborines or bells in an area with mirrors encourages music and movement. Cushions are still important for climbing and tumbling. Encouraging safe movement continues to be very important at this age.

5-6c Book Center

Books should be included in all centers, and book baskets can be placed throughout the center. A book center provides a quiet place where children can listen to a tape recording of a book, sit in a lab to listen to a favorite story, or enjoy looking at a book. Book shelves should be used to display the book with the front cover facing the child. This allows children to remove and return books to the shelf independently. Book centers should be aesthetically appealing. Wall hangings that reflect local and distant cultures are appropriate. Charts with the alphabet can be placed in the center on the child's eye level. Adding puppets, flannel boards, and book props can enhance the interest in the center and stimulate story reenactment.

5-8 The preschoolers in this picture are engaged in constructive play with blocks. Once they begin using symbolism and describing their structure, they will move into dramatic play. The fluidity of the movement between different kinds and types reflects the improvisational nature of play.

5-6d Blocks

Blocks have been a staple of preschool environments for over a century. A variety of blocks should be available. Three-year-olds will enjoy sponge and cardboard blocks; four-year-olds who are almost five will find the wooden blocks more interesting. Adding realistic props such as a bus, barn, or house is essential for increasing the level of play of the younger children. Children who have just turned three still benefit from toys that are more realistic. Safety mirrors and plexiglass tables add to the interest of this area.

The block area should be placed away from through traffic (Photo 5-8). It should be in a place that will allow children to extend play from day to day. Placing the block area in a carpeted area is optimal. If tile is the only option, add a rug to the area or place one on the edge so it can be pulled out during play time. Fill the surrounding walls or furniture with pictures of block structures that others have built in the past.

5-6e Home Center

Preschool children need an area that reminds them of home. This area can include pictures of family members. Children can play in the home center and act out any situation that is causing them concern. The house area should be safe, neat, and inviting.

Montessori (1914) used miniature furniture in a classroom as a way to prepare children to care for their own home. The goal of a home center in a preschool classroom is to encourage sociodramatic play. Realistic props encourage pretense. Children who are experiencing separation anxiety can be comforted by participating in play that includes going home.

5-6f Toy Area

An area for play with puzzles, manipulatives, or toys should be included in all preschool classrooms. Children need a place where they can engage in quiet play with a friend, an adult, or by themselves (Photo 5-9). This area should have bean bags and

5-9 Toys and materials can be used for group or for solitary play. Private places for quiet play and/or reflection are especially needed for children who spend more than four hours each day in a preschool center. Good environments encourage play in a variety of settings.

TeachSource Video Case 5-2

2–5 years: Gross Motor Development for Early Childhood

Gross motor skills are discussed and demonstrated. As the children hop, skip, and toss a ball, they are demonstrating a variety of gross motor skills.

1. Explain why children use their bodies to catch a ball.

2. What are the developmental considerations in planning gross motor activities for young children?

Watch on CourseMate

Did You Get It?

An activity center at a preschool contains two bean bag chairs and a cabinet with shelving. Which center is this likely to be?

a. toy area

b. sociodramatic learning center

c. home center

d. music and movement center

Take the full quiz on CourseMate

comfortable seating arrangements. Some centers use a cabinet without shelves and add padding and curtains to make a safe place for children to be alone. Rotating materials such as puzzles and manipulatives increases interest.

Preschoolers can use puppets. Children younger than three can play with puppets as if they are stuffed animals, but they may not understand the concept of puppet. Preschoolers understand that this is pretend. Puppet play allows children to act out their feelings as they develop a concept of story. Children enjoy finger puppets as much as they do regular puppets. Puppet possibilities are unlimited.

Locomotor skills are developing, and children enjoy running, climbing, and skipping. Their fine motor skills are developing steadily. Blocks, puzzles, and objects that can be manipulated appeal to them. Socially, preschoolers do not like games with complex rules and do not understand when they lose. Therefore, games involving active physical movements should focus on cooperative goals.

5-6g Sociodramatic Learning Center

One area in the room should be designated as the dramatic play area, which is separate from the house area. The sociodramatic center can include themes that range from a dentist office to a flower shop or veterinarian's office. As discussed earlier, prop boxes can be used to store props such as equipment, books, labels, and costumes. Labeling the storage boxes adds to the ease of usage. Prop boxes can be stored in an area away from the classroom so that they can be brought in and out of the classroom. This provides a novel experience that is changed on a routine basis.

5-6h Technology Area

Handheld or stationary computer devices provide an additional source for children to discover the world. It is important to limit the time that children spend using electronic devices, but they should have access to these resources occasionally.

✳ 5-7 Integrative Play Models

Historically, programs for young children started as play programs. Ideas for encouraging play have been presented in this chapter as possible interest or learning centers. Early educators can choose how these are used and what philosophy guides their choices. Several program models are available that offer a framework for programs. These models generally use a philosophical base that promotes one perspective. Some centers will choose one system as a framework for their curriculum, and their choice influences the type of play that occurs. An example of a maturationist approach is the Montessori model (1914), which requires specialized training in a Montessori program. Other programs informed by the Piagetian or Vygotskian philosophy (see Photo 5-10) include the developmental-interaction model, the cognitive-based model, the constructivist model, and the Reggio Emilia approach (Edwards, Gandini, & Forman, 1998). Creative Curriculum (Dodge, Colker, & Heoman, 2002) is presented as a program for professional development that is used throughout the United States. Because some private schools use a curriculum known as the Waldorf model, a perspective of the school is provided by a former teacher and student in the "From the Experts" box located at the end of this section.

5-10 This classroom reflects a traditional approach to preschool. This could be informed by a Piagetian or Vygotskian philosophy.

The advantage of using a program model to inform all classrooms in a center is that children are exposed to a consistent approach. It is more difficult if a child is in a preschool that uses a developmental-interaction approach in one class and a Montessori-based approach in another classroom. High-quality programs use a consistent theoretical approach to guide programs in the child care center. An overview of some common models is provided in the following subsections.

5-7a Developmental-Interaction

The developmental-interaction model is based on enhancing the development of the child through interactions with the world. As was discussed in Chapter 4, the Bank Street School of Education began in the 1900s (Cuffaro, Nager, & Shapiro, 2000).

Bank Street was initially started by Lucy Sprague Mitchell in 1916 as the Bureau of Educational Experiments. Over the years, the school has been influenced by John Dewey's (1919) view of progressive education and later by Erikson's (1950) view of emotional development. The goal was to educate the whole child and included the physical, social, cognitive, emotional, and aesthetic domains. Specific emphasis was placed on progressivism and emotional health.

The Learning Environment. The developmental-interaction curriculum is based on progressivism and experiential learning. The curriculum basically consists of daily living activities. These involve routines and active use of materials throughout the day. Activities include the following:

- Sensory experiences: Sand, water, play-dough, shaving cream, and cooking projects.
- Gross motor activities: Classrooms are set up so children can move in, on, under, over, through, behind, and around objects in the room and so they can be up high, underneath, or hidden. Climbing rooms are used for spatial explorations.

- Blocks: Blocks are a core material in a Bank Street classroom. Like art work, block building with young children emphasizes the process, not the product.

The Curriculum. The curriculum is open and features minimum day-to-day or week-to-week planning. Emphasis is placed on the knowledge and preparation of the teacher, who must understand the overall principles and implement them in the classroom. Children in this program are actively engaged in activities in a democratic classroom. Social studies are the core of the curriculum. In contrast with Lucy Sprague Mitchell's *Here and Now* curriculum, Cuffaro, Nager, and Shapiro (2000) define social studies as "the relationships between and among people and their environments, the world in which we live and our place in it. It concerns the near and far, the past and present" (p. 267). Knowing how to expose the children to both the near and far away requires knowing and understanding the children and the goals of the program. The role of the teacher is to question, plan, provide resources, and assess the relationships.

Bank Street uses the field trip as a way to introduce the child to the world. After the child experiences the field trip, a unit is used as a guide for planning activities and implementing instruction. Another area of emphasis in the Bank Street program is literacy. Children, teachers, and parents are encouraged to read, write, and publish their work. For more information, visit the Bank Street website, which offers an overview of the Bank Street program.

5-7b HighScope

HighScope is a program that originally started as the Perry Preschool project and is the only program that can support its approach with longitudinal research. Based on the work of Jean Piaget, it is designed to provide action-based activities for children that foster the development of key learning experiences (see Photo 5-11). The program has a consistent routine to maximize opportunities for learning. The daily routine includes a **plan-do-review** sequence in the morning. This is a framework for organizing play. First children plan what they are going to do and discuss how they will accomplish their task. Next, they engage in the "do" part of the cycle during work time. During this time, teachers float throughout the room, use questions to scaffold play, and monitor interactions among the children. Clean-up is a part of this phase. Attention is paid to carefully replacing materials on the shelves. Materials are organized so that children learn mathematical concepts when placing materials in their original position. Review is the last part of this cycle. Children review or recall what they have accomplished and represent their work in a variety of ways. Some will dictate stories, some will tell about their work, others will draw pictures. Review provides an opportunity for children to develop their language and literacy skills.

© Cengage Learning 2015

5-11 HighScope programs encourage organized environments, such as this table set for snack, which allow children to develop orderliness and one-to-one correspondence.

Large group time provides a time for children to come together for music and movement. The key preschool experiences in the HighScope program include the following:

- Creative representation
- Language and literacy
- Initiative and social relations
- Movement
- Music
- Classification
- Seriation
- Number
- Space
- Time

Although the HighScope program does not tout itself as a play-based program, the "do" part of plan-do-review that is called work time is very much a time for play. In describing the layout of the room, HighScope recommends four quadrants, with a wet/dry, quiet/loud division and with clear and low boundaries (i.e., boundaries over which the teacher and children can easily climb). Assessment is ongoing and uses an instrument developed by HighScope, the Child Observation Record. One key to effectiveness is maintaining a staffing ratio of no more than 10 children per staff member and group sizes that are limited to 20.

5-7c Constructivist

Many fine constructivist programs exist in the United States. For this text, the program of Reggio Emilia was selected as a model for constructivism due to the recent interest in this approach. The preschools of Reggio Emilia have been recognized by many as the best in the world. Started at the end of World War II by parents with the leadership of Louis Malagozzi, the schools of Reggio Emilia were sponsored by the local municipal government of Reggio Emilia, Italy. Malaguzi was influenced by the teachings of Dewey (1916) and Vygotsky (1978). He believed that children had many ways of knowing the world and described this as *The Hundred Languages of Children* (Edwards, Gandini, & Foreman, 1998). The preschools of Reggio Emilia include a curriculum that reflects the children's interests and expression of their interests as mitigated by adults and the environment. The curriculum is based on an aesthetic approach. Enjoyment of the arts is an important component of the child's world, and play has a major role in the curriculum. A typical center in a room for three-year-olds might include a block center, home area, dress-up or pretend area, computer area, book area, group meeting area, gross motor area, and an enclosed room for art and music. There are two adults in each room. The daily routine is very flexible, with children's interests defining a majority of the activity each day.

Preschoolers in Reggio Emilia engage in a great deal of project work. This concept is based in part on Dewey's notion of progressive education and Katz and Chard's (1989) project approach. The projects can be teacher or child initiated. The preschoolers engage in many field trips. Like the schools of Bank Street, only three or four children participate in an outing at one time. For example, in a video produced by the Friends of Reggio Emilia, a project

The Role of Play and Language Development in Waldorf Education

Deborah F. Carrington, PhD
Caitlin F. Frank, MS, CCC-SLP

Play is at the heart of the Waldorf early childhood curriculum. Not only is play fundamental to developing social, physical, emotional, and cognitive growth, it promotes early language development and emergent literacy skills. The first hour of every morning in the mixed-age prekindergarten and kindergarten is devoted to active, free play. Children aged 3.5 to 6 years engage in a variety of play: solitary, parallel, associative, and cooperative small and large group (Parten, 1932). While playing, young children are actively acquiring language skills: "Play and language develop interdependently and demonstrate underlying cognitive developments" (Owens, 2011, p. 51).

The play environments found in Waldorf kindergartens nurture language development in a variety of ways, encouraging both expressive and receptive language skills. Through a daily rhythmic schedule that includes multiple social activities, story time, songs, finger-plays, rhymes, and chants, children are exposed to a wide variety of language purposes and structures. Children's expressive language grows by learning to express thoughts, feelings, and ideas as well as answer and pose questions. Naming objects and their function and using complex sentences occur during indoor and outdoor playtime. Children also grow in understanding receptive language such as following directions, recalling information and sequencing, retaining details from a story or event, identifying objects, and comprehending complex sentences (Owens, 2011). Daily active, free play serves to reinforce these developing language skills.

The task of the Waldorf teacher is to create an environment that supports the possibility for healthy play and the language growth it nurtures. This environment includes the physical surroundings, furnishings, and play materials; the social environment of activities and social interactions; and the adult's inner spiritual environment of thoughts, intentions, and imagination. The teacher is expected to be strong role model worthy of imitation by young children in every way (Barnes, 1991). To develop oral communication among children, the teacher uses beautiful, articulate speech and rich teacher talk throughout the day. The teacher listens to and responds to what

children have to say; she uses nuanced vocabulary; she converses with children in a variety of settings; she extends children's comments into more descriptive and grammatically mature sentences; and she uses gestures to communicate and augment oral language. The teacher also sings with children, recites poems and finger-plays, and tells stories on a daily basis, thereby developing valuable dispositions that strengthen the children's later literacy interactions with reading and writing.

The teacher also carefully organizes both indoor and outdoor play environments that are worthy of

(Continued)

imitation: environments that are beautiful, rhythmic, purposeful, and inviting (Barnes, 1991). Environments are intentionally nonassertive, meaning that there are no educational objects, devices, or delineated spaces. There is a sensory focus versus an intellectual or didactic focus. Children are allowed space to "make" or "project" versus being passive and receptive. The degree to which children transform their environment with their play is an indication that they are working deeply from within. "The way children think is through their play. It is the way they make the world their own, it is how they make meaning in their life" (Oppenheimer, 2006, p. 71).

What is gained through play stems fundamentally from the self-activity of the child. The following features of a Waldorf inspired prekindergarten and kindergarten support such self-activity:

- **Active play**—one hour every morning, facilitated by the teacher, both indoor and outdoor play

- **Story time**—a daily circle-time story that the teacher initially tells with props, puppets, and/or marionettes, and which the children retell and reenact

- **Natural play materials**—open-ended, unformed toys that are interactive and nonrepresentational to encourage the child's imagination

- **Rhythm**—predictable daily activities planned in harmony with weekly and seasonal changes

- **Home-like environment**—the look and work of "home" that give children opportunities to imitate household tasks

A wide variety of play materials and spaces are made available to children, and great emphasis is placed on natural, open-ended materials in order to provide varied sensory experiences and allow space for the child's imagination and spontaneity: sea shells, rocks, pine cones, branches, roots, large and small pieces of wood, pieces of cloth, buckets and tubs, baskets, simple play stands, empty boxes and boards offer the child an inexhaustible field of activity in which to unfold her creative potential. As Owens (2011) notes, "thought precedes language...children begin to use language expressively to talk about the things they know...world knowledge becomes word knowledge" (p. 50).

With deliberately incomplete play materials, the child's assigning the meaning to the object is the crucial factor. The activity sparked from within transforms into imagination and thinking and forms the foundation for later academic learning in school. "The culmination of play, or the ability to create and hold inner images, is the fundamental prerequisite for all academic learning...it is this very force of the creative imagination that naturally evolves in time into the capacity for conceptual thought" (Oppenheimer, 2006, p. 73).

REFERENCES

Barnes, H. (1991). Learning that grows with the learner: An introduction to Waldorf education. *Educational Leadership, 49*(2), 52–54. EJ 434 784. (Also available: http://www.awsna.org/education-intro.html)

Oppenheimer, S. (2006). *Heaven on earth: A handbook for parents of young children.* Great Barrington, MA: Steiner Books.

Owens, R. E. (2011). *Language development: An introduction. (8th ed.).* Boston, MA: Allyn & Bacon *Communication Sciences and Disorders.*

Parten, M. (1932). Social participation among preschool children. *Journal of Abnormal Psychology, 27,* 243–269.

Deborah F. Carrington, Ph.D., is Professor of Education at James Madison University and is a former Waldorf Kindergarten and Class Teacher.

Caitlin F. Frank, M.S., CCC-SLP, is a clinical educator in Communication Sciences and Disorders at Longwood University and is a former PreK–6 Waldorf student.

about the stone lions on the piazza is discussed. The children might travel to the square to look at the lions, measure the lions with string, and observe the shadows that occur during their visit. This project, which started as a field trip, can extend throughout the month as children make clay lions, paper lions, and three-dimensional lions, and as they develop concepts. They may return to the piazza several times to view the statues before completing their study.

5-7d Creative Curriculum

Creative Curriculum (2002) is a well-known professional development program designed for preschool teachers. Although the program is not affiliated with a lab, school, or university, it uses an eclectic approach. The curriculum framework

> **What do you think?**
>
> Different programs use specific approaches to play. Review the three programs discussed above. Which program reflects your view of how children learn? Can you implement components of any or all of these programs in your current setting? Why or why not?

used by Creative Curriculum (2002) is composed of two areas. The first area is the curriculum framework that includes the following:

1. How children develop and learn
2. The learning environment
3. What children learn
4. The teacher's role
5. The family's role

The second area includes 11 interest areas: blocks, dramatic play, toys & games, art, library, discovery, sand and water, music and movement, cooking, computers, and outdoors. The website for Creative Curriculum has an extensive array of resources for professional development.

5-7e Family Child Care

Family centers can choose any of the program models mentioned in the preceding subsections or use an eclectic model by choosing different components from each program. For example, some early educators choose to use some aspects of the HighScope "plan-do-review" and some parts of the Bank Street program. It is important to align the philosophy of education and the program.

✳ 5-8 Assessment

Assessment for preschoolers is both formative and summative. Formative assessment is also called authentic assessment and reflects the philosophy of the program. Different program models described above use an assessment plan that matches their program philosophy. For example, Bank Street uses an approach that focuses on the child's holistic progress. HighScope uses a Piagetian-based approach that looks at key elements of cognitive development. The HighScope program uses a specific instrument that it created to reflect program goals and objectives. Reggio Emilia uses an assessment system based on a social constructivist view of teaching and learning. Reggio Emilia documents the child's process of learning through documentation panels and portfolios. Reggio Emilia does not look at children in terms of norms. It focuses on children's construction of knowledge within the context of the group. Creative Curriculum does not include an assessment system in its program description. Some preschool programs combine different elements to create their own unique system. Assessment that occurs throughout the year on an ongoing basis is called authentic or formative assessment because it provides information that can be used to guide instruction and interaction.

Summative evaluation is used at the end of each program to determine if the child has met certain objectives and is knowledge in specific areas. Learning that occurs through play can be useful during tests. By its nature, play-based assessment can be either formative or summative. It is formative when it is used in an ongoing way and summative when used at the end of a program to place a child in a different program. The next section discusses play-based assessment and ways to integrate it into the curriculum to create a seamless system.

5-8a Play-Based Assessment

Observing play is relatively easy. Assessing play is much more difficult. The first question that arises in assessment is, "What is the purpose or goal of the assessment?" If the goal of play-based assessment is to understand the child's level of play in order to facilitate the child's development and play skills, then examining the child's play level is essential. One way to accomplish this is to assess the child's play in a specific area such as block play (see Table 5-4).

Another instrument that is designed to measure cognitive and social levels is the Play Observation Scale (Rubin, 1989). This scale provides a profile of the child's play behaviors. This instrument can be used to capture a picture of the child's play at the beginning and end of a specified period of time. For example,

TABLE 5-4 Evaluating Block Play						
Level of Block Play	Day 1	Day 2	Day 3	Day 4	Day 5	Total
Stage One Children carry blocks.						
Stage Two Children build with blocks. They build up (vertically) or out (horizontally).						
Stage Three Children begin putting connecting blocks with other blocks.						
Stage Four Children connect blocks to make completed shapes.						
Stage Five Additions are made to the connected blocks. A great deal of symmetry can be observed.						
Stage Six Children name the structures.						
Stage Seven Children use the structures for dramatic play.						
Additional notes						

For an overview of play in the block center, the number of children engaging in each stage of block play can be tallied. This does not provide information on individual children, but rather provides a profile of what type of play is dominant during the week.

Adapted from Johnson (1933).

it would not be unusual for a preschooler to engage in solitary play sometimes or to engage in constructive play with blocks. In fact, this is very typical behavior. If, however, the child was observed on three different occasions and used the same materials in the same way, then closer observations would be needed. This instrument only shows what the child is doing. It cannot be used for any other purposes.

Observations of block play can occur informally throughout the year to show how the child progressed throughout the year. Another way to examine the quality of play is through the arts. Children can draw their play. Drawing and explaining their play provides a way to practice literacy and communication skills. Another method involves using a mural or large sheets of manila paper (12" × 18") to create play stories. They can also use puppets to act out their play. Another possibility involves drama and is similar to Vivian Paley's (1981) method. The children act out their play. Creative teachers will discover even more ways to understand and capture children's play. Assessment during play provides a natural environment for obtaining information about the child and the child's play. Many teachers have heard of assessments of hopping that indicate that the child cannot hop on one foot, yet the child hopped all over the playground! Play-based assessment has the potential to impact how we think about assessment for preschool children. More research is needed in this area.

There are multiple ways to organize and share the results of play observation and assessment. Three that are commonly used are portfolios, photo essays, and documentation panels. As discussed in Chapter 3, the portfolio is an orderly compilation of the child's growth and development through documented activities and experiences during the time that the child has been in the center. The portfolio can be organized in a variety of ways that reflect either the developmental domains or the overall activities or projects that the child has completed. Artifacts such as work completed in the class can be added to the portfolio; the inclusion of artifacts provides a record for the child, parents, and teacher.

Other informal techniques for include photo essays and documentation panels. Photo essays capture not only an image of the child, but also an interpretation of the child's play. Documentation panels are similar in that they also capture the child at play and add an explanation and interpretation. The difference between a photo essay and a documentation panel is that a photo essay may be on a computer or paper. A documentation panel is generally on a large board, is designed so that others may view it, and is displayed over a period of years. The panel is used to add to the history of a school.

✳ PLAYSCAPE: REFLECTIONS

Juan is in middle of his "play years" and is engaging in very sophisticated play. His construction of blocks involved some sensorimotor play as he carried and stacked the blocks. He appropriated a story he heard earlier and is acting out the story through song and movement. Juan's ability to engage in abstraction is preparing him for instruction in math and literacy. Rosalee knows that not only is Juan enjoying his experiences in the corporate child care center, but he is also receiving a solid educational experience that will prepare him for life and school. Like many of the other parents at the center, Rosalee understands the relationship between play and learning. The teachers are fortunate that the parents of children in this center understand the value of play.

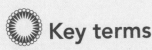

Summary

5-1. List the benefits of play for preschoolers.

Scholars have found that play supports the preschoolers' brain development, self-regulation, and good health.

5-2. Discuss how adult interactions impact preschoolers.

Adults impact preschooler through personal interactions, classroom organization, and meaningful instruction. A proactive voice is especially important when working with children who are English language learners.

5-3. Identify the steps involved in organizing a high-quality play environment.

Steps include planning, organizing, observing, guiding, and evaluating play.

5-4. Explain how play is extended and expanded through art, music, and movement.

When children create art, engage in musical activities, or move, they discover and strengthen their ideas, experiences, and feelings through symbols and symbolism. Play also involves symbols and abstraction. Combining play with art, music, and movement enhances the quality of life for preschool children as they develop their ability to engage in abstract thought.

5-5. Articulate how play supports the content areas of literacy, mathematics, science, and social studies.

Play supports literacy learning for preschoolers when teachers encourage talking, reading, and the use of print and writing materials during play; mathematical learning is fostered through encouraging block play, sand and water play, and play with manipulatives; science learning is nurtured when children engage in explorations, investigations, and outdoor play; and learning in the social studies is fostered when engaging in dramatic play in the house and block areas.

5-6. Design a preschool classroom with at least five learning centers.

Centers include art/messy/dramatic, music/movement, book center, blocks, house, toy, sociodramatic, and technology.

5-7. Compare and contrast play-based preschool models.

HighScope is a model that is based on Piaget's theory of cognitive development and uses a play-based curriculum. Play is also valued in the developmental-interaction approach used by Bank Street but it is informed by Erikison's theory of social and emotional development.

5-8. Describe how to assess play, organize findings, and share results.

Block play scales can be used to assess the quality of the child's play with wooden blocks. Murals provide a way for children to illustrate their play, and drama is an outlet for sharing their interpretation of their play. Remember, these are only a few of the many ways to assess play. These assessments can be organized and shared with others via portfolios, photo essays, and documentation panels. Portfolios are an organized compilation of the child's activities during her time in the child care center. Photo essays provide a way to report the play of children through pictures and text. Documentation panels allow teachers to capture information about children's play through photos and text, and the panels are large and are displayed from year to year.

Key terms

Basic forms stage, 129
Co-play, 126
Co-player, 121
Executive function, 121
Fundamental movement stage, 131
Here and Now curriculum, 134

Logical-mathematical
knowledge, 133
Parallel play, 126
Physical knowledge, 133
Plan-do-review, 140
Play frame, 126

Play tutor, 127
Play years, 120
Preschematic stage, 129
Prop box, 124
Social-arbitrary knowledge, 133
Spokesperson for reality, 127

Technology and Internet Resources

Association for the Education of Children International (ACEI)

http://www.udel.edu/. The Association for the Education of Children International (ACEI) website provides connections to reliable sources of information, experts in the field, and new resources on childhood education.

Centers for Disease Control (CDC)

http://www.cdc.gov/obesity/data/childhood.html The Centers for Disease Control (CDC) provides data on obesity and health issues of preschool children and their families.

Lucille Packard Children's Hospital

http://www.lpch.org The Lucille Packard Children's Hospital at Stanford University Medical Center has an excellent website that includes resources on and encourages play-based preschool programs.

National Association for the Education of Young Children (NAEYC)

http://www.naeyc.org/ The National Association for the Education of Young Children (NAEYC) website provides a wide range of information on preschool children as well as connections to high quality, authentic sources of information. The NAEYC interest group Play, Policy and Practice (PPP) also serves as a source of information about play.

National Association for Sports and Physical Education (NASPE)

http://www.aahperd.org/naspe/ The website for NASPE provides a variety of materials related to the value of physical education. The materials on Play on! designed for parents provide information about backyard play.

Activities

1. Inclass Labs

A. Design a room for preschoolers that reflects the concepts discussed in this chapter. Know the local and state fire, safety, and licensing standards. Also check the state's academic standards. Draw the room on a large 6" × 6" piece of paper. When all the groups have completed their tasks, share the designs in class and display them on the wall.

B. Look at the charts that were placed on the wall. Decide which areas would stimulate cognitive, social, and physical play. Which areas could be used for music, art, and drama? Which areas could be used for functional, symbolic, sociodramatic play, and games with rules? Do you need to address other criteria?

C. Create a prop box outside of class. Include a web of the learning outcomes for children. Share the prop box and web in class.

2. Research and Inquiry

A. Visit a preschool classroom for two hours. Complete a running record of one child's play. Compose a list of the preschool child's characteristics. Identify several physical, social, and cognitive characteristics.

B. How does play in the preschool differ from that in the infant/toddler center?

C. The statement "Play is the child's work" is used in many preschool classrooms. Visit the library and investigate who first made this statement. Bring your answer to class and be ready to share your findings.

3. Service Learning

A. Volunteer to assist in a preschool center for two hours per week. Does the center need additional play materials? Can you assist in creating an environment that fosters play?

B. Volunteer to create a website for a local preschool center.

C. Contact a local child care center and ask if you can present a program on play for one of the center's family night meetings.

4. Family Connections

A. Create a letter that you can send home to parents that will stimulate play. The letter in Table 5-5 can serve as a template. Add information that is unique to your geographic area and local culture. Some of the new templates for newsletters available online can be used to create a visually appealing publication.

TABLE 5-5 Template for Letter to Parents

Dear Parents,

Young children learn as they play. The list below contains some activities that you can use to encourage play at home.

1. Collect the junk mail that comes to your home. Let the children set up a pretend post office. They can draw pictures for relatives or friends and pretend to mail them in the junk mail envelopes.

2. Get some boxes that have been discarded and allow children to use them to build pretend houses. They can drape an old sheet or blanket over the boxes and create a tent. The possibilities are endless.

3. Collect clean grocery boxes and plastic bottles. Let the children set up a pretend grocery store.

4. Let children take coupons to the store. They can locate the item that matches the coupon and pretend to shop while you shop.

5. Blocks are wonderful for play and learning. You can buy a variety of sizes, or you can make blocks by following the directions that are attached to this sheet.

6. Cooking activities are also wonderful for play and learning. A recipe for goop (play dough) requires corn starch and water. Mix together and store any unused portions in a plastic bag in the refrigerator.

Please contact me if you have questions about any of these activities.

Your child's teacher

© Cengage Learning 2015

Digital Download Download from CourseMate

5. Play Advocacy

A. What are the provisions for play programs in your community? Are there any federally funded programs? What state programs are available? What does the local school system fund? Find or start a local group to support play for young children in your area.

B. Ask a local clinic or community center if a display can be set up to distribute NAEYC brochures. Initiate a fund raiser to purchase materials. Select several good brochures that relate to play and other issues related to play-based education.

 Visit CourseMate for this textbook to access the eBook, Did You Get It? quizzes, Digital Downloads, TeachSource Video Cases, flashcards, and more. Go to CengageBrain.com to log in, register, or purchase access.

References

Ashiabi, G. (2007). Play in the preschool classroom: Its socioemotional significance and the teacher's role in play. *Early Childhood Education Journal, 35*(2), 199–206.

Bergen, B. (2002). The role of pretend play in children's cognitive development. *Early Childhood Research and Practice, 4*(1). [Online]. Retrieved on July 17, 2013 from http://ecrp.uiuc.edu/v4n1/bergen.html

Bond, V. L. (2012). Music's representation in early childhood education journals: A literature review. *Update: Applications of Research in Music Education, 31*(1), 34–43.

Boyce, W. T., Obradović, J., Bush, N. R., Stamperdahl, J., Kim, Y. S., & Adler, N. (2012). Social stratification, classroom climate, and the behavioral adaptation of kindergarten children. *Proceedings of the National Academy of Sciences, 109*(Supplement 2), 17168–17173.

Bronson, M. B. (1995). *The right stuff for children: Birth to 8.* Washington, DC: National Association for the Education of Young Children.

Centers for Disease Control and Prevention. (2013) Overweight and obesity. Retrieved on July 3 from http://www.cdc.gov/obesity/data/facts.html

Chalufour, I., & Worth, K. (2005). *Exploring water with young children.* Redleaf Press. St. Paul, MN.

Colbert, P. J. (2010). Developing a culturally responsive classroom collaborative of faculty, students, and institution. *Journal of College Teaching & Learning, 7*(11), 1–10 .

Copley, J. V. (2010). *The young child and mathematics* (2nd ed.). National Association for the Education of Young Children.

Cuffaro, H. K., Nager, N., & Shaprio, E. (2000). The developmental-interaction approach at Bank Street College of Education. In J. P. Roopnarine and J.Johnson (Eds.), *Approaches to Early Childhood Education* (3rd ed.)(pp. 263–274). Upper Saddle River, NJ: Merrill/Prentice Hall.

Denny, J., Hallam, R., & Homer, K. (2012). A multi-instrument examination of preschool classroom quality and the relationship between program, classroom, and teacher characteristics. *Early Education & Development, 23*(5), 678–696.

Dewey, J. (1919). *Democracy and education.* New York: Macmillan.

Downer, J. T., López, M. L., Grimm, K. J., Hamagami, A., Pianta, R. C., & Howes, C. (2012). Observations of teacher–child interactions in classrooms serving Latinos and dual language learners: Applicability of the Classroom Assessment Scoring System in diverse settings. *Early Childhood Research Quarterly, 27*(1), 21–32.

Driscoll, K. C., Wang, L., Mashburn, A. J., & Pianta, R. C. (2011). Fostering supportive teacher–child relationships: Intervention implementation in a state-funded preschool program. *Early Education & Development, 22*(4), 593–619.

Dodge, D., Colker, L., & Heroman, C. (2002). *The Creative Curriculum for Preschool* (4th ed.). Washington, DC: Teaching Strategies.

Edwards, C., Gandini, L., & Foreman, G. (Eds.). (1998). *The hundred languages of children: The Reggio Emilia approach—Advanced reflection.* (2nd ed.). Greenwich, CT: Ablex.

Erikson, E. (1950/2000). *Childhood and society.* New York: W.W. Norton & Company.

Evans, J. (2012). "This is me": Developing literacy and a sense of self through play, talk and stories. *Education 3–13: International Journal of Primary, Elementary and Early Years Education, 40*(3), 315331.

Froebel, F. (1895). *The songs and music of Freidrich Froebel's Mother play* (mutter und kose lieder). New York: D. Appleton.

Gabbard, C. P. (1992). *Lifelong motor development.* Dubuque, IA: Wm. C. Brown.

Gandini, L. Introduction to the fundamental values of the education of young children in Reggio Emilia (adapted from Gandini, L., 2008). Introduction to the schools of Reggio Emilia. In L. Gandini, S. Etheredge, S. & L. Hill (Eds.), *Insights and inspirations: Stories of teachers and children from North America* (pp. 24–27). Worchester, MA: Davis Publications, Inc.

Hanline, M., Milton, S., & Phelps, P. C. (2010). The relationship between preschool block play and reading and math abilities in early elementary school: A longitudinal study of children with and without disabilities. *Early Child Development And Care, 180*(8), 1005–1017.

International Reading Association (IRA) and the National Association for the Education of Young Children (NAEYC) joint position paper. (1998). Learning to read and write: Developmentally appropriate practices for young children. *Young Children, 53*(4), 30–46.

Isbell, R., & Raines, S. (2013). *Creativity and the arts with young children* (3rd ed.). Clifton Park, NY: Delmar.

Isenberg, J., & Jalongo, M. (2009). *Creative thinking and arts based learning* (5th ed.). Columbus, OH: Merrill.

Johnson, H. (1933). *The art of block building.* New York: The John Day Company.

Kamii, C., & Housman, L. (2000). *Young children reinvent arithmetic: Implications of Piaget's theory* (2nd ed.). New York: Teachers College Press.

Katz, L., & Chard, S. (1989). *Engaging children's minds: The project approach.* Norwood, NJ: Ablex.

Kelly, R., and Hammond, S. (2011). The relationship between symbolic play and executive function in young children. *Australasian Journal of Early Childhood, 36*(2), 21–27.

Maslow, A. (1998). *Toward a psychology of being,* (3rd ed.). New York: Wiley (Originally published in 1962)

Mitchell, L. S. (1921). *Here and now storybook.* New York: E. P. Dutton & Company.

Montessori, M. (1914). *Dr. Montessori's own handbook.* New York: Frederick A. Stokes.

Moore, T. (2002). If you teach children, you can sing! *Young Children, 57*(4), 84–85.

National Association for Sport and Physial Education (NASPE). (2011) Physical education is critical to educate the whole child. Position statement retrieved on July 3, 2013 from AAHPERD.org/naspe/

National Geographic Little Kids. (2013). Lady Bug. Retrieved on July 3, 2013 from http://kids.nationalgeographic.com/kids/animals/creaturefeature/ladybug/

Neely, L. (2002). Practical ways to improve singing in early childhood. *Young Children, 57*(4), 80–83.

Oppenheimer, S. (2006). *Heaven on earth: A handbook for parents of young children.* Great Barrington, MA: SteinerBooks.

Paley, V. (1981). *Wally's stories.* Cambridge, MA: Harvard University Press.

PBS Kids. (2013). Dinosaur Trains. Retrieved on July 7, 2013 from http://www.pbslearningmedia.org

Pianta, R., & La Paro, K. (2003). Improving early school success. *Educational leadership, 60*(7), 24–29.

Qu, L. (2011). Two is better than one, but mine is better than ours: Preschoolers' executive function during co-play. *Journal of Experimental Child Psychology, 108,* 549–566.

Rousseau, J. J. (1762/1991). *Emile.* Translated and annotated by Allan Bloom. London: Penguin. (Originally published in 1762.)

Rogers, C. S., & Sluss, D. J. (1999). Revisiting Erikson's views on Einstein's play and inventiveness. In S. Reifel (Ed.), *Play contexts revisited.* Play and culture series (Vol. 2, pp. 3–24). Greenwich, CT: Ablex.

Rubin, K. (1989). *The Play Observation Scale*. Waterloo Canada: University of Waterloo.

Sesame Street (2013). Let's find out. Retrieved from on July 3, 2013 at http://www.sesamestreet.org/parents/topicsandactivities/topics/science

Smith, P. K., & Connolly, K. J. (1980). *The ecology of preschool behavior*. Cambridge, England: Cambridge University Press.

Trawick-Smith, J., & Dziurgot, T. (2010). Untangling teacher–child play interactions: Do teacher education and experience influence "good-fit" responses to children's play?. *Journal of Early Childhood Teacher Education, 31*(2), 106–128.

U.S. Department of Education National Center for Education Statistics. (2012). *Digest of Education Statistics, 2011* (NCES 2012-001), Chapter 2.

Van Hoorn, J., Nourot, P., Scales, B., & Alward, K. (2011). *Play at the center of the curriculum* (5th ed.). Upper Saddle River, NJ: Merrill Prentice Hall.

Vygotsky, L. (1978). *Mind in society: The development of higher psychological processes*. Cambridge, MA: Harvard University Press.

Wallace, A. H., White, M. J., Stone, R., & Kastberg, S. E. (2010). Sand and water table play. *Teaching Children Mathematics, 16*(7), 394–399.

Wellhousen, K. (2002). *Outdoor play every day: Innovative concepts for early childhood*. Clifton Park, NY: Delmar.

Willer, B., (1990). *Reaching the full cost of quality in early childhood programs*. Washington, DC: NAEYC.

Zelazo, P., & Lyons, K. R. (2011). Mindfulness training in childhood. *Human Development, 54*(2), 61–66.

6 Supporting PLAY in Kindergarten Classrooms

STANDARDS COVERED IN THIS CHAPTER
Council of Exceptional Children—Division of Early Childhood (CEC) (DEC)

ECSE 2S1 Apply current research to the five developmental domains, play, and temperament in learning situations

ECSE 3S1 Develop, implement, and evaluate learning experiences and strategies

ECSE 4S1 Plan, implement, and evaluate developmentally appropriate curricula, instruction, and adaptations based on knowledge of individual children, the family, and the community

ECSE 5S4 Structure social environments, using peer models and proximity, and responsive adults to promote interactions among peers, parents, and caregivers

ECSE 7K2 Plan and implement developmental and academic content

ECSE 7S2 Plan and implement developmentally and individually appropriate curriculum

✳ LEARNING OBJECTIVES ✳

6-1 Discuss the relationship between play and kindergarten.

6-2 Interpret the benefits of a play-based kindergarten program.

6-3 Develop a plan that adults can use to increase cultural competence through play.

6-4 Illustrate the role of teachers in implementing a play-based curriculum.

6-5 Describe how Maslow's theory of basic needs informs kindergarten curriculum.

6-6 Contrast an integrative approach to aesthetics with the process of adding songs, art, and movement to the curriculum.

6-7 Develop a plan for using play as a medium for learning literacy, mathematics, science, and social studies.

6-8 Design a play space with play centers found in traditional kindergarten programs.

6-9 Compare a whole-day kindergarten program with a half-day program.

6-10 Evaluate the use of constructivism to inform a traditional kindergarten curriculum.

6-11 Differentiate the HighScope, Bank Street, and Reggio Emilia programs.

6-12 Analyze how toys, puzzles, and materials enhance cultural competence.

6-13 Identify formative and summative assessment strategies that can be used to document how children learn through play

© Cengage Learning 2015

NAEYC Program Standards

4a Understanding positive relationships and supportive interactions as the foundation of work with children

4c Using a broad repertoire of developmentally appropriate teaching and learning approaches

5a Using content knowledge and resources in academic disciplines

5c Using knowledge, appropriate early learning standards, and other resources to design, implement, and evaluate meaningful and challenging curricula for each child

✳ PLAYSCAPE: CASE STUDY

Jamal does not like kindergarten. He likes his grandmother's house and routine. When he's at school, he misses his grandmother and the "stories" they watched every day. Now, he doesn't know what is happening on his grandma's favorite soap opera anymore. He really wants to go home. Tears fall from his eyes as he watches the teacher stack block after block.

"Jamal, would you like to stack some blocks? Can you stack yours higher than mine?" the teacher asks.

As Jamal starts to stack these things the teacher calls blocks, he realizes he can do other things with the blocks. He watches as others build something that looks like a house. He could build one bigger than that!

An hour later, the lights dim to remind everyone that clean-up time is near. Jamal thinks, I don't want to stop. I like blocks! Grandma does not have blocks at her house. As he replaces the blocks on the shelves, he shouts, "I like school!"

Explaining Play Behaviors

The provocation to play in this classroom was the combination of time, materials, and teacher interaction. The teacher allocated over an hour for play; wood units blocks and other materials were well defined and available for use; and the teacher moved throughout the room to facilitate play. Jamal, like some children who come to kindergarten, was not transitioning well. For Jamal, play was cathartic. That is, play provided a place where he could control the situation and gain mastery over his emotions (Erikson, 2000).

A play-based program in kindergarten can facilitate a positive transition into public school. The first day of kindergarten can be overwhelming for some children and adults. If Jamal's grandmother watched daytime television with her grandson for several years, she may be having an equally difficult time adjusting to his absence. The emotional issues surrounding this first step away from home are often complex. For children who have just arrived in America, the new language and different play materials will be equally stressful. Children who have learning difficulties will find the new schedule and names overwhelming. At the same time, the teacher must recognize the needs of children and families who have experienced preschool programs for several years. Play materials and interaction will need to provide an array of interesting, challenging experiences. The teacher must realize the variability of experiences that the children bring to the kindergarten class and provide experiences that foster play for all children. This presents a challenge but can provide lasting, powerful results.

Relationship Between Play 6-1 ✳ and Kindergarten

Play and kindergarten have been synonymous since the inception of kindergarten well over a century ago. Friedrich Froebel (1782–1852), who founded kindergarten, used the German terms "kindergarten" or "garden for children" to describe the curriculum. In his book *The Education of Man* (1887), he wrote the following:

> The mind grows by self revelation. In play the child ascertains what he can do, discovers his possibilities of will and thought by exerting his power spontaneously. In work he follows a task prescribed for him by another, and doesn't reveal his own proclivities and inclinations; but another's. In play, he reveals his own original power. (p. 233)

As discussed in Chapter 1, Froebel thought children should be free to grow and develop like flowers in a garden. He believed that Americans might have more freedom to begin a school for children than he had encountered in Europe, and he was correct. His influence was evident in the first two kindergartens in America, which were started by his students. One student, Margarethe Schurz (1832–1876), is credited with starting the first kindergarten in America in Watertown, Wisconsin; and Caroline Luise Frankenberg started a kindergarten class in Columbus, Ohio even before Froebel opened his own center. Others influenced by Froebel include Elizabeth Peabody, who started the first English-speaking kindergarten, and Susan Blow, who started the first public school kindergarten in St Louis, Missouri (Brostarman, 1997; Froebel 1887/1902).

Patty Smith Hill started as a Froebelian but was influenced by G. Stanley Hall and his scientific approach to studying children. She is credited with creating the traditional kindergarten core (circle with music and movement, play, rest, and outdoor play) that is still found in kindergartens today. She also invented unit wood blocks and wrote the song *Happy Birthday to You*. She was committed to a kindergarten program that emphasized both play and social skills. The kindergarten programs started by Froebel and Hill both were grounded on play. Although they approached it differently, they both viewed play as the basis of the kindergarten program. Today, full-day and half-day kindergarten programs are an accepted part of all public school systems in America. They are publicly funded and situated in public school buildings with primary and elementary schools.

⏸ **TeachSource** Video Case 6-1

© Cengage Learning 2015

2–5 Years: Piaget's Pre-operational Stage

Children who are in kindergarten are in what Piaget referred to as the pre-operational stage. In this stage, children engage in symbolic play and display egocentric thinking. Play as a platform for symbolic thinking is discussed throughout this chapter and in this video.

1. In what ways does this video support a play-based curriculum?

2. Is the play in this clip culturally appropriate? How do you know? What are the indicators?

Watch on CourseMate

Did You Get It?

A kindergarten class spends a significant amount of time playing, but also engages in activities that build social skills. Whose philosophy does this classroom mirror?
a. Patty Smith Hill
b. G. Stanley Hall
c. Erik Erikson
d. Friedrich Froebel

Take the full quiz on CourseMate

✳ 6-2 Benefits of Play in Kindergarten

The role of play in public school kindergarten has been fraught with controversy for the past fifty years (Bishop-Josef & Zigler, 2011). Today, play remains an important component of the curriculum for five- and six-year-olds who are in kindergarten (Roskos & Christie, 2011). Now, however, teachers must use empirical evidence to support a play-based curriculum (Golinkoff, Hirsh-Pasek, & Singer, 2006). Because setting up a study to show that play causes growth and development is difficult (i.e., who gets play and who does not receive play may be questionable or even unethical), it has been difficult to show that play *causes* healthy growth and development. Several research studies, including longitudinal research (studies that occur over several years), have shown the existence of relationships between play and the child's growth and development. For example, the HighScope Perry Preschool study showed that the effects of attending a cognitive-based program that used play as a primary component of the curriculum were still evident decades after preschool (Schweinhart, Montie, Xiang, Barnett, Belfield, & Nores, 2005). Other studies have shown various correlations, such as the one between block play and mathematical prowess in middle and high school (Wolfgang, Stannard, & Jones, 2001). Additional information to support play for children who are in kindergarten classrooms is summarized in the following list.

1. **Play facilitates higher cognitive processing** Research on brain development has found that play is linked to the development of the executive function, which is the area of the brain that controls planning, memory, inhibition, attentional flexibility, organization, and generativity (Bernier, Carlson, Deschenes, & Matte-Gagne, 2012; Kelly, Dissanayake, Ihsen, & Hammond, 2011; Rushton, Juola-Rushton, & Larkin, 2010; Weir, 2011). Vygotsky (2004) argued that "a child's play is not simply a reproduction of what he [sic] has experienced, but a creative reworking of the impressions he has acquired. He combines them and uses them to construct a new reality" (pp. 11–12). From this perspective, pretend play is a bridge to higher cognitive functioning. When children engage in collaborative play that involves a script, a cast of characters, and the use of imaginary props, they are increasing their cognitive capacity. Additionally, Russ and Fiorelli (2010) found that pretend play is associated with long-term gains in creativity. When considered as a whole, play leads to higher-level cognitive functioning.

2. **Play facilitates social and emotional regulation** Brain development affects social as well as cognitive development. The growth of the frontal lobe and the associated prefrontal cortex are linked to increased executive functioning. As these areas of the brain grow and mature, the individual is able to better control her own behavior. Playing allows children to mediate what they do, when and where they do it, and how long they participate or keep the play frame going. Complex collaborative play allows the child to practice self-control, negotiation, and turn taking. All are requisites for social and emotional regulation.

3. **Play enhances the social interactions and sense of self** Children who are involved in collaborative play (symbolic play) use a play script and play frames. When children play, they create and re-create the world according to their view. They have the power to be in or out of the play

What do you think?

Do you agree or disagree with the claim of many professional groups that play is disappearing from kindergarten classrooms? Explain.

frame. They control how the play occurs, who plays, and when and where they play. This helps develop a sense of self.

Social interactions are enhanced as the children interact with each other. The "mirror neurons" allow the child to reflect the emotions of others and to sympathize and empathize with their friends (Rushton, 2011). As children play with others, the mirror neurons enhance children's ability to mirror what others are doing so that they can join the play. The ability to mimic (Piaget's term) and understand others can lead to a better sense of self and others.

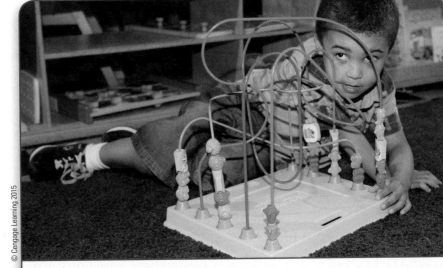

6-1 This child enjoys playing. He does not realize that he is developing his fine motor skills.

© Cengage Learning 2015

4. **Play contributes to fine and gross motor development as well as physical health** Play provides an opportunity to practice and extend fine and gross motor skills (see Photo 6-1). For example, children who are beginning to develop fine motor skills might play in the small block center. As children stack blocks to create a house, they are developing hand—eye coordination and skills necessary for writing. In the same way, play on the playground provides an opportunity for running, jumping, chasing, hopping, and skipping, all of which contribute to large muscle growth and routinized movement that can combat obesity.

5. **Play enhances quality of life** Children at this age enjoy pretend play. Freud's view of play as pleasurable certainly applies when five- and six-year-old children are playing: They wear the play face and laugh joyously at anything and everything. Play is a natural state that children enjoy at home and at school. For some children, the only safe place to play is at school, and these are the children who especially need play and joy in their lives.

Role of Adults in Increasing Cultural Competency through Play 6-3 ✳

Adults who are committed to encouraging play in the classroom must understand and embrace play as pedagogy. That is, play must serve as the medium for learning. If symbolic play dominates the play of five- and six-year-olds, then the teacher's role is to scaffold pretend play in the classroom. To review, symbolic or imaginary play involves the substitution of one object for another in an "as if" fashion. In pretend play, actions, objects, words, and people represent other items or ideas. The acknowledgment that this is not real is the key to the pretend.

In the previous chapters, we talked about the role of the teacher as guide, scaffold, and spokesperson for reality. A study by Jeffery Trawick-Smith (2010) challenges the traditional role of the teacher and warrants a closer look. When children from minority groups or cultures enter the classroom, they are often viewed as having play deficits. The teacher's role is to scaffold them during the play or center time so that they can engage in play with other children. In his naturalistic study, Trawick-Smith spent time in preschool classrooms in Puerto Rico observing children throughout the day. He found that children play in many different ways, so our traditional views of play may need to be expanded. For example, in his data, he identified two major kinds of play: primary play and embedded play. Primary play is viewed as the major activity in which the child is engaged. Embedded play is viewed as play that is located within the primary play but is secondary to the main purpose of the play. Trawick-Smith found that children engaged in play throughout the day and in different ways from those observed in American preschool classrooms. For example, in the Puerto Rican classrooms, no limit was placed on the number of children visiting each center. This reflects the island culture, in which large groups would meet and work together. Children also played with miniature replicas of homes, people, and so on, and these are not a part of the typical classroom on mainland America. The goal of the study was not to find ways of acting that everyone would emulate; rather, the goal was to encourage teachers to investigate the culture of the children who are entering the classroom and to find ways to encourage their native play. This may occur on the playground, in the music class, or, as Trawick-Smith found, during lunch.

✳ 6-4 Role of Teacher in Implementing a Play-Based Curriculum

Teachers who follow the kindergarten tradition place play at the core of the curriculum and generally engage in a recursive cycle similar to the one shown in Figure 6-1.

1. **Appreciate** Teachers must know and value how children in dominant and minority groups engage in play, how these intersect, and the role of play in cultural transmission.

Figure 6-1 Five attributes needed to encourage play-based curricula.

© Cengage Learning 2015

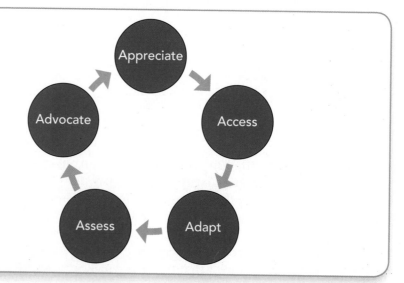

2. **Access**   Teachers must allow children to access play by implementing a play-based curriculum. There must be time and opportunities for indoor and outdoor play.

3. **Adapt**   Teachers must create an environment and activities that support and enhance the quality of play. The teacher acts as observer, stage manager, and encourager.

4. **Assess**   Teachers must evaluate the children's experiences. Do the children engage in repetitive play, or are they engaged in pretend play, with many children assuming different roles?

5. **Advocate**   Discuss the benefits of play so parents will value their children's play.

From the Experts

A New Teacher Talks about Her Experience in the Classroom

Amanda Soenksen, MEd

As a first-year teacher, I wasn't sure what to expect from my sixteen preschool students. Two of these students were identified as developmentally delayed, and seven of these students were English language learners. How was I going to meet everyone's needs? How was I going to focus on our formal assessment tools and teach English/life skills?

What I discovered was the importance of incorporating learning through children's play. Every day we had a full hour of center-based learning. On the very first day of school I taught my students how to play without adult support. Everything was visually labeled in our classroom so that any child could walk in to a center, play with the materials, and know where toys belong for clean-up. I purposely set up the environment to meet the curriculum standards and reinforce the content theme on which we were focusing. These centers included housekeeping, blocks, reading, writing, table toys, art area, water/sand table, science, and math manipulatives. Computers/iPads were also available. There were no limits as to how many students could be at one area at a time, and children were free to go from center to center. At least one teacher-led activity was available each day, but if students didn't want to participate, they didn't have to. My assistant and I supported students as they learned and practiced social skills and problem solving in this academically critical hour.

During this time, I worked one-on-one with students to facilitate and extend their learning and differentiate instruction. I worked with some students on social skills, whereas with other students we read books and began to identify words. During this

© Cengage Learning 2015

one-on-one instruction time, it is crucial to follow the child's lead. I never want to have to pull a student away from an activity in which she is engaged solely for the purpose of working on isolated academic skills or assessment.

I know that I have to teach the academic skills and meet the curriculum standards of my system and state, but this can happen through the way that children learn best—through play and by having meaningful, supported experiences every single day.

Amanda Soenksen, MEd, has a bachelor's degree in early childhood education from the University of North Carolina–Wilmington and a master's degree in early childhood special education from James Madison University.

Did You Get It?

A parent approaches a kindergarten teacher to complain that the children are wasting their time by spending the first hour of class each day playing instead of learning. The teacher responds by explaining the value of play. Which role of the teacher in implementing a play-based curriculum is the teacher fulfilling?

a. assess
b. adapt
c. access
d. advocate

Take the full quiz on CourseMate

Teachers who follow this approach can ensure that all children, especially those who are members of minority groups, have optimal opportunities for play. For example, the teacher begins by making a home visit or invites the child's parent(s) or guardian to a scheduled visit in her classroom after school to better understand the child's culture. The teacher can talk to the parent(s)/adult(s) in the home about their play as a child and encourage them to discuss their favorite games, suggestions for outdoor play, and games for indoor play. The teacher then makes a list of ideas for encouraging play and begins implementing one suggestion each day. At the end of two weeks, the teacher can assess the level of engagement and play observed in the class. The teacher then makes a decision about proceeding with the implementation or altering the approach. This process continues until all children are displaying a high level of play or engagement during play.

Of course, the implementation of any program is contingent on local and state guidelines as well as the educational philosophy of the community, school administration, and teachers. The classroom teacher who must look at societal expectations, governmental regulations, and children's abilities and then develop a kindergarten program. The kindergarten teacher of the past had to be an advocate for the existence of kindergarten. Today's teacher has to be an advocate for the kindergarten curriculum.

✳ 6-5 Using Maslow's Theory to Inform Kindergarten Curriculum

Although the trend is changing, many kindergarten teachers still have the option of creating their own curriculum. The philosophy of the teacher determines how the program operates on a day-to-day basis. The teacher decides which theoretical base is used to influence the classroom. Some theories and curriculum models that influence kindergarten curriculum have been discussed throughout the text. Table 6-1 presents an overview of these theories.

The kindergarten classroom reflects the classroom teacher's interpretation of these theories. Their influence is filtered through the teacher's understanding of how children grow and develop. Each theory has implications for pedagogy. These theories were discussed in earlier chapters, with the exception of Maslow's theory of basic needs. Because Maslow's theory of basic needs is so foundational for kindergarten, it is discussed in the following section.

6-5a Maslow's Theory of Basic Needs

Abraham Maslow (1908–1970) developed a hierarchy of needs basic to all humans (see Figure 6-2). His theory continues to provide the theoretical foundation of many kindergarten programs and includes five levels: (1) need for physical and psychological safety—survival needs (food, shelter, and clothing); (2) need for belonging, love, and acceptance of others; (3) need for approval and recognition from others; (4) need for knowledge and intellectual stimulation; (5) need for aesthetics—beauty and order; and (6) need for self-actualization.

Maslow's hierarchy of human needs provides a way to conceptualize how we approach the overall design of the classroom and curriculum. Safety, health, and respect form the foundation of high-quality programs that view play as a vehicle

TABLE 6-1 Theories that Influence Kindergarten Philosophy

Theoretical Perspective	Scholar	Implications for Impact on Play-Based Curriculum Model
Maturation Perspective		
Maturational Theory	Montessori (1936, 1964) Waldorf (Barnes, 1991)	Emphasis on the child's natural development as they become independent and autonomous individuals.
Theory of Basic Needs	Maslow (1962/1998)	Programs such as the traditional kindergarten program emphasize meeting the child's basic needs of physiological and psychological safety, love and belonging, esteem, approval, and recognition.
Psychosocial Theory	Erikson (1950/2000)	Bank Street program Focus on educating the whole child with an emphasis on social and emotional issues.
Attachment Theory	Bowlby (1988) Ainsworth (1989)	Bank Street has a focus on "easing in" to the center to assure the child and parent that the child will be comfortable in the new setting.
Constructivist Perspective		
Cognitive Development	Piaget (1962) DeVries (1994)	Constructivism is a model that focuses on the child constructing his understanding of the world by actions on objects and through interactions with others.
Sociocultural Theory	Vygotsky (1978)	Reggio Emilia inspired approach is influenced by these theories.
Cognitive Adaptation	Bruner (2009) Edwards, Gandini, & Forman (1998)	Children have multiple ways of constructing knowledge through interactions with more knowledgeable others.
Multiple Intelligences	Gardner (1995)	
Ecological Approach		
Ecological Systems Theory	Bronfenbrenner (1979)	Uses knowledge of the child in the context of the family to inform activities and experiences.
Neurological Approach		
Brain-Based Research	Shonkoff & Phillips (2000)	Uses knowledge of brain growth and development to structure activities and experiences for children.

for meeting the child's needs. Maslow believed that children could not grow and develop until basic survival needs were met. He recognized three levels of basic needs that must be met before growth needs could be considered.

The first basic need for survival is **physiological survival and psychological safety.** Physiological survival includes food/hunger, water/thirst, and shelter/bodily

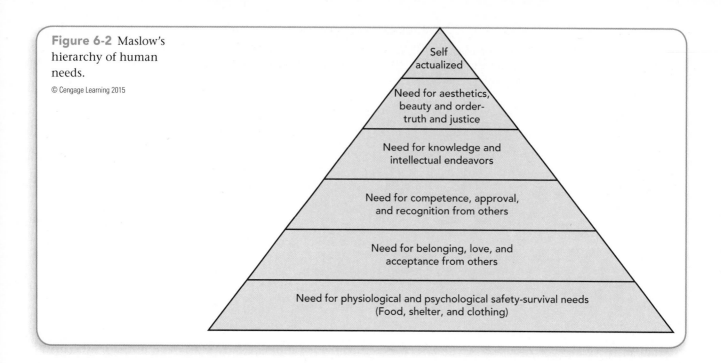

Figure 6-2 Maslow's hierarchy of human needs.

© Cengage Learning 2015

Self actualized

Need for aesthetics, beauty and order- truth and justice

Need for knowledge and intellectual endeavors

Need for competence, approval, and recognition from others

Need for belonging, love, and acceptance from others

Need for physiological and psychological safety-survival needs (Food, shelter, and clothing)

comfort. Both animals and humans have basic survival needs. Children who do not have their physiological needs met cannot move to the next level, and these deficits will impact play. This is very evident in developing countries. Children who do not have sufficient food and water do not have the strength and energy to run and jump. This is also a concern in the United States because many children are hungry and homeless. According to Kids Count (2013), the number of children age five and younger living in poverty has increased from 18% to 26% during the past five years. Schools that serve breakfast and nutritional meals at lunch are providing children with the fuel they need.

Psychological safety includes social and emotional safety. The teacher creates a climate in the classroom that assures the child that he is safe from ridicule, sarcasm, and verbal hostility. The Newtown, Connecticut school shootings have become a part of the national conversation and have created anxiety and concern for many children and their parents. For this reason, psychological safety is as much a concern as physiological safety. Although teachers are not able to control national safety issues, they can create safe zones in their classrooms. Children should feel safe when they go to the restroom, cafeteria, recess, or interact with other.

The second level of basic survival needs is the need for *belonging, love, and acceptance.* The need for emotional security is almost as critical for survival as food and shelter. Children who are experiencing attachment issues because a parent has left the classroom or has moved away from the home will not fully engage in play. Eric Erikson (2000) spent a great deal of time discussing the effect of a death in the family on the play of one child in his classic book *Childhood and Society.* The child's concern that the family would forsake him because he contributed to his grandmother's death permeated his block play. Today's children are equally affected by real trauma and perceived threats. Many teachers have written about changes in play observed after the September 11, 2001, terrorist attacks. Teachers who are inconsistent or irritable create similar concerns for young children. When children experience emotional insecurity, their emotional health is affected.

The third need for survival is a sense of *competence, approval, and recognition* from others. A unique aspect of humanness is the need for approval and recognition (Maslow, 1998). All children want to be a part of a group and, thus, seek the approval of others. This is a basic survival need that develops as children grow. By the age of five, children regularly engage in dramatic and sociodramatic play. Children who direct the play decide who will be chosen and who will be excluded. All children want to be a part of the group selected to ride on the bus or sail on the boat. Those who are left out of the play often end up in tears if the teacher does not intervene. By the end of kindergarten, the need to belong can be observed in play areas when seven or eight children crowd into a center as they engage in sociodramatic play while other play areas are empty. Children who do not believe they belong to a group will cease active participation and watch as others actively engage in social interactions during play. Teachers who use ridicule and sarcasm contribute to the demise of the child's self-esteem. When children lack self-esteem that is based on knowledge of authentic accomplishments, they cannot grow and develop.

The next levels of Maslow's hierarchy are not basic needs for survival but reflect the human need to grow and develop into healthy individuals. Level four deals with the need for *knowledge*. When basic survival needs are met, humans tend to seek knowledge. In the same way, when children have their basic survival needs met, their play flourishes. For example, they may build a school bus, and when an argument erupts about the nature of the bus, they will seek an authority (more knowledge peer, teacher, book, or computer) in their quest for additional information.

The fifth level is the need for *aesthetics, beauty, truth, and justice*. When all the other levels are met, humans seek beauty, truth, and justice. The concern for social justice can even be observed in children's play. Children move through stages of block building—from stacking blocks to balancing blocks on matching structures. When someone does not play fairly, children will protest, "That's not fair." These complex block structures and discussions of fairness do not occur in classrooms until basic survival needs are met so that energy can be channeled in other directions.

The final level of growth is **self-actualization**, toward which all humans are striving but no one—with the exception of exemplary individuals like Mahatma Gandhi, Jesus Christ, and Martin Luther King, Jr.—has attained. Children in classrooms led by caring adults who provide a stable, caring environment are free to take risks. They know that acceptance is not tied to their performance. Even if their block structures fall, they are still accepted as members of the group, so they can figure out why the blocks tumbled. A physiologically and psychologically safe environment provides an optimal environment for establishing self-esteem and autonomy, and this serves as a basis for growing and learning.

An Aesthetics-Based Approach 6-6 ✳ to Kindergarten

An aesthetics-based approach provides opportunities for individual emphasis on music, art, dance, poetry, and drama. Equally important, it values the integration of music, art, dance, poetry, and drama in meaningful activities. An integrated approach is one in which art concepts and practices are combined in relation to broad teaching and learning goals. Making such conceptual and

6-2 Masks allow children to take on a different persona. As the child develops his acting and storytelling skills, he is strengthening his capacity to engage in abstract thought, which is essential for higher-level thinking and problem solving.

© Cengage Learning 2015

process connections involves unifying the disciplines while at the same time recognizing that each of the fields of knowledge is different and distinct, with its own special content. (Wright, 2003, p. 262)

This is different from using a song to teach the days of the week. Rather, it integrates the structural, expressive, and process facets. Poetry and music are created as once. All academic content areas can be expressed through the arts, as products and processes of children's integration through the following:

- Music (listening, improvising, composing, learning musical literature)
- Dancing (imitating, interpreting, choreographing)
- Drama (role-playing, character building, miming, story building)
- Visual arts (using art media and processes to make props, masks, costumes, structures, backdrops; using lighting and projected images) (Wright, 2003, p. 265)

Storytelling can be used as the foundation of an aesthetics-based approach (Nyland & Acker 2012). Because the story has a basic structure that includes a plot, it can be extended to music and art as children create masks, costumes, and music (see Photo 6-2). Storytelling is a basic component of humanity and is found in all cultures. The use of the story as a basic component of the curriculum has been explored by Vivian Paley (1981). Children draw their stories, tell their stories, direct the production of their stories, and enrich their lives as they learn. Paley's books provide a wealth of information in this area.

An aesthetics-based play program encourages the use of the arts during and after play (Korn-Bursztyn, 2012). Music plays during block play. Stories arise and are recorded or drawn for revisiting. Opportunities to paint, sculpt, create, and paint at the easel are a part of daily play. Dance occurs in the music center or sociodramatic center as children don costumes and move to the music. When play is over, children can draw their stories, tell their stories, and act out their stories. Integrating the arts through play enriches both.

✳ 6-7 Play as a Medium for Learning

The push for academics has created a situation in which free or center-time play is being replaced by worksheets and flash cards. In some states, legislatures have even mandated that each day a certain amount of time be spent on specific subjects (Olfman, 2003). *If play is how children naturally learn and symbolic play is at its height at this time, then symbolic play can serve as a vehicle for learning.* Information about how children learn academic content through an aesthetics-based play program is presented in this section.

6-7a Language and Literacy

The variety of languages used in kindergarten classrooms has never been greater. Some children come to school as non–English speakers or with language difficulties. For these children, play provides a risk-free environment where they can play with words and acquire greater language skills. During play, children use words in a variety of ways. They make a variety of sounds as they pretend to fly, knock down blocks, or play dress-up. Literacy develops in the block center when they label their constructions, in the house area when they make up stories, in the art center when they complete visual representations of their world, in the puzzle center when they use visual clues to complete a picture or create a poster, and in the book center when they look at books. Music is a universal language, so children who may not know many words to a song can still enjoy the melody.

Literacy is enriched through this approach. When children act out stories, they are developing their sense of story—a prerequisite reading skill. Children who use puppets to dramatize a story are learning about characterization and plot development in the story. They are also learning the concept of beginning, middle, and end of the story. Children who have opportunities to develop their play simultaneously develop their stories and literacy skills. Language and literacy are supported through play when

- Children draw, tell, and act out their play.
- Play centers encourage language when children talk to each other.
- Play centers encourage literacy when children draw pictures and tell or act out stories about their play.
- Reading and writing materials are available in the home and block areas; costumes and materials are convenient for dress-up and for encouraging role-play. Props to encourage role-play, such as empty cartons and containers, are located in the house area. The availability of reading and writing materials encourages children to become familiar with the writing process, words, letters, and numbers. Adding coupons that can be exchanged also enriches play. Prop boxes with different themes should be rotated on a regular basis.
- Children's language is extended by using appropriate models and giving children opportunities to talk during play.
- Children participate in author's chair (which allows the child to read stories that she has written to the rest of the class), chart making, cooking, drama, documentation panels, finger-plays, guided reading, journals, poetry, reading aloud, shared writing, and storytelling.

6-7b Math

A play environment is a natural math environment. How many children can play at one center? What happens when too many people are in a center? How many plates are needed for dinner? Block center fosters the development of math concepts such as spatial relationships, symmetry, and patterning. Puzzles and toys stimulate critical thinking and problem-solving skills. Mathematic thinking involves the development of logical-mathematical knowledge. When children engage in sociodramatic play, they are creating linkages and relationships that stimulate mathematical thinking. Supporting mathematical thinking through play occurs when

- Play centers encourage mathematical thinking.
- Storage facilities promote storage of dishes, utensils, and other materials in order from smallest to largest.
- Materials include dishes and utensils, the use of which encourages the development of a sense of sets.
- Clean-up time teaches one-to-one correspondence. Shelves are labeled so children can match the block with the label when they are putting them away.
- Different storage bins for manipulatives and other counting materials are available.
- Pattern and bead cards as well as other materials are nearby.
- Props in the sand and water center encourage measuring.
- Clocks, calendars, and schedules are used throughout the day.
- Money is used in different play centers.

6-7c Science

A play environment stimulates science learning (see Photo 6-3). When children play with water in the water table, when they play with bubbles outdoors, when they play with sand and water, or when they paint, they are experimenting. Children are developing basic science concepts as they blow a cotton ball from one side of the table to the other side of the table. Children who carry the thermometer outdoors and back again are learning how to measure temperature. Children who pretend to camp in a refrigerator box that has been painted black and decorated with lights in the shape of different constellations begin to represent the differences between the night and day sky. These basic concepts serve as the foundation for science. When children communicate their science learning (play) through art, music, or stories, they develop a view of science as a part of their world, and this may stimulate some children to pursue a career in science. The arts and play can be integrated to teach basic concepts by ensuring that

6-3 Play and inquiry are intertwined.

© Cengage Learning 2015

- All centers stimulate science and inquiry learning.
- Investigative tools such as magnets, magnifying glasses, and a variety of balance scales are available so children can use them on a daily basis.
- Activities that cause discrepant events are available so children will be challenged to think about the experience and anticipated consequences versus reality.
- Science is encouraged in the sand and water center by using different props.

- Science is encouraged in the block center with pictures of unusual buildings.
- Plants are an ongoing part of the classroom. All plants are required to be nontoxic.
- A variety of musical instruments are available for experimenting with musical sounds.
- Paint and other methods of expression are available for both experimentation and communication.

6-7d Play and Social Studies

Social studies abound in the kindergarten classroom. From the house area to the sociodramatic center to the prop box, the focus is on social studies. Social studies is the study of the relationship between humans and ecology. It includes economics, history, geography, and multiculturalism. Play in the kindergarten classroom lends itself to teaching social studies. Dress-up clothes allow children to try on different roles. Prop boxes with community-based themes provide additional knowledge about their world. Support for social studies occurs through play when

- Play-based curriculum emphasizes a democratic classroom. When children choose their own center, they are a citizen in the classroom with all the rights and responsibilities therein.
- Play-based curriculum explores different topics through themes, units, or projects.
- Children listen to and share books and stories that relate to social studies.
- Children participate in different holiday experiences, such as Martin Luther King, Jr. day.
- Music is used to commemorate and celebrate holidays.
- Art is available as a means of cultural expression.
- Drama is a part of the program.

There is a major push for academics in today's schools, so the content areas of reading, mathematics, science, and social studies are the focus of attention. In 1989, the American Association for the Advancement of Science (AAAS) published the National Benchmarks to delineate content for different grade levels. Along with the Benchmarks, the Association issued a statement emphasizing what children should learn. According to the Association, adults should ask, "Will the proposed content enhance childhood—a time of life that is important in its own right—and not [be used] solely for what it may lead to in later life?" (AAAS, 1989, p. 21). This statement serves as powerful reminder of the importance of the child's quality of life.

Designing Play Spaces 6-8 ✳

Environmental design is second only to adult interaction in terms of influencing play. Indoor environments will be discussed in this section, and outdoor environments will be discussed in Chapter 10. The schools of Reggio Emilia refer to the environment as the third teacher in the classroom (Edwards, Gandini,

& Forman, 1998). Play centers provide a way to include multiple experiences for children. Traditional play centers include block, home, sand and water, art, puzzle, toys and puzzles, and special sociodramatic centers.

6-8a Blocks

Perhaps no other materials are more clearly identified with the kindergarten curriculum than wooden blocks. As mentioned earlier, plain wooden blocks have had a place in early childhood education for over a hundred years. These materials still form the nucleus of the block center.

To encourage play, the block center should be located in an area away from a walkway, low shelves should be available for storing blocks, and shelves should be clearly labeled. A variety of props should be available to stimulate pretense and more complex play. Labeling block constructions, adding writing materials, and placing charts and pictures on the wall can also stimulate learning. Using plexiglass tables and mirrors adds interesting dimensions to the block center.

Constructive play that occurs in this center is a combination of practice play and symbolic play. The child stacks, builds, and creates, then pretends that the construction is whatever she wants it to be. During the process, the child may quickly revert to building. This movement between building and pretense facilitates the child's mental agility.

Block play is valuable for understanding geometry and physics when children get older (see Photo 6-4). Research that supports this premise was conducted by Wolfgang, Stannard, and Jones (2001), who found that children who engaged in high-level block play also achieved higher grades on math tests in high school. Other research supports block play as a valuable activity in the kindergarten classroom.

6-4 Children learn mathematical concepts naturally when they engage in block play. As she builds, she is developing her knowledge of symmetry, patterns, balance, and measurement.

© Cengage Learning 2015

▶❚❚ **TeachSource** Video Case 6-2

© Cengage Learning 2015

2–5: Play in Early Childhood

Levels of social interactions first identified by Parten (1932) are described in the video. See Chapter 3 for a review of these stages.

1. Have you observed children engage in any play behaviors demonstrated in this video?

2. How can the teacher support children who are not involved in play?

Watch on CourseMate

6-8b Home Center

The home center stimulates dramatic play and sociodramatic play. **Dramatic play** occurs when the child uses symbolism to pretend. **Sociodramatic play** differs in that a group of children assign scripts and develop the play together. Kindergarten children are at the zenith of pretend play and can create a variety of play scripts in the home center (see Photo 6-5). Prior to this age, play scripts may be less complex, less developed. **Play script** is a term used to describe the conversations and interactions that occur during sociodramatic play. Children will assign and assume specific roles. The child's knowledge of the world is fully evident during this type of play. To encourage dramatic play by all children, the house area should have materials that reflect the different cultures represented in the class. It is especially important to include dolls with a variety of skin colors even though children of these ethnicities may not be represented in the class.

The house area helps children understand the need for food, shelter, and clothing throughout the world. Equipment for preparing food should be available and may include a stove, refrigerator, and sink. In addition, a table for eating and dishes for serving and sharing meals should be included. Storage for all materials should be available and clearly labeled. Dress-up clothes that encourage pretense should be available and should encourage self-help skills such as snapping, buttoning, and tying. Hooks, hangers, and storage should be available for storing materials.

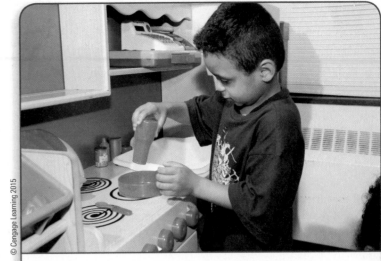

© Cengage Learning 2015

6-5 Dramatic play allows the child to control the play. In play, the child has the freedom to try, to do, to experiment, to fly, or not. It is the child who decides the direction of the play.

6-8c Special Sociodramatic Center

Establishing a special sociodramatic center allows the home area to remain a home area while the special center becomes a dentist's office. This allows children to visit the dentist and return home and, in turn, encourages pretense among a group of children. This center should be changed every two or three weeks as the children's interest waxes and wanes. Some topics that are especially interesting include a doctor's office, dentist's office, restaurant, grocery store, clothing store, hardware store, and veterinarian's office. Setting up centers that are familiar to children encourages pretense. Children can pretend to be a doctor who is taking a pulse or checking a heartbeat with a stethoscope. In this way, the center becomes very cathartic. That is, it helps the child work through an emotion-filled situation such as visiting a doctor or dentist.

6-8d Prop Boxes

Prop boxes are especially beneficial for this age group. A prop box can be used to store materials that stimulate sociodramatic play. A sociodramatic center can be set up in one area of the room, but prop boxes are mobile. A prop box can be taken outside or set up in the book center. Some themes that are especially interesting for prop boxes include a bank, campground, travel agency, and construction site.

6-8e Art Center

Art centers serve as the command center for play in an aesthetics-based program. The art center should provide children with an opportunity to create with paint or other sensory materials on a daily basis. The art center should be stocked with a good supply of paint, different sizes of paper, different kinds of markers, scissors that children can use, different types of play dough, and

6-6 Sensory play is a basic component of kindergarten. Children who play with measuring will develop a natural sense of measurement. The flow of sand facilitates the development of tactile sensory receptors.

© Cengage Learning 2015

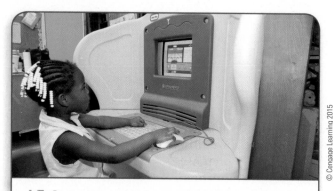

6-7 Computer centers invite children to develop their digital knowledge and skills in a natural environment that allows them to use the computer at their own rate and in their own way.

© Cengage Learning 2015

other materials for creating. Stamps and stamp pads should be available for making posters. The creation of an art center that children can use with and without assistance provides a place that encourages language, literacy, writing, and creativity.

6-8f Sand and Water

Montessori (1936, 1964) was the first to recognize the benefits of sensory materials for young children (Photo 6-6). A water table provides a place where children can experiment with sinking and floating boats of different sizes. The force and flow of water can be studied as water is poured and pumped. Sand provides a soothing material that can be manipulated, poured, and moved. Props can be added to encourage the development of roads and towns. Measuring materials can be used to extend play.

6-8g Toys and Puzzles

This center can be used to stimulate symbolic play and simple games with rules. As the child manipulates a puzzle, a problem is solved. Knowledge of rules is established as the child plays games and lotto. Perceptual and fine motor skills are developed as the child engages in manipulating toys. This center provides a unique setting for facilitating the development of specific skills through one-on-one play with the child.

6-8h Book Center

The book center is especially important in the kindergarten class. Many teachers create a loft area that provides a quiet area for children that physically removes them from the rest of the room. The use of plexiglas provides a safe, translucent barrier. The book center should have a good selection of high-quality books that are changed on a regular basis. The book center can also include DVDs with books, flannel boards with story characters, and metal white boards with metallic alphabet letters. Different books on a variety of levels should be available.

6-8i Computer Center

Most kindergarten centers have at least one computer. This center should be treated like any other center, with children rotating in and out on a regular basis (see Photo 6-7). Otherwise, one or two children will dominate the center. Many games are available, although most kindergarten teachers use the computer for encouraging writing. Children can write or dictate their stories. Pictures can be added, and the children can share their play experiences with their parents and other adults.

Ideas for encouraging play have been presented in terms of individual areas and in terms of interest centers. Teachers decide how these are put together. Several programs are available that can be implemented according to the program's guidelines. These programs generally use a philosophical base that promotes one theoretical perspective. The most common approaches are a traditional kindergarten model, HighScope, Bank Street, Montessori, Waldorf, Reggio Emilia, and approaches used by Head Start. Researchers found that the Head Start program is used more than other models throughout the United States (Walsh & Petty, 2007).

Some centers will choose one system as a framework for their curriculum, and this choice influences the type of play that occurs. Several models are included in this section: a traditional kindergarten, one influenced by constructivism, HighScope, Bank Street, and Reggio Emilia. A traditional American kindergarten model based on an eclectic theoretical stance is provided as the first model. This discussion does not include all available programs but focuses on the ones that are most commonly known and that have been discussed in previous chapters.

6-9a Traditional Kindergarten Program

A traditional model that has developed in America during the past one hundred years includes routines and activities that are familiar to most who have attended kindergarten or who have had children in kindergarten in the past few years. This approach was designed to develop "the whole child" and uses a holistic view of the child that considers cognitive, social, language, and physical development.

The day usually begins with a morning meeting that includes some form of group sharing (show and tell) experience. Songs, finger-plays, and nursery rhymes are usually included in the group meeting. This is followed by play that occurs both indoors and outdoors. Afterward lunch is served at midday, children listen to a story, and then children take a nap. When they get up from naptime, they play, sing songs, and go home with their parents or on a bus when the school day is over. There are different curriculum approaches that emphasize various aspects of the program, but all follow some sort of variation of this approach.

A routine helps children because young children view the routine as the rule. When thinking about the day, some activities can be viewed as routine activities that occur every day. Other activities may be nonroutine activities that require a special plan. Based on Maslow's theory, routines help children establish a sense of safety and security. One caveat: this is not to suggest that a rigid timeline should be imposed in kindergarten. In kindergarten, flexibility is the key. The following is a typical kindergarten schedule:

- Morning greeting
- Morning meeting
- Center play
- Outdoor play

- Lunch
- Storytime
- Rest
- Center play
- Recess
- Evening circle
- Evening farewell

Morning Greeting.   Children should be able to enter the classroom on an individual basis as they arrive at school. When kindergarten children wait in a hallway that does not have seats, they may sit on a cold floor for thirty minutes or more. If they go to a gymnasium with older children, they are seated on bleachers for at least thirty minutes. The same situation occurs when young children go into a cafeteria with older children. These settings may be fine for older children, but are not recommended for kindergarteners. Children should be able to enter the room individually, greet the teacher and other children, put materials in their own cubby labeled with their name, put away outer garments or other materials, and then select a math game, book, manipulative, or other activity. Providing children with a regular schedule facilitates their physiological and psychological safety and contributes to the development of autonomy and self-concept. **Autonomy** is the aim of education (Kamii & Houseman, 2000), and it describes behavior that is independent and self-reliant.

It is important that children are allowed to choose from several activities in the morning. Transitions in the morning and afternoon are the most problematic. Providing children with choices minimizes possible behavior issues and enhances the child's developing self-esteem.

Morning Meeting.   Circle time and sharing time have traditionally been associated with kindergarten. The morning meeting was initially designed to provide a time for children to come together as a group, share their news, show and tell, or discuss the events for the day. Over the years, it has changed, with some morning circles lasting for two hours—much longer than most children can sit still—and focused on memorizing academic content. A morning meeting is more important now than ever before. Children need to come together for a short meeting. They need to have an opportunity to share anything that is on their mind or new in their life (see Photo 6-8). Show and tell is effective and will not digress into "bring and brag" if the teacher sends a letter to parents stating the guidelines for show and tell. (First guideline: toys should not

© Cengage Learning 2015

6-8 Morning meetings provide an opportunity for integrating mathematics and movement.

be brought to school.) However, children should not be made to sit still for a two-hour morning meeting. Limit the meeting to twenty minutes or less. Let the children choose their centers by putting their name by the center. This can be done as they come into the room or as they leave the circle. Move children out of the circle using transition activities. It is never safe to just let a group of children run to their centers, because they will soon learn that the fastest runner gets her favorite center.

Transition Activities.   Transition activities provide a mechanism to move groups of children from one place to another or from one activity to another. Transitions are advantageous because they provide cues about the upcoming activity. Children know what to expect and have a plan for doing so. Some transition activities include calling all children who are wearing certain colors to line up, or giving children the uppercase or lowercase letter and asking for the children's whose first or last names begins with that letter to line up.

Morning Centers.   Play centers should have signs with words and pictures/symbols so the children can see their centers. Programs should also have a system for selecting play centers. Any system will work as long it is systematic and fair. When children have an opportunity to move to centers of their choice, they are engaged and can develop sophisticated and complex play. Centers that are traditionally found in a kindergarten class include block, house, art, sand, water, book, wood, toy and puzzle, computer, and a sociodramatic center that changes through the use of prop boxes. (Prop boxes were discussed earlier in this chapter.) Children should be allowed to stay in the center for an hour. It is never appropriate to ring the bell and require children to move to another center. When children are forced to move frequently, they do not develop concentration skills during play. They learn not to concentrate. At the same time, children should be allowed to move from center to center. Some routines may be needed for clean-up. Some teachers insist that children return to their play center to help clean up at the end of the center time.

During center time, the teacher can float throughout the room. Going from one center to another allows the teacher to monitor and participate in the play. This is also a time that an additional teacher or adult can work with small groups. Small group activities can include cooking, art, painting, and even assessment activities. Some classrooms will have snacks set up for children who are hungry during playtime. Children should not be forced to participate in activities unless they choose. Again, every child does not have to participate in every activity every day. It is more important that children are allowed to choose activities.

Ten minutes before play is over, move throughout the room and begin to give children a warning or signal that play will soon be ending. Also give a five-minute warning, such as announcing, "Children, we will begin clean-up in five minutes." When it is time for clean-up, put on some classical music or other music that is pleasant. Refrain from using a loud sound to signal clean-up because some children may be sensitive to abrasive sounds.

Transition.   When children have cleaned up their centers, they can use the bathroom, wash their hands, and return to the morning meeting area. This is a good opportunity to sing songs and do finger-plays.

Morning Recess. Outdoor play has always been a traditional part of the kindergarten schedule. Children benefit from outdoor play with their friends. They develop physical and social skills when they engage in active play. They also develop cognitively and morally when they participate in games. These are desirable outcomes for children. The teacher should monitor the play and move throughout the playground. It is never appropriate to talk to other adults, supervisors, or teachers while the children are playing. This is a time when accidents can happen quickly. Adults must be vigilant when the children are on the playground. Some centers can be set up on the playground. These are discussed in more detail in Chapter 9. Generally, recess should last for at least fifteen minutes to an hour. *Safety note: Before going outside, children should be checked to ensure that their attire is appropriate for the weather and that they are wearing sunscreen*. The children can keep sunscreen in their cubbies and put it on before going outdoors. Additional information on outdoor safety is available in Chapter 10.

Transition. Always use a signal to move children indoors. For example, using a fun signal such as train whistle or, better yet, moving around the playground like a train provides a fun way for children to join the line and prevents the power struggle that ensues when children fail to join the class line. That is, when the teacher stands at the edge of the playground and puts her hand up as a signal, some children may choose not to join the line to return to the class. When this occurs, the teacher is forced to engage the children in a discussion about going back to the room. This becomes a power struggle, and no one wins. Using a playful approach provides a different way to exit the play area. When children reenter the room, they can use the bathroom, wash their hands, and prepare for lunch. They can draw pictures or write in their journals while waiting for everyone to use the bathroom. Use transition activities to move the children to school-wide meetings, dining facilities, libraries, or other activities throughout the school.

Lunch. Teachers should eat with children. This allows them to monitor and model good eating habits. Some teachers of kindergarten classes in public schools leave the children during lunch for a duty-free lunch hour. Frequently, the issues that they face when they return negate the benefit of being away from the class. Some classes are allowed to eat in the room. When this occurs, the teacher can play music while the children dine, brush their teeth, and then move to journaling, books, or other activities.

Story Time. This is a good time for reading books aloud. This time should last between fifteen and forty minutes, depending on the interest of the children. After the story, children can get their cots or towels and transition to rest time.

Rest Time or Naptime. Rest time or naptime is an important part of the kindergarten day. Children should not be required to maintain a day that is equitable to that of an adult. Rest time provides a time for relaxation. Turn down the lights, play soft music, and allow children to rest with a stuffed animal or doll that they bring from home. This is a good time to play classical music. Some children prefer to look at books during this time. Again, children can have choices, but rest should be encouraged for at least forty minutes.

Gently begin to wake up children who are asleep five minutes before the lights go on. Give children the opportunity to go to the bathroom and get a drink of water.

Afternoon Center Time/Recess. Depending on the length of the day, children will be able to have afternoon centers or afternoon recess or both. Guidelines similar to those used in the morning should be followed.

Afternoon Meeting. The afternoon meeting provides a time for stories, songs, drama, and farewells. The afternoon/evening meeting should not last longer than twenty minutes. Just as each child is greeted individually in the morning, the teacher should bid each child farewell in the afternoon. As the teacher bids farewell, she can remind children to look inside their cubbies for any materials that they need to take home. At the same time, the teacher can take an additional look at the list of those who will be riding the bus, picked up by a parent, or walking home. If a child has a different plan for departure, experienced teachers will place a post-it note beside the child's name. *Be sure to monitor children who have a special restriction on parental or guardian pick-up.* Children should be able to stay in their classroom or play on the playground until they leave for the day. Leaving children in a cafeteria or gymnasium to wait for buses is less than optimal.

The preceding discussion provided an overview of a traditional kindergarten class for one day. The kindergarten schedule is generally adjusted to reflect the philosophy and interests of the teacher, the guidelines of the state, and local school rules. The teacher translates these interests, guidelines, and rules so that the child experiences an appropriate play-based program in kindergarten. Some teachers are influenced by constructivism, which is discussed later in this chapter.

6-9b Half-Day Program

Some activities that are included in the full-day program are also included in the half-day program. For example, activities that are typically found in a half-day program include the following:

- Morning greeting
- Morning meeting
- Center play
- Outdoor play
- Lunch
- Story and circle
- Dismissal

The major difference is that the evening activities don't occur. It is difficult to avoid the wish to include more in a half-day program, but it is advisable to ensure quality experiences rather than quantity. Table 6-2 provides suggestions for encouraging play on the first day of either whole-day or half-day kindergarten.

TABLE 6-2 Tips for Encouraging Play on the First Day of School

1. **Plan for the experienced and novice players.** Some children have attended preschool and are ready for this experience. Others have never stayed away from home for an entire day. Each child in the class brings a cadre of experiences to the class.

2. **Open a limited number of centers.** Too many materials can overstimulate and confuse the children. Play centers that are inviting on the first day include blocks, house, manipulatives and puzzles, and art (play dough). Using a limited number of materials will allow you to monitor the interactions and float throughout the room.

3. **Label each center in the room so the children know where to go.** Hang signs above each center. Make sure the signs are large enough to be seen (14" × 14") and can be suspended by fishing twine. Using white cardboard with pictures of the center is visually appealing. In some schools, fire codes prohibit hanging items from the ceiling. If this is the case, put the signs on the wall near the center.

4. **Take the children on a tour of the centers.** Let them look at the center and examine the materials, and help them develop a list of classroom rules. Help them consider the value of putting materials away when center time is over. Help them understand that this room is their home during the day and that neither teachers nor custodians can pick up toys for so many children. Make sure shelves are clearly labeled so children can easily replace materials when they finish.

5. **Develop a system for moving children to the centers.** If you don't have a transition plan, the children can fall over one another in their rush to get to their favorite center, and disputes can easily erupt over who was at the center first. Establishing routines on the first day can eliminate problems throughout the rest of the year. Some teachers put smaller versions of the center signs on a chart and allow children to select their center. Having a deck of cards with each child's name and picture on it allows children to see a fair system for selecting centers as they establish a democratic classroom. This system allows children to select the first center on a rotating basis.

6. **Ensure that children have at least an hour for play.** Children cannot engage in deep play unless they have uninterrupted time for play. During the first day, the teacher will be able to note who plays well and who watches. Children who are observing but not playing may need additional assistance or time.

7. **At the end of the playtime, go around the room and give the children a ten-minute warning that it is time to end their play.** Then give them a five-minute warning. Finally, give a signal by dimming the lights or ringing a chime that playtime is over for the day. Remind children that they can return tomorrow for more play.

© Cengage Learning 2015

✳ 6-10 Constructivism

Constructivism is based on the notion that children construct knowledge as they interact with their world. Constructivism has three different interpretations: cognitive, social, and symbolic constructivism. **Cognitive constructivism**, based on the work of Jean Piaget, emphasizes the child's internal construction of knowledge. **Social constructivism**, influenced by the writings of Lev Vygotsky, emphasizes the child's construction of knowledge through interaction with more knowledgeable others. **Symbolic constructivism**, informed by the work of Jerome Bruner, focuses on the child's construction of knowledge through symbolic systems such as narratives. Early childhood education has been most influenced by cognitive constructivism based on the work of Piaget. A constructivist model differs little from the traditional kindergarten model described in the preceding section. The kindergarten schedule depends on how the individual teacher interprets and implements it. If a teacher who has a behaviorist view of learning uses the schedule described in the traditional kindergarten, he might be very directive in how he implements the centers and activities. In contrast, a teacher influenced by constructivist pedagogy would focus more on giving the children opportunities to make choices about their centers and activities (see Photo 6-9). Classrooms that use a constructivist philosophy focus on sociomoral and cognitive issues and the establishment of mutual respect and cooperation between the teacher and child. Many teachers who follow a constructivist approach also use the project approach, which is described in the following section.

6-10a Project Approach

The project approach is grounded in a constructivist approach and the belief that children construct knowledge through interactions with the world. Vygotsky's (1978) sociocultural theory serves as a basis for this approach. The focus is on learning through social interactions with more capable peers. The child moves from a point of knowing with the assistance of others to appropriating the information as her own. During the project, inquiry will develop as well as critical thinking skills and creativity. The project approach provides a venue for facilitating social development, cognitive development, and parent involvement.

6-9 A constructivist approach provides opportunities for children to engage in small group play in different centers. The materials in this center can be used as children enter the classroom in the morning, during center time, or during transitional times.

The project is divided into three parts: Phase I, Phase II, and Phase III (Helm & Katz, 2001). The project begins with a provocation, which stems from the adult or child. This can take on many forms. One project began when an adult left an envelope filled with clues on a desk. The children tried to solve the mystery by following the clues, which led them on an exploration of the building. Responsive teachers who listen to children can generally seize the moment when the provocation occurs. For example, in one kindergarten class, the children were looking at a book about bread that someone brought for show and tell. The children were discussing the different kinds of bread that they eat and were amazed at the different types of breads eaten by their classmates. The teacher used this as a provocation and started a KWL (know, want, learn) chart about bread. A KWL chart provides a good instrument for organizing the project because children can see what they know, what they want to know, and what they have learned. Table 6-3 shows a sample KWL chart. The most important aspect of using the project approach with young children is to keep it age and individually appropriate.

TABLE 6-3 KWL Chart		
Phase I	Phase II	Phase III
What do we KNOW about this topic?	What do we WANT to know?	What did we LEARN?

Digital Download Download from CourseMate

Did You Get It?

A kindergarten teacher is careful to always give his students the opportunity to choose their own activities. He follows a _____ point of view.

a. traditional
b. constructivist
c. Eriksonian
d. Freudian

Take the full quiz on CourseMate

For example, after discussing what they knew about bread, children listed questions that they wanted to know about bread. This served as the impetus for the study. The children worked in three groups. One group worked on the first question, the second group considered the second question, and the third group attempted to answer the last question. The first group talked to everyone to find out how many different kinds of bread people in class ate. After they made a list, they decided to make a loaf of bread. The class met and decided on the type of bread. The team that was working on the question "How do you make bread?" was in charge of the cooking project. A field trip to a local bakery and grocery store supplied the materials. A bread center was established where children could create, bake, and sell bread. The children were able to engage in symbolic play as they engaged in role-play and pretend.

After the children began to tire of the center, they reviewed their chart. What did they learn about the bread? What did they learn about the cooking process? What were additional outcomes of this experience? Children can communicate their acquired knowledge through music, art, drama, and stories. Some teachers document the experience through pictures or viedeo. Children can use digital photography to help communicate their knowledge.

✳ 6-11 Commercial Models

Teachers who choose to use a traditional kindergarten or constructivist approach will find a variety of sources and resources available. There are also several well-known commercial models that can be used to structure the program. These include HighScope, Bank Street, and Reggio Emilia approaches.

6-11a HighScope

HighScope was originally developed as a preschool program but has been adapted for kindergarten in many systems. The HighScope program was designed as a cognitively based program. It places more emphasis on cognitive development than on sociomoral development. The HighScope program differs from the traditional program in that it uses a Plan-Do-Review approach. This process was explained in Chapter 5. Research supports the legitimacy of this approach (Belfield, Nores, Barnett, & Schweinhart, 2006). Children in the HighScope program made significant gains over children in programs using a more academic approach. After over two decades, the differences are still evident. Many kindergartens structure their programs around this approach.

6-11b Bank Street

As discussed earlier, the name, "developmental interaction" is generally used to refer to a model that has been used by Bank Street since the 1920s (Walsh & Petty, 2007). Kindergartens that use this approach focus on the democratic views put forth in this program. This program, more than any other program, uses the work of John Dewey (1903) to influence the classroom climate. Respect for the child as a person and citizen is evident in all aspects of the program. The focus is on learning through daily experiences with the indoor and outdoor environments. The indoor environment consists of art, sensory experiences, music, movement, gross motor experiences, blocks, and outings. Outings or field trips are a regular feature of the curriculum and occur in groups of two or three. Although the goals of the Bank Street approach are somewhat similar to a constructivist approach, the influence of Erikson and Dewey is prevalent. The underlying philosophy of Bank Street is developmental-interaction and emphasizes that children develop through social interactions with the world and others. This approach is markedly different from a constructivist approach because the developmental-interaction curriculum is more directive and focuses on literacy.

Kindergarten teachers influenced by the developmental-interaction approach assist the child in establishing social and emotional health. Home visits and the use of attachment objects to ease the home-to-school transition are techniques that have been used in programs directly or indirectly influenced by Bank Street. The source of the Bank Street curriculum is social studies, and this fits well with educational goals for kindergarten. Social studies focus on the "here and now" curriculum for kindergarten, which focuses on the child. For example, units can be developed on the topics, "Me," "My Family," or My Neighborhood." Units provide a venue for teaching social studies and revolve around experiences in the classroom and community. Books created by children and teachers in the Bank Street program reflect authentic experiences used in activities.

6-11c Reggio Emilia

Reggio Emilia is an approach named after a town in northern Italy where it originated and is based on the principles of a social constructivism. The philosophy is based on the work of Dewey and Vygotsky as interpreted by Loris Malaguzzi (New, 2003). At first glance, the program may look like a traditional kindergarten schedule. Children play in centers, play outdoors, eat, rest, and have group meetings. The program is different, however, because the children are not following a routine but are following their interests and research. In addition, interactions between the adults and children are different from those found in most kindergarten classrooms. Children in the Reggio Emilia program receive more scaffolding when completing projects than is typically observed in most kindergarten classrooms (Helm & Beneke, 2003). For example, during center time, the patio door may be open to provide indoor and outdoor play together. If a child is painting a picture of a flower, the child will be encouraged to look closely at the flower to capture the reality of the flower and will be encouraged to redo the painting until it reflects the child's best effort. This is very different from the American kindergarten. Children in the Reggio Emilia program work in groups. Every child does not participate in every activity. The focus is on the completion of the final project by the group.

Assessment in the Reggio Emilia influenced schools is very different from other program approaches and has the potential to impact kindergartens throughout the world. Assessment includes **portfolios** and **documentation panels**. Each child has a portfolio that moves with the child through the program. Portfolios contain samples of the child's best works. Documentation panels can be based on the work of one child or a group. The documentation panel illustrates how the child or group of children developed a project. There are many ways to illustrate how children are constructing knowledge. The schools of Reggio Emilia subscribe to a philosophy that every child has a hundred languages and a hundred ways of knowing. The Reggio Emilia assessment process reflects a hundred ways of assessing and documenting children's knowledge. This reflects a social constructivist approach to assessment and is vastly different from traditional kindergarten, which focuses on developmental norms.

What do you think?

An overview of different models has been presented. Which model do you think is most interesting? Share your views with your classmates.

Did You Get It?

In a kindergarten program, the students regularly take field trips to museums, stores, and other locations where they interact with other people and the environment. Their school follows the _____ model.

a. Bank Street
b. HighScope
c. Project Approach
d. Reggio Emilia

Take the full quiz on CourseMate

✱ 6-12 Toys, Puzzles, and Materials

Toys and materials add depth and breadth to the kindergarten classroom. Toys should provide children with the opportunity to turn knobs, manipulate pieces, and have fun while developing their fine motor, perceptual, and critical thinking skills. Good puzzles stimulate children's problem-solving abilities as they learn the mathematical concept of part to whole. The classroom should have a variety of toys and materials that can be replaced on hooks, labeled shelves, or containers. It is especially important at this age to have a variety of toys that meet the needs of those who are still in sensorimotor play stage, those who are engaged in dramatic or sociodramatic play, and those who are ready for games with rules. Some children will be ready for games like "Hi Ho! Cherry-O" or "Candy Land," whereas others will still need to play with tactile toys. The key is variety.

Cultural competence can be enhanced by including toys, puzzles, and materials that reflect different cultures. This is more evident in classrooms that have diverse populations. It is less apparent in classrooms with one ethnicity, such as all Caucasian, Spanish, or African American. A culturally homogenous classroom population might cause the educator to use dolls and materials that reflect that culture, but children in these rooms need to be exposed to other cultures. They need to see that there are different ways of being human. Books and posters provide a way to facilitate the child's knowledge of different families, communities, and cultures. Children at this age are very aware of gender when selecting materials.

✱ 6-13 Assessment

Unfortunately, the misuse and abuse of evaluation has affected the play of young children more than any other factor in the past decade. Assessment in kindergarten includes a variety of formative and summative instruments. Generally, a **screening instrument** is used at the beginning of kindergarten. A screening instrument is designed to reveal the need for additional evaluation, nothing more. Many young parents will buy materials for their young children based on their belief that these materials will prepare the child for the "kindergarten test." These screening instruments were never intended to be used as entry tests, but sadly, many schools will set a certain score as the entrance score for kindergarten admission. Given that most screening tests are based on the mastery of the items on the test, this is a complete misuse of the instrument. The unfortunate result is that the children who need kindergarten the most are blocked from entrance. Few who originally recommended the use of a quick screening instrument could have imagined this use and abuse of the test scores. Examples of screening instruments include the Gesell, the Brigance, the Lapp, the McCarthy, and the Peabody language screen.

6-4 Illustrate the role of the adult in implementing a play-based curriculum.

Appreciate the role of play in the child's life, provide children with daily access to play, adapt materials and experiences to the level of the child and slightly above, assess play to know how to enhance and expand play, and advocate for play in the life of the child.

6-5 Describe how Maslow's theory of basic needs informs kindergarten curriculum.

Maslow's theory is based on the idea that humans have basic survival needs that must be met. These include (1) physiological and psychological needs, (2) love and belonging, (3) approval and recognition from others, (4) knowledge, (5) aesthetics, (6) self-actualization. Using these six levels to inform curriculum places an emphasis on the whole child, not just the academic concerns.

6-6 Contrast an integrative approach to aesthetics with the process of adding songs, art, and movement to the curriculum.

An integrative aesthetics-based approach looks at how the arts can be used to inform the quality of the program. This contrasts with an approach that adds songs, movement, or art experiences without an overall plan.

6-7 Develop a plan for using play as a medium for learning literacy, mathematics, science, and social studies.

Play provides a platform for learning about the world naturally. Children engage in reading and writing, mathematics, studying the natural world, and understanding the social world as they play.

6-8 Design a play space with play centers found in traditional kindergarten programs.

The design should include block, home, art, sand/water, toys/puzzles, book, technology, and sociodramatic play centers.

6-9 Compare a whole-day kindergarten program with a half-day program.

A whole-day program has more time for play and other activities than a half-day program.

The advantage of the half-day program is that children do not tire as readily as in the whole-day program.

6-10 Evaluate the use of constructivism to inform a traditional kindergarten curriculum.

Constructivism informs the curriculum in two ways: It provides a systematic approach for asking questions about meaning making in the classroom and it facilitates the use of an inquiry approach such as the project approach.

6-11 Differentiate the HighScope, Bank Street, and Reggio Emilia programs.

The HighScope program is influenced by Piagetian theory and uses a Plan, Do, and Review approach. Bank Street is influenced by Eriksonian theory and uses an approach built around theme-based play centers. Reggio Emilia programs are based on the work of Malaguzzi who studied the philosophy of Piaget, Vygotsky, and Bruner (Edwards, Gandini, & Foreman, 1998). The Reggio Emilia program combines an aesthetics approach with the project approach.

6-12 Analyze how toys, puzzles, and materials enhance cultural competence.

Toys, puzzles, and materials must reflect cultural variation found in the classroom and throughout the world. Dolls in the home area must reflect minority cultures so that children can become familiar with different ways of being.

6-13 Identify formative and summative assessment strategies that can be used to document how children learn through play.

Formative assessment provides a venue for organizing observations and providing ongoing feedback. Summative assessment is used to consider where the child is in terms of reaching outcomes.

 ## Key terms

Autonomy, 172
Cognitive constructivism, 176
Constructivism, 176
Dramatic play, 168
Documentation panels, 179
Formative assessment, 181

Play script, 168
Physiological survival, 161
Psychological safety, 161
Portfolios, 179
Screening instruments, 180

Self-actualization, 163
Social constructivism, 176
Sociodramatic play, 168
Symbolic constructivism, 176
Summative assessment, 181

Technology and Internet Resources

American Library Association

http://www.ala.org The oldest and largest library association in the world supports this website. The site is designed to promote the highest-quality library and information services and public access to information. Both teachers and children will find this site helpful.

Bank Street College of Education

http://www.bnk.st.edu The Bank Street College of Education at Columbia University in New York has a website that offers research-based information on activities and experiences. The site also features a book corner with reviews of current publications, recommendations, and activities designed to extend the reading experience.

Montessouri International Index

http://www.montessori.edu Montessouri's methods are explained in detail, and the site provides connections to Montessouri groups around the world.

Smithsonian Museum NASM

http://www.nasm.si.edu/ The Smithsonian sponsors this website, which provides an array of educational materials.

School Improvement Research Series

http://www.nwrel.org The School Improvement Research Series is produced by the School Improvement Program of the Northwest Regional Educational Laboratory under a contract with the Office of Educational Research and Improvement U.S. Department of Education.

Activities

1. InClass Labs

A. In small groups, discuss the current influences that are impacting play in kindergarten classes in your area. Depict these graphically in terms of the microsystem, macrosystem, exosystem, mesosystem, and chronosystem discussed in Chapter 1. Display your chart in the classroom.

B. Discuss the impact of early entry into kindergarten on play. Contrast the impact of delayed entry into kindergarten. How can teachers create play opportunities that ensure challenging experiences for both children?

2. Research and Inquiry Learning

A. Visit a local kindergarten classroom. Watch the children during playtime. What activities are the children selecting? What is the most popular center? What is the least popular center? What factors are contributing to the different levels of interest in the most popular and least popular centers?

B. Interview two kindergarten teachers. Ask them to explain their philosophy of teaching. How are their philosophies alike? How are they different?

3. Service Learning

A. Volunteer in a kindergarten classroom for two hours per week. Are some children more engaged than others in play? Can you facilitate their interaction with others? Were you successful in doing so? Why or why not?

B. Create a toy that might be used in a local kindergarten classroom. What factors affected the design? What safety features were considered?

4. Family Connections

A. Create a letter for parents that discusses at-home play activities. The letter shown in Table 6-4 can be used as a template.

5. Play Advocacy

A. What are your state's and your community's policies for kindergarten attendance? Do children spend a whole day or half day in kindergarten? Are groups in your community advocating for a whole-day kindergarten? Why or why not?

B. Do the schools in your community require tests at the beginning and end of kindergarten? If so, how does this impact curriculum and play?

TABLE 6-4 Template for Letter to Parents

Dear Parents,

Young children learn through play. The list below contains some activities and games that you can use to encourage play at home. Some of these games can be purchased, and others can be made.

Games that can be purchased

Hi Ho! Cherry-O   Candy Land   Uno

Games that can be made

Cover-up   Bingo   Number cards for simple card games

A recipe for simple play dough is included on the back of this sheet.

Please contact me if you have questions.

Your Child's Teacher

© Cengage Learning 2015

Digital Download Download from CourseMate

 Visit CourseMate for this textbook to access the eBook, Did You Get It? quizzes, Digital Downloads, TeachSource Video Cases, flashcards, and more. Go to CengageBrain.com to log in, register, or purchase access.

 # References

Ainsworth, M. (1989). Attachments beyond infancy. *American Psychologist, 44*(4), 709–716.

American Association for the Advancement of Science (AAAS). 1989. *Project 2061: Science for All Americans* (p. 21). Washington, DC: AAAS.

Barnes, H. (1991). Learning that grows with the learner: An introduction to Waldorf education. *Educational Leadership, 49*(2), 52–54. EJ 434 784. (Also available: http://www.awsna.org/education-intro.html)

Bernier, A., Carlson, S. M., Deschenes, M., & Matte-Gagne, C. (2012). Social factors in the development of early executive functioning: A closer look at the caregiving environment. *Developmental Science, 15*(1), 12–24.

Bishop-Josef, S., & Zigler, E. (2011). The cognitive/academic emphasis versus the whole child approach: The 50-year debate. In E. Zigler, W. Gilliam, & W. S. Barnett (Eds.), *The pre-K debates* (pp, 83–88). Baltimore, MD: Paul Brooks Publishing Co.

Bowlby, J. (1988). *A secure base: Parent-child attachment and healthy human development.* New York: Basic Books.

Bronfenbrenner, U. (1997). Ecological models of human development. In M. Gauvain and M. Cole (Eds.), *Readings on the development of children* (4th ed.) (pp. 37–43). New York: Worth Publishers

Brostarman, N. (1997). *Inventing kindergarten.* New York: Harry N. Abrams.

Bruner, J. S. (2009). *Actual minds, possible worlds.* Cambridge, MA: Harvard University Press.

Copple, C., & Bredekamp, S. (2009). To be an excellent teacher. *Developmentally appropriate practice in early childhood programs serving children from birth through age 8.* Washington, DC: National Association for the Education of Young Children.

DeVries, R. (1997). Piaget's social theory. *Educational Researcher, 26*(2), 4–17.

Dewey, J. (1903). *Democracy in Education, IV*(4), 193–204.

Edwards, C., Gandini, L., & Foreman, G. (Eds.). (1998). *The hundred languages of children: The Reggio Emilia approach— Advanced reflections* (2nd ed.) Greenwich, CT: Ablex.

Erikson, E. H. (2000). *Childhood and society* (3rd ed.). New York: Norton. (Originally published in 1950.)

Fosnot, C. T. (1996). *Constructivism: Theory, perspectives, and practice.* New York: Teachers College Press.

Froebel, F. (1887/1902). *The Education of man.* (W. N. Hailmann, Transl.). New York: Appleton. (Originally published in 1826, copyright 1887.).

Gardner, H. (1999). *Intelligence reframed: Multiple intelligences for the twenty-first century.* New York: Basic Books.

Golinkoff, R., Hirsh-Pasek, K., & Singer, D.(2006). Why play = learning: A challenge for parents and educators. In D. Singer, R. Golinkoff, & K. Hirsh-Pasek's (Eds.), *Play= Learning: How play motivates and enhances children's cognitive and social-emotional growth.* Oxford University Press

Helm, J., & Beneke, S. (2003). *The power of projects: Meeting contemporary challenges in early childhood classrooms—strategies & solutions*. New York: Teachers College Press.

Kamii, C. with Housman, L. B. (2000). *Young children reinvent arithmetic: Implications of Piaget's theory*. New York: Teachers College Press.

Katz, L., & Chard, S. (2000). *Engaging children's minds: The project approach*. Stamford, CT: Ablex.

Kelly, R., Dissanayake, C., Ihsen, E., & Hammond, S. (2011). The relationship between symbolic play and executive function in young children. *Australasian Journal of Early Childhood, 36*(2), 21–27.

Kids Count. (2013). The 2013 Kids Count Book. Retrieved on July 11, 2013 from the Annie E. Casey Foundation site, http://datacenter.kidscount.org/files/2013KIDSCOUNTDataBook.pdf

Korn-Bursztyn, C. (2012). *Young children and the arts: Nurturing imagination and creativity*. Charlotte, NC: IAP—Information Age Publishing, Inc.

Maslow, A. (1998). *Toward a psychology of being* (3rd ed.). New York: Wiley. (Originally published in 1962.)

Montessori, M. (1936). *The secret of childhood*. B. B. Carter (Ed.). Calcutta: Orient Longmans.

Montessori, M. (1964). *Montessori method*. New York: Random House Digital, Inc.

New, R. (2003). Reggio Emila: New ways to think about schooling. *Educational Leadership, 60*(7), 34–39.

Nyland, B., & Acker, A. (2012). Young children's musical explorations: The potential of using Learning Stories for recording, planning and assessing musical experiences in a preschool setting. *International Journal of Music Education, 30*(4), 328–340.

Olfman, S. (Ed.). (2003). *All work and no play… How educational reforms are harming our preschoolers*. Westport, CT: Praeger.

Paley, V. (1981). *Wally's stories*. Cambridge, MA: Harvard University Press.

Parten, M. (1932). Social participation among preschool children. *Journal of Abnormal Psychology, 27*, 243–269.

Piaget, J. (1962). The stages of the intellectual development of the child. In S. Harrison & J. McDermott (Eds.), *Child-hood psychopathology* (pp. 157–166). New York: International Universities Press.

Roskos, K. A., & Christie, J. F. (2011). Mindbrain and play-literacy connections. *Journal of Early Childhood Literacy, 11*(1), 73–94.

Rushton, S. P. (2011). Neuroscience, early childhood education and play: We are doing it right! *Early Childhood Education Journal, 39*(2) 89–94.

Rushton, S., Juola-Rushton, A., & Larkin, E. (2010). Neuroscience, play and early childhood education: Connections, implications and assessment. *Early Childhood Education Journal, 37*(5), 351–361.

Russ, S. W., & Fiorelli, J. A. (2010). Developmental approaches to creativity. *The Cambridge handbook of creativity* (pp. 233–249).

Schweinhart, L. J., Montie, J., Xiang, Z., Barnett, W. S., Belfield, C. R., & Nores, M. (2005). *Lifetime effects: The High/Scope Perry Preschool study through age 40*. Ypsilanti, MI: High/Scope Press, 2005.

Shornkoff, J., & Phillips, D. (2000). *From neurons to neighborhoods: The science of early childhood development*. Washington, DC: National Academy Press

Trawick-Smith, J. (2010). Can classroom play ease the transition to a new culture? Applying research on young children from Puerto Rico. *Diaspora, Indigenous, and Minority Education, 4*(2), 92–102.

Vygotsky, L. (1978). *Mind in society: The development of higher psychological processes*. Cambridge, MA: Harvard University Press.

Vygotsky, L. S. (2004). Imagination and creativity in childhood. *Journal of Russian and East European Psychology, 42*(1), 7–97.

Walsh, B. A., & Petty, K. (2007). Frequency of six early childhood education approaches: A 10-year content analysis of *Early Childhood Education Journal*. *Early Childhood Education Journal, 34*(5), 301–305.

Wolfgang, C. H., Stannard, L. L., & Jones, I. (2001). Block play performance among preschoolers as a predictor of later school achievement in mathematics. *Journal of Research in Childhood Education, 15*(2), 173–180.

Wright, S. (2003). *The arts, young children, and learning*. Boston, MA: Allyn & Bacon/Longman.

3 PLAY in School Settings

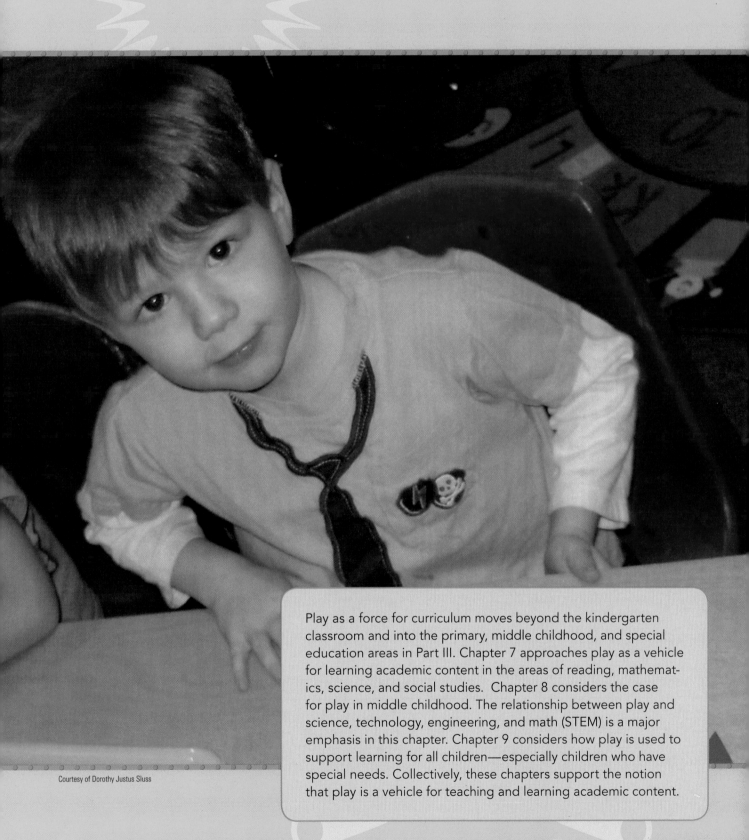

Courtesy of Dorothy Justus Sluss

Play as a force for curriculum moves beyond the kindergarten classroom and into the primary, middle childhood, and special education areas in Part III. Chapter 7 approaches play as a vehicle for learning academic content in the areas of reading, mathematics, science, and social studies. Chapter 8 considers the case for play in middle childhood. The relationship between play and science, technology, engineering, and math (STEM) is a major emphasis in this chapter. Chapter 9 considers how play is used to support learning for all children—especially children who have special needs. Collectively, these chapters support the notion that play is a vehicle for teaching and learning academic content.

7 Supporting PLAY in Primary School

STANDARDS COVERED IN THIS CHAPTER

Council of Exceptional Children—Division of Early Childhood Standards (CEC) (DEC)

ECSE 2S1 Apply current research to the five developmental domains, play, and temperament in learning situations

ECSE 3S1 Develop, implement, and evaluate learning experiences and strategies that respect the diversity of infants and young children and their families

ECSE 4S1 Plan, implement, and evaluate developmentally appropriate curricula, instruction, and adaptations based on knowledge of individual children, the family, and the community

ECSE 5S4 Structure social environments, using peer models and proximity, and responsive adults to promote interactions among peers, parents, and caregivers

✳ LEARNING OBJECTIVES ✳

7-1 List the benefits of play for primary age students.

7-2 Identify strategies that adults can use to support play in primary classrooms.

7-3 Explain the role of play as a medium for learning.

7-4 Name four content areas that can be connected and enhanced through play.

7-5 Develop a plan for implementing inquiry projects.

7-6 Compare and contrast program models for primary school.

7-7 Design a primary classroom with at least five defined areas.

7-8 Describe a play-based assessment system.

© Cengage Learning 2015

ECSE 7K2 Plan and implement developmental and academic content

ECSE 7S2 Plan and implement developmentally and individually appropriate curriculum

NAEYC Program Standards

4a Understanding positive relationships and supportive interactions as the foundation of work with children

4c Using a broad repertoire of developmentally appropriate teaching and learning approaches

5a Using content knowledge and resources in academic disciplines

5c Using knowledge, appropriate early learning standards, and other resources to design, implement, and evaluate meaningful and challenging curricula for each child.

✳ PLAYSCAPE: CASE STUDY

Alana does not want to go to school. She has to go to a new school after recently arriving from Russia. Her English is not good, and she is not happy about the move. But her mother says the move to a new country will give her a new life and more opportunities than she had in her home country. Still, she misses her home and dreads a new school.

When Alana arrives at school, she is greeted by her new teacher, Ms. Johnson, who introduces herself and some of the children to Alana. Then she gives Alana a tour of the room. Alana notices the different areas filled with games and activities. She has never seen a classroom like this. When the tour is finished, she begins playing a game of checkers, which she knows from her home country. The bell rings, the children put away the materials, and they go to the rug area for morning meeting. They sing and dance and play some games. Alana is delighted! Afterward, she spends an hour in centers working on games that involve mathematics, reading, and writing skills. The teacher works with small groups, and soon Alana is able to demonstrate her proficiency in reading English as she reads the items in the restaurant that was set up in the room. After lunch, she goes outdoors for recess and returns to the room to engage in project time. She thinks this might be science, but she is not sure because it involves building a tower with paper towel rolls. She loves this school and is disappointed when the day ends.

She stays in the afterschool program, and when her mother arrives Alana tells her, "Momma, Momma, I love this school!"

"Why do you like this school so much?" her mother asks.

"Oh, Momma, we played all day! It is wonderful!"

Alana's mother is alarmed. "You played all day in first grade? That doesn't seem right!"

Explaining Play Behaviors

Alana's mother is like many parents. She wants the best outcome for her child. Although she wants her child to enjoy school, she may wonder if Alana is receiving the experiences that she needs in this new school. Is the education program rigorous enough? Will Alana be prepared for the higher grades? These are the concerns that she voiced when she met Alana's teacher the next day. How can children play and learn? How will they be prepared for their next level of education? All parents and teachers struggle with these questions as they look at primary curriculum. Today, knowledge of the brain and how it functions confirms scholars' findings that children learn best when play is a part of their life (Rushton, Rushton, & Larkin, 2010). Teachers who have studied the multiple benefits of play are prepared to respond to Alana's mother and to serve as advocates for play in the primary classroom.

Benefits of Play for Primary
Age Students

In first- and second-grade classrooms, children display some of the characteristics found in kindergarten children, but they are beginning to move into another level of development. They are beginning to develop a need for order, a need to belong, and a sense of self (Hughes, 2010). Primary play reflects characteristics typically found in school-age children. In the cognitive domain, the child is developing logical thought and has a *need for order* and structure (Piaget, 1962). Socially, the child wants to be accepted by his peers and has a *need to belong to a group*. The child is in what Erikson described as the industry versus inferiority stage (Erikson, 2000). The child needs to develop confidence and a sense of self, and this need will affect the type of play that occurs in the primary years (see Photo 7-1).

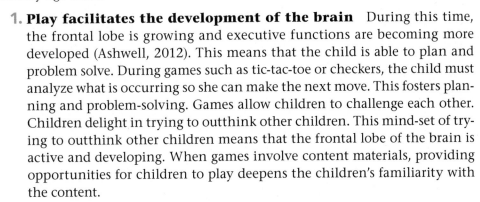

7-1 The need to belong to a group increases during the primary years. Group games are especially powerful and important for this age group.

Symbolic play decreases during the primary years and the use of games with rules increases. Primary play is dominated by games. As children develop a sense of self and become more interested in belonging to groups, games become more important. Using primary play to foster academic development enables children to learn naturally.

Using play and games as pedagogy has many positive outcomes for the primary age child:

1. **Play facilitates the development of the brain** During this time, the frontal lobe is growing and executive functions are becoming more developed (Ashwell, 2012). This means that the child is able to plan and problem solve. During games such as tic-tac-toe or checkers, the child must analyze what is occurring so she can make the next move. This fosters planning and problem-solving. Games allow children to challenge each other. Children delight in trying to outthink other children. This mind-set of trying to outthink other children means that the frontal lobe of the brain is active and developing. When games involve content materials, providing opportunities for children to play deepens the children's familiarity with the content.

2. **Play facilitates the child's developing social system and sense of self** Children are beginning to enter what Erikson referred to as the industry versus inferiority stage. They begin to see themselves as either proficient or deficient. As they play games with others, they learn turn taking, how to follow rules, and how to handle winning and losing. This contributes to their self-control and sense of self.

3. **Play provides an outlet for physical movement and experimentation** Six- and seven-year-old children are experiencing rapid and uneven growth. Although their large muscles may experience rapid growth, their perceptual and balancing skills may not be developing at the same rate. Practicing their locomotor skills, such as running, hopping, skipping, and climbing, facilitates their coordination, movement, and group interaction skills.

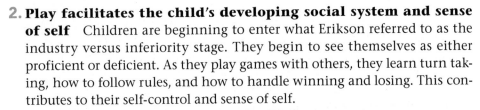

Did You Get It?

A seven-year-old becomes angry and throws his hand of cards on the floor when he loses at a game of "Uno." He is struggling with the stage Erikson described as
a. winning vs. losing.
b. proficiency vs. deficiency.
c. industry vs. inferiority.
d. sharing vs. arrogance

Take the full quiz on CourseMate

4. Play contributes to the child's overall health Children who are in the first and second grade are developing habits for life. This is the time when they make healthy or unhealthy choices about food and movement. These choices contribute to habits that are engrained for life. Children who are allowed to overeat, spend evening time in front of a television or computer screen, or engage in other unhealthy activities will struggle to change these habits as they move into the middle childhood years. Children who spend time during the day and evening playing outdoors with friends experience cognitive, social and emotional, and physical benefits that lead to overall good health (Photo 7-2).

7-2 Although this is not an ideal play space, these children are enjoying the benefits of play.

© Cengage Learning 2015

✳ 7-2 Role of Adults

The role of the teacher changes in the primary grades. They still have a role in supporting play. Creating the context for play requires that adults use their knowledge of children's development and interests to guide program development (Martlew, Stephen, & Ellis, 2011). For example, they must know that children at this age are in the concrete operational stage and that somewhere around the age of six, the child's vision is developed sufficiently to focus on print. Combining a newly acquired focus on text and the development of logical thought enables children to engage in complex cognitive tasks. Teachers must be ready for and capable of supporting and challenging children. Adults support play in the following ways:

- Providing opportunities for budding talents in diverse areas
- Designing games
- Encouraging creative dramatics
- Providing appropriate intervention on playground
- Providing activities that provide legitimate play-based learning experiences (Photo 7-3)

Adding materials enhances the experience and creates new possibilities. Table 7-1 includes a variety of materials that can extend the play for primary age children.

7-3 Young children enjoy games that have a competitive component. Adults foster this play when they provide appropriate games and materials.

TABLE 7-1 Basic Play and Learning Materials for Primary Age Children

- Small figures that may be used in fantasy scenes and constructed models.
- Materials for enacting real-life activities (buying and selling, checking out books, sending letters), and materials (to make props and costumes) for plays and performances (role-play materials). A variety of puppets provided to or made by children (characters appropriate to children in the group) so children can replay familiar stories and give performances and shows.
- A variety of materials for constructing play scenes and models—to be used with blocks and construction materials (ages six and seven)
- A large variety of puzzles (jigsaw, three dimensional), including 50- to 100-piece jigsaws and map puzzles.
- A large variety of specific skill-development materials, including printing and book-making materials, math manipulatives, measuring equipment, materials for learning about money and telling time, science materials (including those related to weather, the solar system, plant and animal life, and basic human anatomy), and computer programs.
- Complex pattern-making materials (mosaic tiles, geometric puzzles) to develop spatial, mathematical, and artistic understanding.
- A variety of games to develop interaction skills, planning skills, skills for using strategies, and an understanding of rule systems. Examples include simple reading, spelling, and math games; guessing or deductive games; memory games; simple card games; and beginning strategy games (games may be created by the children).
- A large variety of art and craft materials, including both graphic and malleable materials appropriate for practicing skills and producing products.
- Recorded music for group singing, moving, and rhythm activities, and equipment for listening and recording.
- A variety of balls and equipment for specific sports activities, such as kickball, and materials for simple target games.
- Complex outdoor and gym equipment (may include climbing gym, swings, slides, ladders, seesaws), especially for ages six and seven, for acrobatics.

Source: Adapted from *The Right Stuff for Children: Birth to 8* (pp. 26, 42, and 81), by M. B. Bronson, 1995, Washington, DC: National Association for the Education of Young Children. Copyright 1995 by the National Association for the Education of Young Children. Reprinted by permission.

✳ 7-3 Play as a Medium for Learning

Looking for play in primary school through the same lens as in preschool may create a situation that provides an incomplete picture of play in the primary classrooms. Play at the primary level involves more inquiry and exploration and less pretend play. The context for play in a preschool classroom might include blocks and a house area, whereas the context for play in a primary classroom might include blocks but may also include materials necessary for conducting science experiments and completing project work (Ortlieb, 2012).

© Cengage Learning 2015

7-4 Classrooms that promote an aesthetics-based approach provide opportunities for movement, music, and art every day.

7-3a Aesthetics

Primary classrooms that use an aesthetics-based approach integrate content that extends the child's learning experience. Combining music and math; art and literacy; movement and social studies; or music and science increases possibilities for neurological connections. Gardner's theory of multiple intelligences suggests that children have many ways of knowing the world (Gardner, 1983). An aesthetics-based approach optimizes opportunities for learning and understanding. When children combine music and movement through play, they can dramatize history by acting out stories from long ago. Children who are able to paint pictures after visiting an aquarium or draw pictures of foliage observed on an outing develop not only knowledge and skills, but also a disposition for learning (Photo 7-4).

7-3b Music

Primary age children are predisposed to enjoy music and can learn through integrating music with other content areas. Budding talents begin to emerge at this age. Children can learn simple tunes, play simple instruments, and develop their talents. They are ready to perform, create, and respond to music. The relationship between music and reading has been discussed on the website of the Music Teacher's National Association. See Technology and Internet Resources at the end of this chapter. The use of symbols for music and symbols for reading requires similar abstract thought. Children who may not read easily may sing easily. This realization has led to the integration of music with different areas. For example, when music plays softly in the background during writing time, children can be observed tapping or nodding to the beat of the music. It relaxes, comforts, and stimulates the child as they write. This is an aesthetic approach that integrates music, writing, and play. Music also bridges cultures. Children who have a special knowledge of a culture or ethnic group can share music and enhance the sense of community in the classroom.

7-3c Movement

Movement and motor development are especially important at this age. Developing gross and fine motor skills enables primary children to develop content-related skills. For example, children enjoy games with movement and learning, such as tossing games that require them to add the number of tosses. Children also enjoy dancing and moving to music. Dance provides an opportunity for children to act out feelings and emotions.

When movement is a part of the curriculum, other benefits are often realized. Obesity rates have doubled since 1970 (Elliott, 2002). The American Heart Association reports that between 1971 and 1974 and between 2007 and 2008, the prevalence of obesity for children in the six- to eleven-year-old range has increased from 4.0% to 19.6 %. Encouraging movement is more important than ever. Outdoor play provides an excellent way to encourage movement and physical activity.

7-3d Art

Appreciating and creating art is an important but often overlooked part of the primary classroom. Children who can begin their day with music and art have opportunities to integrate them into their work throughout the day. Children can paint, draw, use clay and other materials for modeling, drawing, making puppets, creating collages, using paper mache, and engaging in a variety of creative activities. Different opportunities are available when educators use different tools, mediums, and materials. Tools for painting can range from brushes to feathers, sticks or string for painting, or even paintbrushes. Materials that can be used for painting can range from bubble plastic to cloth. The medium can range from paint to glue. Changing the tools, medium, and materials alters the experience and optimizes opportunities.

Curriculum Connections 7-4 ✳

Play can be used to connect four content areas: literacy, mathematics, science, and social studies. This integration provides a reflection of real life and creates a more meaningful learning situation for the children (Sandberg & Heden, 2011).

7-4a Reading

The goal of fostering literacy in primary classrooms is paramount in most school systems. The actions taken to accomplish this goal, however, do not always have the desired effect (Fountas & Pinnell, 2013). Combining play and literacy provides a better approach for encouraging literacy in the primary school. Play is self-motivating to children, in part because they direct it. In the same way, literacy activities should be meaningful to children. This can be accomplished through a play-based literacy program that focuses on meaningful, real-life activities.

In an effective literacy program, children should have the following:

- daily experiences of being read to and independently reading meaningful and engaging stories and informational texts

- a balanced instructional program that includes systematic code instruction along with meaningful reading and writing activities

- daily opportunities and teacher support to write many kinds of texts for different purposes, including stories, lists, messages to others, poems, reports, and responses to literature.

- writing experiences that allow the flexibility to use nonconventional forms of writing at first (invented or phonic spelling) and over time move to conventional forms (Photo 7-5)
- opportunities to work in small groups for focused instruction and collaboration with other children
- an intellectually engaging and challenging curriculum that expands knowledge of the world and vocabulary
- adaptation of instructional strategies or more individualized instruction if the child fails to make expected progress in reading or when literacy skills are advanced (IRA/NAEYC, 1998, p. 42)

The National Association for the Education of Young Children and the International Reading Association have developed a position paper on reading instruction in the primary grades that was mentioned in Chapter 4. Using the arts to extend the reading program optimizes learning for children who have many multiple ways of knowing.

7-5 Opportunities to write using a variety of materials are an important part of literacy experiences for young children.

© Cengage Learning 2015

7-4b Mathematics

Math instruction at the primary level uses a hands-on approach to foster the development of mathematical concepts. As children develop more logical mathematical thinking skills, they become proficient with math. The National Council of Teachers of Mathematics (NCTM) established national standards that are used by many states as guidelines for developing state requirements in math. Clements and Sarama (2009) recommend seeing standards as a vision with guidelines rather than a punitive measure. NTCM recommends an emphasis on number operations and geometry during the primary years. Patterns, measurement, and data collection add to understanding and should be integrated in all activities (Clements & Sarama, 2009). Preparing students to compete in an international marketplace requires that they are competent in mathematics, and this requires informed, competent teachers who understand how to implement a challenging curriculum (Smith, 2012). Play provides a natural venue for creating a challenging, meaningful math curriculum.

There are two ways to approach math instruction through play. One is through planned activities, experiences, and games that stand alone. The other is through an integrated play theme, which is discussed later in this chapter.

Planned activities, experiences, and games must be meaningful, reflect real life, and be appropriate for the primary age child. Math materials should be placed in the room so children can always obtain math manipulatives or games. Blocks should be part of the math program in primary schools because children can see the concepts of geometry and physics. When children are building with triangles and half circles, they are learning geometry through block play. Legos are interesting for both boys and girls. Games placed on a table provide an opportunity for children to play games while waiting for the teacher to start the class. Games provide the best venue for learning for primary age children.

Games can be used to teach first and third graders using the same materials. For example, two children get number cubes (dice) from the shelf and scrap paper from the bin. One child begins by rolling the number cubes. The numbers are 4 and 3. If the child is in first grade, he would write the numbers on the paper and add them together. If in third grade, he might multiply the numbers. When the play time is over, the children can spin a game board that is divided into higher or lower. If the spinner lands on "higher," the child with the highest number wins. If the spinner lands on "lower," the child with the least wins. This provides both children an opportunity to win and lose.

It is important to note that teachers must make a special effort to ensure that math instruction interests and involves girls. In a 2009–2010 data snapshot, girls comprise 36% of the preschool population, 46% of the population in kindergarten, and 49% of the population in elementary school. Although the interest level displayed by girls and boys is very similar in elementary school, there continues to be a discrepancy, with girls trailing in their participation in math classes in the secondary schools, college, and graduate classes (Gender Equity in Education: A Data Snapshot, 2012). Teachers who emphasize math for girls make a difference in ensuring that girls have equal access to a high-quality education.

© Cengage Learning 2015

7-6 When children play math games, they learn math skills as they develop a positive attitude toward mathematics.

7-4c Science

Science and play are linked. Science is a way of experiencing the world. Jarrett and Burnley (2007) found that many scientists describe themselves as playful and view science as their play. One goal of science instruction is to encourage **inquiry** as a way of investigating the world. Inquiry-based learning includes describing objects and events, asking questions, constructing explanations, testing explanations, and communicating results to others. Primary age children are natural scientists who ask, "Why ?" The National Science Education Standards developed by the National Research Council (2012) recognize inquiry as a central tenet of science education. The standards further assert that science education must be developmentally appropriate, interesting, relevant, inquiry based, and integrated with other subjects. Play provides a natural vehicle for understanding scientific principles.

Primary age children have certain attributes that predispose them to science. First, they are naturally curious. They want to know how and why everything works as it does. They enjoy books with titles such as *Everything You Want to Know about the World*—books that answer questions about the color of grass or why the wind blows. Second, they enjoy order and they delight in collecting; they create collections out of almost anything, and they are fascinated by collections of all sorts (e.g., rock collections, seashell collections). As they collect and sort, they are classifying materials. Third, they are developing a sense of self. Many primary age children are developing budding talents that will affect their career choice (Photo 7-7). Recently, in a conversation with this author, Dr. Jim Sluss (2013), who holds a medical degree as well as a PhD in biochemistry, shared that his interest in science was stimulated by a teacher in the second grade who routinely did science projects with the

Courtesy of Dorothy Justus Sluss

7-7 Girls are naturally drawn to science in the primary grades.

class. Fourth, children want to belong at this age, so interacting with each other to solve problems provides a mechanism for developing their negotiation and cooperation skills that are so important for lifelong success.

Science learning can occur through themes, units, or projects, or it can be included in a play program, which is discussed later in this chapter. Themes or units are designed by teachers and feature definite goals, objectives, activities, and evaluations. Projects are open ended and based on emerging knowledge. Projects provide an optimal opportunity for discovery and, thus, for science.

7-4d Social Studies

Social studies, perhaps more than any other content, is intertwined in play. Bank Street and other play-based educational programs in the 1920s used social studies as a basis for the curriculum. Throughout the past century, three approaches influenced the social studies curriculum: (1) the **social skills**, (2) the here and now, and (3) the holiday curriculum (Seefeldt, Castle, & Falconer, 2013). The **social living curriculum** focuses on the development of skills necessary to negotiate the social world. Social skills such as turn taking, self-help skills, and following directions provide a foundation for citizenship. The **here and now curriculum** focuses on providing a curriculum that is meaningful and relevant to the child. This approach can be used to integrate all content areas through play. The here and now curriculum is considered to be the most appropriate approach in primary school. The **holiday curriculum** is built around holidays. Many teachers refer to this as the calendar curriculum, and although it offers the opportunity to familiarize children with national observances such as Thanksgiving, President's Day, and Martin Luther King Day, it has limits. Many who use the holiday curriculum include Christmas and Easter as holidays. These are Christian holidays, not national holidays. If religious holidays are celebrated for one culture, then all cultures represented in the room must also celebrate their religious holidays or none should be observed. Democracy is better served when parents celebrate religious holidays at home and schools celebrate national holidays.

Today, the social studies curriculum is informed equally by the work of Piaget (1962), Vygotsky (1978), Dewey (2008), and the most current work on brain-based learning (Rushton, Rushton, & Larkin, 2010). The social studies curriculum is active, meaningful, integrative, challenging, and value based (Seefeldt, Castle, & Falconer, 2013). Play provides one way to meet the goals of the social studies curriculum by integrating information in units, themes, or projects. For example, setting up a bank in the room allows children to role-play the job of banking employees, understand the process of money exchange, and perhaps develop an interest in economics that will last a lifetime. Children can begin to develop an understanding of needs and wants as they develop basic knowledge of a budget.

✳ 7-5 Inquiry Projects

Inquiry projects allow students to understand the connections and relationships among the content areas of reading, math, science, and social studies. This approach, which encourages children to utilize inquiry and critical thinking skills, was explained in Chapter 6. This section contains information for project implementation at the primary level.

7-5a Phase I: Planning and Organizing

The provocation for a project can come from the children, parents, the teacher, or the community. The media may also influence the children's source of topics. The teacher's role is to guide the process of topic selection. Project topics must be appropriate for the age level, must be meaningful, and must be culturally relevant. For example, children who live in the Northwest area of the United States might find topics related to trees, snow, or ice interesting, whereas children in the southern part of the United States may find topics related to the ocean interesting. Encouraging children to examine topics that are in the here and now also encourages children to learn identification of local flora and fauna, and this is part of many state curriculum guidelines.

KWL. There are several ways to organize project work; one way is to use a KWL chart. The chart basically is divided into three sections that address three questions: What do we know? What do we want to know? What did we learn? The KWL chart helps organize the project and illustrate the learning that occurred. A KWL chart provides a good instrument for organizing the project. Table 7-2 shows a sample KWL chart.

Graphic Organizers. After the KWL chart has been created, the teacher can put the topic of investigation in the middle of the chart and place the children's questions around the topic. Now the class is ready to implement the plan.

7-5b Phase II: Implementing the Project

After the initial planning has occurred, the children can begin an investigation to answer their questions. For example, two questions that might evolve from a study of shells are, "Where do they come from?" and "Are there different types of shells on the beach?" To answer the first question, the teacher may want to secure a set of books about the beach, take the children to the library to research the topic, or invite a guest speaker to talk about the animals that live in shells. To address the second question, the teacher may want to take the children to the beach to explore the vast quantities and varieties of shells on the beach. Children will gain various competencies from this experience, such as sorting and classification, both of which reinforce math skills. Through this experience, they are exposed to the animal's ecological niche, and they have an impetus for learning more about the ocean and beach. This is "scienceing" at its best.

TABLE 7-2 KWL Chart		
Phase I	**Phase II**	**Phase III**
What do we KNOW about this topic?	What do we WANT to know?	What did we LEARN?

© Cengage Learning 2015

Digital Download Download from CourseMate

Developing Areas of Play at Clemson Elementary School

Paul Prichard, EdD

When it came time to build a new school, we were given the opportunity to form a building committee to help with the planning. Our committee not only benefited from the experience of the teachers and community members, but we also gathered information from our students, who knew what they wanted in their ideal school. Children described their desires and also drew pictures of many interesting structures. Children asked for the typical things, like ball field, slides, and swings, but they also had more creative ideas. They asked for climbing walls, outdoor classrooms, nature trails, and petting zoos. We tried to incorporate as many of the children's ideas as possible into the new school plan. Children also suggested theme gardens patterned after some of their favorite books, such as *Peter Rabbit, Alice in Wonderland, A Secret Garden*, and *Harry Potter*.

© Cengage Learning 2015

We believe that the school grounds are an important part of the total school learning environment, so we incorporated many of the children's ideas into our school planning. We welcomed AmeriCorp workers and Eagle Scouts to clear paths and label foliage along the nature trails. Through parent and community fund raisers, we were able to finance playgrounds that were appropriate to each grade level. Kindergarten students were welcomed onto the playground by playground equipment resembling a large panda bear and a turtle. Swings, a sand box, climbing equipment, and slides invited students to free play activities. The first- and second-grade playground starts with jungle climbing equipment guarded by a gorilla and proceeds to a desert with a large lion. Then, children step on lilly pads across a swampy area to escape two alligators. Finally, the children move to traditional climbing and sliding equipment. There is also an open area for running and chasing activities. In another area of the school, athletic fields, basketball hoops, climbing walls, and sidewalk games are available for older children. We

also built a music garden with percussion instruments. To accommodate animals, a barn complete with paddock was readied for animals that come to visit when the curriculum dictates.

The theme gardens offer opportunities for reading, planting vegetables, visiting with a friend, or free play. Our classrooms truly extend to the outdoor environment, thereby offering lots of opportunities for creative activities. For larger group activities, the amphitheater is a wonderful place for puppet shows, singing, and dancing. Build around a 100-year-old oak tree, the ampitheater offers an idyllic source of shade and beauty.

We believe that schools should offer a wide variety of spaces for activities that promote both organized and free play. Schools should be a place where children learn about the complexities of life. Much of what we learn about relationships with others we learn through play. We believe our school makes this possible.

Paul Prichard, EdD, Principal, Clemson Elementary School, Clemson, South Carolina

Project Area. When the children return from a field trip, they can extend their learning in the project area. The project area is an area of the room that is designated for project work. Locating it near a source of water is always a good idea. In the project area, children can work on projects and leave their work until the next project work time. A designated project area is not required, but it does promote the use of projects in the classroom. When children can leave a project and return in three days to work on it, their interest in the project and the depth of learning from the project are both enhanced.

Upon their return from a field trip to the beach, children may want to set up a science lab complete with magnifying glasses, microscopes, science logs, and egg cartons or ice cube trays for sorting and classifying shells. For children at this age, collecting and classifying are pleasurable activities. Adding lab coats to the center increases authenticity. Children who live near the ocean have a different level of knowledge of life at the ocean. They have intimate knowledge of shells, fish, boats, and, in some areas, marine biologists. When children bring their real world into the classroom, their thinking process is enhanced and strengthened. One reason that the projects in Reggio Emilia are so valued is that the projects are intertwined with the local culture and location. They are authentic for the children. For example, children generally visit vineyards during harvest and participate in the stomping of the grapes. This is appropriate in their culture but would be meaningless to a group of children from another area. This is their culture and their world. For this reason, the schools of Reggio Emilia discourage others from trying to replicate their children's experiences. Rather, they encourage early educators to look around their own ecological niche and find areas of interests that are most meaningful and relevant to the children in their classroom.

Children should be involved in planning how to unpack the beach experience in the classroom. They may choose to develop a marine lab, create a beach sweeper, or create a life guard station. Providing guidance in helping the children answer their questions creatively requires the teacher to have both keen observation skills and a strong commitment to inquiry-based education.

Aesthetics. Children can paint murals of their experience, create poems or haiku, or write stories about their experiences. Some may want to create a play or puppet show about fictional characters. Other children may want to know about real people who live near the beach and explore some books about people who live near the beach. Songs and music about the beach extend children's interest in studying the beach. Some children may want to be involved in creating movement to the sounds of the ocean. Making a diorama also provides a way to re-create the experience of being at the beach.

Games. Games provide another avenue for extending project work. Number games can be made with different shells. Rules can be developed that reflect the complexity of the learner's knowledge. Other possibilities include a simple bingo with different shells. Children invent fascinating games when they have the opportunity to do so.

When children begin to tire of the project, it is time to culminate the project; this process of culminating and concluding the project happens in the third and final stage.

7-5c Phase III: Project Conclusion

Encourage the children to look at their KWL chart. What did they learn? They can document on the chart and/or document in other ways what they have learned. For some projects that do not generate much interest, it may be sufficient to record the information on the chart and consider other possible topics for further study. For projects that stimulate interest and involvement, outcomes can be recorded in a variety of different ways. Recording what the project has taught them helps children make sense of the experience and "tell their story" about the project. What did they do first, second, third? What did they learn at each stage of the project? Recording helps children develop a scientific attitude for communicating findings.

In addition, children can write and illustrate books and use digital cameras to capture their experiences and (with assistance) create stories about their experiences. Other options involve performing plays, doing a mock television interview, publishing a book of poems about the experience, or displaying a mural. One class presented its project to the community during an art display, complete with refreshments and a strolling violinist. Opportunities are unlimited. One group of third-graders routinely created PowerPoint™ presentations after a project. A parent uploaded the presentations to the Internet, and the children had an online photo essay of learning that occurred that year.

Project Assessment. Project assessment is difficult and may be one reason why projects are not more popular. Careful collection of data throughout the project can be used to document the child's learning. Assessing individual contributions to group projects is one of the challenges of project work and is an area that needs more study.

Did You Get It?

While working on an inquiry project, a teacher asks a child to consider the trees in her own backyard. On which phase of the project are they most likely working?

a. planning
b. aesthetics
c. implementation
d. assessment

Take the full quiz on CourseMate

✳ 7-6 Program Models

Primary play programs differ from preschool play programs. Although many teachers are familiar with the preschool programs of Bank Street, HighScope, and Creative Curriculum (as described previously in Chapters 4, 5, and 6, respectively), few are familiar with play-based models for primary school. The most well-known play program was designed by Selma Wasserman and is described in her book *Serious Players in the Primary Classroom: Empowering Children Through Active Learning Experiences* (Wasserman, 1990). Wasserman takes the reader through a step-by-step description that details how to establish a play-based program in a primary classroom. In this section, we discuss major program models used in the United States. This list is not exhaustive but includes some of most popular programs available. It includes Wasserman's model, constructivist, developmental interaction such as Bank Street, Creative Curriculum, and Reggio Emilia. As in the previous chapters, the Montessori method is omitted because it requires specialized training.

7-6a Wasserman's Primary Play Model

Based on a book by Selma Wasserman (1990), *Serious Players in the Primary Grades: Empowering Children Through Active Learning Experiences,* this approach identifies itself as a play program. The focus of this model is fostering the development of content "can-do" students through playing, debriefing, and replaying. From Wasserman's perspective, play, debrief, and replay creates a systematic approach to instruction. The goal is to explore and discover the big idea. Play activities are designed to provide opportunities for exploration. Debriefing involves reflecting and reconsidering findings developed during the play experience. Replay involves reexamining and revisiting the materials. An important part of this program involves "breathing out," which is a time in the morning devoted to aesthetically based centers. Many aspects of this approach are similar to those advocated by John Dewey(2008) and many of the activities are very similar to inquiry-based instruction.

7-6b Constructivist Primary Classrooms

A constructivist approach can be established using a framework provided by DeVries and Zan in their book *Moral Classrooms, Moral Children: Creating a Constructivist Atmosphere in Early Education* (1994). This book provides guidelines for teachers interested in establishing a constructivist program. The premise of this approach is "that a sociomoral atmosphere must be cultivated in which respect for others is continually practiced" (1994, p. 1). Like Wasserman's approach, this approach promotes the ideas of a democratic classroom discussed by John Dewey at the beginning of the twentieth century.

John Dewey advocated action that can occur through the arts. Aesthetics can be a part of the primary play program. According to Dewey, "Both play and art have much in common. Both engage imagination, both require reflection, both profit from skill, both seek to generate new forms of experience, both lead to invention, and both are marginalized in the priorities of American education [Photo 7-8]. In my view both children and the cultures within which they live would be better served if art and play had a more prominent place in our schools" (Eisner, 1990, p. 55).

Courtesy of Dorothy Justus Sluss

7-8 Both play and art provide outlets for the child's creativity.

7-6c Developmental Interaction

Developmental-interaction programs for primary schools model their programs on those used at the Bank Street College of Education located in New York City. The primary school developmental-interaction program builds on the developmental-interaction program discussed in Chapters 4, 5, and 6. The program for six- to eight-year-olds is referred to as the middle school, which may be confusing to those who are trying to locate primary-based materials. The curriculum for the Bank Street program includes social studies, reading and writing, math and science, art and shop, music and movement, physical education, and French or Spanish class. The big idea or theme forms the core of the program throughout the program. Children can use materials to build stores, hospitals, or libraries (Photo 7-9).

7-6d Creative Curriculum (Primary Classrooms)

The Creative Curriculum approach is based on the book *Building the Primary Classroom: A Complete Guide to Teaching and Learning*, by Dodge, Colker, and Heoman (2002). The program is based on two parts; the first part includes teaching strategies and the second part involves content. The teaching strategies included in the first part include the following:

© Cengage Learning 2015

7-9 Materials such as blocks can be used to construct the structure that will serve as the foundation for a bank, pet store, or hospital.

1. Knowing the child you teach

2. Building a classroom community

3. Establishing a classroom routine that encourages and facilitates learning

4. Guiding children's learning

5. Assessing children's learning

6. Building a partnership with families

> **What do you think?**
>
> Several models were discussed that can be used to develop primary grade curriculum. Which approach do you find most appealing? Why does this model appeal to you?

The second part includes the content areas of language and literacy, mathematical thinking, social studies, scientific thinking, technology, and the arts. A learning environment using this approach includes the following areas:

1. Meeting areas

2. Arrangement of furniture and tables

3. Organization of supplies and materials

4. Display space

5. Areas for personal belongings and work

7-6e Reggio Emilia

The infant/toddler schools and preschools of Reggio Emilia, Italy are famous throughout the world. Some scholars have suggested using these same principles to inform practice in primary and middle schools. Although valiant efforts have been made, to date there are no program models available to inform primary classrooms. Those who are interested in pursuing the application of these principles to a primary classroom are encouraged to use the basic principles of Reggio Emilia as a starting point.

✳ 7-7 Designing Spaces for Children in Primary School

Primary classrooms present more of a challenge than preschool or kindergarten classrooms. Children still need centers, but they also need space for individual and group work. Aesthetics are equally important for the primary room. Assigning children to water plants, feed fish, or distribute daily mail teaches responsibility and reflects knowledge of the child's need for order, for a sense of belonging, and for a feeling of personal competence. Areas of the room should be arranged to include the following activities or areas:

- **Entry or exit**   The entrance/exit should be safe and free from objects that might serve as a safety hazard. Spaces for hanging coats and placing personal belongings should be close to the entry to ease transition in the morning and evening. In some primary schools, entry/exit doors have designs around them to encourage interest in the room. The room should reflect that children have been involved in the process of creating their learning space.

- **Large meeting space**   All primary classes need a space where children can sit on carpet squares, quilts, or blankets as a group. Many teachers are using risers shaped in a "U"; doing so provides the children with a place where they can sit for class meetings when disagreements need to be resolved. The large meeting space should include a large easel so the responses of the group can be recorded. This space is useful for a variety of activities, including social studies, author's chair, poetry readings, and story reenactments. Placing a class helper chart in this area reminds everyone of daily responsibilities.

Did You Get It?

At the end of each recess, a teacher debriefs her students about their play experiences, asking each about the quality of play, and how they could play differently next time. Whose theory is this teacher following?

a. DeVries and Van

b. Dewey

c. Wasserman

d. Bickart, Jablon, and Dodge

Take the full quiz on CourseMate

- **Small group work places**   Tables can be placed around the periphery of the classroom or flat desks can be pulled together for group work. When children work in groups or teams, they have opportunities to develop their skills in cooperation as well as their sense of self, which is vital for this age group. Learning to negotiate and compromise are important life skills that develop as children work together to solve problems. Small groups can also meet in the large meeting area, on a sofa, at a small group of tables, or on the floor. Carpet remnants provide a defining area for children. Small groups provide a context for games, and children can use games when time permits. They can get them and put them back unassisted. One teacher used coffee can math games. That is, she put a tin coffee can covered with contact paper in the middle of the table and would change out the games every week. The children knew that the games involved two or four people. In the mornings, the children would get the coffee can games, select a carpet remnant, and play until the teacher stopped play and called for morning meeting. One game that the children enjoyed involved number die (cubes with numbers on them work just as well) and a roll of adding machine paper (which is becoming more difficult to obtain because computers have largely replaced adding machines). The rolls of adding machine paper were used because the paper's narrow width minimized the amount of paper the children consumed and because the children enjoyed tearing and cutting the strips of paper. The children would roll the die or number cube and would try to obtain the highest number. They would write their scores on the paper so they could keep a running tally of the game. They could add or multiply when trying to get the highest score that day. If the goal of the day was a low score, children could subtract or divide. The teachers would put a stick in the can that said "low score" or "high score" so the children had opportunities to engage in a variety of operations. No stick in the can meant that the children could decide the criteria for the winner. Children would place their strips in a basket when finished so the teacher could monitor their math skills. This provided a quick assessment of what they could and could not do easily. The setup of materials made it possible for the children to practice their skills in mathematics while allowing the teacher to take care of the morning attendance and other administrative requirements. The children started their day involved in playing and learning with their friends (Photo 7-10).

- **Individual work places**   Because children are developing a sense of order at this age, it is optimal for each child to have a place to hang her jacket, sweaters, and other outdoor wear; a mailbox for materials that are sent home and returned; and an individual desk that can be turned into groups of two, four, or eight desks. Some teachers prefer tables, but individual desks can be used for multiple purposes, and children gain a sense of personal responsiblity from "owning" one desk. They can put their books in the desk and know that they are secure. A place in the room also needs to be designated as a quiet space for one or two children. Some teachers use a decorated refrigerator box as a space ship, whereas others use a bean bag or couch. Bean bags and book baskets create an inviting combination.

© Cengage Learning 2015

7-10 When classrooms are designed to challenge and extend learning, children can be creative and solve problems using a variety of methods.

7-11 These children are able to select their materials without any assistance. The structure and routine encourages children to develop their autonomy and independence.

© Cengage Learning 2015

- **Storage and equipment** Materials should be stored neatly. Labels can be placed on everything in the room so children can develop a sense of independence as they use materials, put away equipment, and collect materials for the next project. Think about how you will handle passing out materials, crayons, and scissors. When children are able to select their own materials, they are encouraged to develop their own autonomy and independence (Photo 7-11). If children keep their materials in a personal space, make sure they can get to them easily. When distributing materials for the entire class, pass them out by table groups or teams. Second and third graders like the use of the word *team*.

  Check the room periodically for clutter and worn-out materials. *Organization* is the key operative term. If materials are placed within the children's work area, they should be available and designated for the children's use. Placing teacher records or materials on the same shelf as materials designated for the children's use creates problems because children do not know which is for their use and which is for the teacher's exclusive use.

- **Aesthetics** A beautiful place for learning can enhance the quality of life and learning for primary age children. Lighting, displays, and room arrangements all contribute to the sense of orderliness and beauty or the sense of chaos. Natural light and lamps can enhance the lighting in a classroom. Painting walls white so hanging plants and pictures are highlighted creates a clean, uncluttered canvas for displaying art.

  Display the children's work thoughtfully. Making fewer projects and displaying them creatively is better than completing daily worksheets. Educational materials purchased from school supply companies may not reflect the children or the culture. It is more appropriate to use student-created work or project pictures, both of which reflect the children, their learning experiences, and their culture. Bringing the local culture into the classroom will add to the children's sense of identity and can be accomplished through interest centers.

- **Interest Centers**

  1. **Blocks and math center** A section of the room set up for blocks and math will reap tremendous rewards. Primary age children benefit from play with blocks, including wood, unit, and Lego blocks. Children need math manipulatives that can be used for counting. Many children do not have regular access to unit cubes or math games, so daily use of these materials can stimulate a greater interest in math. Children who play games can keep up with the games they are playing in a journal; the journal can be used for assessment purposes.

  2. **Book center** The idea of a class library or book center is not new. The idea of creating a comfortable place for children to read is new. Bean bags and wicker baskets filled with books easily create an inviting space for reading. Couches make a great place for sitting and reading.

3. **Project area** Setting aside one area of the room for projects encourages project work. Children can move to this area to work on projects or complete research.

7-7a Toys and Materials

The toys and materials favored by primary age children reflect the characteristics of primary age children (developing a sense of self-esteem, a sense of order and structure, and a sense of belonging) and their dominant play interest, (games with rules). Due to the variability of interests and developmental levels at this age, a wide variety of choices should be available. This is the age when children put on puppet shows for younger children, create props for dramatic productions, and make their own games or collections. Although doll play is waning, dolls are often used to represent human beings in historical re-creations and dioramas. Because children at this age are comparing themselves to others and trying to establish their identity or sense of self, safety concerns revolve around risk-taking behavior such as jumping higher than anyone to touch a shelf and retrieve a game.

▶‖ TeachSource Video Case 7-2

© Cengage Learning 2015

5–11 years: Moral Development in Middle Childhood

Children are developing their sense of morality at this age. The children in the video depict the characteristics of middle childhood. That is, they see everything based on actions or behaviors, and they fail to consider intentions or extenuating circumstances. How can you use this knowledge when developing your classroom?

Watch on CourseMate

Assessment 7-8 ✳

Assessment in primary school looks very different from preschool assessment. Standardized tests are a routine part of primary classes, and test results are used to compare and rate schools and teachers. This is referred to as "high-stakes testing." Many believe that this type of assessment is not appropriate for young children or their teachers. Each subject area has a professional society, and each group has standards; examples include the International Reading Association (IRA), the National Council of Teachers of Math (NCTM), the National Council of Teachers of English (NCTE), the National Council of Social Studies (NCSS), and the National Science Teachers Association (NSTA). Standards recommended by professional associations are not required by law and can be used or ignored by classroom teachers in some localities. However, most states use the specialty standards as a foundation for developing state standards that are mandatory. Some states have developed their standards independent of the guidelines of professional organizations. Add to this the variation in standardized tests from state to state and district to district. The picture is pretty convoluted. Where does play fit into this assessment picture?

Play in the primary grades is different from play in the preschool years. Primary play consists of games with rules, and so play assessment will look different. Assessing play in the primary grades provides information useful in orchestrating instruction and play. Wasserman (1990) ,who proposed a play-based program, also recommended an assessment system based on reflection and dialogue. She also suggested the elimination of letter grades in the primary classroom. Grades would be replaced by dialogues and thoughtful conversations. Although this is an excellent idea, many public school teachers who have a teaching contract that requires them to issue grades cannot implement this system.

Opportunities for developmentally appropriate assessment in primary school are available. Developmentally appropriate assessment reflects the developmental level, age, and culture of the child. Primary age children play games with more structured rules and need to develop self-esteem and a feeling of belonging. If these characteristics are used to structure a play program with an assessment system, then authentic assessment must be included. Authentic assessment is continuous, ongoing assessment and includes games, teamwork, portfolios, and project work. One type of authentic assessment involves the documentation panels that originated in the schools of Reggio Emilia, Italy. The use of authentic assessment provides an excellent way to document play and learning in the classroom.

7-8a Games

Math games provide an excellent venue for assessing math skills. Using open-ended math games allows children to create their own challenge. Children who keep math journals can record their knowledge gains. Math journals can be examined for themes so areas of strength and weakness can be recognized and amelioration provided as necessary. Children at this age enjoy making games. Conducting research to make a social studies game about their town or build a replica of a local historical site brings together play, aesthetics, and content in a creative activity that is beneficial and enjoyable.

7-8b Cooperative Group Work (Teams)

Teamwork offers an opportunity for children who have different skills to work together to complete an assignment. Activities can include reenacting stories, putting on puppet shows for younger children, writing poems about local places, or completing science experiments that are recorded in science journals.

7-8c Portfolios

Portfolios provide a way to document progress. The child and teacher select the child's best work and place it in the portfolio in selected places. For example, after talking about poetry, children can choose to write poetry or conduct research and then record it in a portfolio. A portfolio for language arts is both developmentally appropriate and provides evidence of growth throughout the year.

7-8d Inquiry Work

Inquiry demonstrates knowledge of science and social studies through the language arts, math, art, music, and reenactment. At the end of the experience, students share their findings. Among the skills used in inquiry are research, writing, math and computation, communication, and social interaction.

Creating an assessment program using games, portfolios, cooperative learning teams, and inquiry work provides an overall approach that is aligned with how the child learns. This system provides an optimal way to foster learning in the primary grades.

7-8e Sociograms

A sociogram is a way to collect information about the children's social interactions in the classroom. Ask each child to name three friends that he plays with on the playground or in the classroom. Look at the connections in the classroom. If a child is not mentioned, make a point of including this child in play indoors and outdoors. Look at the groups with the goal of redistributing the groups so that children are interacting with a variety of classmates. Completing a sociogram regularly will provide information about the changing social structure of the classroom.

7-8f Assessing Afterschool Programs

Self-study assessment instruments are available for afterschool programs. The School-Age Environmental Rating Scale (SACERS) (Harms, Jacobs, & White, 1996) is designed to give a quick overview of quality in an afterschool program. Evaluators who use the SACERS must receive training prior to using the instrument. DVDs and podcasts are available to those who choose to use this method. Areas included in the rating scale are Space and Furnishings, Health and Safety, Activities, Interactions, Program Structures, Staff Development, and Special Needs.

Did You Get It?

A teacher asks each child in her class to name three friends, then writes the information in a sociogram. Her goal is probably to

a. subvert the children's play plans.

b. meet state standards.

c. increase the integration of play into the classroom.

d. assess the social structure of the classroom.

Take the full quiz on CourseMate

PLAYSCAPE: REFLECTIONS

In the case study at the beginning of the chapter, Alana enjoyed the games when she first entered the room. She did not realize that the math games were designed to reinforce and strengthen her math skills. As she moved to the songs at morning meeting, she did not know that music and movement were interwoven to introduce her to a different culture. Individual centers included word games, word sorts, drawing, and reading groups. Alana did not know that alternating between learning and playing, between accommodation and assimilation, is designed to help her learn new information and then practice using it during play. Alana's time on the playground allows her to make new friends, chase a boy that tried to grab her jump rope, and enjoy the opportunity to walk around the playground. Ms. Johnson, the teacher, uses a project approach that integrates science and social studies. Alana only knows that playing with the paper towels is fun, and deciding the next step in the project is interesting. She does not know that she is developing skills needed for scientific inquiry. Although the day was filled with what Alana viewed as play, she was engaged in play that was not only enjoyable, but was also designed to facilitate and optimize learning the first-grade content that her mother wants her to learn.

7-1 List the benefits of play for primary age students.

Play provides opportunities for growth and development in the cognitive, social and emotional, and physical domains. Because growth is generally slower but steadier during the primary years, it is especially beneficial for overall health.

7-2 Identify strategies that adults can use to support play in the primary classroom.

Provide opportunities for budding talents in diverse areas; encourage game design and creative dramatics; provide appropriate intervention on the playground; and promote activities that lead to legitimate play-based learning experiences.

7-3 Explain the role of play as a medium for learning.

An aesthetics-based approach can use music, movement, and art to facilitate play as a medium for learning. As children move, create, dance, sing, and play, they rehearse old material or learn new material, which increases neurological connections.

7-4 Name four content areas that can be connected and enhanced through play.

The content areas of reading, mathematics, science, and social studies can be taught through play activities that integrate the core content areas.

7-5 Develop a plan for implementing inquiry projects.

Begin by asking the children what they want to know more about. Use their interest as the topic of the study. Plan the study with the children through the use of KWL, implement the project as a co-investigator, and communicate the findings of the study to others. These basic components can be implemented throughout the year with different groups.

7-6 Compare and contrast program models for primary school.

Five models or approaches discussed in the chapter include the Wasserman primary play model, the constructive primary approach, the developmental-interaction approach, the Creative Curriculum model, and the Reggio Emilia approach. The Wasserman approach is based on the writings of Wasserman, which describe how to encourage a play-based program in primary schools. A constructivist approach is based on the work of Piaget and Vygotsky. A developmental-interaction approach is informed by Erikson's theory, and the Reggio Emilia approach is an example of a constructivist approach that reflects symbolic constructivism. The major difference between Creative Curriculum and other models is that Creative Curriculum is designed as a model for professional development.

7-7 Design a primary classroom with at least five defined areas.

All primary classrooms should have areas that encourage specific activities, including entry/exit area, large meeting space, small group work space, individual workplaces, storage and equipment, as well as interest centers that include blocks/mathematical manipulative, book areas, and project areas. Ensuring that all these areas are available in a classroom is a good first step to ensuring a healthy environment for growing and developing.

7-8 Describe a play-based assessment system.

Play in a primary classroom is assessed using a system that focuses on academic outcomes by looking at games, cooperative group work, portfolios, inquiry work, sociograms, and documentation panels. Afterschool programs can be assessed in the same way.

 Key terms

Technology and Internet Resources

Association for Childhood Education International
http://www.acei.org/
This international association promotes the health, education, and welfare of children from birth to twenty-one.

Bank Street Bookstore
http://bankstreet.edu/school-children
Official site of Bank Street School. The Bank Street Bookstore offers lesson plans, units, and samples of books written by children.

Goldsboro Magnet School
http://teachercenter.scps.k12.fl.us/education
This is the Goldsboro Magnet Elementary School website. Click on Kids Space Station for an overview of the program.

International Reading Association
http://www.reading.org/Official site of the largest professional association dedicated to reading instruction.

National Council of Teachers of English
http://www.ncte.org Official site of the professional organization of English teachers.
Good ideas for second- and third-grade classrooms.

National Council of Teachers of Mathematics
http://www.nctm.org/ Official site of the largest professional organization of math teachers. Provides the most current research and practice for mathematics instruction in the United States.

National Council of Social Studies
http://www.ncss.org/ Official site of the largest professional organization of teachers of social studies.

National Music Teachers
http://www.mtna.org/home.htm Site of the Music Teachers National Association. Includes standards and guidelines for parents.

National Science Standards
http://www.nap.edu/catalog.php?record_id=13165. A free downloadable copy of the book *A Framework for K–12 Science Education* is available at this site.

National Science Teachers Association
http://www.nsta.org/ National professional organization of teachers of science.

Project Approach
http://ecap.crc.uiuc.edu/ Official site of the Early Childhood and Parent Collaborative (ECAP). Information for training on the project approach is available.

Activities

1. InClass Lab

A. Develop a play plan for one curriculum area from first through third grades. For example, a play plan for math might include wood unit blocks in the first and second grade, smaller blocks and manipulatives for all grades, and games at every level. Ways to facilitate math learning through play in the house area or other centers should also be described.

B. Develop a website for a project for second grade. Plan an assessment system that can be used to document learning.

2. Research and Inquiry

A. Make a two-hour visit to a classroom that uses a play-based curriculum in primary school. Now, find another classroom at the same level (grade 1 or 2) that does not use play and visit this classroom for two hours. Compare and contrast your observations in the two classrooms. Based on your knowledge of theories, what theoretical orientation influenced the classrooms? Did this impact the frequency of play in these classrooms?

B. Select a grade such as first or second grade and investigate the curriculum of the same grade in two other countries. How is it similar? How is it different? When looking at the two classrooms, does one include more play than the other? What influences impact their curriculum?

C. Recall the contexts of play explained in Chapter 3. Compare two systems that do and do not use a play-based curriculum. Does the micro-, macro-, exo-, meso-, or chrono-system have the most impact on play? Support your response with data.

D. What is the homework policy in your local school system? Interview teachers from grades 1 to 3. How much homework do they assign?

How does the amount of assigned homework impact afterschool play?

3. Service Learning

A. Volunteer in an afterschool program for two hours a week. What kind of play did you observe? What are the children learning through their play?

B. Create a set of math games that can be used in an afterschool program to reinforce a specific math skill.

C. Visit a local afterschool program. Volunteer to organize a game shelf to encourage play.

D. Develop information sheets that provide directions and rules for noncompetitive games. Distribute these to local afterschool programs.

4. Family Connections

A. Ask if you can organize a Family Night Out for parents and children. Invite parents to attend as a family. They can plan on eating together by bringing a dish for each member of the family. During the dinner, children have time to discuss their projects and display their documentation panels. These panels focus on class projects rather than on individual children's accomplishments. In this way, the panels encourage cooperation and community building among the children.

B. Another Family Night program should involve a presentation on play in the primary grades.

Providing information about development that occurs at this age can assist parents as they deal with the issues of how many extra-curricular activities are too many, when should they monitor interactions with a child's playmate, and how can they block out time for play at home. Be prepared to support your comments with data. Hand-outs with additional information or articles to support your statements should be available.

C. Ask children who have a unique musical heritage to share their music with the class.

D. Plan a Family Night outing to celebrate artistic creations. Invite a local high school or college student musician to provide music for the occasion.

5. Play Advocacy

A. Create a set of games for primary school children that can be played with minimal instruction. Donate the games to a local community agency such as a clinic or homeless shelter.

B. Find out what organizations advocate for children in your state. Who advocates for children in primary school?

C. What state laws affect play in primary school?

D. How does required assessment affect play in local schools? Design an evaluation plan that will assess children's development through games and play.

 Visit CourseMate for this textbook to access the eBook, Did You Get It? quizzes, Digital Downloads, TeachSource Video Cases, flashcards, and more. Go to CengageBrain.com to log in, register, or purchase access.

References

American Heart Association (2013). *Understanding childhood obesity: 2011 statistical sourcebook.* Retrieved on July 13, 2013 from http://www.heart.org/HEARTORG/Getting-Healthy/HealthierKids/Healthier-Kids_UCM_304156_SubHomePage.jsp

Ashwell, K. (2012). *The brain book.* Buffalo, New York: Firefly Books, Inc.

Clements, D. H., & Sarama, J. (2009). *Learning and teaching early math: The learning trajectories approach.* New York:Routledge.

Dewey, J. (2008). *Democracy and education.* Radford, VA: Wilder Publishers, LLC. (Originally published in 1916)

DeVries, R., & Zan, B. (1994). *Moral classrooms, moral children: Creating a constructivist atmosphere in early education.* New York: Teachers College Press.

Dodge, D., Colker, L., & Heroman, C. (2002). *The creative curriculum for preschool* (4th ed.). Washington, DC: Teaching Strategies.

Eisner, E. (1990). The role of art and play in children's cognitive development. In E. Klugman and S. Smilansky

(Eds.), *Children's play and learning* (pp. 43–56). New York: Teachers College Press.

Elliott, V. (2002). Adult options for childhood obesity? Doctors say the high number of extremely overweight young people is serious enough to consider radical interventions. *American Medical News, 45*(20), 27.

Erikson, E. (2000). *Childhood and society* (3rd ed.) New York: W.W. Norton Company.

Fountas, I., & Pinnell, G. (2013). Guided reading: The romance and the reality. *Reading Teacher, 66*(4), 268–284.

Gardner, H. (1983). *Frames of mind*. New York: Basic Books.

Gender Equity in Education: A Data Snapshot. (2012). Office of Civil Rights, U.S. Department of Education. Retrieved from http://www2.ed.gov/about/offices/list /ocr/docs/gender-equity-in-education.pdf

Harms, T., Jacobs, E., & White, D. (1996). *School Age Care Environment Rating Scale*. New York: Teachers College Press.

Hughes, F. (2010). *Children, play, and development* (4th ed.). Washington, DC: Sage.

International Reading Association (IRA) and the National Association for the Education of Young Children (NAEYC) joint position paper. (1998). Learning to read and write: Developmentally appropriate practices for young children. *Young Children, 53*(4), 30–46.

Jarrett, O. S., & Burnley, P. C. (2007). The role of fun, playfulness, and creativity in science: Lessons from geoscientists. *Investigating play in the 21st century: Play and culture studies, 7*, 188–202.

Martlew, J., Stephen, C., and Ellis, J. (2011). Play in the primary school classroom? The experience of teacher supporting children's learning through a new pedagogy. *Early Years, 31*(1), 71–83.

National Research Council. (2012). *A framework for K–12 science education: Practices, crosscutting concepts, and core ideas* . Washington, DC: The National Academies Press.

Ortlieb, E. (2012). The pursuit of play within the curriculum. *Journal of Instructional Psychology, 37*(3), 241–246.

Piaget, J. (1962). *Play, dreams, and imitation in childhood*. New York: Norton.

Peisach, E., & Hardeman, M. (2001). Imaginative play and logical thinking in young children. *The Journal of Genetic Psychology, 146*(2), 233–249.

Rushton, S., Rushton, A., & Larkin, E. (2010). Neuroscience, play and early childhood education: Connections, implications and assessment. *Early Childhood Education Journal, 37*(5), 351–361.

Sandberg, A., & Heden, R. (2011). Play's importance in school. *Education 3-13, 39*(3), 317–329.

Seefeldt, C., Castle, S., & Falconer, R. (2013). *Social Studies for the preschool/primary child* (9th ed.). Upper Saddle River, NJ: Pearson.

Sluss, J. R. (2013). Conversation with a scientist. Oral conversation on March 18, 2013, in Winchester, Virginia.

Smith, S. (2012). *Early childhood methods* (5th ed.). Upper Saddle River, NJ: Pearson.

Vygotsky, L. (1978). *Mind in society: The development of higher psychological processes*. Cambridge, MA: Harvard University Press.

Wasserman, S. (1990). *Serious players in the primary classroom: Empowering children through active learning experiences*. New York: Teachers College Press.

8 Supporting PLAY for Children in Middle Childhood

STANDARDS COVERED IN THIS CHAPTER
Council of Exceptional Children—Division of Early Childhood Standards CEC DEC

ECSE 2S1 Apply current research to the five developmental domains, play, and temperament in learning situations

ECSE 3S1 Develop, implement, and evaluate learning experiences and strategies that respect the diversity of infants and young children and their families

ECSE 4S1 Plan, implement, and evaluate developmentally appropriate curricula, instruction, and adaptations based on knowledge of individual children, the family, and the community

ECSE 5S4 Structure social environments, using peer models and proximity, and responsive adults to promote interactions among peers, parents, and caregivers

ECSE 7K2 Plan and implement developmental and academic content

* LEARNING OBJECTIVES *

8-1 List the benefits of play for middle childhood children.

8-2 Describe the characteristics of play in middle childhood.

8-3 Analyze the impact of context on middle childhood play.

8-4 Explain the role of the adult in supporting play in middle childhood.

8-5 Recognize how play can be integrated in to the core content areas of reading, math, science, and social studies.

8-6 Design a play-based curriculum that utilizes a play-based approach.

8-7 Identify ten play-based learning centers appropriate for middle childhood.

8-8 Discuss the role of play in STEM education.

8-9 Create a plan for implementing a STEM project with a group of elementary children.

8-10 Compare and contrast an inquiry project with a STEM project.

8-11 Develop a play-based assessment system for children in elementary school.

© Cengage Learning 2015

NAEYC Program Standards **naeyc**

4a Understanding positive relationships and supportive interactions as the foundation of work with children

4b Using a broad repertoire of developmentally appropriate teaching and learning approaches

5c Using content knowledge and resources in academic disciplines

5d Using knowledge, appropriate early learning standards, and other resources to design, implement, and evaluate meaningful and challenging curricula for each child

✳ PLAYSCAPE: CASE STUDY

Professors attending a conference on teacher education get on a bus to visit a local middle school considered a "model school." As they travel, they wonder how it will be different from the many schools they have visited throughout the country. When they get out of the bus, they observe that the school looks similar to other schools with the exception of the unusual large dome in the back of the school. They enter the front of the school and don their visitor badges. As they walk through the halls, the rooms look similar to many other schools. What is noticeably different is the work on the walls. Third graders' work related to their studies of different systems in the body is hanging in a hallway. Life-size body drawings of the nervous and circulatory systems cover the walls. Accompanying papers indicate that the children had to prepare a media presentation to explain the visual representation. As a group of experienced educators, the visiting professors question whether third graders could accomplish this type of work. The leader of the group directs them into a winding hallway, and the professors find themselves in the dome section of the building. The area around them is dark, but they are met by student guides and taken into a small auditorium that looks amazingly like a planetarium. The students explain that the professors will see different areas representing ground control, the space shuttle, the moon, and the planet Mars. They advise the professors of guidelines for a successful visit, and the professors follow the students down another dark corridor. As they round the corner, the professors hear this: "Ground control, can we land now?" The guide shares that the astronauts are ready to land.

"The technicians are checking the atmosphere now. Over and out!" responds the ground crew.

Astronauts move about in the space shuttle and prepare for landing. They are checking their pulse, calculating the distance from the shuttle to the landing spot, and checking the air supply needed for exploring on the moon once they have landed.

"Can we land now?"

"Yes, prepare to land. Check all systems."

Although this sounds like a script from NASA, it occurs at Goldsboro Magnet Elementary School in Florida. Students use a model NASA lab that facilitates their play. As they dramatize the entire aeronautical experience, they are playing while they are learning.

Explaining Play Behaviors

The provocation to play is the model NASA station complete with artificial moon for landing, videos, a planetarium, and a computer room that simulates

(Continued)

the one at NASA. The children are engaged in play. It does not look like play in the preschool classroom, but it *is* play. Children use symbolism or imagination when envisioning the flight to the moon and back, constructive play when building places to land on the moon or creating machines to gather data, and games with rules when following or negotiating the rules of the scenario. Play at this age is different and reflects a more sophisticated level of development (Bergen & Fromberg, 2009). Although there is a paucity of research in this area, Manning (1998) defines play in middle childhood as follows:

- voluntary and freely chosen,
- "as if" or symbolic,
- active or requiring participation,
- pleasurable, and
- meaningful.

In this chapter we explore the multiple dimensions of play in the middle childhood years.

Benefits of Play for Middle Childhood 8-1 ✳

The middle childhood years (ages 6–12) are often referred to as the school years because formal schooling and homework dominate the majority of the time when the child is not sleeping (Corno & Xu, 2004). During these years, children are growing and developing in unique ways. The brain and body are growing at a slow but steady pace as they prepare for the explosion of development that will occur in the adolescent years (Feldman, 2012). Play has multiple benefits for this age (Ortlieb, 2010). For example, it allows children to practice needed skills in a safe environment. As in the early years, the benefits of play include cognitive, social and emotional, and physical growth and development, but these look different at this stage (Sandberg & Heden, 2011).

1. **Cognitive development**   The child's brain is growing and developing, although not as rapidly as during the first five years of life. One change that occurs is **myelination**, or the increase or thickening of the **myelin** (the protective coating that surrounds certain parts of the nerve cell). As this insulation increases, so does the speed of travel of the electrical impulses between the nerve cells; this travel of electrical impulses allows for multiple connections between nerve cells. Although many of these connections will be pruned in adulthood, a myriad of connections occur that dramatically increase the information processing speed of the brain. The prefrontal cortex, which controls executive processing, grows at a fast pace; this improves attention, reasoning, and cognitive control (Crone, Windelken, van Leijenhorst, Honomichi, Christoff, & Bunge, 2009; Santrock, 2010). Although most of these changes occur steadily, occasionally some growth spurts occur. The result of steady growth and the occasional brain growth spurt is that the capacity and speed of the brain increase at a fast pace (Ashwell, 2012). Play allows children to use this increased capacity to challenge or test their speed during games

8-1 Children who are in middle childhood need concrete models in addition to abstract ideas.

and competitions with peers or against their own personal best.

Using a Piagetian view, the child moves in and out of the concrete operational stage (Piaget, 1965). The child begins to use logic to solve problems—no longer relying solely on appearance as in the pre-operational stage. Because the child moves between the pre-operational and concrete operational stages, the child needs exposure to multiple ways of developing cognitive capacity in memory and metacognitive processing (Photo 8-1). Games such as Guess Who, Trouble, or Sorry are a good fit for the child's skill level. Legos® provide a wonderful way to use concrete objects to reflect abstract ideas.

Information processing theory is used to explain the child's growing memory and language development. The child continues to develop her theory of mind as she engages in **metacognitive thinking**; that is, thinking about how she thinks (McDevitt & Ormrod, 2013). This can be seen when the child figures out that she can win at checkers if she is the first player to mark a box. Game strategies improve and increase as the child considers different ways to reach the goal. Cognitive development is enhanced through play as children refine and develop memory and language skills in a safe yet enjoyable environment (Thalia & Ellen, 2010).

Howard Gardner's theory of multiple intelligences explains why children develop in different ways during this time (Gardner, 1983). Some children will develop their literacy skills as others develop their dance or music skills. When children play with an activity, they can try it and then leave it. They are playing at learning tennis, they are playing at learning the viola, they are playing at sculpting, or they are playing baseball. Encouraging play during these years allows for the full development of individual talents.

2. **Social, emotional, and moral development** Children who are in middle childhood are in what Erikson described as industry versus inferiority (age 6 to age 12) (Erikson, 2000). Because children are developing a sense of self as competent, playing games that use external rules is extremely important. Because metacognitive skills are developing, children can compare themselves with others. Playing games allows children to develop skills and competencies that add to their self-esteem. These same analytical skills provide a mirror for the child to examine self in terms of how others view him. This is when peer pressure becomes a reality as children become aware of their role in the social milieu that surrounds them. Play provides an arena for developing a sense of self as a competent, independent person who can be a friend while developing a sense of personal integrity.

Piaget believed that game playing contributed to moral development (1965). As children take turns, follow the rules, and interact with others, they develop their own moral code or sense of moral integrity. They learn to negotiate so that they don't alienate the other players. In this way, culture is transmitted to the next generation. Guest (2011) looked at two distinct subgroups in different parts of the world and found that local community values shape peer interactions even though children may be playing far away from adult supervision.

3. **Physical development** Gross motor skills increase as boys and girls become aware of their personal strengths and limitations. Children who have more opportunities to engage in outdoor play will have more developed gross motor skills that will contribute to developing skills in specific areas such as baseball or soccer. Because neurological processing is increasing, fine motor skills are developing rapidly. Children who build with Legos® or use computers to develop media presentations increase their small muscle skills as well as their hand—eye coordination. Play provides a venue for strengthening gross and fine motor skills.

4. **Academic content knowledge** Because these are the school years when the child is well suited to developing academic skills, the focus of school is on learning academic content knowledge. Baines and Blatchford (2011) note that "play can be conceived as a natural inclination of the organism to learn, adapt, or develop the skills required for immediate and eventual later use. That is, play assists with the development and informal education of the child to adapt to their environment and learn the skills that will enable them to survive and succeed" (p. 275). Many local schools have contests such as "Do you know more than a third/fourth/fifth grader?" that place a middle childhood student in competition with an adult. Of course, the young student frequently wins due to the amount of information they are required to know for standardized tests.

When play is a part of the curriculum, children have the opportunity to test new ideas or strategies as well as strengthen their knowledge base as they are exposed to the same content in different venues. For example, many adults recall childhood games that involved games such as "Guess the President." They wanted to know more presidents not because they were interested in the presidents but because they wanted to meet the challenge or win the game. Knowing the presidents was a bonus. The use of this approach ensures not only that the child knows the information, but that it is encoded for life. Another equally important advantage of content knowledge is that the child increases his ability to focus and concentrate on the task at hand. This ability to stay focused and concentrate will allow children to be effective in processing information and completing tasks—which is a goal in many classrooms and schools (Baines & Blatchford, 2011).

What do you think?

Recall your own middle childhood years. Do you remember learning information through play? What play was most memorable for you?

Did You Get It?

Alison, age 10, seems to have slow and steady brain development. She learns new concepts over time, but does not display any growth spurts in her intelligence or understanding. Alison

a. is a slow learner.

b. has a low I.Q.

c. is above her age level in I.Q.

d. is a typical 10-year-old.

Take the full quiz on CourseMate

Characteristics of Play in Middle Childhood 8-2 ✳

As noted earlier, play for children who are in middle childhood is different from that of younger children, but it is also very different from that of past generations. Unique characteristics of middle childhood play today include the types of play, levels of engagement during play, and the quality of play.

1. **Types of play** In Piagetian terms, games with rules dominate this developmental period (Piaget, 1962). Practice play, constructive play, and symbolic play still occur, though not to the extent observed in preschool and kindergarten (Bergen & Fromberg, 2009; Smith & Lillard, 2012). Practice play or repetitive may be seen when children dribble a ball or

8-2 In middle childhood, children engage in and enjoy solitary play for longer time periods.

© Cengage Learning 2015

continue to throw it against a wall or trashcan for no apparent reason. Constructive play occurs when building a card house, Lego® structures, or other activities that require the child to create, build, or design. Symbolic or imaginary play occurs when interacting with scripts, literary materials, or media. Because games with rules dominate during this period, children will create a game out of any activity. As children develop physical and mental skills, they want to test their capacity against others. Middle childhood is a time when lining up for a drink of water can become a game or competitive challenge if no adult is nearby to intervene.

Additionally, social relationships change as the child moves from solitary or associative play to cooperative play. The notion of playing with someone becomes more important. Friendships develop as the child rides bikes, plays ball, jumps rope, or plays hand-clapping games with others. For those in this age range, being with their friends during an activity is play. This is why children at this age enjoy games, parties, and group projects. This is the time when children spend their first night away from home for a sleepover at a friend's house or a sleep-in at the local library.

2. **Play engagement** In the middle childhood years (6–12 years), play is stable and more focused. When children were younger, play was more improvisational. Now, a single play episode may last for an hour or more (Photo 8-2). It is not unusual for children to want to ride bikes, play ball, or jump rope until exhausted. They focus on the play at hand and become totally engaged in the game. Children will play with one game until other activities require their presence. When they engage in play, they spend a great deal of time planning the play, deciding who will do what, and establishing the rules of the game or skit. The rules of the game are enforced because children delight in playing by the rules and winning.

3. **Play quality** In the middle years, children begin to compare themselves with others, and this is evident in play. The young child plays but does not consider how well she plays. The child in elementary school compares her ability to play with that of others. Now, she will talk about how well she played the game and rate her skill level. In middle childhood, children will engage in those games that allow them to be successful and, when allowed, limit their involvement in games that are not well suited for their skills. For example, children will say, "I'm not playing _____ because I never win." This is why it is especially important to provide multiple ways to play that provide multiple opportunities for success.

Children who participate in activities outside of school develop prosocial behavior and social skills. There are numerous benefits associated with afterschool activities, such as lower drop-out rates, higher self-esteem, and better career choices (Howie, Lukacs, Pastor, Reuben, & Mendola, 2010). Because public schools are the major provider of afterschool activities, it is important that educators facilitate high-quality play for middle childhood both during and after school. For example, a third-grade teacher set up math games for children who arrived before school began. She altered the games so that the games on the table focused on increasingly more challenging activities each week. One game that was available throughout the year involved dice and rolls of adding machine paper (which is becoming more difficult to obtain). The children toss one, two, or three dice and they add, subtract, or multiply to get the highest number. At the end of the game, a spinner indicated if the child with the high or low number would be the winner. This involved both skill and luck. When the teacher would ask the children to put the games away, there would be moans and groans because the children did not want to end their games. All children had multiple opportunities to win, lose, and engage in a challenging activity while simultaneously reviewing math facts.

Contexts of Play 8-3 ✳

The impact of the context on play is equally important in the middle childhood years. Contextual settings vary, ranging from suburbs, where children are driven to different activities, to urban areas, where children go directly from afterschool programs into their homes due to the unsafe nature of the streets. Rural areas also provide a contrast because children may be engaged in more natural play. In considering the settings for play, consider places to play, time for play, and materials for play.

1. **Play spaces**   In general, in middle childhood there are more places to play, although they may be unused. At home, children live in neighborhoods that provide areas to explore and investigate, but many parents are reluctant to allow their children to go outdoors alone, so children play indoors. In one study of play in neighborhoods, Othman and Said (2012) found that the sociality of the neighbors was more important than aesthetics in encouraging play.

   This has huge implications for play. In neighborhoods that are inhospitable, children may stay indoors. Indoor play spaces range from large homes with game rooms for billiards and room-size television screens to one-bedroom apartments with minimum space for moving about. The impact of play space affects the kind and type of play that can occur (Photo 8-3).

   Another factor that impacts the context for play is access. Although there are more established play areas for middle childhood, these are not evenly distributed in towns and cities. One national organization investigated access to safe play areas in towns and cities. The investigation found that there are areas in towns and cities where children and families do not have access to safe play areas. The investigators

8-3 Play spaces provide safe spaces for children who want to try out new skills.

call these play deserts. They have targeted play deserts as sites for increasing public awareness about the need for spaces to play and for building new playgrounds (KaBOOM!, 2013).

Schools provide places and spaces that foster play. Places in schools that encourage play include classrooms, libraries and media centers, gymnasiums, and cafeterias. Classrooms include play areas that accommodate games in groups of two, three, or four; spaces for reading and listening to books; music areas; and Lego® block play areas. These areas have tables or carpeted areas near shelves for game storage. Many teachers place a list of games or materials on the wall to help children return the games to the appropriate area. Meeting areas for large group discussions are needed for group play that involves language, linguistics, or large muscle movement. Classroom beanbags invite children to relax as they play games or talk to their friends.

Many libraries offer board games and online games for children. These may be available in the morning or after school. Many communities and schools are teaming up to make gymnasiums available to the community after school. In some communities, gymnasiums are closed and unavailable after school. Gymnasiums provide a context for developing game knowledge about basketball, volleyball, kickball, and dodge ball.

Some schools create a context for dining and playing in their cafeterias. Cushions, beanbags, low tables, and shelves with games and baskets of books surround the perimeter of the room. When children finish with their lunch, they can grab a game or talk about books that they have read.

Other schools have outdoor trails and classrooms. Many afterschool programs include various types of indoor and, especially, outdoor play. Businesses have discovered pay-for-play activities, and many children attend parties and other gatherings at these facilities. The spaces and places for play tend to reflect the economic status of the neighborhood as well as the values of the school and community.

2. **Play time**   Time for play is more limited in middle childhood. Play and social interaction with peers decrease at school (Baines & Blatchford, 2011). When at home, children have a heavy homework load. The average homework load for children aged 6 to 10 years old is 3 hours and 58 minutes per night (Brookings Institute, 2007). Many children spend a great deal of time in afterschool programs or in organized sports. Children in middle childhood may experience longer periods of time involved in organized activities, lessons, and experiences, but time for genuine play is limited (Photo 8-4).

3. **Materials for play**   Materials for play include a variety of materials to encourage creativity. These include but are not limited to the following:

    a. **Board games**   The complexity of board games ranges from checkers to chess. Games such as Tic-Tac-Toe arise and are soon transformed into more complex board or card games. Some common games include Backgammon, Battleship, Bingo, Chinese Checkers, Life, Monopoly or a variation of it, peg boards, Risk, Scabble, Trivial Pursuit, Dominos, Clue, and Walk in the Woods.

    b. **Card games**   Games with cards are central for enhancing mathematical thinking. Popular card games include Seven-Up, Rummy or a variation, Fish, Hearts, Solitaire or a variation, and Uno.

8-4 Afterschool programs provide a variety of activities, such as arts and crafts, and give children time to complete their homework before going home.

© Cengage Learning 2015

c. **Books**   The six-year-old is beginning to develop fluency and comprehension skills that allow him to develop his preference for fiction or nonfiction, sports or science stories. By age ten, the child is an avid reader and is fully aware of his personal preferences. Gender differences are more evident in children's reading selections in middle childhood (boys tend to seek stories about real people, animals, or events, and girls tend to select books about fantasy). Because children are establishing their gender identity, those who are experiencing difficulty accepting a gender role may find solace in books. Boys and girls at this age develop their interests in serial books and begin to select books by specific authors.

d. **Arts and crafts materials**   Children enjoy developing their skills in creating art and producing crafts. Because children at this age are more independent, they can use a variety of tools for creating art, such as pastels, charcoal, oils, and watercolors.

e. **Musical instruments**   Harmonicas, recorders, and drums are instruments that initially interest children. As children experiment with the sounds of music, they will choose more complex instruments. When given the opportunity, it is not unusual for children to select a different instrument every year.

f. **Science equipment**   Backyard telescopes, microscopes, magnifying glasses, magnets, and simple chemistry kits are often given to children at this age, and children use these tools to play out different roles (e.g., astronomer or chemist).

g. **Puppets and marionettes**   Puppets and marionettes are interesting to children at this age. Many children enjoy writing scripts and carrying out plays. In school, this may occur as a script for a play performed for younger classes. At home, this may occur as a play performed in a backyard theater.

h. **Miniatures**   Children enjoy miniatures that they can collect. Because choking is no longer a concern, they can use very small parts and pieces. This fits well with the child's developing capacity for order. Miniatures include dish sets, glass replicas, small cars, trucks, and other transportation/construction vehicles.

i. **Models**   Children can use models that they create to represent the world. Children can assemble dioramas and model racing cars, ships, airplanes, and other facsimiles of their real and imaginary world.

j. **Legos® and blocks**   Interest in building with Legos and other blocks, such as Logicblocks, peak at this age. Many children participate in Lego contests throughout the United States. These contests involve construction and conversation as children design and build their models.

k. **Sports equipment (baseball, football, basketball, soccer, volleyball, jump ropes)**   When children are allowed to choose a sport and enjoy the game for the sake of playing, they have fun. In contrast, if children are forced to be involved in a sport that they do not like, are forced to engage in the sport as a way to build character, or are forced to play a sport in which the focus of the game is on winning, then the game is not enjoyable and little play may occur.

4. Influence of aesthetics (art, music, and movement) The focus on academics during these years decreases the time for the arts. The middle childhood years are the most important years for budding talents in art, music, and dance/movement.

a. **Art** Because the child's small muscles are more developed, she enjoys art activities such as painting with oil or watercolors; drawing with pastels and charcoal; and making figurines and representations of object using paper mache and clay. The ability to complete projects, dioramas, and crafts increases during this time.

b. **Music** Voice as an instrument begins to develop during this time. Children will try out different instruments as they find one that fits their skill and personal interest (Photo 8-5). Some children will combine technology and music as they create music. Listening to music may become part of their play and their music.

c. **Movement** It is difficult to separate music and movement for this age group. Children are developing their abilities in dance such as ballet, tap, modern dance, and gymnastics.

Drama utilizes art, music, and movement and taps the skills of children who are not interested in performing on stage. Some children enjoy writing the script whereas others enjoy creating the props or setting up the stage and lighting. Others might enjoy the aspect of selling tickets, whereas others enjoy performing on stage.

© Cengage Learning 2015

8-5 The children in this picture are playing with a musical instrument, and this initial interest may lead to a lifelong hobby or professional career.

Did You Get It?

Although Jenny lives in a "safe" neighborhood, her parents are reluctant to allow her to play outside. This decision is likely to

a. cause Jenny to have low self-esteem.

b. cause Jenny to have few friends.

c. affect the type of play that can occur.

d. boost Jenny's self-esteem.

Take the full quiz on CourseMate

Role of Adults in Supporting Play 8-4 ✳ in Middle Childhood

The adult is the most important variable in ensuring that high-quality play occurs in middle childhood or elementary school. Teachers who embrace play in middle childhood need to know how to encourage play and learning for this age (Martlew, Stephen, & Ellis, 2011). That is, facilitating play in middle childhood requires a systematic approach that requires the teacher to consider access to play, play materials, play-based curriculum, play relationships and interactions, and play skills; these are discussed in the section that follows.

1. **Access play** The teacher must ensure that children have access to play opportunities. This can be accomplished by looking at the child's day. Are there times for children to play outdoors? Are there times when children can play indoors? Are there learning goals that can be taught through games or play? This is the first step. If the schedule is so rigid or set that children do not have time for play, play will not occur.

2. **Play materials** Adults who work with middle childhood or elementary children must provide materials that are age, stage, and culturally appropriate. These materials allow children to create and explore their world autonomously. Adults can intervene as needed, but setting up the environment to encourage autonomy in securing and replacing materials facilitates the use of the materials (Photo 8-6). For example, one fourth-grade teacher set up a math center that included Legos,® cusinare rods, math games such as Monopoly, cards, Uno, and a variety of manipulatives such as cones, cylinders, and pyramids. The children used the center whenever they had free time because they could access, use, and replace the materials without interrupting other students—the process was seamless.

8-6 Classrooms should be designed to encourage investigation and inquiry.

3. **Play-based curriculum** Consider alternate ways to meet learning objectives and outcomes. Active learning pedagogy provides students with opportunities to engage in meaningful study. The most common types include problem-based, experiential, and inquiry-based learning (Sirinterlikci, Zane, & Sirinterlikci, 2009). These methods provide opportunities for students to learn in a way that is interesting, meaningful, fast paced, and fun.

4. **Play relationships and interactions** Because children are more influenced by peers in middle childhood, the possibility of relational issues must be a high priority. With younger children, moving to the area can often change the play so that all children are included. It is more difficult to intervene with older children, but it is even more important to do so. Conducting a sociogram will provide a great deal of information about the structure of play groups (Figure 8-1). Many studies relate the effects of bullying to isolation during middle childhood. Ensuring that children create a community of players is one of the most important goals for middle childhood.

What do you think?
Do teachers in local schools support play for children in middle childhood and, if so, how do they do it?

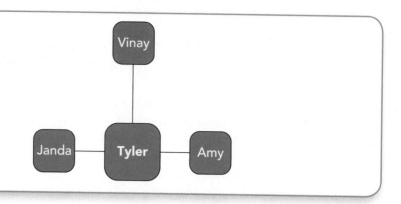

Figure 8-1 A sociogram provides information about the structure of play groups.

© Cengage Learning 2015

Begin by asking any three children who they play with during recess. In the preceding example, ask Janda, Vinay, and Amy about their playmates and write the names of their playmates on the sociogram chart. Connect lines between the names so that all the children are connected. If a child is not included in the relationships, then focus on that child because he is being marginalized either purposefully or unintentionally by the class.

5. **Play skills**   Evaluating locomotor skills on the playground seems rather obvious. It is just as logical to evaluate academic and social skills during the play of elementary children. Watch a mathematics game and you will easily know who still needs assistance with specific skills. Watch children engage in a dramatic production and you will know who does and does not need assistance with reading and language skills. The key to evaluation is a thorough knowledge of what children in elementary school need to know. The adult who knows what the child needs to know can evaluate play so that the play experiences can be changed to ensure optimal play and learning.

✳ 8-5   Play in the Core Content Areas

Play in the middle childhood years can be used to enhance learning in the content areas of reading, mathematics, science, and social studies (Madray & Catalano, 2010). Even though children still engage in some practice, constructive, and symbolic play, games with rules dominate the middle childhood years. If the dominant play is used to guide pedagogy, then games with rules optimize learning in the middle childhood years.

8-5a Reading

The relationship between play and literacy has been confirmed in numerous studies (Christi & Roskos, 2006; Fisher, Hirsh-Pasek, Golinkoff, Singer, & Berk, 2011).

- Constructive play occurs when children create puppets or props for plays.
- Symbolic play is evident when children read books, write stories and poetry, and engage in play that allows them to use imaginative thinking.
- Games with rules are evident when children play board or computer games to learn words (Scrabble, Yahtzee). In classrooms that use a four- or five-block system, the system is a type of game that requires children to follow the rules as they move from center to center.

8-5b Math

Play and mathematics are natural partners. Among the goals that the National Council of Teachers of Mathematics (NCTM) identified for elementary students is ideational fluency (NCTM, 2013). Children who play and pretend or imagine are predisposed to competency in this area.

- Constructive play occurs when children use unit blocks, wooden blocks, three-dimensional models, or attribute blocks, which are three-dimensional plastic blocks in four basic shapes. A longitudinal study found a correlation between mature, complex block play and competency in math class in high school (Wolfgang, Stannard, & Jones, 2001).

- Symbolic play is facilitated when the teacher sets up a bank or a store to teach children about the concept of money. The children role-play working in a bank, playing the customers, writing checks, and depositing and withdrawing money.

- Games with rules provide an optimal opportunity to learn mathematics. Board games give children an opportunity to practice mathematical concepts. Card games create an opportunity for children to develop computational skills.

8-5c Science

Play provides a natural way to learn science. Many elementary students pass tests yet know very little real science. Using play provides a way to encourage meaning making so that children see science at work in their everyday world rather than as just a list of information necessary to pass a test.

- Symbolism occurs as children role-play with magnets, magnifying glasses, and microscopes.

- Games with rules occur as children explore science concepts through learning centers. Allowing children to view a learning situation as a game that they are playing in which they must solve the problem allows them to fully embrace the scientific method.

The Science Circus (SC) is a playful game with rules. The Science Circus is an approach advocated by Janice Koch (2010) to encourage children to participate collaboratively rather than competitively, which occurs when children participate in science fairs. The teacher sets the stage by setting up a series of four or five stations. Each center has an activity card that gives the children directions about what to do or poses problems that the children must solve. When these problems and activities are based on the same topic, such as clouds, the student may begin at a station that includes a book and digital recording, move to a station that focuses on making replicas of clouds, then go to a cloud classification center, and then finally move to a station that allows the child to see how a real cloud is made in a bottle. If the topic is a science process, different topics that all involve one or more of the processes can be used. The key is that there is no one right way to conduct the Science Circus. The goal is for the children to have opportunities to engage in guided play, exploration, and discovery. Many schools set up a Science Circus at night and invite parent(s) to experience the SC with their child. In this way, parents develop their understanding of children's play that includes activities for learning.

8-5d Social Studies

Play provides a natural vehicle for learning social studies. Play is a natural way to set up a democratic community in the classroom.

- Constructive play happens when children make paper mache models.

- Symbolism or imaginary thinking happens when children role-play a mailperson in the classroom and deliver mail to classroom mailboxes. They can role-play the leader of a nation at a mock United Nations to understand the world exchange of goods and commodities. Historical events can also serve as an impetus for role-play. For example, instead of talking about the events that led to the American Revolution, the teacher can provide uniforms for students, give them information to read, and hold a debate in full uniforms at the end of the study.

- Games with rules reflect the essence of social studies. Geography and economics include content that works well for board and computer games.

- The Oregon Trail (Rawitsch, Heinemann, & Dillenberger, 2012) was one of the first computer programs dealing with social studies content and is still a popular website.

Play and playful activities provide opportunities for teachers to create powerful communities for learning academic content.

✳ 8-6 Play-Based Curriculum

A curriculum that embraces play as a medium for learning encourages creativity and autonomy. These are skills that are deemed valuable for the twenty-first century. When children study a topic that they select, they tend to be more interested than if the topic were selected for them (Froiland, Oros, Smith, & Hirchert, 2012). The schedule must be designed to allow children to rotate between periods of learning new information and play (Table 8-1). Play allows children the opportunity to strengthen their knowledge and test new ideas. It promotes what Eleanor Duckworth (1987) calls the "having of wonderful ideas." Once children arrive on the school campus, they should be allowed to go to their rooms.

TABLE 8-1 Sample Schedule for Middle Childhood Classes
Arrival
Morning Meeting
Block One
Lunch
Block Two
Recess
Block Three
Evening Meeting
Arrival

© Cengage Learning 2015

They can put away their materials and then go to breakfast (if available), go to the school store to buy school supplies (if available), go to the library to select books or conduct their research, or use materials in their room to play games. It is never appropriate to have children wait until an adult decides they can enter the room. When they enter the room, they should be able to choose an activity and play until the morning meeting.

1. **Morning Meeting—Creating a Community of Learners** Children need to come together to meet and greet everyone in the room. Sometimes teachers will begin by tossing a ball of yarn to one child, who must introduce herself, say one thing about what she did at home last night, and toss the yarn to another student, who must remember what the previous child said and then repeat before tossing it to the next child. Another idea involves tossing a ball that has questions written on it. Each child responds to the question located on the spot where they caught the ball. There are many additional activities that can build community. Morning meeting is an excellent time to expose students to current events. In addition, teachers can use the morning meeting as a time for framing the day's activities or sharing thoughts and ideas that will lead to questions children may want to study. The morning meeting should not be more than twenty minutes long and should involve a combination of active, passive, and musical activities

2. **First Block—Culture and World** The morning is an open block focused on the acquisition of literacy and social studies knowledge and skills. Available activities include literature circles, dramatic readings, poetry, and theater. Skill groups are directed by the teacher whereas other groups are involved in independent games or activities.

3. **Lunch** Many teachers have a duty-free lunch and eat lunch in an area separate from the children. Although this may seem to be a good situation, it is not. Teachers who stay with their children have the opportunity to engage in rich conversations with their children. It has been observed on numerous occasions that teachers spend at least five to twenty minutes sorting out what occurred in the lunchroom when they return to the class. Additionally, it is optimal for children to have outdoor time at lunch. If this is not possible, then children should be able to play games or look at books between the time that they finish eating their food and return to the room.

4. **Second Block—Curiosity** The focus of the second block is on mathematics and science. The teacher works with a small group while others engage in board and card games, construction with Legos or other blocks, and other mathematics- or science-related activities, such as using magnifying glasses or microscopes; using electronic devices; using measuring tapes and string; or setting up an aquarium.

5. **Recess** Children need at least thirty minutes outdoors during the school day; outdoor recess can take place in the morning or afternoon.

6. **Third Block—Investigation** Students rotate between STEM activities and inquiry projects. Later in this chapter we provide additional information about implementing these activities and projects in the classroom. Teachers who do not want to use inquiry projects can use the project approach, which was discussed in Chapter 7. Learning centers should be available for children who have finished one project but have not started another.

Did You Get It?

A fourth-grade teacher assigns a biography project to her students. Rather than assigning the person to be studied, she encourages each student to select a subject that he or she likes. The students are likely to

a. flounder and feel lost.
b. choose inappropriate subjects.
c. display interest in the topics they choose.
d. feel overly pressured.

Take the full quiz on CourseMate

7. **Evening Meeting—Consolidation**   A group meeting at the end of the day gives the teacher time to review and solidify the day's activities and discuss plans for the next day and week. Afterward, children clean and straighten the room. They can keep card games out until they leave the room.

✳ 8-7 Learning Centers for Middle Childhood

Learning centers that encourage play and learning should be a part of every elementary classroom. When children are in a room that allows them to move to different spaces/centers and engage in activities that they choose, they are more invested in the classroom and thus discipline problems are diminished or minimized. Children who are required to complete worksheets in one seat for the entire day become easily distracted and bored. Heads go down on the desks as children tire of the routine. In contrast, children in classrooms with centers move to those centers, engage in competitive games or thoughtful play with their friends, and return to the next set of activities refreshed. The combination of play and instruction or small group work provides the child with a stimulating environment for learning.

1. **Library**   The library or book center is a staple in most classrooms. This center must be inviting and feature places to sit along with an array of interesting books (both fiction and nonfiction books that reflect the variety of reading levels in the class). Puppets and marionettes encourage the use of oral language, storytelling, and script writing. Before adding puppets and marionettes, discuss how these are used in different cultures found around the world. For example, adults in countries such as Italy and France enjoy puppet and marionette shows. Adding this global perspective expands children's knowledge base of culture and provides materials that they can use to express their feelings.

2. **Games**   It is imperative that games are displayed and labeled so that children selecting and replacing the games can count the pieces that should be in the game before they return the game. Playing games reinforces math facts and concepts. Watching children create the highest numbers through multiplication and addition will give the teacher an idea of who still needs assistance with their multiplication facts. Games can be used to practice needed skills such as multiplication and division. Winning a game is a more powerful motivator than a sticker on a chart listing students who have mastered the times tables.

3. **Technology**   All classrooms need a variety of technological tools in the classroom. A camera provides a way to capture science as it occurs. From watching a weed bloom on the playground to watching milk and water spill on a plastic surface, the camera and printer provide a way to both capture and communicate activities and experiences. Computers open the classroom to the world. Children can access data from around the world, track migration as citizen scientists, and discover the culture of the world. Tablet computers feature educational games that provide a medium for children to learn through play as they track their score on the game they played.

4. **Legos,® blocks, and manipulatives**   Few materials are as versatile as Legos. Placing Legos in the classroom allows children to use them in their own way. They can construct and reconstruct. There should be a place to store ongoing projects that they require a great deal of time to create. Legos and other blocks can be used in a variety of ways. For example, when

teachers allow children to add stickers to the block (using temporary tape), children can communicate their view of complex issues.

5. **Sustainability** There are few issues that are more important than sustainability. The classroom can have a center for collecting paper and plastic recyclables. These recyclables can also be used for art and other projects throughout the year.

6. **Communication** For some children, creative writing is play. Other children see the process of writing the words as their play. The writing center can encourage writing through the inclusion of a variety of instruments for writing, stimulating books and articles, and writings by others in the classroom. When mailboxes are placed in the room, children play out the role of mail carrier as they deliver their mail.

7. **Inquiry** Children should investigate, explore, and engage in inquiry every day. A science center that is complete with goggles, microscopes, magnifying glasses, and so forth and that can be accessed all the time provides the necessary tools for looking closely and thoughtfully at the world.

8. **Arts and crafts** This area is as important for elementary school as for preschool. Children can set up their own paints or materials and can express their creativity while honing their fine motor skills. As with all centers, the arts and crafts center needs to be independently operated and maintained by the students.

9. **Interest center** This center reflects its name. It is based on the ever-changing interests of the children. It might be based on seasonal, political, global, or local issues. The key to this center is that the children select the topic and set up most of the materials.

10. **Current events** Newspapers and magazines are interesting to many children. Many children who are unmotivated to read basal readers enjoy reading a sports page in a newspaper. Some children who are uninterested in other forms of literature find any material about current events relevant. Setting up a center to focus on either local or global current events encourages children to become informed citizens living in a global society.

Role of Play in STEM Education 8-8 ✳

Integrating science, technology, engineering, and mathematics (**STEM**) into the classroom has captured the attention of the educational and political community (Congressional Research Service, 2013–2014) and provides an exciting way to incorporate play into the curriculum. STEM projects, as mentioned earlier, use an activity-based approach that is similar to the project approach discussed in Chapter 7. STEM activities and projects involve inquiry, creativity, and persistence.

Play in STEM education can be examined in two ways. First, during STEM, children try on different roles: scientist, engineer, reporter, designer, creator, and judge. Assuming these roles allows children to play out their interests in different career choices. For example, the children in the case study at the beginning of the chapter assumed the role of astronaut as they engaged in play/tasks that they would do if they actually were astronauts. This type of role-play also provides an impetus for learning new material.

Children's Engineering Taps the Power of Play

Dr. David W. Burchfield

At John Wayland Elementary School, a Rockingham County Public School in Bridgewater, Virginia, "Children's Engineering" (CE) has become an integral and highly valued part of our instructional program. This approach taps the power of play, allowing all of our 550 students, PreK–5, to make creative and relevant connections to the curriculum and to be actively involved in the learning process.

© Cengage Learning 2015

Children's engineering is an integrated instructional approach that draws on interdisciplinary methods such as STEM and Design and Technology Education. It harnesses the design process used in the field of engineering, which challenges the learner to solve a problem, design a solution, construct or build a model, evaluate the product and process, and then share and reflect upon the learning that has taken place. Children are presented with a "design brief" (a description of the challenge: a problem set in a context related to the curriculum), specific requirements for the activity, a list of the limited resources they may use, and often a rubric that gives specific criteria for evaluation.

Eight years ago, our faculty agreed to take a year-long, graduate-level course in Design and Technology Education. This led to the implementation of Children's Engineering as a school-wide initiative and program. Children's Engineering projects and activities take place in both the classroom and in our "Engineering Lab." Some teachers offer "creation stations" in their classrooms, with a variety of materials available to the students for regular, open-ended, creative opportunities.

The Engineering Lab has been outfitted with tools, tables, and materials. Teachers sign up for this space on a monthly calendar posted outside the door for more in-depth and messier project work. Most of the materials in the lab that fuel the projects are donated by parents and members of the community from a "scrounge list" that is sent home a couple of times a year asking for donations. A parent volunteer weekly sorts the materials into bins, which are labeled for easy access. Some funds are needed to purchase tools and consumable materials such as glue sticks and masking tape, but the vast majority of what is used is donated.

In the early years of prekindergarten and kindergarten, ages four to six, the projects are highly creative and design briefs are aimed at making very child-centered and personal connections while at the same time reinforcing skills in the curriculum.

Students may be observed making a creation about the first letter of their name, or crating a fire truck after a field trip visit to the local fire station. Students in the older primary years of grades one through three, age six to eight, are challenged with more detailed and specific requirements for their projects. Students develop a portfolio for their work; the portfolio includes a planning phase, which asks them to draw and plan their solution. At the end of the project, students reflect about what they would do to improve the solution or product.

In the upper elementary grades (grades four and five, age nine to eleven), connections for CE projects are made to the science curriculum so that it is not necessary to carve out more time for another subject in an already crowded schedule. Fourth graders design and build models of roller coasters as they study force, energy, and motion. Fifth-grade students design and construct musical instruments; these instruments demonstrate their understandings of the concepts of volume and pitch.

Feedback from students, parents, and teachers about our Children's Engineering program has been overwhelmingly positive. Parents are thrilled that their children are happy and are learning, but they value even more that their children are developing twenty-first-century learning skills such as problem solving, teamwork, and communication. Teachers enjoy a chance to involve students in learning that is active and engaging rather than just focusing on separate subject areas and test preparation. Students thrive with this approach because they regain a sense of authority and control and they feel a renewed spirit of creativity and playfulness in their learning.

Dr. David W. Burchfield is a Principal at John Wayland Elementary School located in Rockingham County Public Schools, Virginia.

8-7 STEM activities provide a platform for play and learning.

Did You Get It?

A principal who decides that all of her teachers should use the STEM system probably aims to

a. hire only teachers who are state and board certified.

b. create a gender neutral school.

c. incorporate play into the curriculum.

d. integrate the theories of many child development specialists.

Take the full quiz on CourseMate

Additionally, play occurs as the children engage in the tasks and projects (Photo 8-7). The entire process of STEM is a type of game that has specific rules. Children are not really building a tower of paper towels that is a real tower; rather they are building a model of the tower. Children also engage in cooperative play as they decide what problem will be considered and move it through the process to completion. The social interactions that occur allow some children to assume the leadership role and to delegate roles to others. Although the process began in the preschool classroom when children designated others as the parent or child, it continues into the elementary classroom and beyond as children engage in cooperative, collaborative group play.

Develop a Plan for Creating a STEM Project 8-9 ✳

Creating a STEM project is somewhat like problem solving. The children discuss a question or pose a question, gather information about the topic, generate solutions, and share their findings with others. The difference is that in a STEM project, the generation of solutions involves designing and creating a project to solve a problem, testing it, and then reporting the results. The process involves the following:

1. scientific inquiry

2. technology used to discover information and build the project or apparatus

8-8 When children are involved in projects, they are fully engaged in meaningful learning.

Did You Get It?

Two students plan how to build a simple robot. They are implementing the _____ stage of the STEM program.

a. S

b. T

c. E

d. M

Take the full quiz on CourseMate

3. engineering to design and build the project or apparatus

4. mathematics to calculate needed materials and complete the calculations on the design

Placing STEM at the center of the curriculum places the emphasis of the curriculum on inquiry, design, and production. Students engaged in these activities are not sitting passively in a classroom reading books and completing worksheets. Because some parents may be concerned that children are playing in middle childhood (Guest, 2011), it is especially important to embed appropriate play within accepted academic programs. A STEM-based curriculum empowers children to solve problems and create solutions (Photo 8-8). For middle childhood, this is a type of play; it is a game that optimizes lifelong learning skills.

✳ 8-10 Developing a Plan for Implementing an Inquiry Project

When teachers establish a plan to develop an inquiry project, they are engaging in a combination of role-play and games with rules. As children assume the role of investigator, they are playing a role that prepares them for life. As they complete the project, they are engaged in a type of game with rules.

The value of engaging in inquiry learning has been well documented (Falk & Blumenreich, 2005). Inquiry is the basis of science and scientific inquiry. Children who develop the skills necessary to implement an inquiry project are equipped to solve problems and engage in critical thinking. The following is a plan for implementing inquiry projects:

1. First, the project begins when a group of children demonstrates an interest in knowing about a topic. They share the topic with others and inquire about who might want to join the group.

2. Next they *pose a question* that they want answered. The key to inquiry is that the question emanates from the student's interests. For example, they might want to know why dogs are pets but pigs are not.

3. The teacher serves as a guide as the children *gather information* to answer the question. Children can go to the library to secure resources such as books, magazines, newspaper articles, and Internet sites. They make notes about their findings and begin writing about what they are discovering. If they are studying the question about the dog and pig, half of the group might study dogs and the other half might study pigs. Each member of the group will need her own notebook and journal for gathering information.

4. Afterward, the children *conduct the investigation* to answer the question. After the children have studied dogs and pigs, they may want to visit to a farm or pet store where they can see both.

5. Students decide on *which instruments* will be used to collect data. Will they use pictures, measurements, or anecdotal records to capture data?

6. *Data collection* is the next step. All members of the team will collect data. This might consist of taking pictures, writing notes, collecting artifacts, or taking videos.

7. *Data analysis* follows as the student try to understand their findings. Examine the data in terms of how well the question is answered. One method that is used frequently is to read all the information and look for themes. Children can do this by putting major points on index cards that are color coded using markers.

8. Students then *explain the findings*. They discuss what they found by conducting the activity and collecting and coding the data. What do the findings mean?

9. When finished, children *write a summary* of the study and prepare a media presentation about the study.

10. The final step involves the submission or publication of the *final, written report*. Students work together to finish the project. Peer evaluation forms are submitted individually.

Describe a Play-Based 8-11 ✳ Assessment System

Play-based assessment for middle childhood is somewhat similar to that of kindergarten and lower primary school in that it involves utilizing play to understand how the child is progressing in play as well as in other areas of development. For example, a third grader who has a developmental delay may find functional or sensory play more enjoyable than symbolic play or games with rules. Accommodating the need to engage in a different type of play would be part of the child's Individualized Education Plan (IEP). A third grader without developmental delays who does not participate in games warrants special observation and assistance. The child has some issue that is preventing him or her from being a full participant and remediating this at an early age will ensure that this issue does not become a barrier to success in the classroom or life.

Watching children during play can provide a great deal of information about the child's overall cognitive, social, and sometimes physical development. For example, in the inquiry project (Table 8-2) the child's cognitive abilities could be assessed by investigative and communicative skills, the child's social and

TABLE 8-2   Inquiry Project Steps for Children
1. Ask a question.
2. Find out all you can.
3. Try it, do it, or visit it.
4. How do you know?
5. What did you discover?
6. Figure out what it means.
7. Tell and write the story of the study.
8. Share what you found.
9. Publish your work.

© Cengage Learning 2015

Digital Download   Download from CourseMate

emotional development could be evaluated through his engagement and group interactions, and the child's physical development could be observed as he completed the project. Checklists and anecdotal records such as those described in Chapter 3 could be used to capture and report the information.

Although it is helpful when considering the child's development to look at development in terms of age, stage, and culture, the child's overall progress must be considered. This is the true value of a play-based approach in elementary school. Children who sit alone on the playground or cannot engage in prolonged play with others are at risk. Robert Coplan and Murray Weeks (2010) studied unsociability in middle childhood and found that unsociable children—distinguished from shy children—tend to play alone more, and boys experience difficulty with others whereas girls do not have obvious difficulty. The successful resolution of play problems can lead to a more productive adult life, and this is the real goal of play for middle childhood.

PLAYSCAPE: REFLECTIONS

The play described at the beginning of this chapter reflects a view of play that emphasizes play as a legitimate instructional activity—as a medium for learning. Play at this level generally does not follow a program model, but rather it is as individualized as the teachers who set up the programs. The assessment is equally varied. Charting participation in different aspects of the space station and evaluating reports of the play scripts are used as indicators of the student's interaction and learning. There is a sense of trust that if the students have been engaged in play that involves walking on the moon and sending a report back to earth, then the students must know how to communicate and use technology. Rather than measuring isolated skills, the student's overall performance is assessed through play.

✿ Summary

8-1 List the benefits of play for middle childhood children.

Cognitive development is enhanced through play as children refine and develop memory and language skills in a safe yet enjoyable environment. Social development is facilitated because play provides a safe haven for developing a sense of self as a competent, independent person who can be a friend while developing a sense of personal integrity. Play provides a natural venue for strengthening gross and fine motor skills. And play increases knowledge of the academic content.

8-2 Describe the characteristics of play in middle childhood.

In upper primary school, children have more places to play but less time to play. Games with rules dominate, and play with a friend is the preferred social interaction. Stable, focused play occurs as children engage in competitive games that allow them to evaluate their own play with that of a peer.

8-3 Analyze the impact of context on middle childhood play.

The context for play at home and in the community impacts the child's performance at school. Places to play, time for play, and materials available for play all affect how play occurs in different areas.

8-4 Explain the role of the adult in supporting play in elementary school.

The adult must ensure that children have access to play; provide age-, stage-, and culture-appropriate materials; ensure fair treatment during peer interactions; and assess the various levels of play.

8-5 Recognize how play can be integrated into the core content areas of reading, math, science, and social studies.

Play can be integrated by looking at how different types (practice, constructive, symbolic, and games with rules) of play can be used to inform pedagogy in reading, math, science, and social studies.

8-6 Design a play-based curriculum that utilizes a play-based approach.

A schedule for a play-based curriculum might include the following: arrival, morning meeting, block 1, lunch, block 2, recess, block 3, and evening meeting. The room would be equipped with learning stations where children can work together on STEM and inquiry projects.

8-7 Identify ten play-based centers appropriate for middle childhood.

(1) Library; (2) games; (3) technology; (4) Legos, blocks, and manipulatives; (5) sustainability; (6) communication; (7) inquiry; (8) arts and crafts; (9) interest center; and (10) current events.

8-8 Discuss the role of play in STEM education.

Play occurs as children try on different roles in the STEM project. Additionally, the process of STEM is a type of game that has rules the children must follow as they engage in a type of cooperative, collaborative group play.

8-9 Create a plan implementing a STEM project with a group of elementary children.

The process involves scientific inquiry, technology used to discover information and build the project or apparatus, engineering to design and build the project or apparatus, and mathematics to calculate needed materials and complete the calculations on the design.

8-10 Compare and contrast an inquiry project with a STEM project.

STEM projects reflect an emphasis on engineering and building a product, whereas inquiry projects focus more on answering a question through scientific inquiry.

8-11 Describe a play-based assessment system.

A play-based assessment system involves evaluating the child's play in terms of her age, stage of development, and culture. It also involves using the child's play to assess the child's knowledge of specific content information as well as overall development.

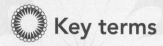
Key terms

Technology and Internet Resources

Middle Childhood Development/National Network for Child Care http://www.nncc.org/ Good source of activities for afterschool activities.

Activities . . . .

1. InClass Labs

A. Think about a classroom that you enjoyed in elementary school. Why did you enjoy the classroom? Now, think about a classroom that you did not enjoy. Why did you dislike about the classroom? Use this information to design a classroom for children who are in upper primary or elementary school.

B. Select a grade in upper primary that you want to teach. Look at the common core curriculum for that grade. Now, design appropriate play that can be used to assist the children in meeting the national standards.

2. Research and inquiry learning

A. Investigate the research behind the use of STEM education. Does the research support the public mandate for STEM education?

B. Examine two articles on STEM education. Compare and contrast one that promotes it and one that views STEM as a deterrent. What is your stance on STEM now? Share your views with the class.

3. Service learning

A. Volunteer in an afterschool program designed for middle childhood (second through fifth grades). Visit the site at least three times. What types of play are available, and what do the children prefer to play?

B. Did you see a connection between learning and play in the afterschool program? Why or why not?

4. Family Connections

Work with a local PTA to create a play night at the local elementary school. Create a list of games that parents can use at home to simulate play and learning.

5. Advocacy

A. Create a brochure that describes the benefits of play for middle childhood. Distribute the brochure throughout the community.

B. Survey play places in your neighborhood. Do middle childhood children have clean, free places to play?

Visit CourseMate for this textbook to access the eBook, Did You Get It? quizzes, Digital Downloads, TeachSource Video Cases, flashcards, and more. Go to CengageBrain.com to log in, register, or purchase access.

References

Ashwell, K. (2012). *The brain book*. Buffalo, NY: Firefly Books.

Baines, E., & Blatchford, P. (2011). Children's games and playground activities in school and their role in development. In A. Pelligrini's (Ed.), *The Oxford handbook of the development of play* (pp. 260–283). New York: Oxford University Press.

Bergen, D., & Fromberg. D. (2009). Play and social interactions in middle childhood. *Phi Delta Kappan. 90*(6), 426–430.

Brookings Institute. (2007). The 2007 Brown Center Report on American Education: How well are American students learning? Retrieved from http://www.brookings.edu/research/reports/2007/12/11-education-loveless

Christi, J., & Roskos, K. (2006). Standards, science, and the role of play in early literacy education. In D. Singer, R. M. Golinkoff, & K. Hirsh-Pasek (Eds.), *Play = learning: How play motivates and enhances children's cognitive and social-emotional growth* (pp. 57–73). New York: Oxford University Press.

Congressional Record Service (2013–2014). HRes. 45, Bill to encourage STEM education in U.S. Retrieved from:http://beta.congress.gov/bill/113th-congress/house-resolution/45

Coplan, R. J., & Weeks, M. (2010). Unsociability in middle childhood: Conceptualization, assessment, and associations with socioemotional functioning. *Merrill-Palmer Quarterly, 56*(2), 105–130.

Corno, L., & Xu, J. (2004). Homework as the job of childhood. *Theory Into Practice, 43*(3), 227–233.

Crone, E., Windelken, C., van Leijenhorst, L., Honomichi, R. D., Christoff , D., & Bunge, S. A. (2009). Neurocognitive development of relational reasoning. *Developmental Science, 12*, 55–66.

Duckworth, E. (1987). *"The having of wonderful ideas" and other essays on teaching and learning.* New York: Teachers College Press.

Erikson, E. (2000). *Childhood and society.* New York: W.W. Norton.

Falk, B., & Blumenreich, M. (2005). *Power of questions: Guide to teacher and student research* (5th ed.). Portsmouth, NH: Heinemann.

Feldman, R. (2012). *Child development* (5th ed.).Upper Saddle River, NJ: Pearson.

Fisher, K., Hirsh-Pasek, K., Golinkoff, R., Singer, D., & Berk, L. (2011). Playing around in school: Implications for learning and educational policy. In A. Pelligrini (Ed.), *The Oxford handbook of the development of play.* Oxford, UK: Oxford University Press.

Froiland, J., Oros, E., Smith, L., & Hirchert, T. (2012). Intrinsic motivation to learn: The nexus between psychological health and academic success. *Contemporary School Psychology, 169*(1), 91–100.

Gardner, H. (1983). *Frames of mind.* New York: Basic Books.

Guest, A. (2011). Cultures of play during middle childhood: Interpretative perspectives from two distinct marginalized communities. *Sport, Education, and Society, 18*(2), 167–183.

Howie, L., Lukacs, S., Pastor, P., Reuben, C., & Mendola, P. (2010). Participation in activities outside of school hours in relation to problem behavior and social skills in middle childhood. *Journal of School Health, 80*(3), 119–125.

Jackson, B. (2007). Homework inoculation and the limits of research. *Phi Delta Kappan, 89*(1), 55–59.

Kaboom! (2013). Map of Play. Retrieved from http://mapofplay.kaboom.org

Koch, J. (2010). *Science stories: Science methods for elementary and middle school teachers,* (5th ed.). New York: Cengage.

Madray, A., & Catalano, A. (2010). The curriculum material center's vital link to play and learning: What's the connection? *Education Libraries, 33*(2), 11–17.

Manning, M. (1998) Play development from eight to twelve. In D. Fromberg & D. Bergen (Eds.), *Play from birth to twelve and beyond: Contexts, perspectives, and meanings* (pp. 154–162). New York: Garland.

Martlew, J., Stephen, C., & Ellis, J. (2011). Play in the primary school classroom? The experience of teacher supporting children's learning through a new pedagogy. *Early Years, 31*(1), 71–83.

McDevitt, T., & Ormrod, J. (2013). *Child development and education* (5th ed.).Upper Saddle River, NJ: Pearson.

National Council of Teachers of Mathematics (NCTM). (2013). Children and Mathematics. Retrieved on July 20, 2013 from http://www.nctm.org/resources/elementary.aspx

Piaget, J. (1962). *Play, dreams, and imitation.* New York: W. W. Norton.

Piaget, J. (1965). *The moral development of the child.* New York: Penguin.

Ortlieb, E. (2010). The pursuit of play within the curriculum. *Journal of Instructional Psychology, 37*(3), 241–246.

Othman, S., & Said, I. (2012). Affordances of Cul-de-sac in unban neighborhoods as play spaces for middle childhood children. *Social and Behavioral Sciences, 38*, 184–194.

Rawitsch, D., Heinemann, B., & Dillenberger, P. (2012). The Oregon Trail. Retrieved on July 12, 2013 from http://www.oregontrail.com/hmh/site/oregontrail/. Minnesota Educational Computing Consortium. Chicago, IL: Houghton-Mifflin/Harcourt Publishing Co.

Sandberg, A., & Heden, R. (2011). Play's importance in school. *Education, 39*(3), 317–329.

Santrock, J. (2010). *Children* (11th ed.). New York: McGraw-Hill.

Sirinterlikci, A., Zane, L., & Sirinterlikci, A. L. (2009). Active learning through toy design and development. *Journal of Technology Studies, 35*(2), 14–22.

Smith, E., & Lillard, L. (2012). Play on: Retrospective reports of the persistence of pretend play into middle childhood. *Journal of Cognition and Development, 13*(4), 524–549.

Thalia, G., & Ellen, W. (2010). Engagement in role play, pretense, and acting classes predict advanced theory of mind skill in middle childhood. *Imagination, Cognition & Personality, 30*(3), 249–258.

Wolfgang, C., Stannard, L., & Jones, I. (2001). Block play performance among preschoolers as a predictor of later school achievement in mathematics. *Journal of Research in Childhood Education, 15*, 173–180.

9 Supporting PLAY for Children with Special Needs

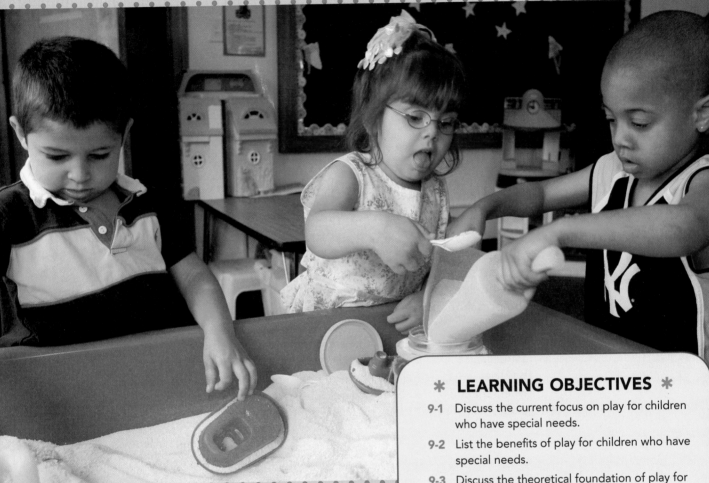

STANDARDS COVERED IN THIS CHAPTER

Council of Exceptional Children—Division of Early Childhood Standards **CEC** **DEC**

ECSE 1K2 Trends and issues in early childhood education, early childhood special education, and early intervention

ECSE 3S1 Develop, implement, and evaluate learning experiences and strategies that respect the diversity of infants and young children and their families

ECSE 5S2 Facilitate child-initiated development and learning

ECSE 5S4 Structure social environments, using peer models and proximity, and responsive adults to promote interactions among peers, parents, and caregivers

ECSE 6S1 Support and facilitate family and child interactions as primary contexts for development and learning

✳ LEARNING OBJECTIVES ✳

9-1 Discuss the current focus on play for children who have special needs.

9-2 List the benefits of play for children who have special needs.

9-3 Discuss the theoretical foundation of play for children who have special needs.

9-4 Explain the role of the adult in fostering play in an inclusive setting.

9-5 List three characteristics of play in inclusive centers.

9-6 Identify the major components of child-focused interventions.

9-7 Evaluate the criteria for models of inclusive program delivery.

9-8 Distinguish the major goals of family-based practice.

9-9 Design a plan to use assistive technology to encourage play in inclusive settings.

9-10 Discuss transdiciplinary play assessment in the classroom.

© Cengage Learning 2015

ECSE 7K2 Plan and implement developmental and academic content

ECSE 7S2 Plan and implement developmentally and individually appropriate curriculum

NAEYC Program Standards

2c Involving families and communities in their children's development and learning

4a Understanding positive relationships and supportive interactions as the foundation of work with children

4b Knowing and understanding effective strategies and tools for early education

5a Using content knowledge and resources in academic disciplines

5b Knowing and using the central concepts, inquiry tools, and structures of content areas or academic disciplines

5c Using knowledge, appropriate early learning standards, and other resources to design, implement, and evaluate meaningful and challenging curricula for each child

---

✳ PLAYSCAPE: CASE STUDY

Sheena is taking Twila to preschool for her first day. Because Twila experienced trauma during birth that resulted in developmental delays, Sheena knows she has been especially protective of Twila and is reluctant to leave her at the preschool. This will be Twila's first group experience, and Sheena wonders how Twila will interact with the other children. Will she have friends? Will the other children play with her? After Sheena drops off Twila, she thinks about calling during the day to check on her, but she doesn't. She knows Twila is in good hands, and she knows that the preschool uses a play-based program. She can't wait to pick up Twila after work.

When Sheena arrives at the preschool after work, Twila is sitting in the same chair that she sat in when she entered the classroom that morning. The ball that Twila is holding is the same one she was playing with that morning when Sheena left. Sheena is concerned. Did her daughter play or did she sit alone? Did she stay in the chair throughout the day? Did she find a friend? What did Twila do all day?

Explaining Play Behaviors

The provocation to play in this scenario could be the ball or other materials in the room. Children are intuitively drawn to toys and materials that can be used for new and creative combinations. In the same way, children who have disabilities can and will play, but they may need additional support or materials to support their play. Today more children like Twila are in inclusive settings. Inclusion is defined as "the philosophy [that] … seeks to include a variety of students with disabilities, including students with severe disabilities, in a general education setting with an opportunity to participate in curricular and non-curricular activities" (Alquraini & Gut, 2012, p. 45). An inclusive setting provides stakeholders with the opportunity to work together to optimize the child's experiences and opportunities within the context of the classroom. Notice that Sheena, like all parents, wants her child to find a friend and play. Perhaps Twila's friend left or perhaps she did not have a playmate during the day. Only the early educator knows. The role of the early educator in facilitating play among children with special needs cannot be overstated and will be thoroughly explored in this chapter.

Focus on Play for Children with Special Needs

Several factors have improved the state of play for young children with disabilities or delays. These include research and scholarship, professional organizations, and globalization.

1. **Research and Scholarship**   For many years, the landscape was dominated by a view that children with special needs should spend their time in direct instruction learning skills rather than spend their time playing (Hanline & Daley, 2002). Today, play is viewed as a medium for learning and for understanding more about the child's ability to use symbolism and language (Thiemann-Bourque, Brady, & Fleming, 2012). The research literature for children who have special needs is replete with studies of play.

2. **Professional Organizations**   The Council for Exceptional Education Division of Early Childhood (CEC-DEC) is the largest professional organization committed to developing policies and practices that enhance the growth and development of young children who have disabilities or delays (Sandall, Hemmeter, Smith, & McLean, 2005). Because the home is a place where the child would be if he did not have a disability or delay, the home is considered a natural environment for an infant or toddler. Professionals visit the child and family in the home and provide coaching to support the child's participation in family activities. Play provides a natural platform for engaging the child within the context of the family and home. Some children are medically fragile and can only play with play therapists or developmental specialists in hospital settings (Photo 9-1). Other children who are stable enough to go home face the challenge of time to play. Too often, traveling from hospital offices to specialized therapy offices such as the one shown in Photo 9-1 does not leave time for play.

© Cengage Learning 2015

9-1 All children, including those who spend a lot of time in hospital settings or in physical therapy, need opportunities to engage in as much unstructured play as possible.

The plan for services is outlined in the Individualized Family Service Plans (IFSPs) or Individualized Education Plans (IEPs) depending on the age of the child. IFSPs (below three years of age) and IEPs (age three and above) regularly include play as a way to acquire required social, cognitive, language, and motor skills and competencies. The recognition of play as a viable medium for learning has legitimized play in the lives of children who have conditions requiring special support.

3. **Globalization**   Another factor influencing play for children who have disabilities or delays is American exposure to the practices in countries throughout the world. For example, the schools of Reggio Emilia, Italy provide a model for interested parents and early educators. These schools have been engaged in inclusion for very young children since the 1970s

Did You Get It?

Clara has Down Syndrome. In her inclusive classroom, her teacher?

a. has her spending most of her time learning skills through direct instruction.

b. gives her extensive play time so she can learn.

c. restricts her activities to a large extent.

d. offers playtime, but has no research to back up the offering of playtime.

Take the full quiz on CourseMate

and are recognized for their approach to working with young children with special needs. Although they do not have as many children in their classes who have delays or disabilities as found in American classrooms, children who have special needs are viewed as special citizens who have special rights—not special needs (Smith, 1998). The Reggio Emilia approach promotes the belief that all children have multiple ways of expressing themselves that are not always evident to adults. They focus on ensuring the child's happiness at school. This is accomplished by accepting the many ways (languages) that children use to express themselves and by delighting in what the child can do. The child is included when he wants to be and not when he is tired or chooses not to do so. Although following the child's lead may be more difficult when the child has a communication delay or other disability, this idea has the potential to change how we view not only inclusion but also the child's right to play in his own unique way.

✳ 9-2 Benefits of Play for Children Who Have Special Needs

The value of play for development and growth for typically developing children has been well documented (Bredekamp & Copple, 2007; Piaget, 1962). Play is perhaps even more important for children who have disabilities or delays (Barton & Wolery, 2010). Because play can serve as a platform for increasing the child's ability to pretend and engage others, some scholars advocate for play as a separate developmental domain (Lifter, Foster-Sanda, Arzamarski, Briesch, & McClure, 2011). Although the benefits of play are unique and specific to the individual child, some common attributes have been identified.

1. **Play supports growth and development in five developmental domains** Professionals in the field of early childhood special education have identified five developmental domains that are deemed important in understanding the child who has special needs. These five development domains are identified as (1) cognitive (thinking and learning), (2) social and emotional (interacting with others), (3) physical (fine and gross motor skills), (4) communication (speaking and listening), and (5) adaptive behavior (self-help skills) (Sandall, Hemmeter, Smith, & McLean, 2005).

2. **Play can lead to increased opportunities for social interaction and cognitive development** The nature of the exceptionality—sensory loss, motoric, cognitive, or emotional—will affect play. For children with mild disabilities, play provides an arena that brings children with and without disabilities together. This may occur at home or in inclusive programs. For children with more severe disabilities, play provides a mechanism for exploring the world, joy for the child and her friends, and a sense of normalcy for the family. This may occur at home, in inclusive preschools, or in special settings. In this way, play affects growth and development in all five domains.

3. **Play is part of a natural environment** A **natural environment** is defined as the place where the child would naturally be if the child were

not disabled. Part C of the Individuals with Disabilities Education Act (IDEA) 2004 provides funding for services to children with disabilities who are under the age of three (IDEA, 2004). For these very young children, natural environments include the home as well as family-based or group child care settings. Play at home or in group care settings is a part of the natural environment.

IDEA (2004) Part B funds services for children three and older and requires that children are educated in the least restrictive environment (LRE). Schools view inclusive classrooms as natural environments or LREs. Play is the method of curricula delivery in many inclusive settings. Although early educators strive to deliver programs that reflect best practices for all children, ensuring appropriate experiences for children who have special needs requires specialized knowledge of the child's delay or disability. For this reason, professionals work together as a team to ensure optimal outcomes for the child.

4. **Play can serve as a bridge for teaching and learning** One professional publication, *The Division of Early Childhood Recommended Practices in Early Intervention/Early Childhood Special Education* (Sandall, Hemmeter, Smith, & McLean, 2005), produced by the Council of Exceptional Children Division of Early Childhood (CEC-DEC), encourages play for children who have disabilities. The Council encourages the adult to use the children's preferences to increase engagement and promote interactions with peers (Photo 9-2). "Play routines are structured to promote interactions, communication, and learning by defining roles for dramatic play, prompting engagement, prompting group

© Cengage Learning 2015

9-2 Children who have mild disabilities may need moderate intervention to ensure that mature play occurs. The amount of intervention is contingent on the child's needs.

What do you think?

This section dealt with the benefits of play for children and their families. But there are other outcomes that were not included in the list. What are some other additional benefits of play for children who have special needs? Are there additional benefits for families of children with special needs?

CEC DEC

Did You Get It?

When planning for the learning needs of a child with a developmental disability, a teacher wants to include play as its own developmental domain. Why would she do that?

a. because for children with special needs, play is more important than skill development

b. because play can increase a child's ability to pretend and engage

c. because children with special needs require help when playing

d. because children with special needs can play better than they can learn

Take the full quiz on CourseMate

friendship activities, and using specialized props. Adults use children's preferences to increase engagement and to promote interactions with peers" (p. 79).

The Division of Early Childhood (DEC) acknowledges the challenge involved in ensuring that activities, play, and assessments are developmentally appropriate for children with special needs (Smith, Hemmeter, & Sandall, 2006). DEC recommendations are provided in terms of direct and indirect services. Direct services include those services that directly involve the child and family. Direct services strands consist of the following:

1. assessment
2. child-focused interventions
3. family-based practices
4. interdisciplinary models
5. technology applications

Indirect services are those that support the delivery of direct services. Indirect supports are comprised of the following:

1. policy
2. procedures
3. systems change
4. personnel preparation

Early intervention occurs when infants and toddlers who have disabilities or delays receive special services to facilitate the child's development and participation in the context of the family. The delivery of both direct and indirect services directly affects early educators who are caring for and educating young children with special needs. Professionals from different agencies provide services to infants and toddlers in the context of the home. Providers who are funded by Part C of IDEA are called Early Interventionists (EIs). Other providers, such as Parents as Teachers, Healthy Beginnings, and hospital-based interventions, are not considered EIs. For example, an EI may show the parent how to assist the child who has a motor delay. The parent tosses the ball to the child so the child can try to toss it back to her. The parent does this at home, and the child begins to respond. Although this is fun and play for the child, it is facilitating the development of the child's gross and fine motor skills, hand—eye coordination, and social interaction. In this way, play connects professionals and family and provides a common platform or bridge for teaching and learning.

✳ 9-3 Theoretical Foundation of Play for Children with Special Needs

Constructivism posits that all children construct knowledge through their actions on objects and interactions with others. Children who have special needs may have transmission problems that keep them from processing the information from their own actions and interactions. They may need special assistance or intervention. For example, put a ball in front of a two-year-old who is typically developing and the child will probably try to throw, hit, or kick the ball. A child who has a disability may or may not react to the placement of the ball in front of him. This is why it is essential that knowledgeable adults facilitate play. The adult must know how to provide support in a way that allows the child to construct his understanding of the world in his own way. Adaptations vary based on the individual needs of the child. Adults who assist the child will need to know the child's diagnosis and possible avenues for encouraging play (Linder, 2008). That is, the child's interests, preferences for play, and new experiences are used to guide the child's play. The work of two constructivists and scholars of human development, Jean Piaget (1962) and Lev Vygotsky (1978), has implications for the field of early childhood special education.

9-3a Piaget

Piaget believed that children learn through play, and that a child's play is a direct reflection of the child's cognitive development (Piaget, 1962). For example, if a child is chronologically age seven, his play should reflect the mastery of skills typical for his age. That is, the child should be engaging in symbolic play and games with rules. If, however, the child is chronologically age seven but mentally age two, the child may benefit more from opportunities to engage in play that are designed for the state that precedes symbolic play (i.e, sensorimotor). Piagetians might recommend exploratory or sensory play as a way to include the child in classroom settings and provide appropriate experiences for the child. For example, the child in the scenario above may be given blocks, simple puzzles, or a tub of styrofoam peanuts for exploration. Although Piaget's scholarship has been criticized, the notion that children exhibit qualitatively different ways of thinking at different ages or levels can inform how appropriate activities are selected to meet the child's unique cognitive needs.

Additionally, Piaget's scholarship has implications for studying social interactions. Piaget found that children transmit social rules and regulations during play. Odum and Brown (1993) found that children who are typically developing do not regularly include children with disabilities in playgroups. In a 2002 study, Brown and Bergen found that children were included only when an adult was present. More recently, O'Connor and Stagnitti (2011) found that teacher intervention made a difference in play behaviors, language, and social skills. Without adult intervention, children who have disabilities or developmental delays may not have the opportunity to benefit from play with other children.

9-3b Vygotsky

In contrast, Vygotsky viewed play differently. He viewed play as a vehicle for learning (1978). He believed that children who play together engage in the highest level of abstract thought prior to formal classroom instruction. Vygotsky believed that during play, children create the zone of proximal development (ZPD). The ZPD is created when the child moves from a state of knowing with the assistance of others to a state of knowing for herself. Anyone who has learned to ride a bicycle has experienced the thrill of riding alone as he moved through the zone. Children who have disabilities create the zone of proximal development during play with the facilitation and support

> **What do you think?**
>
> Constructivism and behaviorism have been used to inform practice for several decades. More recently, brain development research has informed practice. What theoretical approach informs your view of how children who have delays or disabilities think and learn? How will your theoretical view affect your interactions in the classroom?

9-3 An adult actively assists this child in a project. With appropriate assistance, this child will experience success and develop along with his peers.

Did You Get It?

Nory, a three-year-old who has a disability, is repeatedly excluded from play by her classmates. What is the best approach for the teacher to take to change the situation?

a. speak to the parents of Nory's classmates about their behavior

b. reward children who include Nory in their play

c. remain present and involved in the organization of play

d. take Nory aside and play with her one-on-one

Take the full quiz on CourseMate

of adults or peers (Photo 9-3). Children who do not move through the zone of proximal development may remain at a novice level of play. Vygotsky's work has inspired several studies that investigate scaffolding to sustain gains made during interactions with adults or peers. When children play with adults or more capable peers, they model or engage in mimicry—a major component of behaviorism and social learning theory. Although constructivism and behaviorism are vastly different, they can both inform the theoretical framework of inclusion.

9-3c Current Research

All children enjoy play. All children have the innate desire to experience the joy and euphoria of play, but play is more than fun. Play is a medium for learning for all children, including those with disabilities. Research studies have investigated the value of play for typically developing children for over a century. Only recently have scholars begun to examine the benefits of play for children with special needs (Hess, 2006).

During the past decade, the study of pretense and symbolic play among children diagnosed with autism has received the most attention. The increase in research is correlated with the rise in reported cases of autism. The Centers for Disease Control reports that in a sample of 14 sites in 2008 the prevalence of autism occurred once in every 88 births (Balo, 2012). That is, approximately one in every 54 boys and one in every 252 girls in the network were diagnosed with symptoms that placed them on the Autism Disorder Spectrum (ADS) (Balo, 2012). Although this is a sample and cannot be extrapolated to the United States, it does show an alarming increase in the number of cases of ASDs that are identified. Autism is caused by genetic factors, but the diagnosis is based on behavior characteristics that include socialization, communication, and imagination (Jarrold & Conn, 2011). Autism is viewed as a spectrum disorder because it may present as a very mild case to a very severe case. For this reason, it is difficult to make generalizable statements about children who have autism.

Researchers who study brain development have looked at the relationship between autism and the prefrontal cortex of the brain. Many of the executive functions that the prefrontal cortex performs are impaired in children with autism (Jarrold & Con, 2011). This explains why children with autism can engage in functional play, but not symbolic play on their own.

With adult intervention, some children with autism can engage in pretend play. Natalie Porter (2012) has developed a system to scaffold pretend play for children with high-functioning autism through the use of circumscribed interests. "This process involved (1) creating a web, (2) modeling pretend play through use of divergent materials, (3) modeling verbal interaction in pretend play, and (4) providing theme boxes and field trips/excursions" (p. 161). As more techniques are developed, children with high-functioning autism may be able to engage in more sophisticated play. The next decade of research will be instrumental in understanding the unique play of children who have delays or disabilities.

Role of Adults in Child-Focused 9-4 ✳ Intervention

The role of early educators in creating a caring, effective environment for young children with disabilities or delays cannot be overemphasized (Barton & Wolery, 2010). Early educators work with other professionals to develop a plan of action and cooperation; create an environment that facilitates play; intervene to support play; foster interaction among all children; and assess the effectiveness of their actions on the child's development (Sluss, 2000). The quality of the child's life and learning is affected by the adult's competency in carrying out these responsibilities. Strategies for fostering high-quality inclusion are as follows:

1. Remember that children with disabilities are children first. There is no alternative to viewing the child as a young human, a young citizen, and a young member of society.

2. Use children-first language when discussing the child. Never refer to the child by the name of the disability. For example, Twila, who was mentioned in the case study at the beginning of this chapter, should always be referred to as Twila.

3. Identify sources of support in the community and school system. Create a circle of support for the child, family, and teachers. What are the federal resources available? What are the state resources available? What other resources and support are available? Every state has an early intervention network. Find out what resources are available, and create a safe circle of support.

4. Build relationships with family members, guardians, or other adults who care for the child and serve on the Individual Family Service Plan (IFSP) or IEP team. Communication is the key to building a relationship of mutual respect and trust.

5. Maintain confidentiality in all issues at all times.

6. Make appropriate adaptations for the child. Recognize that you do not know everything you need to know to about inclusion or about the child's disability or delay. Each child is unique and each disability is unique. Ask questions about how to adapt the classroom and materials to encourage interaction.

7. Use assistive technology appropriately to facilitate the inclusive process.

8. Support play. An environment that encourages play for all children creates an optimal setting for inclusion.

9. Conduct meaningful assessments and make changes in the program to improve learner outcomes.

10. Remember that children with disabilities are *children first and that all children can play.*

Did You Get It?

A special education teacher and his assistant use their students' disabilities as a reference point when discussing them. They call one, "Down," another, "Asperger's," and so forth. They are

a. promoting a child focused intervention.
b. being clinically cold
c. correct to leave out personal details.
d. diminishing the children as individuals.

Take the full quiz on CourseMate

* 9-5 Supporting Play in Inclusive Centers

Given the recent support for the play of children who have special needs, early educators have an opportunity to provide play-based programs that are developmentally appropriate for all children. This can be accomplished through active participation in the development of the IFSP, the IEP, and specialized knowledge of inclusion. An IFSP, or **Individual Family Service Plan,** describes the child's goals and a detailed plan for meeting these. It is a plan for delivering services to the child and family. The IEP (**Individual Education Plan**) is similar to the IFSP but focuses more on the individual child. Both use a team approach that requires interaction among the teacher, parents, professionals, and early interventionists. Multiple goals and objectives can be met through play when teachers and parents are aware of the benefits of play for all children. As mentioned at the beginning of this chapter, **inclusion** is defined as the inclusion of children with disabilities or delays in settings with typically developing children. **Inclusive settings** are places where children with and without special needs are involved in play and other educational activities. The individual needs of all children are met in inclusive settings or centers.

Early educators must be aware of three major differences in the play of children with delays or disabilities:

1. Children with special needs may not always initiate play. They may not engage in play on their own. Teachers must intervene to encourage play and to foster strategies that will encourage self-generated play.

2. The nature of their special condition will affect their play. For example, a child who has cerebral palsy and is in a wheelchair may need specialized assistance in motor areas but may be able to challenge anyone to a competitive game of checkers if appropriate adaptations are made so that the child can communicate her thoughts to others. A child who has visual impairments may need special assistance to participate in the chess game but can move throughout the room with minimal assistance. Play for children with special needs must be individualized to reflect the child's assets.

3. Their play may not look like the play of their peers. Each child will have a unique way of playing. Teachers must know the child well enough to understand her unique play (Hess, 2006). These ideas are applicable to all developmental levels, infants through primary school.

Next we discuss how to use these techniques with different age groups.

9-5a Infant and Toddler Centers

Inclusion of all children in child care settings begins in the infant/toddler center. Although some children with disabilities or delays are undergoing medical treatment or may be hospitalized, those who can participate in a group setting should be encouraged to do so. The presence of special needs infants and toddlers in the child care center may require some additional knowledge and adaptations on the part of the early educator. Centers that include infants with disabilities or delays may need additional staff to facilitate inclusion. When setting up the placement, the center needs to be fully aware of the child's needs so that his needs can be met.

Did You Get It?

A teacher notices that Ayana, a student with a developmental disability, seems to follow others' play instead of initiating play. The teacher should

a. encourage the other students to follow Ayana's lead.

b. intervene to encourage play.

c. speak to the school's director about her concerns.

d. ask Ayana's parents to encourage her to initiate play.

Take the full quiz on CourseMate

When a parent of a child with a disability places his child in a center, there are several benefits for the child and the family (Photo 9-4). First, doing so provides normalization for the family. They are just like other families when picking up their children from a center. In addition, placing the child at the center allows the parent to work or rest at home. Often, parents of children with disabilities or delays do not receive any respite from 24-hour, seven-day-a-week care. One of the ancillary benefits is that families of typically developing children interact with peers who have disabilities on a regular basis. This fosters interaction between all children and families in a community setting.

9-5b Preschool Centers

Inclusion in preschool centers may be a continuation of involvement in an infant/toddler center or it may be the child and family's first experience in a group setting. A curriculum that is developmentally appropriate for typically developing children may need adaptations for a child with disabilities or delays. The plan for a child who has disabilities must be tailored for the individual needs of the child. The IFSP or IEP should include a plan for transitioning into the public school setting. **Transition** is a term used to describe the process that occurs when the child in an infant/toddler center (birth to age three) that has been under the auspices of federal funding and guidelines is moved to a preschool setting (age three) that is funded and regulated by the state educational system. Sometimes transitions are very smooth as the child moves easily from one system to another. Other transitions are very difficult as the child and family become tangled in bureaucracy. Early educators should take an active role in ensuring that transitions are appropriate and occur in a way that optimizes the child's growth and development.

9-5c Primary Age Settings

It is especially important at this age that teachers take a proactive role in encouraging social interactions among all children. Primary age children have a special need to belong at this age, and children who display differences may not be treated kindly by others who are trying to belong to a specific group. **Relational bullying**, or bullying that occurs when a group of children isolate one child by leaving when the child is near, may occur and may go unnoticed by adults (Stopbullying, 2013). Children with disabilities or delays are sometimes targeted by children who do not understand why they are different (Rose, 2011). Adults must ensure that all children who are in group settings are safe from bullying and abuse.

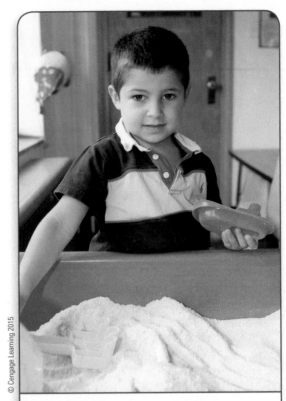

© Cengage Learning 2015

9-4 Smooth transitions occur when all adults involved are aware of the child's special needs and strengths. For example, this child enjoys and benefits from sensory play at the sand table.

© Cengage Learning 2015

▶❚❚ TeachSource Video Case 9-1

5–11 years: Developmental Disabilities in Middle Childhood

The children in this video clip both have disabilities but are experiencing success in their environment.

1. What factors contributed to the success of each child?

2. What is one thing that you will remember about this video clip that will help you in the classroom?

Watch on CourseMate

Play as the "Work" of Children

Jen Newton, PhD

Since play is the work of young children, there are countless opportunities within a child's routine to facilitate, model, and engage in play behaviors. Children with varying abilities benefit from the same language, social, and play experiences as young children who are typically developing because the first five years are a time of constant skill acquisition for all children. Supporting the development of the myriad of skills children gain in this time rests on promoting each child's play by knowing his strengths, preferences, and readiness. Each child has strengths to contribute to his family, his friends, his classroom, and his community. The role of early childhood education is to identify a child's unique strengths and capitalize on them in order to meaningfully include each student, build classroom community, and promote learning outcomes.

Play is central to learning in the early years. Children gain knowledge in all areas—literacy, numeracy, science, just to name a few—and through play and interacting with toys, materials, peers, and caretakers. Although all play skills do not come naturally to all children, each child is motivated by some component of play. Whether it is blinking lights or noises on a cause-and-effect toy, rolling a ball back and forth, or lining up trains on a train track, children will engage in play on some level. The early

© Cengage Learning 2015

childhood community is tasked with extending that play, building on a child's natural instincts for play, and promoting learning through play.

Dr. Jen Newton completed her graduate work at the University of Kansas and currently teaches in the Inclusive Early Childhood Education program at James Madison University, where she is an Assistant Professor and Director of the JMU Young Children's Program.

✳ 9-6 Child-Focused Interventions in Inclusive Settings

Inclusion can be facilitated through child-focused intervention. **Child-focused intervention** is a term that refers to the process of decision making regarding how to design, implement, and monitor the child's experiences and activities to ensure optimal growth in all areas. All aspects of the child's educational program are included in this term. Child-focused intervention involves (1) designing appropriate environments, (2) individualizing and adapting the curriculum, and (3) using systematic procedures to optimize outcomes. These three components are discussed in the following subsections.

9-6a Designing Appropriate Environments

The major goal of environmental design is to ensure that children are active and engaged members of the learning community. This is accomplished by looking at different aspects of the environmental design.

Physical Environment.   The first and most basic requirement involves physical safety and accessibility. Classrooms must meet all guidelines established by the state and local agencies. Children must be able to play in the classroom and on the playground without endangering their health or safety. Children who cannot reach the table cannot play checkers. Children who cannot move a walker on a rug in the block center cannot play with the blocks. Children who are not mobile cannot enjoy the fresh air or enjoy, without special assistance, watching a kite fly up toward the clouds. Safety is a basic need of all children, and children who have disabilities or developmental delays may need extra safety precautions in place when they visit learning labs during recess or center time, when they are in family child care settings, and when they leave indoor settings to go outdoors. Children who have disabilities need play spaces that are physically accessible and safe.

9-5 Materials that optimize interaction are important for children who have special needs.

Additionally, the physical environment must facilitate, not detract from, the child's ability to engage in the task or activity (Photo 9-5). Shelves of potentially distracting materials can be covered or turned away so that the child is not distracted from learning. It is vital to ensure that the environment is a positive influence on learning and a safe place in which to learn.

Social Dimension.   Psychological safety is critically important. The need for physical safety is sometimes obvious, especially when working with children who have physical disabilities. Psychological safety is equally important. As mentioned in 9-5c, children who have disabilities sometimes face a type of relational bullying that may go unnoticed by adults. For example, the other children may choose to leave a center when a child who can benefit from special assistance enters the play area. This may not be obvious to someone who is just looking across a room of children but is obvious to the child who is trying to enter play. Early educators must not allow this abuse to exist or continue in a classroom. Adults must also model positive interactions with children who have special needs. They can provide a safe environment by acknowledging that play may look different. If children are hindered when they attempt to retrieve a ball by reaching for it with their foot, they are less likely to repeat the behavior. This may stop their play. Children who have disabilities need a psychologically safe classroom in which optimal play can occur. This should not be translated as letting the child create chaos. Rather it means that everyone must respect the rights of all children in the classroom. Understanding that play for children who have disabilities or delays may be unfamiliar to other children and adults is a crucial first step in facilitating play for children with special needs.

Play as Curriculum.   The environment must be designed to encourage play and interactions among all children. Many IFSPs will include play activities that can occur in play centers. To facilitate play by all children in the class, the class must be set up to encourage play. This may mean that pictures and words are used together to denote centers so the child who has a reading disability can understand what to do. It may mean that the pictures of centers are

TeachSource Video Case 9-2

Tyler: Augmentative Communication Techniques for a Kindergarten Student with Autism and Language Issues

Strategies for fostering learning are evident in this video. Tyler used PECS (Picture Exchange Communication System) to learn content knowledge.

1. How could you use PECS to foster Tyler's play?

2. What other strategies could be used to foster Tyler's play with his classmates?

Watch on CourseMate

Did You Get It?

When John, who has severe ADHD, enters the block area, three other children who were playing there stand up and leave. This is an example of

a. self-preservation.

b. interactional assessment.

c. premature judgment.

d. relational bullying.

Take the full quiz on CourseMate

large enough for children who are visually impaired, or it may mean that music starts prior to the end of play so children who have difficulty moving to new activities will have a clear indication that play is ending and other activities will occur.

Intervention. The environment must be designed to encourage intervention in a child's natural environment with minimal disruption to the child's schedule. When the child meets with the early interventionist (EI), the EI is responsible for developing an environmental plan that will foster the child's safety and security. Intervention that occurs in a natural setting benefits the child because it is a natural part of the class experience. Creating an optimal environment for inclusion also involves the delivery of instruction, which is discussed in the next subsection.

9-6b Individualizing and Adapting Instructional Practices

Goals for the individual child who has special needs are developed by a team composed of the child's family, early educators, early interventionists, and other specialists based on the child's individual disability or delay. The child's abilities are aligned with state guidelines by team members who develop an IFSP or IEP. Many IFSPs and IEPs include play as a goal or as a means to a goal. A plan for collecting data must also be devised and approved by the team. A summary of the collected data provides a picture of the child in context and is used to guide interactions and instruction during play.

The early educator has an active role in implementing the play activities included in the IFSP. It is the early educator who makes a difference. The importance of adults during interactions among children with and without special needs has been noted in several classic studies. Harper and McCluskey (2003) conducted a study of teacher-child and child-child interactions in inclusive preschool settings. They observed interactions of 24 preschoolers (three to four years old) during free-play time. Half of the children had disabilities and half did not. The proportion of time that preschoolers spent talking to peers and to adults was negatively correlated. Whenever teachers and children initiated conversations or interactions, the child was less likely to initiate or engage in interaction with peers. Early educators who know when and how to talk to children can foster inclusion. On the other hand, those who do not may actually be training the child to interact only with adults. Teachers can avert this situation by fully understanding the concept of scaffolding and implementing different scaffolding techniques on a consistent basis. First, all adults in the setting must understand the difference between helping and scaffolding and know when to use each appropriately. Helping occurs when the adult or more competent peer provides support that enables the child to function in the current context. For example, picking up a toy for a child who is struggling to retrieve the object from the floor may appear to be the appropriate action. This *helps* the child by placing the toy in his hand (see Photo 9-6). This action enables the child to play in the current context. In contrast, scaffolding occurs when the more competent other *assists and guides* the child in developing a better strategy for retrieving the object. Scaffolding is an assistive strategy that can be used in the current context but enables the child to do it on her own in the future. In this way, the zone of proximal development (ZPD) is actualized as the child moves along the continuum of independence.

9-6c Using Systematic Procedures

The most important aspect of the environment is the adult-teacher or interventionist in the classroom. Mature play occurs when knowledgeable adults facilitate play. When Stanley Greenspan (1998) demonstrated a game of catch to parents of a child with autism, he demonstrated a technique that the parent(s) could use to work with their child. As they tossed the bean bag together, they facilitated the child's ability to focus on the bean bag and the child became sufficiently competent to toss and catch the bean bag on his own. The child moved through what Vygotsky calls the ZPD. That is, although he was unable to play alone when he began, he could toss and catch the object without assistance after a great deal of play. Of course, this happened gradually—it did not occur overnight. This process required adults who knew how to enhance play.

Greenspan's seminal work opened the door for additional studies in this area (Greenspan & Robinson, 2004). For example, Murdock and Hobbs (2011) conducted a study to examine the effectiveness of Picture Me Playing intervention. They found that the play dialogue of children with autism spectrum disorders increased after intervention. Additional research will yield even more strategies for facilitating development (Smith, Hemmeter, & Sandall, 2006).

© Cengage Learning 2015

9-6 As he struggles to pick up the blocks, he is developing his balance and coordination skills. Although it is tempting to pick up the blocks and hand them to him, the process of picking them up is valuable. The skilled teacher knows when to observe and when to intervene.

Models of Program Delivery 9-7 ✳

Inclusive programs should reflect program delivery as recommended by the Council for Exceptional Children—Division of Early Childhood. The CEC-DEC (Sandall et al., 2006) recommends an interdisciplinary model that is comprised of the following:

1. Teams, including family members, who make decisions and work together.

2. Professionals who cross disciplinary boundaries. These will be professionals involved in early childhood special education, occupational therapy, physical therapy, and speech-language pathology.

3. Intervention focused on function, not services.

4. Regular caregivers and regular routines providing the most appropriate opportunities for children's learning and receiving most other interventions (pp. 132–139).

9-7 Ensuring that the child is an active member of the class requires assistance from every member of the team.

© Cengage Learning 2015

These strands can be interwoven to create a model for developing a play-based program. First, all adults who interact with the child are considered stakeholders and must be involved equally in decisions and assume responsibility for those decisions. Second, everyone must acknowledge the contributions that everyone on the team makes to benefit the child (Photo 9-7). Third, the intervention must be focused on function, not service delivery. That is, intervention should involve those services that maximize the child's engagement and autonomy in her daily life. If a child needs a piece of equipment to be able to move to the playground, then the entire team should view this as a collective goal. Fourth, learning is holistic, so intervention should be as simple as possible and fit within the context of the group setting. This view values the early educator as an integral part of the child's intervention and values play as a medium for learning. It is therefore imperative that early educators are knowledgeable of ways to enhance and foster play with all children. These guidelines should be evident in all-inclusive programs for young children, as described in the following section.

✳ 9-8 Family-Based Practices

It is imperative that families form partnerships with the adults who work with the child throughout the day and who provide intervention on a weekly basis (Sandall, Hemmeter, Smith, Sandall, & Askew, 2005). These partnerships benefit the child and all adults involved in the process. If a child develops an interest in playing with blocks at school, then the parent(s) may want to encourage block play at home. If the child has been playing with paper that he crushes into a ball at home, this may be viewed negatively at school unless the early educator knows that the child has been playing at home with crushed paper. When families and professionals work together, the child benefits and play progresses.

Focusing on the child's strengths and capabilities instead of what the child cannot do fosters a positive relationship between the family and team members. By focusing on what the child achieves, the child is measured in terms of his own abilities. Instead of using a measure that reflects typical development, the measure reflects the child and the child's individual strengths, abilities, and rate of growth. If developmental levels based on chronological age were used, the five-year-old might be expected to engage in sociodramatic play. When the child could not meet this set goal, both parents and professionals would be disappointed. By looking at the child in terms of his current level of sensorimotor play, a more positive picture is created. Some refer to this as a **strengths-based approach**.

Assistive Technology 9-9 ✳

Assistive technology can be considered for every child. That is, assistive technology includes any equipment or materials that can be used to facilitate the capacity of the individual. Many teachers think of computers and computerized boards when assistive technology is mentioned, but adding knobs to a puzzle so a child can solve the puzzle is also assistive technology. Assistive technology ranges from the very simple to the very complex (Photo 9-8).

9-9a Adapting Toys and Other Materials

Adults can encourage social interaction through the selection of toys. Toys for children who have disabilities may need to be adapted. For example, if an airplane toy requires fine motor skills to manipulate, why not add another airplane that a child who is less coordinated can use? If a truck is available that

9-8 Technology is a tool that can be used to facilitate the child's interaction with the world.

▶‖ TeachSource Video Case 9-3

Assistive Technology in the Inclusive Classroom: Best Practice

Jamie is a five-year-old who has cerebral palsy. The video depicts an instructional activity in the classroom.

1. How can the inclusive facilitator encourage play through the use of assistive technology?

2. What are some low-tech adaptations that can be made to facilitate Jamie's play in the classroom?

Watch on CourseMate

What do you think?

Technology has grown exponentially in the past ten years. Professionals in the field are concerned that very young children will use too much assistive technology and that it will actually impede learning. How do you feel about the use of assistive technology with infants and toddlers, preshoolers, primary age children, and those in middle childhood? Explain any difference or variation in your response to the different age groups.

requires turning a wind-up key, find another truck that can be adapted by adding a larger knob. Adaptations will need to be specific to the child's disability. In general, toys and materials should be *accessible, adaptable,* and lead to *cooperative interaction.*

Accessible. Some toys in the center should be accessible to all children. Preschoolers should be able to access blocks, dolls, books, or balls without a teacher's assistance. One caveat is that some children become overstimulated by too many available materials. If this is creating a problem, rotate toys on a regular basis. A survey of the room can determine the level of accessibility of the toys and play materials. Consider the needs of the individual children. Materials for art should be accessible to children in wheelchairs. If a child has visual impairments, signs with large pictures or signs in Braille can be used depending on the child's degree of impairment. Ensuring that the placement of the shelves and materials is stable will help children navigate the classroom.

Adaptable. Toys can be adapted with low-tech or high-tech changes (Photo 9-9). When most educators think of assistive technology, they think of computers and computerized systems and accessories. These are effective and necessary for some children. When these adaptations are recommended by the IFSP, a professional trained in assistive technology will assist in implementing these systems. On/off switches are also high-technology changes that have positive results. When a switch is added, the child can operate the toy independently. She can experience cause and effect, and this adds to her sense of accomplishment. In addition, the child has a special toy that other children may also enjoy.

9-9 Adapting materials can be as simple as substituting large beads for small beads.

Low-tech adaptations are just as useful and can be done by adults in the classroom. Adaptations that use minimal technology include adding large knobs to puzzles, adding Velcro to blocks, and adding grips to crayons and markers. Simple items such as muffin pans and soft balls can be turned into a game. The muffin pan with soft, multicolored pom-poms is generally recommended as the infant's first puzzle but is equally effective with children who have motor delays. Materials for art can also be adapted for children with visual or auditory impairments. Adding aromas like vanilla to play-dough extends the experience for children who have visual impairments. Putting marbles in a rubber ball allows children with visual impairments to feel the movement of the marbles/objects inside the ball. Again, it is important to emphasize that the changes should reflect the needs of the individual child.

Cooperative Interaction. Toys should be selected that encourage cooperation. Balls encourage interaction between two children when they roll or toss them to each other. Wagons and toys that require two children encourage cooperation. Water play and house play are also designed to stimulate social play. Adults can select toys that facilitate social interaction. For example, if the only blocks available are soft cloth blocks, the child may be content to carry and stack—or even sit on the blocks! Placing different blocks or firefighter hats in the block center provides the child with props that can encourage dramatic or more mature play. It is critically important that children with

Did You Get It?

A teacher notices that a student with special needs has troubling gripping markers. He adds large rubber grips to a group of markers, and presents it to the child. He is using

a. a technique that is likely to embarrass the child.

b. assistive technology.

c. inappropriate methodology.

d. a nice gesture that is unlikely to help the student.

Take the full quiz on CourseMate

disabilities have the opportunity to engage in more mature play with their more competent peers. Adapting materials for children who have special needs fosters inclusion.

When children play together, the play is greater than the sum of its parts. For example, water play encourages physical (gross and fine motor development), social (interactions with other children), and cognitive development (sensory stimulation, language development). But it is also an enjoyable part of the normal day, or normalization, which is one of the goals of inclusion.

Assessing Play 9-10 ✳

Evaluating play involves observation, assessment, and reflection. Early childhood special educators now advocate **transdisciplinary play-based assessment**. This occurs when a team of specialists simultaneously observe a child at play and assess different aspects of the child's play and interactions. In a 2011 study by Lifter, Foster-Sanda, Arzamarski, Briesch, and McClure reported that the second edition of the *Transdisciplinary Play-Based Assessment*, written by Toni Linder (2008), provides a guide for evaluators to use in examining play in terms of a child's sensorimotor, emotional and social, communication and language, and cognitive functioning. This evaluation occurs by observing how the child plays with a familiar adult and how she behaves in a play environment (Lifter, Foster-Sanda, Arzamarski, Briesch, & McClure, 2011, p. 234).

When planning optimal programs for children, begin by focusing on what they can do rather than what they cannot do. In the same way, when planning play, focus on what children can do (Photo 9-10). Begin by valuing the child's unique style of play, and then facilitate movement to a more mature level. In this way, adults enhance not only growth and development, but also the quality of the child's life.

9-10 Communication among stakeholders is basic to establishing good relationships that result in optimal outcomes for children and their families.

Did You Get It?

A psychologist, speech therapist, physical therapist, and teacher simultaneously observe and assess their student at play. They are probably

a. engaging in transdisciplinary play-based assessment.

b. overstimulating the child.

c. displaying unprofessional behavior.

d. writing a research paper about the child.

Take the full quiz on CourseMate

PLAYSCAPE: REFLECTIONS

When she arrived at the center to pick up Twila, Sheena did not know what Twila had experienced during the day. Twila could not clearly communicate that her day was filled with play, including block and sand play. Twila could not tell her mom that she met her new physical therapist, Mary Beth, who provided intervention while she was playing outdoors. She could not tell her mom that she ate lunch with two friends. Although Twila may not be able to tell her mom what happened today, Sheena has a reasonably good idea of what her daughter experienced based on the goals on Twila's IFSP. She will find out exactly how much Twila is gaining from the experiences when Sheena meets with Twila's team in two weeks. For now, she is satisfied that Twila is responsive to her request to leave. She collects her materials, they stop for a hug from her teacher, Tamara, and they travel home. Sheena is satisfied that she made the right choice to place her daughter in an inclusive center that encourages play and friendship.

 # Summary

9-1 Discuss the current focus on play for children who have special needs.

Play is viewed as a universal right for all children. Professionals now view play as a natural environment, and play is included in IEPS and IFSPs. The influence of Reggio Emilia has created a new level of interest in understanding the child's view of the world.

9-2 List the benefits of play for children who have special needs.

A. Play supports growth and development in five developmental domains: (1) cognitive (thinking and learning), (2) social and emotional (interacting with others), (3) physical (fine and gross motor skills), (4) communication (speaking and listening), and (5) adaptive behavior (self-help skills).

B. Play provides a natural environment. Goals listed in the IEP and/or IFSP can be implemented during play in a natural environment, thereby optimizing results.

C. Play provides a medium for teaching and learning. For children who are constantly moving between different settings, play provides a common ground.

9-3 Discuss the theoretical foundation of play for children who have special needs.

Piaget and Vygotsky have long influenced the field of early childhood education, and they are equally important in early childhood special education. Creating an eclectic approach that combines Piaget and Vygotsky, behaviorism, and the most current work on brain development may provide the best approach for inclusive classrooms.

9-4 Explain the role of the adult in fostering play in an inclusive setting.

The adult must respect the child and the child's family within the context of the community. This knowledge must be used to inform practice, program design and delivery, as well as assessment.

9-5 List three characteristics of play in inclusive centers.

(1) Children with special needs may not initiate play, (2) the nature of their special condition will affect their play, and (3) their play may not look like the play of their peers.

9-6 Identify the major components of child-focused interventions.

Child-focused intervention involves (1) designing appropriate environments, (2) individualizing and adapting the curriculum, and (3) using systematic procedures to optimize outcomes.

9-7 Evaluate the criteria for models of inclusive program delivery.

Teams make decisions and work together; professionals cross disciplinary boundaries; intervention is focused on function, not services; and the regular caregivers and routines serve as the basis for receiving all other intervention.

9-8 Distinguish the major goal of family-based practice.

The major goal of family-based practice is to establish a partnership among the adults who work with the child. This allows the creation of a strengths-based approach.

9-9 Design a plan to use assistive technology to encourage play in the inclusive settings.

A plan to use assistive technology can range from simple to complex. It can be as simple as placing a grip on a pencil or a cushion to support the child as they sit in their chair. It can be as complex as adding switches to toys for cause and effect or using computers to communicate so that the child can actively interact with their peers.

9-10 Discuss transdiciplinary play assessment in the classroom.

When planning play, focus on what they can do. Begin by valuing the child's unique style of play and, then facilitate movement to a more mature level.

 ## Key terms

Assistive technology, 257
Child-focused intervention, 252
Early intervention, 246
Inclusion, 250

Inclusive settings, 250
Individual Family Service Plan, 250
Individualized Education Plan, 250
Natural environment, 244

Relational bullying, 251
Strengths-based approach, 257
Transdisciplinary play-based assessment, 259
Transition, 251

 ## Technology and Internet Resources

Office of Special Education Programs (OSEP)

http://www.ed.gov

Official site of OSEP. This site provides information on infants, toddlers, and children with disabilities ages birth through 21. This website has a great deal of information about IDEA and maintains excellent links to other high-quality sites.

National Early Childhood Technical Assistance Center (NECTAC)

http://www.nectac.org

This website is designed for professionals and provides links to a variety of resources. NECTAC is a program of the Frank Porter Graham Child Development Institute of the University of North Carolina at Chapel Hill, funded through the Office of Special Education Programs, U.S. Department of Education.

International Society for Early Intervnetion (ISEI)

http://depts.washington.edu

The ISEI website is produced by the Center on Human Development and Disability at the University of Washington in Seattle, Washington. This site includes links to the ISEI Coordinating Committee, Membership Directory, publications information, and other related resources.

Federation for Children with Special Needs (FCSN)

http://fcsn.org

This site includes a family resource database with information about agencies in Massachusetts and throughout the United States that provide information and/or services to families of children with disabilities.

 ## Activities

1. InClass labs

A. Bring at least one toy to class that can be used by children who are typically developing. How can this toy be adapted to accommodate the needs of children who have specific needs associated with a learning disability or hearing impairment?

B. Look at the classroom design created in Chapter 6. How will this plan work for a child who has a gross motor disability? What modifications are needed for children who are on the autism spectrum?

2. Research and inquiry learning

A. Spend two hours in an inclusive classroom. Complete a running record. What kind of play occurred in the classroom? What did adults do to encourage play?

B. Participate in a local IFSP or IEP meeting. Did you understand all the acronyms that were used? Did you understand all the laws referenced? Was play included in the plan? If so, in what way?

C. Investigate programs for children with special needs in the schools of Reggio Emilia, Italy. Compare the Reggio Emilia program with a generic program in the United States. What factors impact the programs?

3. Service learning

A. Volunteer to help with the local Special Olympics.

B. Contact a preschool teacher in an inclusive classroom. Volunteer to assist in making adaptations in the classroom or adaptations to toys or materials.

4. Family Connections

Interview a parent who has a child with a special need. Volunteer to provide child care for the child one afternoon or evening as a way of expressing appreciation for the interview. Be sensitive to the parent's/parents' rejection of the offer based on their perceptions of their child's needs.

5. Advocacy

A. Attend a meeting of a local Council for Exceptional Children student meeting. What issues are similar to those discussed in other student meetings? What issues are unique?

B. Contact your local newspaper. Does the newspaper feature articles on individuals who have special needs? Are citizens with disabilities visible in your community? Visibility is important; citizens who are not visible in the community can be forgotten and excluded from the flow of community life.

C. Distribute the list of reading materials provided in Table 8-1 at a local teacher's meeting or community meeting.

 Visit CourseMate for this textbook to access the eBook, Did You Get It? quizzes, Digital Downloads, TeachSource Video Cases, flashcards, and more. Go to CengageBrain.com to log in, register, or purchase access.

References

Alquraini, T., & Gut, D. (2012). Critical components of successful inclusion of students with severe disabilities: Literature review. *International Journal of Special Education, 27*(1), 42–59.

Balo, J. (2012). Prevalence of autism spectrum disorders—Autism and developmental disabilities monitoring network, 14 sites, United States, 2008. Centers for Disease Control and Prevention, *Morbidity and Mortality Weekly Report, 61*(3) 2–14. Retrieved on July 22, 2013 from http://www.cdc.gov/mmwr/pdf/ss/ss6103.pdf

Barton, E. E., & Wolery, M. (2010). Training teachers to promote pretend play in young children with disabilities. *Exceptional Children, 77*(1), 85–106.

Bredekamp, S., & Copple, C. (2007). *Developmentally appropriate practice in early childhood programs.* Washington, DC: National Association for the Education of Young Children.

Brown, M., & Bergen, D. (2002). Play and social interaction of children with disabilities at learning/activity centers in an inclusive preschool. *Journal of Research in Childhood Education, 17*(1), 26–37.

Greenspan, S. (1998). The child with special needs: Encouraging intellectual and emotional growth. Paper presented to the OSEP Research Project Director's Conference. Washington, DC, July 1998.

Greenspan, S., & Robinson, R. (2004). Commentary: Improving the prognosis for children with autism spectrum disorders: A comprehensive, developmental approach to intervention. *The Journal of Developmental and Learning Disorders, 8,* 1–7.

Hanline, M., & Daley, S. (2002). "Mom, will Kaelie always have possibilities?"—The realities of early childhood inclusion. *Phi Delta Kappan, 84*(1), 73.

Harper, L., & McCluskey, K. (2003). Teacher-child and child-child interactions in inclusive preschool settings: Do adults inhibit peer interactions, *Early Childhood Research Quarterly, 18*(2), 163–184.

Hess, L. (2006). I would like to play but I don't know how: A case study of pretend play in autism. *Child Language Teaching and Therapy, 22*(1), 97–116.

Individuals with Disabilities Education Act. (2004). Building the legacy: IDEA 2004. U.S. Department of Education. Retrieved on July 20, 2013 from http://idea.ed.gov

Jarrold, C., & Conn, C. (2011). The development of pretend play in autism. In A. Peligrinni (Ed.), *Oxford Handbook of the Development of Play* (pp. 308–321). New York: Oxford University Press.

Lifter, K., Foster-Sanda, S., Arzamarski, C., Briesch, J., & McClure, E. (2011). Overview of play: Its uses and importance in early intervention/early childhood special education. *Infants & Young Children, 24*(3), 225–245.

Linder, T. W. (2008). *Transdisciplinary play-based assessment* (2nd ed.). Baltimore, MD: Paul Brooks Publishing Company.

Murdock, L., & Hobbs, J. (2011). Picture me playing: Increasing pretend play dialogues of children with autism spectrum disorders. *Journal of Autism Developmental Disorders, 41*, 870–878.

O'Connor, C., & Stagnitti, K. (2011). Play, behaviour, language and social skills: The comparison of a play and a non-play intervention within a specialist school setting. *Research in Developmental Disabilities, 32*(3), 1205–1211.

Odum, S., & Brown, W. (1993). Social interaction skills intervention for young children with disabilities in integrated settings. In C. Peck, S. Odum, & D. Bicker (Eds.), *Integrating young children with disabilities into community programs* (pp. 39–64). Baltimore: Paul H. Brooks.

Piaget, J. (1962). *Play, dreams, and imitation in childhood.* New York: Norton.

Porter, N. (2012). Promotion of pretend play for children with high-functioning autism through the use of circumscribed interests. *Early Childhood Education Journal, 40*, 161–167.

Rose, C. A. (2011). Bullying among students with disabilities. In D. Espelage and S. Swearer (Eds.) *Bullying in North American Schools* (pp. 34–44). New York: Routledge.

Sandall, S., Hemmeter, M. L., Smith, B. J., & McLean, M. E. (2005). *DEC recommended practices: A comprehensive guide.* Longmont, CO: Sopris West.

Sandall, S., Hemmeter, M., Smith, B. J., & Sandall, S., Askew, L. (Eds.). (2005). *DEC recommended practices workbook: Improving practices for young children with special needs and their families.* Missoula, MT: Division for Early Childhood.

Sluss, D. (2000). *Towards inclusion in early education (TIES) training manual.* Johnson City, TN: East Tennessee State University (Grant Number HO24B60032-97).

Smith, B. J., Hemmeter, M., & Sandall, S. R. (2006). What do I do with the Division for Early Childhood recommended practices? Tips for using the practices in the early childhood setting. *Young Exceptional Children, 9*(4), 22–33.

Smith, C. (1998). Children with "Special Rights" in the preprimary schools and infant-toddler Centers of Reggio Emilia. In C. Edwards, L. Gandini, & G. Foreman (Eds.), *The hundred languages of children* (pp. 199–214). Greenwich, CT: Ablex.

Stopbullying (2013). *What is bullying?* Retrieved on July 22, 2013 from http://www.stopbullying.gov/index.html, a federal government website managed by the U.S. Department of Health & Human Services, 200 Independence Avenue S.W., Washington, D.C., 20201.

Thiemann-Bourque, K. S., Brady, N. C., & Fleming, K. K. (2012). Symbolic play of preschoolers with severe communication impairments with autism and other developmental delays: More similarities than differences. *Journal of Autism and Developmental Disorders, 42*(5), 863–873.

Vygotsky, L. (1978). *Mind in society: The development of higher mental processes.* Cambridge, MA: Harvard University Press.

4 Beyond the Classroom

Making the case for play in and out of the classrooms is the focus of the final two chapters. Chapter 10 explores the need for and possibilities of outdoor play. Play places and spaces for children are considered in terms of the individual ages and stages. Chapter 11 moves to a different venue by considering the role of professionalism in advocating for play. Chapter 11 looks at the importance of thoroughly understanding current trends and issues, such as the use of technology, before becoming a spokesperson in a public forum.

Courtesy of Douthy Justus Sluss

10 Outdoor PLAY for Young Children

LEARNING OBJECTIVES

10-1 List the benefits of outdoor play.

10-2 Differentiate recess from organized physical exercise classes.

10-3 Distinguish the different roles of the adult in facilitating outdoor play.

10-4 Identify safety concerns and issues related to outdoor play.

10-5 Describe outdoor play for infants and toddlers.

10-6 Describe outdoor play for preschoolers and kindergarteners.

10-7 Describe outdoor play for primary age children.

10-8 Discuss seven types of play spaces.

10-9 Design an assessment for an outdoor environment.

© Cengage Learning 2015

STANDARDS COVERED IN THIS CHAPTER

Council of Exceptional Children—Division of Early Childhood CEC DEC

ECSE 3K2 Explore the impact of social and physical environments on development and learning

ESCE 5S1 Select, develop, and evaluate developmentally and functionally appropriate materials, equipment, and environments

ESCE 5S2 Organize space, time, materials, peers, and adults to maximize progress in natural and structured environments

ECSE 5S3 Embed learning opportunities in everyday routines, relationships, activities, and places

ECSE 5S5 Provide a stimulus-rich indoor and outdoor environment that employs materials, media, and adaptive and assistive technologies that are responsive to individual differences

ECSE 7S7 Develop an individualized plan that supports the child's independent functioning in the child's natural environments

NAEYC Program Standards

1a Knowing and understanding young children's characteristics and needs

1c Using developmental knowledge to create healthy, respectful, supportive, and challenging learning environments

2c Involving families and communities in their children's development and learning

4c Using a broad repertoire of developmentally appropriate teaching/learning approaches

---

✳ PLAYSCAPE: CASE STUDY

As Aiden went out the school doors for recess, he could feel the excitement of the children around him. When Aiden and his classmates reached the outdoor playground, they ran. Some went to the swings, some to the trees, some to the grassy area, and a few to a covered area. Aiden noticed that a few boys were challenging each other to play kickball. They chose teams, and Aiden's classmate Jim was selected as leader. The girls had already started games with jump ropes and the latest jump rope chants. Other children played a game of tag. The morning recess provided just the right break in the morning. Aiden always knew he could make it until lunch if he could just get a chance to play.

Explaining Play Behaviors

The scenario just described could have occurred in any year—1714, 1814, 1914, or 2014. Children need little provocation to play outdoors. High-quality play spaces have always invited children to run, jump, and play. Although culture influences the chants or games and age affects what they choose to play, children naturally gravitate to outdoor play. For example, infants and toddlers enjoy touching and moving everything. Preschoolers want to run, climb, and jump. Kindergartners begin making their own pretend games. Primary age children begin to play exclusively with children of their own gender, pay attention to rules, and develop their own sense of competency in physical areas. Outdoor play is natural for young children. Adults who support outdoor play optimize natural opportunities for play, growth, and overall development (Ramstetter, Murray, & Garner, 2010).

✳ 10-1 Benefits of Outdoor Play

 Playing outdoors has benefits for children in all developmental areas. When children play outdoors, they have more opportunities to run and play with friends (Couper, 2011). Locomotor skills are developed and social interactions are promoted. Young children benefit from fresh air and the opportunity to explore natural environments, touch grass, look at clouds, and watch leaves fall or flowers bloom. Jean-Jacques Rousseau (1712–1778) wrote of the benefits of nature over three centuries ago (Rousseau, 1979). Current scholarship supports the value of outdoor play for growth and development (Council on School Health of the American Academy of Pediatrics, 2013; Frost, Wortham, & Reifel, 2011).

A study that looked at four dimensions of play—physical versus constructive play, change and stability continuum, freedom and control dimension, and differences in adult-child interactions—found that outdoor play is more open or unstructured than indoor play (Stephenson, 2002). This finding supports the need to ensure outdoor play opportunities for all children. In addition, outdoor play is unique in that it does the following:

1. **Encourages physical movement and good health**   One of the most important roles of recess is to improve the level of physical fitness in children. Many children are not getting enough exercise to develop healthy hearts and lungs. Another cause for concern is obesity. The American Heart Association reports that

   - About one in three children and teens in the United States is overweight or obese.

   - Overweight children have a 70 to 80% chance of staying overweight their entire lives.

   - Obese and overweight adults now outnumber those at a healthy weight; nearly seven in ten adults living in the United States are overweight or obese (American Heart Association, 2011, p. 1).

   The White House has been equally concerned about the obesity epidemic and overall health of young children in the United States. In 2010, President Barack Obama signed a Presidential Memorandum creating the first ever Task Force on Childhood Obesity (Task Force on Childhood Obesity, 2013). Michelle Obama organized the Let's Move organization to encourage movement and good health (Task Force on Childhood Obesity, 2013). Other organizations throughout the United States have followed their lead. For example, the American Heart Association and the Robert Wood Johnson Foundation joined together to create the Prevent Obesity website, which provides information on encouraging physical activity (Prevent Obesity, 2013). Outdoor play provides an excellent way to meet the goal of increasing physical activity.

2. **Creates a unique environment for learning that stimulates brain development**   Outdoor play areas create an environment with multiple opportunities for learning (Photo 10-1). It is difficult to understand wind and the movement of clouds from reading a book. The value of real experience for learning was emphasized by Dewey (1930) and has been confirmed by studies of how the brain processes information (Shonkoff, 2009). Studies

© Cengage Learning 2015

10-1 Trees provide natural shade for children, but additional shade is needed on playgrounds that are used throughout the year.

► ‖ TeachSource Video Case 10-1

© Cengage Learning 2015

Elementary Classroom Management: Basic Strategies

Amy Moylan uses a variety of strategies to deal with bullying during recess.

1. What was the strength of the role-playing approach that Amy used in the video?

2. Ms. Moylan suggested developing your own set of guidelines. What are your guidelines or policies for recess?

Watch on CourseMate

---

have substantiated links between recess and academic learning (Blatchford & Baines, 2010). Many schools are creating outdoor laboratories to encourage interaction with natural environments.

3. Encourages different levels of social participation as children self-select playmates Children can choose to play with a group, a friend, or alone. During a game of Frisbee, all children may participate. During a game of jump rope or tag, a smaller group may play in isolation. When children are on the playground, they can freely choose to play with boys, girls, or with no one. This is the richness of outdoor play. Children can disengage if they so desire. They can sit alone and stare at the sky if they choose. They select their level of social engagement.

4. Develops standards of morality during interactions with peers and more competent others Children transmit cultural norms during play with peers. Younger children who play with older children learn the rules of the society and alter them to meet their needs. Although Piaget (1965) first reported observed social interaction on the streets of Geneva, Switzerland, these interactions as a platform for cultural transmission have been studied by Artin Göncü and Suzanne Gaskins (2007). Piaget found that children who did not know the rules at the beginning of games learned them as they interacted with others. Sometimes the rules changed, but the children knew who could and who could not change the rules and when.

Outdoor play provides a context that encourages children to compromise and collaborate as they become members of the group. The mechanism for transmitting cultural norms during outdoor play occurs through chants, rhymes, and rituals used during games. In their classic studies of children during outdoor play, Opie and Opie (1959) found that children used chants and rhymes that dated back to the seventeenth and eighteenth centuries even though adults had not shared these with them. Children on the playground transmit their songs, chants, and rhymes to others. These are not transmitted from adults to children, but rather from child to child. Outdoor play creates a special context for the transmission of children's culture (Baines & Blatchford, 2011).

5. Provides opportunities to engage in freely chosen play Children can choose when and where they play during outdoor play. Although adults control indoor activities, children can freely choose their outdoor play. They can choose rough or tumble, pretend, or games with rules. This may be the only time during the day when they can control their activity level. Some organizations, such as the International Play Association (IPA) (2013), see this as a basic human right.

The term **recess** is generally applied to a block of time when children are allowed to go to a defined area and engage in self-selected physical play for a specified amount of time. Recess allows children to choose to play, or not; to talk, or not. Many children choose to play with their friends, so recess represents a time of social bonding for many children (Photo 10-2). Recess is the child's personal time when she chooses what she does; this is different from physical education classes, which involve following an instructor's directions.

Despite the importance of recess, over the course of the last two decades, recess has disappeared in many schools throughout the United States (Burriss & Burriss, 2011). In 1989, over 90% of the principals in districts throughout the United States reported having recess in their school. Ten years later, only 40% of principals reported having recess (Kieff, 2001), and a decade later, a study involving 11,000 third graders found that 30% had less than fifteen minutes of recess per day (Barros, Silver & Stein, 2009). In 2013, Lounsbery, McKenzie, Morrow, Monnat, and Holt found a national trend of decreased access to recess. Where did it go and why?

The focus on academics has created a situation that eliminates any activity that cannot be tested. Music, art, and movement are not included on standardized tests and have been the first areas eliminated from the schedule. Recess is not a test item, so it has been eliminated in many schools. In her research, Olga Jarrett (2003) found that recess occurred every day in affluent suburban schools but was eliminated in urban schools with an African American, low socioeconomic population. Another study by Beaulieu, Butterfield, and Pratt (2009) found a similar trend. That is, Caucasian children in more affluent school divisions located in rural areas were more likely to have recess than children of other ethnicities in poorer urban areas.

> ### What do you think?
>
> Many parents are concerned that children are not receiving recess on a regular basis. At the same time, they are even more concerned that children are not spending enough time on academics. As a professional educator, how would you resolve this dilemma in your classroom?

© Cengage Learning 2015

10-2 When children play outdoors, they have opportunities to engage in turn-taking behavior, which is needed for good citizenship.

A Child's Right to Play Outdoors

Dr. Olga Jarrett, PhD

I am a strong advocate of recess! Both from my own research and my review of the research done by others, I am convinced of the many benefits of recess. I also know that many children are not getting it.

There is evidence from brain research cited by Jensen (2005) that breaks improve concentration. Our research found that children were more on-task as well as less fidgety when they had about 20 minutes of recess in mid-morning (Jarrett, Maxwell, Dickerson, Hoge, Davies, & Yetley, 1998). Recess is also a time when children can learn social skills and develop a sense of fairness. They learn to be effective leaders and followers, how to organize games, how to be good winners and losers, and how to decide who is "it." Astute supervisors and children trained as peer mentors can help train children to not bully or exclude others. Our research found that children in a low income school engaged in almost no negative behavior while playing on the playground equipment, chasing one another, and making up their own games during recess (Jarrett, Farokhi, Young, & Davies, 2001).

Another benefit from recess is the opportunity to be physically active. Childhood obesity is a serious problem resulting both from eating habits and from lack of exercise. Research (Kahan, 2006) suggests that children are more active during recess than during Physical Education (PE) classes, and the children who are less active during the day are also less active after school (Dale, Corbin, & Dale, 2000). According to the National Association for Sport and Physical Education (NASPE, 2006), both PE and recess are needed.

Recently, a small survey I conducted with new teachers (unpublished data) found that half the teachers did not have recess on a given, beautiful day and that over half of the teachers with recess deprived at least one child of recess as punishment either for misbehavior or for not finishing their homework or classwork. What do you think? Is recess an educational benefit that is a right for all children, or is it a privilege for well-behaved children who do their work efficiently?

© Cengage Learning 2015

REFERENCES

Dale, D., Corbin, C. B., & Dale, K. S. (2000). Restricting opportunities to be active during school time: Do children compensate by increasing physical activity levels after school? *Research Quarterly for Exercise and Sport, 71* (3), 240–248.

Jarrett, O. S., Maxwell, D. M., Dickerson, C., Hoge, P., Davies, G., & Yetley, A. (1998). The impact of recess on classroom behavior: Group effects and individual differences. *The Journal of Educational Research, 92*(2), 121–126.

Jarrett, O. S., Farokhi, B., Young, C., & Davies, G. (2001). Boys and girls at play: Games and recess at a Southern urban elementary school. In Stuart Reifel (Ed.), *Play and Culture Studies, Vol. 3: Theory in context and out* (pp. 147–179). Westport, CT: Ablex Publishing.

Jensen, E. (2005). Teaching with the brain in mind, 2nd Edition. Alexandria, VA: ASCD.

Kahan, D. (2008). Recess, extracurricular activities, and active classrooms: Means for increasing elementary school students' physical activity. *Journal of Physical Education, Recreation & Dance, 79*(2), 26–31.

Recess for elementary school students (2006). National Association for Sport and Physical Education. Retrieved from http://www.aahperd.org/naspe/standards/upload/Recess-for-Elementary-School-Students-2006.pdf

Olga S. Jarrett, Ph.D. received her bachelor's and master's degrees from the Pennsylvania State University and her doctorate from Georgia State University. Her research interests are on recess, the role of play in science, and service learning. In 2010, she received the Brian Sutton-Smith award for lifetime contributions to play research. She is currently a professor of Early Childhood Education and Science Education at Georgia State University.

The American Association for the Child's Right to Play (International Play Association/USA, 2013) has launched a movement to support the child's right to play outdoors every day. A recent study found that 87% of the states do not have a policy that requires or promotes daily recess or outdoor exposure (Slater, Nicholson, Chriqui, Turner, & Chaloupka, 2012). This is important because children in states without policies are less likely to have physical activity that those in states with recess and/or physical movement policies in place. NAEYC supports the reinstatement of recess and notes that recess benefits instruction in the following ways:

1. Recess is an appropriate outlet for reducing stress in children.

2. Recess allows children the opportunity to make choices, plan, and expand their creativity.

3. Recess gives children a release of energy.

If these benefits sound familiar, revisit the classical theories of play discussed in Chapter 1. The innate nature of play suggests that the need to play is a biological need, and eliminating recess does not eliminate the child's need to play. It only eliminates an appropriate context for play. Pelligrini (2011) reported the results of an empirical study that found that recess breaks optimize children's attention in classes and interactions with classmates. More frequent, shorter breaks may be better for younger children, whereas older children may do better with breaks that give them ample time to talk with friends or listen to music. The National Association of Early Childhood Specialists in State Departments of Education recommends the following advocacy actions (2003):

- Support policies that require recess time to be part of the preschool and elementary school curriculum.

- Ensure and support additional research on the effects of recess on the developmental domains (social, emotional, physical, and cognitive), and on the effect of recess on academic achievement.

- Develop policies and resources necessary to support an awareness of the importance of recess and of active, free play in the development of the young child.

- Support research on the benefits of recess and its possible restorative role for children with attention disorders.

- Support research and professional development that facilitate every educator's skills in observation and assessment of the developmental growth of children through the play process.

Role of the Adult 10-3 *

Adults have a major role in fostering outdoor play. They may serve as a source of information for chants during jump rope, keeper of the rules for tag or basketball, or guide as children discover how to climb up and down safely. Adult roles can be categorized into four areas: organizer, observer, supervisor, and evaluator (Johnson, Christie, & Wardle, 2005; Seefeldt & Barbour, 1998).

Above all, the adult is responsible for the health and safety of the children on the playground.

10-3a Organizer

Organizing materials for outdoor play involves surveying the area, observing play, and considering goals for outdoor play. Plans for moving materials in and out will be necessary when setting up additional activities. Children should have appropriate materials and sufficient time for play. In some climates, organizing to go outside may require time to put on boots and coats. In other climates, sunscreen may be needed. Some teachers take play crates outside. Play crates contain materials that can be used to stimulate play. For example, one play crate might be filled with different balls, whereas another might contain different kinds of sheets and coverings for pretend buildings. Other teachers will set up a special project outside, such as using water to "paint" the building. Offering a variety of activities provides choices for children.

10-3b Observer

Observing provides the teacher an opportunity to look at the total picture. As a skilled observer, the teacher will see many levels of play skills. Some children will be engaging in a great deal of symbolic play. Others may be just walking around the playground. Another child may be engaged in associative play, and yet another child may play alone. By observing and recording the action that is occurring, the teacher will know where and when to act. Taking time to watch outdoor play is an important and often overlooked responsibility.

10-3c Supervisor

Keeping children safe and healthy is, of course, critically important. Someone must be assigned to routinely check and perform maintenance on the playground and any equipment used by the children. Ensuring that children are using materials in a safe manner is of paramount importance. Table 10-1 provides a checklist that can be used to inspect the playground for unsafe equipment or materials. Physical safety is the first basic need recognized by Maslow (1972) and is necessary for high-quality play.

Adults charged with children's safety must monitor the overall play scene. Are the perimeters safe? Are there any adults near who should not be on the playground? Does litter need to be removed? Is the equipment safe? As supervisor, the adult can walk around the playground and both observe and interact with children on a one-to-one basis. Pushing a child on a swing, helping a child climb a slide, and interacting with children agitated over ownership of a ball all add to the richness of the play experiences (Photo 10-3).

Adults should avoid talking to other adults when supervising groups of children on the playground. If an accident occurs, the adult in charge will need to provide a description of the incident, and this is difficult to do if the accident was not observed.

TABLE 10-1 Consumer Product Safety Commission Public Playground Safety Checklist

Is your public playground a safe place to play?

Each year, more than 200,000 children go to U.S. hospital emergency rooms with injuries associated with playground equipment. Most injuries occur when a child falls from the equipment onto the ground.

Use this simple checklist to help make sure your local community or school playground is a safe place to play.

Public Playground Safety Checklist

1. Make sure surfaces around playground equipment have at least 12 inches of wood chips, mulch, sand, or pea gravel, or are mats made of safety-tested rubber or rubber-like materials.

2. Check that protective surfacing extends at least 6 feet in all directions from play equipment. For swings, be sure surfacing extends, in back and front, twice the height of the suspending bar.

3. Make sure play structures more than 30 inches high are spaced at least 9 feet apart.

4. Check for dangerous hardware, like open "S" hooks or protruding bolt ends.

5. Make sure spaces that could trap children, such as openings in guardrails or between ladder rungs, measure less than 3.5 inches (for guardrails) or more than 9 inches (for ladder rungs).

6. Check for sharp points or edges in equipment.

7. Look out for tripping hazards, like exposed concrete footings, tree stumps, and rocks.

8. Make sure elevated surfaces, like platforms and ramps, have guardrails to prevent falls.

9. Check playgrounds regularly to see that equipment and surfacing are in good condition.

10. Carefully supervise children on playgrounds to make sure they're safe.

From the Consumer Product Safety Commission

http://www.cpsc.gov/en/Safety-Education/Safety-Guides/Sports-Fitness-and-Recreation/Playground-Safety/Public-Playground-Safety-Checklist

© Cengage Learning 2015

10-3 When adults interact with children on the playground, they have a different context for knowing the child and understanding the child's view of the world.

10-3d Evaluator

Evaluating play can provide insights that may be less obvious in the classroom. Children who cannot skip when asked to do so in a semiformal assessment have been observed skipping and hopping during recess. Outdoor play provides early educators with opportunities to observe, monitor and assess, evaluate, and then develop new plans for more complex play.

One approach that has been implemented at the Frank Porter Graham Center involves dividing the playground into zones and assigning individual supervisors to monitor each zone. In this way, individual children can be monitored carefully and scaffolding can be delivered in a way that can be evaluated closely (Kern & Wakeford, 2007).

✳ 10-4 Safety Issues for All Children

Safety issues are especially important for infants and toddlers. The American Academy of Dermatology recommends special caution with infants and toddlers. Minimize exposing infants under the age of six months to direct sunlight. A covered pram is recommended for outings. Older infants and toddlers should be covered with sunscreen thirty minutes prior to going outside. Be sure to check for allergic reactions before using the sunscreen. Parents can be asked to provide their child's sunscreen. Recommended sunscreen for this age is a UVA- and UVB-absorbing or UVA- and UVB-blocking product with an SPF of at least 15 (Chambers, Roorda, & Wang, 2007). Encourage children to wear hats, sunglasses, and sun protective clothing (Photo 10-4). Schools in some climates may want to limit outdoor time between 10 a.m. and 4 p.m. Overexposure to the sun is a major concern at this age, so monitor carefully how long children are exposed

10-4 All children need sunscreen and shaded structures to protect them from sun damage.

to direct sunlight. Additional information is available on the website of the American Academy of Dermatology.

10-4a Playground Safety

Play areas must be safe havens for children. Playgrounds should be fenced in, with sturdy, safe equipment and shock-absorbent surfaces. No climbing structures should ever be placed on asphalt. The unique needs of the children must be considered. If children are allergic to bees, another adult, such as a teacher, paraprofessional, parent volunteer, or playground monitor, should be present with necessary supplies, such as an auto-injector with a dose of medicine. See Bee Stings (2013). Too often, children who have allergies are forced to stay inside the building. Adults must take responsibility for ensuring that all children can experience the outdoors. Some teachers ask parents to come by the school for the outdoor time, and parents will plan their work schedule so they can ensure their child has a safe experience. By working as a team, the child's safety needs are met (National Playground Program Safety, 2013). Safety needs can vary according to age group, and the following sections discuss age-specific safety measures. Just as indoor play is different for infants and preschoolers, outdoor play is equally unique for the developing child.

Did You Get It?

A child is extremely sensitive to bees. What should his teachers do during outdoor playtime?

a. one teacher should remain inside with him

b. have an extra adult on the playground with any needed supplies

c. insist that he do what all the other students are doing, regardless of his sensitivity

d. allow him to sit inside near the doorway, so he can watch the other children at play

Take the full quiz on CourseMate

Designing Outdoor Play Environments 10-5 ✳ for Infants and Toddlers

naeyc
CEC DEC

Infants and toddlers need fresh air every day. Outdoor play allows them to experience a different learning environment. Grass and natural materials are intriguing to toddlers. Slides and tunnels provide opportunities for movement that might not be possible in the indoor environment. Infants and toddlers need the benefits of daily outings and outdoor play.

Play spaces for infants and toddlers should be separated from preschoolers' play spaces. The area must be partially shaded to prevent overexposure to sun and must feature a covered structure, such as a pavilion, to allow for play on rainy days. The area should include sensorimotor activities such as sand and water. Placing a sheet on grass creates a sensory experience for infants and toddlers. Activities such as painting, bubbles, and play-dough are enjoyable activities that can occur outdoors. The play area should be small and secure so children feel safe and comfortable. The ground cover should include a variety of surfaces. Equipment with low ramps and stairs permits children to practice their walking and climbing skills and improve their gross motor skills. Based on the work of Joe Frost (1992), Karyn Wellhousen (2005) describes four principles for designing outdoor spaces:

1. **Safety and comfort** are the most important aspects to consider when looking at play spaces. Infants and toddlers who are just developing vertical stability should be separated from preschoolers.

2. **Provide for a large range of movements** Frost (1992) advocates play areas that are "gentle for crawling, kind for falling, and cool for sitting" (p. 260). Infants and toddlers need places that allow them to develop in a safe environment. Play areas that include places for both low-mobile and high-mobile children generally include a variety of coverings, including grass, sand, and indoor/outdoor carpet.

3. **Plan for sensory stimulation** Nature provides abundant sensory stimulation for infants and toddlers: wind, sunshine, grass, rocks, and trees. When the outdoor play space lacks natural features, use sand and water experiences, wind chimes, and art activities.

4. **Offer a variety of novel and challenging activities** Adding empty boxes that children can safely climb into is always interesting. Scarves allow children to catch the wind. Play centers that are moved outside are always exciting.

10-5a Examples of Infant/Toddler Play Places

Infant/toddler play areas should be separate from those designed for older children. Infant/toddler playgrounds should include the following features:

- Shady area
- Sandbox
- Grassy area
- Place for locomotor play such as running, climbing, and rolling
- Mounds
- Blankets or soft materials for sitting on grassy areas
- Empty boxes

10-5b Types of Play on Infant/Toddler Playgrounds

The outdoor playground encourages a different kind of play than that found inside. Play happens as toddlers run, jump, climb, crawl, and slide down. Climbing is a primary interest of toddlers. Outdoor play areas can provide a safe place for climbing and exploring. Toddlers also enjoy running and engaging in rough and tumble play. Infants engage in exploratory, practice, and locomotor play outdoors. Infants and toddlers do not initiate group play at this age. They tend to play alone or interact with a caregiver. Interactions that occur generally are caused by intersections—that is, they run into or encounter each other as they are engaged in their own play rather than mutual reciprocity.

Climbing is a natural, yet seldom valued, activity that older infants and toddlers engage in as often as possible. By taking advantage of the child's interest in climbing, we can use the child's natural interest to enhance developing motor skills. Climbing requires a certain combination of thoughts and motions. First, the child must have the desire to climb. Some children are more interested in climbing than are others. Children who enjoy climbing need little motivation other than structures higher than ground level. Second, children must have the skills and strength to pull themselves up and then push their larger head and body onto the supporting structure. By the age of two, almost all children are able to climb (Readdick & Park, 1998). Playgrounds that have climbing structures, low slides, and low stairs with handrails encourage children to develop climbing skills. Of course, a soft padded surface is necessary to ensure safety. Readdick and Park (1998) recommend that heights be limited to 1 foot for each year of life. So a climbing structure for a 12-month-old would be a stair that is 1 foot high. Structures for two-year-olds would be no higher than two feet. Because children love to climb, never place climbing equipment near fences that would enable children to climb over the fence. Although many fences are made

Did You Get It?

At a child care center for newborns through age five, there is one outdoor play area for all the children to share. This

a. is inadvisable, as teachers cannot supervise more than one age group at a time.

b. is advisable, as it saves both money and space.

c. is advisable, as it gives opportunity for children of all ages to interact.

d. is inadvisable, as play spaces for infants and toddlers should be separated from those for preschoolers.

Take the full quiz on CourseMate

of chain links, wood is a better choice for infant/toddler playgrounds because wood fences create a feeling of intimacy and a smaller area. In addition, many educators and parents are concerned about the safety of chain fences because many of these fences have sharp points on the bottom of the fence or have worn areas that can injure curious children.

10-5c Safety for Infants and Toddlers

Be aware of sun safety. Infants under six months should not be exposed to direct sunlight. Young children should have a play area that has a shelter or tent covering the area to prevent direct exposure to the sun's rays. Infants and toddlers must be carefully supervised and should never be left unattended outside.

Designing Outdoor Play Environments 10-6 ✳ for Preschoolers and Kindergarteners

Preschoolers and kindergarteners need outdoor time and fresh air every day. Children in this age group benefit from outdoor play as they acquire competency in locomotor abilities, problem solving, negotiation skills, and social interactions (Photo 10-5). They enjoy acrobatic activities that are difficult to do inside. Playgrounds also provide opportunities for different types of play. Preschoolers have moved beyond the need to climb and are beginning to engage in rough and tumble play. The key element that distinguishes rough and tumble play from aggression is the play face or facial expressions, which include eyes and mouth with upturned corners and laughter (Tannock, 2008). Rough and tumble play may also include running, chasing, fleeing, wrestling, jerking, and open-hand tag or beat, in which children go by and tap one another with their open hand (Pelligrini & Boyd, 1993; Tannock, 2011). Preschoolers are only beginning to engage in rough and tumble play, and this type of play occupies less than 10% of their play time (Pellis & Pellis, 2011; Smith, 1997). It is important not to confuse rough and tumble play with aggressive behavior. Rough and tumble may be frowned on inside but acceptable outside, whereas aggressive play is not acceptable in either setting.

© Cengage Learning 2015

10-5 Playgrounds provide places for children to explore the limits of their physical capacity as they climb, crawl, and explore.

During social interactions, children can choose playmates. Interventions are necessary when children purposefully exclude other children. Responsive teachers are careful to intervene without interfering. For example, when a child is being excluded from a group, the adult can physically move over to the group and join the group play. The teacher brings the excluded child into the group play and then watches for an appropriate time to exit the play.

Preschoolers need room to run, jump, skip, hop, gallop, and play with their friends. The space should be enclosed with a fence to ensure safety. An adult should be assigned to check the equipment and play area on a daily basis. A shelter is needed to shield the children from the sun and to serve as a play place on rainy days. Equipment should include tire swings, low slides, climbing apparatus, sand boxes, water tables, and equipment with wheels for pulling, pushing, and riding. The space should include a variety of surfaces and a paved riding area for tricycles, wagons, and pull toys. Large blocks also work well outside. Old tires make wonderful swings when attached correctly and can be used to signal areas for climbing and sitting.

10-6a Play Spaces for Preschoolers

Areas for preschoolers should be more complex and challenging than those for infants and toddlers. The complexity level should be greater and should allow for more diversity and independent play. Table 10-2 lists seven preschooler play zones recommended by Esbensen (1990).

10-6b Types of Play on Preschool Playgrounds

The most dominant play during the preschool years is pretend. Although some rough and tumble play may be evident, pretend play is at its peak. When children are outdoors, they can pretend that they are flying like birds, running like dogs, or rescuing someone from a monster. Preschool children are egocentric (egocentrism is a normal aspect of development as children develop a sense of their own identity) but will engage in associative and co-operative play during this time. Rudimentary games may be evident but are short lived due to the episodic nature of play at this age.

10-6c Safety Issues

Although preschoolers need less supervision than infants and toddlers, they still need supervision. Children at this age are testing their abilities and do not have the necessary skills to assess risks. It is incumbent upon teachers to ensure their safety during outdoor play. As with younger children, preschoolers need appropriate clothing and sunscreen when outdoors. Many schools give children snacks and ice cream at this time, but it is unwise to do so because if children use their time eating, they miss their play time. Their hands may be sticky when

TABLE 10-2   Seven Playground Zones for Preschoolers
Different zones provide interests and challenges.
1. Manipulative/creative_____
2. Projective/fantasy_____
3. Focal/social_____
4. Social/dramatic _____
5. Physical_____
6. Natural_____
7. Transition (to tie zones together)_____

© Cengage Learning 2015

they finish eating, and sticky hands can cause accidents when using equipment. In addition, when ice cream and food are eaten and papers are deposited outdoors in trash cans, bees and other insects are attracted. This can make outdoor play risky for children who are allergic to bees as discussed previously. Keeping snacks and ice cream indoors minimizes these problems.

Designing Outdoor Play Environments 10-7 * for Primary Age Children

Primary age children need equipment for swinging, sliding, and climbing with their friends. They are beginning to play group games and need space for playing jump rope and group chase games. They can still benefit from sand boxes and enjoy spaces that allow them to dig in the dirt.

10-7a Play Spaces

Although equipment should be more complex and challenging than that used for infants/toddlers and preschoolers, primary age children need opportunities within the seven zones listed in Table 10-2. Playgrounds for primary age children should have more space for group games that include running and throwing. Adults should also ensure that girls and boys have access to equal space. Too often, boys tend to dominate the space on the playground and girls spend their time in one corner of the playground.

10-7b Types of Play on Primary Playgrounds

Typically developing primary age children are capable of playing structured games and enjoy doing so. They can concentrate on play for a longer length of time than can preschoolers, and they can select group leaders. The dominant play at this age involves games and exploration. Many activities are games, and the games evident on the playground may include running games like tag, touch football, or soccer. Other games that are popular include jumping games with ropes, clapping games with chants or rhymes, and hopscotch.

Teachers must pay attention to those children who are not included in the games. Instead of forcing children to play and forbidding them to exclude others from their play, teachers must be creative in how they foster opportunities for all children to participate in outdoor play (Photo 10-6). For example, teachers can encourage play among different children by giving specific children new play materials such as bats and balls or Frisbees. The novelty of the new materials will attract children to the child with the materials.

10-7c Safety Issues

Safety issues are a concern at every age. Children at the primary age are establishing their self-esteem. In an attempt to demonstrate their skills, they will sometimes take risks that place them in danger. Children also need to be protected from the sun and should wear appropriate footwear and appropriate attire when outside.

10-6 Group play gives children opportunites for group membership that may not be available in the classsroom.

10-7d Afterschool Programs

Afterschool programs hold a special challenge for educators. Because many schools end before the parents' work day ends, many children need alternative opportunities for child care when the school day ends. A report by the Afterschool Alliance found that in 2009, over one in four children (26%) or fifteen million children needed care after school because one or both parents were working (Afterschool Alliance, 2009). Creating an interesting afterschool curriculum is challenging because children have been in classrooms during the day and are now joining a new group of children who are not always age mates or classmates. Nonetheless, effective afterschool programs are especially valuable in today's society. If these programs were not available, many children would be in self-care or would be "**latchkey children.**" *Latchkey children* is a term used to describe children who are at home without adult supervision for an hour or more before their parents return from work. Planned programs with proper adult supervision are a better alternative to leaving a child alone at home.

High-quality afterschool programs offer unique opportunities and benefits for the child. For example, many afterschool programs utilize the facilities of outdoor classrooms or natural areas. Other programs offer classes in sports or lifetime recreation so children can gain special skills. Parks, arboretums, and museums provide activities and classes in a variety of areas. College students pursuing degrees in early childhood education often volunteer as mentors for children who are in afterschool programs. With the support of federal, state, and local agencies, today's afterschool programs offer children high-quality experiences and opportunities that challenge children and optimize growth and development.

Selecting Play Spaces 10-8 *

Although outdoor play seems natural and spontaneous, the quality of play can be enhanced through high-quality, inclusive playgrounds and the support of adults. The quality and characteristics of a community or school play space provide a mirror of the community. Some areas have play spaces that reflect the most current research and equipment. They invite children to enter, to run, and play. Other regions have playgrounds with two or three pieces of equipment on an asphalt surface or no equipment at all. Children play there because there are no other places to play. Even worse, some communities have no places that are safe for young or old. Cars parked on vacant lots, drug dealers on the corner, and unsafe streets cause children to stay indoors behind locked doors. These children only see the outdoor world as they travel to and from their homes. If we are to create an educated citizenry appreciative of nature and the natural environment, children must have outdoor experiences that enrich their lives. The nonprofit group KaBOOM! is developing a map of playgrounds throughout the United States. KaBOOM! members have identified **play deserts**, where no safe and accessible play places are avail-

© Cengage Learning 2015

10-7 Outdoor play provides for personal time. Children choose their activities, friends, and level of involvement. All children need opportunities for outdoor play.

able for children. They are working with communities to ensure that these play deserts disappear as new playgrounds are installed.

Outdoor play areas range from unstructured open spaces where children happen to gather to fenced-in, heavily supervised playgrounds (Photo 10-7). The full continuum is described in the following subsections.

10-8a Natural Play Spaces

Natural play spaces are identified as those areas that are not defined by adults but provide a space for children to play. For example, a local park may have open areas that are not defined as playgrounds but that children use for running, tumbling, and chasing. The National Park Service has many open areas that provide space for play but that are not specifically designed as playgrounds. Too often, outdoor play is equated only with outdoor playgrounds. High-quality playgrounds provide a well-defined, safe environment for children but should not define how we view outdoor play. Many modern schools are including outdoor areas that expand their classroom activities. Although these do not fit the definition of a playground per se, play occurs.

10-8 Communities that are challenged to find space for play can create playgrounds on top of buildings. The location of the play space does not restrict the children's play or joy.

© Cengage Learning 2015

10-8b Defined Play Spaces

Defined play spaces are areas set aside for children's play (Photo 10-8). They are the precursor of the traditional playground. Defined play spaces are used by groups like the !Kung tribe in Africa. Adults throughout the world realize the child's need to play, and some societies set aside space for play. David Elkind (1981) warned of the disappearance of play spaces and playgrounds in urban areas. Defined play spaces still exist in some communities, but too often defined play spaces have given way to soccer fields, tee-ball and Little League fields, and fields for other sports activities. In America, noncompetitive play does not enjoy the same level of support as do competitive sports.

10-8c Traditional Playgrounds

Traditional playgrounds first appeared in the United States in the 1920s (see Frost, 1992). G. Stanley Hall (1844–1924) is considered the founder of the American playground movement (Hall, 1902). He believed children should be encouraged to play out their natural evolution from monkey to human by swinging on equipment like the monkey bars. Although spaces with equipment can encourage play, too often playgrounds include monkey bars, a slide, and swings over asphalt surrounded by a chain link fence. This type of playground only encourages limited movement. More often than not, these playgrounds encourage accidents. The National Program for Playground Safety (NPPS) reports that over 200,000 children are injured on playgrounds every year (O'Brien, 2009). Adults need to be especially observant on older playgrounds with older pieces of equipment that may have broken or missing parts. The most common type of injury on the playground is incurred during and after a fall; adults need to monitor climbing equipment and tall slides to minimize injuries.

10-8d Contemporary Playgrounds

Contemporary playgrounds encourage a great variety of play (Photo 10-9). These playgrounds generally have diverse ground coverings and an assortment of equipment designed for a variety of ages and developmental levels. Contemporary play structures are generally made of wood and have tire swings; slides with platforms at the top; climbing ropes; driving areas for tricycles, wagons, and buggies; and shaded areas (i.e., canopied or roofed areas); in addition, contemporary play structures provide a variety of physical challenges. Some modern designs look very colorful and contemporary but on closer inspection are very traditional. Playgrounds that are the most appropriate for children have the following characteristics:

- They have been checked for safety using the NPPS guidelines, which can be found on the NPPS website.

- They include a variety of ground coverings that meet safety standards.

- They create multiple opportunities for movement.

- They encourage play for all children who have multiple skill levels. Slides have a variety of levels, and ladders with platforms and steps are available.

- They facilitate different kinds of movement. The child can move up and down, sideways, tumble, climb, crawl, and jump.

10-9 Contemporary playgrounds invite the child to climb, move, and play with peers.

- They encourage creative pretense. Good equipment is open ended and encourages sociodramatic play.

- They include materials that are translucent and provide places where children can look at and talk to other children through a variety of openings.

10-8e Community or Adventure Playgrounds

The **community or adventure playground** movement started after World War II in the Scandinavian countries and spread throughout Europe; it reached England in the 1960s. Today, Denmark and other Scandinavian countries still lead the world in adventure playgrounds, but England is making headway. In contrast, there are very few adventure playgrounds in America today.

The adventure playground movement started in Copenhagen, Denmark. These playgrounds provided spaces that allowed children to build, tear down, and build again. Adventure playgrounds employ an adult who is the play leader.

The leader is available to assist in the play and ensure a supply of materials. The area for the playground ranges between a half acre and four acres. Wild and domesticated animals live in many of these playgrounds, and some adventure playgrounds resemble a small farm complete with flower and vegetable gardens and greenhouses. The children and adults are encouraged to work in these areas, and many families grow vegetables there.

Unlike playgrounds with either a chain link fence or no fence, adventure playgrounds are enclosed by a wooden fence that has a gate wide enough for a truck to enter. These fences do two things: first, they shield the public from messy play because when children are building, the playground may be cluttered. Second, they provide privacy for children at play. A building for storing materials and rainy day play is always available, and bathroom facilities are located within the building.

10-8f Inclusive Playgrounds

A recent trend in America has been the establishment of **inclusive playgrounds** designed for children with disabilities or delays. Although the American with Disabilities Act of 1990 and the 1997 IDEA amendments were authorized in the 1990s (IDEA—The Individuals with Disabilities Education Act, 2012), it has taken two decades for the Act to become a reality in terms of access to playgrounds. All children have the right to access any public facility. As public areas, playgrounds should be free and open to everyone. All playgrounds should be inclusive; inclusivity is set aside as a separate category in IDEA because, in addition to offering full access to all activities, new playgrounds are designed to allow simultaneous play with typically developing peers. Inclusive playgrounds are designed to allow children with disabilities or delays to access areas so they experience play with other children. Paved walkways are parallel with steps for climbing. This allows friends to move along the playground together. Similarly, sand boxes are built so that children in wheelchairs can play alongside others in the sand. Several nonprofit groups, such as Boundless Playgrounds (Boundless Playgrounds, 2013), Can-Do Playgrounds (Can-Do Playgrounds, 2013), and KaBOOM! (2013) are dedicated to establishing inclusive playgrounds.

10-8g Theme-Based Parks

The term **theme-based** (or *pay for play*) is sometimes used to refer to commercial parks such as Disneyland. It is also used by manufacturers of playground equipment to describe large pieces of equipment that depict a theme, such as a pirate ship. Commercial theme parks are designed for entertainment and provide a different type of playground experience. One advantage is that theme-based parks provide opportunities for families to spend time together engaged in activities that appeal to the entire family.

Some concerns related to businesses that host pay-for-play spaces involve safety and sanitary issues. Dr. Carr-Jordan, a professor of child development, investigated indoor play areas in restaurants and found various safety concerns due to equipment with broken or protruding parts. Additionally, she found a variety of bacteria and even feces in some of the play areas (Carr-Jordan, 2011). There have been a multitude of newspaper reports throughout the United States about the lack of oversight for indoor play areas, but to date, there are no regulations. Given the lack of required oversight, safety and sanitary issues in these areas should be expected.

Another disadvantage is the cost of pay-for-play facilities, which can limit who can play in those facilities.

Assessing Outdoor Play 10-9 ✳

Outdoor environments provide an optimal opportunity for assessing play and the child's development. Assessment can be used to evaluate physical, social, and cognitive development by examining play taxonomies discussed in Chapter 1. These include physical development (gross and fine motor skills), social interaction (solitary, parallel, associative, and group play), and cognitive development (sensorimotor or functional, constructive, pretense or dramatic play, and games with rules). These taxonomies provide tools to examine different aspects of the child's play. Combining methods can provide a profile of the child's play.

10-9a Planning for Assessment

The first step involves planning. Decide how you will use the information. Appropriate assessment is conducted for a purpose. The data collected should be used to change or improve programs for young children. Next, decide if you are observing skills. If so, do you plan to make changes based on your assessment? If you choose to observe the child's play level, always focus on play that is dominant for the child's age group. For example, if you are observing four-year-olds, the dominant play should be pretend play, although some practice and constructive play will be occurring. You may even see some rough and tumble play. If you only see sensorimotor play, then you may want to look at the playground again. What are the impediments?

Outdoor assessment provides a unique context for observing play. The playground is different from the indoor classroom. When beginning informal assessment, limit assessment to one or two behaviors per class, or limit observations to one child. If you are assessing skill development such as jumping, use a check list to write down the names of all the children in the class. Then slip a one-inch-by-two-inch pack of yellow memo notes and a pencil in your pocket. As you walk around the playground, pay attention to who is jumping. When you see someone jumping, write the name on the memo slip. Later in the day, check off the child's name. Some teachers choose to put a square for each child on a file folder and place sticky notes on the file folder. Some teachers will take a picture of the behavior. Either system works. If this is done throughout the week, the entire class can be assessed for jumping skills without a single test situation. Deciding what and how you will assess is the first step. The next step involves assessment.

10-9b Play Assessment

If you are assessing play behaviors, use the Play Scale (Table 10-3) to record play behaviors for five minutes. Do this for two weeks and average the data. When this is done throughout the year, it provides a powerful picture of the child's play.

The process of watching one child involves watching his movements during one outdoor play period. Doing this requires another adult on the playground to supervise the other children. This is a valuable process for several reasons. First, by focusing on observation and assessment only, the adult can more fully analyze the child's total play and combine the physical, social, and cognitive behaviors for a total picture of the play experience. This is especially valuable for

TABLE 10-3 Play Scale

	Sensorimotor Play	Symbolic: Constructive	Symbolic: Dramatic Play	Games	Other
Unoccupied					
Onlooker					
Solitary					
Independent Play					
Parallel Play					
Associative Play					
Cooperative Play					
Rough and tumble play_____					
_____					

Adapted from Piaget (1965), Parten (1932) and Rubin (1989).

children who have play problems or are exhibiting other atypical behavior. The process proceeds as follows:

1. **Physical movement** First, examine the child's physical play (Photo 10-10). All children should engage in movement outside. Is the child's level of movement congruent with his age, stage of development, and culture? Can children move, climb, run, skip, hop, jump, and move in a variety of directions? Does the child have a sense of balance, or does he seem to be unstable at times? Does the child engage in smooth, fluid movements, or are his movements jerky and uneven? If there are signs of inconsistencies with his age mates, then an additional report requesting further testing might be needed.

© Cengage Learning 2015

10-10 Locomotor skills are best assessed on the playground, where children are strengthening their existing abilities and developing new skills.

2. **Social interaction** Second, consider the child's social play. Outdoor play provides a perfect place for assessing social interaction. Again, set up a system for either class observations or individual observations. If you select two children per day, look at their play with their peers. Do they have friends or are they playing alone? Can they play with other children or are they constantly seeking

adult attention? Children who report behaviors of others (what is called tattling) are often seeking adult attention and approval. Find out why the child needs adult interaction. Can you assist the child in finding playmates? Are some children demonstrating leadership skills by organizing games? Have you seen these behaviors in the classroom?

3. **Cognitive development** Although it is more difficult to observe cognitive skills than physical and social skills, cognitive skills are also manifest on the playground. Very young children should engage primarily in practice or functional play on the playground. The infant/toddler playground will be filled with children engaging in practice play, such as emptying sand buckets over and over, climbing up and over a low ramp, and repeatedly moving in different ways. This is typical behavior for this age. Preschoolers will begin to engage in pretend play. Place a large empty box on the infant/toddler playground and the children will fill it with materials. As soon as it is filled, they will empty it again. Place the same large box on a preschoolers' play area and it becomes a boat, a car, or a space ship. The element of pretense has begun. Take the same box to the primary playground and it becomes a club house, and only those who follow the rules can enter. Look at the child's play. Engaging in practice play in preschool is fine, but when children are still exhibiting this type of play in primary school, there may be a reason for concern. Use the Play Scale table 10-3 to get an overall sense of the child's play.

10-9c Multiple Measures

Other data collection techniques are available. These include running records, check lists, narratives, portfolios, and documentation panels. Refer to Chapter 7 for a review of portfolios and documentation panels. Narratives and running records are discussed in the next section. A **running record** is exactly what the name implies; it is a running record of observed behaviors. After watching the children to develop a sense of their physical, social, and cognitive play levels, take a look at each child for one play period. As indicated earlier, this will require another adult on the play space. Complete a running record on the child. That is, write down everything you see the child do during the play period. This will provide an in-depth view of the child's social interaction with peers, communication skills, and play level. Information can be gained from this technique that cannot be garnered using any other method. Running records are used to write narratives of the child's play experience.

10-9d Assessing Primary Play

Assessing primary play is more difficult than assessing preschool play. A system for observing primary play has been developed by Anthony Pelligrini (1998) based on the work of Humphries and Smith (1987). Pelligrini used the following behaviors in a matrix:

Passive/non interactive

Passive/interactive

Adult directed

Adult organized

Did You Get It?

When assessing children playing on a playground, a teacher notices an increase in rough and tumble play. She should

a. look for the exceptions.

b. assume that she is watching an unusually active group of children.

c. research the impediments to other types of play.

d. immediately end outdoor playtime.

Take the full quiz on CourseMate

Aggressive

Rough and tumble play

Vigorous behavior

Games

Object play

Role-play

These behaviors can be used to record observations and frequency of children's behaviors. Watching behaviors over a period of time can provide a powerful tool for understanding children.

PLAYSCAPE: REFLECTIONS

Aiden, like many other children of his age, was excited to be outside. The playground provided a good variety of appropriate choices. As in years past, the girls continue to occupy a smaller amount of space on the playground than the boys. Although Aiden could not speak English as well as others in his class, he excelled on the playground in games of competition. He found a way to be accepted by the other children in the class. When the children return to the class they are more likely to sit and concentrate. Although Aiden may not excel indoors, he excels outdoors. Children have always benefited from outdoor play, and all children should continue to benefit from outdoor play on a daily basis.

 Summary

10-1 List the benefits of outdoor play.

A. Encourages physical movement and good health.

B. Creates a unique environment for learning that stimulates brain development.

C. Encourages different levels of social participation as children self-select playmates.

D. Develops standards of morality during interactions with peers or more competent others.

E. Provides opportunities for freely chosen play.

10-2 Differentiate recess from organized physical exercise classes.

The term *recess* is generally applied to a block of time when children are allowed to go to a defined area and engage in self-selected physical play for a specified amount of time. Physical education class is directed by an adult who directs the activity.

10-3 Distinguish categories of adult interaction on the playground.

Teachers have four different roles on the playground: organizer, observer, supervisor, and evaluator.

10-4 Identify safety concerns and issues related to outdoor play.

Although the primary concern for young children is overexposure to the sun, sun safety is important for everyone, including early educators who are going outdoors with young children. Allergies prevent many children from going outdoors so parent(s) should be involved. For these children, other activities should be developed. Playground equipment and ground coverings can contribute to injuries.

10-5 Describe outdoor play for infants and toddlers.

Infants and toddlers need a play space that is safe, partially shaded, and comfortable; provides a large range of movements; encourages sensory stimulation; and offers a variety of novel and challenging activities.

10-6 Describe outdoor play for preschoolers and kindergarteners.

Preschoolers and kindergarteners need a safe, partially shaded play space that increases locomotor abilities, problem-solving skills, negotiation skills, and social interactions. Preschoolers enjoy acrobatic activities that are difficult to do inside.

10-7 Describe outdoor play for primary age children.

Primary age children need a safe, partially shaded play space with equipment for swinging, sliding, and climbing with their friends. They are beginning to play group games and need space for playing jump rope and group chase games such as soccer football, or kickball. They can still benefit from sand boxes, and they enjoy spaces that allow them to dig in the dirt.

10-8 Discuss seven types of play spaces.

1. Natural play spaces allow children to experience and enjoy the natural environment.
2. Traditional playgrounds were first developed in the early 1900s. They feature steel equipment placed on grass. Injuries are often associated with these playgrounds.
3. Contemporary playgrounds have wooden or plastic structures with ground coverage to deter injuries from falls.
4. Community or adventure playgrounds provide an opportunity for children to engage in construction and dramatic play.
5. Inclusive playgrounds are designed so that all children can use the facilities. Children in wheelchairs can play alongside children who are mobile.
6. Theme-based playgrounds have a theme that is predominant throughout the playground.
7. Pay-for-play playgrounds provide jumping and bouncing opportunities in an indoor environment. Safety and sanitary issues are problematic in these spaces.

10-9 Design an assessment for an outdoor environment.

Make a plan to systematically collect information on the physical, social, and cognitive development of the child on the playground. This can be done by observing one child closely or by watching a group. The most important aspect is that when you are observing the child for assessment purposes, you must continue to scan the playground for safety issues. It is optimal to have another adult on the playground.

 ## Key terms

 ## Technology and Internet Resources

Afterschool Programs

http://www.afterschool.gov

Good site on afterschool programs. Sponsored by the federal government and designed for educators, the site contains links for children as well as for educators.

California Early Childhood Protection Curriculum

www.dhs.ca.gov

The California Early Childhood Protection Curriculum is available for use by early educators and can be accessed via this website.

Centers for Disease Control and Prevention

http://www.cdc.gov

U. S. Department of Health and Human Services, Centers for Disease Control and Prevention. *School Health Index for Physical Activity and Healthy Eating (Elementary School): A Self-Assessment and Planning Guide.* (The document can be downloaded from the CDC website)

International Play Association

http://www.IPA.org

Includes information to support the right of the child to play. Links to other information about recess included.

National Program for Playground Safety

http://www.uni.edu

National Program for Playground Safety Web page. The site includes information about playground safety.

Playground Design

http://www.ecdu.gov

Good site designed by educators that includes the necessary information for planning and developing safe play spaces for young children.

Play Space Assessment

http://www.aahperd.org

Forum created by Head Start to evaluate outdoor play spaces for young children.

Safe Kids Worldwide

http://www.safekids.org

Global organization committed to protecting children from unintentional injuries, the number one cause of death among children in the United States.

Skin Cancer News

www.aad.org

This site is sponsored by the American Academy of Dermatology. A fact sheet is included that can be shared with parents.

 Activities . . . .

1. InClass Labs

A. Design at least three play activities that can be used for an infant/toddler, a preschool, and a primary play area. Be sure to include some art and water activities. How will you set up the area? Consider clean-up. How will clean-up be implemented?

B. Think about the activities that you planned in part (a) of this exercise. How will you store and or transport materials to the playground?

2. Research and Inquiry

A. Visit a local primary school during recess. Complete a time sample of one minute each for three boys and three girls using the Play Scale in Table 10-3 (on p. 287). Compare and contrast their play.

B. Visit and describe at least three different playgrounds. What factors contribute to making them different?

3. Service Learning

A. Visit a local playground. Use the check list in Table 10-2 (p. 274) to inspect the playgrounds for safety. Report any safety concerns to the playground supervisors.

B. Volunteer to help clean up a playground on a community clean-up day.

C. Make a list of safety precautions that teachers should follow to ensure safety on the playground. Include information about sun safety. Create brochures or order brochures from the National Program for Playground Safety (NPPS). Distribute the materials to local PTAs.

4. Family Connections

A. Contact the International Play Association for information on the International Play Day.

B. Present the information you received from the International Play Association to a local parents' group, student group, or community group, and invite the community group to sponsor a play day in the community.

5. Play Advocacy

Survey local schools concerning recess in your community. If recess is at risk in your community, join an action group that is supporting school recess.

 Visit CourseMate for this textbook to access the eBook, Did You Get It? quizzes, Digital Downloads, TeachSource Video Cases, flashcards, and more. Go to CengageBrain.com to log in, register, or purchase access.

 References _____

Afterschool Alliance. (2009). *Uncertain times 2009: Recession imperiling afterschool programs and the children they serve*. Retrieved from Afterschool Alliance on July 24, 2013 at Alhttp://www.afterschoolalliance.org.

American Heart Association. (2011). *Understanding children: Statistical sourcebook*. Dallas, TX: National Center for American Heart Association.

Baines, E., & Blatchford, P. (2011). Children's games and playground activities in school and their role in development. In A. Pelligrini (Ed.), *Oxford handbook of the development of play* (pp. 260–283). Oxford, UK: Oxford University Press.

Barros, R., Silver, E., & Stein, R. (2009). School recess and group classroom behavior. *Pediatrics, 123*(2), 431–436.

Blatchford, P., & Baines, F. (2010). Peer relations in school. In K. Littleton, C. Wood, & K. Staarman (Eds.), *International handbook of psychology in education* (pp. 227–274). Bradford, UK: Emerald Group Publishing.

Bee Stings. (2003). Bee Stings: Treatment and Drugs. Retrieved from the Mayo Clinic website on July 24, 2013, at http://www.mayoclinic.com/health/bee-stings/DS01067/DSECTION=treatments-and-drugs

Beaulieu, L., Butterfield, S. A., & Pratt, P. (2009). Physical activity opportunity in United States public elementary schools. *ICHPER-SD Journal of Research, 4*(2), 33–36.

Boundless Playgrounds. (2012). Boundless Playgrounds. Retrieved on July 24, 2013, from http://www.boundlessplaygrounds.org

Burriss, K., & Burriss, L. (2011). Outdoor play and learning: Policy and practice. *International Journal of Education Policy and Leadership, 6*(8), 1–12.

Can-Do Playground. (2013). Can-Do Playground. Retrieved on July 24, 2013, from http://www.candoplayground.org

Carr-Jordan, E. (2011). The dangers of indoor play areas. Retrieved from CNN Health on July 24, 2013. Posted November 21, 2011 at http://thechart.blogs.cnn.com/2011/12/03/the-dangers-of-indoor-play-areas/

Centers for Disease Control and Prevention. (2010). *The association between school based physical activity, including physical education, and academic performance*. Atlanta, GA: U.S. Department of Health and Human Services.

Chambers, V., Roorda, H., & Wang, P. (2007). "SUN SAFE SAFARI": a unique method of educating school age children about sun safety. *Oncology Nursing Forum, 34*(2), 491.

Council on School Health of the American Academy of Pediatrics. (2013). The critical role of recess in schools. *Pediatrics, 131*(1), 131–183.

Couper, L. (2011). Putting play back into the playground. *Kariaranga, 12*(1), 37–42.

Daniels, S., Jacobson, M., McCrindle, B., Eckel, R., & McHugh Santer, B. (2009). American Heart Association conference proceedings, *American Heart Association Childhood Obesity Research Summit Executive Summary,119*(15), 2114–2123. Retrieved on July 22, 2013 from http://circ.ahajournals.org/content/119/15/2114.full

Dewey, J. (1930). *Democracy and education*. New York: Macmillan.

Elkind, D. (1981). *The hurried child: Growing up too fast too soon*. Reading, MA: Addison-Wesley.

Frost, J. (1992). *Play and playscapes*. Clifton Park, NY: Delmar.

Frost, J., Wortham, S., & Reifel, S. (2011). *Play and child development* (4th ed.). Upper Saddle River, NJ: Merrill/Prentice Hall.

Göncü, A., & Gaskins, S. (2007). An integrative perspective on play and development. In A. Göncü & S. Gaskins (Eds.), *Play and development: Evolutionary, sociocultural, and functional perspectives* (pp. 3–18). New York: Lawrence Erlbaum Associates.

Hall, G. S. (1902). Some social aspects of education. *The Pedagogical Seminary, 9*(1), 81–91.

Humphreys, A. P., & Smith, P. K. (1987). Rough and tumble, friendship, and dominance in schoolchildren: Evidence for continuity and change with age. *Child Development, 58*, 201–212.

IDEA—The Individuals with Disabilities Education Act. (2012). National Discrimination Center for Children with Disabilities. Retrieved on July 24, 2013, at http://nichcy.org/laws/idea

International Play Association. (2013). *International Play Association*. Retrieved on July 24, 2013, form http://IPA.org

Jarrett, O. (2003). Urban school recess: The haves and have nots. *Play, Policy, & Practice Connections. Newsletter of the Play, Policy, and Practice Interest Forum of the National Association for the Education of Young Children, 8*(1), 1–3,7–10.

Johnson, J. E., Christie, J. F., & Wardle, F. (2005). *Play, development, and early education*. Allyn & Bacon. Needham Heights, MA.

KaBOOM! (2013). KaBOOM! Retrieved on July 24, 2013 from http://ourdreamplayground.kaboom.org

Kieff, J. (2001). The silencing of the recess bells. *Childhood Education, 77*(5), 319–325.

Kern, P., & Wakeford, L. (2007). Supporting outdoor play for young children: The zone model of playground supervision. *Young Children, 62*(5), 12–18.

Task Force on Childhood Obesity. (2013). Let's Move: America's Move to Raise a Healthier Generation of Kids. Retrieved on July 22, 2013 from http://www.letsmove.gov/white-house-task-force-childhood-obesity-report-president

Lounsbery, M., McKenzie, T., Morrow, J., Monnat, S., & Holt, K. (2013). District and school physical education policies: Implications for physical education and recess time. *Annals of Behavioral Medicine, 45*, 131–141.

Maslow, A. H. (1972). *The farther reaches of human nature*. Anna Maria, FL: Maurice Bassett Publishing.

National Association of Early Childhood Specialists in State Departments of Education. Retrieved on October 12, 2003, from http://ecap.crc.uiuc.edu/websites/naecs.html

National Center for Health Statistics. *Prevalence of overweight among children and adolescents: United States, 1999–2000*. Retrieved on January 10, 2004 from www.cdc.gov/nchs/products/pubs/pubd/hestats/overwght99.htm

National Program for Playground Safety (2013). Retrieved on July 24, 2013, at http://playgroundsafety.org

O'Brien, C. (October 2009). *Injuries and investigated deaths associated with playground equipment, 2001–2008.* Washington, DC: U.S. Consumer Product Safety Commission.

Parten, M. B. (1932). Social participation among pre-school children. *The Journal of Abnormal and Social Psychology, 27*(3), 243.

Pellegrini, A. D. (2011). The development and function of locomotor play. *Oxford handbook of the development of play, 172–184.*

Pelligrini, A. (1998). Play and the assessment of young children. In O.Saracho & B. Spodek (Eds.), *Multiple perspectives on play in early childhood education* (pp. 220–239). Albany, NY: SUNY.

Pelligrini, A, & Boyd, B. (1993). The role of play in early childhood development and education: Issues in definition and function. In B. Spodek (Ed.), *Handbook of research on the education of young children* (pp. 105–121). New York: Macmillan Publishing Company.

Pellis, S., & Pellis, V. (2011). Rough- and-tumble play: Training and using the social brain. In A. Pelligrini (Ed.), *The Oxford handbook of the development of play* (pp. 245–260). New York: Oxford University Press.

Piaget, J. (1965). The stages of the intellectual development of the child. In B.A. Marlowe & A.S. Canestrari 's (Eds.), *Educational psychology in context: Readings for future teachers,* pp. 98-106. Thousand Oaks, CA: Sage

Prevent Obesity (2013). Prevent Obesity. Retrieved on July 24, 2013 at http://preventobesity.net

O'Brien, C. (October 2009). *Injuries and investigated deaths associated with playground equipment, 2001–2008.* Washington, DC: U.S. Consumer Product Safety Commission.

Opie, I., & Opie, P. (1959). *The lore and language of school-children.* Oxford: Claredon Press.

Ramstetter, C., Murray, R., & Garner, A. (2010). The crucial role of recess in schools. *Journal of School Health, 80,* 517–526.

Readdick, C., & Park, J. (1998). Achieving great heights: The climbing child. *Young Children, 53*(6), 14–19.

Rousseau, J. J. (1979). *Emile, or On education,* trans. Allan Bloom. New York: Basic Books,

Rubin, K. H. (1989). *The play observation scale.* Unpublished coding manual, Department of Psychology, University of Waterloo.

Seefeldt, C., & Barbour, N. (1998). *Early childhood education: An introduction.* Columbus, OH: Merrill.

Shonkoff, J. (2009). Mobilizing science to revitalize early childhood policy. *Issues in Science and Technology.* Retrieved on July 24, 2013 from http://www.issues.org/26.1/shonkoff.html

Slater, S. J., Nicholson, L., Chriqui, J., Turner, L., & Chaloupka, F. (2012). The impact of state laws and district policies on physical education and recess practices in a nationally representative sample of US public elementary schools. *Archives of pediatrics & adolescent medicine, 166*(4), 311.

Slater, S., Nicholson, L., Chriqui, J., Turner, L., & Chaloupka, F. (2012). The impact of state laws and district polies on physical education and recess practices in a nationally representative sample of US public elementary schools. *Archives of Pediatrics and Adolescent Medicine, 166*(4), 311–316.

Smith, P. K. (1997). Play fighting and real fighting. *Perspectives on their relationship.* In A. Schmitt, K. Atzwanger, K. Grammar, & K. Schäfer (Eds.), New aspects of human ethology (pp. 47–64). New York: Plenum Press, NY

Stephenson, A. (2002). Opening Up the Outdoors: Exploring the Relationship between the Indoor and Outdoor Environments of a Centre. European Early Childhood Education Research Journal, *10*(1), 29–38.

Tannock, M. (2011). Observing young chidlren's rough-and-tumble play. *Australasian Journal of Early Childhood, 36*(2), 13–20.

Tannock, M. T. (2008). Rough and tumble play: An investigation of the perceptions of educators and young children. *Early Childhood Education Journal, 35*(4), 357–361.

Wellhousen, K. (2005). *Outdoor play every day: Innovative concepts for early childhood.* Clifton Park, NY: Delmar.

11 Current Trends and Issues

STANDARDS COVERED IN THIS CHAPTER

Council of Exceptional Children—Division of Early Childhood Standards CEC DEC

ECSE 9K1 Understand legal, ethical, and policy issues related to educational, developmental, and medical services for infants and young children and their families

ECSE 9K2 Advocate for professional status and working conditions for those who serve infants and young children and their families

ECSE 9S3 Respect family choices and goals

ECSE 9S7 Advocate on behalf of infants and young children and their families

ECSE 10S1 Collaborate with caregivers, professionals, and agencies to support children's development and learning

NAEYC Program Standards

6a Identifying and involving oneself with the early childhood field

* LEARNING OBJECTIVES *

11-1 Identify major trends that affect children's play.

11-2 Describe four issues that currently impact play.

11-3 Explain the evolution of play research in terms of current practice.

11-4 Create and implement a policy on play and a plan for play advocacy.

© Cengage Learning 2015

6b Knowing about and upholding ethical standards and other professional guidelines

6c Engaging in continuous, collaborative learning to inform practice

6d Integrating knowledgeable, reflective, and critical perspectives on early education

6e Engaging in informed advocacy for children and the profession

 PLAYSCAPE: REFLECTIONS

As the teacher walks over, Sierra and Adriel look up from their block play. They have just finished putting the finishing touches on their block structures. The electronic grass blocks are glowing a bright shade of green against the bright buildings. As Adriel puts the last grass block in place, he tells Sierra, "Put the e-blocks here, Sierra."

"Okay, turn on the day lights, not the nighttime lights," Sierra responds. As the teacher watches, she contemplates how much she should interject into their play.

"You know you don't see as much grass in the cities," the teacher says. "Sidewalks and highways are more common. If you want to change the environment block from grass to concrete, you can push this button. Do you want to look at some tech samples of cities?"

Both Adriel and Sierra shake their heads. "This is a pretend city," Sierra says. "Let's just pretend the grass blocks are concrete. Let's just pretend the skylights are on and the night lights are off."

"Yeah. We're just pretending!" Adriel says.

"Okay," says the teacher. "But let me know if you want to look at some samples." As their teacher walks away, Adriel and Sierra smile and continue playing.

Explaining Play Behaviors

The children in this scenario are engaged in block play. The blocks in this scenario serve as an impetus for play as the teacher attempts to guide the children's play. However, the types of electronic blocks described in this scenario do not currently exist. Perhaps new technologies will create blocks such as those depicted in the case study that allow children to create different environmental systems. Perhaps not. The future impact of technology on materials and how they are used is unknown. What we do know is that new materials and toys can encourage activity or passivity based on what is available and how it is presented to children. For example, some classrooms have a varied assortment of wooden, cardboard, and cloth blocks designed to stimulate play. These classrooms have cameras that allow the teacher to record block play and create e-books about play in the block center. Teachers in these settings are optimizing learning by integrating technology into the curriculum. In contrast, some classrooms have computers with programs that depict blocks but no access to real blocks, whereas other classrooms have no access to either blocks or technology. Children will always be fascinated by new materials and will always engage in pretend play. Or will they? Some have expressed concerns about the influence of today's culture on the young child's play (Campaign for a Commercial-Free Childhood, 2007/2009/2010). This chapter is designed to examine current trends and issues that will impact play in the twenty-first century.

In Chapter 1, the contexts of play were examined using an ecological lens. This approach discussed in Chapter 1 considered the political and economic forces that impact young children and their play. This chapter returns to that perspective in an examination of global, national, regional, and community trends and their subsequent impact on play.

11-1a Global Trends

The impacts of war, disease, poverty, and violence are factors that influence play throughout the world. Children in countries that are being ravaged by war, disease, poverty, or violence have limited opportunities to play. For example, children who live in countries where the peril of stepping on land mines is a daily reality must choose not to play outdoors or to face consequences that may result in the loss of a limb or life. Diseases such as AIDS affect young children in many countries in Africa and impact their daily activities. Still, children will use their last energy to engage in play. After touring refugee camps, Liv Ullman noted that "children who are too sick to move, who must be carried out of their house, will still play in the dirt. With their last breath, they play" (Rogers, 1989). Maggie Fearn and Justine Howard (2012) looked at the impact of adversity on children who were in the bombing of Beirut, orphaned in Romania, or abandoned to the streets of Rio de Janeiro. They found that, "given the opportunity, children interact with and influence their environment through play and that this process provides a resource to meet the challenge of adversity ... play appears to be a key factor in supporting the development of emotional resiliency" (Fearn & Howard, 2012, pp. 456 and 465). Although many children do not experience the horror of war, they may still experience the reality of violence in a way that impacts their childhood.

Children in more affluent nations have many opportunities to play. Mobility and communication provide access to information at an unprecedented rate and in a sense create a global village. In addition, those who teach children have more opportunities than ever before to learn about play. For example, early educators in countries throughout the world travel to different locations to study play for young children. Teachers from over forty-four countries have visited the schools in Reggio Emilia, Italy (Photo 11-1). Others travel to Norway to study programs for infants.

During a program that the author attended with Constance Kami, teachers from America sat next to teachers from Japan, and the teachers from both countries talked with each other about how young children make sense of the world through play with games. Now, teachers and children communicate via the Internet. As teachers and children acquire new information and perspectives,

© Cengage Learning 2015

11-1 Environmental changes that capture and reflect light reflect the influence of the Reggio Emilia programs.

11-2 The use of light to highlight colors and shapes is another example of how a school on one continent can impact daily activities on another continent.

change occurs in their classrooms and the play that occurs therein. The interface between countries and cultures continues to evolve and to influence play as we experience the reality of the global village (Photo 11-2).

11-1b National Trends

Over the past decade, the demographics of children under age eight has made a major impact on early education. The 2010 U.S. census found that 48.4% of households list their marital status as married, and of these, only 20.2% report that they have children. Today, 9.6% of homes have single parents at the helm (Timmermann, 2013). More children than ever before are entering the United States from different countries and bringing with them different cultures and styles of play. Many children are non–English speakers, and ESL (English as a second language) education is a standard part of many classrooms. As these changes continue to unfold, teachers must fully embrace diversity and multiculturalism if they are to implement a curriculum and environment appropriate for all children.

An informational trend is also affecting play. Organizations such as the National Association for the Education of Young Children, Association for Childhood Education International, Association for the Child's Right to Play, and the National Program for Playground Safety provide information about play. Anyone seeking information can find research and support within a matter of minutes. At the same time, incorrect and inappropriate information is equally available. It is important that educators have access to lists of and guidelines for appropriate resources.

At the same time, a national crisis is occurring in the health of our youngest citizens. As mentioned in Chapter 1 and Chapter 10, obesity is decreasing slightly after continuously increasing for the past five years. This may be due to the national emphasis on the topic of obesity. For example, a national discussion was spearheaded by the First Lady, Michelle Obama. Her initiative influenced other organizations to join the promotion of play (Photo 11-3). Even though the focus on the physical benefits of play will, most likely, decrease within the next five years as the rate of obesity decreases, the semiotic relationship between children's health and play will continue to impact state and local programs.

11-3 Play and physical activity are major components of a healthy lifestyle that prevents obesity.

11-1c Community Trends

Changes in neighborhoods and families have changed the nature of play. Some of the changes are positive and some are negative. The cumulative nature of the changes has made a difference in how play occurs in neighborhoods and families (Sluss, 2008).

Neighborhood. In the past, children played in neighborhoods after school often without adult supervision. Today's neighborhoods may not always be safe, and in unsafe neighborhoods young children are supervised by adults at all times. They watch television, play computer and video games, or participate in organized activities. The days of roaming through the neighborhood, climbing trees, and wading through a stream have disappeared in most areas of the United States. Children who climb, play with mud, or visit sites in the neighborhood do so under the watchful eye of a parent or early educator. In both high-income and low-income areas, parents or other adults accompany children to playgrounds due to safety issues. The influence of this constant adult supervision on the transmission of children's games, songs, and chants is yet unknown.

To combat this trend, many neighborhoods are developing play places for young children. Neighborhood groups throughout the nation are involved in building playgrounds. As mentioned in Chapter 10, KaBOOM! is a nationally recognized group dedicated to establishing playgrounds. KaBOOM! is committed to promoting active play and is especially interested setting up playgrounds in locations considered "play deserts," where there is little access to outdoor play spaces.

Families. The changing structure of families has an impact on play. In the past, young children played with members of the family or siblings. Young children now live in a variety of familial structures, including nuclear, single, extended, and blended families. As compared with 1960, the number of children living with one parent or in single-parent homes has doubled. Over a third (35%) of all American children live in a single-parent home, and single-parent families tend to be underfunded families (Kids Count, 2011). Additionally, children who are raised in families without male role models may not experience the benefits of rough and tumble play (Photo 11-4). Today's family also tends to be smaller, with the average family unit being 2.58 people (U.S. Census Data, 2011). For this

11-4 Adult males in the classroom serve as powerful role models for young children.

© Cengage Learning 2015

Did You Get It?

A four-year-old usually plays with her older brother, younger sister, or her parents. She is
a. emulating play trends of the past.
b. in accordance with national trends.
c. in the minority, because she comes from a two-parent household.
d. unlikely to learn from play with siblings.

Take the full quiz on CourseMate

reason, many parents are developing play-groups that meet two or three times a week. Other changes in the family unit include the increase in the number of grandparents serving as parents or support partners (Harper & Ruicheva, 2010). When the adult in the household is an older adult or even octogenarian, the care that the child receives changes along with the play that he experiences (DPhil & Ruicheva, 2010). As family structures continue to morph, play will also change.

From the Experts

Play and the Future: Gesell Institute of Child Development's Perspective

Marcy Guddemi

The study of early childhood education has produced some extraordinary findings as of late. The most exciting finding is in the area of brain research, executive functioning, and pretend play. Through the use of MRIs (magnetic resolution imagery) of the brain, we find that pretend play of young children helps develop the part of the brain that enables a child to have executive functioning skills, which in turn leads to learning, self-control, flexibility, creativity, persistence, engagement, self-motivation, connection making, and risk taking. Children who have ample opportunities to practice pretend play have higher test scores in both reading and math. A recent study in New Zealand of executive functioning found that children who could better regulate their impulses and attention were four times less likely to have a criminal record, three times less likely to be addicted to drugs, and half as likely to become single parents. In many dimensions of successful, healthy living, the level of executive functioning was more predictive of adult outcomes than either IQ scores or socioeconomic status.

Arnold Gesell, PhD, MD (1880–1961) was a ground-breaking researcher of child development. He carefully documented growth and development over time using cinematography (a new technology at the time). He took thousands of photographs and movies, and he took copious notes. He was an observer of children. "If we use effective tools, the child reveals himself to all who will stop and listen to what he says, and who, with seeing eyes, will watch what he does" (Guddemi & Gessell, 2010). Gesell found that all children travel on the same path of development; however, some go faster, some go more slowly, and all have spurts and setbacks along the way. The Gesell Institute of Child Development, having just completed a nationwide study of three- to six-year-olds, has found that children are not developing faster today.

In fact, children are reaching the major developmental milestones at about the same time as they did when Dr. Gesell first started collecting data over 100 years ago. The Gesell message to educators is that each child has his own pace on the path of development that must be respected in the classroom and that play is the vehicle of child development.

The future of play is in the hands of the researchers and technology. Just as Dr. Gesell used the most cutting-edge technology of his day to study child development in the early part of the twentieth century, today's twenty-first-century researcher is using science and technology to discover and sometimes confirm what we once just had "gut-level" feelings about. Research now shows that pretend play, the charming and hallmark feature of the child's world, helps develop the part of the brain that is critical for learning. Pretend play is not just something

(Continued)

all children do to have fun; pretend play is essential in child development. As more cutting-edge research rolls in, the role of play in child development and learning will be preserved and perpetuated into the future. And cutting-edge research will validate what philosophers and educators have said for centuries: "Do not…keep children to their studies by compulsion but by play" (Plato).

REFERENCES

Guddemi, M., & Gesell, A. (2010). The eole of play in an overly-academic kindergarten. Gesell Institute of Human Developmen, New Haven, CT. NAEYC

Washington, DC, 2009. http://www. NAEYC2009/ Play/Handout. pdf. Downloaded May 3, 2013.

MacIntyre, A. (1994). Plato: The Republic. *Plato, 1*, 41.

Dr. Marcy Guddemi, PhD, MBA, is President and CEO of the Gesell Institute of Child Development on the Yale University campus. She is a widely recognized expert in early childhood education, assessment, and learning through play. She earned a PhD in Early Childhood Curriculum and Instruction at the University of Texas at Austin and an MBA from Golden Gate University in San Francisco.

Current Issues 11-2 *

Young children are experiencing changes in their culture that will affect how they view the world. Notice a four-year-old using a computer that his grandmother will not touch. Watch the five-year-old use her grandmother's cell phone or digital camera. Walk through an exhibit filled with art based on the Newtown, Connecticut school tragedy. How will these changes impact children's play? Some are concerned that changes in technology and constant media coverage of all topics are creating a culture that threatens to erode childhood. At the same time, technology provides a link between children and grandparents that offers possibilities never before imagined. Early educators must be informed and serve as both a conduit and filter for information.

Four issues that are currently creating concerns among educators and the public are (1) technology, (2) media influences, (3) toys, and (4) violence.

11-2a Technology: Ready or Not

Perhaps no other area has created as much conversation and consternation in the early childhood education community than technology. Viewpoints range from complete avoidance to a computer-based curriculum. Early educators are faced with questions: Should I encourage computer usage? Should I refuse to place a computer in my classroom? Will children be forced to choose between computers and play? These are real issues that teachers are currently struggling to answer. The impact of technology on play is a major concern and is already evident in children's play. One colleague shared the following story:

> A grandmother reminisced about her experience as a child of watching one of the first telephone operators use a headset and telephone. She recalled that as a child the operator let her put the headset on and dial numbers. She never forgot the magic of that moment. She said she wanted her grandchild to have a similar experience. She was elated when she found a headset that looked like the one she remembered from her childhood. Her granddaughter was equally delighted when she opened the gift. The grandmother later observed the child at play. She had the headset on and was engaged in pretend play. As the grandmother moved closer to the granddaughter, she heard her say, "Hello, Welcome to McDonald's. Can I take your order, please?"

Those who work with young children understand the child's use of headphones. The child was engaged in pretend that reflected her knowledge of reality. In Piaget's terms, she subordinated reality to fit her schema. Vygotskians might point to her social knowledge. The child's experiences with headphones had occurred at fast food restaurants. Even though the grandmother had shared her stories about operators and headphones, the child was more familiar with McDonald's restaurants. This child's pretense reflected her understanding of her world.

The difference in technology at the beginning of the twentieth century compared to the beginning of the twenty-first century is startling. At the beginning of the twentieth century, technology included new inventions such as telephones, cars, and airplanes, which were reserved for the very few wealthy. At the beginning of the twenty-first century, technology includes televisions, computers, and cell phones, which are commonly used by a majority of Americans. In 2003, 69% of homes had a computer, but in the 2010 United States Census, 77% of households reported having a computer in the home (U.S. Census Bureau, 2010). The numbers for adults between the ages of 18 and 44 owning a computer was the highest, ranging from 78% to 82%. When over half of all children have computers in their home, technology is a daily part of a child's life (Photo 11-5). The rapid transformation in technology has occurred over the past fifty years and will continue into the foreseeable future. These changes will, no doubt, impact play.

Current State of Technology. The impact of technology on children can be either positive or negative. It is negative when children access unsafe websites or when teachers isolate children in front of a computer screen for a long period of time. On the other hand, the impact of technology is very positive when children can take pictures of their play, write about their play, and access additional information that extends their activity. The teacher's knowledge of how to use technology appropriately makes the difference.

In 2010, the Campaign for a Commercial Free Childhood (CCFC, 2007/2009/2010) sent a letter signed by seventy child advocacy organizations to encourage the National Association for the Education of Young Children to set a policy for limited computer screen time for young children (Narey, 2010). In 2012, the National Association for the Education of Young Children (NAEYC) and the Fred Rogers Center for Early Learning and Children's Media at Saint Vincent College developed a position paper outlining their views on the appropriate use of technology and interactive media with young children (Schomburg, Donohue, Parikh, Buckleitner, Johnson, Nolan, Wang, & Wartella, 2012).

Techniques for using technology appropriately have been suggested by Douglas H. Clements and Julie Sarama (2009). They recommend planning, creating the environment, and instructing students in the proper use of technology. The first

© Cengage Learning 2015

11-5 Technology impacts children's experiences in and out of school. The extent of the influence will depend on adult attitudes and professional development in technology.

step involves professional development. Complete the course(s) before selecting equipment and materials. After the professional development has been completed, select curriculum modifications, software, and hardware. Review software for the best interactive material. Recognize the limitations of educational technology, and move at a steady, incremental pace.

The second step involves the classroom environment. The number of children in the classroom will determine the number of computers needed. That is, the child/computer ratio is generally at least 10/1. Locate the computers in the center of the room so accessibility is enhanced. Set up the computers so that they are close to each other and so at least two children can work together at one time.

Finally, focus on teaching as an interactive activity. Use large group discussion appropriately along with open-ended questions, activities, and software. When working with individual children, especially those with special needs, monitor social interaction to ensure that children with special needs are involved as an active member of the group (Clements & Sarama, 2009).

Technology and Play.   Technology can be used to extend, expand, and document play. Documentation panels created in the schools of Reggio Emilia used technology to capture the essence of play. These panels also illustrate the joy involved in play and provide evidence of learning that occurs when children play. Many schools in America are starting to use this concept to inform how teachers capture the child's learning through play as they create documentation panels for display.

In the schools of Reggio Emilia, the notion that children have multiple ways of expressing themselves—or, as Reggio Emilio educators say, children have a hundred languages—informs how they interact with children and technology (Edwards, Gandini, & Forman, 2012). Reggio Emilia educators view the use of technology as a way the child can share her view of the world. Putting children and technology together provides a powerful mode of expression for children.

Strategies to enhance the appropriate use of technology to support play and development are listed as follows:

1. **Integrate technology into the classroom**   It is optimal to place a computer in the writing center so children see the computer as a means of communicating. A separate computer center can also be established. If the computer center is in a separate center, treat it like a center. A digital camera should be available throughout the day to capture play and learning. Many children see pictures as a natural part of their activity. Some schools have limited funds but are using disposable cameras. Others have encouraged children to take cameras home and record what they do at home. It is easier for children to share their view of the world when using technology.

2. **Select appropriate hardware and software**   Use funds wisely. Many companies will donate used equipment. A list of websites is included in this text at the end of each chapter. Check the ratings on any program before using it with students. Also, review the commentaries on the programs to ensure that children will be challenged appropriately.

3. **Use computers appropriately**   Time is important. It is not appropriate to force children to stay at the computer station. At the same time, children who are engaged in interactive play with the computer should not be stopped after ten minutes. Time spent in front of a computer screen or television is often called **screen time** and should be limited. The effect of overexposure to computer screens is not known, but the effects of passive

TABLE 11-1	Recommended Computer Use: Infants through Third Grade
Infants and Toddlers	Infants and toddlers can benefit from the adult's use of technology to create books and posters and to document growth and learning through portfolios.
	Children under two should **not** use computers or view television (Schomburg, Donohue, Parikh, Buckleitner, Johnson, Nolan, Wang, & Wartella, 2012).
Preschoolers	Like infants and toddlers, three- and four-year-olds can benefit from the adult's use of technology. Creating books, documenting play, and creating learning portfolios are valuable activities. In addition, adults can create a record of group activities. Preschoolers can use cardboard replicas of computers in their house area. If a computer is available, some games can be used with four-year-olds on a limited basis.
Kindergarten/First Grade	Five- and six-year-olds can use computers for creating books, playing games, and writing stories. The computer should be a center that is available as needed.
Second/Third Grades	Children who are seven and eight years old are ready to use the computer on a regular basis to create books, play math games (such as Millie's Math House, Edmark Corp., Redmond, Washington; or Thinkin' Things, Edmark Corp. Redmond, Washington [Li, Atkins, & Stanton, 2006]), write stories, and conduct simple research.

© Cengage Learning 2015

activities are well documented. It is alarming to know that some companies are targeting babies as an audience for products. Recommended computer use for each age is given in Table 11-1.

It is important to recognize that technology should reflect best practices. Using a computer with two-year-olds is not appropriate but may be appropriate for kindergarteners. Sackes, Trundle, and Bell (2011) conducted a longitudinal study that found "that the availability of computers in kindergarten could help close the initial gap in children's computer skills due to socioeconomic status and lack of computer access prior to entering school. Supplying kindergarten classrooms with adequate computers could positively contribute to children's long-term development of computer skills" (p. 1698). When technology is used, it must be developmentally appropriate for the age, stage, and culture of the child.

4. **Integrate technology in the curriculum** Include pictures of computers and digital cameras in pictures boxes. Include technology props in prop boxes and house areas. What are programs that develop skills in math, science, literacy, and social studies?

5. **Involve parents** Many classrooms are setting up websites so children can show their parents what they did at school that day. This is a wonderful way to connect the family to the classroom. In the same way, some classrooms have a camera in the classroom to provide live streaming so parents can see their children throughout the day.

6. **Continually update your knowledge** Computer literacy depends on staying current. Those who thought they would wait until the fad passes are in trouble. Computers are a part of everyday life. Keeping current involves reading the latest information and participating in training workshops. Teachers who use computers on a regular basis and explore a variety of programs are more knowledgeable and can help their students become comfortable with new experiences and learning opportunities.

Impact of Technology on Play. The impact of technology on play has the potential to be very positive. Like all innovations, technology can be misused.

The teacher is the key to effective use of technological innovations. Knowing what is and is not appropriate and how much to use and when to use it is essential. At this time, data indicate that technology can enhance learning outcomes for young children when used appropriately (Sackes, Trundle, & Bell, 2011). As the database continues to grow, knowledgeable teachers will use this information to inform their decisions in the classroom.

11-2b Media

The impact of media in today's world is unparalled. News from New York can be heard and seen in rural California in a matter of minutes. Television has transformed our culture. A 2009 Nielson Company survey found that children between the ages of two and five spend more than 32 hours a week in front of television screens (Levin, 2010; Linn, 2012). Although some parents use parental control devices to monitor what their children watch on television, others do not. For this reason, it is important that teachers use media appropriately in the classroom. The American Academy of Pediatrics, the American Public Health Association, and the National Resource Center for Health and Safety in Child Care and Early Education joined together to establish guidelines for screen time in early care and early education settings (2011). They recommend that children under age two not be exposed to any media (television, videos, or DVDs) or computers. Additionally, they recommend the following:

1. For children two years and older in early care and early education settings, total media time should be limited to not more than 30 minutes once a week, and the media time should be for educational or physical activity use only.

2. During meal or snack time, TV-, video-, or DVD-viewing should not be allowed.

3. Computer use should be limited to no more than 15-minute increments except for homework and for children who require and consistently use assistive and adaptive computer technology.

4. Parents/guardians should be informed if screen media are used in the early care and education program.

5. Any screen media used should be free of advertising and brand placement. TV programs, DVDs, and computer games should be reviewed and evaluated before participation of the children to ensure that advertising and brand placement are not present.

Impact of Media on Play. Overexposure to violence in the media may be affecting how some children play. Diane Levin (2010) expressed her concern that children who are exposed to violence at an early age engage in play that reflects these themes, and this has a ripple effect on the play of the other children in the classroom. Children transmit their moral code through play (Piaget, 1965). Watching others play games has always provided a venue for learning games. Children who are overexposed to violence are developing a moral code from the media that is based on a culture of violence. The outcome may be a change in society and culture resulting in activities that occur in the context of the macrocosm over which teachers have little control.

The power of the media in shaping culture cannot be denied. This can, however, be a positive influence. Fred Rogers influenced generations as Mr. Rogers in *Mr. Rogers' Neighborhood*. One story bears repeating. A well-known professor shared that as a child, he came home every evening to an empty house. Reared in a single-parent home, he watched *Mr. Rogers* every evening until his mother returned from work. Mr. Rogers served as the male influence in his life. When he learned of the September 11, 2001, attack, he went home and, after being overcome by disbelief and grief, he turned to *Mr. Rogers' Neighborhood* just as he had done so many times as a child. Just sitting and listening to Mr. Rogers's soothing voice made it easier for him to cope with the violence. The calming effect and wisdom of Fred Rogers was transmitted through the media of television. Similar stories were shared about the influence that Mr. Rogers had on both viewers and on those who knew him personally. His wisdom transcends generations and is now recorded for future generations. This is the positive influence of the media.

naeyc
CEC DEC
Early educators must be knowledgeable about the impact of the media. Mr. Rogers would encourage teachers to find ways to use the media in appropriate ways.

Another issue closely linked to the media is toys, which are discussed next.

11-2c Materials and Toys

Materials that children use during the day—such as toys, educational materials, furniture, and outdoor equipment—reflect the values of society. Today, the Internet allows parents and teachers to access the best educational materials in the world. In well-funded classrooms, materials and toys reflect the latest in technology, safety, and research. Early educators who travel throughout the world bring the most current information back home with them to the classroom. For example, after travels to Scandinavia and Italy, many teachers added baskets that older infants could crawl in and out of, different floor textures, materials for softness, and wooden toys that challenge the infant and toddler to engage in exploration and play (Edwards, Gandini, & Forman, 2012). For example, the schools of Reggio Emilia, Italy, inspired the use of plexiglass to provide safe, translucent barriers in elevated spaces, and now this is a standard feature in many preschool classrooms.

Some are concerned, however, that the media is having a negative effect on children's materials and toys (Linn, Almon, & Levin, 2012). Since the Federal Trade Commission deregulated the manufacture of toys related to movies and television shows, the market for such toys has grown exponentially. Many of the top toys have a movie or television show attached to promote sales (Levin, 2010). When a new movie is released, new toys are produced, and new ad campaigns are launched to sell toys at fast food restaurants. Children play out this reality during play in the house area. Children whose parents wisely avoid eating at fast food restaurants and/ or buying these toys may be left out of the group during conversations and play. This creates a culture of consumerism based on the latest movie and advertisements. Teachers who want to negate the effects of commercialism aimed at children must be vigilant and intervene when necessary.

Another concern inherent in the manufacturing of toys is the nature of the toys themselves. Toys that are **uni-dimensional** have only one focus and can only be used in predetermined ways. This can be positive. That is, puzzles are considered one dimensional but add to the child's development (Photo 11-6). In contrast, toys

11-6 Puzzles are uni-dimensional materials that are valuable for development.

© Cengage Learning 2015

that are developed specifically for a movie or television show have only one use. It is difficult to do very much with an action hero figure other than play out scenarios that involve action heroes. For this reason, many centers limit the types and kinds of toys that children can bring to school.

Throughout this book, **multi-dimensional toys** or open-ended toys such as blocks, house items, sand, water, and art materials have been discussed (Johnson, Christie, & Wardle, 2005). Open-ended materials can be used for any purpose. The only limit is the child's imagination (Photo 11-7).

Classrooms should have a mixture of materials and toys that are multi-dimensional or open ended and uni-dimensional or close ended. The following list of toys and materials begins with open-ended materials and toys and progresses to uni-dimensional or close-ended materials and toys.

1. **Natural or real materials** are real and exist outside the realm of play; examples include mud, water, clay, dirt, sand, wood, and rocks (Photo 11-8).

2. **Construction materials** are materials that can be used to build and create. These include wood unit blocks; hollow blocks; sponge blocks; cardboard blocks; Tinker Toys™; interlocking plastic units; wood-working tools (wood, nails, and hammers); art materials such as paint, play-dough, and paper; and

11-7 Dramatic play materials are multi-dimensional materials that can be used in a variety of ways to extend and expand play.

11-8 Natural materials are open ended and allow children to engage in endless play opportunities.

11-9 Large wooden blocks enhance creativity and play. Because they are made of wood, they are virtually indestructible, so once a set is purchased, it can be used for decades.

© Cengage Learning 2015

11-10 The children are using educational materials. Although they are playing, they are developing fine motor skills, math skills, hand—eye coordination, and social skills.

© Cengage Learning 2015

recyclables or reusables such as newspaper, plastics, boxes, cardboard, and any other materials that can safely be repurposed (Photo 11-9).

3. **Toys** are materials that stimulate play and include replicas of people and animals, vehicles, and homes and places. Wagons, bicycles, and wheeled vehicles are included in this category.

4. **Educational materials** are materials that facilitate skills such as stringing beads, puzzles, nesting materials, books that talk to children, computer programs, and robots (Photo 11-10).

Toys that reflect media themes are designed for more structured play than the toys discussed in the preceding list, and this is one reason why educators are so concerned about the prevalence of these media-influenced toys.

Toy Safety. Another current concern is toy safety. The National Safe Kids Campaign found that the rate of unintentional injuries decreased by 55% from 1987 to 2010 (Safe Kids, 2013). The United States Consumer Product Safety Commission (CPSC) reported that in 2011, an estimated 262,300 children under the age of 15 were treated in hospital emergency rooms for toy-related injuries (Tu, 2011). Data indicate that 23% of deaths of children under

15 involved balloons, small marbles or balls, games, and accessory parts. The biggest danger continues to be latex balloons for children under three. Riding toys are responsible for the most injuries of children between ages three and fourteen.

The United States CPSC reports the following major causes of death related to toys and materials:

1. Choking hazards from latex balloons, small marbles or balls, games, and accessory parts or plastic film that comes on toys. Keep all of these away from children under three.

2. Strings and straps can strangle children. Don't give these to children, and keep all cords higher than the child can reach.

3. Ingested magnets can cause intestinal injuries. Children have died from ingesting button magnets.

4. Caps from toy guns can burn children if they fire them in their pant pockets or put them in their pockets after firing them.

5. Electrical shock can be caused by faulty batteries or wiring in toys. Ensure that children have the correct batteries for their toys and that they know how to use electric-powered toys safely.

A major safety point to remember is that children need the right toy for the right age. Children are less likely to suffer a toy-related injury if they have access solely to toys that are age appropriate and are well maintained and checked regularly for hazards and wear.

11-2d Violence

Perhaps no other issue is impacting children more than violence. Violence transcends political and national borders. It is a concern from Miami to Washington, DC, to Los Angeles; and it is a problem in neighborhoods, schools, and homes in both rural and urban America. Since the Newtown, Connecticut attack, few are exempt from the reality of violence and its subsequent impact.

Children who grow up in violent neighborhoods, attend dangerous schools, and go home to abusive parents/caregivers are at risk to grow into abusive, violent adults (Finkelhor, Hamby, Ormrod, & Turner, 2009). But even children who live in safe neighborhoods, attend safe schools, and grow up with caring and nonviolent parents may be at risk. When children are surrounded by violence on television, play with toys that encourage violence, and play computer games depicting violence, they experience violence indirectly (Bushman & Anderson, 2001; Gentile, Saleem, & Anderson, 2007).

There are a multitude of resources available online that provide guidelines for working with young children who are exposed to violence. For example, the Safe Start Center (2013) website provides research, evidence, and information related to children and violence. To combat the effects of violence on children, Levin (2003) suggest guidelines to help children use play to work out violent and disturbing content:

- Watch children as they play to learn more about what they know, what worries them, and what they are struggling to understand.

- Remember that for many children it is normal and helpful to bring into their play graphic aspects of what they have seen and heard.

Did You Get It?

A fourth-grade teacher places a computer in the class writing center. Her overall goal is probably

a. to have the children view the computer as a means of communication.

b. to have the children learn to type.

c. to teach children how to research online.

d. to use it as an assistive device for children who have special needs.

Take the full quiz on CourseMate

- If the play gets scary or dangerous, gently intervene and redirect it. For example, ask children, "How could people help each other?" Or provide toys such as rescue vehicles and medical equipment.

- Help children come up with ways for extending play. For example, ask children, "Now, what can we do after this occurs?" Try to follow the children's lead in the roles that you take; don't try to take over the play.

- After the play, talk to children about what they played. Reassure their safety. Answer questions simply. Clear up confusions.

- If children are bringing violence to the play, try to teach alternatives to the harmful lessons children may be learning at home, in their neighborhoods, or via media.

Some children will need additional intervention and can benefit from play therapy. By working together, professionals can better meet the needs of young children who are under stress.

✳ 11-3 Play Research

At the beginning of the twentieth century, play research was influenced by the emphasis on empirical research and focused on the physical and social aspects of play. During the second half of the century, research examined the benefits of play in terms of development. Cognitive development and social pretend dominated the literature during this time. In the twenty-first century, the study of play is being influenced by new information in the area of research methods, cognitive development, social and emotional development, and physical development.

1. **Research Methods** The state of play research was dealt a blow by omission from the fifth edition of the *Handbook of Child Psychology* (Eisenberg, 1998). Although play held a prominent role in the fourth edition of the *Handbook of Child Psychology* (Mussen, 1983), it is markedly missing from the fifth edition. Those interested in play theory must turn to the *Oxford Handbook on the Development of Play* (2011), which is edited by Anthony Pelligrini.

    A movement away from the laboratory and into the classroom started during the past decade and is continuing to gain momentum. The focus on the teacher as researcher is continuing to affect how some teachers view their role in the classroom. Naturalistic settings provide rich environments for gathering data and are gaining in popularity. These settings affect research and the data that are gathered.

    Another change in research is the role of play in research studies. In the past, many studies looked at behaviors that occurred during play. More recent studies are using play as an intervention for performance outcomes in the areas of social interaction, math, and literacy.

2. **Cognitive Development** Research on **Theory of Mind** (TOM) has changed some previously held beliefs about the child's ability to understand concepts. Theory of Mind refers to research that looks at the child's ability to understand what others are communicating in terms of intentionality. Research in this area emphasizes the role of culture on cognitive development.

    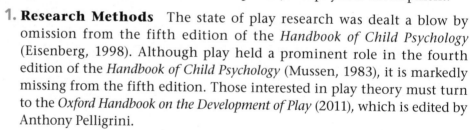 Another area of interest is **brain-based research**. The latest findings confirm the plasticity of the brain. Children have over 100 trillion synaptic

connections at eight months of age but lose these as they interact with culture. By the age of ten, the typical child has 500 million connections (Shonkoff, 2009). Those that were not used were eliminated. As research studies glean more information about the brain, we will understand with greater clarity the role of play in establishing neurological connections. This presents an exciting area of research.

3. **Social and Emotional Development**   Information regarding social interaction and emotions is changing in terms of play. The use of play as a way to assist children who are experiencing cognitive, social, or physical difficulties or delay continues. Studies today are examining ways to encourage safe play to ensure that no child is a victim of intentional harm or bullying.

4. **Physical Development**   Health issues are on the forefront of concern among scientists and laypeople alike. Many organizations are turning to play as a way to decrease the number of obese children. Another aspect of health and physical development involves risk taking. Some scholars are beginning to question the effects of the lack of risk taking in children's play (Little, Sandseter, & Wyver, 2012). Has the focus on health and safety removed an element of risk from play and, if so, what are the effects?

    Another area that is impacting development is the number of children who are living with grandparents. Children who live with octogenarians are certainly affected by their physical limitations. How do the physical limitations of elderly caregivers affect the physical development of children who are living with them? The need for intergenerational studies has never been greater.

5. **Early Educator Professional Development**   One new area of research involves the engagement of adults in sustained play or play with manipulatives that occurs over several hours (Nell, Drew, & Bush, 2013). Sustained play provides adults with an opportunity to experience play in the same way that children do, and this has implications for professional development.

Play Policy 11-4 *

When early scholars of play discussed the benefits of play, they based their comments on their studies of previous research and personal observations. In the twenty-first century, we know more about the benefits of play than at any other time in history. Indeed, Brian Sutton-Smith has spent a lifetime studying play and stated that play is probably necessary for survival (1997). The recent plethora of research has validated the real benefits of play. Although we know more about the value of play for young children, early educators are being challenged to focus on skills that can be measured on tests and to eliminate outdoor play. Changing the public's perception of play begins with developing sound play policy that can be used to guide play advocacy efforts. Ideas initiated in Chapter 1 serve as a foundation for developing play policy. These include the following:

- Play is important in the lives of young children.

- Play and development are reciprocal and progressive. Play contributes to growth and development, and these, in turn, enhance play. Both follow an orderly progression from simple to complex.

- Play promotes good physical and mental health.
- All children should have play places that are safe and support play.
- All children have the right to play, as stated in Article 31 of the United Nations Convention on the Rights of the Child.

Although these ideas may seem repetitive to those who have read this book, they can be used to develop a play policy that can inform the public about the benefits of play in childhood development. Basic advocacy steps include awareness, research, and action (Kieff & Casbergue, 2000). Students who are equipped with knowledge are ready to make a difference in the world. The steps discussed in the following subsection provide information that will assist in changing public perceptions about play.

naeyc
CEC DEC

11-4a Steps for Play Advocacy

1. **Awareness**   Develop an awareness of the needs and available resources
   - **Investigate**   What is the current state of play in your area?
2. **Research**
   - **Find out which professional organizations promote play**   Many organizations are dedicated to supporting play. International groups include the National Association for the Education of Young Children (NAEYC), Association for Childhood Education International (ACEI), International Play Association (IPA), The Association for the Study of Play (TASP), and the Parent Teachers Association (PTA). State and local groups are available throughout the United States.
   - **Find out what other communities are doing**   Investigate what other communities that are close to your area are doing. Find ways to emulate what they are doing or, better yet, join them in their efforts.
3. **Action**
   - **Consider what steps are needed to make a difference, and take them**
     a. **Plan activities that will inform parents about play**   Parents who are informed are supportive. Make a point to keep parents informed about the benefits of play in the classroom and at home.
     b. **Make prescheduled home visits**   Discuss the value of play during home visits.
     c. **Invite parents to group meetings**   Present the benefits of play based on research studies.
     d. **Prepare and share newsletters**
        i. In newsletters sent to parents, include articles and statements that supporting play.
        ii. Include pictures and stories relating the children's progress through play.
     e. **Design and build a class Web page**   Many classrooms have a Web page. Teachers take pictures of children at play and explain what they are gaining from this experience. Links are included that connect parents to Internet sites that support a play-based curriculum.

f. **Plan or participate in a local play day** Every year, IPA sponsors an international play day, and on that day many communities host activities for young children that focus on the child's need to play.

g. **Be politically active** Know your local representatives, and discuss with them the child's need to play and the potentially negative impact of legislating learning mandates for children.

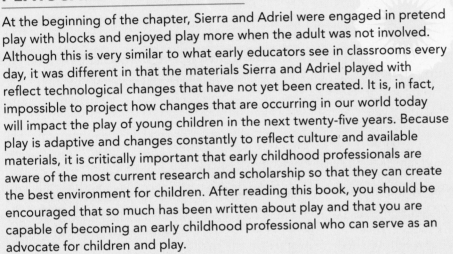

PLAYSCAPE: REFLECTIONS

At the beginning of the chapter, Sierra and Adriel were engaged in pretend play with blocks and enjoyed play more when the adult was not involved. Although this is very similar to what early educators see in classrooms every day, it was different in that the materials Sierra and Adriel played with reflect technological changes that have not yet been created. It is, in fact, impossible to project how changes that are occurring in our world today will impact the play of young children in the next twenty-five years. Because play is adaptive and changes constantly to reflect culture and available materials, it is critically important that early childhood professionals are aware of the most current research and scholarship so that they can create the best environment for children. After reading this book, you should be encouraged that so much has been written about play and that you are capable of becoming an early childhood professional who can serve as an advocate for children and play.

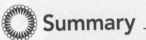 Summary

11-1 Identify current trends that affect children's play.

War, poverty, disease, and violence are influences throughout the world. In the United States, changing demographics, technologies, and health issues are major concerns. Neighborhoods are experiencing changes that are both positive and negative in terms of space and time for children to play. Family structures are smaller, and more children are growing up in single-parent homes that may have limited economic resources.

11-2 Describe four issues that currently impact play.

Four issues that are currently creating concerns among educators and the public are as follows: (1) technology, (2) media influences, (3) toys, and (4) violence.

11-3 Explain the evolution of play research in terms of current practice.

Whereas the study of play was once restricted to the laboratory and articles were read exclusively in libraries, the Web has created a plethora of research available on play. Additionally, many websites offer free articles about various topics related to play.

11-4 Create and implement a policy on play, and a plan for play advocacy.

Be aware of the current state of early childhood education in your area, investigate sources of information so that you are fully informed, and take action to change the situation or contribute to the conversation and thus help bring about meaningful changes in the future.

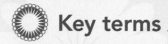

Key terms

Technology and Internet Resources

National SAFE KIDS Campaign

http://www.safekids.org/

This site is sponsored by the National SAFE KIDS Campaign, which is a national nonprofit organization dedicated to preventing unintentional deaths in children age fourteen years and younger.

Consumer Product Safety Commission

http://www.cpsc.gov/

Click on Safety Education and Safety Guides for numerous resources about toy safety. Guidelines are divided by age and category.

National Association of School Psychologists

http://www.nasponline.org/

This site is a good source of information for helping children cope with violence.

Activities . . . .

1. InClass Lab

What issues are affecting play in your community? How do you know that these issues are affecting play? Choose an issue that is responsible for a negative change in play, and list three actions that your group can take to make a change. If this issue is responsible for a positive change in play, how can your group supply additional support or encouragement?

2. Research- and inquiry-based learning

A. Select one area of interest. For example, choose recess, pretend play, or sand play and locate a research study that dealt with it at the beginning of the twentieth century and one that deals with it now. What are the similarities? What are the differences?

B. Spend four hours on a Saturday morning in front of a local toy store. Ask shoppers, "What toys did you purchase? Why did you buy these toys?" (Special note: Contact the store owners/managers to find out if they will allow you to talk to shoppers entering and exiting their store. In some malls, permission may be needed from the mall administrators.)

C. Use the Internet to discover how children are playing in other parts of the world.

3. Service learning

Contact a local women's shelter. Ask if you can volunteer to survey and repair toys and other materials that are available to the young children of women in the shelter.

4. Family Connections

Ask parents to survey their children's toys and donate any unwanted toys in good condition to local charity organizations such as homeless shelters.

5. Play Advocacy

Find out how you can support play in early childhood education in your local area.

Are there local groups that conduct activities during the Week of the Young Child (WOYC)? The National Association for the Education of Young Children sponsors the Week of the Young Child every year (NAEYC, 2013). Most communities have annual activities and events that coincide with this week. Does your community sponsor a WOYC celebration? If so, find out how you can be involved in the activities. If not, find out what you can do to help sponsor a WOYC celebration. In this way, you will become a local advocate for children's play and you will be affiliated with state and national organizations.

Visit CourseMate for this textbook to access the eBook, Did You Get It? quizzes, Digital Downloads, TeachSource Video Cases, flashcards, and more. Go to CengageBrain.com to log in, register, or purchase access.

References

American Academy of Pediatrics, American Public Health Association, National Resource Center for Health and Safety in Child Care and Early Education. (2011). *Caring for our children: National health and safety performance standards; Guidelines for early care and education programs* (3rd ed.). Elk Grove Village, IL: American Academy of Pediatrics; Washington, DC: American Public Health Association.

Bushman, B. J., & Anderson, C. A. (2001). Media violence and the American public: Scientific facts versus media misinformation. *American Psychologist, 56*(6–7), 477.

Campaign for a Commercial-Free Childhood. (2007/2009/2010). Take Action. Campaign for a Commercial-Free Childhood. Retrieved on July 15, 2013, from http://www.commercialfreechildhood.org

Clements, D., & Sarama, J. (2011, online). *Engaging young children in mathematics: Standards for early childhood* (print, 2004). Mahwah, NJ: Lawrence Erlbaum Associates.

DPhil, S., & Ruicheva, I. (2010). Grandmothers as replacement parents and partners: The role of grandmotherhood in single parent families. *Journal of Intergenerational Relationships, 8*(3), 219–233.

Edwards, C., Gandini, L., & Forman, G. (2012). *The hundred languages of children: The Reggio Emilia experience in transformation* (3rd ed.). Santa Barbara, CA: Praeger.

Eisenberg, N. (Ed.). (1998). *Social, emotional, and personality development.* Volume 3 in W. Damon (Series Ed.), *Handbook of child psychology* (5th ed.) (pp. 839–842). New York: Wiley.

Fearn, M., & Howard, J. (2012). Play as a resource for children facing adversity: An exploration of indicative case studies, *Children & Society, 26,* 456–468.

Finkelhor, D., Turner, H. , Ormrod, R., Hamby, S., & Kacke, K. (2009). Children's exposure to violence: A comprehensive national survey. National Survey of Children's Exposure to Violence, *Juvenile Justice Bulletin,* pp. 1–11.

Finkelhor, D., Hamby, S. L., Ormrod, R. K., & Turner, H. A. (2009). Violence, abuse, & crime exposure in a national sample of children & youth. *Pediatrics 124*(5), 1–14.

Gentile, D. A., Saleem, M., & Anderson, C. A. (2007). Public policy and the effects of media violence on children. *Social Issues and Policy Review, 1*(1), 15–61.

Harper, S., & Ruicheva, I. (2010). Grandmothers as replacement parents and partners: The role of grandmotherhood in single parent families. *Journal of Intergenerational Relationships, 8*(3), 219–233.

Johnson, J., Christie, J., & Wardle, F. (2005). *Play, development, and early education.* Upper Saddle River, NJ: Pearson.

Kids Count. (2011). Data Center. Kids Count. The Annie E. Casey Foundation. Retrieved on July 15, 2013, from http://datacenter.kidscount.org

Kieff, J., & Casbergue, R. (2000). *Playful learning and teaching: Integrating play into preschool and primary programs.* Boston, MA: Allyn and Bacon.

Levin, D. (1998). *Remote control childhood? Combating the hazards of media culture.* Washington, DC: NAEYC.

Levin, D. (2003). *Teaching young children in violent times.* Washington, DC: NAEYC.

Levin, D. (2010). Remote control childhood: Combating the hazards of media culture in schools. *New Horizons in Education, 58*(3). 14–25.

Li, X., Atkins, M. S., & Stanton, B. (2006). Effects of home and school computer use on school readiness and cognitive development among Head Start children: A randomized controlled pilot trial. *Merrill-Palmer Quarterly, 52*(2), 239–263.

Linn, S. (2012). *Healthy kids in a digital world: A strategic plan to reduce screen time for children 0–5 through organizational policy and practice change.* A report by the Campaign for a Commercial-Free Childhood for Kaiser Permanente Community Health Initiatives Grants Program. Retrieved on July 12, 2013 at http://www.commercialfreechildhood.org/healthykidsdigitalworld

Linn, S., Almon, J., & Levin, D. (2012). *Facing the screen dilemma: Young children, technology, and early education.* New York: Campaign for a Commercial-Free Childhood and the Alliance for Childhood.

Little, H., Sandseter, E., & Wyver, S. (2012). Early childhood teachers' beliefs about children's risky play in Australia and Norway. *Contemporary Issues in Early Childhood, 13*(4), 300–316.

Mardell, B., & Carpenter, B. (2012). Places to play in Providence: Valuing preschool children as citizens. *Young Children, 67*(5), 76–78.

Narey, T. (2010). *One thing leads to another: Evolution, play and technology.* Education Research Information Center. Retrieved from July 10, 2013 from http://www.eric.ed.gov/ERICWebPortal/search/detailmini.jsp?_nfpb=true&_&ERICExtSearch_SearchValue_0=ED521381&ERICExtSearch_SearchType_0=no&accno=ED521381

Nell, M., & Drew, W. (2013). *From play to practice: Connecting teachers' play to children's learning.* Washington, DC: NAEYC.

Piaget, J. (1965). *The moral judgment of the child.* New York: Free Press.

Pellegrini, A. D. (Ed.). (2011). *Handbook of the development of play.* New York: Oxford University Press.

Rogers, C. (1989). Personal Interview with Liv Ulman, Recorded for PBS pilot, *To Play.*

Sackes, M., Trundle, K., & Bell. R. (2011). Young children's computer skills development from kindergarten to third grade. *Computers & Education, 57,* 1698–1704.

Safe Kids. (2013). Safe Kids Worldwide in the United States. Retrieved on July 24, 2013, from http://www.safekids.org/united-states

Safe Start Center: Children's exposure to violence, it's everyone's responsibility. (2013). Retrieved on July 25, 2013 from http://www.safestartcenter.org

Sarama, J., & Clements, D. (2009). *Early childhood mathematics education research: Learning trajectories for young children*. New York: Routledge.

Sarama, J., & Clements, D. H. (2009). "Concrete" computer manipulatives in mathematics education. *Child Development Perspectives, 3*(3), 145–150.

Schomburg, R., Donohue, C., Parikh, M., Buckleitner, W., Johnson, P., Nolan, L., Wang, C., & Wartella, E. (2012). *Technology and interactive media as tools in early childhood programs serving children from birth through age 8*. Joint position statement by the National Association for the Education of Young Children and the Fred Rogers Center for Early Learning and Children's Media at Vincent College. Retrieved on July 25, 2013, from http://www.naeyc.org/content/technology-and-young-children

Shonkoff, J. (2009). Mobilizing science to revitalize early childhood policy. *Issues in Science and Technology.* Retrieved on July 25, 2013 from http://www.issues.org/26.1/shonkoff.html

Sluss, D. (2008). Dangerous and Daring Books for Boys and Girls: Artifacts of the Changing State of Childhood *The Journal of Developmental Processes, 3*(1), 66–75.

Sutton-Smith, B. (1997). *The ambiguity of play.* Cambridge, MA: Harvard University Press.

Timmermann, S. (2013). What ever happened to the nuclear family? Impact of a changing America on financial services. *Journal of Financial Service Professionals, 67*(1), 27–29.

Tu, Y. (2011). Toy-related deaths and injuries calendar year 2011. U.S. Consumer Product Safety Commission. Behtesda, MD. Retrieved on July 25, 2013 from http://www.cpsc.gov/PageFiles/133613/toymemo11.pdf

U.S Census Data. (2010). Computer and Internet Use in the United States. *Population Characteristics United States Census.* Issued May 2013 P20-569. Retrieved on July 24, 2013 from http://www.census.gov/prod/2013pubs/p20-569.pdf

U.S. Census Data. (2011). United States Census Bureau. Retrieved on July 22, 2013 from http://www.census.gov.

Glossary

A

accommodation—Term used by Piaget to describe the process that occurs when children adjust their schemata or mental structures to accept new knowledge. This generally occurs during instruction when children acquire new information.

adventure playground—Adventure playgrounds allow children to engage in open-ended play or adventures as they design and build different structures. Materials and tools are available for building the play structure.

anecdotal record—A procedure for recording information about a child's behavior in a variety of contextual settings (classrooms, hallways, playgrounds, dining areas, field trips, nature classrooms, etc.) Anecdotal records capture an event in a story format that includes a beginning, middle, and ending.

assimilation—Term used by Piaget to describe the process that occurs when the child fits information into existing mental structures or schemata. Piaget thought that play was almost pure assimilation. For Piaget, play strengthened and solidified schematic structures.

assistive technology—Any adaptation that facilitates an individual's ability to function. Frequently used to refer to computer assistance provided to individuals who have special needs. Assistive technology can range from low-tech changes, such as adding knobs to puzzles, to high-tech changes, such as adding switches or using computers to communicate.

associative play—Play that occurs when a child plays with another child. The children may talk to each other, exchange toys, and play near one another, but they do not have defined roles or shared goals.

attachment—A strong emotional tie that exists between a baby or young child and caring adult who is part of the child's everyday life. The child's attachment to the adult can affect play. Children who are secure that the adult will return can engage in complex play, whereas children who are concerned that the adult will not return may not engage in play at all.

authentic assessment—Assessing children using an ongoing, continuous process. Generally conducted in the classroom or on the playground on a daily basis, it is used to provide information about the child's development and involves the child, parent, and teacher in a collaborative process designed to facilitate learning.

autocosmic play—This term was coined by Erikson to describe what he viewed as the first level of play that occurs in the first year of life when the child explores, experiences, and investigates his own body and discovers that he is separate from other people. Autocosmic play involves a lot of repetitive play—shaking hands, shaking feet, and pulling hair.

autonomy—Typically refers to the notion that individuals are independent and self-reliant. That is, peer influences are minimal and behaviors are based on reason, not popular opinion. Piaget believed that facilitating the development of autonomy should be the aim of education.

B

basic forms stage—A stage in the development of writing when children move beyond *controlled scribbles* and can repeat their marks on paper. This typically occurs between the age of three and four. It is not unusual to see a child at this age fill a complete page with similar marks.

behavioral disposition—Term used to describe the child's overall approach to a specific event or occurrence. In their classical definition of play, Rubin, Fein, and Vandenberg (1983) use the term, behavioral disposition, as one of the three descriptors of play.

behavior samplings—Behavior samplings provide a way to record the frequency of specific behaviors or actions. Behavior samplings provide information about small units of behavior that can be used to create a picture of patterns of behavior.

C

chase—Involves one child running after another child.

checklist—An instrument created to record information about what the child can do at the time of the observation. A checklist can provide a record of the child's social interactions during play, a record of the child's competence in specific skill areas such as hopping and skipping, and a quick profile of class skills.

child-focused intervention—Child-focused intervention includes all aspects of the child's educational program: (1) designing appropriate environments, (2) individualizing and adapting the curriculum, and (3) using systematic procedures to optimize outcomes.

child study movement—A period of time in the first three decades of the twentieth century when a group of scholars simultaneously began using scientific research methods to study children. A great deal of their work still informs research today. Example: Mildred Parten's study of social interaction is as beneficial today as it was in 1932 when it was published.

children-first language—Refers to the use of language to acknowledge and respect the child with special needs first as an individual. It is never appropriate to refer to a child by her diagnosed medical condition or disability. The child is always a child first.

choice boards—Boards that provide an array of play choices available in the classroom. Children may place a clothespin, picture, or symbol/name tag next to the area to show that this is their play choice for the day. Choice boards present a procedure that is understandable and fair for the young child. Choice boards also provide a venue for developing independence that leads to autonomy.

choke tube—A tube used to check the size of a toy. If the toy fits inside the tube, it could fit inside the child's throat, become lodged, and cause an infant or toddler to choke to death. Toys that are too big to go through the choke tube are considered safe. Choke tubes vary according to the child's age.

chronosystem—In Bronfenbrenner's ecological theory, the chronosystem refers to the impact of sociocultural and sociohistorical factors on the child. Examining the impact of factors over a period of time provides insight that may not be available otherwise. For example, the impact of computers on play can be observed in children who have been exposed to computers since birth.

co-play—The adult slides into the child's play to extend and expand it. As a co-player, the teacher does not take the lead, but rather follows the child's lead.

cognitive constructivism—A type of constructivism that emphasizes the child's internal construction of knowledge as the source of information. Piaget is the primary source of inspiration for this approach.

community playgrounds—Started in Europe after World War II and known as adventure playgrounds. In America, the term frequently refers to a playground built through a community-initiated effort.

concrete operational stage—Piaget used this term to refer to the stage when children begin to develop an organized view of the world. Conservation and logical thought develop during this time, which generally occurs between seven and eleven years old.

constructive play—Play that occurs when children use materials to create, invent, or construct something; occurs more than any other kind of play in the classroom and leads to the development of skills and creativity.

constructivism—Educational approach based on the notion that children construct knowledge as they interact with their world.

contemporary playgrounds—Defined areas that have diverse ground coverings and an assortment of equipment designed for a variety of ages and levels. Contemporary playgrounds generally have structures made of wood and feature tire swings, slides with platforms at the top, and climbing ropes that provide a variety of physical challenges. Specific areas for tricycles, wagons, and scooters are available. Shaded areas provide a place for rest and quiet play.

context—The social, cultural, political, and environmental factors that impact behavior. The context influences and affects play behaviors.

controlled scribbles—Type of drawing that young children make when they can control the direction of the pencil or crayon. Controlled scribbles can be observed during play in a variety of settings.

cooperative play—Term used by Parten to describe play that occurs when two or more children engage in interactive play with a common goal. This is a complex level of social play in which children may assign roles and scripts.

coordination of secondary schemes (eight to twelve months)—Piagetian term used to describe a level of cognitive development that occurs during the first year of life. The child tries known actions in new situations. Because mobility is increasing, the child moves quickly from one action to another. That is, she uses a previously learned behavior in a novel setting and does so rather quickly. Examples include pushing and pulling objects, putting hats/materials on her head, and filling and dumping.

creeper-crawler—An informal term sometimes used to describe older infants who are beginning to crawl.

D

DAP—Acronym for developmentally appropriate practice (DAP). DAP is based on a consensus of experts. This perspective encourages children to make choices, values the child's interest, and emphasizes play and enjoyment as best practice for young children.

DEC—The Division of Early Childhood (DEC) is a division of the professional organization, Council of Exceptional Children (CEC). Whereas CEC is committed to working with disabled individuals, DEC specifically focuses on young children with special needs and their families.

decentration—Moving from focusing on self to awareness that others exist. This generally occurs within the first two years of life. Piaget viewed this as the first step in the development of symbolic play.

decontextualization—Representing objects and actions symbolically with other objects and actions. Piaget viewed this as the second level of symbolic play. For example, an older infant may lay his head on a pillow as though he is going to sleep. He realizes he is not sleeping and may look at observing adults and smile because he knows he is pretending.

developmental-interaction approach—Program model that combines Dewey's view of progressive education with Erikson's view of emotional development. The goal is to educate the whole child by fostering development through social interactions. Bank Street is the original model and is located at Columbia College in New York City.

documentation panels—Large boards that are used to display evidence of children's learning, play, and other behaviors through both pictures and narratives. Idea originated in the schools of Reggio Emilia, Italy. These panels are displayed for a number of years so others can see what children are gaining from the program and understand the history of the program.

dramatic play—A type of play that involves symbolism in which one thing represents or stands for another. For example, children might choose to let a set of blocks represent a hotel or plastic teddy bears serve as money. Pretend is the essential element.

E

early intervention—Services provided for children with disabilities or delays (birth to age three) and their families. The goal of early intervention is to provide services in the most natural setting for the child (that is, in the place or setting the child would be in if he were not disabled). For some children who have mild disabilities, the most natural setting may be in the local child care center. Others who are medically fragile may receive services in a hospital setting.

ego mastery—A term used to describe a benefit of play. Ego mastery occurs when emotions can be "played out" and anxiety reduced through play.

electronic portfolio/e-folio—Similar to a regular portfolio, the e-folio provides a record and interpretation of the child's experiences in school using a computer program such as PowerPoint™.

endogenous stimulation—Stimulation from internal factors such as neurological growth that is a part of a dynamic process that results in infant brain growth and development.

event samplings—A sample of the child's behavior that focuses on observing a specific behavior. The observer may watch a child for thirty minutes and note how many times the child responds appropriately to a question or comment from another child. Event samplings can provide a record that confirms or disconfirms a teacher's assessment that a child is engaging in a specific sort of behavior.

exact imitation of reality—Piaget viewed this as one of three components of stage two, symbolic play, that occurs between the ages of four to seven. During this stage, the child focuses on the specific details of the materials and script used in creating the play setting so that it reflects their own view of reality. This is a precipitating factor of conflict for this age group.

executive function—The executive function includes planning (conceptualizing what may occur in the future), working memory (ability to process and store incoming information), inhibitory control (capacity to monitor and control actions), goal setting (establishing objectives that will be met), and attentional flexibility (the ability to easily move from thinking about one topic or subject to another).

exogenous stimulation—Stimulation from external factors that is a part of a dynamic process that results in infant brain growth and development.

exosystem—In Bronfenbrenner's ecological model, the larger social system that surrounds the child. Although the child is not directly impacted, the child is indirectly influenced. For example, changes in child care regulations by the local government or the elimination of the parent's job will impact the child's life by affecting the microsystem. As another example, if a state eliminates recess, the child will be directly influenced even though he has no direct contact with or control over the system.

exploration—Exploration involves gaining information: the child engages in activities that are stereotypical, require deep concentration, and have a neutral effect. Inquiry-based learning and the project approach are based on exploration.

exploratory play—Although purists reject this term, some use it to describe the young child's play when it is rapidly moving between play and exploration. Exploratory behaviors occur in tandem with play during the first two years of the child's life, and some scholars and educators refer to this process as exploratory play.

expressive speech—When children talk, their speech to others is considered expressive speech. That is, they express themselves to others

F

fine motor skills—Motor skills that develop small-muscle coordination. Generally, play that involves working on puzzles, using manipulatives, stringing buttons, and dropping clothespins into a plastic containers develops these small muscles.

formative assessment—Assessment that occurs throughout the year or at a set time period and uses instruments and methods to provide feedback that can be used to guide behaviors or curriculum.

fortuitous combinations—Piaget viewed this as the second level of *practice play*. The child begins to put new combinations together. For example, the child can put toys in and take toys out of the basket.

functional play—Sensory and motor exploration of people, materials, and toys; appears in infancy and is evident throughout the first two years. Smilansky used the term to describe the first level of play, similar to practice play described by Piaget. The terms *functional play* and *practice play* tend to be used interchangeably.

fundamental movement stage—This is a stage that occurs during the preschool years. Children are developing skills that provide a foundation for movement throughout their lives.

G

games with rules—According to Piaget, the third stage of play. Children develop games with rules as they become more capable of using symbolism and external rules to guide play. The rules can be changed with group consensus and can be transmitted to others orally.

graphic organizers—A method of organizing thought processes by drawing a picture with words that depicts how the person is thinking about a topic. This is sometimes referred to as mind mapping.

gross motor skills—Motor skills that develop large-muscle coordination. Outdoor play provides a good arena for developing large-muscle coordination through hopping, running, skipping, and riding tricycles.

H

here and now curriculum—A social studies curriculum developed in the early 1920s at Bank Street that focuses on what is close or relevant to the child. It is designed to help children understand their world.

Holiday curriculum—A social studies curriculum based on celebrating national holidays. Some educators refer to this as the calendar curriculum when teachers use this to the exclusion of any other approach. If this approach is used, religious holidays should be omitted.

I

inclusion—Placement of children with disabilities or delays in settings with nondisabled children. Inclusion should occur in natural environments where a child would be placed if she did not have a disability or special need.

inclusive settings—Term used to describe places such as classrooms or playgrounds where children with and without special needs are involved in play and other educational activities. The individual needs of all children are met in inclusive settings.

inclusive playgrounds—Play areas designed to allow children with disabilities or delays to access all areas so that they experience play with all children.

indiscriminant (or *stereotypical play*)—A term used by Piaget to describe object play that occurs when the child uses an object in an indiscriminant way. For example, the child bangs the cup or throws the bottle.

Individualized Education Plan (IEP)—An IEP for children ages 3–21 is designed to provide a blueprint for the child's educational experiences.

Created by the educational team that includes parent(s), teacher (s), special education teachers, specialists, and other stakeholders; it includes objectives, activities that occur to meet these objectives, and a timetable for meeting required social, cognitive, language, and motor skills and competencies.

Individualized Family Service Plan (IFSP)—A written plan that describes the goals for a child and her family and indicates how these will be met through the delivery of services.

infant-directed speech (IDS)—A term used to describe speech that infants use to engage adults and others.

infant/Toddler environmental rating scale (ITERS)—Scale developed by Thelma Harms to rate the environment of an infant/toddler center.

integration—Piaget used this term to describe a stage in which the child uses a combination of several single schemes in a multiple-scheme play experience. For example, the child pretends to put a doll in a bed. The doll and bed are signifiers and the process of putting the doll in the bed involves the scheme of singing the doll a song, placing the doll in the bed, and covering the doll and leaving the play area. These three schemes are integrated into one event.

intentional combinations—Piaget used this term to describe the third level of *practice play*. During this time, the child engages in repetitive behaviors that are more complex than in the second stage, and these foster new play experiences in which new behaviors are deliberately combined.

inquiry based learning—An investigative instructional approach that allows children to use exploration and discovery to answer questions that they or others pose. In the process, children acquire deep knowledge about their topic and the content areas of reading, math, science, and social studies.

K

KWL chart—A chart used to organize children's thinking during project work or other class activities. It provides a graphic representation of what the children want to **K**now, what they **W**ant to learn, and what they **L**earned. This is frequently used in project work to organize the children's activities.

L

lap babies—A term caregivers sometimes use to describe an infant that is not mobile.

latchkey children—Children who are at home alone without adult supervision for an hour or so before parents return from work. These children typically carry a key with them so they can unlock the door in the afternoon; hence the name *latchkey*.

locomotor skills—Skills involving movement such as running, jumping, hopping, climbing, skipping, rolling, creeping, crawling, climbing, stepping up and down, bounding, and galloping: the list is endless.

logical-mathematical knowledge—The type of knowledge that is developed when children construct a mental relationship between two objects; it is developed through play as children develop relationships between materials as they set the table, put the block on top of a stack, or complete a puzzle.

M

macrosphere—Erikson described this as the second level of play development. It begins when the child enters the social realm, which involves interactions with others beyond the primary caregiver. Children develop a shared view of the world as they engage in sociodramatic play and games.

macrosystem—In an ecological systems model, the culture in which the child lives, including the beliefs, behaviors, and other patterns that are handed down from one generation to another. The child's culture will impact his play, and the child's play will be further impacted when the child brings his culture from home (macrosystem) to the child care center (microsystem).

mere practice play—This is the first stage of *practice play* and involves simple repetitive activity that the infant engages in for pleasure.

mesosystem—In an ecological systems model, relationships between two systems, such as family and school.

metacognitive—The mental process that occurs when an individual analyzes their own thought processes.

microsphere—Erikson referred to this as a stage where children gain mastery over their world as they gain mastery over their toys. *Solitary play* is the primary social mode of play, and pleasure is derived from managing and manipulating toys.

microsystem—In an ecological systems model, this is the setting in which the child lives; composed of the child's family, neighborhood, schools, peers, and other factors that directly impact the child.

motherse or parentese—The high-pitched voice that adults often use when talking to infants.

mother-ground—In some parts of Africa, a term used to refer to a special area set aside for children to play.

multi-dimensional toy—Toys that are open-ended or have a variety of ways to encourage play. For example, blocks are multi-dimensional in that the child can create anything with the materials.

myelin—Refers to the protective coating that surrounds certain parts of the nerve cell.

myelination—The process that occurs when the myelin or protective coating that surrounds certain parts of the nerve cell thickens which allows electrical transmissions to travel quickly.

N

natural environment—Describes the location in which the child would be if he was not disabled. The goal of the amendments to the Individuals with Disabilities Education Act (IDEA) is to encourage natural environments for children with disabilities or delays.

natural play spaces—Areas that are not fenced or defined by adults but provide a space for children to play and run freely.

newborns—Term used to refer to infants between the time of birth and four months of age.

O

object play—Object play begins around four months of age, when the infant's interest moves from self to play with others and objects. Interaction with objects is called object play whereas interactions with adults is called social play.

observable behavior—Typically used to describe behavior that can be observed during play. Observable behavior is used interchangeably with characteristics of play.

onlooker behavior—The child watches, asks questions, and talks to other children. She is observing, but she fails to play. She is more engaged than in unoccupied behavior, but she is not playing. Although some onlooker behavior is normal, if this behavior occurs on an ongoing basis, intervention is needed.

orderliness—The development of a sense of order or organization in developing the play script and in the placement of materials used in the play scenario.

Ounce scale—The Ounce scale provides an interactive system of documentation, monitoring, and evaluation of development for Early Head Start programs; early intervention programs, including children at risk or who have special needs or disabilities;

and other home- or vendor-based infant, toddler, and preschool child care in the community.

P

parallel play—A type of social play identified by Mildred Parten in which the child plays independently alongside other children but does not engage in conversation or play with them. Some children who are entering a new play setting will engage in this kind of play.

pay-for-play—Commercial playgrounds located in businesses and entertainment parks designed around popular culture.

photo essay—A technique that captures the child's play through a set of pictures that may or may not include explanations. Photo essays present a message through visual imagery.

physical knowledge—Knowledge gained by observing the physical traits of an object. Young children rely on physical knowledge to help them understand the world. For example, they believe that a penny is worth more than a dime because it's bigger.

physiological survival needs—Basic need for food/hunger, water/thirst, and shelter/bodily comfort. Maslow used this term to describe the survival needs of both animals and humans.

plan-do-review—An approach used by HighScope to structure children's play experiences. Children plan what they will play, then they play, and afterward they discuss or review what they did and represent this work by talking about it, drawing pictures, or dictating stories. In this way, children develop skills for planning and communicating their actions.

play desert—Areas in urban areas were no safe or accessible play grounds are available for children and their families.

play frame—The term *play frame* has been used to describe an episode of play that has a definite beginning point and a definite ending point. The play frame begins when children shift from reality to pretend play, and it ends when children shift back to reality. Children use signals to communicate the beginning and ending of play.

play rituals—Rituals that occur during play that transmit cultural values through aesthetically satisfying behaviors. For example, children transmit jump rope/clapping chants on the playground through other children, not through adults.

play script—Script is used to refer to a mental structure for actions or events. Play scripts are organizing structures that store play events in the young child's memory. Young children store only short play scripts, so even though they may play for an hour, they will explain the activity in a sentence. This is their play script. This term is also used by teachers to describe the conversations and interactions during sociodramatic play.

play tutor—A play tutor serves as a play leader or model who scaffolds the child or children to a higher level of play. This technique is used mostly in therapeutic settings or with children who have disabilities or delays.

play years—The play years occur from the age of two to six, when play informs the child's view of the world and pretend play reaches its peak. Fantasy and pretend play are dominant during this time.

playfulness—An attitude or disposition characterized by joy, humor, and spontaneous action. It is important to note that play and playfulness are not the same.

pleasure principle—The theory that children play because they are motivated to seek pleasure and avoid pain. Viewed by Freud as a primary motivator for play and recognized by others as an outcome of play.

portfolios—This term was first used to refer to folders or containers for projects used by artists to store and display their best projects. It is now used to describe a system of storing and displaying children's work in the class. Most teachers use notebooks, but boxes can be used also. Some schools use computers for storing electronic versions of the portfolio (e-folio). The portfolio provides a venue for capturing a sample of the child's best work or most interesting play over a period of time.

practice play—Term used by Piaget to describe the first stage of play, which dominates the first two years of life. The child engages in repetition of an experience for the sheer joy of doing so. Although this is the first stage of play, it can also occur during symbolic play and games with rules. For example, when a child creates a play scene with miniature cars, they begin by racing the car down the track. Then continue the same sequence for the next twenty minutes. The game involves symbolic play but it is also practice or repetitive play.

pre-operational thinking—Second stage of Piaget's stages of cognitive development. Children develop the ability to internally represent sensorimotor actions, yet they do not engage in operational or logical thought.

preschematic stage—Stage of artistic development that occurs from ages four to seven and involves the use of symbols to represent ideas, thoughts, experiences, or feelings.

primary circular reactions (one to four months)—First stage of infant development in which primary circular reactions develop. During this time, touching becomes important as the infant develops the ability to use circular actions when grasping and reaching for objects. This is when the infant discovers cause and effect.

prime time—The period when the brain is especially efficient at specific types of learning.

project approach—A curriculum approach that utilizes projects as a way to organize the curriculum. Projects are divided into three sections: Phase I (introduction), Phase II (investigation), and Phase III (communication). This has been popularized by the recent interest in the schools of Reggio Emilia, Italy, because they use them for all age levels.

prop box—Box or plastic container used to store materials or props that are related to a specific theme. Example: artificial flowers, ribbons, pots, and Styrofoam™ can be used to create a flower shop. Pictures and words on the outside of the box increase ease of access. Both teacher and children can easily find the material that will support play.

psychological safety—Used to describe social and emotional safety.

R

rating scale—An instrument used to rank the child's level of accomplishment on a specific skill. Can be used to develop a quick class profile.

receptive speech—Refers to understanding what others have communicated

recess—A block of time when children are allowed to go to defined play areas and engage in self-selected physical play. This is not the same as physical education. All children should have daily recess.

reflexive stage (birth to one month)—Reflexes rule this age, and newborns spend their time watching, observing, and reacting instinctively. Brain research tells us that the child is developing and pruning synapses during this time.

relational bullying—Occurs when two or more children leave play centers or stop playing rather than engage in social interactions with a specific child/victim.

rough and tumble play—Rough and tumble play includes a combination of activities such as making play faces, running, chasing, fleeing, wrestling, and using an open-hand beat in which the child uses an open hand to hit another child.

running record—A running record is a record of observed behaviors. The adult watches the child or targeted behavior for a specified period of time, (5, 10, 15 minutes, or whatever amount of time was previously established) and writes down everything that is observed. Objective observations should be included in a narrative style. Subjective observations or personal interpretations should not be included.

S

scaffold/scaffolding—A verbal support provided by the teacher or adult to move the child to a higher level of understanding. For example, scaffolding occurs when the more competent other assists and guides the child in developing a better strategy for retrieving the object.

screen time—Time children spend in front of a computer, game, or television screen.

screening instruments—An assessment tool designed to provide a quick screening of the child's development in order to identify children who need additional tests. Common screening instruments include the Lapp, Brigance, and McCarthy screening tests.

scribble stage—A stage of artistic development that occurs when the child begins to hold a pencil and make random marks.

secondary circular reactions stage—The time between four and eight months when infants develop reaching and grabbing skills. The joy of causing an effect is evident in laughter. Doing something for the pleasure of doing it evolves at this age.

self-actualization—Term used to describe final level in Maslow's hierarchy of basic needs. When achieved, the individual has a sense of wholeness or fulfillment.

sensorimotor period—Piagetian term used to describe the first two years of the child's life. During this time, practice play occurs when the infant is engaged in pleasure-producing behaviors that involve exercising sensorimotor schemata.

sitting and "lap" babies—Term used to refer to young infants who have very little mobility. Generally defined as the period from birth to one year.

social-arbitrary knowledge—Knowledge developed during social interactions with others. Includes knowledge transmitted from other generations and other cultures. Numbers, writing, and language are all examples of information acquired as social-arbitrary knowledge.

social constructivism—One type of constructivism that emphasizes the construction of knowledge during social interactions with more capable others. Social constructivism is greatly influenced by Vygotsky's sociocultural perspective.

social skills curriculum—A social studies curriculum that is based on developing social skills necessary to navigate the social world. Many still see this as the primary goal of preschool and kindergarten.

social toxicity—A term coined by James Garbarino to describe the presence of social and cultural "poisons" in the world of children and youth. Poisons refer to the profanity, sexuality, and violence routinely viewed on television and in the media.

sociocultural theory—A theory of cognitive development that considers the impact of social, cultural, and historical factors on the construction of knowledge during interactions with others.

sociodramatic play—The highest level of symbolic play in which children engage in symbolism and mutual reciprocity as they assign and assume roles. Children must agree to put the goals of the group above their own individual goals during sociodramatic play.

solitary play—The child plays alone or independently and does not interact with others. In solitary play, the child concentrates on individual play. Although Parten initially saw this as a lower level of play, others view it as worthwhile and valuable.

special rights—A term used in the schools of Reggio Emilia, Italy, to describe the status of the child who in the United States would be described as having special needs.

spokesperson for reality—A role the adult assumes to add depth to play by extending and expanding it. Paradoxically, the spokesperson for reality can also stop play.

stander and mover (one year to eighteen months)—Term used by caregivers to describe a child who is a toddler and can stand alone but has low mobility.

STEM—Refers to an approach that emphasizes science, technology, engineering, and math altogether.

stereotypical play—Occurs when the child uses the object in an indiscriminate way—using the rattle for shaking but also for throwing.

strengths-based approach—Approach used in early intervention (EI) and special education that uses the child's individual strengths, abilities, and rate of growth as a measure for planning instructional goals.

summative assessment—Assessment procedure used to provide information about how much the child has learned over a period of time; it occurs at the end of a period of time and is generally used to determine if the child has met certain objectives and has gained knowledge in specific content areas.

superhero play—Play that combines pretend play and rough and tumble play. In this play, children choose to assume roles of superheroes that they watch on television or in the movies. Sometimes a group will work together to develop a theme around a common superhero.

switch—An electrical device that can be added to toys to enable children with limited dexterity to manipulate them. Kits for adding switches are commonly available in most rural and urban areas and can be ordered through the Internet.

symbolic constructivism—Type of constructivism that emphasizes the construction of knowledge through language and symbols. Bruner's work provided the impetus for this approach.

symbolic play—According to Piaget, the second stage of play; occurs when a child uses an object or action to represent or stand for another; usually begins within the first two years of life.

T

tertiary circular reaction (one year to eighteen months)—Coordination of actions that enable the infant to use active experimentation to discover new uses for materials. Example: putting a key in an electrical outlet.

theme-based playground—Playground developed around a theme with specific learning outcomes in mind. The idea is that children will enjoy the outdoor play and learn content material incidentally.

theory of mind—A line of research that examines how young children develop their understanding of their own internal mental state alongside their knowledge of the internal mental states of others.

transdisciplinary play-based assessment—This occurs when a team of specialists simultaneously observe a child at play and assess different aspects of the child's play and interactions.

transition—1. Term used in special education to describe the process that occurs when a child in a setting under the auspices of one governmental agency moves to a program operated by a different system. Generally refers to moving from programs for children under three to programs for children three and older. 2. Refers to activities used by teachers to seamlessly move children from one activity to another or from one place to another.

U

uncontrolled scribbles—Stage of artistic development that occurs when the child first begins to hold a pencil and make marks: the child cannot control the direction of the marks.

unoccupied behavior—The child moves around the room or playground but does not participate in play. Behavior does not appear to have a goal.

uni-dimensional toy—Toys that have only one focus and can only be used in predetermined ways. For example, many of the toys that accompany movies or television shows can only be used in one way.

Z

ZPD—A term used by Vygotsky to refer to the zone of proximal development. In the ZPD, the child moves from knowing with the assistance of others to knowing with no assistance. Vygotsky believed that instruction and play create the ZPD and that play allows children to reach their maximum potential.

Index

Note: Page numbers followed by "f" and "t" indicate figures and tables respectively.

C

Campaign for a Commercial Free Childhood, 302
Cannella, Gail, 22
Card games, 222
Carrington, Deborah F., 142–143
Case studies, 76–77
Chase, 48, 51
Checklists, 62, 62t
Child care centers
    adult facilitation, 88–89
    context for play, 87–88
    evaluation of, 114
    teacher turnover rate, 88–89
Child-focused intervention, 252–255
Children's museums, 5–6
Children with special needs, 241–261
    adult role, 249, 254–255
    benefits of play, 244–246
    child-focused interventions, 252–255
    cognitive development, 244, 247
    distinctive play characteristics, 250
    family-based practices, 256–257
    global approaches, 243–244
    inclusive settings, 250–255
    infants and toddlers, 250–251
    instructional practices, 254–255
    observation and assessment, 257, 259
    play environment, 252–254
    playgrounds, 286
    preschoolers, 251
    primary age children, 251
    professional organizations, 243
    program models, 255–256
    recommendations for high-quality inclusion, 249
    research on, 243, 248–249
    safety concerns, 253
    social development, 244
    theoretical foundations, 246–249
    value of play for, 26
Choice, importance of children's having, 101, 104, 135, 172, 207, 270
Choice boards, 135
Choke tube, 109
Chronosystem, 61
Classroom decoration, 206
Classroom organization, 122
Cognitive adaptation theory, 21
Cognitive constructivism, 17, 176
Cognitive development
    children with special needs, 244, 247
    infants and toddlers, 35, 87, 107–108
    kindergarten, 156, 178
    middle childhood, 217–218
    observation and assessment, 65–73, 70t
    outdoor play, 269–270
    outdoor play assessment, 289
    play-based curriculum, 87, 121, 156, 191
    preschoolers, 42, 121, 140–141
    primary age children, 48–49, 191
    recent research, 310–311
Collective symbolism, 69

Commercialization, 8, 306
Communication skill development.
    See Language development
Communication theory, 20–21
Community playgrounds, 285–286
Competence, 163
Computers and technology
    access to, 302
    appropriate use, 302–304, 304t
    assistive technology, 257–259
    cameras, 230
    current trends and issues, 301–306
    impact of, 26, 302, 304–305
    kindergarten, 170
    media, 305–306
    middle childhood, 230
    observation and assessment, 71, 181
    play centers, 138
    preschoolers, 138
    STEM education, 231, 233–234
Concrete operational thinking, 48, 218
Constructive play, 44–45, 67, 220, 227, 228
Constructivism
    cognitive, 176
    infants and toddlers, 108
    kindergarten, 176–178
    preschool, 141, 143
    program models, 203
    social, 176
    symbolic, 21, 176
    theory of play, 17–18
Consumerism, 8, 306
Consumer Product Safety Commission, 308–309
Contemporary playgrounds, 285
Content learning
    kindergarten, 164–167
    middle childhood, 219, 226–228
    preschoolers, 131–135
    primary school, 195–198
Controlled scribbles, 99
Convention of the Rights of the Child, 4
Cooperative group work, 208
Cooperative interaction, with children with special needs, 258–259
Cooperative play, 43, 74, 220
Co-play, 126–127
Co-players, 121
Corsaro, William, 21
Council for Exceptional Education Division oof Early Childhood (CEC-DEC), 243, 245–246, 255
Co-watching media, 7
Creative Curriculum, 108, 143–144, 203–204
Cultural competence, 157–158, 180
Cultural influences
    classroom decoration, 206
    music, 94–95, 130–131
    play materials, 169, 180
    types and value of play, 7, 94–95, 157–158
Current events, 231